Law and the Disordered

An Exploration in Mental Health, Law, and Politics

George C. Klein

University Press of America,® Inc.
Lanham · Boulder · New York · Toronto · Plymouth, UK

This book is dedicated to all the

patients and prisoners
cops and crooks
judges and juries
lawyers and legislators
psychiatrists and psychopaths
and
caseworkers and clients

who assisted me
(and to whom I promised anonymity).

It is also dedicated to
Susie
and the kids.

"For all our white-walled asylums and all our dark-walled courtrooms, overheated district stations and disinfected charity wards, where the sunlight is always soiled and there are no holidays."

Nelson Algren
(1961: 58)

"Perhaps the most fruitful distinctions with which the sociological imagination works is between . . . personal troubles . . . and . . . public issues."

(Mills, 1959: 8)

Contents

Preface
The Politics of Mental Health

Science is driven by theory. Or, so I was taught in college. This may be true in physics or chemistry, but I am not convinced that this is true in the social sciences. I probably feel this way because I was originally trained as an anthropologist. As an anthropologist one must develop a theory and test it. However, what one *really* needed to do was to find a tribe that no one had ever studied. Then you would travel to a distant land and conduct fieldwork on this exotic people. This entire enterprise struck me to be more about *curiosity* than theory.

So, in 1971, with an anthropologist's heart, but a sociologist's interests, I began to study the mental health court in Chicago. I was interested in the intersection of mental health and criminal justice. In other words, I was *curious* about how these two institutions intersected.

I thought my court research would go quickly. However, it took three years – off and on. I then moved on to the state hospital's admissions services and from there I rode with the police to study their handling of the mentally ill. I also wondered what influence the state's department of mental health had on the court. So I conducted a study of that department. And, since the department was an arm of state government, I went on to examine the legislature and the governor, also. This all took 15 years.

In 1986 I returned to graduate school for my doctorate. I was told that if I published the book I could not use any of the data for my dissertation. So, I put off publishing the book and used the court chapter for my dissertation.

In the mid-1990's I returned to my study. I found much of the original manuscript out of date; so I tossed half of it out. I then began a restudy of each topic. This took about 10 years. I flirted with the idea of writing a book on each topic. However, this seemed "excessive." So, I condensed the material in to one tome.

Along the way I stumbled upon organizational theory and I found it to be useful in structuring my book. However, more broadly, this book is about the meshing of institutional imperatives, professional ideologies, budgetary considerations, and time constraints that drive the functioning of the institutions that were studied. In other words, it is about the compromises, the deals, within, and among, the institutions that I studied. However, compromises and deals are the essence of politics. So, most broadly, this book is about the *politics of mental health*.

I teach at a community college. Because of this I had no student aides, research assistants, graduate students, or colleagues with time to spare to assist me with this book. Its success or failure rests solely with me.

However, this book would not have been possible without all the patients, police officers, physicians, judges, administrators, legislators, and many other who let me observe, interview, and pester them. They are too numerous to mention; and, I have guaranteed anonymity to most of them. So, simply, let me thank them for their time and patience.

Also, this book would not have been possible without the help of my four secretaries: Linda Gelb, Lisa Palminteri, Diane Rabey, and Rosann Scalise. And I certainly could not have completed this book without the tolerance of my wife, Susie, and the kids who allowed me to spend endless hours riding, observing, interviewing, and writing. To them I owe my greatest thanks.

I *Theory*

1 *Congeneric Analysis*
On the Emergence of an "Accidental" Methodology

1. Introduction

I had long been interested in the intersection of the mental health and criminal justice. So I began observing the mental health court in Chicago in 1971. I found that "everyone" was committed. I then moved on to the state hospital's admission service. There I found that "everyone" was admitted. Many of those brought into the admissions services were in police custody. I then rode with the police in order to examine police apprehension of the mentally ill. I found that the "real" decisions were made on the street. The rest of the system was relatively automatic. So, I realized that in order to understand the court I had to study "down" to the street.

During my research I saw that the court's decision making was dominated by the physicians. They represented the Illinois Department of Mental Health. So, I conducted a study of that agency. However, the agency was a creature of state government. So, I then examined the state legislature and the governor's office. I concluded that to study *all* the major influences on the court I also had to study down to the street, as well as, "up" in to the centers of power.

My field research had taken over ten years. I finally finished the manuscript in 1986. However, I was unable to publish it because I returned to graduate school for my Ph.D. I then wrote a book on Romanian adoption (Klein, 2007).

After I had completed my adoption book I felt compelled to finally publish my mental health study. So I conducted a restudy of each topic I had analyzed earlier. I realized that about half of my original material was dated. I then added my new data. However, I retained my original theoretical orientation from the 1970s and early 1980s because I felt that my original vertical perspective (studying down/studying up) might still be valid. I will examine this issue in the final chapter.

As I wrote the updated version of my manuscript I realized that in some of the chapters (the court, admissions, and the Illinois Department of Mental Health) there was a "discontinuity." That is, there had been so much change in the system that those chapters did not cohere. On the other hand, the state legislature had not changed significantly. In order to accommodate these discontinuities I considered reorganizing the manuscript and presenting the material by decade. However, I felt this would produce too much repetition in the text. Also, I wanted to keep my original vertical perspective and to see if it was still valid thirty years after its formulation.

So, let me begin with the original idea, and the original theoretical perspective, for this study.

2. Helping

I had long been interested in the intersection of mental health, law, and social control. In order to satisfy this curiosity I began to observe the local mental health court in 1971. I had not gone to the court with a formal hypothesis to test. Instead, in the tradition of C. Wright Mills, I had begun my research with a "why" question (see: Rapoport, 1964:6; Crozier, 1972). That is, I asked: Why, and how, are individuals involuntarily committed to state mental hospitals? I had gone to the court expecting to find a type of human service organization called a "people processing organization." This type of organization classified and labeled its clients. Such organizations were to be differentiated from "people changing organizations" and "people sustaining" organizations (see: Hasenfeld, 1980, 1983; Hansfeld and Cheung, 1985).

The description of people-processing organizations as simply "classification and disposition" quickly proved to be inadequate. For example, the law stated that an individual may be committed only if he or she was found to be a "person in need of mental treatment." That is, they could only be committed if they were a threat to themselves or others or were unable to take care of their basic bodily needs. I had assumed that such commitment decisions were straightforward and based upon medical diagnosis. The court personnel, however, did not see the court as functioning in such a mechanical fashion. In fact, they did not see the court as a court at all. Instead, they thought of it as a social service agency which existed "to help people." That is why they worked to commit those that "needed help" and to free those that "don't need to be in the hospital." However, since most of those who came before the court were sad, pathetic souls, the courts' decisions were almost uniformly to commit. That is why the Mental Health Division of the Circuit Court was simply called, "the commitment court." Most of the "patients," never defendants, who appeared before the court were poor and often black. They were frequently terrified, angry, and overmedicated. They suffered from a variety of social and psychiatric problems—all of which were aggravated by a lack of services and poverty. These individuals had been picked up by the police for disorderly conduct or for "safekeeping;" or, they had been brought to the hospital by relatives, friends, or neighbors after a disruptive act.

Over the three-year period that I initially observed the court (1971-74) almost all of those who were brought before the court were found to be "in need of mental treatment" by the hospital physicians. The judge, assistant state's attorney, and public defender usually accepted the doctor's recommendation and committed the individual to the hospital. In this manner they were able to "help"; that is, they could help the patient, while still protecting society.

3. People Processing Organizations

Our initial analysis of the court was that it was a type of human service organization. Hansenfeld (1972; 1983:4-7) has distinguished three types of such organizations: people processing, people sustaining, and people changing organizations. He has described each of these three types:

   a. People processing organizations: These types of organizations attempt to transform their clients by labeling them with a public status that evokes predetermined reactions from other organizations. They do not attempt to directly alter the individual's personal attributes. This is accomplished through a system of classification and disposition. By means of such labels other human service organizations respond to such clients in a predetermined manner (providing psychotherapy or placing a child in a special class).
   b. People sustaining organizations: These types of organizations attempt to prevent, maintain, or retard the deterioration of an individual. They do not, however, attempt to change that person's personal attributes. Nursing-homes and income maintenance programs illustrate this type of organization.
   c. People changing organizations: These organizations attempt to directly alter the personal attributes of their clients in order to improve their well-being. These organizations employ technologies such as psychotherapy, education, and medical treatment.

Human service organizations are frequently plagued with ambiguities about their objectives. For example, while public aid departments claim that their primary purpose is to produce productive individuals, their critics argue that they merely sustain people. Similarly, while the advocates of the juvenile courts argue that their aim is to change the behavior of juvenile offenders many point out that these courts are preoccupied with client processing and not treatment.

By cross-classifying these types of organizations according to the type of client they serve (normal or abnormal) Hasenfeld (1983) arrived at a six cell typology of human service organizations (see: Table 1-1). Each one of these types of organizations encounters unique dilemmas as it attempts to meet its mandate. For example, people processing organizations (Type I) must demonstrate that their processing technologies identifying client attributes and matching them with appropriate dispositions. An example of this is credit-rating bureaus. They must convince financial institutions that they are able to differentiate between good and bad credit risks. And, college admissions offices must assure university officials that they can identify potentially successful students.

Table 1-1
A Typology of Human Service Organizations

Type of Client	People Processing	People Sustaining	People Changing
Normal Functioning	Type I:	Type III:	Type V:
	College admissions office	Social Security	Public school
	Credit rating bureau	Retirement home	YMCA
Malfunctioning	Type II:	Type IV:	Type VI:
	Juvenile court	Public assistance	Hospital residential treatment center
	Diagnostic clinic	Nursing home	

(Hasenfeld, 1983:6)

It is advantageous for Type I organizations to exclude certain individuals from its pool of acceptable clients. However, the obverse is true for Type II organizations. This is because Type II organizations have jurisdiction over deviant clients. Therefore, they must demonstrate that they are capable of effectively identifying all deviants. Therefore, these organizations tend to be cautious and conservative; that is, they have a tendency to designate clients as deviant rather than normal. Similarly, physicians prefer to commit the error of diagnosing a person as ill rather than healthy.

People sustaining organizations (Types III and IV) must first demonstrate that their clients are entitled to care and sustenance. In order to do this they must develop criteria for eligibility. However, such distinctions may be arbitrary. After an individual is found to be eligible they are granted the services or cash they are entitled to receive.

Also, both types of people sustaining organizations must determine an acceptable level of care. However, ideological and fiscal considerations tend to pull these organizations in opposite directions. This is particularly true when there is little agreement on what constitutes an adequate level of care. For example, what is a desirable level of support for welfare recipients?

People changing organizations (Types V and VI) are plagued with problems in distinguishing between normal and abnormal clients. In addition, they must operate with "technologies" that produce uncertain outcomes (e.g., psychotherapy or psychotropic medication). Further, there is often no consensus about the desired outcome. For example, correctional institutions are torn between punishment and rehabilitation.

Since we are interested in the mental health court let us examine people processing organizations in details. Hasenfeld (1983:135-137) has pointed out that people processing has one central purpose; that is, to confer on a client a particular label, position, or status. This then produces a predetermined response from other groups or organizations. The core activities of such a technology are based on a system of classification and disposition. Such a system is composed of a set of procedures that guides the staff in one organization in assigning labels to clients and then linking them to other organizations. Staff activities consist of interactions with clients, the creation of dossiers, assignment of labels, and the movement of clients to other organizations. If other organizations fail to respond to these labels the very rationale of the organization is jeopardized. Therefore, this labeling process is constrained by the recipient of the clients.

The linking of the client to other units is a primary managerial concern of people processing organizations. The ability to ensure a smooth flow of individuals in and out of the processing unit is a major factor in shaping the activities of the organization. To achieve this objective an organization may employ several mechanisms to make the organization function efficiently: First, the staff usually uses categories which are acceptable to the receiving units. Second, efforts are made to simplify the processing by reducing the range of categories. This has the effect of limiting the amount of information needed from the client. Third, common sense categories often emerge which enable the staff to quickly, and routinely, assign clients to predetermined slots. This reduces the need for extensive probing or the consideration of a client's personal history. For example, Sudnow (1965) found that public defenders attempted to make defendants' attributes fit those of a "normal crime" rather than trying to ascertain all the facts of a particular situation. Such categorization then permits a rapid and smooth movement of a case through the court (see also: Kemeny, 1978).

The emphasis on staff-client interaction is minimal in this type of technology. That is because staff-client interaction is used primarily to gather information. Therefore, organizational concerns about client control are limited and center upon ensuring that clients provide valid information. Compliance is most often attained by the use of threats. Some organizations have acquired the legal authority to force their clients to document their personal histories (juvenile courts), while others may threaten not to process the client application unless access to such information is granted (credit bureaus). Internally, the organization's primary concern is to ensure staff compliance to the prescribed classification-disposition scheme. However, Prottas (1979) has found that the ability of an organization to enforce such compliance is problematic. That is because the front line staff have a monopoly over the client information. Therefore, the front line staff members become the key decision-makers in people-processing organizations.

Hasenfeld and Cheung (1985) have pointed out that the focus of research on such organizations has been to identify the organizational determinants of client processing. Studies have ranged from schools (Rosenbaum, 1976), to general and psychiatric hospitals (Coe, 1970; Strauss, et al., 1964), to welfare departments (Prottas, 1979; Street, Martin, and Gordon, 1979), to courts, and to correctional programs (Emerson, 1969). These studies have attempted to isolate the specific organizational variables which explain the differential responses of these organizations to their clients. Hasenfeld and Cheung (1985) have concluded that "these studies have tended to be nontheoretical." That is, "they have had no . . . explicit organizational theories or perspectives" (p. 801-2). Therefore, this body of research has tended to identify disparate organizational variables such as professional ideologies, client-processing technologies, organizational resources, and conditions of work. Let us briefly review this research.

Some studies of people processing organizations have attempted to demonstrate that patterns of client processing are shaped by professional ideologies. Roth (1972), for example, has noted that the differential handling of patients in medical emergency rooms reflected the physicians' values concerning the social worth of individual patients. Also, Rist (1970) has found that teachers gave preferential attention to children displaying attitudes and behaviors compatible with the teachers' middle-class values.

Some studies have shown that organizational responses to clients are sometimes determined by the client's fit with its client-processing technologies. For example, several studies on the selection of patients for psychotherapy have noted that preference is given to persons who are young, articulate, and motivated. These are the attributes which are considered to be best suited for a successful outcome in psychotherapy (Schofield, 1964; Lorion, 1973; Link and Milcarek, 1980).

Other studies have shown that clients may be handled differently according to their potential contribution to that organizations resources. Scott (1967), for example, has noted that agencies for the blind prefer young persons because they evoke the public sympathy needed to stimulate charitable contributions to the agencies.

Research on people-processing organizations have also focused on the effects of working conditions on the line staff in their processing of clients. For example, Lipsky (1980) and Prottas (1979) have suggested that line staff process clients in a manner which protects or improves the staff's working conditions. Therefore, welfare workers, operating under conditions of severe time pressures and limited resources, give preference to cooperative clients. Similarly, nurses are said to respond more favorably to patients who are submissive (Lorber, 1975).

4. Theory

In the beginning of my research I was driven by curiosity. The "why" question. However, since I am a social scientist I soon began to look for a theory to explain the phenomena I was examining. "People processing" was my initial answer. However, people processing was a "small" theory. It did not explain the big picture. However, it did provide a clue to a more useful theory. People processing organizations are tied to other organizations because they receive clients and pass them on to other organizations. Therefore, in order to study the court one had to examine organizational theory.

Originally, organizations were viewed as rationally organized instruments created to attain specified goals. From this perspective, environmental forces were ignored and each organization was seen as a self-contained entity. The next stage of organizational theory was dominated by a conceptualization of organizations as "natural systems." From this point of view organizations were perceived of as collective systems bent on survival. Here, the environment was seen as a hostile force determined to subvert the organization's goals. However, today, theorists employ an "open systems" approach. From this perspective organizations are viewed as being intimately tied to their environments. This is because of functional necessity or as part of a geographic community (Scott, 1983; Meyer, 1978, 1979; Lauman, et al., 1978; Morrissey, 1982a: 170-1).

Although the open systems model is a more realistic view than earlier organizational theories it comes with a vexing new problem. How far does an organization's environment extend? Simply, where do we draw the line? And, is this line arbitrary? This is not merely a technical question. Rather, it is a substantive one. That is because *the definition of an organization's environment will often predetermine the answer one receives to the theoretical question which has been asked.* How have organizational theorists handled this problem?

Aldrich (1979) has argued that an understanding of an organization and its environment can only be obtained when we consider "the aggregate of all [of the] relations and transactions involved" in its functioning. However, Aldrich adds that limits to an organization's environment are crucial because without specific criteria to circumscribe an organizational aggregate "relations between . . . organizations could be extended . . . indefinitely" (p. 279; see also: Freeman, 1978). The solution to this problem has been the creation of three concepts: organizational set, action set, and network. Let us review these formulations.

An organization set has been defined as a focal organization and the direct links it has with other organizations (see: Merton, 1957:368; Evans, 1966:177; Linton, 1936:113-114; Scott, 1981:279; Blau and Scott, 1962:195; Caplow, 1964). These links are identified by contact between boundary spanning personnel or by the flow of resources (Aldrich, 1979:280; see also: Boje and Whetten, 1981; Evans, 1966). However, Caplow has noted that such a set can be "nebulous." He concluded that "the problem lies not with our categories but with the nature of reality" (1964: 223-224).

The second concept that has been used by researchers to categorize organizational environments has been the action set. Such sets are defined as a group of organizations which have been temporarily allied to achieve a particular goal (Boissevian, 1974: 170-205; Mitchell, 1969: 39; see also: Van de Ven, et al., 1974:119-126). However, the problem with such sets is that they are unstable because of shifting goals and affiliations (see: Barker and Jansiewicz, 1970).

The third concept researchers have employed in analyzing organizational environments has been the interorganizational network. Such a network is defined as all of the organizations that are linked by a specified relationship. However, Aldrich has pointed out that such networks are "purposively created constructs of an investigator" (1979:28; see also: Mitchell, 1973; Wellman, 1983; Mulford, 1984). Further, most studies of such networks have been narrow, quantitative studies (see: Aldrich, 1979; Lauman and Pappi, 1976:19). Qualitative researchers, however, have dealt with more complex relationships (Boissevian, 1974:170-205; see also: Mitchell, 1969, 1973; Banck, 1973; White, Boorman, Breiger, 1976). After analyzing the research in this area Aldrich (1979) and Whetten (1982) have both concluded that most of the quantitative studies have not been successful. However, the qualitative studies, which have relied upon an investigator's intimate knowledge of the network studied, have produced better results.

The most serious problem with the research on organizations and their environments has been that they have assumed that the population they have selected for study is theoretically meaningful. However, such groupings often appear to be quite arbitrary (Aldrich, 1979:284; see also: Barnes, 1969, 1972; Whetten, 1982:114; Burt, 1980; Gronovetter, 1979a, 1979b; Benson, 1982; Noble, 1973; Cook, *et al.*, 1983; Tichy, 1981; Scott, 1983; Cook, 1977; Boissevian, 1974; Mitchell, 1969, 1973; Banck, 1973; White, Boorman, and Breiger, 1976).

This has led Scott (1981) to take a different tack. He has proposed that organizational research can examine the individual (psychosocial), organizational (structural), or collective (ecological) levels. This last level is often referred to as the interorganizational field or network (see: Hawley, 1950; Warren, 1967; Emery and Trist, 1965; see also: Jurkovich, 1974; Marrett, 1971; Phillips and Conviser, 1972; Kimberly, 1976; Levine and White, 1961).

Hannan and Freeman (1977) have examined populations of organizations at the ecological level. Such populations consist of aggregates of organizations that were alike in some respect. Here, a "population" was analogous to a species in biology. However, biologists have been able to specify exact criteria for a species; social scientists, however, have not been able to specify the particular criteria to define an organizational population (see: Scott, 1981:27-54). The primary difficulty with all these types of categorization is the manner in which one specified the population under study. That is because *the categorization of the population predetermined the solution* which one received to the research problem. A good example of this was Stinchcombe's (1965) analysis of the evolution of industry. His study, from the pre-factory to the modern stage, employed a U.S. Census Bureau classification scheme in which railroads and air transportation were placed in different categories. This led Stinchcombe to conclude that the structural characteristics of railroads had changed very little. However, Scott (1981) has noted that if Stinchcombe had decided to focus on "transportation" his conclusion would have been "quite different" (p.172). This has led Aldrich and Pfeffer (1976) to conclude that the specification of the field was often arbitrary (p. 99-100; see also: Starbuck, 1976:1077, 1099; Van de Ven, et al., 1974:120; Aldrich and Whetten, 1981:386-7, 400-01).

Hall and Clark (1974) found that their "first methodological problem was, on the face of it, very simple. We had to decide who was in and who was out." However, "the inclusion of all organizations . . . would result in ever increasing circles of organizations which would not stop until *all* organizations were included." Therefore, "tactical decisions must be made in any interorganizational research about which organizations to include and which to exclude" (pp.49-50, emphasis in the original; see also: Pennings, 1981; Zeitz, 1974; Morrisey, et al., 1982b; Madow, 1980; Weiner, 1980; Maldonado and Knowles, 1981; Goldman, et al., 1980; Milward and Rainey, 1983; Hopkins, 1980; Raelin, 1980; O'Toole and O'Toole, 1981). For example, Turk (1970), while conducting a study of local organizations, found that "extra local" variables usually predicted the activity level of the local interorganizational networks (see also: Warren, 1967; Lewin, 1951: 24; Aldrich and Whetten, 1981; Galaskiewcz, 1979).

This has led Freeman (1978) to conclude that researchers often miss the true "locus of causation." That is why he argued that if one conducted a study only at the local level one might be "missing the most important causal variables." Therefore, *"misspecifying the unit* [of analysis] *leads to misspecifying the model used to analyze the data"* (p. 338, emphasis in the original).

Further, Hall and Clark (1974) have noted that "there is virtually no work on . . . government agency relationships. This is a surprise since they concern the distribution of power in society" (p. 46; see also: Whetten, 1982:107, Scott, 1983).

In their studies of public agencies several theorists have attempted to devise proper group boundaries as a first step in their research. However, Hood and Dunsire found it difficult to even define what constituted a department within the British government. This occurred even though they realized that such a definition was of "fundamental methodological importance." Ultimately, they concluded that such a seemingly straightforward question was "a deep legal (indeed a philosophical)" problem because what counted as "a government department" varied "between one list and another" (1981:52, 40). For example, the civil service listed 61 departments, whereas, the Treasury Department listed 70 departments. However, these differed from the approximately 100 "blocks for cash control" that the government funded. And, a still different list of 450 "audit accounts" existed. This differed, further, from the 480 "separate bodies" which the Parliament funded each year. One list even cited as many as 787 departments in the British government (1981:41). Hood and Dunsire concluded that the definition of a department was "remarkably slippery phenomena" (1981:37, 52; see also: Kimberly, 1976:591; Argyris, 1972; Pennings, 1981; Knocke, 1993; Knocke and Lauman, 1982).

Meyer, in his study of state finance departments had less difficulty in creating an acceptable definition of a department. However, he concluded that separating the departments from their environments was counterproductive. This was because these agencies were "nested" in larger governmental structures. Therefore agencies were not truly separate entities (1979:32-4; see also: Scott, 1983:140). In order to circumvent this problem he suggested that we examine the "program networks" and constituencies within which agency leaders operated (see: Milward and Rainey, 1983: 143; Warwick, 1975; Scott, 1985).

In their attempts to define group boundaries, some researchers have gone in another direction. They have focused on the mechanics of governmental programs. This allowed them to study programs directly run by the Federal government, as well as, those funded through Federal and state grants. Since such grants constitute as much as 20 to 30 percent of the budgets of many agencies, Milward and Rainey (1983) have argued that we are creating the "contract state." Wolfe (1977) has labeled the same phenomena the "franchise state" and has portrayed it in an ominous light. For Wolfe, the key factor in this arrangement is that many state functions are assigned to private interests through quasi-public bodies. The organization then carries out these state functions for private gain. Since many private interests are given control over small pieces of the state apparatus the franchise state operates on a strategy of "massive co-optation." The result of such an arrangement is that substantive policy conflict comes to be seen as merely "interorganizational conflict." And, when class struggle or racial antagonism emerged, these, too, become merely another form of "administrative difficulty."

Salamon (1981) has taken a different perspective and has argued that social scientists needed to analyze the "generic tools of governmental action." He suggested that we should examine mechanisms such as grants-in-aid, loans, loan guarantees, regulations, taxes subsidies, governmental corporations, interest subsidies, and insurance. Such "tools" were important because they were the underlying mechanisms of governmental control. However, since each program had its own "unique political economy" the choice of any particular tool was not simply an arbitrary decision. Instead, it was a carefully negotiated political decision (p. 260).

Hjern and Porter (1983) used still another alternative to conceptualize interorganizational relations. They proposed that the unit of study should be the "implementation structure." Such structures are composed of bundles of programs and their supporting administrative organizations. These non-hierarchical structures function as self-organizing entities for the implementation of public programs (p. 275).

Another approach has come from Ostrom and Ostrom (1965). Ostrom and Ostrom have pointed out that in the past government has been seen as either a "self-sufficient public firm" or as a collection of fragmented, and often ineffective, programs. The Ostrom's, however, argue that governmental services should not be conceived of as either of these two carica-tures. Instead, they believe that governmental services should be viewed as "public service industries." That is, agencies should be grouped together if they share similar production methods, technologies, or information. Therefore, just as there are automobile, electrical, and oil industries, so too, there would be educational, law enforcement, and tax collection industries (p. 139; see also: Ostrom and Parks, 1981; for a similar notion, see: Scott and Meyer, 1983).

Benson has taken a different approach and suggested that we examine multilevel "policy sectors." Such sectors are clusters of organizations which are the product of public policy decisions and are connected to each other by resource flows (1982:148). Such sectors con-sist of the administrative apparatus which runs the programs, the interorganizational ties through which resources are acquired and dispersed, the power relations which permeated it, and the values that motivate its participants. The holders of power in each sector are usually a complex mix of program recipients ("demand groups"), suppliers of financial and political resources ("support groups"), and others.

Such a formulation is useful because it forces us to explicitly examine the political, as well as, the administrative influences on a program. This helps us to avoid seeing such programs as merely the product of routine administration. Instead, we can see them as the product of politically and institutionally directed resources (Benson, 1982:164; see also: Karpick, 1977, 1978).

Benson has concluded that researchers in interorganizational relations have ignored such considerations and have attempted to create a context-free theory. He has argued that the result of this has been the creation of an ideology, and not a theory. Implicit in this ideology has been the belief that complex societies such as ours are faced with "no funda-mental structural problems or contradictions." Therefore, these problems were merely or-ganizational and could be solved by administrative fixes. From such a point of view, critical structural problems become merely "resource blockages" or "domain conflicts." He con-cluded that such a viewpoint promoted limited change; change which did little to diminish the structural tensions of society. The consequence of this was that the interorganizational perspective had become little more than a rationalization for technocrats. And, as a socio-logical theory it was hollow and incomplete (1982:146-7).

An example of such an apolitical and technocratic approach is Warren's (1982) study of mental health and the law. In her research on involuntary civil commitment she included a chapter entitled, "The Court and the Interorganizational Network." In the chapter was an excellent mapping of the social world Warren had studied (see: Figure 1-1). However, in her discussion of that social world she concluded:

The relationship between governmental resource allocation and organizational aspects of decision making is of great significance, but at the same time it is quite difficult to study empirically (because it is expensive and difficult, if not impossible, to obtain the necessary

Figure 1-1
The Mental Health Law Interorganizational Network

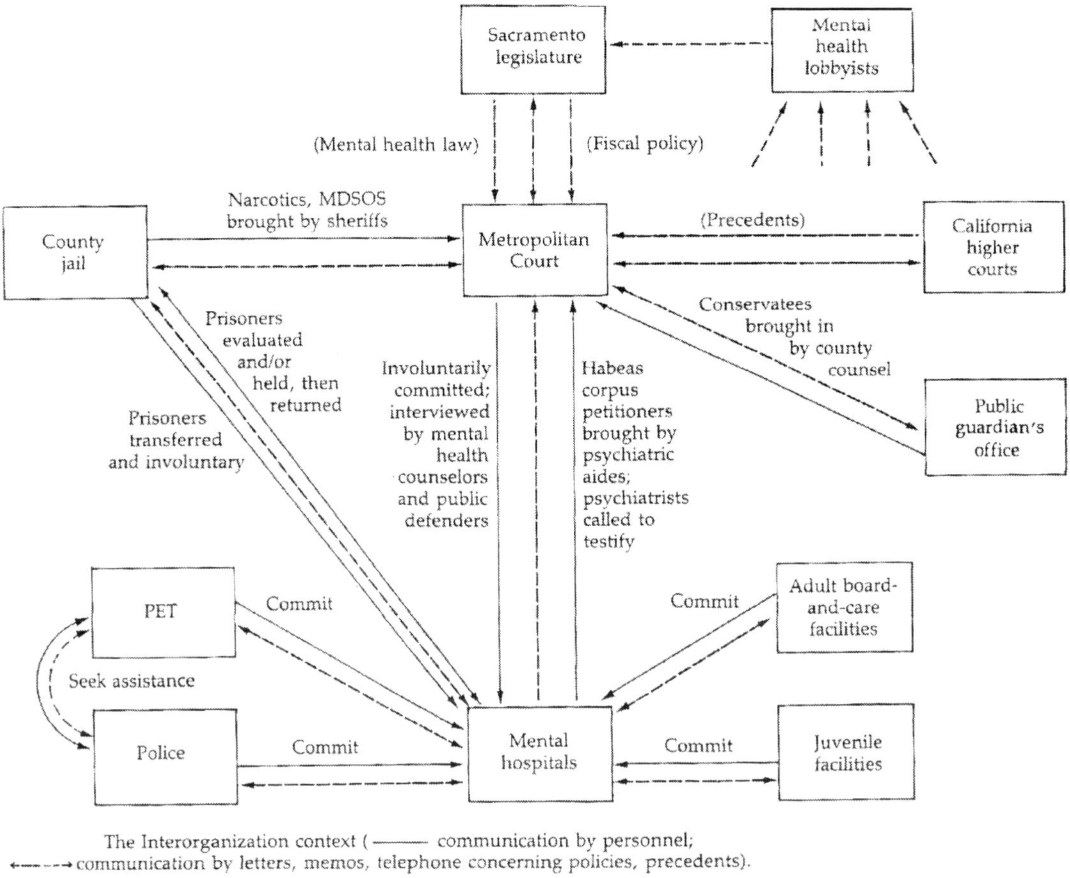

(Warren, 1982:72)

budgetary data) and to make causal connections between resource allocation and decision making (because only correlations can be made at this macro level of analysis). (1982:181)

Such a statement is striking. That is because Warren has made three errors in one long sentence. Her first mistake is her statement that it was always "quite difficult" to tie governmental resource allocation to organizational decision making. In fact, it is often quite easy. Her second error is her assertion that it is "expensive and difficult, if not impossible" to obtain budgetary data. Such data is, in fact, usually available on the internet or simply by placing a telephone call. And her third mistake is her argument that "correlations" were the only method social scientists have available for this type of research. Therefore, what Warren has done in her chapter on interorganizational relations is to conclude that research on interorganizational relations is impossible. Such a conclusion is probably the result of her own idiosyncratic conception of her research problem. However, it brought to mind Benson's warning that interorganizational analysis produced a formal theory which was "devoid of content." This occured because it is "difficult to escape the grasp of the interorganizational" paradigm. For, "even potentially radical departures" often are "caught within it." More importantly, interorganizational analysis diverts attention from "fundamental issues of context and structure." Therefore, only when one is involved in "untangling the connections" to the "deeper structures of interest and power" does a meaningful analysis occur (1982:138, 143, 146, 153; see also Duster, 1991; and Kemeny, 1976).

In my own research I stumbled upon a technique that allowed me to explore this tangle of mental health, law, and politics. Let me explain how this occurred:

In my initial research on the mental health court I found that almost everyone was committed. Although this research had been interesting, it had not produced the results that I had anticipated. I had begun my study expecting to find that the court was the crucial gatekeeper to the mental health system. However, I found just the opposite. This realization led me to conclude that the "real" decision must be made elsewhere. Since every patient who appeared before the court had to pass through the admissions service I moved my study to that office. I had expected to find the admissions service to be a highly selective gatekeeper. Instead, I found just the opposite. They took virtually everyone. So, again, I realized that the "real" decision must be made elsewhere.

The next step in the research came from my observations of who brought individuals into the admissions service for hospitalization. About two-thirds of the patients were brought in by friends or relatives. However, the other third arrived in police custody. Since research had been conducted on families and mental illness (Kreisman and Joy, 1974) I decided to ride with the police and observe their handling of the mentally ill. I found that the police saw most of the mentally ill people they dealt with as victims rather than criminals. However, the police did arrest the mentally ill when they were creating a public disturbance and no caretaker could be found to take them. At the conclusion of my field research I realized that the "true" decision was made by friends, relatives, or police officers on the street. The remainder of the process was relatively automatic.

At the completion of my police research I wondered if there were other significant, though indirect, influences on the court. That is, I asked myself: If I had already studied "down" (to the street) did I also now need to study "up" (to the political institutions that influenced the court)? Since the answer to this question was problematic, I returned to the court to conduct an "experiment."

I began by asking the public defender whether changes in the present court procedures might alter the commitment rate. He commented: "I think some changes would alter the rate. For example, the average patient receives only one psychiatric evaluation, and that usually lasts only ten to fifteen minutes. In some cases I'd like another, more extensive exam, but the judges don't like the delay involved in a second exam. That's because the judges have large caseloads and they feel they have to move the cases at a relatively quick pace in order to hear all of them in a reasonable length of time. The judges also know that the *mitimus* [holding] ward often gets severely overcrowded and they feel they can't exacerbate the situation by returning defendants to the ward. An extra exam might prove fruitless, anyway, because all of the physicians attached to the court are foreign born, speak broken English, and simply are not competent. Besides, the doctors are not even psychiatrists, but only regular MD's. In fact, they're not even 'regular MDs' since most of them are 'permit physicians' who have been unwilling, or unable, to pass the state licensing exam. And, even if they wanted to hire real psychiatrists the cost would be prohibitive.

"Money also contributes directly to my inability to do what I feel is a competent job. Because of a shortage of public defenders I'm the only one available for the commitment court; and I'm only assigned here on a half-time basis. Due to this time restriction, and a heavy caseload, I'm only able to investigate a few cases. Therefore, I have to rely, almost entirely, on the social workers attached to the ward for any investigations. Because of this severe time restriction I'll often have only five or ten minutes on the day of court to prepare a defense for a client. I'd also like to have a psychiatrist on my staff to do independent evaluations. That's because we have to rely, *completely*, on the hospital physicians." He paused and then shrugged in disgust. "It's so frustrating, and so awful. If somebody could really find out!" With a wistful look on his face, he concluded: "Ultimately, the problem is simply one of money."

I asked if he thought it might be useful to speak to the public defender's office concerning the staff situation. He agreed, and referred me to one of the office's administrators.

In an interview the next day, Mr. A., who supervised over half of the office's seventy-five attorneys, said that "the public defender's office is tremendously overloaded and understaffed. I feel I could use twice the staff I have. The public defender at the commitment court could use a psychiatrist and support staff, but a lack of money prohibits anyone but the one public defender from working at the court."

"If money is the problem," I asked, "would it be useful to discuss the matter with the County Board" (the public defender's funding body)? He agreed and referred me to Mr. B. at the Board.

Later that morning Mr. B. explained how he arrived at a funding level for the public defender's office: "My office reviews the budget requests of the various county agencies under the board's jurisdiction and makes recommendations for the allotment of funds. These budget evaluations rest upon criteria such as expenditures last year versus requests for this year, justifications for requests, and performance, that is, output versus work load. This year the public defender's office received a little over 1% of the county budget. They did very well for themselves. In fact, they received several extra positions for the upcoming year. However, these personnel decisions are not made in my office, but by a judges' conference." I mentioned that Mr. A., of the public defender's office, had said that he felt he could use twice as much staff as he had. Mr. B. was shocked. However, his mood quickly turned to indifference. He then said: "It really doesn't matter what he thinks he needs because the Board's money comes from property taxes. Therefore, nothing can be done." He then shrugged and added, "I don't think people give a damn if they need more public defenders. The public just doesn't care." He then said that if I wished to explore the personnel situation further I should contact Mr. C., an administrator with the judge's conference.

In an interview that afternoon Mr. C. explained how personnel levels were set for the public defender's office: "The judges make decisions on manpower and then pass those recommendations on to the County Board. The Board usually accepts those recommendations." I then asked what criteria were used to decide how staff positions were allocated to the public defender's office each year. He explained the "the public defender's office makes a request and then that request has to be weighed in the light of the rights of the indigent versus the rights of the taxpayer. The indigent deserves the best possible legal assistance the taxpayer can provide; but how much can the property owner take? If I were a taxpayer with a modest income and a wife and two kids I would be paying a *lot* of money a year in property taxes. If those taxes are raised much higher, homeowners are going to run away to another country!" He then settled back into his chair and added: "Everyone in government needs something, but someone has to reach a balance between the taxpayer and public services. The average taxpayer, if given a choice, might well say, 'Piss on the services'." He then leaned forward and stared at me intensely. "There is a taxpayer's revolt going on and the budget process ultimately resides with the taxpayer. The taxpayer! I can't stress that enough."

My "experiment" led me to realize that just as I had been forced to study "down" to the street in order to understand some of the significant, though indirect, influences upon the court, I also had to study "up" in order to comprehend the other significant, though indirect, forces on the court (see: Nader, 1969). This led me to again rethink the focus of my research: Although the judge was legally empowered to commit individuals, he almost always deferred to the decision of the physician. Why was the situation like this? Since the physicians were representatives of the state's Department of Mental Health (DMH) I began a study of that department. However, since the department was a creature of the state legislature, I followed the DMH study with a one year examination of mental health legislation and budgeting in the state legislature and the governor's office. In the end, I concluded that the court, like a landing between two escalators, had forces converging on it from above and below; forces that were direct, as well as, indirect.

In conducting my research I had employed ethnographic field methods and interviewing. I had used these methods in order to avoid creating a study of what Bennis has called an "organization without people" (1959:263). The result was that my monograph resembled the work produced by symbolic interactionists. Interactionists had frequently been criticized for conducting studies which were astructural (Davis, 1975: 166, 173, 183; Liska, 1981:141; Burrell and Morgan, 1979; Stryker, 1987, Buroway, 1991). However, they had, in fact, produced several excellent analyses that overcame this problem. And I saw my new technique as a way to add to this body of work.

Within interactionism my approach most closely resembled negotiated order theory. This perspective focused on the never-ending adjustive processes that occurred as organizational participants negotiated the rules that governed their everyday lives (Strauss, et.al. 1963; Strauss, et. al., 1964; Bucher and Strauss, 1961; Maines, 1977; see also: Couch, 1986). Such negotiations consisted of individuals striking bargains, making verbal agreements, and achieving implicit understandings. Such arrangements constituted the organizations "negotiated consensus" (Strauss, et al., 1964:301). Since this consensus changed over time as individuals actively reworked it, negotiated order theory was a perspective which focused on social process. Strauss and his colleagues, in their lengthy study entitled, *Psychiatric Ideologies and Institutions*, describe such a negotiated order:

> We might define the "structure of the hospital" at any point in time as the total of all its rules, agreements, and understandings—of whatever kind. Some are so transitory, however, that one might well be reluctant to call them aspects of structure; when the researcher looks

for them, they have disappeared almost before he can observe them. But of course even the firmest rules and concordance are eventually subject to change. Whether one chooses to call the totality of agreement by the name of "structure" or reserves the term only for the most stable or universal features one nevertheless must focus upon the negotiative and bargaining process. For these processes are of the utmost importance: not only because the work of the hospital gets done largely through them, but because, through them, personnel and organization both become prepared for change—indeed change "in process." (1964:16)

In this study Strauss and his colleagues, for the first time within the negotiated order perspective, had recognized outside influences as relevant to the negotiations within an organization. For them the hospital was seen as an arena to which staff members brought their professional commitments. Because of this, the boundaries of the hospital had to be "extended outward," and, "if we were to view the hospital realistically as 'a social system', these outside commitments" had to be included (Strauss, et al., 1964:15).

One particular outside influence was keenly felt, that of state government: "'Springfield' [the state capital] hovers in the air, the mysterious source of the means for survival, frustration, and even punishment. Requisitions disappear into an administrative maze leading to Springfield. The lack of understanding of and control over this maze engenders a sense of hopelessness among the personnel: 'Nothing can be done about it,' becomes a familiar refrain, while they 'make do' with what is actually available" (1964: 99; see also: Fine, 1993; 94; Clark, 1983; 130; Farberman, 1975b:436). In other words, *outside institutions circumscribe the limits of negotiation* within the hospital (see: Fudge and Barrett, 1981; Kleinman and Fine, 1979; Maines, 1982; Fine, 1991; Hall, 1995:399).

In the same year Glaser and Strauss published a paper on "awareness contexts." Such contexts were structural units which were larger than the interaction under study. They "surrounded" and "effected" the interaction. They included organizations, communities, societies, or, even, nations. With such a formulation Glaser and Strauss hoped to create a theoretical scheme which encompassed "the twin, but often divorced, sociological concerns" of "social structure and social interaction" (1964: 470, 670, 678).

In the following year, Glaser and Strauss (1965) focused their research more narrowly. They transformed awareness contexts into "structural process" and used it to study the social context of dying in hospitals. They found that as a patient moved through the "dying trajectory" the structure of the ward, its "moving equilibrium," changed. For example, as the patient's condition deteriorated, so did the staff's morale. After the patent's death, the staff recovered. However, this new equilibrium was somewhat different than the one that had existed before the patient had arrived. The result of taking such a process-oriented view led one to realize that a ward, hospital, or any other institution was not an inflexible structure. Instead, it was a "structure in process" (see also: Glaser and Strauss, 1967:239-42; Glaser, 1976).

In a similar study Fagerhaugh and Strauss (1977) examined "the politics of pain management." They found that research restricted to a few wards in a hospital was too confining. So, they urged other sociologists to examine the multiple "social worlds" which impinged on any hospital. This led Strauss (1978b) to propose that researchers needed to trace the processes, strategies, and consequences that tied these worlds together (see also: Moore, 1973:720). Later, Strauss called this interaction "processal ordering;" that is, the "working out" of these arrangements. This ordering, however, was more than just negotiations. It also included exchange, bargaining, compromising, brokering, collusion, and coercion (1993 254-255).

Strauss also pointed out that what one should study was not always clear. Therefore, he argued that "we should be interested in *discovering* relevant structural conditions and analyzing their linkages" for "limits require exploration" (1978a:259, emphasis in the original; see also: Bucher and Stelling, 1969; Stelling and Bucher, 1972; Hall, 1972).)

One of the few researchers to have done this, that is, tied micro-level behavior to macro-level structures, has been Friedson. In his examination of the medical profession he has pushed beyond the usual confines of such a study to include a vertical context. For example:

> The most strategic and treasured characteristic of the profession—its autonomy—is . . . owed to its relationship to the sovereign state from which it is not ultimately autonomous. And the autonomy of the individual practitioner exists within social and political space cleared and maintained for his benefit by political and formal occupational mechanisms. (1970a:23-4; see also: Freidson, 1970b, 1973, 1975, 1976; Starr, 1982; Scott, 1987:508-9)

Another study which included a vertical context was Denzin's research on the American liquor industry. What Denzin found was a tiered system of distillers, wholesalers, distributors, retailer, tavern owners, drinkers, and enforcement agencies. These tiers intersected "along moving and shifting lines of accommodation, acceptance, cooperation, tolerance, . . . retention, and open hostility." Sometimes there was overt competition, at other times these groups banded together to coopt the public. Corruption, payoffs, and deals were the lubricants of this system. The result of all this was a "consensual world of understanding whose central focus" was the alcoholic beverage (1978:89, 99-100). This was a particularly valuable study since it provided "a way of mapping the distribution of problematic situations and their resulting negotiations. Moving from the local level to the state, regional, and national levels, the problematics of the drinking transaction" became "less and less problematic" (Maines, 1977:252; see also: Gerson, 1977; Ritzer, 1990; Hage, 1980; Hagan, 1989; Clark, 1983:130; Scott, 1985).

A third study which tied micro-level behavior to macro-level structures was Faberman's (1975a) examination of the automobile industry. He focused on how the institutional structure of the industry forced dealers and salesmen to become part of a "criminogenic market structure." He argued that this occurred because the manufacturer imposed a pricing policy on new car dealers which required high volume and low per-unit profit. This initiated a downward spiral of illegal activities which inclined the new car dealer to engage in a number of illegal activities. Farberman concluded that in an economically concentrated industry "a limited number of oligolopolist manufacturers" could create a market structure that caused dealers "to engage in patterns of illegal activity. Thus, criminal activity, in this instance," was "a direct consequence of [a] legally established market structure" (1975a:455-6). Although Friedson's and Denzin's works were excellent, they did not explain *why* they chose to expand their studies beyond the usual focus in their fields. Farberman, however, *did* explain how his research evolved:

I did not start out to study a criminogenic market structure. Rather, I wanted to follow up on a speculative hypothesis which grew out of some previous research on low income consumer[s] . . .

My interest in the systematic nature of occupational crime developed without my realizing it . . . [S]ometimes, while I wrote up notes in the office after watching a sales transaction, I would vaguely overhear or observe the sales manager and customer "write-up" the deal. I began to notice that occasionally the customer would make out a check as *well* as hand over some cash. This was accompanied by the customer's saying how "taxes were killing the little man" and "if you didn't watch out, the Governor would bleed you to death." Out of simple curiosity I began *deliberately to observe* the "write-ups . . ." It was at the "write-up," however, that a new research problem emerged, because [of] what I had witnessed— and what, in fact, led me off in a new direction—was an instance of "selling short," or "a short-sale," an illegal act which constitutes the first link in a chain of activity that goes back to Detroit. (1975a:441-2; emphasis in the original)

Such "short sales" occurred when the salesmen reduced the selling price on the bill of sale. Although such deals produced only a few dollars in savings for the customer, they produced much more for the dealer; they produced "a lot of money; more precisely, a lot of *unrecorded* money" which the dealer used primarily as "kickbacks in order to get more used cars." This led Farberman to ask:

"So, you have to pay them to get cars. You mean something under the table?"

"Yeah, the 'vig'."

"The what?"

"The grease, the commission, the kickback. How am I gonna stay in business with no cars? You tell me." (1975a:442-2)

The dealer was forced to do this because the profit margins on car sales were kept artificially low. A dealer explained:

"It boils down to investment—return ratios. The factory has us on a very narrow per unit profit margin [on new car sales]. But if I had the money and the cars I could use my capital more effectively in used cars."

"In other words, G.M. establishes how much profit you can make on each new car you sell?"

"Just about. And more than that, they more or less determine how much [new car] inventory I have to carry, and the composition of that inventory. So you have to take what they give you—even if you don't want or need it." (1975a:450)

Farberman then reminded us that such an analysis was the product of an accident:

Although my initial research problem situated me so that I luckily *tripped over* and *recognized* a *new problem*, the new problem actually links to the old problem so that my understanding of the dynamics of customer/salesman interaction is enlarged by my understanding of the systemic dynamics of "short sales." *In fact, deliberate—as opposed to accidental—problem transformation may be integral to the methodologic of contextual, vertical analysis.* (1975a:442n; emphasis added)

With this in mind, how then, should we analyze the functioning of such middle-level gatekeepers as the court personnel? We should *not* do it as Farberman and I had done; that is, by stumbling upon an answer. Instead, we should create a *deliberate methodology*. A deliberate methodology which *required* us to trace the strands of influence or power from organization to organization, institution to institution. For example, a study in sports sociology might lead us to drug use among sports figures and eventually to drug dealing by organized crime. The crucial element in such studies would be *to follow wherever our data leads us* (see: Strauss and Corbin, 1990:158-175; 1991:455-463). Such a technique I have termed "congeneric analysis." The term "congeneric" is derived from the French "congener," which is a person or thing resembling or *suggesting* something else (see: Gove, 1981; Dewey, 1910:117-118; see also: Blumer, 1969:40; Bar-On, 1990). The essence of such an analysis would be for the researcher to explore, or at least consider, all the *significant direct*, and *indirect*, forces affecting a problem or organization under study. Therefore, a congeneric analysis would be *holistic*, that is, it would be *vertical* and *contextual*.

Thus, the researcher must appreciate that the behavior present in one institution is the product of the behavior of other institutions at different levels (see: Hagan, 1989: 117; Heinz and Manikas, 1992:832; Emerson, 1991; Hall, 1995; Lammers; 1988; Becher and Kogan, 1980:1-25; Clarke, 1990b:16; Fennell and Warnake, 1988). That is, one could say that "macro-realities are . . . in effect someone else's micro-reality" (Prendergast and Knottnerous, 1993:164; see also: Collins, 1981:989; Gilmore, 1990; Clarke, 1991b:136; Fine, 1991). So, in order to conduct this type of study we must create *a connected series of ethnographies* (see: Duster, 1981; 1990:130-136). A series of ethnographies that stretches from the street to the centers of power (see: Van de Graaff, 1978: 179, 186-7; Becher and Kogan, 1980:1-25).

Included in such a congeneric analysis should be the history of the organization. This is because once historical choices have been made they often predetermine future organizational choices. That occurs because "change follows a branching model." Once a particular path is chosen "it is very difficult to get back on a rejected path" (Krasner, 1984:225; see also: Almond, 1973; 22-4). In such an analysis one must also include the cultural context. However, frequently, this has not been done. That is because researchers have routinely focused on the structural and technical functioning of an organization while slighting, or even ignoring, the role of cultural values and beliefs (see: Krasner, 1984: 230-3; Milner, 1980; Kahne and Schwartz, 1978: 462, 464). Therefore, traditionally, organizations have been seen as tied by budget allocations and chains of command. However, they are also interrelated through "larger cultural systems involving . . . normative elements [such] as legitimacy" (Scott, 1983:156; Evans, 1972:182; 1966; Meyer, 1979:31-41, 200-1). It is through the fulfillment of these normative expectations that an organization justifies its right to exist (Maurer, 1971:361; see also: Thompson, 1967; Dowling and Pfeffer, 1975; Galaskiewicz, 1985; Meyer and Scott, 1983).

With such a vertical and contextual focus we believe that congeneric analysis can be a useful methodology. That is because it allows us to overcome the problem of the definition of one's universe of study. We can do this by examining all those who hold power over an organization. In other words, our universe of study is an organization's *polity*. Such a polity includes "the whole web of groups and individuals, internal or external to an organization, that possess resources to sanction decisions." Therefore, included in the polity are those having an "active and . . . organized influence on the process of decision-making." This includes the power, influence, and characteristics of the organization's members, as well as, its suppliers and consumers (Zald, 1970:229-30; see also: Sharkansky, 1981; Mijs, 1992; Fligstein and Freedland, 1995: 31; Hurst, 1991: 192-3).

Only a handful of such vertical and contextual analyses have been undertaken. An early example of one of these was Vidich and Bensman's (1958) study of a small town in the U.S. In their research they did not simply conduct a "community study." Instead they explored how a small town was influenced, and even controlled by, the "mass society." Because of such external controls the townspeople felt powerless and dependent. And, while the agents of the larger society were respected, their very existence devalued the importance of the inhabitants' rural existence.

A more recent study was Jacobs chronicle of the history of Stateville prison in downstate Illinois. In this work Jacobs found that between 1925 and 1975 the prison passed through several stages: anarchy, charismatic dominance, drift, crisis, and restoration. In the first decade that was studied the prison was mired in the political spoils system; this produced institutional anarchy. Then, for the next twenty-five years one warden dominated the institution. In the 1960s the civil rights movement and the Black Muslims entered the prison and brought on a period of prisoner militancy and administrative drift. As the 1960s progressed programmatic opportunities shrank while administrative and judicial reforms loosened internal controls. Violence was the result. Eventually, this produced a restoration of a more authoritarian, albeit corporate, model of management. Jacobs concluded that since 1925 the prison had been characterized by the movement of the general society's values into the correctional setting. Therefore, rather than viewing the prison in isolation he saw the prison's place in society as moving "from the periphery toward the center" (1977:6).

A third example of such a study was Walmsley's (1969) examination of the selective service system. What was striking about this study was the researchers' placement of the organization in a web of contradictory influences. Walmsley and Zald (1973) believed that the study of such public organizations illustrated that they were part of a policy subsystem. Such a "subgovernment" consisted of an arena of individuals, groups, organizations, and "relevant others" which were affected by, and interested in, a given policy. Therefore, interest groups, competing public organizations, political superiors, appropriation subcommittees, subject matter committees, and staff agencies all comprised the environment of such a public agency (see: Figure 1-2). These organizations could be "competitive, cooperative, hostile, overseeing, reviewing, [or,] controlling, but regardless of their role they shape[d] the mandate and the conditions of existence for a public organization" (p. 27; see also: Cater, 1964:26-48; Truman, 1968:437-78; Freeman, 1965:22).

Figure 1-2
The Environment of the Selective Service System

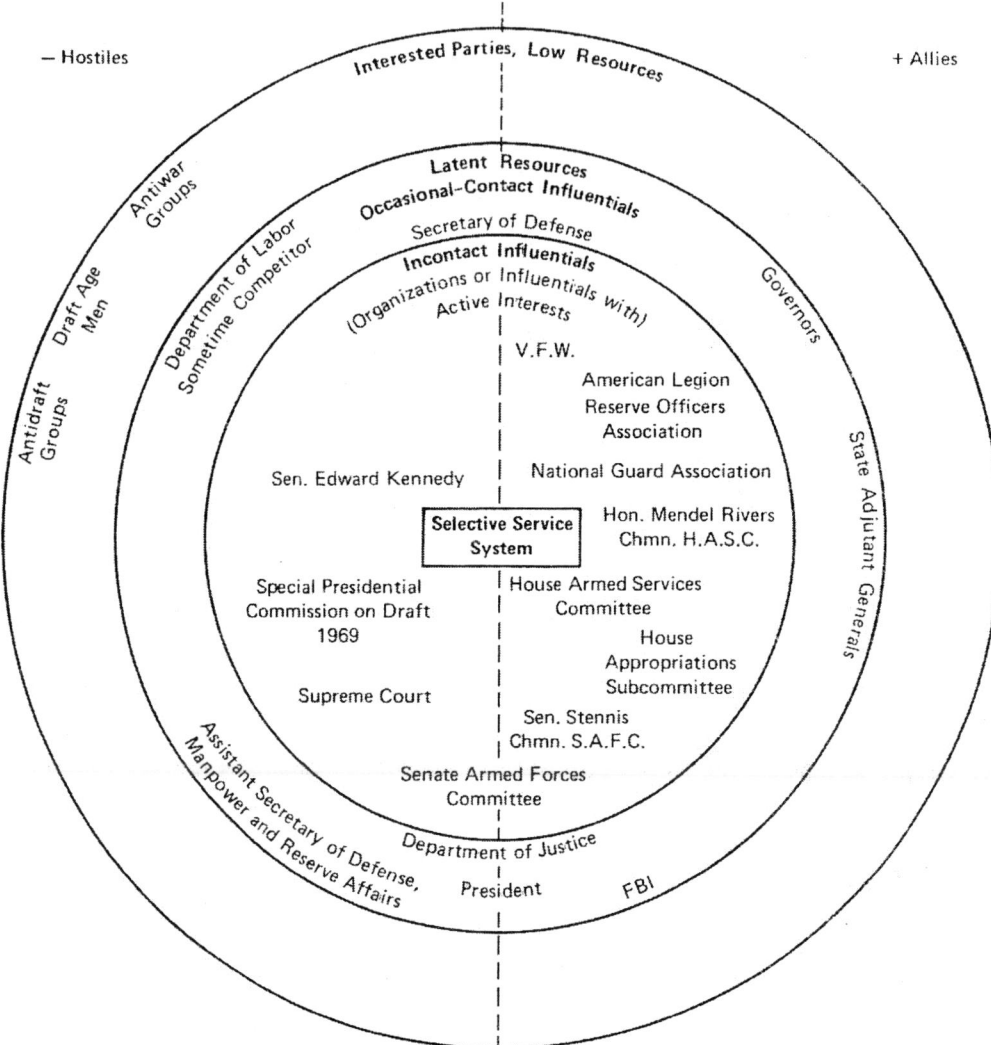

(Walmsly and Zald, 1973:29)

If we return to symbolic interactionism we can site several studies which show a similar contextual perspective. For example, Busch (1980, 1982) has conducted research on the ties between farmers, agribusiness, government, and various interest groups. Busch employed the negotiated order perspective in order to explain the evolution of the relationships among these groups. In a 1980 paper Busch discussed policy making among agricultural researchers, administrators, and interest groups. He explained how each used their political and economic clout in attempting to prevail. Busch's purpose was to show "the dynamics that occur within [the] structure" (1980:31; see also: Prendergast and Knottnerus, 1993:178).

In his 1982 article Busch described the rise of the agricultural sciences as a social movement in the late 1800s and early 1900s. Here, farmers, scientists, and the U.S. government sought to remake rural America. Through legislation they hoped to create "a new farmer." However, Busch concluded that although a law may create a government agency, social structure only emerged from the "sediment" of earlier negotiations (see: Prendergast and Knottnerus 1993: 177-8).

Another study that attempted to go beyond traditional interactionism was Sharon Mast's (1983) examination of the social organization of television drama. Based on her work as an actress, Mast explained how the aesthetic and technical requirements of television constrain television drama. For example, in order to appeal to a mass audience television producers felt they must conventionalize characters and plots. In theater and film, however, experimentation was far more acceptable. Also, in the theater an actor may "rant and roar." However, in television frequent close-ups force the actors to be more contained ("naturalistic"). In television out of sequence acting (to allow for editing), and the lack of an audience, also made television acting different from theater acting. In the theater the actors were in control. However, in television, the director, through his or her control of the technology, was dominant.

With its focus mass entertainment Mast concluded that television drama had no "social imperative" (1983: 81). However, there *was* a social imperative that she overlooked. She mentioned that writing for television dramas was "a corporate enterprise" (1983: 73; see also: Overington and Mangham, 1982: 184). This is exactly the point she should have explored further. The point is that television dramas existed in order to sell products. And such consumption is at the heart of our capitalistic system (see: Scott, 1996; Klady, 1998).

Another attempt to expand beyond traditional interactionism was Faulkner's (1983) examination of the career patterns of Hollywood composers. He found that in order to protect themselves producers repeatedly used only a handful of composers who had a proven record of success. Therefore, "Big Hollywood—the matching of top-level projects to the . . . circle of name composers" narrowed the range so that participation was "permanently restricted to a chosen few" (1983: 170). This occurred because proven composers produced a "stabilizing force for *profit seeking enterprises.*" This was particularly true when a film was produced for national distribution and was "subject to extraordinary levels of . . . uncertainty" (Faulkner, 1983: 43, 101, 170-177, emphasis added; see also: Prendergast and Knottnerus, 1993: 169, 180). In other words, filmmaking, like all other business enterprises, is driven by *financial decision making*. And unless one studies investment and financial practices in the film industry one could never attain a *comprehensive* understanding of that industry.

Another researcher who has attempted to incorporate structure into symbolic interactionism was Adele Clarke (1987, 1990a, 1990b, 1991a, 1991b). Clarke analyzed the emergence of modern biological research. Her historically oriented studies employed a "social world" perspective. Social worlds were groups with commitments to certain activities who shared resources in order to achieve their goals. She saw social worlds as the fundamental building blocks of collective action and were "the principle affiliative mechanism" through which people organized social life. Therefore, she saw society as a "mosaic of social worlds that . . . touch and interpenetrate" each other (see: Kemeny, 1976: 743). Clarke believed that these social worlds were the structural units within which a negotiated order was constructed (1990b; 12-20, 1990a: 30). Such social worlds came together around various issues in "arenas." Here, alternative courses of action were fought out. This she termed "processual ordering" (Strauss, 1993: 226, 230, 254-5; see also: Strauss, 1984, 1985; Gilmore, 1990; Ulmer, 1995; Katovich, 1986; Hall, 1987:12).

Using this perspective Clarke (1987) analyzed the process by which experimentation overtook description as the primary activity of American physiologists. This process, which occurred between 1890 and 1920, brought on a change in the structure of the science. Early description in anatomy and morphology required extensive collections of specimens, but only a few of each type. Amateur researchers often collected these specimens. They were then shared among networks of collectors and scientists. Later, experimental research required large quantities of live specimens or fresh cadavers. Eventually, "biological farms" were established in order to meet this new demand. The large costs of these "farms" forced scientists to turn to private capital, foundations, and the government for funding. Thus, there was a shift from amateur collecting to research institutions. This produced a change from informal networks to formal markets. The result of this was the emergence of "big science."

In another study Clarke (1991a) asked: Why were the reproductive sciences so late to emerge? Clarke provided two answers. One was that genetics and developmental embryology had to develop their techniques before reproductive science was "doable." The other was that where their work touched upon human sexuality it lacked public legitimacy and financial support. These two problems were overcome with the development of the Pap Smear. This technique was developed in 1917 and become available to women in the 1930s. It gave reproductive science public legitimacy and external support. As a result of this reproductive science grew from the 1930s until the 1960s. However, in the 1960s the field was buffeted by political controversy when the birth control pill and abortion became available.

5. Premises

Defining the larger social structures surrounding an organization are often difficult (Prendergast and Knottnerus, 1993: 176). In order to avoid such a problem let us make the methodological and theoretical premises of congeneric analysis explicit:

One perspective described earlier was negotiated order theory. This theory was not included simply because it "resembled" congeneric analysis. Instead, it was chosen because I, as well as most negotiated order researchers, employ ethnographic field methods. Such methods are open-ended and flexible. That is, they begin with a preliminary model or a checklist of points to explore. Then field workers proceed by feel and improvisation rather than a plan. Thus, through hunches, or even serendipity, researchers attempt to gain a comprehensive knowledge of a subject. The monographs produced by these studies are descriptive and they focus on the interpretation of the group or organization under study (Eckstein, 1975:81-2; see also: Sanday, 1979; Emerson, 1981; Geertz, 1973; Shankman, 1984; Pelto and Pelto, 1973; Stake, 1983, 1985, 1986).

Weiss (1966) has argued that such a methodology is qualitatively different from the experimental method. That is because the experimental approach stresses the isolation or linking of a small number of elements or variables. Ethnographic research, however, investigates complex situations in a holistic manner. That is, researchers see a complex situation as containing a system of interrelated elements. Thus, rather than focusing on particular relationships between independent and dependent variables, the researcher seeks to identify the nature of the *system*. Therefore, ethnographic research is different from experimental studies (see: Light, 1980; Sanday, 1979; Emerson; 1981).

There are four characteristics typical of this type of research: First, ethnographic researchers resist explanations that refer to a few simple postulates. Instead, they concentrate on the interpretations of complex situations by participants. Second, since relations between parts of the social system are not logical, unknown parts can not simply be deduced from known data. Because of this the investigation of unknown portions of the system becomes a key focus of the research. Third, explanation is never complete because of the emergent character of social life. And, fourth, the social patterns being described are subject to change since new data is constantly being uncovered (Diesing, 1971; see also: Mason, 1976:129-311).

Just as the data is emergent in such studies, so too, is the theory. In these studies there is an ongoing process of hypothesis formation, data collection, testing of the hypothesis, more data collection, and so on. Because of this process ethnographic research operates from the bottom up, rather than from the top down. It is "recursive" in nature because each investigative decision is contingent upon on those that preceded it (Light, 1980; Borman, et.al., 1986:54; Schwartz and Jacobs, 1979:270). Such a research methodology is "heuristic;" that is, it stimulates the formation of theory through constant feedback. Hopefully, the result of this type of process is the discovery of new problems and innovative theoretical solutions. That is because "theories do not come from a vacuum, or fully and directly from data. In the final analysis they come from the theorists' imagination" (Eckstein, 1975:104-108).

Eckstein's emphasis on the emergent character of theory has been formalized by Glaser and Strauss (1967) as "grounded theory" (theory grounded in data). Such a formulation is built upon a process of constant feedback; that is, "theory as process." Such a process allows theory to become "rich, complex, and dense" (Glaser and Strauss, 1967:21-43). Glaser and Strauss (1967: 21-43) see this process of grounded theory beginning with the emergence of hypotheses out of a preliminary analyses. However, such a hypothesis is more like a suggestion than a formal theory. Such an approach functions in a feedback manner in order to produce higher and higher levels of scientific abstraction (Eckstein, 1975, 108-112).

Because of the nature of this research process the researcher is not simply the passive receiver of their data. Instead, the scientist is drawn into "actively generating and verifying . . . hypotheses." As this process continues, questions of sampling become part of the research process. That is because the further collection of data cannot be planned in advance of the emerging theory (as is done so carefully in traditional experiments). Eventually, the emerging theory points to the next step. This process ends with "theoretical saturation." That is, the research ends when the production of additional data leads to a theoretical dead-end (Glaser and Strauss, 1967: 40-1, 47, 61-2; see also: Cavan, 1974; Denzin, 1977; 1970, 1978; Fine, 1992).

Beyond such methodological concerns, the use of ethnographic research has theoretical implications. For example, by employing ethnographic field methods no explicit decision is made concerning a theoretical orientation. However, implicitly, the use of ethnography (the micro-analysis of human behavior) forces the researcher to focus on day to day social interaction. This creates, in effect, the same theoretical orientation as symbolic interactionism (Burrell and Morgan, 1979:79; see also: Morgan, 1984; Estes and Edmonds, 1981).

Since symbolic interactionism was the de facto theory of our study, let us examine this perspective in more detail. We do this so that, again, we may make our implicit premises, explicit. Symbolic interactionists emphasize psychosocial processes as the primary element in social life. Drawing from the work of Mead and Blumer, interactionists shun biological, structural, or narrowly psychological explanations of human behavior. Instead, interactionists focus on the open-ended, situational construction of reality in which meanings or symbols create social life. Through this process the self is seen as an emergent social object and not just a set of traits. Thus, human nature is perceived to be essentially social. Through such a microscopic approach, society and the self, become a reciprocal process. As a consequence of this symbolic interactionists do not see individuals as molded by society. Instead, they view them as actively defining and interpreting reality. This gives fluidity to social processes and sometimes causes social structures to become residual or to virtually disappear in a monograph (Davis, 1975:170-1; see also: Fine, 1984, 1993; Maines, 1981).

This focus on social process produces studies which tend to define reality in terms of the actors subjective definition of the outside world. Thus an individual's reality sometimes comes to be seen as if it were separated from any social organization. Davis has concluded that "while the work of this school is often highly insightful and imaginative, the theory has been largely astructural, ahistorical, and noncomparative, promoting a sociology of the segmental, the exotic, and the bizarre" (1975:173,182; 1977).

Davis' critique of symbolic interactionism is incorrect. That is because while interactionists may ignore social structure explicitly, they include it, implicitly. A good example of this is Bittner's research on police work in the mid-1960s. At that time Bittner conducted a study of police order maintenance activities ("peace keeping") on Skid Row in two large American cities. He found that the police considered this area to be divorced from the larger society. Since there was almost no judicial or administrative control over the officers on Skid Row their discretion in handling street incidents was broad. As a result of this their work was governed only by their own "wisdom, integrity, [and] altruism." These officers viewed the citizens on Skid Row as ripe for exploitation by each other. They saw their task as the protection of individuals from one another. Overall, their hope was to keep Skid Row inhabitants from sinking deeper into misery. In their daily encounters on Skid Row the officers found that gratuitous violence was common. They dealt with these situations by applying the most expedient methods available. Questions of culpability or just desserts were usually irrelevant (1967:700, 707, 711).

Burrell and Morgan have pointed out that Bittner emphasized that the officers on Skid Row had a great deal of freedom of action in handing their jobs. However, they noted that Bittner was "at pains" to point out that Skid Row was "unusual in that the men who patrol[ed] it" were "not subject to 'any system of social control'." Thus, Burrell and Morgan emphasize that Bittner, while baring social structure through the front door, admitted it through the back door (1979:263-64; see also: Crozier, 1972).

Just as Bittner implicitly accepted social structure in his research, so did we. This occurred by adopting the concept of polity as a way to define our universe of study. By doing this we accepted the need to examine the whole web of groups and individuals that possessed resources to affect organizational functioning. Also, by explicitly adopting the concept of polity we implicitly adopted its larger theoretical context, the political economy model. Let us describe this school:

This theoretical orientation focuses on the mobilization of power, legitimization, and economic resources by organizations. Here, interest groups compete and negotiate over control of the resources of the organization. In trying to dominate the organization each group within the organization attempts to control the resource allocation process. Eventually, through competition, bargaining, and compromise, a dominant coalition emerges (Hasenfeld and Cheung, 1985; Hasenfeld, 1980, 1983; see also: Benson, 1977, 1982; Astley and Van de Ven, 1983; Karpik, 1977, 1978; Mizruchi and Galaskiewicz, 1993; Baxter and Lambert, 1991; Knocke, 1993).

In the political economy school four sets of structural variables are seen to shape organizations. They are the external polity, the external economy, the internal polity, and the internal economy. Let us briefly describe each of these. The external polity refers to the exchanges between the organization and external units for control over legitimization, resources, goal definitions, and the channels for the exertion of influence. The external economy refers to conditions which affect the supply of resources to the organization and the demand for its services. The internal polity refers to the internal structure of authority and the dominant elite's values and goals. The internal economy refers to the ways the organizational tasks are accomplished. This encompasses the production system, the rules governing it, and the resources allocated to it (Walmsley and Zald, 1973). Most importantly, the political economy model is merely a variant of Talcott Parsons' traditional functionalist approach (Bates, 1970:262). Therefore, we may conclude that our study combines the microanalysis of behavior (ethnographic field work/interactionism) within the institutions of a functioning social structure.

This orientation is made explicit in Burrell and Morgan's (1979) analysis of the different paradigms that shape sociological theory (see: Figure1-3). By arraying their scheme along two axes, subjective-objective and regulation-change, they have created four paradigms: functionalist, interpretive, radical humanist, and radical structuralist. These four paradigms have different premises. The funtionalist paradigm is based upon common sense notions about the world which generates positivist and systems-oriented explanations of social life. The assumptions of the interpretive paradigm produces phenomenology and focuses on how reality is socially constructed. The radical humanist paradigm produces critical theory and attempts to reveal the dimension of power underlying our social institutions. And, the radical structural paradigm gives rise to Marxian or conflict approaches that focuses on domination and the contradictions inherent in a social system.

Morgan points out that "the knowledge generated by all paradigms must be regarded as ideological." That is because there are "no independent reference points for determining validity" (1984:312). So, our choice is to explore (micro)interaction with the context of a social system. That is our premise.

Figure 1-3
The Four Sociological Paradigms

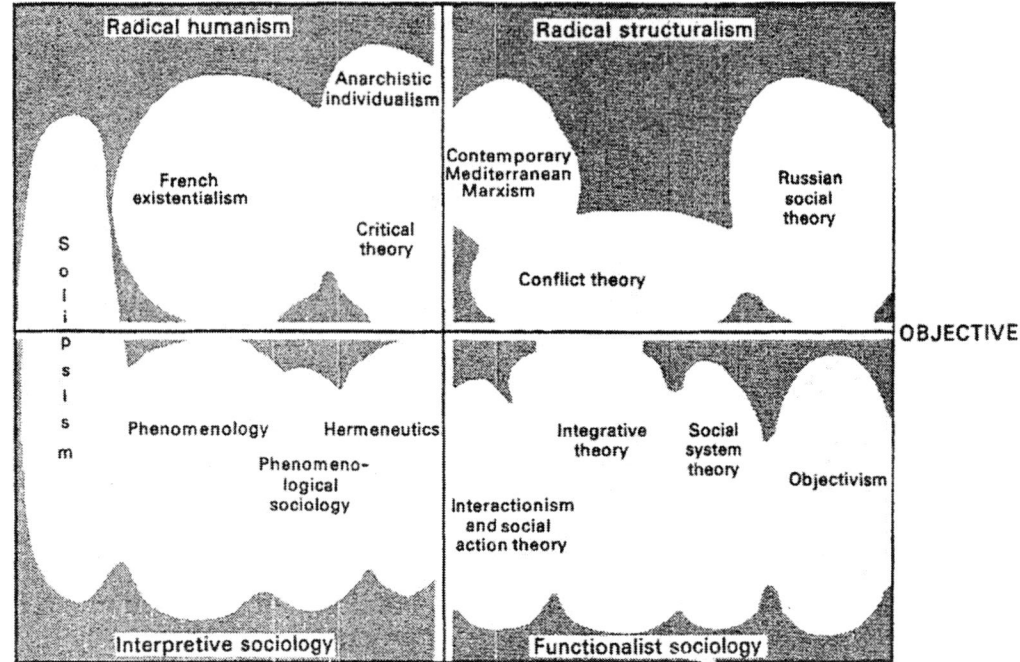

THE SOCIOLOGY
OF RADICAL CHANGE

Radical humanism

Anarchistic individualism

French existentialism

Critical theory

S
o
l
i
p
s
i
s
m

Radical structuralism

Contemporary Mediterranean Marxism

Russian social theory

Conflict theory

OBJECTIVE

Phenomenology   Hermeneutics

Phenomeno-logical sociology

Integrative theory

Social system theory

Objectivism

Interactionism and social action theory

Interpretive sociology   Functionalist sociology

THE SOCIOLOGY
OF REGULATION

(Burrell and Morgan, 1979:29)

6. Conclusions: There Is No View Without a Viewpoint

Scientific research usually begins with a hypothesis (see: Scott and Meyer, 1983; Sawyer and Gamm, 1981; Knoke and Lauman, 1982). This study, however, began with a "why" question: Why, and how, are individuals involuntarily committed to state mental hospitals? The answer to this question eventually produced a methodological innovation. An innovation that we will test—congeneric analysis. The benefits to us for such an innovation are significant. Let me explain.

The emergence of congeneric analysis was not accidental. In fact, it was *inherent* in the methodology of the study. However, normally, scientists do not encounter such problem transformations. That is because they focus their research on the methodology or the data they have gleaned (from within a specific conceptual framework). However, such practices produce too narrow a vision. That is because serendipitous innovation tends to be shut out. Congeneric analysis avoids this problem and allows our analysis to encompass both process and structure within functionalism (see: Barber and Fox, 1958; Pelto and Pelto, 1973:243).

Theoretically, congeneric analysis was also not an accident. However, one might ask: Would another observer have produced the same study from the same observations? Becker (1968:236) has answered; yes, but only if they had used the same theoretical framework and worked on the same problem. That is because "neither the theoretical framework nor the major problem chosen for study is inherent in the group studied." Or, as Robert Lynd (1939) has put it, there is no view without a viewpoint (see also: Rapoport, 1964).

Congeneric analysis also helps us to avoid the problem of misspecifying our universe of study. We were able to avoid this complication because we did not predetermine the environment of the organization under study. However, once tentative relationships were established then a more focused analysis was pursued.

Also implicit in congeneric analysis was the assumption of the penetration of political forces in to our organizations under study. However, such a penetration may not exist. For example, one analysis of the criminal justice system found a doughnut shape for the set of relationships in the field. There were no central political brokers or mediators. And, a national study of the agriculture, energy, health, and labor policy areas also found no political mediators. The researchers called this structure a "hollow core" (Hagan, 1989; Heinz and Manikas, 1992; Heinz, et al., 1990, 1993). Therefore, our assertion that politics molds or constrains organizational actors must be *verified* through empirical research.

Lastly, congeneric analysis, which is simply a methodological innovation, allows us to recapture the focus of early functionalist research: structural process. This type of orientation was characterized by the work of Radcliffe-Brown. Radcliffe-Brown employed this perspective because he believed that many functionalist researchers had overdone the organismic analogy of society. He believed that there were three problems with the functionalist perspective. First, he felt that it was possible to study living structures independently of their functioning in nature; however, in society, individuals cannot be understood without considering the larger social context. Second, although societies were able to elaborate and change their structures, organisms could not. Third, functionalism was based upon the assumption of the functional unity of society. Since this was not a proven fact, it was merely a hypothesis that needed to be tested (1952:181). Burrell and Morgan (1979) felt that these cautions had been forgotten; and the notion of structure, and not process, had become paramount (see also: Silverman, 1970; Colomy, 1992).

So, let us begin our study with the court. We will then move "down" to the admissions office and then to the police. After that we will move "up" to the state's Department of Mental Health and the state legislature and the governor's office.

By including both the direct, and the indirect, influences which effect involuntary civil commitment we can broaden our viewpoint to look beyond the legal and psychiatric perspectives usually taken in such research. In this way our examination of involuntary civil commitment does not become just another study. Instead, it becomes an *exploration* in mental health, law, and politics. That is, by using a vertical and contextual analysis, we can begin to link personal troubles to public issues. In that way, we can begin to employ our sociological imaginations.

References

Aldrich, Howard E.
1979	*Organizations and Environments*. New Jersey: Englewood Cliffs.
—— and Jeffrey Pfeffer.
1976	"Environments of Organizations." *Annual Review of Sociology*. Palo Alto, California: Annual Review Press.
—— and David A. Whetten.
1981	"Organization-Sets, Action-Sets, and Networks: Making the Most of Simplicity." In *Handbook of Organizational Design*, Paul C. Hystrom and William H. Starbuck, eds. 1: Oxford: Oxford University Press.

Algren, Nelson
1961	*Chicago City on the Make*. Oakland, California: Angel Island Publications.

Almond, Gabriel, et al.
1973	*Crisis, Choice, and Change*. Boston: Little Brown.

Argyris, C.
1972	*The Applicability of Organizational Sociology*. Cambridge: Cambridge University Press.

Astley, W. Graham, and Andrew H. Van de Ven.
1983	"Central Perspectives and Debates in Organization Theory." *Administrative Science Quarterly* 28: 245-273.

Banck, Geert A.
1973	"Network Analysis and Social Theory: Some Remarks." In *Network Analysis: Studies in Human Interaction*. Jeremy Boissenain and J. Clyde Mitchell, eds. The Hague: Mouton.

Barber, Bernard and Renee C. Fox
1958	"The Case of the Floppy-Eared Rabbits: An Instance of Serendipity Gained and Serendipity Lost." *American Journal of Sociology* 64; 128-136.

Barker, Lucius, and Donald Jansiewicz
1970	"Coalitions in the Civil Rights Movements." In *The Study of Coalition Behavior*, S. Groennings, et al., eds. New York: Holt, Rinehart, and Winston.

Barnes J.A.
1969	"Networks and Political Process." In *Social Networks in Urban Situations*, J. Clyde Mitchell, ed. Manchester: Manchester University Press.
1972	"Social Networks." *Module Publication* 26. Reading, Massachusetts: Addison-Wesley.

Bar-On, Arnon A.
1990	"Organizational Resources Mobilization: A Hidden Face of Social Work Practice." *British Journal of Social Work*. 20: 133-149.

Bates, F.L.
1970	"Comment: The Political-Economy Approach A Perspective." In *Power in Organizations*, Meyer Zald, ed. Nashville: Vanderbilt University Press.

Baxter, Vern and Charles Lambert
1991	"Competing Rationalities and the Politics of Interorganizational Regulation." *Sociological Perspectives* 34: 183-203.

Becher, Tony and Maurice Kogan
1980   *Process and Structure In Higher Education*. London: Heinemann.
Becker, Howard S.
1968   "Observation." In *International Encyclopedia of the Social Sciences*, David L. Sills, ed. Vol. 11. New York: Macmillan Free Press.
Bennis, Warren
1959   "Leadership Theory and Administrative Behavior." *Administrative Science Quarterly* 14: 259-301.
Benson, J. Kenneth
1977   "Innovation and Crisis in Organizational Analysis." *The Sociological Quarterly* 18: 3-16.
1982   "A Framework for Policy Analysis." In *Interorganizational Coordination*, David L. Rogers and David A. Whetten, eds. Ames: Iowa State University.
Bittner, Egor
1967   "The Police on Skid Row—A Study of Peace Keeping." *American Sociological Review* 90: 801-824
Blau, Peter M. and W. Richard Scott
1962   *Formal Organizations*. San Francisco: Chandler.
Blumer, Herbert
1969   *Symbolic Interactionism*. Englewood Cliffs, New Jersey: Prentice-Hall.
Boje, David M., and David A. Whetten
1981   "Effects of Organizational Strategies and Contextual Constraints on Centrality and Attributions of Influence in Interorganizational Relations." *Administrative Science Quarterly* 26: 387-395.
Boissevain, Jeremy
1974   *Friends of Friends: Networks, Manipulators, and Coalitions*. Oxford: Basil Blackwell.
Borman, Kathryn M., et al.
1986   "Ethnographic and Qualitative Research Design and Why It Doesn't Work." *American Behavioral Scientist* 30: 42-57.
Bucher, R., and A. Strauss
1961   "Professions in Process." *American Journal of Sociology* 66: 325-34.
Bucher, R., and J. Stelling
1969   "Characteristics of Professional Organizations." *Journal of Health and Social Behavior* 10: 3-15.
Burrell, Gibson and Gareth Morgan
1979   *Sociological Paradigms and Organizational Analysis*. London: Heineman.
Buroway, Michael
1991   "Reconstructing Social Theories." In *Ethnography Unbound*, Michael Buroway, et al., eds. Berkeley: University of California Press.
Burt, Ronald S.
1980   "Models of Network Structure." *Annual Review of Sociology*. Palo Alto: Annual Reviews Inc.

Busch, Lawrence
  1980   "Structure and Negotiation in the Agricultural Sciences." *Rural Sociology*. 45:
          26-48.
  1982   "History, Negotiation, and Structure in Agricultural Research." *Urban Life* 11:
          368-384.
Caplow, Theodore
  1964   *Principles of Organization*. New York: Harcourt, Brace, Jovanovich.
Carter, Douglas
  1964   *Power in Washington*. New York: Vintage.
Cavan, Sherri
  1974   "Seeing Social Structure in a Rural Setting." *Urban Life and Culture* 3: 329-346.
Clark, Burton R.
  1983   *The Higher Education System*. Berkeley: University of California Press.
Clarke, Adele E.
  1987   "Research Materials and Reproductive Science in the United States." In *Physiol-
          ogy in the American Context, 1850-1940*, Gerald R. Geison, ed. Bethesda: Ameri-
          can Physiological Society.
  1990a   "Controversy and the Development of Reproductive Sciences." *Social Problems*
          17: 18-37.
  1990b   "A Social Worlds Research Adventure: The Case of Reproductive Science." In
          Theories of Science in Society, Susan E. Cozzens and Thomas F. Gieryn, eds.
          Bloomington: Indiana University Press.
  1991a   "Embryology and the Rise of American Reproductive Sciences, circa 1910-1940."
          In *The Expansion of American Biology*, Keith R. Benson, et al., eds. New
          Brunswick: Rutgers University Press.
  1991b   "Social Worlds/Arenas Theory." In *Social Process*. David R. Maines, ed. New
          York: Adline De Gruyter.
Collins, Randall
  1981   "On the Microfoundations of Macrosociology." *American Journal of Sociology*
          86: 984-1014.
Colomy Paul
  1992   *Introduction. In The Dynamics of Social Systems*. Paul Colomy, ed. London:
          Sage.
Cook, Karen S.
  1977   "Exchange and Power in Networks of Interorganizational Relations." *The Socio-
          logical Quarterly* 18: 2-82.
Cook, Karen S., et al.
  1983   "The Distribution of Power In Exchange Networks: Theory and Experimental
          Results." *American Journal of Sociology* 89: 275-305.
Couch, Carl J.
  1986   "Structural Conditions of Intergroup Negotiations." In *Studies In Symbolic In-
          teraction*, Supplement 2 (Part B), Carl J. Couch, et. al, eds. Greenwich, Conn.:
          JAI Press.

Crozier, Michael
   1972   "The Relationship between Micro and Macrosociology." *Human Relations* 25:
           239-251.
Davis, Nanette
   1975   *The Sociological Construction of Deviance*. Dubuque: Brown.
Day, Robert, and Jo Anne Day
   1977   "A Review of the Current State of Negotiated Order Theory: An Appreciation
           and a Critique." *The Sociological Quarterly* 18:126-142.
Denzin, Norman K.
   1970   "The Methodologies of Symbolic Interaction: A Critical Review of Research
           Techniques." In *Social Psychology through Symbolic Interaction*, Gregory P.
           Stone and Harvey A. Farberman, eds. Waltham, Massachusetts. Xerox College
           Publications.
   1977   "Notes on the Criminogenic Hypothesis: A Case Study of the American Liquor
           Industry." *Sociological Review* 42: 905-920.
   1978   "Crime and the American Liquor Industry." *Studies in Symbolic Interaction* 1:
           887-918.
Dewey, John
   1910   *How We Think*. Boston: Heath.
Diesing, Paul
   1971   "Patterns of Discovery." In *The Social Sciences*. Chicago: Aldine.
Dowling, John, and Jeffrey Pfeffer
   1975   "Organizational Legitimacy: Social Values and Organizational Behavior." *Pa-
           cific Sociological Review* 18: 122-36.
Duster, Roy
   1981   "Intermediate Steps between Micro- and Macro-Integration: The Case of Screening
           for Inherited Disorders." In *Advances In Social Theory and Methodology,* K.
           Knorr-Cetina and A.V. Cicourel, eds. Boston: Routledge and Kegan Paul.
   1990   *Backdoor to Eugenics*. New York: Routledge.
Eckstein, Harry
   1975   "Case Study and Theory in Political Science." In *Strategies of Inquiry*, Fred I.
           Greenstein and Nelson W. Polsby, eds. Reading, Massachusetts: Addison-Wesley.
Emerson, Robert M.
   1981   "Observational Field Work." *Annual Review of Sociology*. Palo Alto: Annual
           Reviews, Inc.
   1991   "Case Processing and Interorganizational Knowledge: Detecting the "Real Rea-
           sons" for Referrals." *Social Problems* 38: 198-212.
Emery, F.E., and E.L. Trist
   1965   "The Causal Texture of Organizational Environments." *Human Relations* 18:
           21-32.
Estes, Carroll and Beverly C. Edmonds
   1981   "Symbolic Interaction and Social Policy Analysis." *Symbolic Interaction* 4: 75-
           86.

Evans, William M.
    1966   "The Organization-Set: Toward a Theory of Interorganizational Relations." In *Approaches to Organizational Design*, James D. Thompson, ed. Pittsburgh: University of Pittsburgh Press.
    1972   "An Organization-Set Model of Interorganizational Relations." In *Interorganizational Decision Making*, Matthew Tuite, et al., eds. Chicago: Aldine.

Fagerhaugh, Shizuko and Anselm Strauss
    1977   *Politics of Pain Management*. Menlo Park, California: Addison-Wesley.

Farberman, H.
    1975a   "Criminoginic Market Structure: The Automobile Industry." *The Sociological Quarterly* 16: 438-57.
    1975b   "Symposium on Symbolic Interaction: An Introduction." *The Sociological Quarterly* 16: 435-37.

Faulkner, Robert R.
    1983   *Music on Demand*. New Brunswick, New Jersey: Transaction Books.

Fennell, May L. And Richard B. Warnecke
    1988   *The Diffusion of Medical Innovations*. New York: Plenum.

Fine, Gary Alan
    1984   "Negotiated Orders and Organizational Cultures." *Annual Review of Sociology*. Palo Alto: Annual Reviews, Inc.
    1991   "On The Macrofoundations of Microsociology: Constrairist and the Exterior Reality of Structure." *The Sociological Quarterly* 32: 161-177.
    1992   "Agency, Structure, and Comparative Contexts; Toward a Synthetic Interactionism." *Symbolic Interaction* 15: 87-107.
    1993   "The Sad Demise, Mysterious Disappearance and Glorious-Triumph of Symbolic Interactionism." In *Annual Review of Sociology*. Palo Alto: Annual Reviews, Inc.

Fligstein, Neil and Robert Freedland
    1995   "Theoretical and Comparative Perspectives on Corporate Organization." In *Annual Review of Sociology*. Palo Alto: Annual Reviews, Inc.

Freeman, John H.
    1978   "The Unit of Analysis in Organizational Research." In *Environments of Organizations*, Marshal W. Meyer, et al., eds. San Francisco: Jossey-Bass.

Freeman, J. Leiper
    1965   *The Political Process*. New York: Random House.

Friedson, Elliot
    1970a   *Profession of Medicine*. New York: Dodd and Mead.
    1970b   *Professional Dominance*. New York: Atherton.
    1973   *The Professions and Their Prospects*. Beverly Hills: Sage.
    1975   *Doctoring Together*. New York: Elsevier.
    1976   "The Division of Labor as Social Interaction." *Social Problems* 23: 304-13.

Fudge, Colin and Susan Barrett
    1981   "Reconstructing the Field of Analysis." In *Policy and Action*, Susan Barrett and Colin Fudge, eds., London: Methuen.

Galaskiewicz, Joseph
   1979   *Exchange Networks and Community Politics*. Beverly Hills: Sage.
   1985   "Interorganizational Relations." In *Annual Review of Sociology*, Ralph Turner, ed. Palo Alto: Annual Reviews.
Geertz, Clifford
   1973   *The Interpretation of Cultures*. New York: Basic.
Gerson, E.
   1977   *Negotiations and Structure: A Comment on Benson and Day*. Unpublished. San Francisco: Pragmatica Systems.
Gilmore, Samuel
   1990   "Art Worlds: Developing the Interactionist Approach to Social Organization." In *Symbolic Interaction and Cultural Studies*, Howard S. Becker and Michael M. McCall, eds. Chicago: University of Chicago Press.
Glaser, Barney
   1976   *The Patsy and the Subcontractor*. New Brunswick, New Jersey: Transaction Books.
Glaser, Barney and Anselm Strauss
   1964   "Awareness Contexts and Social Interaction." *American Sociological Review* 29: 669-79.
   1965   *Awareness of Dying*. Chicago, Aldine.
   1967   *The Discovery of Grounded Theory*. Chicago: Aldine.
Goldman, Howard H., et al.
   1980   "Integrating Primary Health Care and Mental Health Services: A Preliminary Report." *Public Health Reports* 95: 535-39.
Gove, Philip
   1981   *Webster's Third New International Dictionary*, ed. Springfield, Massachusetts: Merriam.
Granovetter, M.
   1979a   *Getting a Job*. Cambridge: Harvard University Press.
   1979b   "The Theory Gap in Social Network Analysis." In *Perspectives on Social Network Research*, P. Holland and S. Linehardt, eds. New York: Academic Press.
Hagan, John
   1989   "Why Is There So Little Criminal Justice Theory? Neglected Macro- and Micro-Level Links Between Organization and Power." *Journal of Research in Crime and Delinquency* 26: 116-135.
Hage, Jerald
   1980   *Theories of Organizations*. New York: Wiley.
Hall, Peter M.
   1972   "A Symbolic Interactionist Analysis of Politics." *Sociological Inquiry*. 42: 35-75.
   1987   "Interactionism and The Study of Social Organization." *The Sociological Quarterly* 28: 1-22.
   1995   "The Consequences of Qualitative Analysis for Sociological Theory: Beyond the Microlevel." *Sociological Quarterly* 36: 397-423.

Hall, Richard H. and John P. Clark
    1974   "Problems in the Study of Interorganizational Relationships." *Organization and Administrative Sciences* 5: 45-65.
Hannan, Michael T. and John Freeman
    1977   "The Population Ecology of Organizations." *American Journal of Sociology* 82: 929-64.
Hasenfeld, Yeheshel
    1972   "People-Processing Organizations an Exchange Approach." *American Sociological Review* 37: 256-263
    1980   "Implementation of Change in Human Service Organizations: A Political Economy Perspective." *Social Service Review* 12: 508-520.
    1983   *Human Service Organizations*. Englewood Cliffs, New Jersey: Prentice-Hall.
Hasenfeld, Yeheshel, and Paul P.L. Cheung
    1985   "The Juvenile Court as a People-Processing Organization: A Political Economy Perspective." *American Journal of Sociology* 90: 801-24.
Hawley, Amos
    1950   *Human Ecology*. New York: Ronald.
Heinz, John P. and Peter M. Manikas
    1992   "Networks among Elites in a Local Criminal Justice System." *Law and Society Review* 26: 831-861.
Heinz, John P., et al.
    1990   "Inner Circles or Hollow Core? Elite Networks In National Policy Systems." *Journal of Politics* 52: 356-390.
    1993   *The Hollow Core*. Cambridge: Harvard University Press.
Hjern, B. and D. Porter
    1983   "Implementation Structure: A New Unit of Administrative Analysis." In *Realizing Social Science Knowledge*. I. Holzer, ed. Wein: Physica-Verlag.
Hood, C. and A. Dunsire
    1981   *Bureaumetrics*. Farnborough: Grover.
Hopkins, Michael
    1980   "The Documentation of Intergovernmental Organizations: A Critical Survey of Supply and Demand Situations in the United Kingdom." *International Social Science Journal* 32: 371-82.
Hurst, Leslie
    1991   "Mr. Henry Makes a Deal: Negotiated Teaching in a Junior High School." In *Ethnography Unbound*, Michael Buraway, et al. eds. Berkeley: University of California Press.
Jacobs, James B.
    1977   *Stateville*. Chicago. University of Chicago Press.
Jurkovich, Ray
    1974   "A Core Typology of Organizational Environments." *Administrative Science Quarterly* 19: 380-394.

Kahne, Merton J. and Charlotte G. Schwartz
  1978   "Negotiating Trouble: The Social Construction and Management of Trouble in a College Psychiatric Context." *Social Problems* 25: 461-475.
Karpik, Lucien
  1977   "Technological Capitalism." In *Critical Issues in Organizations*, Stuart Clegg and David Dunherley, eds. London: Sage.
  1978   "Preface." In *Organization and Environment*, Lucien Karpik, ed. London: Sage.
Katovich, Michael A.
  1986   "Temporal Stages of Situated Activity and Identity Activation." In *Studies in Symbolic Interaction*, Carl J. Couch, et al., eds. Greenwich, Connecticut: JAI Press.
Kemeny, Jim
  1972   "People Processing Organizations: An Exchange Approach." *American Sociological Review* 37, 256-63
  1976   "Perspectives on the Micro-Macro Distinction." *The Sociological Review* 24: 731-752.
Kimberly, John R.
  1976   "Organizational Size and the Structuralistic Perspective: A Review, Critique, and Proposal." *Administrative Science Quarterly* 21: 571-597.
Klady, Leonard
  1998   "H'wood's B.O. Blast." *Variety*. January 5: 2.
Klein, George C.
  2007   *The Adventure: The Quest for My Romanian Babies*. Lanham, Maryland: Hamilton Books/Rowman and Littlefield.
Kleinman, Sherryl and Gary Alan Fine
  1979   "Rhetorics and Action in Moral Organizations." *Urban Life* 8: 275-284.
Knocke, David
  1993   "Networks of Elite Structure and Discussion Making." *Sociological Methods and Research* 22: 23-45.
Knocke, David and Edward O. Lauman
  1982   "The Social Organization of National Policy Domains." In *Social Structure and Network Analysis*. Peter Marsden and Nan Lin, eds. Beverly Hills: Sage.
Krasner, Stephen D.
  1984   "Approaches to the State: Alternative Conceptions and Historical Dynamics." *Comparative Politics* 1: 223-46.
Kreisman, Dolores E. and Virginia D. Joy
  1974   "Family Response to the Mental Illness of a Relative: A Review of the Literature." *Schizophrenia Bulletin* 10: 34-57.
Lammers, Cornelius J.
  1988   "The Interorganizational Control of an Occupied Country." *Administrative Science Quarterly* 33: 438-457.
Lauman, Edward O. and Franz U. Pappi
  1976   *Networks of Collective Action*. New York: Academic Press.

Lauman, Edward O., et al.
  1978   "Community Structures as Interorganizational Linkages." *Annual Review of Sociology*. Palo Alto: Annual Review, Inc.
Lewin, Kurt
  1951   *Field Theory in Social Science*. New York: Harper.
Levine, S. and P. E. White
  1961   "Exchange as a Conceptual Framework for the Study of Interorganizational Relations." *Administrative Science Quarterly* 5: 583-601.
Light Donald
  1980   *Becoming Psychiatrists*. New York: Norton.
Link, B. and B. Milcarek
  1980   "Selection Factors in the Dispensation of Therapy." *Journal of Health and Social Behavior* 21: 279-90
Linton, Ralph
  1936   *The Study of Man*. New York: Appleton-Century-Crofts.
Lipsky, M.
  1980   *Street-Level Bureaucracy*. New York: Sage.
Liska, Allen E.
  1981   *Perspectives on Deviance*. Englewood Cliffs, New Jersey: Prentice-Hall.
Lorber, J.
  1975   "Good Patients and Problem Patients: Conformity and Deviance in a General Hospital." *Journal of Health and Social Behavior* 16: 213-25.
Lorian, R. P.
  1973   "Socioeconomic Status and Traditional Treatment Approaches Reconsidered." *Psychological Bulletin* 79: 263-70.
Lynd, Roberts.
  1939   *Knowledge for What?* Princeton: Princeton University Press.
Madow Michael R.
  1980   "Communication in a Community Mental Health System." *Psychiatry* 43: 324-332.
Maines David R.
  1977   "Social Organization and Social Structure in Symbolic Interactionist Thought." In *Annual Review of Sociology*, Alex Inheles, ed. Palo Alto: Annual Review, Inc.
  1981   "Recent Developments In Symbolic Interactionism." In *Social Psychology Through Symbolic Interaction*, Gregory P. Stone and Harvey A. Farberman, eds. New York: Wiley.
  1982   "In Search of Mesostructure." *Urban Life* 11: 267-279.
Maldonadow, Ernest and Lyle Knowles
  1981   "Inter-Communication between Police Patrol and Detective Personnel." *The Police Chief* 48: 53-55.
Marrett, Cora B.
  1971   "On the Specification of Interorganizational Dimensions." *Sociology and Social Research* 56: 83-99.

Mason, Graham A.,
   1976   "You Have To Have Been There: The Method of Naturalistic Inquiry." In *New Directions in Sociology*, David C. Thorns, ed., Totowa, N.J.: Rowman and Littlefield.

Mast, Sharon
   1983   "Working for Television: The Social Organization of TV Drama." *Symbolic Interaction* 6: 71-83.

Maurer, J. G.
   1971   *Readings in Organizational Theory*. New York: Random House.

Merton, Robert K.
   1957   *Social Theory and Social Structure*, rev. ed. New York: Free Press.

Meyer, John W. and W. Richard Scott
   1983   *Organizational Environments: Ritual and Rationality*. Beverly Hills: Sage.

Meyer, Marshal W.
   1978   *Environments and Organizations*. San Francisco: Jossey Boss.
   1979   *Change in Public Bureaucracies*. Cambridge: Cambridge University Press.

Mijis, A.A.
   1992   "Genesis and Viability of Inter-Organizations: An Institutional Approach." *The Netherlands Journal of Social Sciences* 28: 155-169.

Mills, C. Wright
   1959   *The Sociological Imagination*. London: Oxford University Press.

Milner, Murray, Jr.
   1980   *Unequal Care*. New York: Columbia University Press.

Mitchell, J. Clyde
   1969   "Networks." In *Social Networks in Urban Situations*, H. Clyde Mitchell ed. Manchester: Manchester University Press.
   1973   "Networks, Norms, and Institutions." In *Network Analysis*, Jeremy Boissevian and J. Clyde Mitchell, eds. The Hague: Mouton.

Milward, H. Brinton and H. G. Rainey
   1983   "Don't Blame the Bureaucracy." *Journal of Public Policy* 3.

Mizruchi, Mark S. and Joseph Galaskiewicz
   1993   "Networks of Interorganizational Relations." *Sociological Methods and Research* 22: 46-70.

Moore, Sally F.
   1973   "Law and Social Change: The Semi-Autonomous Social Field as an Appropriate Subject of Study." *Law and Society Review* 7: 719-746.

Morgan, Gareth
   1984   "Opportunities Arising From Paradigm Diversity." *Administration and Society* 16: 306-327.

Morrissey, Joseph P., et al.
   1982a "Assessing Interorganizational Linkages Toward a Systems Analysis of Community Support Programs at the Local Level." In *The Chronically Mentally Ill*, Richard C. Tessler, et al., eds. Cambridge, Massachusetts: Ballinger.
   1982b *Interorganizational Relations*. National Institute of Mental Health, Washington, D.C.: National Institute of Mental Health.

Mulford, Charles L.
    1984   *Interorganizational Relations*. New York: Human Sciences Press.
Nader, Laura.
    1969   "Up the Anthropologist—Perspectives Gained from Studying Up." In *Reinventing Anthropology*, Dell Hymes, ed. New York: Random House.
Noble, Mary
    1973   "Social Networks: Its Use as a Conceptual Framework in Family Analysis." In *Network Analysis Studies in Human Interaction*, Jeremy Boissevain and J. Clyde Mitchell, eds. The Hague, Mouton.
Ostrom, Elinor and Roger Parks
    1981   "Complex Models of Urban Service Systems." *Urban Affairs Review* 21.
Ostrom, Elinor and Vincent Ostrom
    1965   "A Behavioral Approach to the Study of Interorganizational Relations." *The Annals of the American Academy of Political and Social Sciences* 359: 137-46.
O'Toole Richard and Anita O'Toole
    1981   "Negotiating Interorganizational Orders." *The Sociological Quarterly* 22: 28-41.
Overington, Michael A. and Jain L. Mangham
    1982   "The Theatrical Perspective in Organizational Analysis." *Symbolic Interaction* 5: 173-185.
Pelto, Pertti J. and Gretel H. Pelto
    1973   "Ethnography: The Fieldwork Enterprise." In *Handbook of Social and Cultural Anthropology*, John J. Honigman, ed. Chicago: Rand McNally.
Pennings, Johannes M.
    1981   "Strategically Interdependent Organizations." In *Handbook of Organizational Design*, Paul C. Nystrom and William H. Starbuck, eds. New York: Oxford University Press.
Phillips, David P. and Richard Conviser
    1972   "Measuring the Structure and Boundary Properties of Groups: Some Uses of Information Theory." *Sociometry* 35: 235-254.
Prendergast, Christopher and J. David Knottnerus
    1993   "The New Studies in Social Organization: Overcoming the Astructural Bias." In *Interacationism: Exposition and Critique*, Larry T. Reynolds, ed. Dix Hills, New York: General Hall.
Prottas, J. M.
    1979   *People-Processing*. Lexington, Massachusetts: Heath.
Radcliffe-Brown, A.
    1952   *Structure and Function in Primitive Society*. London: Cohen and West.
Raelin, Joseph A.
    1980   "A Mandated Basis of Interorganization Relations: The Legal-Political Network." *Human Relations* 33: 57-68.
Rainey, H.
    1990   "Public Management: Recent Development and Current Prospects." In *Public Administration*, N. B. Lynn and A. Wildansky eds. Chatham, New Jersey: Chatham House.

Rapoport, Anatol
   1964   "The Scientific Relevance of C. Wright Mills." In *The New Sociology*, Irving
           Louis Horowitz, ed. Oxford: Oxford University Press.
Rist, R. C.
   1970   "Student Social Class and Teacher Expectations: The Self-fulfilling Prophecy in
           Ghetto Education." *Harvard Educational Review* 40: 411-51.
Ritzer, George
   1990   "Micro-Macro Linkage in Sociological Theory: Applying a Metatheoretical Tool."
           In *Frontiers of Social Theory*, George Ritzer, ed. New York: Columbia Univer-
           sity Press.
Rosenbaum, J. E.
   1976   *Making Inequality*. New York: Wiley.
Roth, J. A.
   1972   "Some Contingencies of the Moral Evaluation and Control of Clientele: The
           Case of the Hospital Emergency Service." *American Journal of Sociology* 77:
           839-56
Salamon, Lester M.
   1981   "Rethinking Public Management: Third Party Government and the Tools of Gov-
           ernment Action." *Public Policy* 29: 255-75.
Sanday, Peggy Reeves
   1979   "The Ethnographic Paradigm(s)." *Administrative Science Quarterly* 24: 527-538.
Sawyer, Darwin O. and Larry D. Gamm
   1981   "Latent Structures of Vertical Control in Intergovernmental Relations." *Social
           Science Research* 10: 314-336.
Schofield, W.
   1964   *Psychotherapy*. Englewood Cliffs, New Jersey: Prentice-Hall.
Schwartz, Howard and Jerry Jacobs
   1979   *Qualitative Sociology*. New York: Free Press.
Scott, Matthew S.
   1996   "Are You Ready to Invest In The Film Industry?" *Black Enterprise* 27: 5, 66.
Scott, Richard W.
   1967   "The Selection of Clients by Social Welfare Agencies: The Case of the Blind."
           Social Problems 14: 248-57
   1981   *Organizations: Rational, Natural, and Open Systems*. Englewood Cliffs, New
           Jersey: Prentice Hall.
   1983   "The Organization of Environments: Network, Cultural, and Historical Elements."
           In *Organizational Environments*, John W. Meyer and W. Richard Scott, eds.
           Beverly Hills: Sage.
   1985   "Systems within Systems." *American Behavioral Scientist* 28: 601-618.
   1987   "The Adolescence of Institutional Theory." *Administrative Science Quarterly*
           32: 493-511.
Scott, W. Richard and John W. Meyer
   1983   "The Organization of Societal Sectors." In *Organizational Environments*, John
           W. Meyer and Richard W. Scott, eds. Beverly Hills: Sage.

Shankman, Paul
    1984   "The Thick and Thin: On the Interpretive Theoretical Program of Clifford Geertz."
            Current Anthropology 25: 261-279.
Sharkansky, Ira
    1981   "Intergovernmental Relations." In *Handbook of Organizational Design*, Paul C.
            Nystrom and William H. Starbuck, eds. New York: Oxford University Press.
Silverman, Daniel
    1970   *The Theory of Organizations*. London: Heineman.
Stake, Robert E.
    1983   "Stakeholder Influence in the Evaluation of Cities-in-Schools." In *Stakeholder-
            Based Education*. San Francisco: Jossey-Bass.
    1985   "A Personal Evaluation." *Educational Evaluation and Policy Analysis* 7: 243-44.
    1986   "An Evolutionary View of Educational Improvement." In *New Directions in
            Educational Evaluation*, Ernest House, ed. London: Falmer.
Starr, Paul
    1982   *The Social Transformation of Medicine*. New York: Basic.
Starbuck, William H.
    1976   "Organizations and Their Environments." In *Handbook of Industrial and Orga-
            nizational Psychology*, Marvin D. Dunnette, ed. Chicago, IL: Rand McNally.
Stelling, J. and R. Bucher
    1972   "Autonomy and Monitoring on Hospital Wards." *Sociological Quarterly* 13:
            431-46.
Stinchcombe, Arthur L.
    1965   "Social Structure and Organizations." In *Handbook of Organizations*, J.G. March,
            ed. Chicago: Rand McNally.
Strauss, Anselm
    1978a   *Negotiations: Varieties, Contexts, Processes, and Social Order*. San Francisco:
            Jossey-Bass.
    1978b   "Social World Perspective." In *Studies in Symbolic Interaction*, Norman Denzin,
            ed. Greenwich, Conn.: JAI Press.
    1984   "Social Worlds and Their Segmentation Process." *Symbolic Interaction* 5: 123-
            139.
    1985   "Work and the Division of Labor." *The Sociological Quarterly* 26: 1-19.
    1993   *Continual Permutations of Action*. New York: Aldine De Gruyter.
Strauss, Anselm and Juliet Corbin
    1990   *Basics of Qualitative Research*. Newbury Park: Sage.
    1991   "Tracing Lines of Conditional Influence: Matrix and Paths." In *Creating Socio-
            logical Awareness*, Anselm Strauss, ed. New Brunswick, New Jersey; Transac-
            tion Books.
Strauss, Anselm, L. Schatzman, D. Ehrlich, R. Bucher, and M. Sabshin
    1963   "The Hospital and Its Negotiated Order." In *The Hospital in Modern Society*, E.
            Freidson, ed. New York: Free Press.
    1964   *Psychiatric Ideologies and Institutions*. New York: Free Press.

Street, D., G. T. Martin, and L. K. Gordon
  1979   *The Welfare Industry*. Beverly Hills: Sage.
Stryker, Sheldon
  1987   "The Vitalization of Symbolic Interaction." *Social Psychology Quarterly* 50: 83-94.
Sudnow, D.
  1965   "Normal Crimes: Sociological Features of the Penal Code In a Public Defender's Office." *Social Problems* 12, 255-76.
Thompson, James D.
  1967   *Organizations in Action*. New York: McGraw Hill.
Tichy, Noel M.
  1981   "Networks in Organizations." In *Handbook of Organizational Design 2*, Paul C. Nystrom and William H. Starbuck, eds. Oxford: Oxford University Press.
Truman, David
  1968   *Politics and Government in the United States*, 2nd ed. New York: Harcourt, Brace, and World.
Turk, Herman
  1970   "Interorganizational Networks In Urban Society: Initial Perspectives and Comparative Research." *American Sociological Review* 35: 1-19.
Ulmer, Jeffrey.T.
  1995   "The Organization and Consequences of Social Pasts in Criminal Courts." *The Sociological Quarterly* 36: 587-605.
Van de Graaff, John H., et al.
  1978   *Academic Power*. New York: Praeger.
Van de Ven, Andrew H., et al.
  1974   "Frameworks for Interorganizational Analysis." *Organization and Administrative Sciences* 5: 113-129.
Vidich, Arthur and Joseph Bensman
  1958   *Small Town in Mass Society*. Princeton: Princeton University Press.
Walton, Kenneth P. and Patrick Murphy
  1981   "Joint FBI/NYPD Task Forces: A Study in Cooperation." *FBI Law Enforcement Bulletin* 50: 20-3.
Walmsley, Gary L.
  1969   *Selective Service and a Changing America*. Columbus, Ohio: Merrill.
Walmsley, Gary L. and Mayer N. Zald
  1973   *The Political Economy of Public Organizations*. Bloomington: Indiana University Press.
Warren, Carol A. B.
  1982   *The Court of Last Resort*. Chicago: University of Chicago Press.
Warren, Roland L.
  1967   "The Interorganizational Field as a Focus for Investigation." *Administrative Science Quarterly* 12: 396-419.
Warwick, D.
  1975   *A Theory of Political Bureaucracy*. Cambridge: Harvard University.

Weiner, Ronald I.
  1980   "Managing the Interorganizational Environment in Corrections." *Federal Probation* 44: 16-21.
Weiss, Robert S.
  1966   "Alternative Approaches in the Study of Complex Situations." *Human Organization* 25: 198-206.
Wellman, Barry
  1983   "Network Analysis: Some Basic Principles." In *Sociological Theory*, Randall Collins, ed. San Francisco, Jossey-Bass.
Whetten, David A.
  1982   "Issues in Conducting Research." In *Interorganizational Coordination*, David L. Rogers and David A. Whetten, eds. Ames: Iowa State University Press.
White, Harrison C., Scott A. Boorman, and Ronald L. Breiger
  1976   "Social Structure from Multiple Networks: Blockmodels of Roles and Positions." *American Journal of Sociology* 81: 730-780.
Wolfe, A.
  1977   *The Limits of Legitimacy*. New York: Free Press.
Zald, Mayer N.
  1970   "Political Economy: A Framework for Comparative Analysis." In *Power in Organizations*, Mayer N. Zald, ed. Nashville: Vanderbilt University Press.
Zeitz, Gerald
  1974   "Interorganizational Relationships and Social Structure: A Critique of Some Aspects of the Literature." *Organization and Administrative Sciences* 5: 131-139.

II The Court

2 *The Mental Health Court*
The Beginning

1. Introduction

My research began in 1971 on involuntary civil commitment of the mentally ill. I spent three years observing the mental health court where this process occurred. A new mental health code was written in the late 1970s. So, a restudy of the court was undertaken in 1983. A final examination of the court was made in 2004.

The chapter will begin with a brief review of the history of the treatment of the mentally ill. Then there will be a brief overview of the issues involved in involuntary civil commitment. We will begin our description of the process of commitment in the 1960s by Rock (1968) and others. I will then follow this by my own fieldwork from the 1970s, 1983, and 2004.

2. History and the Mentally Disordered

In the Sixteenth Century the deranged were expelled, shipped off, or executed; In the Seventeenth Century the insane were locked up in jails and houses of correction; In the Eighteenth Century madmen were confined to mad houses; In the Nineteenth Century lunatics were sent to asylums; In the Twentieth Century the mentally ill are committed to hospitals; In the Twenty-first Century . . .

K. Jones (quoted in Kittrie, 1971:50)

In ancient times, the laws that governed the mentally ill were taboos and tribal customs (Biggs, 1955; Deutsch, 1949). Until the Golden Age in Greece the prevailing explanations and cures of such illnesses were magical. In the fourth century B.C. Hippocrates recognized mental disorders as natural phenomena. He suggested that the mentally ill should be confined in comfortable, sanitary, and well-lighted housing. Similarly, the Romans believed mental disorders were medical, rather than religious, phenomena.

During the Middle Ages there was great intolerance towards madness. Widespread poverty, disease, mass population movements, and religious fanaticism made the populace of the time fear that the world itself was going mad. In order to stem this tide those who feared a "secret invasion" of madness felt it necessary to persecute those already possessed by devils (Foucault, 1965). Later, strict controls were placed upon the "furiously insane" as well as upon a great many others. Unable to subsist without begging or becoming public charges, the mad, the wretched, the infirm, the retarded, the senile, and the lazy, were all regarded as threats. In Europe, the mad were often chained, thrown into prison, or even executed. Some were driven from the cities to roam the countryside. Still others were sent on pilgrimages to holy places. A common practice in northern Europe was to charter ships and to drop off the mad in uninhabited places. The ships were called *Narrenschiff* or "Ships of Fools."

In the Renaissance hospitals replaced ships as the solution to mental illness (Foucault, 1965: 10-11, 35). This change was not a chance development. Because of the gradual disappearance of leprosy, 19,000 leprosaria were left vacant. These vacated institutions provided the facilities for what Foucault calls "the great confinement." In the *ho'pitaux ge'ne'raus* (general hospitals) of France, *Zuchthausern* (houses of correction) in Germany, and the Bridewells' of England, the poor, unemployed, idle, vagabonds, and insane were all confined. Also incarcerated were the debauched, spendthrift fathers, prodigal sons, blasphemers, and libertines. However, these houses of confinement did not serve as hospitals. Instead, they were for the provision of charity, the maintenance of order, and for moral uplift. These institutions existed because social uselessness was seen as morally reprehensible; and the insane were the most useless of all (Foucault, 1965).

During the Renaissance the "madhouse" was created. In these madhouses the "frenzied and ranting" were confined. Also, confined were the "melancholic," "mad drunks," "madmen deprived of memory and understanding," "madmen benumbed and half-dead," and "madmen of giddy and empty heads" (Foucault, 1965:35-6). In the seventeenth and eighteenth centuries the mad were perceived to be possessed by uncontrolled passion and bestiality. This caused society to turn to discipline and brutality to control the mentally ill.

At this time, however, medicine began to explore the causes of mental illness. At first it was thought that an imbalance of bodily humors was the cause. Later "diseases of the nerves" became the explanation.

In the nineteenth century, madness became a subject of scientific study. With the emergence of "scientific psychiatry" came a shift in the meaning of madness. Madness was transformed from a societal threat to an individual malady. Extreme behavior had to be contained; but "reasonable" restraint and confinement could be employed. This could be done in newly created "asylums" (Foucault, 1965: 247). With the coming of Freud and psychoanalysis this trend was magnified.

The treatment of the mentally ill in America followed that in Europe. In early America the mentally ill were treated in one of two ways. If they were "men of property" their personal finances were used to help support their treatment within a family setting. However, if the person had neither family nor finances they often joined transient bands of drifters. In the strongly Puritanical temper of the times, such vagabonds were considered immoral because of their refusal to work. So charity was not available to them (Deutsch, 1949).

When the mentally ill were violent forcible restraint was used to control them. The constable or sheriff detained them and confined them in a local jail. The first formal statute legally codifying the restraint of the mentally ill was a 1676 Massachusetts law which ordered the town's selectmen to confine "dangerously distracted" persons and others of questionable morality. A Connecticut statute promulgated in 1727 was typical of the laws of the day. It read that "all rogues, vagabonds and idle persons going about in town or country begging, or persons . . . feigning themselves to have knowledge in physiognomy, palmistry, or pretending that they can tell fortunes . . . common drunkards, common nightwalkers, pilferers, wanton and lascivious persons . . . and also persons under distraction and unfit to go at large, whose friends do not take care for their safe confinement" would be confined by the state (Kittrie, 1971:63). With the establishment of asylums in the eighteenth century medicine began to deal with the mentally ill (Rock, 1971).

In early America most mentally ill individuals were confined in poorhouses. In May, 1751 Pennsylvania passed an act written by Benjamin Franklin to establish a general hospital for the treatment of the poor and the mentally ill. In 1773 Virginia erected the first mental hospital. Although a few of the mentally ill began to be housed in asylums, most still lived in poorhouses.

In 1833 an examination of a typical poorhouse, the Boston House of Industry, concluded:

> Instead of being a house of industry the institution has become at once, a general infirmary—an asylum for the insane and a refuge for the deserted and most destitute children of the city. So great is the proportion of the aged and infirm, of the sick, insane, idiots and helpless children in it, that nearly all of the males, is required for the care of those who cannot take care of themselves. (cited in Deutsch, 1949:129)

As the 1800s progressed more and more of the mentally ill were shifted to asylums. The superintendents of some of these asylums began to claim cure rates of over 90 percent. Although these rates were probably greatly exaggerated this spurred the building of more asylums and dispelled the previously held belief that insanity was incurable. However, as quickly as hospitals were constructed, they were filled; and the much-heralded cure rates never materialized:

> Hardly were hospitals opened than their capacities became overtaxed by the never ceasing flow of patients. Overcrowding soon forced upon authorities the problem of selection. Faced with the necessity of admitting a certain number of applicants and excluding others, authorities naturally favored the admission of recent cases over chronic and incurable cases. Gradually then, there developed the custom . . . of sending only acute cases to institutions for the insane while the chronics (sometimes euphemistically called the "surplus insane") were to be confined in poorhouses . . . jails or else supported in the homes of friends or relatives. (Deutsch, 1949:230)

In the 1840s this system began to change (Deutsch, 1949:420-422). In 1845 a habeas corpus action was instituted on behalf of Josiah Oakes. He had been detained on the allegation that he suffered from hallucinations and displayed unsoundness of mind in conducting his business affairs. The charge grew out of the fact that Oakes, an elderly and ordinarily prudent man, had become engaged to a young woman of "unsavory character" a few days after the death of his wife. He sought his release from the McLean Asylum in Massachusetts on the grounds that he had been illegally committed by his family. The court acknowledged that the United States Constitution prohibited the detention of anyone against their will. The only exception to this was if they were deprived of their liberty by the judgment of their peers or the law of the land. The court went on to state:

> The right to restrain an insane person of his liberty is found in that great law of humanity, which makes it necessary to confine those whose going at large would be dangerous to themselves or others . . . And the necessity which creates the law, creates the limitation of the law. The question must then arise in each particular case, whether a patient's own safety, or that of others, requires that he should be restrained for a certain time, and whether restraint is necessary for his restoration, or will be conducive thereto. The restraint can continue as long as the necessity continues. This is the limitation, and the proper limitation. (quoted in Brakel and Rock, 1971:7)

In the 1860s and 1870s state legislatures began to enact statutes which protected the rights of those alleged to be mentally ill. In so doing they were reacting to the abuses of the day. During this period a hospital trustee reportedly remarked: "It seems as if the public believed that every man connected in any way with the hospital for the insane had entered into a conspiracy to deprive the patients of all their rights and do violence to all the relations of life" (quoted in Deutsch, 1949:427).

Public fears of just such a conspiracy were verified by the case of Mrs. Dorothy Packard. She had been confined to an Illinois mental hospital by her husband. However, she claimed that she was not mentally ill and that her husband had merely wanted to get rid of her. Eventually, she was released. Later, through her efforts, many states enacted laws which required jury trials in all commitment cases. Many of these laws were later repealed. However, the legacy of these reforms was that citizens must be dealt with fairly when being involuntarily confined. That is, procedural due process was required (Rock, 1968:17-18).

3. Involuntary Civil Commitment: An Overview

When an individual is in need of mental treatment, but refuses to voluntarily accept such treatment, the state may civilly commit them to a mental hospital (see: Brakel, Parry, and Weiner, 1985). In such cases, mental illness is more than the agony of an individual's madness. It becomes a medical, governmental, administrative, and legal problem, as well. Therefore, the analysis of the involuntary commitment of mentally ill persons is a complex matter.

When involuntarily hospitalizing a mentally ill person the various interests of the community often conflict. Among these opposing forces is the interest of the community in protecting itself from irresponsible or dangerous acts; the interest of individuals in protecting themselves from wrongful or unnecessary confinement; and the general social interest that mentally ill persons receive treatment.

The conflict between these three concerns is minimized in a voluntary hospitalization. In such cases, the patient accedes to a physician's judgment and the decision to hospitalize falls within traditional medical practice. However, if compulsion is required, then the act of hospitalization becomes a medical and legal morass.

The medical decision of whether to hospitalize or not is based, at least theoretically, upon a rather straightforward diagnosis of illness. The legal component in a decision to involuntarily hospitalize an individual rests upon a more complicated base. Within our legal system, compulsion against a person can be exercised only for good reason; and then only in a procedurally fair and reasonable manner. The substantive justification for such compulsion is the exercise of the police power of the state to protect society or its *parens patriae* power to protect individuals unable to protect themselves. The police power of the state has been defined as "that inherent and plenary power in the state over persons and property which enables the people to prohibit all things inimical to the comfort, safety, health, and welfare of society." Compulsory hospitalization and commitment have long been a legitimate recourse of the state when mentally ill persons behave in a manner that is dangerous to themselves or others. *Parens patriae* power, however, concerns the state's duty to protect persons with a disability. It is this justification which allows for guardianship, juvenile court laws, and, commitment statutes. The doctrine of *parens patriae* differs from that of the police power of the state because its focus is based upon the interest of the individual rather than the interests of society (Rock, 1968).

The problem of the involuntary hospitalization and commitment of individuals centers on defining mental illness in a way that is both legally and medically intelligible. Legally, the overriding problem is to define the circumstances under which public power and authority may be used to involuntarily detain and confine a person who has not broken any of the state's laws. The problem that arises in such a decision is that contemporary psychiatric diagnosis is intuitive. If this were not the case then drafting a statute for commitment would be no more formidable than drafting a law for measles quarantine. However, at this point in medical history, diagnoses which fully satisfy legal requirements cannot be provided. The laws governing involuntary hospitalization and commitment of the mentally ill, can, at best, therefore, only approximate a desirable standard of legal precision. For example, in his survey of commitment statutes, Rock concluded that none of the statutes' definitions were satisfactory. That was because "they do not specify independent, objective distinctions between those who require intervention and those who do not. All of them are either so vague that they fail to provide a helpful working . . . definition or they merely beg the question." Rock, however, noted that "practices that are at odds with statutes are not ipso facto right or wrong." Instead they "may simply represent the best accommodation that can be made between large caseloads, . . . limited medical and judicial capabilities, . . . and the principle embodied in the statutes." For "*statutes, after all, are no more than rough blueprints for institutional processes*" (1968:11, 20; emphasis added).

4. The Chicago Court: The 1960s

In the early 1960s there was no workable emergency hospitalization procedure for the mentally ill in Chicago (Cook County). There was also no adequate county treatment facility. When an individual was mentally ill they were brought to the Cook County Mental Health Clinic. It was not a treatment facility. It was at "its best . . . a facility for making diagnoses on an inpatient basis and at its worst . . . [was] simply a detention facility." As a result of this, the clinic functioned as a processing and classification center. Admission to the clinic was contingent upon the presentation of a properly executed petition for commitment and a supporting certificate from a physician. If these documents were presented, admission was automatic; if they were not, then admission was denied (Rock, 1968:174).

In 1960, the clinic processed 8,237 petitions for admission. About 85 percent of the petitions resulted in commitment. Because of the lack of alternatives the only way to receive inpatient treatment was through commitment. And since there were few treatment alternatives, virtually all committed patients were sent to state hospitals. The clinic's administrator blamed the situation on rigidities in the law. However, Rock (1969) concluded that the situation was attributable to fiscal, rather than, legal constraints. Neither Cook County nor Chicago had been willing to finance an appropriate mental health system. The result of this was that all mental health treatment became the state's responsibility. Because of this commitment became nothing more than a mechanical gateway to the state hospital system.

Rock (1968) described the commitment process in the 1960s:

Admitting for the clinic took place in a drab 15 by 15 foot prison-like room. Here, the clerk would explain that no admission could begin without a physician's certificate. Also, no responsibility for the ill person was accepted until the documents were in order. As a result of this the prospective patient was often either left unattended or accompanied by the petitioner as he or she wandered from office to office to complete the paperwork. Hardly anyone was admitted without a physician's certificate. However, doctors were warned: "If not an emergency . . . disregard." As a result of this warning most physicians were reluctant to get involved in the commitment process.

Although the clinic's primary function was diagnostic, it was understaffed even for this function. Rock (1968) found that although the clinic admitted 160 patients per week, it had only four staff psychiatrists. Since two-thirds of the psychiatrists' time was devoted to paper-work and court appearance, only a gross judgment of psychosis could be made in the few minutes each psychiatrist had with each patient.

After the intake interview the patient was examined by a commission of two court appointed physicians who were not affiliated with the clinic. Upon the completion of this examination the judge saw the individual in court. The judge almost always concurred with the physicians. Therefore, the commitment decision was, in practice, a medical one. In these examinations patients were seen for less than five minutes. In not one of the 500 cases observed by Rock was the physician's commitment decision overruled (1968:181).

The hearings were held in a courtroom on the clinic grounds. The courtroom was simply a large room about 20 by 35 feet containing a long table. During the hearings, the judge sat at the center of the table. The ward psychiatrist, an assistant state's attorney (prosecutor), and two court clerks were also seated at the table. A member of the clinic's social service staff was also present in the courtroom. Opposite the judge were additional chairs for the petitioner or witnesses. At one end of the room was a chair for the patients. They were allowed in one by one as their cases were called. Along the walls were several benches which were usually occupied by student nurses or interns. Members of the public were barred from the hearing room. This was justified on the grounds that there was no space available (Rock, 1968).

The court's atmosphere was informal. Neither the witnesses nor the petitioner were sworn before testifying. Sixty cases were heard each day. Each hearing took only a few minutes. The opening question was usually directed towards the patient: "What's the trouble?," "Why are you here?," or "How do you feel now?" A few questions followed that related to the incident which had precipitated the petition. After the patients had completed their testimony they were removed from the room. Then the petitioner and witnesses, if any, were called in from a small waiting room outside the court. Most of the hearing was taken up by the psychiatrist's testimony. It was usually directed towards demonstrating the patient's symptoms to the court. Upon the completion of the psychiatrist's testimony the judge rendered a decision. If the decision was for commitment, the judge asked the relatives about preferences regarding hospital placement (Rock, 1968).

Patients who were believed to be "troublesome" were seen on the ward. Since the court did not wish to upset or provoke these patients, these hearings were brief. In an interview in the early 1970s one nurse described these hearings to the researcher:

> When I was a student nurse I attended the commitment hearings. There was this very old judge who teetered from bed to bed with an assistant state's attorney and a clerk trailing behind him. He'd look each patient in the eye and go, 'Hmmm.' Usually, the patient would mumble something incoherent and the judge would commit them. But no matter what the person said, and no matter how lucid they were, the judge committed them. If each one of these "hearings" took 30 seconds then that was unusual. It was amazing. He treated every patient the same; and I mean that in a negative sense. I was just a student nurse then and I didn't know anything about civil rights, but it was obvious that there was no consideration for the human beings involved. It was like a factory production line—inhuman and impersonal.

Since the admitting and commitment processes were so perfunctory, mistakes sometimes occurred. Kutner (1962) described one such case:

> On October 5, 1960, Mrs. Anna Duzynski, a recent Polish emigrant who lived with her husband on the northwest side of Chicago discovered that $380 in cash had been stolen from her apartment. Suspecting that the money had been taken by the building janitor, the only other person who had a key to the apartment, Mrs. Duzynski rushed to his flat and demanded that the money be returned. The janitor in turn called the police, and upon their arrival stated that both Mr. and Mrs. Duzynski were insane and should be committed to a mental institution. Without any further examination, the police seized both Anna and Michael Duzynski, neither of whom spoke English, and took them in handcuffs to the Cook County Mental Health Clinic. At the Mental Health Clinic, unable to answer questions in English and thereby defend themselves, the Duzynskis were duly pronounced mentally ill and committed to the Chicago State Hospital. Six weeks later, Michael Duzynski still had less idea why he had been imprisoned than he had when thrown into a Nazi concentration camp in World War II. Finally, in desperation, he hanged himself. [When] the gross injustice of the entire affair [was] thus vividly pointed out to them, hospital officials hurriedly released Anna Duzynski the next day.

So, in the 1960's there was merely an "illusion of due process" (Kutner, 1962).

5. The Chicago Court: The 1970s

For the intake worker each new patient was just another case. However, most of those who entered the hospital had been tricked or forced into coming in to the hospital. Erving Goffman (1961) has explained how the routine process of admission becomes a process of "identity stripping" for the patient:

> The recruit comes into the establishment with a conception of himself made possible by certain stable social arrangements in his home world. Upon entrance, he is immediately stripped of the support provided by these arrangements. In the accurate language of some of our oldest . . . institutions, he begins a series of abasements, degradations, humiliations, and profanations of self. His self is systematically, if often unintentionally, mortified. (p. 14; see also: Garfinkel, 1956)

For those who had to appear in court, still another week of anxiety existed. Between the trauma of admission and the ritual of commitment was the dreariness of the *mitimus* (holding) ward.[1] The ward was a limbo where persons waiting for their court hearings were held. The ward itself was shabby. There was a locked door which opened on to the hallway between the two halves of the ward. To the left was the sparsely populated women's section. To the right was the often overcrowded men's section. If you turned towards the right you caught sight of the locked doors of the ward social workers. They interviewed patients singly, and they always kept their doors locked for fear of attack by the patients. If you continued down the hall you reached the locked gate which defined the limits of the patient's living space. The two dormitories were locked during the day. So the men often lay littered about as they slept on the hallway floors. Some men wandered about aimlessly while others sat and stared ahead oblivious to those around them. A few of the inmates performed for their new visitor while most seemed to ignore him. The room itself was painted a sickly municipal green. Rows of chairs were pressed against its walls. "This is just a holding ward," the staff explained, "we just give medication." "How much?" Some staff answered: "A lot." Other staff answered: "Not too much." (However, I did remember a few patients falling off their chairs in court from being overmedicated.) The ward was often overcrowded and it was common for a patient in court to beg not to be sent back up to the *mitimus* ward "because that place can drive you crazy!"

One supervising nurse who had worked on the *mitimus* ward for several years described it as follows:

---

1. A few patients who appeared in court did not come from the *mitimus* ward. These were patients who had entered voluntarily and had been placed on the regular wards. If they wanted to leave, but the staff felt they were too sick to be discharged, the staff then had to "file a petition" and take the individual to court. Also, if patients wanted to leave, but the staff objected, the patient could file a "five day notice" in order to have a hearing. However, most five day notices were withdrawn when the patient was "convinced" by the staff to do so. In such circumstances it was common for the staff to say: "If you cooperate you'll be out of here in a couple weeks. But if you make me go to court, you'll *never* get out of here!" (see: Lewis, *et. al.*, 1984, 1987.)

Mitimus is a hellhole. Ninety percent of the staff have been kicked out of other services. They're "individualistic" and have "strong personalities." They have strong pluses and minuses; and if you can utilize their pluses, you're okay.

The *mitimus* ward has been here for years. For a long time all intake was through here. Until two years ago *mitimus* had the worst reputation of any service at the hospital. The patients and the staff both were violent. From 1950 to 1970 the same administrator ran the place. But he was afraid of his staff. The result was "monolithic anarchy."

Recently, we received a special 10 percent raise. Now security therapy aids make $530 a month rather than $380. But to tell you the truth, I'd put the staff, as well as the patients, in jail!

On the first floor of one of the state hospital buildings was the courtroom.[2] It was a typical courtroom with a judges' bench and a six person jury box. The seats in the jury box were usually occupied by social workers or physicians. A long table was parallel to the judge's bench. Here, the patient, physicians, attorneys, and witnesses sat. There were also about 50 spectator seats behind the rail. The courtroom was open to the public. The seats were usually occupied by students. The patients were called before the court one at a time. Those patients that were waiting their turn usually sat in the first row of the spectator seats. When the case ended the patients were brought through the gate and sat towards the right side of the table. To the immediate right of the patient was their public defender or a private attorney. In the middle of the table were the chairs for the witnesses. To the left sat the ward social worker and the physician. To the far left was the assistant state's attorney (prosecutor).

Between 1971 and 1974 the researcher observed several thousand cases which came before the court. Most cases followed a typical pattern: As each hearing began the clerk handed the patient's court record to the judge. Meanwhile the uniformed bailiffs hovered behind the patient. The defendants were usually poor or black. They were often disheveled, confused, angry, or terrified. Some appeared to be overmedicated. They had either been arrested for disorderly conduct or had been brought to the hospital by relatives or friends for treatment after a disruptive act.

Before the hearing began the patient was usually asked to sign a voluntary admission form. About 10 percent of the patients agreed to this. Otherwise the hearing began. All present were sworn. The physician began by testifying about the examination that he or she had given the patient. The physician usually found the patient to be disoriented in time, place, or person. The patients often suffered from delusions or hallucinations. Many patients possessed paranoid tendencies and some were described as disruptive, violent, or suicidal. A diagnosis of schizophrenia was common. The physician usually concluded that

---

2. Three days a week the court met at one state hospital. Two days a week they met at another state hospital. However, there were few cases heard at the second state hospital. The court would also occasionally have a "private hearing" at a private hospital. However, the vast majority of cases were heard at the primary court. Also, the hearings, no matter where they were held, were essentially the same.

the person was "in need of mental treatment." The state's attorney seldom explored, and the public defender seldom challenged, the doctor's testimony with more than a few perfunctory questions. The social worker from the ward then usually presented a brief social history. The social worker usually ended with a note on any previous psychiatric hospitalizations. If any friends, relatives, or other interested parties were present, they were then allowed to speak. Lastly, the patient was allowed to make a statement. At the conclusion of this process the judge ruled on whether or not to commit the patient. Commitment was common.

Over the three-year period that the researcher observed the court almost all of those who were brought before it were found to be "in need of mental treatment." For example, in a random sample of thirty-three cases that were observed the judge followed the doctor's recommendation in almost every case. However, in about a third of these cases the physician's testimony was vague; therefore, it was not clear if the patient had met the legal requirements for commitment. In another forty percent of the cases, usually lasting a minute or two, the patient had already agreed to a voluntary admission or the judge convinced the patient to sign a voluntary admission form in court. In another randomly selected sample of eighty-eight cases that the researcher observed almost ninety percent of the cases produced a commitment. In most of the remaining ten percent of the cases the individual was remanded to the custody of the sheriff (to stand trail on criminal charges—all misdemeanors). In this sample the hearings were brief, even cursory. They lasted from one to twenty-six minutes; the average hearing was about seven minutes. A third random sample contained twenty-six cases. In thirteen of these cases the patients were white and an equal number were black. There were no Hispanics. Twenty-one of the individuals were male. The white males, twelve in number, were between twenty and fifty years of age. The black males, ten in number, were predominately in their twenties. The females of both races were mostly in their twenties (four out of the five).

A few typical cases follow:

Sarah D.,[3] a sixteen-year-old white female, was seated at the table and the hearing began. The doctor testified that Sara has been "quiet, withdrawn, and slow. She did not communicate or interact with others on the ward although she had been cooperative. She was delusional, showed fragmentary thinking, conceptual disorganization, and had bizarre delusions about controlling Sonny and Cher. The devil controls her mind and she hears his voice," he said. "She is also suicidal," he added.

"She has shown a gradual improvement in the hospital but she still retains an underlying despair which is brought on by being lost and forsaken by her family and friends. The patient's reality is harsh because of her social, family, situation. She must stay in the hospital," the doctor concluded.

The doctor then added: "She is oriented in time and place but is schizophrenic with paranoid trends or is schizo-affective. She is currently receiving medication."

---

3. All patients' names are fictionalized.

The public defender asked if it was possible that she was "just talking" and meant little of what she said. "Yes," the doctor said, "but . . . when she came in she had been in an acute psychotic state, but now she is better."

The judge then called on the ward social worker to testify. The social worker said that "none of Sarah's relatives wanted to come to the hearing. Her husband is in jail and her child has been placed in a foster home. She has had previous hospitalizations. Her behavior on the ward has been unpredictable and she has said she is controlled by others. I doubt whether she is able to take care of herself."

The judge then asked Sarah to speak on her own behalf. She explained in a lucid and reasonable manner that she had been arrested while standing in front of a hospital to which she had been trying to gain admission. She said she did hear voices. However, she denied any suicidal tendencies. The one exception to this was once, long ago, but she had not acted on that occasion. She went on to explain that "Sonny and Cher are part of me but I don't feel I control them, not as much as before." She concluded that she had been previously hospitalized but now wanted her freedom.

The doctor then somewhat defensively added, "She fluctuates, sometimes she's good and sometimes she's bad. But she's better in court today than ever before."

The public defender then asked for another examination. "No," the doctor said, "I've seen her almost every day; that won't be necessary."

The judge committed her.

Robert B., a thirty-year-old black male, was led into the courtroom at 10:54 a.m. The doctor said that Robert was in need of treatment and that a voluntary admission would be acceptable to him. The social worker added that Robert had had a hospitalization three months ago. The judge nodded, Robert signed the form, and he left the courtroom. It was 10:55 a.m.

Albert A., a middle aged man, was led to his chair and he sat down. The doctor testified that Albert was an alcoholic and mentally ill. The doctor noted that he had delusions about atomic bombs. The patient then spoke coherently and sensibly about his situation, except for his mention of atomic bombs.

The judge leaned forward in his chair and asked:

"How long have you been here?"

"Since Thursday."

"How many days is that?"

"Six," the patient correctly replied.

"Where are you?"

"The state hospital."

The judge leaned back in his chair. "I think you've got to stay in the hospital. I find you in need of mental treatment."

The hearing began as the doctor testified concerning the condition of Jack L., a 26-year-old white male. The doctor said that she had examined Jack on two separate occasions. "During the first examination Jack had been very restless, agitated, preoccupied, and had difficulty in concentrating on the conversation. He had wanted to be cooperative but hadn't been able to." She added that he had broken a window early in his hospitalization. The doctor went on to explain that "during the second examination Jack had heard voices and had hallucinations. Two weeks previous to this hospitalization Jack's father had thrown him out of the house. This had made him angry and had eventually led to his hospitalization. He has told me: 'I am going crazy with my girl pretty face.' Furthermore, he has been on drugs for five years and has told me: 'My mind is slipping and my memory is poor.' The patient had been depressed with suicidal feelings during the interview, although he had denied any attempts on his life. He manifested inappropriate affect." She concluded that "he is schizophrenic, chronic undifferentiated, and is currently suffering an acute psychotic episode." She paused. "Jack has been passive on the ward but has seemed anxiety ridden and fearful. Jack seems to respond to external stimuli that are not present. He has shown no improvement since the beginning of his hospitalization." The doctor concluded that he was unable to take care of himself.

The ward social worker then testified that "Jack has four previous hospitalizations and was last released a month ago. He has told me that he had been living on the street for the last two weeks. He had begun using drugs while away at college. Since returning he worked for three years. However, he has not worked for the last two years." The social worker concluded that "Jack had been very well behaved on the ward, but very quiet and withdrawn."

The patient, in a somewhat loose and rambling manner, testified that "my mother is 54 years old and senile. She upsets me sometimes so I come to the hospital and stay here a while. I've used drugs and sometimes I have hallucinations about seeing nice, pretty people. I sometimes get lost in my mind."

The judge asked if he had broken the window.

"No," he replied.

"Did a voice tell you to break the window?" the judge asked.

"I don't hear voices." He paused. "I won't remember this day."

The judge committed him.

Individuals can only be committed if they are found to be a "person in need of mental treatment." That is, a person may be committed only if they are mentally ill and a threat to themselves or others. Specifically, the Illinois Mental Health Code states that "any person afflicted with mental illness, not including a person who is mentally retarded," may be committed if, "as a result of such mental illness, [he or she] is reasonably expected at the time the determination is being made or within a reasonable time thereafter to intentionally or unintentionally physically injure himself or other persons, or is unable to care for himself so as to guard himself from physical injury or to provide for his own physical needs. This term does not include a person whose mental processes have merely been weakened or impaired by reason of advanced years" (Section 1-11).

In implementing the statutes the court's legal responsibility is to protect those unable to protect themselves and to insure public order. In performing these functions the court is legally obligated to adhere to both the statutes and procedural due process. The decision as to who fulfills the criteria for commitment is in the judge's hands. In practice, however, the judge commits when the examining physician decides the person is in need of treatment and releases the patient when the physician concludes that they are no longer in need of treatment. Because of this reliance on the physician, and the medical model in the decision-making process, the legal "niceties" of due process are often overlooked or circumvented. When a question of the lack of due process arises, the court personnel explain: "We are merely involved in a civil hearing to ascertain the facts. We are not trying a criminal case."

Kutner has noticed "a great discrepancy between the theoretical (statutory) and the practical ways in which persons are committed to mental institutions. The legal profession laboriously constructs elaborate provisions to guarantee that no person shall be committed without 'due process of law'; then the medical profession quietly circumvents much of this procedural 'red tape' because of the requirements of medical propriety" (1962:384; see also: Lemert, 1945, 1946; Warren, 1977).

In fact, in Chicago, the mental health court is not conceived of by the staff as a court at all. Instead, it is seen by the court personnel as a social service agency established "to help people." The state's attorney once said: "This is not an adversary hearing. We're all here just to help the patient; I don't prosecute, and the public defender doesn't defend, it's not an adversary procedure. It's 'a hearing'." The assistant state's attorney's role, as part of the "helping team," is to represent the hospital staff and to push for commitment if there is any hint of violence in the record. In this way the public is protected and the state's attorney's office is "covered." The public defenders hold similar attitudes: "I often find myself 'prosecuting' people just to keep them in the hospital; that way the person who needs help can stay here a couple of weeks and then be discharged." When an individual has been committed to a state hospital, the criminal charges against them are usually dismissed or "stricken with leave to reinstate." Therefore, the public defender, or even the judge, may recommend to a person who "needs help," but who they feel does not meet the criteria for hospitalization, that they "sign themselves in" in order to avoid the criminal charges. Although such practices are of dubious legality, they are appropriate for a "helping agency" (see: Gilboy and Schmidt, 1971; see also: Lindman and McIntyre, 1961; Brakel and Rock, 1971; Brakel, Parry, and Weiner, 1985; Warren, 1977; Lewis et al. 1984; Treffert, 1973, 1985: Zimmerman, 1982).

A few typical examples of such cases follow:

The patient, Fred H., a 35-year-old male, was led in to the courtroom. The hearing began with the doctor's testimony. The doctor felt the patient was definitely psychotic. He was "schizophrenic with chaotic delusions. The patient feels persecuted and he is autistic. However, he is not dangerous to himself or others."

The patient then said that he wanted to go back to jail. The doctor injected that Fred could take care of himself. "You would be better off signing a voluntary," the judge advised. "No," the patient replied, "I want to go back to jail." The judge shook his head and discharged the case. He remanded the man to the custody of the sheriff.

Alfred L., an elderly black male, took his seat in the courtroom. The hearing began as the doctor testified that Alfred was alert, aware of time and place, and in superficial contact with reality. However, the doctor observed that during the interview the patient had presented some "implausible" information. The doctor said that Alfred had been drinking for years. The doctor then noted that there had been gradual improvement since his arrival at the hospital but it was evident that he was "a chronic, low grade schizophrenic" whose condition was complicated by alcoholism. She felt he was not a threat to himself or others. Therefore, she recommended his discharge.

The judge was dumbfounded. "You mean a man in his condition can take care of himself?"

"He's psychotic, but he can."

"If he's psychotic, he should be in a hospital."

"He can function in a limited environment."

The judge turned to the patient. "You were born in 1910?"

"Yes."

"Do you have a job?"

"Yes, as a day laborer."

"Where have you been living?"

"On the Southside in a vacant house."

"How many times have you been in a hospital?"

"I lost count."

The judge turned back to the doctor. "Why can't a man like this go over to geriatrics?"

"He's too young, you must be 65."

"Where would he go?" the state's attorney asked. The judge looked disgusted.

"I have no choice but to discharge him to the sheriff. Somebody has to take care of him."

A handsome, but poorly dressed, 70-year-old man entered the courtroom and took his seat next to the public defender. The hearing began as the patient, in a French accent reminisce of Maurice Chevalier, explained that he needed a place to stay. He explained that he was a musician but had fallen on hard times. He gave a brief description of his life and told several vignettes from his career. Everyone in the courtroom was charmed. Finally, the judge called on the doctor to testify. He said the patient was disoriented in time but knew his age and date of birth. "There's no mental illness," the doctor said, "only senile dementia. There's just no one to take care of him." He signed himself into the hospital. Everyone was pleased.

A poor, shabby looking elderly man sat down at the witness table. The social worker began the hearing by testifying that Mr. D. had "acted out towards the manager of his boarding home."

"Sure I did, he called me a bastard," the patient retorted.

"Where will you go if you're released?" the judge asked. The patient shrugged.

The doctor testified that the patient was "passive-resistive and schizophrenic, chronic-undifferentiated." The doctor's testimony had not sounded very convincing. After a long pause, the judge concluded: "This is really a social problem." The judge paused again. After some thought, he committed the man.

The court's decisions are made "to help." However, public order is also on the judge's mind. That is why the elderly, drug abusers, alcoholics, and young offenders are all commonly committed. In this way, they are "helped" and "kept off the street." For example, in a study of commitment in California, Maisel found that "reluctance to release 'bad actors' is merely a more flamboyant instance of the wide range of extra psychiatric factors which govern decisions to [commit or] release patients—as any hospital social worker will freely admit. Living accommodations, jobs, helpful relatives or friends, [and] financial solvency enter into such calculations" (1971:359n; see also: Whitmer, 1980; Warren, 1977).

One place where social factors would play an appropriate role is in the decision on what type of placement or form of treatment a patient required. For example, the Illinois Mental Health Code requires that the judge "as part of the hearing shall consider the alternative forms of care or treatment which are desirable for and available to the patient, including but not limited to hospitalization" (Section 9-6). However, the judges seldom do this. At the end of every hearing in which someone was committed the judge routinely asked, "What hospital?" A social worker then responded with the name of a state hospital. That ended the proceeding.

Of all the court personnel involved in the commitment process it is the public defenders who find themselves in the most awkward position. They reject the role of advocate, whose function is to contest commitment. Instead, they take on the role of a counselor, whose job it is to determine what appears to be in the client's best interest. However, when lawyers act as counselors in the ordinary lawyer-client relationship, they assist in the clients' pursuit of their own goals. However, at the mental health court many of the patients are unable to define their own interests. As a result of this the public defenders, as well as the prosecutor, have decided that their goal is "to help." Therefore, when their clients are "sick" they try to help them by getting them into the hospital (see: Wexler, 1981; Lewis, et al., 1984). Gilboy and Schmidt found a similar attitude among the attorneys they studied. One attorney commented:

> You know that this court proceeding is not like other criminal proceedings. This is not an adversary proceeding, where you want your case off no matter what. Here they need care. You understand? Sometimes I have to fight to keep them here. So you do not want them to leave. They could blast their head open [at the jail]. (1971:448n; see also: Morris, 1978:422-6)

In defending their clients the public defenders could ask for an independent psychiatric examination or an in-depth investigation. In Los Angeles Rock (1968) found that the public defenders used the threat of a jury trial to force a closer examination of borderline cases. In Chicago, however, the public defenders was part of the "helping team" who "worked with" the doctor, assistant state's attorney, and judge to help put people into the hospital who were sick. As part of "the team" the public defender appeared to actively discourage jury trials because it disrupted the functioning of the court. Also, most of the public defenders who served in the court were young and eager for "real" trial work. They privately commented that they found the commitment hearings routine, dreary, and emotionally exhausting. One public defender commented that "after six months it begins to wear on you so that you want to run away!" As a result of this, most public defenders applied for transfers after a relatively short period of time at the mental health court. During their waiting period they usually would "go along with the program." Some public defenders had taken the position at the court as a favor to their supervisors and filed for a transfer a few days after arriving.

Under such circumstances the public defenders did not wanted to "rock the boat" for the few months they served at the court. Those public defenders that stayed at the court for some time were usually older and felt comfortable in their "helping" role.

Irrespective of a particular public defender's attitude the practical limitations of the job circumscribed their advocacy. For example, each morning before the court met, the public defenders went up to the *mitimus* ward to interview the 10 to 20 patients they were to defend that day. Because of time limitations they seldom had more than a few minutes with each patient. Also, if they were available, the public defender reviewed the patient's records and any information concerning the patient's arrest. However, they did not have the patient's medical file available before the interview. Because of this, they were not able to review the doctor's report, the nursing notes, or the social investigation before the court hearing.

While conducting interviews on the ward, the public defenders identified themselves to the patients and informed them of their right to a private attorney. Since most of the patients were indigent the public defender defended them. The public defender then took a brief history focusing on the arrest or precipitating incident that led to the hospitalization. The public defender might then ask, "Why don't you sign yourself in?" Little further explanation was given concerning voluntary admission.

In other jurisdictions the public defenders were also often young, inexperienced, and had little training in mental health. Gilboy and Schmidt quoted one public defender as saying: "We had a patient that put a baby in a tub of water and put the hot water on the baby. The baby was scalded badly and the woman did not immediately take it to the hospital . . . In the court she stated that she wanted to go back to her baby. A real human emotion. But you know, you just don't know" (19781:448n).

Occasionally, private or Legal Aid attorneys would defend patients. On such occasions the patients were vigorously defended. For example:

The patient, a slightly built black woman in her twenties, and her Legal Aid attorney, sat jovially chatting before court convened. The judge called the court to order and began the hearing with the doctor's testimony.

The doctor explained that the patient had arrived one week ago. She had one hospitalization two weeks prior to her current admission but had been released after a jury trial. The doctor testified that the patient, Andrea L., "had been restless, agitated, angry, and hostile on the day of her admission." Although the patient denied it, the doctor felt Andrea had been taking drugs immediately preceding the hospitalization. Two days later the doctor had seen her again when she refused to take medication. Four days after that, however, the patient was well-oriented, cooperative, and completely different.

"I was no different," the patient angrily broke in.

The doctor continued. "I have detected no indications of hallucinations or delusions and the patient has denied any knowledge of the reason for her arrest. I feel the patient has been evasive, callous, and has shown inappropriate affect. In my opinion the patient is covering up a deep depression and an uncontrollable rage."

"I object to 'rage'," the Legal Aid attorney angrily interjected. "Sustained," the judge ruled.

"What did Miss L. say which led you to these conclusions?" the Legal Aid attorney asked the physician.

"Well," the doctor paused and deeply inhaled, "actually, she wouldn't talk to me." The Legal Aid attorney slammed his hands against the table as he turned away in disbelief.

The doctor then hurriedly concluded that "the patient is schizophrenic, paranoid type with sociopathic trends. I feel the patient can't take care of herself and is a threat to others. She is, therefore, in need of a 'short hospitalization' to control her rage."

The Legal Aid attorney, in a sarcastic tone of voice, asked if the doctor had passed her psychiatric boards. "No," she answered, "but in Illinois an M.D. becomes a psychiatrist after practicing in a state hospital for a year. And I've been here 17 years!" she triumphantly concluded.

The judge intently leaned forward. "Is she psychotic?"

"Maybe," the doctor answered.

The social worker then testified that "the patient has been divorced twice and has three sons. She doesn't know why she was brought here and feels she doesn't need hospitalization." The social worker thought that the patient had been picked up on a warrant and brought to the hospital. Then the social worker added that "the patient has told me that her mother had signed her into the hospital the last time so she could 'get a rest'."

Two of the patient's friends then testified. One commented that "there was an altercation at a party and Andrea was wrongfully arrested." The other friend said that "Andrea is a good mother and has never done anything out of the ordinary."

The social worker then noted that "the patient has worked at the Post Office for the last six years. She has been a career employee but was injured on the job and has not worked for the last six months." She stated that the patient had told her that she was "anxious to get home and take care of her children."

The patient then spoke in a coherent manner about her job and the medications she took. She said that she had medication for her "nerves and pain" but does not take the "nerve medicine." The patient stated that she had been transferred to the hospital from the House of Correction. "I request a directed verdict," the Legal Aid attorney asked.

"Discharged, back to the House of Correction," the judge concluded.

Some time later I spoke with two Legal Aid attorneys who handle commitment cases. "As lawyers," one of the attorneys explained, "I believe in a presumption of innocence and so forth. And I oppose the idea that the psychiatrist knows best. I see myself as a legal overseer of the medical process. I'm a 'patient advocate'."

"It's a pretty even match between a good lawyer and good psychiatrist," the other attorney continued, "but at the commitment court, the doctors aren't so hot." He paused. "Psychiatrists aren't good at predicting dangerous behavior, and the commitment court's doctors, even less good. I feel that unless there's been some evidence of a recent overt act, a mere prediction by a permit physician isn't good enough to take someone's liberty away."[4]

"It's not a question of good intentions," the first attorney added, "it's that abuses begin to develop."

---

4. See below for a discussion of permit physicians.

"The real issue is an ethical one." The other lawyer added: "What is the lawyer's responsibility? Lawyers shouldn't be forced to second guess what's good for their clients. A lawyer should simply talk the case over with their client and if the client wants out, then the lawyer should try and get him out. The public defenders are a prime example, an exemplary case, in how to go about this thing in the wrong way. They 'selectively defend' their clients. They have told me that they are willing to 'take a fall' because they've 'got to be responsible.'" The attorney shook his head. "My job is to warn the patient that anything they say to the psychiatrist could be used in court. I'm sure the public defender doesn't do that. You know, sometimes the public defender even brings out psychoses in the courtroom. 'Tell me about the radio waves'." He smiled. "I know they feel they're just trying to bring out the facts, but . . . There was even this epileptic that the public defender let them commit because the guy didn't have any place to go. Most of the public defenders in the commitment court are just out of law school and they get hustled. Also, there's no reinforcement for being tough or innovative. However, Legal Aid lawyers like to win, and innovation is important for us."

The other lawyer broke in. "It's sort of sick that the public defender, the assistant state's attorney, and the judge all ride around together and are all chummy." He then got up and began to pace the room. The first one went on. "There's also a problem with time. Some of the patients are held too long before being brought to court. One of the judges once admonished the Department of Mental Health on that, but another one said, 'What are you crying about, you and the patient are here.' Another point is all these 'voluntaries' that get signed, that's just like plea bargaining."

Suddenly the other attorney spoke up. "As a lawyer I believe in all this stuff about rights, and I do my job, but as a person, these people need help!"

Since the attorneys usually do not play a crucial role in the court proceedings, the two key actors in the process are the physician and the judge. The decision to commit or discharge a patient is by law in the hands of the judge. However, in reality, the decision is the doctor's. If they say "commit," the judge must either commit the patient or ask for a second examination. Asking for a second opinion requires the judge to send the patient back to the overcrowded *mitimus* ward. This is not considered to be a viable alternative. One judge explained: "It's not my job to procrastinate. I can't create a backlog." The judges also follow the physician's recommendation when they find that a patient is not in need of mental treatment. The only time a truly independent judicial decision is reached is when the physician equivocates. Most of the time, however, the judges simply follow the physician's recommendation. For example, after months of observing one judge sit placidly before the court, the following incident occurred:

During the testimony of one of the physicians the judge suddenly exploded. "What studies confirm that paranoid people are dangerous?"

"A certain percentage of paranoid people injure themselves or others."

"What percentage?"

"Even if it's only nine-tenths of one percent then that should be considered."

The judge did not seem convinced. "Do we hospitalize everyone in this class? Are they all dangerous?"

"Depends on the patient," the doctor meekly replied.

The judge then settled back in his chair and the testimony continued.

The patient in that case was diagnosed as paranoid schizophrenics. The judge committed him.

The physicians at the court were all foreign born. Many spoke broken English and most of them were working there because they had been unable or unwilling to pass the state licensing exam. They were called "permit physicians" and they were allowed to practice only in state hospitals run by the Illinois Department of Mental Health. However, the law stated that any physician who worked for one year in a state hospital was then considered to be a psychiatrist. In spite of this, few of these physicians had any training in psychiatry. And what training they did have came from the in-service seminars that were provided by the state's Department of Mental Health (see: Wexler, 1981:101-106).

In interviews each of the foreign born physicians confided to the researcher that they felt that all the *other* foreign born physicians at the hospital were only marginally competent. And it was common for these physicians to shake their heads in disbelief at another foreign born physician's testimony at a commitment hearing. However, it was also common for the situation to reverse itself a few cases later.

Concerns about the quality of the permit physicians reached a crisis in 1977. The state legislature had passed a law that mandated that all permit physicians pass the state licensing examination. The Department of Mental Health employed 330 physicians at the time. Many of these physicians had private practices and worked for the department only a few hours a week. However, almost the entire ward level staff at most state hospitals were full-time permit physicians. After the statue was passed the department's 158 permit physicians were required to take the licensing examinations. Thirty-one of the physicians refused. For the remaining 127 physicians a special examination was made up. Questions were drawn from state licensing examination in the fields of psychiatry, neurology, and internal medicine. Outside physicians privately admitted the questions were among the easiest that could have been offered. To make the examination even easier, it only included questions that 92 percent of the doctors taking the complete test had passed. The examination was also curved. The best possible score was 800 points. When the examination was given these physicians averaged about 235 points. Some physicians scored as low as 5 points. All of the 127 permit physicians who took the examination failed (Parachini, 1977a, 1977b).

An extreme example of the quality of permit physicians employed by the department appeared in a front-page article in a local newspaper under the title: "Eccentric or Insane? Mental Health Court Anguish":

Myrtle R. mutters to herself a lot, but she's been able to hold down a job in the packing company for 25 years.

Should she be put in a mental hospital? Floyd D. thinks he's Irving Berlin. He doesn't work, but sits around home humming his tunes. He lives with his mother and sister, who say he's a gentle soul.

Should he be forced to go to a mental hospital?

Questions like these confront the Mental Health Court every day, and attorneys for the Legal Aid Society are unhappy with many of the answers.

"People are forced to undergo the anguish and indignities of mental commitment only because they are eccentric," says a legal aid attorney.

Both Myrtle and Floyd were committed to state hospitals, although no evidence was submitted in either case to indicate they were dangerous or couldn't care for themselves—the only grounds for commitment.

In both cases, the physicians who recommended commitment were not licensed to practice medicine in the state.

The two doctors were trained in Eastern Europe and hold temporary permits to practice at state hospitals. They examine a majority of [the] 2,200 commitment cases appearing annually before the court.

Temporary permits are supposed to be in effect only long enough for foreign-trained doctors to take brush-up courses so they can pass state licensing examinations. But one of the court's doctors had held her temporary permit since 1955 and the other has had hers since 1967.

Neither has taken state licensing tests and neither would be admitted to the staffs of private hospitals.

Issuing temporary permits to foreign-trained doctors seems to be the only way the state Mental Health department can staff the hospitals. As a result, there often is a severe language barrier between psychiatrist and patient.

In one recent case involving a Vietnam veteran, a doctor was trying to tell the judge what he had learned about the young man in an interview.

"With the danger we have today in our society . . . Now, this man drinking and being a paranoid individual has delusions of grandeur.

"My diagnosis schizophrenia, paranoid type. Present condition severe by the history. Impairment of motor rate too severe."

At this point the public defender interrupted: "I didn't understand that."

The doctor replied, "I am sorry. I am a Cuban I do not speak English fluent that you can't understand it."

The judge suggested that the young veteran be reexamined.

The doctor seemed insulted. "But I talk only a few words with a patient and I know immediately what the patient is."

The judge said, "The order will be that there be an additional examination, and by another doctor."

In another case, a man brought to the hospital by his wife was extremely upset when a physician testified he had a fetish for burning paper.

The doctor said, "He told me, 'I burn paper on the stove. That is my business, burning paper.' "

The man insisted, "I don't know anything about that. I don't burn paper."

Finally the doctor said: "I saw two patients that are in court today. Now, it is possible the next patient may have said this."

Except for the paper-burning fetish, the doctor did not have much to say about the man. He was "negativistic," he showed "thought disorder" and he felt his wife "plotted" to get him into a mental hospital.

His wife, in her testimony, said he had threatened to "hurt" her. He never had actually struck her, she said, but she was frightened.

A judge denied the public defender's motion for a mistrial or a new trial and the man was committed to a mental hospital. (Wille and Sodomka, 1973)

The court is officially titled the "Mental Health Court." However, almost everyone who works there simply calls it "the commitment court." The persons who are brought before it are always called "patients" and never "defendants." Implicit in the actions of the physician is the belief that anyone who is ill is a person "in need of treatment" (hospitalization). Warren has concluded that the consideration of individual rights and the protection of society have been displaced "by considerations of the relief of family tensions and the smooth functioning of the mental health system" (1982:175; 1977; see also: Luckey and Berman, 1979.) Similarly, Applebaum and Ham (1982) found that the key variables in commitment were mental illness, a place to live, and support on the outside (see also: Bachrach, 1976, 1980; Chase, 1973).

In Illinois, when a physician finds a patient who "needs to be in a hospital" they will urge the court to commit that person (see: Rothman and Dubin, 1982). However, if the physician's testimony is unconvincing the public defender may challenge it. If pressed by the public defender it is fairly common for a physician to stammer that "a person is dangerous to himself . . . in the sense that . . . he may get into situations . . . in which people may misunderstand him . . . and therefore . . . in those types of situations . . . he could get hurt." In desperation physicians have even blurted out: "Of course he's dangerous, he was arrested, wasn't he?"

In such a system the judges feel trapped. They must be careful because they can not release an individual who will leave the court and commit a murder. For example, McGarry (1981) has pointed out that in the court he observed patients were committed if they displayed "harmful behavior." However, on the average such behavior had occurred 18 and a half weeks before the hearing. In spite of this, the judges took threats of violence very seriously. Warren (1977, 1982) found that threats were alleged in nearly half of the cases she observed in a California court. In Pennsylvania "threats" were eliminated as a basis for commitment in a 1976 reform of the mental health law. At the same time, a new category, "need for treatment" was added. Surprisingly, Munetz and his associates (1980) found that there was little change in the number of those committed after the law was rewritten. In comparing pre- and post-reform patients, the researchers found that "the clinicians seemed to have identified highly similar patients as needing involuntary admission." As a result of this "there was remarkably little . . . change found in the clinical characteristics of the patients committed" (p. 92; see also: LeBuffe, et al., 1979). However, Hiday (1981) found that dangerousness itself explained only a portion of the variance in a study of civil commitment in North Carolina. She concluded that the patient's condition at the time of the hearing, as well as the availability of alternatives to involuntary hospitalization, played key roles in the decision to commit.

Although judges are concerned with dangerousness they also do not want to keep people in the hospital who do not fit the statute's criteria of a committable individual. However, they are leery about releasing anyone against medical advice. One judge explained to the researcher that he did not want a reporter to come up to him after an "incident" and ask, "Well judge, how many years of medical school have you attended?" In the end, the judges, like the patients, are in Bruce Ennis' (1972) words, "prisoners of psychiatry" (see also: Wexler, 1981:102).

To get a better idea of how this medically dominated process occurs let us examine some findings from our data. In a random sample of 33 cases, only 2 cases clearly fell within the statutes of the person being a threat to themselves or others. In 14 cases, usually lasting a minute or two, the patient had already agreed "to sign a voluntary" or was "convinced" to sign one by the judge in court (see: Warren, 1977). In these cases, the threat of a commitment was certainly a motivating factor in signing "voluntary papers." Also, most of the persons brought before the court had misdemeanor charges pending against them in other courts. These were usually dropped upon the signing of a voluntary admission form. And, after a week or so of confinement, some individuals may have felt that it was easier to simply sign in voluntarily than to fight for a hopeless cause (see: Spradley, 1970; Wiseman, 1970).

Also, the lawyers and the judges frequently stressed to the patient that the signing of voluntary admission papers was considered to be a private matter. Therefore, no public record of a commitment would exist. The signing of such voluntary papers often took place with only agreeable nods by the doctor, the lawyers, and judge. Therefore, it was impossible to ascertain how many of these persons had actually met the statute's requirements. In fact, it is unclear if these individuals were even aware of exactly what they were signing (see: Gilboy and Schmidt, 1971:449).

In nine of the other 33 cases observed it appeared that the individuals did not meet the requirements of the statute. In all these cases, however, the patients were committed. In many of these nine cases, the physicians seemed to "stretch" their testimony in order to gain a commitment. In eight other cases the patients were discharged and remanded to the custody of the sheriff to stand trial on criminal charges (all of which were misdemeanors). Only

3 of the 33 patients were given their freedom. These were an epileptic, an alcoholic, and a woman who was emotionally upset about a recent divorce (see: Warren 1982:164).

Gilboy and Schmidt (1971) found a similar situation in the 110 cases they analyzed. They found that 56 persons were committed and 28 signed voluntary admission papers. Of the remaining number, 5 cases were continued, 8 were returned to jail, and 5 individuals were released to the care and custody of others. Only six of the patients were released outright (see: Warren, 1982:155).

Warren (1977, 1981) has pointed out that the sponsorship of family members willing to care for the patient was a significant factor in avoiding commitment. That is why the commitment rate was only 50 percent in California.

However, the rejection of the patient by the family was an important factor in producing a commitment. In fact, she heard one judge say that the individual was "not gravely disabled if returned to relatives." Alternately, the hospital served as a safety valve for families who could no longer tolerate the behavior of family members. This can be seen in the fact that Warren found that half of all commitments were initiated by family members (see also: Greenley, 1972; Steadman and Cocozza, 1974:127-127; Mosher and Gunderson, 1973; Rachlin, et al., 1975; LeBuffe, et al., 1979; Spensley, et al., 1974; Stone, 1975:46; Brakel, 1985:80; Lewis and Hugi, 1981).

The speed in which the cases are handled is also interesting. In a study by the California Legislature (1966) the average hearing lasted only 4.17 minutes. On a randomly selected day on which the researcher observed the Chicago court the average case lasted 7.2 minutes. However, if the 3 longest cases (26, 23, and 19 minutes) were eliminated from the 20 cases heard that day, the average hearing took only 4.5 minutes. Also, 7 cases took one minute or less and 14 cases averaged about 3 minutes each. In contrast, the 6 longest cases averaged about 19 minutes each.

The pretrial psychiatric evaluations were also usually brief. The average evaluation session seldom lasted more than 20 or 30 minutes; and they often were quite a bit shorter. Similarly, Scheff (1964a, 1964b) found that medical evaluations were brief (10 minutes) and commitment was recommended in 196 of the 196 cases he reviewed. In a second random sample of my data there were 11 dismissals in 88 cases. Since such a high percentage of the individuals brought before the court were committed (87.5 percent) one may assume that there is a presumption of illness (Scheff, 1964b; see also: Scheff, 1964a; Weinberg, 1967). This led Lewis and his associates to comment that "madness in the mental health court, like guilt in the criminal court, is not in question" (1984:634; see also: Burstein, 1980).

Ideology is a potent factor in any decision to commit. Scheff (1964b) found that implicit in psychiatric doctrine were the following assumptions:

1. The condition of mentally ill persons deteriorates rapidly without psychiatric assistance.
2. Effective psychiatric treatments exist for most mental illnesses.
3. Unlike surgery, there were no risks involved in involuntary psychiatric treatment, it either helped or was neutral, it could not hurt.

4. Exposing a prospective mental patient to questioning, cross examination, and other screening procedures exposed them to unnecessary stigma. These procedures may well do further damage to a patient's mental condition.
5. There was an element of danger in most mental illnesses. Therefore, it was better to risk unnecessary hospitalization than to take a chance by not hospitalizing a patient.

He, and some mental health professionals, question the validity of these statements. For example:

1. The assumption that psychiatric disorders usually get worse without treatment rests on very little evidence. And the evidence that does exist is often of an anecdotal nature.
2. It is still not clear whether most psychiatric interventions are any more effective than no treatment at all.
3. There is evidence that involuntary hospitalization may negatively affect the patient's life. There is also some evidence that too hasty an exposure to psychiatric treatment may convince patients that they are "sick." This may then prolong an otherwise transitory episode.
4. The assumption that a court proceeding may traumatize an individual is correct, as far as it goes. But it is misleading because it fails to consider the negative reaction to an involuntary commitment without a means of redress.
5. The element of danger is usually exaggerated among psychiatric patients. For example, in a psychiatric survey of new patients admitted to a state mental hospital, danger to self or others was mentioned in about a fourth of the cases. Furthermore, in those cases where danger was mentioned, it was not always clear that the risks involved were greater than those that would be encountered in ordinary social life.

After examining the role of the psychiatrist in commitment hearings Scheff has concluded that the psychiatrist is "the key agent of social control" (1964b:413). Similarly, Maisel has concluded that "the medical model of mental illness ultimately controls the flow of patients to and from the hospital" (1971:356). Therefore, the medical (psychiatric) approach, rather than the judicial one, is dominant in commitment hearings.

Although the medical perspective is dominant, it is not absolute. That is because psychiatric opinion is occasionally overturned and patients are sometimes released. When this occurs it is usually in routine cases. However, sometimes there are dramatic occurrences which reinforce the physician's opinion that the judges who sit in the mental health court are "wild-eyed civil libertarians." An example of such a case occurred one morning:

William B., a shabbily clothed 35-year-old man, was led to the witness table and seated. After all were sworn the hearing began. "Mr. B.," the doctor testified, "had manifested memory loss, had been unkempt, talking to himself, and disoriented in time and place when he was first admitted. Also, he had spoken in broken sentences and had acted like an automaton during the intake interview. During his second interview, a few days later, Mr. B. was better." The doctor went on to state that he believed that the patient's memory loss was due to possible brain damage. This was complicated by alcoholism and a poor diet. He diagnosed the patient as "schizophrenic with a substratum of brain damage." He concluded that "the patient is not dangerous to others but is dangerous to himself. Therefore, hospitalization is recommended." The doctor added that "there have been hints during the interviews that the patient is an escapee from a Texas psychiatric hospital."

The patient, looking bleary-eyed, testified that he had come to Chicago from Texas looking for a job. He said that he had a previous psychiatric hospitalization. He explained that he had had trouble finding jobs because he had been injured in the Navy and was not able to work at full capacity.

"He's rather coherent now," the judge commented. "Do you have a friend here in town?" the judge asked.

"No."

"He's alright now," the doctor then injected.

"Could he be an outpatient?" the judge queried.

"Yes," the doctor responded.

The judge then asked Mr. B. the time and place. He replied correctly.

"There's a Texas sheriff willing to come and get him," the ward social worker suddenly commented. The judge seemed surprised and continued the case. This was to allow the social worker to contact the Texas authorities.

A few days later William B. was again brought before the court. He still looked glassy-eyed and a bit lost. The doctor began his testimony with a diagnosis that Mr. B had chronic brain syndrome. However, this was reversible. The patient was now oriented in time, place, and person the doctor concluded. He was still a chronic schizophrenic but was now in remission and had been recovering with proper diet. "However," the doctor cautioned, "I would play it safe by keeping him in the hospital until we know more medical information."

The judge then asked why the social worker was not present. "She's either sick or has a day off," a staff member replied. The judge became disgusted and the public defender quickly volunteered to call Texas. He left the courtroom and a few minutes later returned. He said that he had had no luck in contacting the appropriate Texas authorities.

The judge asked the doctor if Mr. B. could take care of himself on the outside since he was currently "in remission."

"I don't know," the doctor answered.

The doctor, state's attorney, and public defender all settled back in their chairs as the judge pondered the case for a moment. They all appeared to expect a continuance or commitment because it was "obvious" that Mr. B. "needed help."

"I find Mr. B. not to be in need of mental treatment." The judge's pronouncement stunned the courtroom.

After court the two horrified attorneys rushed to the judge's chambers. "Why was he discharged?" the attorneys kept asking. The judge, with some annoyance, explained that "I'm not merely an administrative officer, but a judge. I have to follow the law. Sure, I'm concerned about this poor man, but he didn't deserve to be in the hospital." The attorneys shook their heads in disbelief and walked from the judge's chambers.

Although the commitment ratios do not differ between the three judges who sit in the weekly rotation before the mental health court, their attitudes do differ. For example, the same judge who had released Mr. B. had promised at an initial hearing that he would release a Polish immigrant, who was unquestionably psychotic, because no one at the hospital spoke Polish; therefore, she could not be treated. The case, however, came up for a rehearing when another judge was presiding over the court. It appeared that the woman would be committed. However, the case was postponed when it was found that the woman was to be deported for lying on her immigration papers. At the conclusion of the hearing the judge commented: "Don't worry, we'll work this legal thing out." He put his pen down and shaking his head added, "That Judge _____, he's a bug on social service. That's not appropriate here."

6. The Outlying Chicago Court: The 1970s

At a state hospital on the fringe of the Chicago metropolitan area another mental health court presided at a state hospital. However, here the tone and the decisions were often quite different from the city court. This court, which was outside of Cook County, was held in the state hospital's auditorium. The "courtroom" was nothing more than a few tables which had been pushed together. The judge, who wore a suit but no robes, chain-smoked his way through the dozen or so cases he heard each Friday morning. The patients were usually white working-class individuals from the suburbs, small cities, or towns in the area. There were few minority group members. There was no overcrowded *mitimus* ward. The patients were examined by foreign born physicians. However, the court personnel generally felt that these physicians were competent.

In this court, like the other, the physicians found most persons to be "in need of mental treatment." However, this judge reacted differently than did the city judges. Instead of committing the borderline cases he often continued these cases for a week or two and told the physician or social worker, "Help find Mr. X a job," or "Help Mrs. Y to get out on her own."

A typical case involved a patient who was "troublesome":

The patient, a white male about 30 years old, had caused "some trouble" in a drug store and tavern. He had then been brought to the hospital by the police according to the father's testimony. The judge asked if the father wanted to take his son home. "Not right away because I'm afraid he would begin drinking again." The social worker testified that the patient had been "having problems for the last six years. He's manic-depressive and he had been receiving lithium treatments during his last hospitalization here. After being released, he moved to Mississippi and had gotten into trouble there when he blocked traffic on a railroad crossing. As a result of this he had lost his job. Recently, he had been in a nearby town and had gotten into trouble there, too. He drinks and that aggravates his problem." The father added that "once he even smashed up his own car with a hammer." The patient countered by saying that he had merely been fixing it.

The judge asked the patient where he would go if he were released. "I want to go back to Mississippi."

"The patient's a threat to others," the social worker countered. The physician agreed and added that "the patient has acted in a bizarre manner and, besides, he's only got $5 to get back to Mississippi."

"And he's had police problems before," the social worker self-righteously intoned.

"How long would it take to stabilize his medication?" the judge asked.

"Two weeks."

"Well then, let's continue the case two or three weeks."

The biggest difference between the two courts was the treatment of potentially violent persons. City courts always committed patients when there was any hint of violence. The outlying court, however, did not commit individuals if the violence had been situationally produced and the patient appeared to be in good contact with reality when they appeared before the court.[5] Therefore, cases in which a son had been fighting with his parents or a man had been creating a disturbance at his ex-wife's apartment did not necessarily produce a commitment. If the judge felt the individual could function outside of the hospital he would release them with a warning such as: "Stay away from your parents or next time I'll commit you," or "Don't go near her or next time you'll go to jail." For example:

A 35-year-old woman had been brought to the hospital after a fight with her husband. The social worker testified that the patient had been drinking with her husband. They had had a fight in which she struck him. She had broken his wrist, some ribs, and he had sustained head injuries. The patient explained that she had been drinking and had recently stopped taking her medication. She promised to begin taking it again if she were released. The doctor said that she was alright now but needed help with her alcoholism. The patient said she would like to be discharged and go to a clinic for treatment. "Get some counseling and get off the booze," the judge warned.

"But where would she stay?" the social worker asked.

"She's a big girl. Discharged."

Since the city judges treat even the hint of violence very seriously a city judge probably would have committed both the patient and the judge in the following case:

The admissions service was alerted that a serious case was about to arrive with the police. They were told that the prisoner had pulled a gun at a mall in a nearby city. The police had been called and a tense stand-off had ensued. The man repeatedly pointed the gun at the officers. Finally, the man put the gun down, officers tackled him, and then cuffed him.

---

5. Dangerousness in psychiatric patients has become a major focus of study (see: Monahan and Steadman, 2001, 1994; Hawk and Fitch, 2001; Hidday, 1983, 1988; Nicholson, 1986; Holstein, 1993; Steadman and Cocozzo, 1974; Halleck, 1967; Monahan, 1981; Blackburn, 1983; Brooks, 1984; M. Cohen, et. al., 1978; ENKI, 1972; Hunt, 1968; Kozol, et. al., 1972; McGuire, 1976; Megargee, 1970; Pfohl, 1978, 1979a, 1979b, 1984; Sadoff, 1978).

The police report, which arrived before the patient, stated that he was very powerful and "when he flapped his arms like a bird the officers flew off." While they waited for the police the intake workers anxiously scurried around the office rearranging the furniture; this was so they could flee if the man attacked them. When the police brought the man in he was in handcuffs and leg irons. He was a large black male, well over 6 feet tall and 250 pounds. He shuffled into the office and immediately began to apologize for all the trouble he had caused. His intake summary stated:

> Mr. Gregory G., a 38-year-old black married male, was brought to our hospital by the County Sheriff's Department. He was arrested for pointing a loaded weapon at the police officers.

> A petition and order for detention and examination accompanied Mr. G. His legal rights were explained to him. He preferred not to sign any forms and so remains on emergency status. [The incident which brought him to the hospital is as follows:]

> This morning, while at the mall with his wife and three children he was approached by the police. They had been summoned to investigate a report that there was a person with a mental problem. When they arrived he stated, "I am a federal lawyer and I will stay here until this mall pays me for all the sign designs they stole from me." He pulled out a carbine and pointed it at the officers. He was asked to put down the gun and he did. However, after several other officers were called, he again picked up the gun. This time, however, his wife was able to persuade him to hand it over to her. With great difficulty they then transported him to jail. According to the police report, he has great strength; with three officers on each arm he would merely thrash his arms and brush them off. After obtaining the petition signed by Mr. G.'s father, he was brought here . . .

> Upon arrival, Mr. G. was handcuffed and in leg restraints. After being released, he requested, and was granted, a phone call. After the phone call his legal rights were explained to him. It was dubious if he was able to comprehend his rights. . . .

> Mr. G. appeared to be oriented but only in superficial contact with reality. He was quite delusional. He denied having ever pulled a gun, quarrelling with the officers, etc. However, he did state that he was a federal lawyer, that his print designs were stolen, and that he has federal copyrights and patents on dramas and plays. He contended that he was a Reverend and a minister of the Pentecostal faith. He appeared to be very lucid about some of these matters and displayed a fairly good vocabulary. It appeared that he had little insight into his condition and very poor judgment. He presented no behavior problems on the ward. He was seen by Dr. _____ .

Nine days later in court Mr. G.'s hearing began with a statement from his mother. She explained that her son had been "sick" while in the Army. She went on to say that "he's been acting paranoid lately and he claims that his patents for special printing techniques have been stolen." The doctor then testified that "the patient has told me that he has filed a suit against the federal government for taking his patents. The patient is in good contact with reality and has not done anything dangerous on the ward."

The social worker added that he was fine except for his paranoid ideation.

Mr. A.'s wife then testified that they had eight children and he provided for his family.
"How does he support you?"
"He's an exterminator."
The patient, wearing a suit and tie, explained that "I have contracts waiting to be filled if I'm released from the hospital."
The judge replied:
"Keep away from confrontations with the police. Discharged."

There were other significant differences between this court and the city court. For example, the outlying court heard only about a dozen cases a week, whereas the Chicago court often heard 70 to 100 cases a week. In the outlying court the judge had personal knowledge of many of those who appeared before him from previous hospitalizations or hearings. In Chicago, however, the process was anonymous. At the outlying court many of the patients had financial or social resources to fall back on. In Chicago, most of the persons who appeared before the court were indigent. In the outlying court the pressure against releasing patients was not great, whereas in Chicago, the pressure was substantial.

The city judges are aware of many of the shortcomings of the mental health system in Chicago. One judge explained that "the police usually take mentally ill persons to jail rather than the hospital, and I don't understand why they do it. After they are incarcerated, they must often wait, five, seven, or even nine days for a psychiatric exam at the jail. If they are certified by a physician, they are then shipped to the hospital for five more days and a second examination. The person may end up being confined from ten to fourteen days and then found not to be in need of treatment. If he had been found guilty of the disorderly conduct charge that he had initially been picked up on he would have paid a small fine and soon would have been free." When asked why he didn't remedy the situation through a court order he explained: "One of the other judges [the Chief Judge of the Mental Health Division] does some of that, and in individual cases, I try and do the right thing. But we're just big fish in a small pond. We can't go sticking our necks out and telling the police and the Department of Mental Health how to run things."

The Chief Judge of the Mental Health Division does, in fact, occasionally force changes upon the Department of Mental Health. Because of these efforts he is widely regarded as a champion of the rights of the mentally ill. And he has gained a national reputation as a reformer and civil libertarian in the mental health field. In a recent conversation he explained that a major shortcoming of the current system was that it was rigid and mechanical and produced no dynamic understanding of the patients or their conditions. Also, he was not pleased with the quality of physicians at the mental health court and he felt that "if they're not qualified to practice on Michigan Avenue, then they're just not qualified." He concluded with the comment that "the medical model has not served us very well" and that we should consider alternatives.

In specific cases he has curtailed, at least temporarily, some abuses by the Department of Mental Health. For example, he reduced the use of restraints and drugs on patients, ordered that a young boy be removed from a closet he was being held in and given treatment, and required that all inpatients have individualized treatment plans. He has also agreed to a number of procedural reforms for the court, urged the establishment of a patient advocacy system, and been appointed by the governor to chair a committee to rewrite the Mental Health Code.

These reforms have all been substantial and important. However, most of them have been the result of newspaper exposes or Legal Aid court suits. In most cases the chief judge has been a "passive reformer" allowing situations to exist for years until they were challenged from without. He is widely regarded as one of the most knowledgeable persons in the state on mental health and has been widely acclaimed for having "cleaned up" the commitment court. That court, in his words, had been "a perfunctory, mass thing, without legal safeguards." He was brought in to reform the system "because it had become a source of embarrassment. Now I'm stuck here because there's no problems."

7. The Chicago Court: 1983

A wave of reform swept the U.S. in the 1960s and early 1970s. In mental health it began in 1969 with the Lanterman-Petris-Short Act in California (Miller, 1987; Holstein, 1993; Chu and Trotter, 1974: 42-3). In the 1970s Illinois revised its Mental Health Code. Officially, the law was Chapter 405 of the Illinois Revised Statutes. Its title was, Act 5 Mental Health and Developmental Disabilities Code (last amended, January, 2004). We will refer to it as the Mental Health Code, or simply, the Code.

The new code states that when an individual wishes to voluntarily enter a mental health facility for treatment the states primary concern is that the individual falls within the definition of mental illness as defined by the Code. Under the code the definition is:

> "Mental illness" means a mental or emotional disorder that substantially impairs a person's thought, perception of reality, emotional process, judgment, behavior, or ability to cope with ordinary demands of life, but does not include a developmental disability, dementia or Alzheimer's disease absent psychosis, a substance abuse disorder, or an abnormality manifested only by repeated criminal or otherwise antisocial conduct. (Chapter I – Section 1-129)

Article IV of the code describes the voluntary admission of adults. The article states that any person who is 16 years old or older may be admitted as a voluntary patient if the facility director deems that person to be clinically suitable for admission. The application for admission can be executed by the individual themselves, if 18 or older, any interested party, 18 or older, at the request of the person seeking admission, or by a minor, 16 years or older. If the individual gives written notice he or she may be discharged at the earliest appropriate time, not to exceed 5 working days. After giving written notice to be discharged the hospital must release the individual unless it files a petition and 2 certificates are filed with the court asserting that the individual is in need of involuntary admission. A court hearing then must be held. No staff member may say to that person that an involuntary admission may occur unless the individual signs a voluntary admission.

Article VI describes an emergency (involuntary) admission. In such an admission the Code spells out the criteria through which the state must comply in order to hospitalize an individual against their will:

(1) A person with mental illness and who because of his or her illness is reasonably expected to inflict serious physical harm upon himself or herself or another in the near future which may include threatening behavior or conduct that places another individual in reasonable expectation of being harmed; or

(2) A person with mental illness and who because of his or her illness is unable to provide for his or her basic physical needs so as to guard himself or herself from serious harm without the assistance of family or outside help. (Chapter I – Section 1-119)

Article VI also states that when a person 18 years or older is in such a condition that immediate hospitalization is necessary for the protection of that person or others from physical harm any person 18 years of age or older may present a petition to the director of a mental health facility or their designee. The petition shall include a detailed statement of the need for an involuntary admission. This shall include the signs and symptoms of the mental illness and the description of any acts, threats or other behavior supporting the petition. The petition shall be accompanied by a certificate executed by a physician, clinical psychologist, or qualified examiner (a clinical social worker, registered nurse, or professional counselor). The petition shall contain clinical observations, other factual information, and a statement that the individual was advised of their rights. No person can be held for more than 24 hours unless a second certificate is executed.

Also, upon the receipt of a petition a police officer may take an individual into custody and transport them to a mental health facility. Or, a police officer may take a person into custody if he or she observes injurious behavior and believes the individual is subject to involuntary hospitalization.

Article VII states that a court may order a temporary hospitalization under the same grounds. In either case a psychiatrist must examine the individual within 24 hours of hospitalization. However, the psychiatrist can not be the same examiner who executed the first certificate.

Article VII details the requirement of a hearing for an involuntarily detained individual. In an involuntary admission the person must have a hearing within 5 working days. If the hearing can not be held within 5 working days the judge may continue the case for 15 more days. The continuance may not extend beyond 15 days except by the request of the individual. The person who is subject to an involuntary admission may request a (6 person) civil jury trial for his or her hearing. Also, every person subject to involuntary admission must be represented by counsel. The court may commit the individual to a mental health facility only if there is clear and convincing evidence of the need for such treatment. If the person is found to be in need of treatment the court must order the confinement of the person to the least restrictive environment available. An individualized treatment plan must then be created. The initial order for hospitalization is for a period of 90 days. After 90 days a hearing must be held. The court may then continue the original order, modify it, or discharge the patient (Article VIII – Section 3; Article IX – Section 3-910).

The code also allowed individuals to refuse treatment. If the hospital believed that treatment was necessary it had to file a petition with the court. A hearing must then be held on that petition (Chapter 2 – Section 2-107). In order for the hospital's petition to be granted it must prove that the benefits of the treatment outweighed the harm (Chapter 2 – Section 2-107.1).

When a petition has been filed the examiner must inform the individual that they do not have to speak to the examiner. Also, they must be informed that any statements they make may be disclosed in court (Article II – Section 3-208). And, if a patient is to be transferred and objects to that transfer they have a right to a court hearing (Article IX – Section 3-910).

In 1983 the researcher conducted a restudy of the mental health court in Chicago. The hearings were held in the same courtroom as before. And, as before, the defendants were poor or black. They often seemed lost and overmedicated. They had been arrested for minor crimes or had been brought to the hospital by family or friends after a disruptive act (see: Lewis, et al., 1987).

The hearings began with a physician or clinical psychologists testifying. The physician or psychologist usually found the person to be disoriented in time, place, or person. The individual was often found to have hallucinations and delusions. Some were disruptive, violent, or suicidal. A diagnosis of schizophrenia or affective disorder (manic-depressive illness) was common. However, under the new code the public defenders behavior was more aggressive. They often brought up family conflicts or housing problems that led to the hospitalization. They also sometimes challenged the clinician regarding their diagnosis. Also, social workers were frequently present to amplify the details of familial or other problems that brought the individual to the hospital.

Observations were made of the Chicago mental health court on seven randomly chosen days in 1983. Thirty-eight cases were observed. The judge committed 21 of the defendants. Two patients signed voluntary admission papers in the court. And four were discharged. The major change was that in 11 cases, almost a third, were continued so that familial, housing, or mental health treatment problems could be solved. Once these difficulties were overcome the patient would usually be discharged by the hospital and the court case would be dropped.

In the 1970s hearings lasted from one to twenty-six minutes; the average hearing was about seven minutes. In 1983 the hearings lasted between one minute and two hours and thirteen minutes. The average was about twenty-two and a half minutes. However, if the three longest cases from 1983 were dropped, the average was about fifteen and a half minutes. The three longest hearings (2 hours and 13 minutes, 1 hour and 35 minutes, and 1 hour and 23 minutes) were considered to be exceptional by the court personnel. And they would have been inconceivable under the old system. The three longest cases were the result of testimony concerning the social factors that led to the hospitalization. When these issues were brought up a continuance was often the result. In the 1970s these factors were not considered to be relevant. Only the diagnosis of the physician was relevant at those hearings.

Out of the 38 cases observed in 1983, 24 defendants were white and 14 were black. There were no Hispanics. Twenty-nine of the defendants were male and 9 were female. The average age of defendants was about 28 years old.

Also, the availability of new programs, housing, and cash after discharge were significant influences on the judges' decisions.

A few typical cases follow:

Mary H., an eighteen-year-old white female was brought before the court. A social worker testified she had come from a private hospital. She had been taken there because her friends believed that she was suicidal. She had been transferred from the private hospital because she was out of control. A review of her medical history indicated that she had four previous hospitalizations in Illinois Department of Mental Health facilities. She had also been in a drug rehabilitation program. She reportedly used "speed" and LSD. However, a recent test revealed no drugs in her system.

The physician stated that the patient had an anxiety disorder. When she became "panicky" she entertained suicidal thoughts. He also believed she had a borderline personality disorder.

The judge asked the patient: "What are we going to do?"

The patient replied, "I don't know."

The judge then asked: "Do you want to do it [suicide]? Some day you'll succeed." He continued the case for two-weeks. "Let's find a program for her," the judge concluded.

Joan M., a forty-five-year-old black woman was brought before the court. The case had been continued for a progress report. The nurse testified that the staff would like to place her in shelter care. However, since she had been transferred from another state hospital her Social Security check was going to the wrong address. The nurse also stated that she had been taking her medication on the unit. However, the nurse believed she was paranoid when she refused to go to a workshop. The nurse concluded that the patient would like to be discharged but she has no money and no place to stay.

A treatment plan was then handed to the judge and then passed to the attorneys.

A law student, assisting the public defender, argued that the treatment plan was invalid since it was not signed by a psychiatrist.

The judge stated that this was not required by the mental health code.

The law student then argued that since a psychiatrist did not sign the treatment plan a psychologist should have signed it.

The judge noted that there was a letter from the psychiatrist and overruled the law student.

The states attorney asked if the patient had hurt anyone on the unit and was she taking her medication?

The staff stated that the patient had not injured anyone on the unit. And the patient had been taking her medication. However, she was only attending one-third of the activities set up to promote her independence.

"How often did she see a psychiatrist?" the assistant states attorney asked.

The staff replied that she had seen a psychiatrist twice and a psychologist once. She had not seen a social worker or counselor.

The patient added that her life on the unit was "routine. I get up, wash up."

The assistant states attorney then asked if the patient was getting any help in securing her check. No, the staff replied. However, they were trying to find her a halfway house in the city for a placement.

The patient then added: "I'll take my medication if I'm released. And I'm not Mayor Harold Washington. I'm not director of the CIA. I've not seen any Nazis on TV and I'm not in combat with Nazis."

The assistant states attorney asked, "The police brought you here?"

"Yes."

The judge then asked: "What are the parties seeking here. Should she stay here?"

The assistant states attorney then stated that the patient was not able take care of herself. She was confused. She did not attend her workshop. However, if she cooperated he felt she could be discharged quickly. The assistant states attorney then added that the patient was not a danger to herself. However, he was concerned that she would not be able to take care of herself. The assistant states attorney said he had called about the Social Security check but they were unresponsive since the patient was undomiciled. However, he agreed that it was true that she was receiving few services at the hospital.

The judge then noted that the psychiatrist's letter said the patient was not dangerous to herself or others. "So why not release her?" he asked.

The assistant states attorney replied: "No halfway house will take her. They [the staff] did their work. Besides, she's still confused and needs help with her Social Security. She needs a plan."

"But what if it takes 6 months or a year?" the judge asked. "I can discharge her, but to where? We have a responsibility. She needs a plan. I'm hesitant to release. I don't want her freezing to death. We need a plan."

The assistant states attorney then replied: "Let's define some services and set a deadline. But getting her benefits might be difficult; but, the hospital has done little."

The judge then said: "I know what the department will do. They'll discharge her and then what will we do? What does your client want?"

"I want a discharge," the patient said.

"To where?" the judge asked. "Let's go to chambers and come up with an agreed order."

There was a three minute recess. When the judge returned he said: "The conference has reached an agreement. Continued for two weeks for placement. But the patient must cooperate. OK? Stay on your medication."

"She's acting much better today," a staff member added.

Jim W., a 29-year-old black male came before the court. The public defender began by stating that the patient wished to sign a voluntary admission form.

The assistant states attorney objected. However, he had no witnesses and this was the second time this case had come up.

The judge commented that a voluntary petition may be a bad idea but the patient may not be committable. He then asked the social worker to testify.

The social worker stated that the patient had eight prior admissions. His last discharge was three weeks earlier to the county jail. After his release from jail he was again arrested and returned to the hospital. He had been arrested for battery. It was charged that he had punched his father and chocked him with telephone cord. On the ward he had told the staff that he hit his father 25 years ago. He also had stated hat he was a judge, supreme commander of U.S. forces, was on a secret mission to D.C., his mother was a transsexual, and that he had a transmitter in his molar. He refused to take any medication. The staff concluded that he needed to go to another state hospital for long-term treatment.

The judge asked if the patient would be treated differently if he were a voluntary or a committed patient.

No, the doctor answered.

However, the social workers added that if he signed in voluntarily and asked to leave the staff would then have to sign a five day petition; and they would be right back in the court.

The physician then said that there was no doubt that the patient was mentally ill. The patient was not taking his medication and the patient wanted to sign himself out. And the patient was very delusional. The doctor concluded that the patient was schizophrenic, chronic undifferentiated. The doctor then added that the patient had been in jail six or seven times.

The judge asked how long the patient would need to be in the hospital.

Four to eight weeks, the doctor believed. That, was, if he took his medication.

The assistant states attorney then said a commitment was appropriate in this case. He believed it was appropriate for the patient, as well as, to protect society from someone who was dangerous.

The public defender responded that he felt that a voluntary admission would be appropriate. And if the hospital wished to keep him they could bring him back to court or send him back to jail. Also, the public defender noted that the father was not present to testify about the attack; therefore, there was no proof that the patient was dangerous.

The judge then wondered out loud if a voluntary petition or commitment would allow the patient to better accept his treatment.

The public defender objected to the judge's "leading question."

The judge laughed. "I'm the court. You can't object."

The judge than said: "The code is applicable here. It's in the best interest of the patient and the public to not accept a voluntary. It's not appropriate here."

The patient than said: "I'm on a 25-year mission to check drugs. I have a transmitter in my teeth. I got a home in Lake Forest."

The judge committed the patient.

After the hearing the public defender said: "I didn't say he wasn't nuts. But the testimony was lousy. He's a conservative judge."

"Oh come on," the assistant states attorney moaned.

The attorneys and judges are more activist than in the previous decade. However, they are constrained by the functioning of the state's department of mental health and the services available for patients upon discharge. For example:

Marion A., a 42-year-old white male came before the court. The physician testified that he had three previous hospitalizations at this hospital and seven elsewhere. The patient was suspicious and reluctant to respond to him. The patient was currently mentally ill and his behavior outside the hospital was also abnormal. His parents had told the doctor that the patient had been discharged to their care. But he would walk away from their home, sit in alleys, and look at the sky. He would not bathe and slept in the corner of various rooms in the house during the day. He also refused to take his medication. The doctor concluded that the patient had no hallucinations but was schizo-affective with paranoid overtones. The doctor felt that if the patient were released he would harm himself or freeze to death. He needed long term care with behavior modification.

The judge then asked: "Why was he released a month ago?"

The doctor replied that there had been a slight improvement so they "gave him a chance." However, he had been violent at home. So now he needed to go for long term care.

The public defender than asked: "What would be different now? Won't they just release him?"

"They shouldn't. But, we can't do anything with him now. He has lice," the doctor explained. "Maybe he can go to the V.A.," the doctor added.

The social worker then said: "The V.A. didn't work out last time. He was resistant to therapy. And he threw lighted cigarettes on the floor."

The patient then injected that he didn't need to be in the hospital. He had gone to a hotel and the police had picked him up. "I'm a little confused here," he concluded.

"About what?" the judge asked.

The patient didn't respond.

The judge then said: "Exactly the same as before. He's not getting help. Why was he discharged last time?"

"They'll just let him go," the public defender concluded.

"I'm dissatisfied with the statute," the judge stated. "Committed."

8. The Outlying Chicago Court: 1983

A restudy was also conducted of the outlying Chicago area court in 1983. The court was still held in the hospitals auditorium with the same judge presiding. The judge still wore a suit and still chain smoked his way through the proceedings. The patients were still mostly white working class males from the suburbs, small cities, or towns in the area. There were few minority patients.

Forty-seven cases were observed. Ten years earlier many of the cases were continued. Now almost all the cases were continued. For example, out of the 47 cases observed only two commitments occurred; and no voluntary petitions were signed by the patients. There were nine discharges. There were also four review hearings of committed patient who had been in the hospital for 90 or 180 days. What was most striking about the 47 cases observed was that 32 out of the 47 cases were continued; and each case was dispatched quickly. The average case took less than 3 minutes.

There were 35 male patients, 8 black, and 3 Hispanic. There were 7 females. The average age of the patients was about 29 years old. The judge knew many of the patients from previous hospitalizations or court hearings.

Just like the Chicago court in 1983, there was more emphasis on the social factors that led to the hospitalization. There was also more concern with the availability of services upon discharge.

A few typical cases follow:

Matilda B., a 50-year-old white female, came before the court. The social worker testified that she had barricaded herself in an apartment with a knife. She had been apprehended by the police. She had not been taking her medication. Her apartment was full of rotten food and liquor.

The judge asked the patient: "Did you go back to drinkin'?"

"Not too much," she replied.

The physician then testified that the patient was schizophrenic, chronic undifferentiated.

"And your determination?" the judge asked.

"She can't take care of herself," the physician answered.

"Does she have any income?" the judge asked the social worker.

"Yes, Social Security."

"And, an apartment?"

"Yes, a rented apartment."

"How long will it take to stabilize her?" the judge asked.

"More than two weeks, I'm afraid," the physician answered.

"I'm afraid so. You've got to cooperate," the judge told the woman.

"Continued," the judge ruled.

James A., an 18-year-old white male appeared before the court. The social worker stated that this had been an emergency admission. The mother had signed the petition. The patient had been talking to his fingers and toes. On the unit he had had hallucinations and delusions. He believed his food was poisoned. He paced on the ward. His eating habits were extremely poor. The mother, who was not present, wanted her son kept in the hospital for 3 to 4 weeks.

The judge, concluded: "We'll give it two weeks. Keep on your meds. OK doc?" The physician nodded.

Jane J., a 40-year-old white female, was brought in to the courtroom. The social worker testified that the patient had been upset and left her placement. She had been wandering the streets wearing inadequate clothing in 20 degree temperatures. She was not properly clothed because someone had thrown away her clothes at her placement. The social worker felt these were "extenuating circumstances in this case." So, what the patient needed was a new placement.

"Let's give it two weeks," the judge said.

Damien B., a 28-year-old white male, came before the court. The social worker stated the patient wished to go back to jail. He had been arrested for criminal trespass to his ex-girlfriend's residence. At the hospital he had stated that he was agitated and angry. And he did not understand why his girlfriend did not want him. He felt he did not have any control over himself. The social worker stated that the patient had been involved in a paternity suit with the ex-girlfriend six years earlier. But that had been dropped. Now he was making death threats to her and he had been physically aggressive towards her.

A police officer stated that the patient had entered the ex-girlfriend's apartment with a hatchet and a rope. He had made death threats to the ex-girlfriend. He had threatened the police, as well as, others.

The physician then quickly added that he was paranoid schizophrenic and dangerous.

"I'm being railroaded!" the patient asserted.

"Are there any plans?" the social worker asked.

"Stay away from the girlfriend and find a place to stay" the judge said.

Then the judge asked: "Do you want to stay?"

"No. But I've been out of control since I got here."

"Let's set this over for three weeks," the judge concluded.

Suzanne H., a 20-year-old white female appeared before the court. The social worker testified that she had several previous hospitalizations. She had been confused, disoriented, and incoherent during her stay on the unit. Her husband had not contacted her since she had been hospitalized.

The patient stated that her husband wanted to get her.

The social worker added that the patient had refused to take her medications.

"Continued one week. Have your husband get you," the judge stated.

After the patient left the judge whispered to the staff: "Sounds like the old man dumped her."

Samuel S., a 25-year-old white male was brought before the court. The social worker testified that he had been transferred from the jail. He had had an argument with his roommate. He had hit the roommate and been charged with battery. He had been hostile and paranoid at the jail so he was transferred to the hospital.

"What happened?" the judge asked.

"The social worker stated it pretty well," the patient replied.

The social worker then said that the patient denies any hallucination, delusions, or suicidal tendencies.

The public defender then asked: "Can you handle it in jail?"

"Yes."

The doctor then testified that the patient became psychotic while on amphetamines. The doctor concluded that the patient could hurt someone.

The Judge then said, "It's up to you. Do you want to help yourself?"

"I want to go back to jail."

"O.K. Back to jail," the judge concluded.

Frank S., a 21-year-old white male was brought in to court. The social worker testified: "We were ready to discharge him but then he began bending silverware, mooning the nurses, and threatening suicide. He had been appropriate all week. He wants to live with a former female patient."

The physician testified that he had "many suicide attempts. And that he was playing a very dangerous game."

"He seems to be able to control it," the judge observed.

The public defender then asked: "Does he have a personality disorder?"

"Yes, borderline," the doctor answered.

"We'll give you a chance then. Good luck. Discharged," the judge ordered.

Implicit in the decisions of the judge in outlying court were four characteristics: First, by continuing the cases the judge was placing the patient in the hands of the physicians. Just as in a commitment. He was also expecting the hospital to solve the patients' problem, whether it was behavioral, social, or programmatic. Second, he minimized the violence in many cases. The judge appeared to believe these episodes were situational or transitory; or, simply part of the human condition. Third, since these were hearings and not trials, Chicago judges usually accepted written statements from various persons. However, the judge at the outlying court sometimes felt he needed testimony to substantiate a situation or problem. Or, the judge needed the presence of a family member or friend to help resolve the case. And, lastly, in Chicago the physician's testimony was central. However, at the outlying court the social worker's testimony was often more influential. In fact, in some cases the physician never even spoke.

9. The Mental Health Court: 2004

By 2004 the new code had produced dramatic changes in the functioning of the mental health court. Each day the court would begin with "read ins." These were cases where the respondent had already been discharged, the case was being continued, the respondent had signed a voluntary admissions form, or the case was "passed" because of a problem. The process would begin as the clerk called each case. If the respondent had been discharged the assistant states attorney would intone, "motion, state dismissed." The judge would then sign the papers. If a voluntary admission had occurred the clerk would say, "voluntary, we have papers" or "voluntary, papers attached." The assistant states attorney would again say, "motion, state dismissed." The judge would reply, "so ordered," and would then sign the papers. Some cases were continued because the attorney's agreed that further evaluation or case preparation was needed. In court they would say, "further evaluation and trial preparation" required. However, the state was allowed only one continuance. So, if the state had asked for the continuance the judge would say, "First time up, so ordered."

Sometimes there were a few read ins; sometimes there was two dozen. Since each one usually took 20 or 30 seconds, the read ins I observed took a total of between 4 and 14 minutes. If there were no hearings or trials that day the court then adjourned. The researcher attended sixteen days of court in 2004. Twelve days had read ins and then hearings. Four days had only read ins. The researcher would have spent more time at the court but skipped several days because there were no hearings.

As a result of the changes in the Mental Health Code the hearings before the court had become much more legalistic. For example, the individuals appearing before the court were no longer called patients. They were now always referred to as "respondents." Also, in Cook County (Chicago) the respondents were often defended by the state's Guardianship and Advocacy Commission (GAC) attorneys. An assistant states attorney privately complained that with these attorneys there was "too much advocacy." However, he added that in the past, when public defenders represented patients, they usually "went along, unless they felt the patient was being railroaded. Then they got feisty."

Because of the new mental health code the mental health court now heard more than commitment cases. There were also writs in which someone requested that the police bring an individual in to the hospital for an examination. Also, there were hearings regarding continued hospitalizations.

Some typical cases follow:

a.) A commitment hearing

The hearing began at 10:17 a.m. The assistant states attorney began by stating the petition was flawed and he would refile it. The doctor was then asked to testify. He stated that Jane M., a 40-year-old black female, was paranoid schizophrenic. She was delusional, her thoughts were disorganized, her emotions were labile, and she was agitated. She often did not understand what was occurring around her and as a result of this she became threatening. She also had a sexual preoccupation. She had become aggressive and confrontational before coming to court that day. A deputy sheriff has been forced to intervene. A second physician testified that she had threatened him and had been pounding on a door on the unit.

Ms. M. testified that she had been kidnapped and that a policeman had hit her. She did not believe she was mentally ill. She said "I worked in the fields. I'm nothing. My house is haunted. I had a cut on my feet when I was little. I'm a lawyer. They're raping me and taking my money. I've been working in my house."

The judge ordered her committed. It was 10:27 a.m.

b.) A writ hearing

The hearing began at 12:11 p.m. A friend of Eleanor K. stated that Ms. K., a 70-year-old black female, had been hospitalized four or five years ago for a psychiatric disorder. Currently she was not eating properly and some days she would not eat at all. She said that Ms. K. had stated that Mayor Daley was her son. She had also threatened to kill her niece last year.

A social worker then testified that Ms. K. was a pleasant woman. However, sometimes she became forgetful and as a result she became agitated. Ms. K. had told her that she had changed her race. And that she had millions of babies. In the past she had suffered from a vitamin B-12 deficiency. At the moment, however, she was eating adequately.

The judge signed the writ at 12:17 p.m. and ordered that Ms. K. be brought to the hospital for an examination.

c.) A 90 day hearing for continued hospitalization

The doctor testified that Mr. Terrance D. had refused to come to court. The Guardian and Advocacy Commission (GAC) attorney agreed to waive the respondent's presence in court.

However, in order to convince Mr. D. to attend the hearing the court moved to a conference room on the ward. In spite of this Mr. D. still refused to attend. The hearing in the conference room began at 1:25 p.m. The doctor presented his credentials and the attorneys agreed that he was an expert witness. The doctor then testified that the patient had been admitted almost three months ago. He had been on his current unit for two weeks. The doctor stated that he saw the patient every day. He also interviewed him twice a week. During those interviews Mr. D. was often uncooperative. He had two previous hospitalizations. The doctor believed Mr. D. was bipolar with psychotic features. That is, he had hallucinations, delusions, and a thought disorder. He was currently manic and psychotic. The doctor said that the patient talked a great deal and had high energy levels. He was also paranoid and grandiose. The patient had stated that the doctor had killed his mother in San Diego. Mr. D. told the doctor that he was concerned about being poisoned. Mr. D. also stated that he had won $700 million on television and that he believed that he was a doctor and a lawyer. The doctor also said Mr. D. was aggressive. On three separate occasions he had attacked patients or staff. Twice he had to be put in restraints. He also had to be prompted to eat his meals. The doctor added that when Mr. D. did not take his medication his aggression and agitation increased. Also Mr. D. always wore a cloth band on his head and aluminum foil on his neck. Mr. D. told the doctor that was because he had a skull fracture. The doctor believed this was a delusion. The doctor concluded that Mr. D's. judgment was impaired, he had no money, no friends, and no ability to seek medical attention. Therefore, discharging him would be a mistake.

The GAC attorney asked if the least restrictive environment he could be in was the hospital? "Yes," the doctor replied. The doctor was then asked for a treatment plan. He stated that the patient needed medication, as well as, individual and group counseling. However, Mr. D. had attended few group sessions and was refusing to take his medication. The doctor felt another 90 days of hospitalization was needed.

The GAC attorney asked about Mr. D.'s medication. The doctor said he needed antipsychotics and mood stabilizers. However, Mr. D. often refused his medication.

The GAC attorney asked if Mr. D. could live in a nursing home. That is, could he take care of his basic physical needs? "No," the doctor stated. His "diagnosis was permanent." However, his symptoms could be controlled with medication. Then he could live alone.

The GAC attorney then asked for a directed motion since there was no clear and convincing evidence of physical harm to himself or others. Also there was no proof he was unable to get medical attention for his fractured skull. The GAC attorney also stated: "Maybe he can take care of himself. He needs to be in a nursing home. The aggression is not relevant." The judge took a recess. It was 2:30 p.m.

The court reconvened at 3:02 p.m. The judge denied the GAC attorney's directed motion. He then ruled that there was clear and convincing evidence that Mr. D. suffered from a bipolar disorder and he was psychotic. He also felt he could cause physical harm to himself and others. And he was not convinced he could protect himself. He also ruled that the least restrictive environment for Mr. D. was the state hospital. He ordered hospitalization for another 90 days. And a forced medication hearing would be scheduled next week. The court adjourned at 3:30 p.m.

d.) A commitment hearing

Mrs. M., a 70-year-old Asian female, was brought before the court. It was 11:28 a.m. A Korean translator was present since Mrs. M.'s English was limited. The hearing began when the doctor was asked to present his credentials. He stated that he had been a psychiatrist for 15 years. However, he was not board certified. He had attended medical school in India. He had served as an expert witness in over 50 court cases. And he had treated over 1,000 patients. The lawyers agreed that he was an expert witness.

The doctor began by testifying that the patient had been transferred from a private hospital about a week earlier. He had reviewed the documents sent by the sending hospital. He had also seen her on the ward almost every day since she had been admitted. His diagnosis was that she was "psychotic not otherwise noted." However, he felt that she might also be bipolar. He believed that she was currently psychotic. She had hallucinations, delusions, and a thought disorder. She was also paranoid. She had written a letter to Al Gore. Since he had not written back she planned to sue him. The doctor concluded: "She jumps from topic to topic, she's incoherent, and manic."

The patient then suddenly said: "I don't need a translator."

The judge then said: "You asked for one last time. Listen to the interpreter."

Then the patient asked: "Why am I here today?"

"Because of an involuntary petition," the judge answered.

The judge then said to the attorneys: "I've got to know if she understands the interpreter. Ask if the dialect is correct." However, the interpreter did not understand English well enough to answer the judge. The family then said that there was only one dialect of Korean.

The patient again asked: "Why am I here?"

The judge asked: "Do you understand English?"

"No," she replied.

"Then go through the interpreter," he said.

"I'm practicing English, but I need an interpreter," the patient explained.

"Check if there is a Korean doctor here," the judge said.

The GAC attorney then asked where the discharge papers were from the previous hospital. The judge dismissed this as "a technical issue." However, the GAC attorney said that a hearing should have been held at the private hospital. Instead the patient had been dumped at the state hospital. The GAC attorney noted that a major focus of the new Code was to stop such dumping. He argued that the Code mandated that a hearing should have been held at the private hospital. Also there was no second certificate from the private hospital. The judge took at recess. It was 12:02 p.m.

The court reconvened at 12:28 p.m. The assistant states attorney stated that Mrs. M. had been taken to the psychiatric unit from the emergency room. That was why there was no second certificate. He then withdrew his petition for hospitalization. The judge dismissed the case and freed the patient. It was 12:31 p.m.

The Mental Health court in Chicago sat in a courtroom at the state hospital. (The same courtroom the researcher had been attending since 1971). Most of its cases were heard there. However, in 2004 it traveled to a second state hospital in the far south suburbs to hear cases. There were still hearings at the outlying hospital. The previous judge had retired and a formal courtroom had been built. A new judge now sat in that mental health court.

The city court heard most of the cases. For example, on one randomly chosen day there was one legally complicated case concerning an interstate transfer of a patient. There were two hearings on the case that took a total of 15 minutes. Then there were two commitment hearings (now usually called "trials" by the staff). They averaged 45 minutes each. There were four cases that concerned discharges. They averaged 5 to 6 minutes each. Two of these cases were continued. One was 8 minutes long the other lasted 45 minutes. One writ was heard. It took 3 minutes. And two medication hearings lasted 48 and 60 minutes, each. The average for all these cases was twenty minutes.

At the south suburban court there were few cases. On one randomly chosen day one hearing was required because a violent patient was being transferred within the hospital from a civil unit to a forensic one (that is, to a more restrictive environment.) The hearing lasted 24 minutes. Two cases were continued for a total of 3 minutes. One commitment hearing occurred. This lasted 93 minutes. One patient had filed a petition for release. Another hearing that resulted in a discharge lasted 53 minutes.

At the outlying court there were also few cases. On one randomly chosen day there were two cases where individuals signed voluntary papers. These lasted 1 and 6 minutes, each. Two other cases were continued. Two commitment hearings lasted 10 and 44 minutes, each. And three writs were heard. These lasted 3, 3, and 6 minutes, each. The average of these cases that day was 7.3 minutes.

However, the outlying court met for almost four and one-half hours on one case. This last case was interesting since it highlighted the legalistic nature of the new mental health code. That is, how "hearings" had evolved into "trials." A summary of thc case follows:

Mr. Atrim A., a 37-year-old white male patient, was led in to the courtroom by the bailiff. He was seated at the far left seat of a table in front of the judge's bench. The family and an assistant states attorney were to the right.

The hearing began at 10:47am when Mr. A.'s sister testified that she and her brother had lived together in their parents house from 1992 to 2002 and then for three months before his recent hospitalization. She stated that he had worked as a computer technician until 1996. He then became mentally ill and stopped working. She stated that he believed that the government wanted him to turn himself in. And he believed that there were cameras and electronic listening devices coming through tunnels into his home. Also, George Bush had talked to him through the TV. He had two previous psychiatric hospitalizations in 1996 and 2002.

She went on to state that he had become a recluse since 1996 by closing himself off in his room in the family home. Also, in 1997 or 1998 he had burned his belongings in the fireplace. In 1997 he also had pushed her against the wall. She stated that she is still afraid of him. She is also frightened because she found lighter fluid under his bed. She feared that he would set fire to the house. She also found 50 feet of rope and gauze in the bathroom. She thought that he might hang himself. She added that they were Bosnian Muslims and that she felt he had an extremist view of Islam.

She went on to say that in 2002 he had moved out of the family home and had lived in a motel until 2004. When his money had run out he had moved back home. However, from 2002 to 2004 he did come home once a week to wash his clothes and boil his food. In fact, she noted, everything he ate had to be boiled. She thought that this behavior was bizarre. The family had recently signed a petition for hospitalization because they felt he had not eaten in over a week and was starving himself.

The patient, acting as his own attorney, asserted that he was not paranoid and does not know why he was hospitalized in 1996. In 2002 he was hospitalized because he was fearful he might hurt others because of the war in Iraq. He denied burning anything in the fireplace and he denied pushing his sister. Also, the lighter fluid in his room was for ordinary purposes. And the gauze was to clean his possessions.

Various family members stated that he had been verbally abusive towards them. And that he listened to the television but never looked directly at the screen. He denied these assertions. The court recessed at 12:07.

At 12:12 the hearing resumed. The patient's brother testified that from 1998 to 2002 he had worked at the family's liquor store. However, in 2002 he would not follow orders and swore at customers and a delivery man. He also avoided anyone who was not a Muslim. In 2002 he was hospitalized. After his discharge he refused to take his medication. Because of this he was not allowed to work at the store. After his 2002 hospitalization he lived in a motel. However, he frequently visited the house. During those visits he was verbally abusive. He also appeared to have lost a great deal of weight.

The patient denied any problems at home or that he had done anything wrong at work. However, he did admit that he had pushed his father and bumped his brother in 2000. He added that he had been in a gang as a youth. And that he had been incarcerated. He was still fearful that a gang-member might attack him. He said he did boil water and kept bottles of "holy water" at work.

The states attorney pointed out that that the patient had admitted to two acts of physical violence.

Then there was a discussion as to why an interpreter was not present. The patient eventually allowed a family member to interpret. The court recessed at 12:49 for lunch.

The court reconvened at 1:29. The mother, with the patient's brother acting as the interpreter, testified. She testified that he was not currently working and had locked himself in his room. Also, he had not eaten for a week before his current hospitalization. She also felt he was dangerous because of the lighter fluid, rope, and gauze he kept in his room. She was afraid he would kill himself or others. Also, she thought he might kill her with a knife. She added that when he crossed the street he was constantly looking around. Recently, his hygiene had been poor and he kept body hair, toe and fingernail nail clippings, and toothpicks in a bag in his room.

The patient denied most of his mother's allegations. However, he did admit to pushing his sister in 1997. He also stated that he constantly looked around outside because he feared a gang attack. He then stated that the real problem was that he wanted his independence from his father. Also, his brother was judgmental and a "power freak" at work. He had stopped taking his psychiatric medication because he felt better after a few pills. He also asserted that he was eating regularly; and that he would never hurt himself or anyone else. He said that he studied Islam in his room and never watched the "idiot box." He concluded that he was not a threat to himself or society.

The doctor then testified that he was a paranoid schizophrenic. He could harm himself. He had already pushed his sister and was verbally aggressive. And, since he had lighter fluid and gauze he could burn the house down. The doctor argued that causing a fire was a "big issue" and that "you don't have to wait for him to burn down the house. That's the case law."

The patient responded by denying he was mentally ill. And, again, that the lighter fluid, rope, and gauze were for ordinary purposes.

The judge recessed the court at 3:10 to review his notes.

At 3:48 the judge returned. He stated that there was clear and convincing evidence that the patient was schizophrenic. However, there was not clear and convincing evidence that he would harm himself. Also, there was no testimony that he had harmed anyone in the last four years. There was also no clear and convincing evidence that he could not take care of himself. He ordered the defendant released. It was 3:56pm.

In 2004 the researcher observed 24 hearings at the three courts. The average case took 37 minutes. Eighteen of the respondents appeared in court. There were nine females. Five of them were black, three were white, and one was Asian. Nine males appeared in court. Five of the males were black, four were white. The females' ages ranged from 30 to 72 and averaged 62 years of age. The males' ages ranged from 25 to 84. Their average age was about 35. Although age differences between males and females were striking, it is difficult to draw any conclusions since the numbers were small and the individuals were in court for various reasons. No Hispanics appeared before any of the three courts.

10. Conclusions

I began my research on the mental health court in 1971 because I was interested in the intersection of mental health and criminal justice. As an ethnographer I entered the court, as I would have entered a village, assuming that I knew nothing. What I found at the court in the 1970s was a medically dominated system where patients who were "sick" and "needed to be in the hospital," were committed.

After my initial research the mental health code was rewritten. Numerous rights and protections were added for the protection of the patients. This dramatically changed the functioning of the mental health court (see: Millen, 1987). In the 1971 to 1974 period it was common to have 70 to 100 commitments a week. By 2004 the number of any type of case in the mental health court was no more than a handful.

This shift in the functioning of the court was not simply the result of the new mental health code. It was also the response of the state's Department of Mental Health to the new code. The department found the new code to be too legalistic; and, too cumbersome to deal with. That is, it was time consuming, troublesome, and a drain on their scarce resources. So their response was simply to avoid the court. That is, the department's response was to avoid commitment and to create, in practice, a voluntary system (see: Lewis et al., 1987, 1988; Bursztajn, et al., 1986:172).

Now, let us return to the initial idea that prompted this study:

I had begun my research with the assumption that the court was the key gatekeeper in the mental health system. In my initial research I realized that "everyone" was committed. So, my initial assumption was incorrect. Since the court received patients from the admissions service the next step in my research in the 1970s was to conduct a study of the admissions office. Since the admissions office received individuals "off the street" I assumed *it* was the true key gatekeeper in the mental health system. After my 2004 research I again studied the admission process. Although the mental health system had changed dramatically I believed it was worthwhile to test my vertical and contextual analysis, again. So, in the next chapter we begin the process of "studying down."

References

Applebaum, Paul S. and Robert M. Hamm
  1982   "Decision to Seek Commitment." *Archives of General Psychiatry* 39: 447-451.
Bachrach, Leona L.
  1976   *Deinstitutionalization: An Analytical Review and Sociological Perspective.* Rockville, Maryland: National Institute of Mental Health.
  1980   "Is the Least Restrictive Environment Always the Best? Sociological and Semantic Implications." *Hospital and Community Psychiatry* 31: 97-103.
Bigges, John, Jr.
  1955   *The Guilty Mind.* New York: Harcourt, Brace, and Co.
Blackburn, R.
  1983   "Psychometrics and Personality Theory in Relation to Dangerousness." In *Dangerousness*, J. W. Hinton, ed. London: Allen and Unwin.
Brakel, Samuel Jan
  1985   "Involuntary Hospitalization." In *The Mentally Disabled and the Law*, 3rd ed., Samuel Jan Brakel, John Parry, and Barbara A. Winer, eds. Chicago: American Bar Association.
Brakel, Samuel J., John Parry, and Barbara A. Winer
  1985   *The Mentally Disabled and the Law*, 3rd ed. Chicago: American Bar Foundation.
Brakel, Samuel J. and Ronald S. Rock
  1971   *The Mentally Disabled and the Law*, 2nd ed. Chicago: University of Chicago Press.
Brooks, Alexander D.
  1984   "Defining the Dangerousness of the Mentally Ill: Involuntary Civil Commitment." In *Mentally Abnormal Offenders*, Michael Craft and Ann Craft, eds. London: Bailliere Tindall.
Burstein, Carolyn
  1980   "Criminal Case Processing From An Organizational Perspective: Current Research Trends." *The Justice System* 5: 258-273.
Bursztajn, Harold, et al.
  1986   "Process Analysis of Judges Commitment Decisions: A Preliminary Study." *American Journal of Psychiatry* 143: 170-174.
California Legislature
  1966   *The Dilemma of Mental Commitment in California: A Background Document.* Sacramento.
Chase, J.
  1972   "Where Have All The Patients Gone?" *Human Behavior* 14.

Cohen, M., et al.
  1978   "The Clinical Prediction of Dangerousness." *Crime and Delinquency*, 28-39.
Chu, Franklin and Sharland Trotter
  1974   *The Madness Establishment*. New York: Grossman.
Deutsch, Albert
  1949   *The Mentally Ill in America*, 2nd ed. New York: Columbia University Press.
ENKI
  1972   *A Study of California New Mental Health Law*. Chatsworth, California.
Ennis, Bruce J.
  1972   *Prisoners of Psychiatry*. New York: Harcourt, Brace, Jovanovich.
Foucault, Michael
  1965   *Madness and Civilization*. trans., Richard Howard. New York: Vintage Books.
Garfinkel, Harold
  1956   "Conditions of Successful Degradation Ceremonies." *American Journal of Sociology* 61: 420-424.
Gilboy, J. A. and J. R. Schmidt
  1971   "'Voluntary' Hospitalization of the Mentally Ill." *Northwestern University Law Review* 66: 429-453.
Greenley, James R.
  1973   "Alternative Views of the Psychiatrists Role." *Social Problems* 20.
Halleck, S.
  1967   *Psychiatry and the Dilemmas of Crime*. New York: Harper and Row.
Hawk, Gary and W. Lawrence Fitch
  2001   "Community Forensic Evaluation: Trends and Reflections On The Virginia Experience." In *The Evolution of Mental Health Law*, Lynda E. Frost and Richard J. Bonnie, eds. Washington, D.C.: American Psychological Association.
Hidday, Virginia
  1981   "Court Discretion: Application of the Dangerousness Standard in Civil Commitment." *Law and Human Behavior* 5: 275-289.
  1983   "Judicial Decisions In Civil Commitment: Facts, Attitudes, and Psychiatric Recommendations." *Law and Society Review* 17: 517-530.
  1988   "Civil Commitment: A Review of Empirical Research." *Behavioral Sciences and the Law* 6: 15-43.
Holstein, James. A.
  1993   *Court-Ordered Insanity*. New York: Aldine de Gruyter.
Hunt, Robert C. and David E. Wiley
  1968   "Operation Baxstrom After One Year." *American Journal of Psychiatry* 124.
Illinois
  1968   Mental Health Code. Effective January 1, 1968. As Amended 1969-71. Springfield.
  2004   Revised Statutes. Chapter 405, Act 5. Mental Health and Developmental Disabilities Code. Last amended, 2004. Springfield.
Kittrie, Nicholas N.
  1971   *The Right to be Different*. Baltimore: Johns Hopkins University Press.

Kozol, H., et al.
   1972   "The Diagnosis and Treatment of Dangerousness." *Crime and Delinquency* 18: 371-391.
Kutner, Lois
   1962   "The Illusion of Due Process in Commitment Proceedings." *Northwestern University Law Review* 57: 383-399.
LeBuffe, Francis P., et al.
   1979   "The Virginia Commitment Law: Clinical Characteristics of Patients Hospitalized Involuntarily By Court Order." *Bulletin of The American Academy of Psychiatry and Law* 7: 411-421.
Lewis, Dan A. and Rob Hugi
   1981   "Therapeutic Stations and the Chronically Treated Mentally Ill." *Social Service Review* 55: 206-220.
Lewis, Dan A., et al.
   1984   "The Negotiation of Involuntary Civil Commitment." *Law and Society Review* 18: 629-649.
   1987   *State Hospital Utilization in Chicago: People Problems and Policy*. Evanston, Illinois: Center for Urban Affairs and Policy Research, Northwestern University.
Lindman, Frank T. and Donald M. McIntyre, eds.
   1961   *The Mentally Disabled and the Law*. Chicago: University of Chicago Press.
Luckey, James W. and John J. Berman
   1979   "Effects of a New Commitment Law on Involuntary Admission and Service Utilization Patterns." *Law and Human Behavior* 3: 149-161.
Maisel, Robert
   1971   "Decision Making in a Commitment Court." *Psychiatry*.
McGarry, A. Louis, et al.
   1981   *Civil Commitment and Social Policy: An Evaluation of the Massachusetts Mental Health Reform Act of 1970*. Cambridge: Laboratory of Community Psychiatry, Harvard Medical School.
McGuire, J.
   1976   *Prediction of Dangerousness in a Federal Correctional Institution*. Ph. D. Dissertation. Department of Psychology, Florida State University.
Megargee, E.
   1970   "The Predication of Violence With Psychological Tests." In *Current Topics in Clinical and Community Psychiatry*, C. Spielberger, ed. New York: Academic Press.
Miller, Robert D.
   1987   *Involuntary Civil Commitment of The Mentally Ill In The Post-Reform Era*. Springfield, Ill.: Thomas.
Monahan, John
   1981   *Predicting Violent Behavior*. Beverly Hills: Sage.

Monahan, John and Henry J. Steadman
  1994 "Toward the Rejuvenation of Risk Research." In *Violence and Mental Disorder*, J. Monahan and H. Steadman, eds. Chicago: University of Chicago Press.
  2001 "Violence Rich Assessment: A Quarter Century of Research." In *The Evolution of Mental Health Law*, Lynda E. Frost and Richard J. Bonnie, eds. Washington, D.C.: American Psychological Association.
Morris, G.
  1978 "Conservatorship for the 'Gravely Disabled': California's Nondeclaration of Nonindependence." *International Journal of Law and Psychiatry* 1: 395-426.
Mosher, L. R. and J. G. Gunderson
  1973 "Special Report: Schizophrenia." *Schizophrenia Bulletin* 7: 12-52.
Munetz, Mark R., et al.
  1980 "Modernization of a Mental Health Act: Commitment Patterns." *Bulletin of the American Academy of Psychiatry and Law* 8: 83-92.
Nicholson, Robert A.
  1986 "Correlates of Commitment Status in Psychiatric Patients." *Psychological Bulletin* 100: 241-250.
Parachini, Allan
  1977a "Mass Failure on Psychiatrist Test." *Chicago Sun-Times*. Feb. 27:4.
  1977b "Thompson Got Warning on Doctor Crisis." *Chicago Sun-Times*. March 18:3.
Pfohl, Stephen J.
  1978 *Predicting Dangerousness*. Lexington, Massachusetts: Lexington Books.
  1979a "Deciding on Dangerousness: Predictions of Violence as Social Control." *Crime and Social Justice* 11: 28-40.
  1979b "From Whom Will We Be Protected? Comparative Approaches to the Assessment of Dangerousness." *International Journal of Law and Psychiatry* 2: 55-78.
  1984 "Predicting Dangerousness: A Social Deconstruction of Psychiatric Reality." In *Mental Health and Criminal Justice*, Linda Teplin, ed. Beverly Hills: Sage.
Rachlin, Stephen, et al.
  1975 "Civil Liberties Versus Involuntary Hospitalization." *American Journal of Psychiatry* 132: 189-192.
Rock, Ronald S., with M. A. Jacobson and R. M. Janopaul
  1968 *Hospitalization and Discharge of the Mentally Ill*. Chicago: University of Chicago Press.
Rothman, Marc and William R. Dubin
  1982 "Patients Released After Psychiatric Commitment Evaluation: Comparison With the Committed." *Journal of Clinical Psychiatry* 43: 90-93.
Sadoff, Robert L.
  1978 "Indications For Involuntary Hospitalization Dangerousness or Mental Illness?" In *Law and the Mental Health Professions*, Walter E. Barton and Charlotte J. Sanborn, eds. New York: International Universities Press.
Scheff, Thomas
  1964a "Social Conditions for Rationality: How Urban and Rural Courts Deal with the Mentally Ill." *American Behavioral Scientist* 8: 21-24.

1964b   "The Societal Reaction to Deviance." *Social Problems* 2: 401-413.

Spensley, James, et al.
    1974   "Involuntary Hospitalization: What For and How Long?" *American Journal of Psychiatry* 131: 219-222.

Spradley, James P.
    1970   *You Owe Yourself a Drunk*. Boston: Little, Brown.

Steadman, Henry J. and Joseph J. Cocozza
    1974   *Careers of the Criminally Insane*. Lexington, Massachusetts: Lexington Books.

Stone, Alan A.
    1975   *Mental Health and Law: A System In Transition*. Rockville, Maryland: National Institute of Mental Health.

Treffert, Harold A.
    1973   "Dying With Their Rights On." *American Journal of Psychiatry* 130: 1041-1042.
    1985   "The Obviously Ill Patient in Need of Treatment: A Fourth Standard for Civil Commitment." *Hospital and Community Psychiatry* 36: 259-264.

Warren, Carol A. B.
    1977   "Involuntary Commitment For Mental Disorders: The Application of California's Lauterman-Petris-Short Act." *Law and Society Review* 11: 629-649.
    1981   "New Forms of Social Control: The Myth of Deinstitutionalization." *American Behavioral Scientist* 24: 724-740.
    1982   *The Court of Last Resort*. Chicago: University of Chicago Press.

Weinberg, S. K.
    1967   "The Commitment of Patients to the Mental Hospital." In *The Sociology of Mental Disorders*, S. K. Weinberg, ed. Chicago: Aldine.

Wexler, David B.
    1981   *Mental Health Law*. New York: Plenum.

Whitmer, Gary E.
    1980   "From Hospitals To Jails: The Fate of California's Deinstitutionalized Mentally Ill." *American Journal of Orthopsychiatry* 50: 65-75.

Wille, Lois and Dennis Sodomka
    1973   "Eccentric or Insane? Mental Health Court Anguish." *Chicago Daily News*. Feb. 3-4:1.

Wiseman, Jacqueline P.
    1970   *Stations of the Lost*. Englewood Cliffs, New Jersey: Prentice Hall.

Zimmerman, Joel
    1982   *Civil Commitment in Chicago*. Denver: National Center for State Courts.

III Studying Down

3 Admissions
"I Don't Reject Anybody . . . I'm Protecting Myself"

1. Introduction

In the original study we moved from the court to the admission's service because "everyone" was committed. Therefore, we assumed that the real decision-making point in the system was admission's service.

In this chapter we begin with a brief overview of mental illness and help seeking behavior. We then describe the mental health system in the 1960s in Chicago from the work of Rock (1968) and Gilboy and Schmidt (1971). We then present our data from the 1970s. We restudied the admission's process in 2005. That data is compared to our earlier research.

2. Overview

Almost 15 percent of the U.S. population uses mental health or addiction services in the average year. This includes about 6 percent in the mental health sector, about 6 percent in the general medical sector, and about 3 in the human services sector. An additional 4 percent seek out voluntary support networks. However it is estimated that 70 percent of those with mental disorders do not receive any services at all (Howard, et al., 1996; Reiger, et al., 1993; Carey, 2005).

In the last 20 to 30 years the number of organizations treating mental illness has more than doubled. However, the number of beds available for the treatment of mentally ill has been halved. In other words, there has been a dramatic shift in the treatment of mental illness from inpatient to outpatient services. For example, in 1955 inpatient care comprised the majority of mental health care. However, in 1992 inpatient care shrank to one-third of all treatment; however, outpatient care rose to 68 percent of the 8.8 million treatment episodes (Mannersheid and Sonnenschein, 1996).

Epidemiological studies indicate that about 28 percent, or approximately 44.7 million people, have a mental illness or addictive disorder. Twenty-two percent, or approximately 35 million people, suffered from a mental illness. For treatment of these problems 5.6

percent of the population visited specialty mental health practitioners as outpatients and another 6.4 percent were treated by general hospitals as outpatients. Another 12 percent saw other professionals (teachers, clergy, etc.). Others received assistance from self help groups, family, and friends. Only 1 percent received impatient hospital care (Narrow, et. al, 1993). One could conceive of the mental health treatment as four separate systems of care: the medical or mental health professionals; the human or social service system, the folk system of religious advisors or alternate healers; and the lay system of friends and family (Larson, et. al, 1998; Pescosolido, et al., 1998; Pescosolido, et. al, 1999; Polgar and Morrissey, 1999).

How do individuals seek out the mental heath services that they want? (see: Pescosolido and Boyer, 1999; Avison, 1999). Research shows that mentally ill individuals enter treatment by one of three pathways: choice (46 percent), coercion (23 percent), or by stumbling into treatment through a suicide attempt (32 percent) (Pescosolido, et al. 1998; Gerson and Bassuk, 1980).

Individuals who seek help often have a different sociocultural and attitudinal profile than those who do not seek help. For example, women, Jews, those with low religiosity, residents of urban and suburban areas, and individuals with higher income and education tend to seek out professional help (Greenley and Mechanic, 1976a, 1976b). Since the 1950s help seeking behavior has increased. Now psychiatrists and psychologists are more likely to be consulted than in the past. However, today most people who seek help consult a general practice physician (Veroff, et al., 1981). However, men are more reluctant to seek help than women. And the poor tend to be isolated from services and use prayer more than affluent individuals (Cockerham, 2000:206; Kadushin, 1969).

The greatest gap between need and use of services is among blacks and Hispanics (Hough, et. al, 1978; Padgett, et al., 1994; Sussman, Robins, and Earls, 1987; Wells, et al., 1986; Wells, et al., 1988). Among minority groups there are greater economic barriers, as well as, suspicion of institutions. This prevents them from receiving treatment (Rogler and Cortes, 1993; Rogler, 1989).

Age shows a curvilinear relationship to receiving outpatient mental health treatment. Younger and older groups have the lowest rates of use, where 25- to 64-year-olds have the highest rates (Horgan, 1984; Shapiro, et al., 1984). This is just the opposite of treatment for physical illnesses (Anderson and Anderson, 1972).

Social class has long been studied in regards to mental health care (e.g., Farris and Dunham, 1939; Hollingshead and Redlich, 1958; Srole, et al., 962; Ryan, 1969). It has been found that the upper socioeconomic groups are more likely to seek treatment than the lower groups. However, if "class" is broken down by education (Greenley, Mechanic, and Cleary, 1987; Veroff, Kulka, and Dounan, 1981) and insurance coverage (i.e., income) this appears to explain the lack of treatment by lower socioeconomic groups (Wells, et al., 1986). When individuals seek out services they are usually driven by "distress" (Greenley and Mechanic, 1976; Mechanic, 1978; Gurin, et al., 1960; Leaf, et al., 1985; Portes, Kyle, and Eaton, 1992; Scheff, 1996; Ware, et al., 1984; Cleary, 1989; Pescosolido and Boyer, 1999: 400-11; Kadushin, 1969). However, social and cultural factors are the most important in deciding where to seek help. What is likely to be the most important factor in a decision to seek help is the degree of psychological distress an individual is suffering.

Troublesome feelings and interpersonal difficulties also contribute to help seeking (Thoits, 1985; Whitt and Meile, 1985; Perucci and Targ, 1982). So, some individuals go directly to professionals, whereas, others seek out help within their social networks (Gursky and Pollner, 1981; Perrucci and Targ, 1982; Veroff, et al., 1981).

In an important study Clausen and Yarrow, (1955) found that wives attempted to normalize their husband's mental illness. This process had five stages:

1. The wife's first recognition of a problem depended on the accumulation of behavior which was not readily understandable or acceptable to her.
2. This recognition forced her to adjust her expectations for herself and for her husband to account for his deviant response.
3. The wife's interpretation of the problem shifted back and forth from seeing the situation as normal to seeing it as abnormal.
4. She tended to make continuous adaptations or build defenses to the behavior while waiting for new behaviors that would either confirm her definition of his illness or lead her to a new one.
5. She reached the point at which she could no longer sustain a definition of normality and cope with her husband's behavior (see also: Karp, 1996; Goffman, 1971; Lemert, 1972; Thoits, 1982; Denzin, 1984).

Family and community members also often try to normalize mentally ill behavior. Only when that behavior becomes so extreme that it can no longer be tolerated is a person removed from the community (Goffman, 1971). This inability to tolerate mentally ill persons may be based upon a complicated interaction of factors: inability to perform appropriate role behavior, increasing social visibility of disturbed behavior, changes in family situations that bring on crises in formerly stable relations, the exhaustion of other resources, or, a suicide attempt. So, prior to the public phase of the crisis, and often again after it, the illness of the patient is contained within a family or community setting. It is the collapse of the accommodative patterns between the individual and their interpersonal network which renders the situation unmanageable and ushers in the public phase of the crises (Sampson, et al., 1961).

It is this disruption of social relationships that is the key to the individual being forced into treatment (Cockerham, 2000: 233-4; Rosenberg, 1984). And, it is estimated that 40 to 50 percent of all "voluntary" psychiatric admissions are coerced by family, friends, social agencies, or the police (Pescosolido, et al., 1998; Dennis and Monahan, 1996).

3. Seeking Help

The initiation of the hospitalization of a mentally ill person is viewed as a mysterious process by most individuals (Rock, 1968: 77-8). Rock arrived at this conclusion after conducting an experiment in which he made a number of "blind inquiries," much as an average citizen might, concerning psychiatric hospitalization. A call to the emergency service of the local medical society produced only a referral to the county hospital psychiatric division. This medical society explained that no referral could be made directly to a physician because it did this only in cases of physical emergencies. They further explained that the medical society did not have any specific information available about mental hospitalization. He next called the county hospital's psychiatric division which handled 8,000 mentally ill persons per year. The following conversation ensued:

Researcher:	"I have a friend who needs mental hospitalization. What should I do?"
Admission Worker:	"Well, you'll have to get a doctor's certificate."
Researcher:	"What is that?"
Admissions Worker:	"It's a certificate from a doctor that says your friend needs mental treatment. Call any doctor in the city and he will prepare it for you."
Researcher:	"Well, what do I do when I get it?"
Admissions Worker:	"Bring him down here and we will have him committed."
Researcher:	"Does that mean that he has to go to court?"
Admissions Worker:	"He will have to if he wants mental treatment."
Researcher:	"Well, he wants mental treatment but he doesn't want to go to court. He just wants to come in and have the hospital take care of him."
Admissions Worker:	"That makes no difference—he will have to be committed."
Researcher:	"He doesn't want to go to court—isn't there any other way he can do it?"
Admissions Worker:	"No, if he wants treatment, he will have to be committed." (The admissions worker had incorrectly stated that voluntary admission was impossible.) (Rock, 1968: 77-9)

Rock (1968) made additional calls to a number of social service agencies and most simply referred him to the county hospital's psychiatric facility. However, the city's social referral agency did provide information which was more adequate. A call to the local police elicited the advice that only a doctor's certificate was necessary and that any doctor in the community would be willing to prepare one. The experiment was repeated in several other cities with similar results.

Rock's (1968) experiment had been conducted in the early 1960s before much of the community mental health movement had begun. There were indications in Rock's description of his initial calls that Chicago was the city used in his experiment. Therefore, I repeated his experiment in the spring of 1974 by trying to secure assistance from various Chicago agencies on an early Monday morning.

At 4:30 a.m. I began to look up telephone numbers. I started with the largest sectarian social service agencies in the city. I called each one but none answered. I looked up the number of a large non-sectarian social work agency and called it. Again, no one answered.

I was sure that the Illinois Department of Mental Health had a clinic in the neighborhood. So I began looking for its number. I opened the city directory and began leafing through it: Illinois . . . Mental Health . . . Rogers Park . . . Clinic. But, I couldn't find it. I then took out the neighborhood telephone book: Rogers Park . . . Clinic . . . Mental Health . . . Emergency Services . . . Crisis Line . . . I tossed the book on the table in annoyance.

I thought for a moment while I tapped my pen against the kitchen table. I remembered that the local medical society had an emergency medical service number. Although one of their doctors had allegedly allowed a patient to die the previous week because the caller could not immediately pay a $30.00 cash fee, I called them. I was told: "There are no psychiatrists on call until nine a.m." I asked, "Is a regular physician available?" "I don't think so," she answered. "Do you have a family physician?" "No." There was a long pause. "Your best bet would be to call the Department of Mental Health's crisis intervention number." I thanked her and hung up.

I called the crisis intervention number. I asked: "Do you give help to people with psychiatric crisis?" "Oh, no," the woman responded in a pleasant voice. "I'm just the switchboard operator but a counselor from the service wouldn't answer the call unless the person who is mentally ill comes to the phone." "But what if they won't come to the phone?" "Well then, you better call the state hospital's admitting office." I hung up. I looked at the clock. It was almost 5:00 a.m.

I picked up the phone and called the state hospital. I asked how I would get a mentally ill person into the hospital. The woman said: "You can bring him in yourself, in a cab, on a bus, or call the police, that's all I can advised you to do." "But," she suddenly added, "bring him in during the morning, not now." "Why?" "The doctor only admits emergencies at night. Anyway, there's more staff here during the day." She then hung up.

I didn't know what to do next. I picked up the phone and called the fire department. I asked if they sent ambulances out for the mentally ill. "No, we never handle mentals, that's a matter for the police department, entirely," the fire fighter on the phone said.

I wearily pressed the phone's arm down, released it, and dialed the police department's number. "Do I need some type of doctor's certificate before you can take a person to the state hospital?" I asked. "Yes, you've got to have a doctor's certificate or they won't even touch him," the officer explained. "How do I get a doctor?" "Do you have a family doctor?" "No." "Well, then . . . there's a doctor's service . . . but they probably won't come." After a long pause the officer said: "Ya' know, they won't even let us in the gate at Chicago-Read without a certificate. And if they don't take him then we're stuck with him. That's why we've got to have a doctor's certificate or a court order." I waited several seconds for the officer to volunteer information on how to get a court order. When he remained silent, I thanked him and hung up. It was 5:30 a.m.

The next morning at 3:00 a.m. I called the police again. I asked the officer how I could get a court order so that they would transport a person to the state hospital. "Truthfully, I don't know . . . But a relative can sign the person in. Or, we could send a wagon over. But, first, call the desk sergeant at the district station." I called and asked the desk sergeant how someone could get a court order so they could pick up a person and take them to the state hospital. "You can't get a court order at 3:00 in the morning." However, he suggested that I could call back downtown and have them send out a wagon so that officers could talk the person into coming to the hospital. I thanked him and hung up.

So, over a decade after Rock's experiment the emergency psychiatric assistance available to an average citizen in Chicago was no better than it was in the early 1960s. It appears that receiving assistance was still a mystery. The response to an average citizen's call for help may consist of nothing more than the knowledge and good will of the officer who answer the phone.

A public aid caseworker described his involvement with the police in the earl 1970s when he tried to get help for a mentally ill client:

"I worked at an office on the Southside of Chicago. Early one summer morning the phone rang at 8:35. The woman calling said: 'This is Mrs. Jones. Billy's got the nerves. Can you come and see him?' 'O.K.' I drove to the house. It was a two flat and they lived on the second floor. I rang the bell and the wife let me in. I found her husband on all fours in his underwear on the bedroom floor. His head was leaning against the bed and he looked like a lost puppy. And he was obviously psychotic. So I called the medical unit in my office. I said, 'This is Mr. Johnson. I have a psychiatric emergency and I need an ambulance.' 'O.K.,' the person on the other end of the line said. 'Fill out a T-98 ambulance form and then we'll consider sending an ambulance.' 'No, you don't understand. I'm in the *field*, not in the office, and I need an ambulance for a psychiatric emergency.' 'I understand,' she coolly replied, 'come back to the office, fill out a T-98 ambulance form, and *we* will decide if you need an ambulance.' I slammed down the phone. Now, that's not the official agency policy, but it is the *real* agency policy. Just because a caseworker asks for an ambulance doesn't mean they're going to send one.

"So, I called the police and they said they'd send a squadroll. Now, if an average citizen calls they might, or might not, respond. But, if a doctor, lawyer, teacher, or social worker calls, they assume everything else has been tried, so they send a unit.

"While I had been on the phone my client had gotten up, pulled on some pants, and gone in to the bathroom. I walked over and saw the door was partially open. He was ritually washing his hands over and over again. But, as long as he didn't try to cut himself, then that was O.K. After half an hour he walked into the kitchen, sat down on a chair in the middle of the room, and stared blankly ahead.

"A little later the police arrived. I remember them quite distinctly. There was the 9 foot tall black officer and his young-Polish-assistant. It was the big, liberal integrated team on the Southside, I thought. I also thought that they must do this every day. And my ego was less important than my client's health. So I stepped aside and let them do their job. Well, they talked to him, joked with him, and cajoled him for half an hour. But there was no response. They were getting tired and I was afraid they were going to MACE him and drag him out the door. So, finally, I stepped between them and said, 'C'mon Mr. Jones, lets get dressed and go see the doctor. If everything is O.K. you'll be home by lunch.' I repeated that over and over in a soothing voice as I dressed him. I then touched him on the elbow; he stood up, and walked towards the door. 'Oh, O.K.,' the officers said as they walked out the door. I helped my client into the squadroll. Then his wife got in and they drove off. They took him to Cook County Psychiatric, they admitted him, bombed him with medication, and released him two weeks later.

"After he got home I visited him and he was the nicest guy in the world. Two weeks later I visited the house again. He watched me suspiciously from the corner. 'Is he taking his medicine?' I asked the wife. 'No.' 'He's *got* to take his medicine. You're here 24 hours a day, I'm not. You've got to get him to take his medicine.' 'O.K.' Two weeks later I visited again. He hid in the bedroom and watched me through a crack in the door. 'Is he taking his medicine?' 'No.' The first, and the hardest thing, I learned on this job is that there's lots of people you can't help. So, since he wasn't taking his medicine, there was nothing I could do for him. So, I washed my hands of the case.

"Several weeks later I got a call at the office at 8:35am. It was his wife. 'Billy locked me out of the house all night. I called the fire department three times. They came and asked, 'Did he have a heart attack?' 'No.' I said, 'he's got nerves.' 'Can't take him,' they said. Then I called the police three times. They asked, 'Did he commit a crime?' 'No.' I said, 'he's got nerves.' 'Can't take him,' they said. So, I called the police again and they sent the same two policemen from earlier this summer. And they said, 'Call Mr. Johnson, maybe he can talk him out.' 'So, can you come?' 'O.K.'

"So, I drove to the house. I got there at 9:00 a.m. It was an early September day and it was already 90°. 'Go talk to him,' the black officer said. So, I went upstairs. I said, 'Mr. Jones, Mr. Jones, lets go to the hospital and get some medicine.' I saw the door was ajar and the chain was on. I saw him pacing back and forth in the frontroom. But he ignored me. So I went back to the two officers. I looked up at the 9 foot tall black officer and said, 'We've got to take him'—volunteering myself to go in with them. Then I remember, quite distinctly, the black officer looked down at me and said, 'Man, I ain't hasslin' with no crazy dude.' 'Call the sergeant!' the young Polish-assistant said. So, they called the sergeant. He arrived at 10 a.m. It was now 95°. He got out of his squad and said to me, 'schizophrenic, right?' 'Yes.' 'So, he could be better in 5 minutes, right?' 'Or, he could murder somebody in 5 minutes,' I replied. 'Call the lieutenant!' he countered.

"In the meantime I went upstairs twice more and got no response. The lieutenant arrived at 11 o'clock. It was now 100°. He got out of the car, gave me a dirty look and walked away. So, I chased after him and explained the situation. In his best bureaucratese he replied, 'I'm not endangering the life and limb of my officers for a mentally ill person who has not broken the law. Call County and have them send out a doctor to give him a shot.' So I walked over to a neighbor's house and called Cook County Hospital's Psychiatric Admitting office. I explained the situation and asked them to send out a doctor. The woman on the other end of the line laughed and laughed and said, 'We don't send doctors out for *that*. Sign a disorderly conduct complaint. Then they've got to take him.' So, I sauntered back to the lieutenant and said, 'We'll sign a disorderly conduct complaint.' 'Damn!' he yelled as he pounded his fist on to the hood of the patrol car. He then had the wife sign a blank form, tossed it on the front seat of the squad, and called for assistance.

"Just then his best friend wandered by. 'Talk to him,' I implored. 'O.K.' We went upstairs and the door was still ajar on the chain. And he was still pacing back and forth. 'Hey Billy, come on, lets go to the hospital. Come on Billy.' There was no response. The friend then turned to me and said, 'Ya' know how it is, you marry an older woman, you don't get it regular, and you go a little nuts. Gotta go.' And he left.

"A little later someone told me a retired physician lived down the block. So, I knocked on his door. A 110-year-old man answered. I said, 'Are you a physician?' 'Yes.' I explained the situation and said, 'Well, I understand that if you sign a paper you can get my client in the hospital?' 'Yes,' So he took his prescription pad out and wrote something like, 'Put this man in the hospital.' He handed it to me. Then he screamed, "And never bother me again!' I walked over to the lieutenant and handed him the note. He laughed and tore it up.

"At noon the lieutenant said, 'We're ready, but go talk to him once more.' So, I went upstairs. This time the door was closed. Suddenly, it flew open and Mr. Jones stood there with a raised screwdriver. 'I am goin to die,' I thought to myself. Just as suddenly he yelled, 'police!', and slammed the door.

"A little later six officers, the lieutenant, and I went to the back door. They broke down the door. They grabbed Mr. Jones. Suddenly he began screaming, 'I'm not going! I'm not going!' Then he fell silent. They cuffed him, he walked out the door, down the stairs, through the gangway, and in to the squadroll. They drove off to Cook County Psychiatric Admitting. The wife got in my car and I drove to Cook County Psychiatric Admitting. We got there at 1 o'clock.

"I explained the situation to the admitting clerk. She said, 'I can't admit him without his admitting number.' I explained that I was a public aid worker and I had no idea what his admitting number was. However, I emphasized that he *was* psychotic and needed to be in the hospital. She refused to admit him. We stood there and argued about this for one hour. Finally, I insisted on speaking to a doctor. Soon a doctor came out and said, 'Ah, Mr Jones is back. Can't take him.' 'Why?' 'He has a special care and custody order. God damn ACLU always screwin' around in mental health. Take him to jail!' 'Wait!' I yelled. 'He's sick, he needs to be in a hospital.' 'Ok . . . Ok . . . I'll call a judge,' the doctor said. Two hours later the doctor returned. 'Its Friday afternoon, the judges are all fishing in Wisconsin. Take him to jail.' So, they took him to jail.

"The next morning I picked up the wife and we drove to court. My client was sitting in the back row, handcuffed. Eventually, they called the case. They judge said to the wife, 'Why did you sign this?' 'I just want to get Billy in the hospital.' The judge shrugged. The clerk said to the judge, 'sign this, sign this, sign this.' The judge signed the documents, shrugged, and said 'next!' The bailiff then took my client away. After court I asked the clerk what he had done. He said that Mr. Jones would be sent to the police hospital and if he needed treatment he would then be transferred to the state hospital and be committed. I was relieved and thanked him. I drove the wife home and said goodbye since it was my last day at the agency.

"Several months later I met my old deskmate. I asked, 'What happened to Mr. Jones?' 'He was paranoid. He got in a fist fight with someone at the police hospital and poked him the nose. So they sentenced him to jail for 30 days. Now he's back out on the street.' That's mental health in America!"

4. Psychiatric Admitting: The 1960s

How then do people get in to the hospital? Rock (1968) studied hospital receiving centers in Chicago for a twelve-month period in 1960-1961. He found that half of all admissions in Chicago were initiated by the patient themselves, their family, or their friends.

Table 3-1
Number of Patients Brought to Chicago Mental
Health Clinic (Year Ending April 1961)

Intake Source	Number of Patients	Percent
Family or friends	3,867	47.5
Police	1,228	15.1
Municipal court psychiatric facility	1,171	14.4
Other hospitals	847	10.4
County hospital	407	5.0
Self	315	3.9
Social agencies	206	2.5
Other	97	1.2
Total	8,138	100.0

(Rock, 1968: 83)

The police, however, have a more significant role to play than is obvious at first glance. For example the "municipal court psychiatric facility" in the chart was the local court's diagnostic service. Persons who were brought before the court on criminal charges and whose conduct was believed to be the result of mental illness were referred for a preliminary psychiatric exam. Those who were charged with misdemeanors and were found to be mentally ill were then transferred to the state hospital for a commitment hearing. Most of those persons who were transferred to the state hospital from the courts became involved in the criminal justice system through police action. If we also assume that about half of the transfers to the state hospital from other hospitals (including the county hospital) and from social service agencies began with a police action, we may conclude that at least one-third of all persons who were brought to the state hospital have been in contact with the police. A Pennsylvania study also found that the police there have contacts with one-third of all psychiatric hospital admissions (see: Table 3-2). The referrals in Table 3-2 from "component units" (19 percent) were patients who came to the reception center at the direction of the nearby state hospital for admissions. It seems probable that a large number of these referrals followed the same initial patterns as did those for the other Pennsylvania admissions. Therefore, the Chicago data appears comparable to that of Pennsylvania.

Table 3-2
Intake Source, Receiving Center 1960

Intake Source(First Admissions Only)	Number of Patients	Percent
Hospitals:		
Component units	597	19.0
Other hospitals	468	14.9
Police, courts, prisons	742	23.8
Social agencies	215	6.9
Private physicians	350	11.2
Outpatient clinics	23	0.7
Nursing homes	22	0.7
Families and friends	360	11.5
Selves	299	9.5
Unknown	57	1.8
Total	3,133	100.0

(Rock, 1968: 84)

Thus, we may conclude that over 80 percent of all psychiatric admissions in the early 1960s in Chicago were the result of the patient themselves, their family, friends, or the police. All other governmental institutions, social service agencies, and independent professionals assisted in only 20 percent of all psychiatric admissions to state hospitals.

Further, as we noted earlier, in the early 1960s the psychiatric admitting facility for the Chicago area was focused on involuntary admission and commitment. The Chicago Mental Health Clinic, which was then the city's admitting facility, was ostensibly also a treatment facility. However, in practice, it was a diagnostic and custodial institution. Rock (1968) found that all persons brought to the clinic were eligible for admission to a state hospital only if they had been involuntarily confined and committed. The medical staff at the receiving center viewed involuntary commitment as a sure means of achieving admission. They found this procedure to be considerably easier to administer than voluntary admission. That is because it routinized the procedure and discouraged vacillation by the patient or their relatives. It also shifted all responsibility for formal decision making to the court. Further, the court viewed the involuntary procedure (petition by a citizen, medical examination, and a formal public hearing) as the only means of recognizing a patient's rights.

This attitude changed in the late 1960s when a new mental health code was written. As a result of this commitments dropped in Chicago from over 8,000 per year in 1960 to 3,400 per year in the early 1970s. In fact, involuntary admissions soon fell to only about one-third of the total.

This shift from involuntary to voluntary admission was seen as a positive step by both the medical and legal profession. By making the patient volunteer for their own treatment, rather than be committed against their will, it was believed that this increased both the patients feeling of self-worth and their receptivity to psychiatric treatment. Voluntary admission also avoided a formal judicial hearing and an involuntary commitment. This was thought by physicians to be psychologically damaging. Legal opinion also looked favorably upon voluntary admission because it was seen to be a way of avoiding the morass of constitutional issues raised by compulsory commitment.

Gilboy and Schmidt (1971) however, found considerably more coercion involved in "voluntary" admission than one would have anticipated (see also: Palmer and Wohl, 1972). Under Illinois law (Illinois Mental Health Code, 1968, Articles 4 and 5) there are two different procedures for voluntary admission to a mental hospital. An individual may enter a hospital as an "informal admission." Under this procedure they do not have to make a formal application and they are free to leave at any time during normal working hours. However, those patients entering as voluntary admissions must execute a formal application. If they wish to leave they must file a notice. The staff then has five working days to decide if they wish to release them or bring them before a court for a hearing.

Proponents of voluntary admission assume that a person seeking such an admission arrive at the hospital with friends, relatives, or a physician. However, Gilboy and Schmidt (1971) found that half of all persons had been brought to the facility in police custody. For example, in February and March of 1971, 358 of the 723 voluntary admissions had arrived in police custody.

In Illinois, the police may bring a person to a mental hospital on the basis of an "emergency petition" signed by any citizen over 18 years old alleging that "immediate hospitalization is necessary for the protection from physical harm of such person or others" (Illinois Mental Health Code, 1968, Article 7). Also, the police may bring an individual to a hospital on the basis of a "certificate of a physician." This certificate must state that a person is "in need of mental treatment" and it must be signed both by a physician who has personally examined the individual as well as by some other person (Illinois Mental Health Code, 1968, Article 6). The police may also transport a person to the hospital of their own initiative, at the request of another person, or by the individual themselves.

In 1973 it was reported that for the Chicago-Read Mental Health Center, which serves much of Cook County, there were 24 informal admissions, 115 physicians' certificates, 4,204 voluntary admissions, and 2,391 emergency admissions for the year (Mental Health Statistics For Illinois, Fiscal, 1973).

Gilboy and Schmidt (1971) found that the staff of the admissions office felt that their options were severely limited because of practical considerations. The office was badly understaffed. A substantial majority of the police cases arrived at night and on weekends. During most of that time they were the only psychiatric admitting facility open in the area. In the winter of 1971 the office was staffed by a single intake worker and one physician. However, people frequently arrived in bunches. On one night 19 people arrived between 5:00 p.m. and midnight. To complete the clerical work on each person and to transport each patient to a ward took 15 to 20 minutes each. This created strong pressures to screen patients quickly.

Because of this pressure admissions became bureaucratic routine: Once the individual was brought in to the admitting office an application was filled out by the person's friends or relatives. If the individual was brought in by the police the application was usually filled out by the officer or a staff member. An interview was then conducted by an intake worker in an attempt to ascertain why the individual had been brought in and whether the case was serious enough to require hospitalization. A social history was then taken and the appropriate intake forms were filled out. If the intake worker believed that the person was ill enough to be hospitalized they tried to convince the individual to sign a voluntary admission form. Since the admissions office was often busy, there was strong pressure to screen people quickly and to complete the paperwork as quickly as possible. If a person "signed themselves in" the paperwork was reduced, the screening process was sped-up, and the physician avoided the responsibility of certifying the individual for an involuntary admission.

After the screening by the intake worker the person was sent to a physician. The physician was usually foreign born. He or she may or may not have been a psychiatrist. This physician gave the individual a brief physical and psychiatric exam. This often perfunctory examination determined whether the person would be held or not. If the physician felt that the person should be hospitalized they were asked to sign a voluntary admission form. If the person refused and the physician felt the individual needed to be in the hospital they were admitted as an "emergency admission." They had to be brought before a court for a hearing within five working days.

In the day to day operations of the office the staff preferred voluntary admission over the involuntary admissions since it was quicker and simpler. Moreover, voluntary admissions were favored because the physicians could then avoid assuming the responsibility of signing a certificate and involuntarily confining a person against their will. Much of this problem could have been avoided by refusing to admit police cases. However, the admissions staff was quite aware that the police bring in people who "need to be arrested." Further, to deny the police officer's request would force the staff and physician to make an independent decision which could eventually bring them grief. For example, one intake worker commented, "What if you let them go and they murder five nuns?" So, everyone "goes along with the program." As a result of this the hospital admitted 86 percent of the police cases (531 out of 614) in February and March of 1971. In that same time period they admitted only 53.5 percent (577 out of 1077) of the non-police cases (Gilboy and Schmidt, 1971).

Another source of admissions is transfers from the courts. In 1972 judges made about 5,800 referrals of misdemeanant cases to the Psychiatric Institute, which is attached to the courts. Of those 5,800 referrals about 2,000 persons were "certified" and transferred to the state hospital for a second examination and a commitment hearing. Since these individuals had already been seen by a physician there was little concern about these cases in the admitting service.

Although the social worker I interviewed at the Institute spoke in glowing terms about the Institute's work, a number of other mental health professionals I interviewed were highly critical of its functioning. Several claimed that the Institute certified far too many individuals who could stand trial and quickly be freed. Two of the mental health workers interviewed caustically commented that the Institute "certifies everybody." One supervising nurse with ten years of experience working with committed patients shook her head in disbelief as she thumbed through a number of the Institute's certificates. She pointed out that there were only a couple of sentences scrawled under each of the form's categories. She felt that such certificates were inadequate.

A Legal Aid attorney who handled commitment cases commented that "the average judge has no real understanding of mental illness. The judges feel that the mentally ill are dangerous and need to be confined. Although a person may have been only picked up for 'safekeeping' high bonds are routinely set so that they can be held for examination at the Psychiatric Institute. One judge usually sets a $1,000 recognizance bond for disorderly conduct cases. For the mentally ill however, he sets a $5,000 cash bond so that they will be unable to leave. It's a mill."

Gilboy and Schmidt (1971:430) in their study of voluntary admissions concluded: "In a majority of cases voluntary admission is utilized to hospitalize persons who are already in some form of official [police] custody. Voluntary admission avoids procedural complexity and the need for officials to assume responsibility, both inherent drawbacks to compulsory commitment from the official's point of view. Individuals are therefore, induced to voluntarily commit themselves with the threat of involuntary commitment as the principal means of persuasion." Therefore, they ask: Is this "voluntary" at all?

5. Psychiatric Admitting: The 1970s

In the late 1960s a new mental health code was written and passed by the legislature in Illinois. In order to examine the changes in the admission process the researcher conducted a study at an outlying state hospital in the Chicago metropolitan area in the summer of 1973. The researcher observed the admission of, or analyzed the written intake summaries of, 120 persons. The hospital studied drew its patients from a diverse area including some of Chicago's suburbs, small industrial cities (100,000 population), towns, and rural areas. Therefore, the data is not strictly comparable to an urban situation but it will give us a basis upon which to draw some conclusions on the functioning of the state hospital's admissions office and the changing patterns of admissions since the 1960s.

Of the 120 persons who sought help from the state hospital almost all received some assistance. Eighty-seven percent were admitted to the hospital and only 13 percent were turned away ("deflected"). This seemed like an unusually high percentage of admissions since the literature argued that over half of all persons seeking admission could be handled in the community.[1]

In order to examine the hospital's admissions policy I interviewed the physician who did most of the hospital's admitting. He was slightly built middle-aged man with a European accent and an engaging smile. I began the interview by asking the doctor to describe his job. He said that he was the only physician on the hospital grounds during most of 4 p.m. to midnight shift. He said with a sigh that there was simply too much to be done for one physician. During his shift he was responsible for the health and welfare of the hospital's 1400 patients. I asked if the pressure of his duties made him cut corners on his admission interviews. He replied that "on every admission I check the person's mental condition and problems." He said, "I usually take 10 to 15 minutes per interview though with some

---

1. One psychiatrist that was interviewed concluded that hospitalization was not needed for 46 of the 47 patients he assessed if alternative social services had been available at night.

alcoholics and mental patients I speed things up." I said that this seemed a rather short time for such an important interview. He nodded in agreement. "It's very difficult to do an evaluation in a very shout time, but a thorough mental exam might take hours or days." He shrugged. "I'm not perfect. I just put my impressions on paper." He added that in most cases background information was sparse. "I have only the direct information from the patient," he concluded.

"How do you handle the borderline cases?" I asked "There are no borderline cases here. We keep everybody. We keep people because they need help." "Do you deflect [turn away] anyone?" I asked "I don't reject anybody," he said, "I'm protecting myself. If I reject somebody and then something happens. You know, it has happened in other places." He settled back in his chair. "Of course I deflect a few persons," he added, "but not many. When I do, however, they go home with a friend or the police take them, but they don't just wander off. If someone needs to be deflected, let the ward physician do it the next day." "I hear Dr. A., on the midnight shift, deflects a lot of people," I said. "She's been here only a year and doesn't have enough experience; that's why she does it," he answered. "How long have you been here?" "I've been in this country for over 13 years and I've worked this shift at the hospital for eight or nine years. I'm originally from Estonia, but I fled to Sweden. And after seven years there, I came to the United States in 1958. I did my internship in Chicago and then specialized in dermatology and urogenital problems. But that all was a long time ago," he said wistfully as he seemed to drift off into his memories for a moment.

"Psychiatry is a funny business," he said. "We say alcoholics are mentally ill and let them into mental hospitals, but they know what they're doing; they're not mentally ill." He leaned forward. "There was this fellow whose wife died. He sent flowers to the wife's grave in Arizona every month. Then one day he drove down to Arizona, dug her up, brought the body back, and put it in his freezer for a year. He's a classic schizophrenic according to orthodox Freudian psychiatry, but when I interviewed him, he was perfectly fine, except that he said he had to take his wife home. There are *many* people here like that—murderers and such, who are really fine." He settled back into his chair. "Psychiatry is the darkest specialty in medicine," he said shaking his head, "because you really don't know," pointing to is temple, "what's going on up here."

After the interview I wandered backed towards the admissions office and sat down among a circle of intake workers. "Do most of the persons who come in here *really* have a psychiatric problem?" I asked. "This is impressionistic," the admissions director said, "but most of them seem to have medical or police problems." He paused. "Almost everybody who comes in here is admitted; and we do get 20 to 30 people a month who are 'referrals'. They come in and say, 'I'm confused, where do I get help?' On weekends we get people who wander in and are admitted because they have nowhere else to go. We have a smattering of deflections, but not many. Normally, we just automatically admit everybody on a petition. During the day shift admitting is handled by the ward physicians. Hardly anyone, 1 in 100, is ever rejected on a ward. However, Dr. A. is different. She doesn't 'chop-chop,' admit everybody, but explores alternatives and so forth. But because of her hours, she hardly ever sees a patient." Heads began to nod. "She's gusty," one worker commented. "She's the most militant," another added.

"The thing is we're here to help people," one intake worker said. "We take everybody, because if we don't, they won't get any help. They'll fall through the cracks in the system if we don't let them in here. That's especially the case with alcoholics. Anyway, we have to take everybody. We can't lose people to the Department of Corrections!" All nodded in agreement. "We're just here to be problem solvers." Everyone nodded again. The admissions director turned and rummaged through a folder stuffed with intake summaries. "Here, read these." He handed me some typical admitting summaries.

Lynne B.,[2] a white, 29-year-old single female was brought to Central Admissions at about 12:45 p.m. this afternoon by an employee of the Salvation Army. Lynne was referred to the Salvation Army by the Mission. Apparently, Lynne has no place to stay. The Mission said they did not have room for her, the Salvation Army could not keep her, so we were contacted for possible assistance. Ben B. of Community Placement is coordinating a possible placement for Lynne.

While at CAS (Central Admissions Service) Lynne appeared to be in contact with reality, oriented, was cooperative, and polite. Apparently the only obstacle to Lynne being an excellent candidate for sheltered care or other moderately supervised placement is her reported promiscuity. Lynne was formerly a patient at the State School, admitted and was most recently a resident of ____, given a discharge for unauthorized absence there on ____. Apparently, Lynne is unable to take care of herself adequately, and her family will have nothing to do with her. Lynne stated that she did feel she needed help in finding a place to stay. She has most recently been staying with a friend. Lynne did not wish to undergo any type of treatment here. She stated that she only wanted to be here as long as it takes to find a suitable place to stay elsewhere.

Vivian S., a 39-year-old female was returned here at approximately 8:00 p.m. tonight by the police. She was admitted here on ____; she went UA (Unauthorized Absence) on ____; and on ____ she was given an absolute discharge. Apparently Vivian was picked up wandering about and appeared to be lost. When the police stopped her, she apparently indicated to them that she was still a patient here. When she arrived at Central Admissions she wanted no part of voluntary or informal admissions. She didn't have any money or any place to stay. Several calls were made in an attempt to find a temporary place for her to stay. Mr. S. (her father-in-law) refused to have anything to do with her. Since she didn't have any money, she could not get a hotel room. Vivian's intentions were to go to her father-in-law's home and get her money that he had. She decided that she would rather return to a residence where she apparently had been staying since she left the hospital. Vivian was taken there by two intake workers.

While at Central Admissions she was very talkative and a little upset because she felt that her father-in-law was taking her money from her unfairly (he is her conservator). She did however, appear to be oriented and in fair contact.

---

2. All names have been changed and some of the details of each case have been fictionalized to protect the privacy of the individual. The researcher observed a number of the cases cited below.

"What if someone comes in who just needs a place to stay?" I asked. "We would put in a couple of dollars each and got her a room." "What if that kind of situation occurred several times in one evening and you ran out of money?" Everyone shrugged and there was a long silence. "We just can't put people out on the street!" one intake worker stated. Everyone nodded in agreement.

The admissions director went on to explain: "Our real problem is not deflections, it's that other agencies dump on us. Probably one quarter to one third of all our admissions shouldn't occur. For example, a lot of old people unnecessarily spend a few days here between nursing homes. Outpatients at mental health clinics sometimes can't get appointments when they're upset or need their medication changed—so they end up here. Nursing homes and shelter care facilities routinely send us 'dangerous' people. They're usually fine but got mad when the place refused a reasonable request of theirs or simply didn't deliver any services. The police and jails dump on us to avoid charging someone or if they act out in the slightest way. Then bang, we get them. And they just love to bring us alcoholics and drifters. Kids who get in trouble with agencies or the Department of Children and Family Services (DCFS) get put in here, too. We also get kids with meticulously documented physician's certificates from some agencies; but frankly, I don't believe half of them. Private hospitals routinely send people to us if they're 'confused,' 'uppity,' troublemakers, or run out of money. And of course, runaways from other psychiatric hospitals are brought here. If the police find an ex-patient, even if he's been out forty years, we get him. He's branded. 'Once a mental patient, always a mental patient.'"

"Talkin about dumping on us, read these." He handed me some other case summaries.

Sheila N., a 17-year-old female was transported here tonight by personnel from an emergency child care center in Chicago. Sheila has been in their facility since Friday and has been upsetting the center's residents. According to the workers that accompanied her, Sheila has physically abused other residents and generally caused trouble at the center. Sheila has been placed at the center four different times this past year and bounced in and out of several other placements, none of which have worked out. The center is an "open living" environment and apparently this is too much for Sheila to handle. Sheila is 6 months pregnant, also.

The CAS (Central Admissions Service) office had been notified that Sheila would be brought back for readmission. When the Center people arrived with Sheila, they stated that we should have had a call from the Department of Children and Family Services (Sheila's legal guardian) authorizing Sheila's admission as a voluntary minor admission. However, we had not received any such call. The staff from the center signed an emergency petition so we could hold Sheila while they made arrangements for the voluntary minor authorization. Finally, after not receiving any call from DCFS, I contacted their Springfield office and talked with Director's secretary. She refused to give authorization for a voluntary minor admission due to the fact that the child care center had not had Sheila seen by a doctor to have admission to a DMH (Department of Mental Health) facility recommended. She stated that perhaps it was a good idea to have Sheila committed so she would not be bounced from placement to placement and could finally get some consistent help. So Sheila remained admitted as an emergency.

Helen H. a 56-year old white married female, was brought to CAS from the hospital via ambulance. Her husband also accompanied her and was willing to sign a petition on Helen, but she chose to sign in voluntarily. Helen has been here on one previous occasion and was discharged on ____ .

Helen is a short plumpish woman who, while at CAS, was accommodating in every aspect. She was in superficial contact with reality but displayed no insight whatsoever into her current situation. She was very talkative and rambled on and on. She was pleasant and displayed a good sense of humor. Her husband was going to sign a petition but could not state any reason why Marion would be a danger to herself or others. In fact, Mr. H. seemed quite distant, taking the admission process as some kind of weird joke, laughing most inappropriately.

Evidently Helen was taken to the hospital because of an asthma condition but because of Helen's confused behavior, it was decided that she should be brought out here. Apparently Helen would become violent at times, striking out at her husband with a rubber hose. When confronted with this, Helen freely admitted to "giving old Ray a bop." She states that he drinks too much quite often and she was trying to straighten things out. Mr. H. admitted that he did drink quite heavily. When Helen and her husband were together they seemed to get along fine although they're whole conversation made little sense whatsoever. It is my opinion that Helen is just an extremely eccentric lady. It seems to me that most of Helen's behavioral problem stems from her marital relationship, although asserting what type of relationship they have will be a difficult task.

Richard R., a 26-year-old single white male, was brought to CAS at 9:30 A. M. by his step-father, David. Richard signed voluntary papers. Richard has had one previous admission here, AD (admission date) on ____ . After his discharge Richard was taken to the _____ , a private hospital. Richard was discharged yesterday after a 10 month hospitalization. According to Dr. Z. Richard was making "gradual improvement but lately his progress had remained stationary." Because Mr. R. has spent most of his savings for Robert's hospitalization, it was necessary to have Richard transferred here.

While at CAS, Richard was rather inappropriate. He constantly paced the floor, and not once did he sit in a chair. When asked a question, Richard responded by only nodding his head; and often times he would not respond at all. Usually, Mr. R. had to prod Richard before he would answer. Richard appears to understand where he is, but it is doubtful if he has any insight into his situation. Mr. R. brought along many of Richard's medical records. These records more adequately explain his recent behavior.

According to Mr. R. Richard had an average childhood. But at the age of 16 he was struck by a train. Both legs, both hands, and many ribs were broken, and he was in traction for 11 weeks. According to Mr. R. it was after this accident when Richard lost all motivation, became apathetic, and "just didn't care about anything." He quit school, quit his job, and got into trouble with the law by stealing for which he was convicted and sent to prison. Dr. Z's impression is that Richard has a "behavior disorder due to brain injury."

The admissions service also handles the readmission of those who are UA (unauthorized absence). For example, one worker told me the following story: Some patients are granted grounds passes and allowed off of their wards. Sometimes they wander off or escape. Other patients escape from their wards. In discussing this problem staff often say, "this is a hospital, not a jail." When these patients are found they are returned to the admissions service. The hospital is located on the edge of town. There are cornfields behind it. When patients wander off farmers often call the admissions service to pick them up. For example:

One fall day a farmer called and said a patient was wandering in his fields and the admissions service should pick her up. Two intake workers drove a mile west of the hospital. They saw the farmer who had called and he pointed down a lane. They turned left and drove down the lane with 8 foot high corn on either side. Soon they entered a clearing. Wandering in the clearing was a 50-year-old woman babbling in Polish. The intake workers pulled up and walked over to the woman. One worker said, "Hi Zelda, how ya' doin'?" She then threw her arms around the other worker and began kissing and hugging him. Since she seemed harmless the second worker allowed her to kiss and hug him. After about five minutes the second worker said, "O.K. Zelda lets go back to the hospital." The intake workers ushered her in to the car and drove back to the hospital. They pulled up to the ward and had her get out of the car. The first worker unlocked the door, pushed her on to the unit, and locked the door behind her.

"What was all that?" the second worker asked. "That's the famous Zelda. . . ." "Wait, before you tell me; her hands and face were covered in chocolate; does she have a chocolate fetish?" "No, that's the famous Zelda, she eats her own feces."

The admissions director began to walk off but turned and said, "You shouldn't just study us, That is, people who get to the admissions office. You should take a look at what some of the outpatient and community services are like, that hopefully keep people out of here. Most of the community agency reps are talking to ladies tea groups rather than doing important things, like the police. But, go talk to Will, he's the outpatient program director for one of the areas."

I walked over to the program office and found William R. I introduced myself and I asked him to explain his job. He said that "our service handles recidivists in order to avoid hospitalization. We also run group activities for discharged patients, handle deflected persons for our area, and often meet with patients before discharge. We run a bowling thing on Friday nights for ex-patients and we try to do some family therapy." "Do you work with the police or send people out into the community to give treatment in emergencies?" I asked. "We're not working with the police or doing that kind of thing. Although one of our nurses has given a couple of shots in the community, but that's it. In spite of that we still like to consider ourselves a crisis center." "Are you a 24 hour center?" "No, 13 hours a day, seven days a week, now." He paused. "When the need is established, we'll be 24 hours a day." "When will that be?" "When the community learns to trust the hospital and the administrators. And when the 'powers that be' decide there is a need."

"Are there other crisis centers in the community?" "Yes, but they close their phones at nine p.m." He paused again. "If there were a lot of crisis calls to admissions, then we'd open up." "There aren't? Why not?" "Because there's no community visibility and therefore, nobody calls. However, we're in the 'investigative stages' of a community based, 24 hour emergency service."

He then went on: "For the last two years we've been trying to set up a network of crisis services that would serve the mentally retarded, mentally ill, alcoholics, drug abusers, etc. I presented a package of funding, crisis intervention, medical backup, central information clearing house, and a consumer's referral service." "And how about the police?" I asked. "No, there's no relationship with the police. That's the weakest point in the system."

"If a police department were to call you now, would you send your people out?" "Yes, but they don't call often. We have a good relationship with one department but we don't relate to the other 15 or 20 departments in the area. We're really just an outpatient center."

The researcher conducted five weeks of observation in the admissions service. It produced the following data:

Fully 40 percent of those admitted to the hospital did not suffer from a psychosis. Of this group, 28.5 percent were alcoholics, 2.5 percent had drug related problems, and 8.5 percent were admitted because of "behavior problems" (nudity, eccentricity, etc.), physical or medical problems, or a lack of housing. Some admission summaries follow:

Fred F., a 56-year-old married male came to Central Admission and requested admission. Fred has been hospitalized on two previous occasions, the last admission and discharge being _____ to _____. Charles signed voluntary papers. For the last two months, since discharge, Fred has been living on the riverbank. According to him, all the time that he was there he was drinking daily, eating and sleeping whenever and wherever he could. When asked why he requested admission he stated that he wanted to dry out and stay for the 30 day program. Fred added that on his two previous admissions he only stayed for several days. He did this because he had money, he wanted out, and he wanted to get a drink. He promises this time to stay for as long as it takes him to straighten himself out.

On arrival to Central Admission, Fred was in poor physical appearance. His clothing was very dirty and it would seem that it has been some time since he last had a bath. Although he was moderately intoxicated, he appeared to be oriented and in fair contact with reality. He was shaky and unsteady on his feet. His speech was very slurred and garbled.

Fred was admitted.

Francis F., a 51-year-old married white male, came to Central Admissions this afternoon requesting admission. Francis has been a patient here before. He signed voluntary admission papers. After seeing the doctor, Francis was taken to the ward.

Francis is here for purposes of detoxification. He has remained sober for two and one-half years, since the time of his last discharge from here. He has been attending AA meetings regularly, both in town and in the hospital here. His wife left for a class reunion this past week, and during her absence, Francis began drinking again. He has been drinking for under a week, about ten shots of whiskey per day. Francis expressed some shame at returning here since he has been somewhat instrumental in aiding other alcoholics at this hospital.

Henry Y., a 33-year old single white male, came to Central Admissions this evening requesting a place to sleep. I explained to him that this is not a hotel, and that the hospital does not admit people on a one-night basis. He accepted this and explained that he had an employment interview in the morning and only needed some sleep prior to the interview. He was not interested in signing into the hospital at this time. Henry left and apparently slept for several hours on the grounds of the hospital, for he returned about three hours later looking rather sleepy. Henry talked with the CAS staff for several minutes, and during the course of the conversation began to shake. Henry states that he hasn't ever really experienced DT's, but didn't think that the trembling which he was experiencing was due to the DT's. However, his physical condition worried Henry to a sufficient extent that he decided that it would be best if he postponed his job interview in the morning and signed in until his condition improved. Henry has been a patient once before. He states that he has been drinking every day since his discharge, although not always to excess. He has been drinking beer and vodka. Henry signed voluntary admission papers. After seeing the doctor, Henry was taken to the ward.

Nathan R., a 16-year-old, single Negro male, came to CAS at 10:50 a.m., accompanied by his mother and sister. Al had one previous admission and was discharged in _____. Because he is a minor, Mrs. R. signed the voluntary admission form.

Upon admission, Nathan appeared to be well oriented and in contact with reality. He didn't have much to say, other than that he didn't think he was going to like being here.

According to Mrs. R., Nathan has quite a behavior problem. He has not been going to school and has been in trouble with the police. Mrs. R. said that with her working, she finds it impossible to do anything with Nathan.

After filling out the necessary admission forms, Nathan was taken to the ward.

Since the hospital was in an outlying area of Chicago, 87 percent of the persons in the sample were white (see: Table 3-7). Half of the sample was between 20 and 39 years old. Another one third of the sample was between forty and fifty-nine years old (see: Table 3-3). There were few elderly persons because of the large number of individuals in nursing homes and other residential facilities in the area. Sixty-eight percent of the individuals were single, divorced, separated, or widowed (see: Table 3-4). Almost two-thirds (62 percent) were male (see: Table 3-5). Almost 60 percent had a hospitalization within the last year (see: Table 3-8). Patients were cooperative 70 percent of the time and 70 percent were in contact with reality (see: Table 3-9 and Table 3-10). Almost everyone was admitted (87 percent) (see: Table 3-11).

Table 3-3[3,4]
Age Range

Age Range	Number	Percentage
1-9	0	0
10-19	11	50
20-29	28	25
30-39	27	25
40-49	20	18
50-59	17	15
60-69	8	7
70-79	2	2
80-89	1	1
Total: 113		100

(Table 3-3 was statistically significant at the .01 level.)

Table 3-4
Marital Status

Status	Number	Percent
Single	35	43
Married	26	32
Divorced	15	18
Separated	2	2.5
Widowed	4	5
Total: 82		100

(Table 3-4 was statistically significant at the .01 level.)

---

3. For most admissions complete data was not available. The charts reflect all the data available in each case. Percentages have been rounded in some cases.

4. A chi-square (x2) test was applied to each table. The chi-square test determines if the distribution in the table is a matter of chance (not statistically significant) or not likely to be the product of chance (statistically significant.) If the test was statistically significant it was measured at a 90 percent level of certainty (.10 level), a 95 percent of certainty (.05 level), or a 99 percent level of certainty (.01 level).

Table 3-5
Sex

Sex	Number	Percent
Male	70	62
Female	43	38
Total: 113		100

(Table 3-5 was statistically significant to the .05 level.)

Table 3-6
Time of Admission

Time of day	Number	Percent
Morning (6 a.m. – 12 noon)	16	28
Afternoon (12 noon – 6 p.m.)	21	36
Evening (6 p.m. – 9 p.m.)	8	14
Night (9 p.m. – 6 a.m.)	13	22
Total: 58		100

(Table 3-6 was statistically significant at the .10 level.)

Table 3-7
Race

Race	Number	Percent
White	86	87
Black	9	9
Hispanic	4	4
Total: 99		100

(Table 3-7 was statistically significant at the .01 level.)

Table 3-8
Previous Hospitalizations

Hospitalizations	Number	Percent
None Previous	18	19
Recently (within 1 yr.)	55	58.5
Not Recently	21	22
Total: 94		100

(Table 3-8 was statistically significant at the .01 level.)

Table 3-9
Patient Cooperation

Cooperation	Number	Percent
Cooperative	30	70
Passive/non-protesting	6	15
Protesting	6	15
Total: 42		100

(Table 3-9 was statistically significant at the .01 level.)

Table 3-10
In Contact With Reality

Contact	Number	Percent
Yes	37	70
Somewhat	11	21
No	4	9
Total: 52		100

(Table 3-10 was statistically significant at the .01 level.)

Table 3-11
Admissions and Deflections

Admitted/Deflected	Number	Percent
Admitted	104	87
Deflected	16	13
Total: 120		100

(Table 3-11 was statistically significant at the .01 level.)

Table 3-12
Admission Type

Type	Number	Percent
Voluntary	51	64
Emergency/Involuntary	27	33
Physical Certificate/Direct	2	2
Informal	1	1
Total: 80		100

(Table 3-12 was statistically significant at the .01 level.)

Table 3-13[5]
Primary Presenting Symptom

Symptom	Number (%)	Aggregate Percentage
Aggression	38 (25)	25
Alcohol	44 (28.5)	31
Drugs	4 (2.5)	
Depression	10 (6.5)	
Anxiety/Agitation	24 (16)	31
Hallucinations/Delusional	13 (8.5)	
Other	13 (8.5)	8.5

Total: 154

(Table 3-13 was statistically significant at the .01 level.)

Table 3-14
Intake Source

Source	Number (percentage)	Aggregate Number (Percentage)
Self	13 (10.5)	46 (37)
Family	27 (22)	
Friend	6 (5)	
Social Services	20 (16)	47 (38)
Nursing/Shelter/Homeless	20 (16)	
Hospitals	7 (6)	
Police	31 (25)	31 (25)
Total: 124 (100)		124 (100)

(Table 3-14 was not statistically significant.)

Some typical case summaries follow:

John K. is a 45-year-old married white male. He was brought to Central Admissions at 8:00 pm by his wife and son. Mr. K. has been hospitalized here on twelve previous occasions; he received his last discharge on _____.

---

5. When co-occurring illnesses were diagnosed, such as depression and alcoholism, both were counted.

Mr. K. initially refused to enter CAS, and just sat in his son's car trying to finish a fifth of Beefeaters. In the interim Mrs. K. signed a petition, citing John as endangering his own life by drinking, and as being a danger to others because he had threatened her.

After an hour of coaxing, John finally entered the building, only to leave a few moments later because he wanted to get sick outside. He then left. Security was notified and within the hour he was found heading towards town. John was taken directly to the ward and no further intake was attempted.

Anna A., a 60-year-old, single, white female, was brought to CAS by ambulance at 10 A.M. She was accompanied by her mother, Adelle J., who signed an Emergency Petition to have Anna hospitalized. Anna was hospitalized. Anna had one previous admission here from _____ to _____. At the time of admission Anna would not sign any papers.

Anna has been living with her mother since she received her discharge. According to Mrs. J., for the past few weeks, Anna has refused to take her medication, and recently she has not been eating.

Due to her extreme agitation and her refusal to come in to the office to talk to anyone Anna was taken directly to the ward. Anna did not seem to be well-oriented and appeared to be only in superficial contact with reality. She spoke of loving everyone and saving the world from their sins.

Betty B., a 38-year-old white, divorced female, arrived at CAS at 2:30 p.m., accompanied by her mother, involuntarily, which prompted her mother to sign an Emergency Petition, admitting her involuntarily. This is her third admission, last on _____.

The petition stated that Betty is endangering her health by refusing her medication and also refusing regular meals. She had been going to the local mental health clinic, but today walked out refusing to take any medication. Her family then brought her to the Outpatient Services here, in which she also refused to take part.

Betty had been living with her grandmother for the past year. Her grandmother passed away about a week ago, which has upset her to a great extent. She has been divorced for 1-2 years, and her ex-husband died about a week after the divorce. Their only child, a daughter was just home for the grandmother's funeral. Apparently Betty's depression and withdrawal began shortly after her daughter's departure. Mrs. J., Betty's mother, stated that Friday, Betty broke down crying and asked for professional counseling. Presently, she has given up the idea that she needs help, and wants to move so she can be with her daughter.

Mrs. J. also said that after the loss of her grandmother, Betty became secluded, refused to eat, started pulling all the shades in her house, lengthening the hems on her dresses, and generally exhibiting unusual behavior. Supposedly Betty has a friend who has been talking her into eating only health foods, and "informing" her as to the dangers of all medication.

Upon admission, the patient was quiet and seemingly depressed, although oriented. She saw no reason why she should be admitted, repeating that she will not take any medication because she doesn't need it. She was not willing to give any information and generally was uncooperative. She refused a ride to the ward, insisting on walking to the ward by herself (although she did not know where it was located). After some time, she walked to the ward with an intake worker.

In situations where physical aggression has occurred or when people were found "wandering the streets" or "acting funny" in public, the police were likely to be called. Frequently an involuntary hospitalization is the product of such a call. Twenty-five percent of all calls involved the police. For example:

John J., a 26-year-old, white, single male, was brought to CAS by his father at approximately 11:00 A.M. John who has had one previous admission, refused to sign the voluntary admission form. John's status is presently EMERGENCY, since his father signed a petition to have him hospitalized.

Since his discharge from here John has been living at home with his parents. According to Mr. J., John has recently started "acting funny" once again. He goes on long walks at all hours of the day and night and talks to trees. He has also begun talking to himself. Mr. J. said he has received several phone calls from the local police and one from another department, because people have been calling to complain about John's "strange" behavior. The last time the local police called Mr. J., they warned him that if they receive any more complaints about John, they would be forced to take John to jail, and he would no doubt end up there. At this point, Mr. J. said he had better bring John in for observation. (When asked whether or not John had been going to an out-patient clinic since his discharge, Mr. J. said that John went to the local clinic a couple of times right after he was discharged, but then he stopped going because, according to John, the medicine he was getting was making him sleepy all the time.)

While at CAS, John was fairly well-oriented, but only in superficial contact with reality. It was very difficult to understand him or to carry on much of a conversation. For example, I asked John what it was he enjoyed doing, —his reply was, "Dance—no! Movies—yes!" When what kind of movies he enjoyed, he said, "space stories—no! Mysteries—yes!"

Although John seemed quite irritated at being back at the hospital, he remained cooperative throughout the intake.

Edmond D., a 22-year-old, white, single, male was brought handcuffed to Central Admissions around 1:00 A.M. by police. His father also accompanied him. A CAS staff member was needed to help bring Ed into the building. He refused to sign any papers: Mr. D. signed a Petition for Hospitalization which stated that Ed had threatened several people and had attempted suicide with a knife. This was Ed's first admission to a DMH facility.

While at admissions, Ed was intoxicated, very agitated, verbally abusive, and combative. He attempted to kick the police officer and threatened to kill his father. He offered no relevant information other than expressing fear of this hospital.

Mr. D. explained that Ed has had psychiatric problems for 10 years and was previously hospitalized. Ed has been seeing a social worker for the past 2 or 3 months.

According to Mr. D., Ed has been using both drugs and alcohol heavily for the past two years. Ed generally drinks everyday and often to excess. While intoxicated, Ed becomes hostile and combative. Mr. D. related several incidents when Ed had to be physically restrained from hurting himself or others. About two months ago, Ed began acting-out and kicked his father. Mr. D. then "decked" Ed and had him arrested. Charges were pressed and Ed was put on probation. The court also suggested that Ed seek treatment and subsequently Ed began his involvement with the social worker. Ed has also attempted to burn the family home down.

Although the social worker recommended antibuse, Ed took it for just a few weeks. He continued his usual pattern of drinking. According to Mr. D., the episode tonight began when he returned home from work and found Ed drinking. Ed then left the house for his car. A few hours later, Ed was involved in a minor traffic accident. Rather than press charges, the police officer decided to accompany Ed to his home. Upon arrival, Ed went immediately to the kitchen and grabbed a knife. He attempted to stab himself and was stopped by a younger brother. The police remained and agreed to transport Ed here. The social worker was contacted and made arrangements to have Ed admitted. (He can be contacted for further information.)

Security was necessary to transport Ed to the ward. Once there, Ed calmed down. (Apparently he discovered his fears were unfounded.) Mr. D. stated that Ed will probably be cooperative in the morning.)

Tables 3-12, 3-13, 3-14 indicate a common cause of involuntary hospitalization was when a person was perceived by a relative or friend to be acting strangely, not eating properly, drinking, taking drugs, or not taking their medication. Almost 60 percent of all admissions were persons who had been recently discharged (within one year) from a psychiatric hospital.

Table 3-13 is quite interesting. Thirty-one percent of all admissions were for drug or alcohol problems. Another 31 percent were for psychiatric symptoms (depression, anxiety, hallucinations, or delusions). However, fully 25 percent were for "aggression." Although this is not a diagnostic category (mental illness) this was the reason for the admission. In other words, the hospital was an alternative to jail. It was an asylum. And, the intake worker was correct, "We can't lose people to the Department of Corrections!"

Tables 3-12, 3-13, 3-14 also indicate dramatic changes in the functioning of mental health agencies since the 1960s. At that time the majority of persons entering state hospitals were involuntary confined. In the early 1970s however, almost two-thirds of all admissions were voluntary. As significant as this change is, some of it is more apparent than real. For example, since involuntary admissions have dropped from 80 percent to 33 percent we might assume a significant drop in police involvement with the mentally ill. In fact, that is not the case. Table 3-14 indicates that 25 percent of all admissions involve the police. Table 3-14 also indicates that 38 percent of all intakes were from social service facilities. However, we must keep in mind that many of these intake sources are secondary; that is, persons were placed in them (nursing homes, shelter facilities, etc.) after admission and screening at the state hospital. Therefore, we can add several percentage points to the police intake figures. In the early 1960s police contact involved about one-third of all admissions; a similar percentage apparently holds true today. Therefore, after a decade of community mental health programs, it seems that the system still lacks the means or the interest to adequately prevent or cope with the "disorderly" mentally ill.

6. Psychiatric Admitting: 2005

Since the 1973 study the admissions process has changed dramatically. Few individuals are directly admitted to state hospitals any longer. Most persons are screened at local hospital emergency rooms. Only if they do not have insurance and they need to be hospitalized are they sent on to the state hospital.

In 1973 there were 25,731 admissions to state hospitals in Illinois. In 2004 there were only 9,760 admissions to state hospitals (Illinois Department of Mental Health, 1973; Illinois Department of Mental Health and Developmental Disabilities, 2004). That is a decline of approximately 62 percent. However, during the same period the population of the state of Illinois rose from approximately 11,260,000 to approximately 12,714,000 (www.census.gov). The only exception to this decreasing admission rate is at Chicago-Read Mental Health Center in Chicago. One Department of Mental Health administrator explained that this occurs because "we're the only state hospital that has a bus stop at the front door."

In order to examine the new method for admitting psychiatric patients a study was conducted in the summer of 2005 at a private hospital in Chicago. The hospital was chosen because it routinely handled psychiatric cases. It also was a designated drop off point for the mentally ill for the Chicago Police Department.

The hospital had contracted out the psychiatric screening in its emergency room to a local social service agency.[6] The director of the screening unit explained the functioning of his program: "We do triage. That is, risk assessment and management. The process usually begins when the patient is seen in the emergency room and is medically cleared. If there is no medical problem the person may be brought directly into our unit by the police. They sign a log and we ask them to make out a petition so that we can hold them for a psychiatric screening. Some officers are leery of signing a petition. But we're usually able to convince them to do so.

"However, in about 5 percent of the cases they refuse. In those cases we call in a sergeant and he or she solves the problem. We than take a brief history from the officer and then help them fill out the petition. This is important because the petition must contain only the behavior they witnessed. The officers are then allowed to leave. Most importantly, the unit has a no refusal policy so that officers can be assured that they will not be 'stuck' with a mentally ill person that no one will accept."

Approximately 250 persons a month are screened in the unit. Most are admitted. If they have insurance they "go upstairs" to the inpatient psychiatric unit, are medically admitted, or are transferred to another community hospital. If they are "unfunded" then they are transferred to a state hospital.

---

6. In 1963 the Community Mental Health Centers Act stipulated that emergency psychiatric treatment must be included as one of the five essential services in all federally funded community mental health centers. As the number of family physicians fell in many poor neighborhoods emergency rooms replaced them. Thus emergency rooms became the "poor man's doctor." However, psychiatric patients are often seen as an intrusion in the busy work of an emergency room (Merson and Bassuk, 1980). The hospital that was studied handled this problem by shifting such cases to a "separate" entity (located within the emergency room).

The unit's director estimated that about five percent of the individuals they see each month are homeless. "We try to give them what they need," the unit director commented. If that need is primarily housing then they will often call the Chicago Department of Human Services (DHS) to pick them up and take them to a shelter. However, one intake worker explained that "the DHS van often takes six to eight hours to get here, or they never come." A further complication is that the van will take the individual to a shelter with an available bed. This could be anywhere in the city. When homeless persons hear this they often simply leave.

The unit director estimated they see 40 to 50 substance abusers or intoxicated individuals a month. Since it may take 10 to 12 hours for these individuals to detoxify the emergency room often acts a defacto detoxification facility for them.

One physician commented that the unit's work was "an afternoon thing." So, the researcher observed from 3 to 11 p.m., Wednesday through Sunday for six weeks in the summer of 2005. One hundred and fourteen "patient contacts" were observed. Fourteen of these contacts were "SASS calls" (Screening, Assessment, and Support Services) from agencies or parents to assess a child for psychiatric admission. Upon the receipt of these calls a specially trained SASS worker is dispatched. Since these are merely referrals, and the patients are rarely seen in the ER, these fourteen calls were omitted from the sample. Also, the unit handles crisis line calls. These are either requests for information or "frequent callers." Since these individuals were not seen in the unit these 12 contacts were also omitted from the sample. Therefore, 88 contacts were analyzed.

In the 1973 data 87 percent of the sample was between the ages of 20 and 59 (see: Table 3-1). In 2005, 83 percent of the sample was in the same age range (see: Table 3-16). This would indicate that much of the elderly population that used to be housed in state hospitals were already in nursing homes or other institutions by the early 1970s.

The male/female ratio was almost identical for both samples. It was 62 percent males in 1973 and 64 percent males in 20005. Females were 38 percent of the sample in 1973 and 37 percent of the sample in 2005 (see: Tables 3-5 and 3-15).

The outlying hospital studied in 1973 covered an area that included small cities, suburbs, and rural areas. The racial composition of the 1973 sample was 87 percent white, 9 percent black, and 4 percent Hispanic (see: Table 3-5). The city hospital was located in a white area of the city. However, Hispanic neighborhoods were nearby. Relatively few blacks lived in the area. The social breakdown of the 2005 sample was: 60 percent white, 31 percent Hispanic, 11 percent black, and 2 percent other (see: Table 3-17).

In 1973 87 percent of the patients were admitted (see: Table 3-11). And most of those who were deflected received some type of assistance. In 2005 39 percent of the patients were admitted to the hospitals inpatient psychiatric unit. Another 12 percent of the sample was medically admitted. In these cases the patients refused psychiatric care so a "medical admit" was used to circumvent their resistance and have them receive the psychiatric care that the physicians felt that they needed. Overall, 74 percent were admitted to a hospital or other treatment facility. And, another 11 percent were given referrals to mental health facilities for outpatient care. So, again, almost everyone received some type of assistance. For example:

A 67-year-old white female was left alone in a car for 2 days by her brother. She was treated and sent to a nursing home.[7]

A 72-year-old white female hit her husband of 40 years in the face with a plate. Both were brought to the hospital by the police. The husband needed numerous stitches to close the wound. Their children were called. The police told them that she needed to sign herself in or she would be taken to Cook County Jail. Her children pleaded with her to sign herself in. The staff felt the woman was depressed and perhaps suicidal. They told her, "Cook County Jail is no place for a 72-year-old woman." She agreed and signed herself in. She was sent upstairs to the psychiatric ward.

The great change here is that 53 percent of the 2005 sample were admitted directly to private hospitals and another 10 percent were transferred to nursing homes, group homes, or detoxification facilities. Only 9 percent of the patients were transferred to the state hospital. However, in 1973 87 percent were admitted directly into the state hospital (see: Table 3-11 and Table 3-20). For example:

A white female, 60 years old, was brought in by a Chicago Fire Department ambulance and accompanied by her family. Her daughter stated that she was acting paranoid and delusional. They had built her a new house in the suburbs but she refused to move there because she felt that the daughters would steal her old house. She was also not sleeping, eating, or taking her diabetes or psychiatric medications. This caused them to be concerned about her diabetes since she had lost a toe to the disease, already. When asked to sign a voluntary petition for psychiatric care she vehemently refused and spent several hours endlessly, and loudly, lecturing the intake workers on how her daughters were trying to steal her money. The doctor spoke privately with the daughters. When he returned he said he was not comfortable certifying her since financial issues were involved. After several more hours it was suggested that she be admitted to have her diabetes treated. She immediately agreed and was taken upstairs to a medical unit.

A 62-year-old white female was brought in by family members. They said that she was bipolar and schizophrenic. She stated that she had hiccups for 30 years. She said that she had been gulping air for 3 months. She had been to several hospitals but they had not been able to help her. She hoped this hospital could help her. The family said that she was suicidal and depressed. And she compulsively drank huge amounts of water every day. The doctor concluded that she had developed hyponatremia, an electrolyte psychosis. He told her he thought he could help her so she signed a voluntary admissions form. Since she had private insurance she was sent upstairs to the psychiatric unit.

A 32-year-old Hispanic female was brought in to the Emergency Room by Fire Department ambulance. There were no treatment rooms available in the ER so she was put in a

---

7. The researcher observed all the cases cited in the 2005 study. The cases are slightly fictionalized to protect the privacy of the individuals.

corner of the ER and a screen was put around her. Her alcohol level was .275 and her wrists had been cut. She was placed in restraints. Since her alcohol level was high the emergency room staff had to wait seven hours until it fell to a normal level before they could interview her. She had several bruises on her face. When she was interviewed she stated that she was the victim of domestic abuse. And that this had not been the first time her boyfriend had hit her. She admitted to having gotten a DUI and attended AA. However, she felt that the meetings had been a waste of time. Although she had several cuts on her wrists, she denied that she was suicidal. The boyfriend, who was home watching their child, was called. He said that they had had a fight. He stated that she was drunk and suicidal and had cut her wrists. He said that she was pregnant with their child but he would not let her come home. The patient denied any problems, except domestic abuse, and wanted to go home. The doctor concluded that she was suicidal. Further, she now had nowhere to go. He certified her. Since she had no insurance he sent her to the state hospital.

In 1973 25 percent of all admission were diagnosed as "aggression" (see: Table 3-13). However, now the American Psychiatric Association's Diagnostic and Statistical Manual IV of mental illnesses (DSM-IV) is closely followed; and aggression is not a diagnostic category. Therefore, there were no admissions for aggression.[8] However, 3 percent of the 2005 sample was diagnosed as "homicidal" (see: Table 3-18). In 2005 59 percent of the diagnoses in the sample were for psychosis (excluding 3 percent for dementia). In 1973 only 31 percent fell into this category. In 1973 alcohol and drug problems were 31 percent and in the 2005 sample they were 23 percent of the sample (see: Table 3-18 and 3-27). The single largest category was for depression or a suicide attempt (32 percent). This is similar to the national statistic of 38 percent of psychiatric hospitalizations for such behavior (Stefen, 2006: 28).

The screening unit kept its own statistics (see: Table 3-29). It did not categorize individuals by diagnosis. However, it did admit 704 of the 2,672 individuals it handled for psychiatric treatment in 2005. It is reasonable to assume all these individuals were psychotic. It also admitted 297 persons (11 percent) for alcohol detoxification or substance abuse. The unit admitted 94 individuals for medical reasons (3.5 percent). It is likely that many of these individuals needed psychiatric care. Thirty-six individuals (1.3 percent) suffered from domestic violence and were not admitted. Seven-hundred and twenty-five were referred for outpatient care. Three hundred and twelve persons (27.1 percent) were transferred to state hospitals. And 139 (5.2 percent) were homeless and picked up by city vans and taken to shelters. So, 48.9 percent were admitted or transferred to a state hospital for psychosis or alcohol or substance abuse. For example:

A 32-year-old black female was brought in to the unit. She had thrown away her psychiatric medication and had relapsed into drug use. She said that she had been taking heroin and marijuana and that she said that she felt "really crappy." She also said that she felt "worthless and hopeless" and that she wanted to kill herself. She was asked if she had a plan to kill

---

8. However, studies show that up to one-half of all admissions to psychiatric inpatient programs may be the result of "interpersonal conflicts" (Stefan, 2006: 20-1; Rhodes, 1991: 37).

herself. Yes, she said. She had a .38 revolver at home. However, she added that she was homeless since her roommate was a drug dealer. However, she said she could not go back to her apartment because she was afraid she would get arrested. She emphasized that she had never been to prison although she had 3 DUI's, 2 orders of protection against her, and 6 domestic violence arrests. In fact, she said that she had once kidnapped her husband and forced him into the car trunk. "I used to be a violent alcoholic," she concluded. She added that she had OD'ed in 2000 and attempted to commit suicide in 2002. "I used to have highs and lows. I used to be manicy," she added. However, she said she had been "low" for the last 3 weeks. Also, lately, she had been irritable, anxious, and sad. She concluded that "I'm having thoughts I'm gonna explode." The physician certified her and sent her up to the psychiatric unit.

A 52-year-old American Indian male came into the unit. He said that he had been drinking all day. His blood alcohol level was .397. He said that he had fallen down some stairs in a park and a Fire Department ambulance had brought him to the hospital. He did not feel his injury was severe because he had been a gang-banger and he had had broken arms and legs. Also, he had been in prison 4 times. He said that he was not suicidal or psychotic but had been unable to get in to a detox program that night. It was decided to keep him overnight and to call a detox program in the morning.

In 1973 self, family, and friends accounted for 37 percent of all intake sources (see: Table 3-13). In the 2005 sample the percentage was 41 percent. In 1973 social service agencies or nursing homes accounted for 38 percent of all intake sources. However, in the 2005 sample this had fallen to 13 percent. (Nationally, 2.4 percent of all emergency room visits in 2002 were from institutions such as nursing homes [Stefan, 2006: 28]). In 1973 the police were involved in 25 percent of the intakes and in the 2005 sample it was 30 percent. However, if we add in Chicago Fire Department ambulance intakes this rises to 41 percent (see: Table 31-19).[9]

The screening unit's statistics for 2005 indicate that 25.4 percent of all the individuals they saw were there because of self referral or having been brought in by family or friends (see: Table 3-29). Referrals by the emergency room were 39.4 percent of all cases seen by the unit. However, if we assume this number masks a 25 percent self referral or those brought in by family and friends the percentage rises to 35 percent. Similarly, emergency room referrals may mask transfers from mental health clinics and community placements. If we apply these percentages to the emergency room referrals we get 19.5 percent. And if we apply the same method to police and fire referrals that rises to 32 percent. For example:

A 52-year-old white male was arrested for breaking into someone's house. He said that he was Commander Gorbachev. He had apparently escaped from a nursing home. He was diagnosed a schizoaffective and sent up to the psychiatric unit.

---

9. In New York City alone 24,798 emotionally disturbed persons (EDP's) were escorted to hospitals in 1999 by the police (Stefan, 2006: 30).

A 21-year-old black male had been walking through Sears "bothering customers" and then screaming in the street. When the police arrived he requested that he be taken to a hospital. When he arrived in the ER he began screaming and was put in restraints. "He's responding to internal stimuli," the doctor observed. Later, he became unresponsive. He was sent up to the psychiatric unit.

A 54-year-old white male was found lying in the street by a Fire Department ambulance. He was brought to the ER. He was agitated, screaming, and acting paranoid. He was put into restraints. He had overdosed on cocaine. It was decided to let him detox for the night and to then send him back to his drug program.

A 26-year-old black make had been wandering in the street. A Fire Department ambulance had been called and he was brought in to the ER. He said that he was suicidal and had wanted to overdose. He said that he had not eaten or slept for 5 or 6 days. He said that he was homeless and that he had been walking all that time. His feet were blistered and swollen. Later, he became agitated and said that he wanted to kill everyone. He was given an injection of Ativan to calm him down and Benadryl to reduce the swelling of his feet. He was sent up to the psychiatric ward.

In 1973 approximately 32 percent of the sample was married. The other individuals were single, divorced, separated or widowed (see: Table 3-4). In the 2005 the crisis workers did not solicit information concerning marital status. Therefore, the sample is quite small (only 9) and not comparable (see: Table 3-28).

In 1973 approximately 60 percent of the sample had a previous hospitalization (see: Table 3-8). In 2005 only 36 percent had a previous hospitalization. However, if we add in those admitted from nursing homes and other similar facilities the percentage rises to 52 percent (see: Tables 3-22 and 3-19). For example:

A 72-year-old Hispanic male was brought into the ER. He had been sent by a nursing home. The staff attempted to interview him but he was unresponsive. They concluded he suffered from dementia. They called the nursing home in order to make plans to return him to the facility.

A frail 80-year-old white male was brought into the ER. He spoke only Polish. An ER technician acted as a translator. The staff had been told that he had attempted to smother a female patient at the nursing home. When the staff attempted to interview him he either spoke incoherently in Polish or explained that he was "in the game." When asked about the incident at the nursing home he explained that it had not happened because "it was in the game." The staff was unsure if he suffered from dementia or a psychosis so they sent him up to the psychiatric ward.

In 1973 85 percent of the patients were cooperative or passive (see: Table 3-9). In 2005 the percentage was 66 percent (see: Table 3-24). For example:

A 52-year-old white male walked into the ER. He said that his wife had died three days ago. He stated that he had been depressed for three weeks. He was now homeless and he wanted to die. When asked if he had a plan to kill himself he said, yes. He said that he had planned to slash his writs. He added that he had 5 previous suicide attempts, several previous hospitalizations, and was schizophrenic. He said that he wanted to sign a voluntary admission form. He did so and was sent up to the psychiatric unit.

In 1973 70 percent of the patients were in contact with reality. Another 21percent were somewhat in contact with reality (see: Table 3-10). In 2005 45 percent of the patients were in contact with reality. And another 34 percent were somewhat in contact (see: Table 3-25).

In 1973 64 percent of the admissions were voluntary (see: Table 3-12). However, in 2005 that number was only 31percent (see: Table 3-27). In 1973 only 33 percent were involuntary or emergency petitions. Whereas in 2005 the percentage was double that amount (60 percent).

In 1973 all patients were admitted or deflected without any discussion of insurance coverage. However, in 2005 insurance coverage was always discussed. In 2005 77 percent of the sample patients had public funding and another 6 percent had private insurance. Only 12 percent were unfunded (see: Table 3-23). As a result of this 74 percent were admitted to a private hospital or other private facility. Only 9 percent of the patients were transferred to state hospitals.

In 2005 the screening unit recorded insurance information on 2846 individuals (see: Table 3-31). Thirteen hundred and eighty three (48.7 percent) were publicly funded. Four hundred and thirty-nine had private insurance (15.4 percent). And one thousand twenty-four (35.9 percent) had no insurance.

In 1973 no statistics were kept of whether the patient was domiciled or undomiciled. In 2005 84 percent of those seen had a residence. However, 16 percent were homeless (see: Table 3-21). On January 27, 2005 a one day, point-in-time count of the homeless was undertaken in Chicago. The study found 6,715 homeless persons. Of these 4,988 were sheltered whereas 1,727 were unsheltered (Chicago Department of Human Services, 2005). If we take the number of unsheltered individuals and divide it by the Chicago population (approximately 3,000,000) we get a percentage of about .06 percent of the population in Chicago as being homeless and unsheltered. Yet, our ER sample had a 16 percent homeless rate. Therefore, homeless people are heavily overrepresented in their usage of emergency rooms and emergency psychiatric services.[10] For example:

A 42-year-old black male was brought in to the unit by his son. His son said that he had been wandering in traffic, would not take his psychiatric medications, and had not bathed in a year since he was homeless. When asked about this he replied: "I will kill black people." The son then said that he had called the police the previous day but his father had left by the time they had arrived. The son said his father was delusional. The father then said that he had no legs and that he can not see through a TV screen. He concluded that other than that,

---

10. The homeless only tend to become involved with the mental health system during emergency room visits (Belcher, 1998).

he had no problems. He refused to sign a voluntary admission form. The physician signed a certificate and involuntarily hospitalized him on the psychiatric unit.

The literature indicates that 40 to 50 percent of all voluntary admissions are coerced. If we combined this estimate with the involuntary admissions (see: Table 3-26) we can conclude that in actuality about 75 percent of all admissions are involuntary. Alternately, if we use the same estimate for the chart on cooperativeness (see: Table 3-24) then, again, about 75 percent of the sample was coerced in to entering the hospital.

In 1973 and 2005 income or job status was not elicited by the workers unless directly relevant to the admission. However, if we analyze the 2005 data we find that if we combine those individuals on public assistance (Medicaid), Medicare, unfunded, or receiving EPS funds (see: Table 3-23) we have a total of 94 percent. This is an indirect indicator that the vast majority of patients seen in the unit were poor.

Table 3-15
Intake Source

	Number	**Percent**
Male	54	(64)
Female	31	(37)

Total Number: 85

(Table 3-15 was statistically significant at the .05 level.)

Table 3-16
Age

Age	**Number**	**Percent**
1-9	0	0
10-19	2	2
20-29	13	15
30-39	21	24
40-49	16	18
50-59	23	26
60-69	6	7
70-79	2	2
80-89	4	5

Total number: 87   100

(Table 3-16 was statistically significant at the .01 level.)

Table 3-17
Race

	Number	(Percent)
Black	9	(11%)
White	50	(60%)
Hispanic	23	(31%)
Other	2	(2%)

Total Number: 84

(Table 3-17 was statistically significant at the .01 level.)

Table 3-18[11]
Diagnosis

	Number	(Percent)
Schizophrenia	22	(15%)
Depression/Suicide	33	(32%)
Bipolar	8	(8%)
Alcohol	7	(7%)
Drugs	12	(11%)
Alcohol& Drugs	5	(5%)
Borderline Personality Disorder	1	(1%)
Domestic Violence	1	(1%)
Mental Retardation	1	(1%)
Brief Psychotic Episode	1	(1%)
Drug-induced Psychotic Episode	1	(1%)
Impulse Control	1	(1%)
Homicidal	3	(3%)
Anxiety	4	(4%)
Paranoid	2	(2%)
Dementia	3	(3%)

Total number: 105 (100%)

(Table 3-18 was statistically significant at the .01 level.)

---

11. When co-occurring illnesses were diagnosed, such as depression and alcoholism, both were counted.

Table 3-19
Age

Source		Number	(Percent)
Self		24	(32%)
Family		7	(9%)
Nursing Home[12]		13	(17%)
Police		23	(30%)
Ambulance[13]		8	(11%)
	Total:	75	(100%)

(Table 3-19 was statistically significant at the .01 level.)

Table 3-20
Disposition

	Number	(Percent)
In-Hospital Psychiatric Unit	32	(39%)
In-Hospital Medical Unit	10	(12%)
State Hospital	7	(9%)
Eloped	1	(1%)
ER	1	(1%)
DHS	2	(2%)
Nursing Home	5	(6%)
Released	1	(1%)
Referral	9	(11%)
Other Hospital Psychiatric Unit	2	(2%)
Refused Treatment	1	(1%)
Group Home	2	(2%)
Transferred	1	(1%)
Left	3	(4%)
Detox Facility	2	(2%)
Home	3	(3%)
Total:	82	(100%)

(Table 3-20 was statistically significant at the .01 level.)

---

12. And other community based residential facilities or social service agencies.
13. Chicago Fire Department

Table 3-21
Domiciled/Undomiciled

	Number	(Percent)
Domiciled	74	(84%)
Undomiciled	14	(16%)

Total number: 88

(Table 3-21 was statistically significant at the .01 level.)

Table 3-22
Previous Hospitalization

	Number	(Percent)
Previous	74	(84%)
No Hospitalization	14	(16%)

Total Number: 88

(Table 3-22 was statistically significant at the .01 level.)

Table 3-23
Funding Source

	Number	(Percent)
Public Aid Medicare	40	(58%)
Medicare	8	(12%)
Public Aid & Medicare	3	(4%)
Private Insurance	4	(6%)
Unfunded	8	(12%)
EPS[14]	2	

Total Number: 69

(Table 3-23 was statistically significant at the .01 level.)

---

14. EPS Funding is state monies which can be used for unfunded patients for medication, hospitalization, or transportation. However, the funds can only be used if the individual lives in the hospital's service area (LAN or local area network), the admission is voluntary, the patient has not taken drugs or alcohol, the patient has not had a psychiatric hospitalization in the last year, and the patient is certifiable. During the research period only 2 persons received EPS funding. And, these were only used to fund prescriptions for psychiatric medication.

Table 3-24
Cooperativeness

	Number	(Percent)
Cooperative	52	(60%)
Passive/Non-Protesting	5	(6%)
Protesting	29	(34%)

Total number: 86

(Table 3-24 was statistically significant at the .01 level.)

Table 3-25
Contact with Reality

	Number	(Percent)
In Contact	40	(45%)
Somewhat	30	(34%)
Not In Contact	18	(20%)

Total number: 88

(Table 3-25 was statistically significant at the .01 level.)

Table 3-26
Admission Type

	Number	(Percent)
Voluntary	18	(31%)
Emergency/Involuntary	35	(60%)
Physicians CertificateDirect Admission	5	(9%)

Total number: 58

(Table 3-26 was statistically significant at the .01 level.)

Table 3-27
Drugs and Alcohol

	Number	(Percent)
Drugs	7	(29%)
Alcohol	12	(50%)
Both	5	(20%)

Total number: 24

(Table 3-27 was not statistically significant.)

Table 3-28
Marital Status

	Number	(Percent)
Single	1	(11%)
Married	3	(33%)
Divorced	—	—
Separated	—	—
Widowed	1	(11%)
Living Together	4	(44%)

Total number: 9

(Table 3-28 was not statistically significant.)

Table 3-29
Screening Unit
All Dispositions—2005

	Number	(Percent)*
psychiatric (admit)	704	(26.3%)
detoxification (admit)	76	(2.8%)
substance abuse (admit)	221	(8.2%)
medical (admit)	94	(3.5%)
domestic violence	36	(1.3%)
outpatient referral	725	(27.1%)
transfer (state hospital admit)	312	(11.6%)
other	209	(7.8%)
shelter	139	(5.2%)
no service	39	(1.5%)
respite	3	(0%)
refused service	94	(3.5%)
Total:	2,672	(100%)

* rounded

(Table 3-29 was statistically significant at the .01 level.)

Table 3-30
Screening Unit
All Source of Referral—2005

	Number	(Percent)*
police	519	(17.9%
fire	72	(2.5%
family	281	(9.7%
self	456	(15.7%
emergency room	1,140	(39.4%
mental health clinic	182	(6.2%
other	206	(7.1%
community placement	40	(1.3%
Total:	2,896	100%

* rounded

(Table 3-30 was statistically significant at the .01 level.)

Table 3-31
Screening Unit
Funding for All Patients—2005

	Number	(Percent)*
EPS	28	1%
EPS (medication only)	24	1%
Medicare	206	7%
Medicaid (public aid)	793	27.8%
Medicare and Medicaid	309	10.9%
Veterans Administration	23	1%
Private Insurance	439	15.4%
None	1,024	35.9%
Total:	2,846	100%

* rounded

(Table 3-31 was statistically significant at the .01 level.)

7. The Function of Emergency Rooms

Emergency rooms provide a crucial service to families, providers of mental health services, and the police—all of whom are overburdened and underfunded. Since emergency rooms are accessible 24 hours a day, and impose no eligibility requirements, they "solve" both individual and systemic problems. That is, other agencies can save money by not providing services while knowing that there is always a backup service available. And, families and the police can unburden themselves of "burdensome" individuals (Stefan, 2006: 143-6).

Families, the police, and social agencies use the emergency room for both treatment and detention. These two functions are inextricably intertwined. As Stefan points out, those who use emergency rooms for this dual purpose "are not evil or malicious; they are *desperate.*" They use emergency rooms "to solve pressing problems for which no other solutions exist in the community" (emphasis added, 2006: 144-6). For example:

A VA hospital intake worker who worked in psychiatric admitting was interviewed. He described how desperate individuals often ended up in the emergency room or his service:

"A patient took PCP, which makes you organically psychotic. He thought his tongue felt funny in his mouth so he took a scissor and cut it off. He quickly realized that he had made a mistake; so he decided to walk over to the VA for treatment. Because of significant blood loss he collapsed in the street. He fell near the curb, between two parked cars. Because it was in the middle of the night no one noticed him until dawn. A police squadroll then picked him up and brought him to the ER. The ER doctors stitched up his tongue. But since he was a 'psych patient', they were frightened of him; so they sent him to us. By the time we got him the PCP was through his system and he was O.K. What he needed was reconstructive surgery. So, we sent him back to the ER. Shortly thereafter, they returned him to us. Since there was nothing wrong with him, and he needed reconstructive surgery, we sent him back to them. Since they were frightened of him they sent him back to us, again. Since there was nothing psychiatrically wrong with him at that time, we discharged him."

"In an admitting service or a walk-in clinic you can be swamped or it can be dead. So, you always bring reading material. Early one morning I was sitting in my office reading with my feet up on the desk. My door was partially open—you always leave your door open so you know what is going on. I heard the pitter-patter of little feet. 'Some kids running down the hall,' I thought to myself. But, I realized there were no kids at the VA. So, I walked around the corner to my boss' office. There I saw this guy screaming and flailing his arms in the air. I quickly moved behind him, put my hands on his shoulders, and forced him down into a chair. I held him there while he screamed. A minute later a security guard arrived. He and I each grabbed an arm and twisted them behind him. We pulled him out of the office and we dragged him down the hall. He was screaming, struggling, and trying to kick our feet out from under us. We dragged him down the hall, through the lobby, into the ER, and then in to the 'quiet room'—which is an empty room with a gurney bolted to the floor. Immediately five other security guards rushed in and we tied him to the gurney with leather restraints. A doctor then came in and bombed him with Haldol. However, it had no effect on him and he screamed for four more hours. Eventually, he fell asleep.

"By 4 p.m. the PCP was out of his system and the Haldol had worked. So, he was 'fine'. Actually, he looked like shit, but he wasn't psychotic anymore. So, my boss said, 'Give him a good talking to and let him go.' I went in to the quiet room and undid the restraints. I said, 'You can't . . .' He interrupted me and said, "Thank you for being so gentle.' 'No,' I replied, 'that's not the point. You can't be going around and. . . ." Again he interrupted and said, 'Thank you for being so gentle.' 'I was just doing my job,' I responded. 'But, that's not the point,' I continued. If you do this in front of a policeman you might get killed.' He looked at me and said, 'Ya know the last time I did this, when I was directing traffic on the expressway, the police weren't so gentle.' 'You *really* need to come in for help'," I said. He smiled, walked out, and we never saw him again.

"This woman brought in her brother. He was a 50-year-old Hispanic male. He was flamboyantly dressed with his shirt open to his navel and lots of gold chains . . . very macho. We had treated him before and given him Xanax, a mild anti-anxiety medication. The sister then told us: 'I can't stand it any more. He walks around the house all day naked and masturbating. Then he goes out at night and has two or three hookers. He says, 'No one woman could ever satisfy a real man.' Then he sleeps for 2 hours and does it all again. I'm going crazy!' 'Oh!' I blurted out, 'he's hypersexual, he's manic! Why didn't you just tell us that before?' So, we sent him up to the ward and they bombed him with lithium."

"Admitting offices or walk-in clinics often have 'repeaters.' For example, a guy came in, who was well known to us, and said, 'I have a cold.' 'O.K.,' I said, 'but this is psychiatric admitting.' 'But, I've had the cold for six months.' So, in my usual sing-songy way I use in these cases, I said, 'Did you take your medication today?' 'No.' 'So, go home and take your medication.'

"Another day a patient, well known to us, came in. He said, 'I'm going to China on vacation!' 'Wow, how are you getting there?' 'Via Du Page County!' So, I said, 'Did you take your medication today?' 'No.' 'Then go home and take your medication.'

8. Conclusions

In 1973 87 percent of all patients seen in the state hospital's admission's service were admitted. However, in 2005 only 9 percent of the patients were transferred to the state hospital. However, 74 percent of those seen at the private hospital were admitted to the hospital or other treatment facility. In 1973 the police were involved in at least 25 percent of all admissions. In 2005 it was at least 30 percent. So, the police still play a significant, and undiminished, role in psychiatric admitting.

The premise of our original study was that "everyone" was committed by the court. That is no longer true. Now, "no one" is committed. The original study found that self, family, friends, and the police were the primary sources of intake of psychiatric admitting. The same conclusion holds true in 2005.

We had originally studied the police because research had been conducted on families in the admitting process (e.g., Yarrow, 1955). A great deal of research has been conducted on self and family admission since then (Yarrow, et al., 1995). So, let us return to the police and reexamine police apprehension of the mentally ill. With such a study we can see if police practices have changed. We can also see if our notion of a vertical analysis from the court to the street is a valid technique.

References

Anderson, O. W., and R. Andersen
   1972   "Patterns of Use of Health Services." In *Handbook of Medical Sociology*, 2nd ed., H. E. Freeman, S. Levine, and L.G. Reeder, eds. Englewood Cliffs, New Jersey: Prentice-Hall.

Avison, William R.
   1999   "Family Structures and Process." In *A Handbook for the Study of Mental Health*, Allan v. Horowitz and Theresa L. Scheid. Cambridge: Cambridge University Press.

Belcher, John R.
   1988   "Rights Versus Needs of Homeless Mentally Ill Persons." *Social Work* 33: 398-402.

Carey, Benedict
   2005   "Most Will Be Mentally Ill at Some Point, Study Says." *New York Times*. June 7:17.

Chicago Department of Human Services
   2005   "Summary Findings of the Point-In-Time Count of Chicago's Homeless." June.

Clausen, J and M. R. Yarrow
   1955   "The Impact of Mental Illness on the Family." *Journal of Social Issues* 2.

Cockerham, William C.
   2000   *Sociology of Mental Disorder*, 5th ed. Englewood Cliffs, New Jersey: Prentice Hall.

Dennis, D. L. and J. Monahan
   1996   *Coercion and Aggressive Community Treatment*. New York: Plenum.

Denzin, Norman K.
   1984   *On Understanding Emotion*. San Francisco: Jossey-Bass.

Department of Mental Health and Developmental Disabilities
   1973   "Mental Health Statistics for Illinois Fiscal, 1973." Springfield, Illinois.
   2004   "Statistics, Fiscal, 2004." Springfield, Illinois.

Erlich, Eugene, et al.
   1980   *Oxford American Dictionary*. New York: Oxford University Press.

Farris, Robert E. and H. Warren Dunhem
   1939   *Mental Disorder in Urban Areas*. Chicago: University of Chicago Press.

Gerson, Samuel and Ellen Bassuk
   1980   "Psychiatric Emergencies: An Overview." *American Journal of Psychiatry* 137: 1-11.

Gilboy, Janet A. and John R. Schmidt
   1971   "Voluntary" Hospitalization of the Mentally Ill. Northwestern University Law Review. 66.

Goffman, Erving
   1971   *Relations in Public*. New York: Basic Books.

Greenley, James R., and David Mechanic
   1976a "Patterns of Seeking Care for Psychological Problems." In *The Growth of Bureaucratic Medicine*, D. Mechanic, ed. New York: Wiley.

1976b   "Social Selection in Seeking Help for Psychological Problems." *Journal of Health and Social Behavior* 17: 249-62.

Greenley, J. R., D. Mechanic, and P. D. Cleary
1987   "Seeking Help for Psychological Problems." *Medical Care* 25: 113-28.

Grusky, Oscar, and Melvin Pollner, eds.
1981   *The Sociology of Mental Illness*. New York: Holt, Rinehart and Winston.

Gurin, G., Joseph Veroff, and S. Feld
1960   *Americans View Their Mental Health*. New York: Basic Books.

Hollingshead, A. B., and F. C. Redlich
1958   *Social Class and Mental Illness*. New York: Wiley.

Horgan, C. M.
1984   *Demand for Ambulatory Mental Health Services from Specialty Providers*. Rockville, Maryland: National Center for Health Services Research.

Hough, R. L., J. A. Landsverk, M. Karno, A. Burnam, D. M. Timbers, and J. I. Escobar
1978   "Utilization of Health and Mental Health Services by Los Angles Mexican Americans and Non-Hispanic Whites." *Archives of General Psychiatry* 44: 702-9.

Howard, K. I. Cornille, T. A., Lyons, J. S., Vessey, J.T., Lueger, R. J., and Saunders, S. M.
1996   "Patterns of Mental Health Service Utilization." *Archives of General Psychiatry* 53: 696-703.

Kadushin, Charles
1969   *Why People Go to Psychiatrists*. New York: Atherton.

Karp, David A.
1996   *Speaking of Sadness*. New York: Oxford University.

Larson, D. B., A. A. Hohmann, L. G. Kessler, K. G. Meador, J. H. Boyd, and E. McSherry
1988   "The Couch and the Cloth: The Need for Linkage." *Hospital and Community Psychiatry* 39: 1064-9.

Leaf, P. J., M. M. Livingston, G. L. Tischler, M. M. Weissman, C. E. Holzer II, and J. Myers
1985   "Contact with Health Professionals for the Treatment of Psychological and Emotional Problems." *Medical Care* 23: 1322-37.

Lemert, Edwin M.
1972   *Human Deviance, Social Problems, and Social Control*, 2nd ed. Englewood Cliffs, New Jersey: Prentice Hall.

Mandersheid, R. W. and Sonnenchein, M. A.
1996   *Mental Health, United States, 1996*. Washington, D. C.: Center for Mental Health Service.

Mechanic, David
1978   *Medical Sociology*, 2nd ed. New York: Free Press.

Narrow, W. E., et al.
1993   "Use of Services by Persons with Mental and Addictive Disorders: Findings from the National Institute of Mental Health Epidemiological Catchment Area." *Archives of General Psychiatry* 50: 95-107.

Nolan, Joseph R. and Jacqueline M. Nolan-Haley
1991   *Black's Law Journal*, 6th ed. abridged. St. Paul, Minnesota: West Publishing.

Padgett, D. K., C. Patrick, B. J. Burns, and H. J. Schlesinger
   1994   "Ethnicity and the Use of Outpatient Mental Health Services in a National Insured Population." *American Journal of Public Health* 84: 222-6.
Palmer, Albert B. and Julian Wohl
   1972   "Voluntary Admission Forms: Does The Patient Know What He's Signing?" *Hospital and Community Psychiatry* 23.
Perrucci, Robert and Dena B. Targ
   1982   "Network Structure and Reactions to Primary Deviance of Mental Patients." *Journal of Health and Social Behavior* 23:2-17
Pescosolido, Bernice A., et al.
   1998   "How People Get Into Mental Health Services: Stories of Choice, Coercion, and Muddling Through From First-Timers." *Social Science and Medicine* 46: 275-86.
Pescosolido, Bernice A. and Carol A. Boyer
   1999   "How Do People Come to Use Mental Health Services? Current Knowledge and Changing Perspectives." In *A Handbook for the Study of Mental Health*, Allan V. Horowitz and Theresa L. Scheid. Cambridge: Cambridge University Press.
Pescosolido, Bernice R., et al.
   1999   "The Social Dynamics of Responding to Mental Health Problems." In *Handbook of the Sociology of Mental Health*, Carol S Aneshensel and Jo C Phelan. New York: Kluwer/Plenum.
Polgar, Michael F. and Joseph P. Morrissey
   1999   "Mental Health Services and Systems." In *Handbook of the Sociology of Mental Health*, Carol S. Aneshensel and Jo C. Phelan. New York: Kluwer/Plenum.
Portes, A., D. Kyle, and W. W. Eaton
   1992   "Mental Illness and Help-Seeking Behavior Among Mariel Cuban and Haitian Refugees in South Florida." Journal of Health and Social Behavior 33: 283-98.
Reiger, Darrell, et al.
   1993   "The de Facto Mental and Addictive Disorder Service System: Epidemiological Catchment Area Perspective 1-Year Prevalence Rates of Disorders and Services." *Archives of General Psychiatry* 50: 85-94.
Rhodes, Lorna A.
   1991   *Emptying Beds*. Berkeley: University of California Press.
Rock, Ronald S. with M. A. Jacobson and R. M. Jonopaul
   1968   *Hospitalization and Discharge of the Mentally Ill*. Chicago: University of Chicago Press.
Rogler, L. H
   1989   "The Meaning of Culturally Sensitive Research in Mental Health: Issues of Memory in the Diagnostic Interview Schedule." *Journal of Nervous and Mental Disease* 146: 296-303.
Rogler, L. H., and D. E. Cortes
   1993   "Help-Seeking Pathways: A Unifying Concept in Mental Health Care." *American Journal of Psychiatry* 150: 554-61.

Rosenberg, Morris
    1984   "A Symbolic Interactionist View of Psychosis." *Journal of Health and Social Behavior* 25: 289-302.
Ryan, William
    1969   *Distress in the City*. Cleveland: Case Western Research University Press.
Sampson, Harold, Sheldon Messinger, and Robert Towne
    1961   "The Mental Hospital and Marital Family Ties." *Social Problems* 9:141-55.
Scheff, Thomas J.
    1996   "Users and Nonusers of a Student Psychiatric Clinic." *Journal of Health and Social Behavior* 7: 114-21.
Sexton, Christine Jordan
    2007   "Florida Adopts Plan For Mentally Ill Inmates." *New York Times*. January 11:23.
Shapiro, S., E. Skinner, L. Kessler, M. V. Korff, P. German, G. Tischler, P. Leaf, L. Benham, L. Cottler, and D. Regier
    1984   "Utilization of Health and Mental Health Services: Three Epidemiologic Catchment Area Sites." *Archives of General Psychiatry* 41: 971-8.
Srole, Leo, et al.
    1962   *Mental Health in the Metropolis*. New York: Harper and Row.
Stedman, Henry J., et al.
    1998   "Violence by People Discharged From Acute Psychiatric Inpatient Facilities and By Others In the Same Neighborhood." *Archives of General Psychiatry* 55: 393-401.
Stefan, Susan
    2006   *Emergency Department Treatment of the Psychiatric Patient*. New York: Oxford University Press.
Sussman, L. K., L. N. Robins, and F. Earls
    1987   "Treatment-Seeking For Depression by Black and White Americans." *Social Science and Medicine* 24: 187-96.
Sykes, Gresham and Robert K. Merton
    1978   *Criminology*. New York: Harcourt, Brace, Jovanovich.
Thoits, Peggy, A
    1985   "Self-Labeling Processes in Mental Illness: The Role of Emotional Deviance." *American Journal of Sociology* 91: 221-49.
Ware, J. E., W. G. Manning, N. Duan, K. B. Wells, and J. P. Newhouse
    1984   "Health Status and the Use of Outpatient Mental Health Services." *American Psychologist* 39: 1090-1100.
Wells, K. B., J. M. Golding, R. L. Hough, A. Burnam, and M. Karno
    1988   "Factors Affecting The Probability of Use of General and Medical Health and Social/Community Services For Mexican Americans and Non-Hispanic Whites." *Medical Care* 26: 441-52.
Wells, K. B., W. G. Manning, N. Duan, J. P. Newhouse, and J. E. Ware
    1986   "Sociodemographic Factors and the Use of Outpatient Mental Health Services." *Medical Care* 24: 75-85.

Veroff, Joseph, Richard A. Kulka, and Elizabeth Douvan
  1981 *Mental Health In America.* New York: Basic Books.
Website
       www.census.gov
Whitt, Hugh P. and Richard L. Meile
  1985 "Alignment, Magnification, and Snowballing: Processes in the Definition of Symptoms of Mental Illness." *Social Forces* 63: 682-97.
Yarrow, M., C. Schwartz, H. Murphy, and L. Deasy.
  1995 "The Psychological Meaning of Mental Illness in the Family." *Journal of Social Issues* 11: 12-24.

4 The Police
"How Do You Talk a Mentally Ill Person Out of Being Mentally Ill?"

Introduction

The best way to understand behavior is to understand its context. So we will begin this study of the police apprehension of the mentally ill with a brief historical review of policing and then an examination of the role of the police in modern urban America. We will then present our data on police apprehension of the mentally ill.

1. The Policeman and His Job History

Our system of policing grew out of the British experience during the early industrial revolution. The police, as a formal bureaucratic organization, only came into existence in the 19th century in London. This was in response to earlier, and unsuccessful, attempts to maintain order. Before 1500 the earliest forms of policing were watchmen. They were charged with "maintaining the King's peace." This consisted of enforcing regulations concerning the prevention of plague, fire, commercial fraud, and the maintenance of order.

Each area of London chose its own watchmen. However, they soon became known for their timidity. Later, in the 1500s, "bellmen" were appointed to guard against fire but this "watch and ward" did not improve matters. The watch and ward soon became an organization of old men. They were known as "Charlies." These Charlies were often terrorized by rich young men. So, each citizen was responsible for his or her own protection. Persons of property either armed themselves or traveled with bodyguards. So, the rich were able to protect themselves whereas the poor were the common victims of crime (Mather, 1959:75-95).

A supplement to the watch and ward was the Yeomanry. The Yeomanry consisted of small, rural landowners who employed the saber charge as their typical tactic against mobs and riots among the emerging urban working class (Silver, 1967:9).

These early attempts at order maintenance proved acceptable to the ruling classes until gin was introduced. Agricultural interests saw great profit in changing the drinking habits of lower-class Londoners from beer, ale, and wine to hard liquor. By 1725 there were at least seven thousand gin shops in London. For a penny one could drink all day and get a straw mat on which to sleep it off. By 1743 the consumption of gin had increased six-fold to eight million gallons a year in less than twenty years. The result was an unprecedented crime wave with riotous mobs a common occurrence. The governments reaction to this disorder was inadequate and the rich began to flee the city. In the 1770s and 80s the Lord Mayor of London, the Duke of York, and the Prince of Wales, were all robbed in the street. These occurrences led to the creation of the London "preventive police" in 1829 (Rubenstein, 1973:5-10). Although the military was capable of putting down large scale rioting they were unable to act in small dispersed units throughout civilian society on a permanent basis. So, the police were organized for that specific purpose (Silver, 1967:8-14).

Those who urged the government to establish the preventive police argued that they would reduce and ultimately eliminate crime. The police, it was hoped, would also bring more humane treatment for criminals. Thus, the police were seen as a civilizing force (Rubenstein, 1973:10).

The first police commissioner, Colonel Charles Rowan, created the "New Police." He organized them territorially. For the first time the entire city was to be continuously patrolled by men assigned to specific areas and whose "beat" was bureaucratically determined. To produce the required discipline to carry out this task Colonel Rowan chose the British military as his organizational model. The plan was not an immediate success. On the department's first day many of the constables were drunk; others brought umbrellas to protect themselves from the rain. The Colonel forbade drinking and banned umbrellas. However, many of the officers performed poorly and he fired many of them in the early years (Reith, 1943:193-5: Mather, 1959:97). In spite of this the New Police concept became popular. Between 1830 and 1860 every major city and town in the United States adopted a similar system (see: Lane, 1967). Over the years technological innovations such as call boxes, radios, and patrol cars enhanced the functioning of the police. However, the core of police work has remained the same: "Policing has been and will remain a personal service. Law enforcement is almost totally concerned with the problems of people" (Wilson and McLaren, 1972:51).

2. The Police and the Law

Although we would all agree with Wilson, most people would say that what a policeman really does is maintain law and order. However, what this means is ambiguous. A policeman is charged with maintaining order through the use of the criminal laws. These laws contain both a substantive and a procedural component. The substantive law consists of the norms of society. And it spells out the punishment if one violates that code. The procedural law regulates the conduct of officials who process suspected criminals. Procedural law involves such matters as search and seizure, arrest procedures, questions of proof, the right to counsel, criminal accusation, and the fairness of a trial. These rules stress the protection of a citizen's liberties. In practice, substantive law and procedural law often conflict. Inherent, then, in the practical application of the "rule of law" is a constant tension (Skolnick, 1966:6-10; Barth, 1963).

A further complication is the concept of order. For example, within a few miles of each other are the UCLA campus, the Watts ghetto, and Beverly Hills. Do these three areas all possess the same quality of order? In practice, the maintenance of order is influenced by a complex set of factors. They are the substance of the criminal law, the level of danger in the community, the community's political complexion, the social makeup of the population being policed, the influence of police policies, and the rate of social change. Therefore, the legal order is not static; and the policing of that order is a complex process—an "enterprise" (Skolnick, 1966:9-12; Fuller, 1964).

The essence of that enterprise is discretion, the decision to arrest or not to arrest. These low visibility decisions are seldom reviewed by higher authority. Since police resources are inadequate for enforcing all the laws, discretion must be exercised in the allocation of the available resources. First, through the budgetary process, the public and the legislature influence the absolute level of policing that they are willing to accept and pay for. Second, the police administration allocates officers based on its perception of need. And, third, at the individual level, the decision to arrest is based upon an individual officer's attitudes towards right and wrong, as well as, about conserving police resources. That is why the police often do not arrest individuals for trivial offenses such as traffic violations, minor juvenile offenses, or drunkenness. The police may also not arrest individuals when they view conduct as conforming to the norms of the group involved, when the victim is not seriously interested in prosecution, or when the victim's plight is the product of his or her own misconduct. The police may also not arrest if they believe that there is no likelihood of prosecution or conviction, if the predictable punishment is thought to be either too strict or too lenient, or if the police feel the criminal process cannot provide the appropriate solution. A good example of this is the discretion used in routine order maintenance situations. Most criminal laws define acts such as murder, rape, speeding, and so on. However, "disorderly conduct" is often indefinable. Simply put, what constitutes order is a matter of opinion. A further complication is that the police cannot arrest individuals in many states unless an offense has occurred in their presence or the victim is willing to sign a complaint. Also, the police are taught not to rush into situations. And they learn from experience to "not stick their necks out" and to "keep their noses clean." For all these reasons police tend to act conservatively and to under-enforce the law (Goldstein, 1960; LaFave, 1965, 1962a, 1962b; Wilson, 1968:21-24, 48-50).

3. The Police Officer's Working Personality

Police officers develop a "working personality." The police officers' working personality begins to form at the police academy. Harris (1973, 1978) observed that the academy instilled in the cadets masculinity, defensiveness, professionalism, and depersonalization. It also fostered group solidarity, a propensity to cut corners, and a cops-and-robber's mentality. Gross (1991) found that cadets feared physical danger. But they also feared organizational sanctions and court appearances. Harris (1973) noted that the academy instilled a code of silence and fraternal bonding. This occurred in order to avoid departmental reprimands. Van Maanen (1973) observed that most recruits found the academy to be a required, but tedious, stage in their police careers. This stage required cadets to give absolute obedience to departmental rules, endure rigorous physical training, and tolerate dull lectures (see also: Van Maanen, 1972, 1975, 1978a, 1978b).

The academy also began the process of creating attitudes which are highly authoritarian, conventional, moralistic, domineering, rigid, and hostile (Adlam, 1982). Autsin (1987) and Klopsch (1983) have argued that such personality types self-select themselves for police work. However, research on police socialization has shown this not to be the case. Most police recruits are similar to other members of their cohorts. However, intensive socialization in the academy funnels recruits into a narrow ideological perspective (Hopper, 1977; Conti, 2000: 141, 217). Tenerowicz (1992) found that the academy made the officers more aggressive, defensive, controlling, domineering, rigid, and insensitive. Also, police officers came to identify themselves with power figures and were preoccupied with issues of dominance, strength, and leadership. Conti (2000) observed that most of the idealistic cadets or those merely curious about a police career dropped out of the academy. He found that the majority of the cadets who completed the academy had a "realistic" perspective on police work which they had gained from previous law enforcement experience (see also: Hopper, 1977). However, Maghan (1988) found in his research that cadets were not just trained to be authority figures. Instead, they were also trained to be service oriented. In this process the recruits had to learn to decide the "amoral issue" of when to render service and when to enforce the law.

The police subculture at the academy stressed mission, macho attitudes, an us-versus-them mentality, and cynicism. However, what also developed were the twin foci of the police role: sensitivity to danger and the taking on of the authority role. And this authority was ultimately based upon coercion (Paoline, 2001).

Although the academy may be important in police socialization, Neiderhoffer has a different view: "When the recruit finally meets older members of the force . . . the more experienced men tell him that in order to become a real policeman, he will have to forget everything he learned at the academy" (1967:162). Similarly, Wilson has reported that learning the craft of policing occurred by on-the-job apprenticeship (1968:283). And, Van Maanen noted that new police officers learned their profession from their field-training officers. These new officers were tested on "hot" or "heavy" calls. Such calls required "real police work" and were "the measure of the man" (1973:413).

Real police work, then, involves avoiding danger, asserting authority, and the willingness to use coercion (Bittner, 1978). That is, the officer's job is to control a situation and gain compliance or control. He or she does this through force. However, such force can be verbal, non-verbal, psychological, or physical. Verbal force can range from requests ("Please sit down.") to commands ("Drop the knife!"). Non-verbal communication may consist of body position or hand movements. Psychological force may be the officer's office, badge, uniform, or equipment. And, physical force can range from a light touch to the use of deadly force (see: Rubenstein, 1973:221, 233, 260).

One point that is rarely appreciated by outsiders is that citizen encounters with police officers are almost always *reactive*. That is, officers respond to the cues or actions of the citizen. A citizens actions can vary widely. They can consist of:

a) verbal or non-verbal danger cues;
b) unwillingness to comply with an officer's directions,
c) refusal to move;
d) pulling away from or pushing an officer;
e) physically attacking an officer;
f) attempting to disarm an officer; or
g) attacking an officer with a weapon.

The officer's response, in either words or actions, is governed by a "use of force continuum." This takes into account both the subjects actions and a "reasonable force response" by the officer. The officer's response will escalate as the resistance or threat increases. Depending upon the situation the officer's response will be:

a) officer presence (body position or stance);
b) verbal and non-verbal requests or directions;
c) taking control of or escorting an individual away;
d) "soft control" techniques (pressure points, arm locks);
e) OC (oleoresin capsicum) spray or the use of a Taser;
f) baton strikes: or
g) deadly force (Barker, 1999:67; Truncale and Smith, 1994:1-3, 181-188).

The first step in this process is gaining citizen compliance through command presence. Command presence is a quality that conveys authority and the physical ability to back it up. Command presence, coupled with weapons skills, allows officers to control almost all situations. It is this control that allows officers to do their job. An officer commented that all you need on the street is "the brains God gave you, your gun and command presence. If it came right down to it, you could do without the brains and the gun, but God help you if you don't have command presence" (Barker, 1999:69-70; see also: Rubenstein, 1973: 267-8, 295-6). In an interview one officer commented: "When I'm dealing with someone, no matter how nice or how stern I am, I have to convey to them-through body position, tone of voice, or words—that if things go sour I'm going to knock them on their ass."

Police officers, because they regularly deal with difficult people and difficult situations, develop a set of attitudes; this is their "working personality." The police officer's working personality is shaped by the constant threat of danger, his or her own awareness of their position as an authority figure, and the continual pressure to perform efficiently. The police officers response to danger is suspicion. This leads to isolation from the public (see: Piliavin and Briar, 1964). The requirement to enforce laws representing morality (drinking, gambling, prostitution, etc.) further alienates the officer from the public. And the necessity of policing routine public activity, such as traffic violations, isolates the policemen even more from the public. Further, the enforcement of morality, which the officer and the public often do not subscribe to, creates cynicism (see: Westly, 1951, 1953; Niederhoffer, 1967).

The core function of the police officer is to protect the community from violence. Because of this he or she becomes extremely sensitive to potentially dangerous situations and persons. The policeman may perceive threat in the arrogance of a teenager, a person who is either too casual or too nervous in his or her presence, the loitering of an individual near a public restroom, or an individual wearing a coat on a hot day (Piliavin and Briar, 1964; Adams, 1963:28). Since such encounters are frequent, threat is constantly present in an officer's work.

Threat creates caution, but it also creates excitement. This is one of the major enticements of police work. One of the reasons individuals become police officers is their dislike of confining and routine jobs. Few police officers enjoy desk jobs except as a reward for many years on the street. "Street cops" often disparage "inside" or "staff cops" for losing sight of the "real" job. Street officers think of police who work inside as bureaucrats more concerned with statistics, public relations, or politics, than police work. However, 80 to 90 percent of the average patrol officer's job is *not* "real police work."

Instead, it is answering service calls. Family fights, disturbances, lost children, traffic incidents, drunks, the mentally ill, and loud parties are the vast majority of their calls. They are routine. Officers have told me that they are considered to be "just the usual bullshit," that is, "ubs calls."[1] The police respond to these routine service calls because they must, but few enjoy them. I once asked an officer why policemen don't go crazy with all the routine calls they handle. "We just don't talk about it," he somberly replied.

However, the policeman's working personality is too broad to fully explain police behavior. Broderick (1977) found four types of police roles that an officer may take on. One is the "enforcer." This role emphasizes law enforcement at all costs. The second is the "idealist." The idealist aspires to make policing a profession. Third is the "realist" who sees both society and policing as a shambles. And fourth is the "optimist" who derives his or her pleasure from helping people in trouble.

Walsh (1977) takes a different tack. He sees three types of police officers. One is the "street cop" who becomes a police officer because it is a secure job. Second are "middle class mobiles" who are attracted to the status of the job and the chance for career advancement. Third, are "action seekers" who are lured by the prospect of excitement (see also: Reiner, 1992; Muir, 1977; Wilson, 1968; Paoline, 2001).

In spite of their orientation, for the average patrol officer, routine is the watchword of policing. To the policeman the unknown or the disorderly raise anxieties about their personal safety. Policemen, therefore, seek out regularity and predictability. McInnes points out: "The true copper's dominant characteristic, if the truth be known, is neither those daring nor vicious qualities that are sometimes attributed to him by friend or enemy, but an ingrained conservatism, and almost desperate love of the conventional. It is untidiness, disorder, the unusual, that a copper disapproves of most of all, far more, even than of crime which is merely a professional matter. Hence, his profound dislike of people loitering in streets, dressing extravagantly, speaking with exotic accents, being strange, weak, eccentric, or simply any rare minority." In other words, "anything that can not be safely predicted" (1962:74).

---

1. These are the officer's words, but the researchers acronym.

And Peter Connel notes: "The time spent cruising one's sector or walking one's beat is not wasted time, though it can become quite routine. During this time, the most important thing for the officer to do is notice the *normal*. He must come to know the people in his area, their habits, their automobiles, and their friends. He must learn what time the various shops close, how much money is kept on hand on different nights, what lights are usually left on, which houses are vacant . . . only then can he decide what persons or cars under what circumstances warrant the appellation `suspicious'" (quoted in Skolnick, 1966;48).

The social isolation of the police officer is almost as powerful as his or her need for regularity and predictability. The social distance of the policeman from the policed is described well by McInnes: "The story is all coppers are just civilians like anyone else, living among them . . . but you and I know that's a legend for mugs. We *are* cut off: we're *not* like everyone else. Some civilians fear us . . . some dislike us but no one—well, very few indeed—accepts us as just ordinary like them. In one sense . . . we're just like hostile troops occupying an enemy country. And say what you like, at times that makes us lonely" (1962: 20).

James Baldwin expresses the same isolation for the ghetto policeman: "The only way to police a ghetto is to be repressive. None of the Police Commissioner's men, even with the best will in the world, have any way of understanding the lives led by the people they swagger about in twos and threes controlling. Their very presence is an insult, and it would be, even if they spent their entire day feeding gumdrops to children. They represent the force of the white world, and that world's criminal profit and ease, to keep the black man corralled up here, in this place. The badge, the gun in the holster, and the swinging club make vivid what will happen should his rebellion become overt.

"It is hard, on the other hand, to blame the policeman, blank, good-natured, thoughtless, and insuperably innocent, for being such a perfect representative of the people he serves. He, too believes in good intentions and is astounded and offended when they are not taken for the deed. He has never, himself, done anything for which to be hated—which of us has? And yet he is facing, daily and nightly, people who would gladly see him dead, and he knows it. There is no way for him not to know it: there are few things under heaven more unnerving than the silent, accumulating contempt and hatred of a people. He moves through Harlem, therefore, like an occupying soldier in a bitterly hostile country; which is precisely what, and where he is, and is the reason he walks in twos and threes" (1962: 65-67).

The reasons for police isolation are not only the product of the policeman and his job. They are also the result of civilian attitudes towards the police. The police are tainted. Police are seen as the fire it takes to fight fire. Because of their duties, police must inflict harm on other persons; but the citizen prefers to see the policeman as an automaton. If the citizen sees the police as his or her representative, then the citizen becomes implicated in the very taint he or she fervently tries to avoid. One New York detective from the 1850s is quoted as saying: The police officer is "the outgrowth of a diseased and corrupt state of things, and is, consequently, morally diseased himself" (George S. McWatters quoted in Lane, 1967:69).

Physicians are praised by society for their work, although they must often deal with disagreeable people or disagreeable matters. But police officers can only accomplish something for someone by proceeding against another person. Or, the police officer must stand between people and decide subtle human conflicts, profound legal questions, and ponderous moral issues without being allowed to give the subtleties and profundities the consideration they deserve. This, then, makes their job crude. Their only option is to arrest or not to arrest. This limited choice exists even though the police are charged by society with all the human conflicts and misery with which the other agencies of government are unwilling or unable to cope. Further, police work is concentrated where crime is most likely to occur; that is, among the young, the poor, the black, and the Hispanic. Originally, the police were organized to suppress crime among the "dangerous classes" (Silver, 1967). Today, however, enforcement is based on statistics and crime rates. However, in practice the result is the same (Skolnick, 1966:54; Bittner, 1970:6-14).

Police officers are conservative. That is because their job is to enforce the (current) laws; that is, to maintain the status quo. Most police officers do not possess rigid, authoritarian personalities. However, they do have what Skolnick (1966: 61) calls "conventional personalities." Brooks notes: "Cops are conventional people. All a cop can swing in a milieu of marijuana smokers, interracial dates, and homosexuals is the night stick. A police officer who passed a lower east side art gallery filled with paintings of what appeared to be female genitalia could think of doing only one thing—step in and make an arrest"(1965, 29-30).

In conclusion, embedded in a police officer's working personality is a combination of danger, authority, routine, and convention. Danger is the most pronounced of these. And when danger threatens, legal niceties may be forgotten.

4. The Patrol Officer's Job

The most basic police function is performed by the patrol officer. He is not a "law enforcement officer" but a "peace officer." Law enforcement officers, such as detectives, perform punitive or inquisitorial functions. Patrol officers, however, are concerned with maintaining order and working within the moral consensus of the community (Banton, 1964:6-7; Skolnick, 1966; Cumming, Cumming, and Edell, 1965). The patrol officer's job is to prevent disorder. The patrol officer uses the law as a *tool* to maintain order. The officer is concerned with keeping the peace, determining who is to blame for some action, and restoring order. He or she is often not concerned with "enforcing the law." A patrol officer uses phrases such as "knock it off," "break it up," or "go home and sleep it of," more commonly than, "you're under arrest." A patrol officer is "typically . . . expected to maintain order on the street, to keep a `clean beat', to disperse mobs, to remove `undesirables', whether or not legal tools for accomplishing these results are available" (The President's Commission on Law Enforcement and Administration of Justice, Task Force Report: The Police, 1967:179). In order to accomplish this task the officer must often ignore formal justice. He or she is concerned with an outcome that is neither right nor wrong. Instead, the officer is there to restore order and punish the guilty. However, when a patrol officer arrives, the people he encounters are often dirty, angry, rowdy, obscene, dazed, savage, or bloodied. Under such circumstance restoring order may be possible. But, determining who is guilty is often guesswork.

However, even "restoring order" in such circumstances is problematic. First, the police officer must decide whether to intervene. Then he or she must decide how to intervene. This is not always obvious because officers are routinely called to make quick decisions about individuals. This often leads officers to "pre-judge" people based upon their appearance. This makes the line between professional and personal opinion ("prejudice") thin (Wilson, 1972:3538). Therefore, the patrol officer may restore order; however, he or she may be unjust in the process.

A further complication is that there are three distinct styles of policing (Wilson, 1968). One style is the watchman style in which the department ignores minor violations and uses the law to maintain order rather than to regulate conduct. The legalistic style deals with everyday situations as if they were matters of law enforcement rather than order maintenance; this will produce a high proportion of juvenile offenders, a high rate of ticketing, active enforcement against illicit enterprises, and a large number of misdemeanor arrests. This will occur even when the public order has not been breached. The service style is common in homogeneous middle class communities and takes seriously all requests for either law enforcement or order maintenance (unlike departments with a watchman style). However, unlike the legalistic system, the police are less likely to respond by making an arrest or otherwise imposing a formal sanction. Service oriented departments are concerned with maintaining public order according to the community consensus and in dealing with trouble from "outsiders." They are also concerned with directing traffic, regulating juveniles, and providing service.

5. Police Apprehension of the Mentally Ill: 1973[2]

a. Introduction

In the course of daily life in modern America, citizens become involved in problems or situations which they cannot control. When this happens they "call the cops." It does not matter if the situation is civil or criminal. What is important is that the police are the only agency of government which is available 24 hours a day to solve problems (Bittner, 1970: 36-47). The most common call a police officer gets is a "disturbance call." Disturbance calls are a catch-all designation which describes family fights. drunks, loud parties, or teenagers on a street corner. They are routine calls in which the officer quickly restores the peace and seldom makes an arrest.

b. Considerations

On a disturbance call the police will sometimes find someone who is mentally ill. The police are not concerned with the illness, per se, but are interested in whether the situation will get out of hand if they ignore it. Therefore, the police are not concerned about mental illness; instead, they are concerned about danger to life, health, property, and order in public places.

---

2. The research of this chapter is based upon the work of Bittner (1967a) and my own participate-observation field research for six months in the summer and fall of 1973 with three Midwestern police departments. Two of these departments were in cities of 100,000 population with significant minority populations. The other department was in a suburban community that possessed approximately a 50 percent minority population. All these communities were within the Chicago metropolitan area and were considered by most of the officers I rode with to be miniature versions of Chicago.

In spite of these concerns, police are often reluctant to apprehend a mentally ill person. They do not consider themselves experts in psychopathology. Since they are involved in situations of high stress and anxiety for the citizen, they will often shrug off a case as "just another nut."

One officer I rode with said "mental illness is irrelevant to my job. If a person breaks the law, they're charged with a crime, period. Police can't decide if a person is mentally ill; so that never enters my mind. I can't even pick up someone for safekeeping because there would be no reason to hold them. I'd be violating their civil rights. If they are committed and escape, then it's alright to take them back, but otherwise, it's not. You, as a cop, just can't decide their mental condition for fear of the repercussions. In court, all the guy's lawyer has to ask is, 'Are you a psychiatrist?' I would have to say, 'No', and then I was in trouble. Police simply can't get involved because we have to protect ourselves from legal repercussions."

Also, the police are particularly careful not to be exploited in unknown situations in which they possess only fragmentary information. Further, police officers confront perversion, disorientation, misery, irresoluteness, and incompetence much more often than any other social agency. They can easily point to large numbers of persons who, to all appearances, need to be in a psychiatric hospital. However, they seem to lead lives which require neither aid nor intervention. Against this background the requirement that one should have a good brain and an even temper belong to the same category of wishes that one should have a good income and a pretty wife. Thus, making psychiatric apprehensions is, in a sense, simply a matter of economy. Lower the standards somewhat and the number of apprehensions might be greatly multiplied. Similar considerations apply to making various other types of arrests. Though the police could easily multiply the total number of arrests, they seem to produce just enough cases to keep the courts busy and the jails full. And similarly, they help bring in just enough people to keep the hospitals busy (Bittner, 1967b:280-281).

Although the police readily admit that dealing with mentally ill persons is an integral part of their job, they believe it is not a proper task for them. Not only do they lack training and competence in this area, but such apprehensions are incompatible with their perceptions of their role as crime-fighters. Police officers commend each other for a "good pinch"; and departments encourage vice arrests and other "activity" (pedestrian and car stops). However, apprehending or transporting mentally ill persons is nothing more than another routine assignment (see: Rubenstein, 1973).

Officers complain that taking someone to a psychiatric hospital is usually a tedious, cumbersome, and uncertain procedure. They may wait for hours in the admitting office and are occasionally obliged to explain situations that appear to question the officer's judgment. They must also consider the possibility of being turned down by the physician. Police officers are mystified by the seemingly erratic behavior of psychiatric admitting offices. Because of this many officers have given up on taking individuals to mental health facilities. They simply charge mentally ill people with DC (disorderly conduct). Further, since hospital admissions often consume great amounts of time police officers are often reluctant to get involved. "Let's hurry it up and get back on the street," is probably one of the most common phrases spoken by police supervisors.

In my initial research, none of the police officers I rode with were aware that Illinois law (Sections 7-1 and 7-2 of the Mental Health Code, 1968) allowed anyone over 18 years old to sign an emergency petition for admission to a mental health facility when a person is "in need of mental treatment and (is) in such a condition that immediate hospitalization is necessary for the protection from physical harm of such person or others." In fact, the police I rode with were at a loss to know how to handle mentally ill persons. For example, typical comments were:

"We try to back off mental cases."

"I can't sign a certificate. I don't have any authority."

"They just let them go after a doctor talks to them."

"They say they don't want them, they're full."

"We really don't have enough time to handle a case, talk to them, find out what their problem is, etc."

"You can get stuck with one. What are you gonna do? They didn't do anything."

"There's no procedure for handling mentally ill persons. I have no authority to take them to a hospital unless a supervisor or relative tells me to. Otherwise, they have to be booked as drunk and disorderly. They're then bonded out quickly and right back where they started from."

"When mentally ill persons call, we send a car by, as we do for all calls; but for `regular callers', we recommend that they call a priest or minister, Alcoholics Anonymous, dial a prayer, etc."

"All I was ever told in training was that they were strong, fighters, and that you needed a back up man to help you."

"During training we didn't learn anything about dealing with people, just different forms and case law."

"I just go along with the program, that's all."

"I just keep talking and hope they get in the car."

"Mentally ill people cause trouble. The hospital won't take them and the judge won't convict them so they're right back on the street. Someone is bound to get hurt because these people carry knives and other weapons. I think the situation is just plain lousy!"

One officer from a nearby Wisconsin city told me that "policemen have a great tool available to them in dealing with mentally ill persons. All that's needed is two signatures on a petition to get someone admitted to a hospital." He added that "some of the guys are unaware of this and, they try to get the person angry enough so that he begins fighting and then can be arrested on disorderly conduct and taken to the hospital." A few minutes later I saw a lieutenant from the same department and asked him what the procedure was for handling mentally ill persons. He laughed and said that he didn't know. A court case had recently invalidated the state's commitment laws and they didn't know what to do with mentally ill persons. After an arrest they had been calling a local judge and asking him to come down and look at the prisoner if they thought he was mentally ill. If the judge decided that the person was mentally ill then he would sign the commitment papers and they would then be able to take them to the hospital. Later, another officer explained: "We used to be able to get people committed by calling up a local psychiatrist and having him agree to commit someone after the officer explained the situation over the phone. He retired and the practice ended. But, now everybody is looking for a chance to sue so now we have to go before a judge. However, the problem with this is that if the person is picked up on a Friday, we have to put him in a cell until court convenes on Monday." I asked him how the person was cared for in the lockup. "We sit a jailer in front of the cell and if the guy starts up the jailer sits on him until he is calm or the jailer calls for help." Later that evening I asked one of the department's best young officers how he handled mentally ill persons. "It's a gray area," he said. "Once in a while the department issues an order on the handling of mentally ill persons. We try them and they never work; so now we just play it by ear. We take them to the hospital, if that doesn't work, we try to get a relative, or . . .?" He shrugged and asked himself: "How do you talk a mentally ill person out of being mentally ill?"

c. Street Contacts and Caretakers

The police have frequent contacts with mentally ill persons. However, most of these contacts begin and end in the field. When an officer encounters a mentally ill person on a call he does not automatically take him or her to jail or to a hospital. Unless the person has committed a serious crime or is violent and cannot be restrained, the officer usually tries to turn them over to a caretaker in the community. These caretakers may be relatives, friends, landlords, or hotel clerks. Police officers do not uncritically "dump" mentally ill persons, for that would eventually mean more calls and more trouble; and such an officer would be considered a poor craftsmen by the other officers. What a police officer tries to do is to find a solution with some permanency so that the problem will be "solved." In such cases other social agencies are usually not involved. That is because they function on a 9 to 5, five-day-week schedule and are not available when most police business occurs; that is, on evenings and weekends. Therefore, if the problem isn't solved by the police, it simply isn't solved.

Few middle class persons who are mentally ill become involved with the police. Most of these persons are kept within a stable social environment and use medical, social, or legal professionals to assist them in their crises. Lower class persons, however, have few of these resources available; therefore, they are more likely to become involved with the police. Since their place in the community may be tenuous, it is often necessary for the police to use the "informational network" in their communities to find a caretaker for these ill persons. Such a network consists of the officer's knowledge of the semipublic members of the community such as barbers, newsstand operators, hotel clerks, and merchants. Their knowledge of the community, plus their sources of information, usually are sufficient to produce results. As a last ditch resource YMCA's or old hotels can be used as temporary shelters for those in need of a place to stay and a watchful eye. It is the officer's grasp of the stable aspects of the community in slums, transient areas, or business districts that allows them to find alternatives to hospitalization (Bittner, 1967a).

Officers also apply what Bittner (1967b) calls "psychiatric first aid." Police officers are not mental health professionals. But they are concerned with helping a person move from an emotional crisis to one of relative calm. Most police officers are untrained in handling mentally ill persons, just as they are untrained in handling family disturbances, or most other service calls (Parnas, 1971; Sullivan, 1968). All the officers I rode with said that in non-criminal cases they were told: "Use your common sense." For example:

A woman called the station and said she was being controlled by radio waves. She said that people were telling lies about her selling dope and creating problems in the neighborhood. After about five minutes of listening to her story, the sergeant told her to call back if she had any more trouble. He hung up with a look of relief on his face and told me he had learned her husband's business address and would call him to speak to her. Later that evening the sergeant said that the woman had come in to the station with further complaints. He said he had then called her husband to the station. The husband then picked her up and had her committed.

In handling calls involving mentally ill persons, police officers use the same procedures they would in handling any other routine call. They begin by removing the person from the immediate situation. This is good police practice and allows the officers to reduce emotions and gain control of the situation. This also allows the officer to make decisions without outside pressures interfering. In dealing with a mentally ill person the officer usually tries to establish and maintain an air of normalcy and routine. All of the person's remarks, allegation, or complaints are treated as routine police business. The police attempt to ignore extreme remarks, or even extreme behavior, and treat the situation as just another routine call.

One type of mentally ill person officers encounter is the "neighborhood nut." These are people who are chronic callers and are thought to be mentally ill. However, they live in stable situations and the police take no action in such cases beyond what they would do for any other similar call. After the appropriate report is taken or advice given, such as, "Call us if this happens again," or "We'll pay special attention to your home tonight," the police quickly depart. These calls are considered to be "unfounded" or "just bullshit." However, the officers answer them in order to reduce the person's fears and "to keep them from going really nuts." For example:

One evening we received a call of an attempted burglary. We drove to the address and found a tiny, elderly woman who said that some boy from the neighborhood had beaten on her cellar door while yelling to be let in. The officer checked the door and found no damage. The woman then began babbling about a man who had been walking by and how she had asked him to call the station about the man upstairs (she lived in a barren room in a basement). She said the man upstairs had gotten rid of his Polish wife for an Italian one (or vice versa) and now he wanted to evict her. She also talked about her schizophrenic son and how she has received nothing but harassment for the last two years from the neighborhood kids. The officer checked the other door and walked away from the lady as she babbled on. "Call immediately if the kid comes back," he said. "And we'll keep a close eye on the house tonight." We drove off and never went near the house again that night.

Police also run into chronic schizophrenics, the retarded, or senile persons during their regular duties. The officer's dealings with these persons are determined by the person's condition and the situation. These people usually have a long standing relationship with the officer. Like "psychiatric first aid," these encounters are structured by the officer's tendency to disregard pathological material, to act matter-of-factly, and to move the person away from others. Bittner describes such an encounter:

A young man approached an officer in a deteriorating business district of the city. He voiced an almost textbook-type paranoid complaint. From the statements and the officer's responses, it could be gathered that this was a part of a sequence of conversations. The two proceeded to walk away from an area of high traffic density to a quieter part of the neighborhood. In the ensuing stroll, the officer inspected various premises, greeted passers-by, and generally showed a low level of attentiveness. After about twenty-five minutes the man told the officer good-bye and said that he would be going home now. Later, the officer stated that he ran into this man quite often and it was usually on the same spot. He always tried to lead the man away from the place that apparently excited his paranoid suspicions. The officers inattentiveness was calculated to impress the person that there was nothing to worry about (Bittner, 1967b:290).

Police officers usually try to solve or alleviate the immediate problems of a mentally ill person. However, sometimes, officers treat mentally ill persons, as if they were "just drunks." For example:

A woman in her mid-fifties had called the station and had claimed that she had been threatened. The woman, who had been drinking, told the responding officers that she had been threatened and wanted protection. The incident was considered to be untrue by the officers and they told her to go up to her room and to lock the door until tomorrow morning. The officers laughed as they walked away. One officer commented that the woman was under "active psychiatric treatment."

In another incident the squad was stopped at a stoplight when a girl in her twenties, who was well known to the officers, came up to the car. She said hello and told the officers that she was working as a maid and that she liked her work. She acted silly and childish and the officers teased her although she didn't know it. After a few minutes, we said good-by and drove off. As we turned the corner, one of the officers informed me she was a former mental patient.

d. Assisting

Some contacts with mentally ill persons straddle the line between a field contact and a formal apprehension. On such calls the officer is asked to assist in the moving of a recalcitrant person from their home to a mental health facility. In such cases the officers accompany the person down the stairs and into a waiting auto. Beyond such assistance, the police remain in the background. However, they do stay until the move is completed to show that they are serious about the individual complying with the move. In such circumstances they keep their conversation with the person to a minimum. When they do speak they usually confine their comments to asking the individual to be more cooperative or to assure him or her that the move is legitimate and in their best interests. The officers may be the only ones on the scene who listen to the person and who use the leverage of trust to facilitate the move. Through such cases do not involve police initiative, and involve no active police decisions, the successful accomplishment of these moves is dependent upon police presence. For example:

We received a call of a mentally ill person that needed to be hospitalized. When we arrived, a black woman in her thirties came out of her home and said that her father had to be taken to a hospital but he didn't want to go in a squad car. She said she would try and get him to go in one of the family cars. The sergeant said that that was fine but to call if they needed assistance.

Later that afternoon we received a call to return to the house. The officers went up onto the porch where the man was sitting on a swing. His wife whispered that he had refused to go to the hospital and asked if we could help. The sergeant, who was white, tried to talk to the man, but he ignored him. One of the black officers tried to strike up a conversation and the man soon responded. In a few minutes the man had agreed to go to the hospital in the family car. The wife, a daughter, the man, and the black officer got into the car and drove to the hospital. We followed them and met them at the entrance. We then walked them into the admissions office and left.

The next day we received a call that the man had escaped from the hospital and was at his daughter's home. The dispatcher told us to apprehend the man and to return him to the hospital in a squad. When we arrived at the address the patient and the relatives were ready to leave in their car for the hospital. One of the officers told the family to take him to the hospital and we would meet them there. On the way to the hospital, the officer said that in Chicago, and even some of the officers on his own department, would have simply have grabbed him and tossed him into the squad. However, by letting him go in his own vehicle "the job got done with no hassle and the dispatcher will never be the wiser." When we arrived at the hospital we turned the man over to two three-hundred-pound security guards and left.

e. Apprehension

Although patrol officers are reluctant to apprehend mentally ill persons they do so at a rate equivalent to the total number of arrests for murder, manslaughter, rape, robbery, aggravated assault, and grand theft. The result is that 25 to 40 percent of all psychiatric admissions to public hospitals are the product of police apprehensions (Bittner, 1967b:282, Rock, 1968:87).

One call that almost always results in an apprehension is that of an attempted suicide. If the officer feels a serious attempt has been made the officer will almost always transport the person to a hospital. Although such incidents are significant, they are handled routinely. For example, in one department I studied they treated cases of attempted suicide as merely a "transport to the hospital" call. A report was filled out and the officer would then leave the hospital. Any further decisions were "purely medical" and of no concern to the department. In another department that was studied individuals who had attempted suicide were taken to the psychiatric ward of a nearby general hospital "if there were any marks." However, "if the psychiatrist doesn't admit him, we book him for disorderly conduct and keep him overnight. The next morning we release him and drop the charge."

In one case two officers were called to the hospital to take a report on an attempted suicide. The officers thought the attempt was fraudulent because the patient claimed he had put his head in an oven with the gas on but had not died. However, the officer's opinions were irrelevant since this call was considered to be a call for a report. The officer took the needed information from a nurse and began to leave. As they passed the man he whispered, "I didn't know it was so hard to die."

While on patrol one evening we received a call of an attempted suicide. As we neared the address a teenage girl ran towards the squad waving hysterically. "My father . . . I'm afraid he's gong to kill himself, but please don't say that I called." "It's Johnnie, the shoemaker," one officer said as we pulled up to the house. We knocked on the door and a voice replied, "It's open." We walked in and to our left was Johnnie crumpled in an old chair. "Hi, Johnnie," one officer said, "How ya' doin'?" He shrugged. The officer sat down on the couch but Johnnie didn't seem to notice. "Been havin' any trouble?" "This alimony, it's been eatin' my gut out." Johnnie may have been crying but it was difficult to tell because his face was partially hidden by his hand. "Did you try anything tonight, Johnnie?" "No. I wouldn't do anything stupid." "Can we look around?" "Sure." We glanced into the bathroom but nothing seemed out of place. We went down to the basement. "What are you looking for?" I asked the officer. "A rope, clothesline, anything like that." The basement was dark and dirty. We turned on a small light. We looked for a rope or razor but we didn't find anything. The officer turned on another light and saw that the ceiling was laced with a plastic clothes line as if it were a spider's web. The officer stood there for a moment and with a look of frustration. He swiped at the clothesline, shrugged, and turned towards the stairs. We went back upstairs.

"What happened today, Johnnie?" "Jan had a bunch of her friends over and they were making a hell of a racket. I finally couldn't stand it so I threw them all out." "Anything else?" "No, I've been stupid once already . . . I'm not going to humiliate myself again." "Want a cigarette?" Johnnie nodded. "Ya' know Jan needs you." "I know, and I promise I won't do anything foolish."

The officer talked to Johnnie a couple of more minutes. Johnnie never ever looked up. "Well?" I asked. "He'll be okay." "You know him?" "Sure, he's lived in the neighborhood for years." "Has anything like this ever happened before?" "Yeah. He's okay tonight, but he tried to kill himself yesterday." We drove off.

Police apprehensions will usually occur when the police answer a call and find a person who shows distorted thoughts or emotion and a peculiar physical appearance, unknown injuries, seizures, odd posturing, nudity, extreme dirtiness, or having soiled one's clothing (Bittner, 1967b). If the situation appears to be more than a brief lapse of control, and the individual is not a "bum" or a "drunk," he or she will be taken to the hospital. However, repeated encounters with an alcoholic will lead to the conclusion that he is mentally ill and "needs help." For example:

It was about 4 p.m. and we were heading north from downtown when we saw Rudy lying on the sidewalk. The officer sighed. We made a left turn and pulled the van up next to him. "This must be the one-hundredth time I've picked him up. When he's sober, he's supposed to be a terrific mechanic, but he's never sober." We called the station and told them we were bringing Rudy in. We got out of the van and helped him up. "Fuck you, fuck America, fuck the police. I thought this was a free country. This is like Poland, fuck the President, fuck you!" "Sure, Rudy, just come on, right, into the van, now sit down, okay?" "Fuck America, fuck you, fuck the sergeant!" The officer laughed as he slammed the van door. We drove into the station and deposited Rudy in the drunk tank. The lieutenant was disgusted. "He's been in the state hospital dozens of times, but it doesn't help. Damn! We'll go over their heads!" He walked away shaking his head. Back on patrol, the officer said that Rudy had once set a house on fire and the department had wanted to send him to a state prison farm for a special one-year alcoholism treatment program. "The judge, however, had thought the incident was a big joke and had released him. So now he's right back on the street."

Police apprehensions also often occur when employers or professionals, that is, doctors, lawyers, or teachers, request assistance. Although the police have not witnessed the incident they will usually take the person to the hospital. The assumption is that all other options have been explored and a solution was not found. However, the same request from a friend or relative of the individual may be refused. For example, a severely depressed person probably would be taken to the hospital from his job if his employer or a doctor requested it. However, if a relative were to make the same request they often would be advised to take the person to the hospital themselves (Bittner, 1967b:284-285).

It is common for the police to make an apprehension when they find a mentally ill person causing a disturbance or making a nuisance of themselves. If the individual is agitated or violent, and cannot be pacified, they will be apprehended. Also, if a person is confused or disoriented and might injure themselves or be victimized, they are picked up for "safe keeping" and charged with disorderly conduct. The individual is then either brought in to the station or taken to a hospital. Individuals are only picked up, however, when no caretaker or other facility can be found. For example, the local mental health center in one of the cities that I rode in had an excellent working arrangement with the police. If someone needed psychiatric help the department would call the clinic and they would send a physician or social worker to the scene or the jail to examine the person. However, the clinic was only open 9 to 5, Monday through Friday. However, most police calls occur on evenings and weekends.

One afternoon we received a call for transport at a local hotel. The officers said the hotel was for "nuts, whores, and criminals." When we arrived one of the hotel residents, who was well known to the department for his frequent trips to the state hospital, was led to the van. "What's happening?" I asked. One officer said, "He was preaching in the hotel lobby when we arrived. He had some money in his pocket and to stop him from being robbed by some mean drunk we picked him up."

In another incident we received a call that there was a fire, plus "something else," at a local housing project. As we turned the corner the fire engine was just pulling away. We stopped and some of the project's residents came up to the squad. They explained that a woman had been creating a disturbance for the last two days and had just set fire to a bean bag chair inside someone's van. The officer asked if they wanted to sign a complaint. A young black man, about 23 years old, stepped forward he said that it was his van. He said that he was mad and that he would sign a complaint. Two officers tried to talk to the woman but each time they approached her she ran off. This went on for about ten minutes.

The chase finally ended when the woman gashed the palm of her right hand. She told a friend to get some water to wash out the cut. Her friend returned with several bottles of water. The woman plopped down and began pouring the water over her hand. The officers walked over and asked if she would get in the squad car so they could talk to her. "No," she said, "I want to go in the wagon." One officer walked over to the squad and called for the wagon. In a couple of minutes the wagon and three or four other squads arrived. She suddenly jumped up and said she wanted to go in to the house. She then ran towards an apartment. Two officers ran after her and grabbed her as she tried to go in the back door. They then led her to the wagon. She suddenly began resisting. The other officers swooped down and grabbed her and dumped her onto the floor of the wagon. They locked the doors and drove off.

During the ten minutes the officers had chased the woman people from the project had gathered on their stoops and verbally taunted the officers. Each time someone said something the officers would simply laugh or answer the taunt with a wry smile. Everyone within ear-shot would then laugh for they knew it was all a game; and the officers knew that the residents of the all black housing project were just trying to "slick them." Later, one of the officers said that it appeared the residents enjoyed the humor of two white officers being made fools of by this crazy black woman.

At the station she was taken from the van and brought into the booking area. "Have you ever been to the state hospital, Martha?" one officer asked. "Yes," she said, "but I'm not crazy!" The officer sat down and began making out the arrest form. "What's she here for?" the sergeant asked. "Criminal damage to property and . . . safekeeping, I guess." While the officer made out the forms she sat down on the floor. She said that she needed medicine for her nerves but had left it back at the apartment. She asked if they could go back and get it. The officer said, no.

She was given some change and she tried to call a friend in Indiana collect for her $25 bail. She was unable to reach him. After her phone call she plopped back down on the floor and sat there for a few minutes. She then said that she didn't have a home or real friends in town. She suddenly began laughing wildly. After another few minutes she said she wanted her picture taken so people would know where she was. But first she said she'd have to take off her blouse to fix it. The officer agreed to take her picture so we all had to turn away until she had fixed her blouse. She was then led through the door and they took her picture. She laughed again and acted silly throughout much of the time she was in the station. One officer motioned another over and suggested that since she didn't have a home or friends they'd take her up to the state hospital. The other officer agreed. They asked her if she would sign a "voluntary" if they took her to the hospital. "Yes," she said. The officer then called the admissions office and explained the situation. They said they would take her; and, if she refused to sign a voluntary when she arrived the officers could sign an emergency petition. Before we were ready to leave she suddenly became very anxious and began crying and sobbing. "Get her out of here before she goes off the deep end!" one of the sergeants yelled. In a couple of minutes she stopped crying and we walked out to the squad car.

The officers got into the front seat and Martha and I got into the back. I had not thought that the seating arrangement was odd but later I remembered that an officer was required to sit in the back seat of a squad with a prisoner. It later struck me that the officers must have been at a loss to understand her behavior and had sat her with me because I was a "mental health expert."

On the way to the hospital Martha demanded that the radio be turned up, and then down, and then up again. She became restless and insisted that she be given cigarettes and one of the officer's sunglasses. He agreed to her demands for it appeared he did not know what else to do to keep her quiet. In twenty minutes we arrived at the hospital. We led the woman into the admissions office where she agreed to sign a voluntary admission form. She signed the form and the officers left as quickly as possible.

6. Police Apprehension of the Mentally Ill: 1995–2002[3]

A restudy of police apprehension of the mentally ill was conducted from 1995 to 2002. As before, we will put this data into context. However, since we have covered much of the qualitative data on police apprehension of the mentally ill we will focus on quantitative data here.

The researcher observed 1,338 police-citizen encounters over a seven-year period.[4] The 1,338 police-citizen contacts were divided into ten categories: traffic incidents, the investigation of suspicious persons or incidents, reports, disturbances, assistance calls, warrant service, other arrests, juvenile apprehensions, miscellaneous, and handling the mentally ill.

In brief, these ten categories of police-citizen encounters produced the following results: Traffic incidents (including traffic stops) produced 520 police citizen encounters. Thirty-one arrests resulted from these incidents. There were 287 calls of suspicious persons or incidents. No arrests resulted from any of these calls. Seventy-six reports were taken. There were 154 disturbance calls. Sixty-one of these were family disturbances. These produced 5 arrests. There were 93 non-family disturbances. Three individuals were arrested in these incidents. There were 104 assistance calls. Most of these were to assist citizens with motor vehicle problems. There were no arrests from any of these calls. There were 28 arrests for warrants. And, there were 49 people arrested for other reasons (these were usually for retail theft, alcohol intoxication, or drug possession). There were 40 juvenile apprehensions. Eleven of these juveniles were ticketed and 15 were arrested. All but one was turned over to their parents. And there were 53 miscellaneous calls or duties (administrative assignments, carnivals, parades, 4th of July celebrations, etc.). There were 12 incidents involving mentally ill persons. All of those individuals were released, turned over to their families, or transported to a hospital by paramedics.

The details of these 1,358 police-citizen encounters are not what one would expect. The police are usually perceived of as crime fighters who rush from call to call. It sometimes is said that police officers are "slaves to their radios." However, this does not appear to be the case. Five hundred and twenty police-citizen contacts were for traffic incidents (39 percent

---

3. Data for this section was collected when the researcher served as an auxiliary (part-time) police officer and auxiliary sergeant in a Chicago suburb from 1995 to 2002. The suburb was primarily a white, middle class community. However, it was located near one of the small industrial cities studied earlier.

4. Personal conversation between officers and civilians were not included. Officers frequently checked the license plates of suspicious vehicles through their computers. This was called "running plates". However, only if such a check produced a vehicle stop was it included in the data. If a motorist was ticketed and arrested, only the arrest was logged. And, if more than one ticket was issued only one was noted under "tickets". If an officer attempted to stop a vehicle for speeding but lost it in traffic, there were half-a-dozen of these instances, it was not included. Frequently an officer would check on another officer who was conducting a traffic stop. If they received a "thumbs up" they would continue on patrol. These were not counted. Regular training sessions were excluded. Carnivals, parades, and 4th of July celebrations were counted as one each since they did not involve individual calls.

of all police-citizen encounters). These included 24 traffic accidents, 62 calls to back-up another officer on a traffic stop, and 6 calls to remove traffic obstructions. These were all dispatched by the radio. However, officers made 428 traffic stops on their own initiative (32 percent of all police-citizen encounters). These stops were for traffic infractions or suspicious vehicles. These stops produced 259 verbal warnings, 63 warning tickets, 75 formal tickets, and 31 arrests. That is, traffic stops produced serious enforcement actions (arrests) in only 7 percent of all these traffic stops.

There were 287 calls of suspicious persons or incidents. No arrests were made on any of these calls. That was because the individuals were GOA (gone on arrival), the situation was innocuous, or the persons were given a verbal warning and sent on their way.

Seventy-six reports were taken. A few of these were passed up to the investigators. However, most were merely filed away.

There were 154 disturbance calls. Fifty-six of these were family disturbances. These calls were treated seriously because of their potential for violence. Even through blows were struck in a number of these cases only 5 arrests occurred. That was because these incidents were usually seen as the product of long standing disputes between family members or intimates that could only be solved by the persons involved. (In some states there are mandatory arrest statutes if violence has occurred in a domestic disturbance. However, in Illinois the decision to arrest in such situations is left up to the discretion of the officer). On such calls the individuals were separated, calmed down, counseled, and a resolution was usually reached when one party agreed to leave the scene. Other disturbances such as loud parties or teenagers throwing firecrackers were handled more routinely (there were 90 of these calls). They produced only 3 arrests.

There were 104 assistance calls. Nine of these were to assist the fire department or paramedics and 14 were to assist other police agencies. Eighty-one of these calls were to assist a citizen. These were usually the result of a vehicle lockout or break down. The department expected the officers to respond to these calls since the chief stressed that the department was a service-oriented agency.

There were 28 warrant arrests. In many of these cases the warrant was used as a tool to remove an individual from the street when the officers lacked enough evidence for an arrest.

There were 49 other arrests. These included retail theft, intoxicated individuals, or young adults carrying small amounts of drugs.

Forty juveniles were apprehended. Fifteen juvenile arrests were made and tickets were issued to eleven other juveniles. Thirteen juveniles were not charged and were released to their parents. One youth was turned over to a state affiliated social service agency for foster care placement. All these calls were considered to be a nuisance by the officers. It was common for officers to say that juvenile apprehensions were a waste of time since "nothing ever happens to these kids."

Fifty-four calls were listed under "miscellaneous." Twenty of these were for routine administrative functions such as vehicle repairs or the delivery of reports. Also included in this category were carnivals, parades, and 4th of July celebrations. Some officers considered these assignments to be fun since they could "meet and greet" the public. Other officers considered them to be tedious. In either case, they did not involve individual calls; instead they consisted of non-criminal functions such as crowd control and traffic direction.

Twelve mentally ill persons were apprehended. None of these individuals had committed a serious crime. Instead, they had come to police attention because they had been "disorderly." Since they were not considered to be criminals they were released without charge or transported to a hospital by paramedics for evaluation and treatment.

Since there were only a dozen cases let us briefly describe each one.

1) A mentally ill woman, who was drunk, was "tearing up" her house. She was restrained, turned over to the paramedics, and transported to the hospital.

2) A woman attempted suicide. The police assisted the paramedics by helping put her on the gurney. She was taken to the hospital.

3) A woman was found in a parked car by the river after a suicide attempt. "She's still alive," one officer observed. The police blocked the park entrance and stood by as the paramedics worked on her. She was then transported to the hospital.

4) Two police officers responded to a routine "assist the fire department" call and arrived at the home of a woman who had attempted suicide. The woman had taken Prozac and drunk rum. She had then vomited up the concoction. When the paramedics were finished they asked one of the officers to help them lift the woman on to the gurney. He did. Then one of the paramedics said, "Oh, I didn't know you didn't have gloves on." "That's O.K.," the officer jauntily replied, "it was only vomit."

5) Two officers responded to a call that a teenager had sent a suicide note to a friend on the internet. In front of her parents and the officers the teenage girl denied that any suicide note was sent. She said she was fine. As the officers left one turned to the other and quietly said, "If she won't admit it, we can't help her."

6) Two officers were called to a house where a 12-year-old girl had sent two suicide notes to a friend on the internet. She admitted that she had been depressed and admitted to sending the initial suicide message. However, she said she was fine now and she denied that she had sent the second message. The officers informed the parents of what the girl had told them and left. Later that night the officers filed a report on the incident.

7) Officers were called to a family disturbance. A woman told the officers that her 10-year-old daughter had been fighting with her brother and had put a knife to his throat. The girl had recently been discharged from a psychiatric facility after a 7 day admission. The officers spent half an hour talking to the girl. She seemed indifferent to the officers. Finally, one of the officers said, "You know we're really here to help your mom out." The other officer asked, "Are you listening?" The girl did not respond. The officer then said, "The next time we'll take you to jail, if you don't end up back in the hospital." The officers left.

8) Two officers responded to a call of a woman wandering in the street. When the officers arrived they found a woman, who was well known to them, standing near the curb in front of her house. They asked her if she had been wandering the streets. No, she said, she was just standing in front of her house. She was

drunk and threatened the officers. They ignored her threats and suggested that she go inside. She agreed and the officers left. Later, the same two officers responded to a call involving the same woman. The woman was quite drunk and was wandering the street in front of her home. She again threatened the officers and they again ignored the threats. They told her that she should go inside. She agreed. As they drove off one officer turned to the other and said, "She's 10-96." (The police call number for a mentally ill person.)

9) The police were called to a family disturbance. This was the second call of the day. (An earlier shift had handled the first call.) When the officers arrived they found a woman who was emotionally upset. Her husband said that she had attempted suicide one month earlier. She was now upset because she had recently given up her baby and the state had taken her 8-year-old. After discussing the situation with the husband he agreed to stay home with her and the other children for the day. The officers left.

10) Two officers were called to a family disturbance. Two adult sisters were fighting. After much back and forth one of the officers said, "How do we solve the problem, *tonight*?" One of the sisters, who had told the officers she was on psychiatric medication, agreed to leave. As the officers drove off one turned to the other and said, "They're both loony."

11) There was a call to "check the welfare" of a woman at a local bowling alley. When the officers arrived they found a woman standing outside the bowling alley. She told the officers that she had been thrown out of the bowling alley because she was drunk. Also, she had not been taking her diazepam (Valium). The officers suggested she call someone to pick her up. She said that her mother was not home. The officers then suggested that she call a cab. She said she didn't have any money, and besides, she preferred to walk. Since she was relatively steady on her feet the officers shrugged and let her go. She walked off. Later, the officers received a call that the same woman was wandering down a busy street. When they arrived a passerby said that the woman had been given a lift by a trucker. The officers left.

12) One night an officer was sitting on a residential street writing a report. He looked up and saw a woman wandering down the sidewalk stripping. He jumped out of the squad, grabbed her, and began to retrieve her clothes. A second unit was called. When the second unit arrived, one of the officers said, "I know her, that was the woman who tried to kill herself two weeks ago with Prozac and rum." The officers asked the woman what was her problem. She said she was bipolar and had not taken her medication. The initial officer said, "I'm not going to arrest you but you can't walk around doing this. Do you wan to go to the hospital?" No, she said. Another officer who knew her asked if they could call her parents to pick her up. She said, yes. The parents were called and they picked her up. They apologized and explained that she had not been taking her medication. They drove her home.

How do we analyze these twelve calls? The four suicide attempts were seen by the officers as merely assistance calls for medical situations. The officers were there to provide security and to "lend a hand." The two internet calls could be considered to be "check the welfare" calls. Since the parents were home and there was no obvious problems, they were treated routinely. The other six calls could be considered "disturbances." They could be broken down into four different responses. First, officers spent half-an-hour speaking with the 10 old girl because they felt this was a call in which a juvenile needed counseling. Second, the woman wondering in front of her home and the woman ejected from the bowling alley were treated as "drunks." Third, the emotionally upset woman and the two sisters fighting were treated as a family disturbance that needed to be "solved." And, fourth, the woman who was stripping was seen to be mentally ill, but harmless. In conclusion, all twelve of the calls were considered "routine." *The police did not think of these calls as "mental health calls." Instead, they were merely situations to be "handled;" just like the other 1,358 calls they handled.*

Let us compare our research to Teplins (1984) on the police apprehension of the mentally ill. Her work is considered to be the benchmark for such studies. However, before discussing her study let us look at the work of other researchers on factors affecting the police apprehensions of the mentally ill.

Deinstitutionalization, more stringent commitment criteria, and the underfunding of community-based centers has increased the frequency of encounters between the police and the mentally ill (Skull, 1977; Teplin, 1983; Wachholz and Mullaly, 1991; Silver, 2000b; Bonovitz and Bonovitz, 1981; Menzies, 1987; Teplin and Pruett, 1992; Borzecki and Wormith, 1985).

Most researchers have concluded that the mentally ill are arrested in disproportionate numbers; that is, they are "criminalized" (Abramson, 1972; Steury, 1991; Steadman, et.al., 1984). This conclusion stems from numerous studies that show that persons who are mentally ill are over-represented in prisons and jails (Fisher, et.al., 2000; Lamb and Weinberger, 1998; Bureau of Justice Statistics, 1999; Lamb and Grant, 1982; Palermo, et.al., 1991; Teplin, 1990). Also, the arrest rates of the mentally ill tend to be higher than the average population (Rabkin, 1972; Link, et.al., 1992). The implication of the criminalization hypothesis is that the police are inappropriately arresting the mentally ill. However, since there is a lack of available community services, the police are constrained in their choices (Engel and Silver, 2001:228; Cohen, 1996; Travin, 1989; Green, 1997; Cooper, Mc Clearen, and Zapf, 2004:307). Also, individuals with mental disorders are more likely to engage in dangerous behavior or be under the influence of drugs or alcohol than average citizens (Link, et.al., 1992; Swanson, 1990; Steadman, et.al., 1998; Kaminski, DiGiovanni, and Downs, 2004). Thus, other factors, and not the mental illness, itself, may produce the arrest.

This is reinforced by studies that indicate that intoxication and demeanor increase the chance of arrest of non-mentally ill individuals (Engel, et.al., 2000; Ricksheim and Chermak, 1993; Worden, 1989; Worden and Shepard, 1996; Worden, Shepard, and Mastrofski, 1996; Engel and Silver, 2001: 242; Silver, 2000a). Further, situational factors, such as the relationship between the victim and the suspect, the preference of the victim, and the presence of bystanders, all influence the chance of arrest (Matrofski, et.al., 2000; Ricksheim and Chermak, 1993; Smith and Visher, 1981; Worden, 1989). Also, arrest was more likely if the individual fought with another citizen, attacked the officer, or possessed a weapon (Engel and Silver, 2001:242). With these factors in mind let us examine Teplin's (1984) research.

Teplin (1984) analyzed 1,382 police-citizen encounters. This is close to our number of 1,338 encounters. She states that she conducted her study in a "large northern city." I believe this was Chicago. The data was collected "in two busy urban police precincts, which included residents ranging from the lowest socioeconomic level to the very wealthy." She goes on to state that "these two precincts are fairly typical of this particular city and are fairly generalizeable to any large northern urban area." (p. 797) However, in another publication of hers she states: "Specifically, the data collection site included two 'deviant ghettos' . . . i.e., neighborhoods which contained a number of halfway houses and residential hotels housing former mental patients" (1986:31). From her description I believe this area to be several neighborhoods on the Northside of Chicago along the lakefront. This area, and the Uptown neighborhood in particular, has been considered a "dumping ground" for the Illinois Department of Mental Health. So, it is not clear if her results are as generalizable as she claims.

In her study, Teplin (1984) over-sampled by riding evenings and weekends. She, and her five graduate students, observed for 2,200 hours over a 14 month period during 1980-81.

I rode in a suburb of Chicago from 1995 to 2002. I rode approximately 2,500 hours. I too over-sampled by riding evenings and weekends. Since this was a suburb, my data may be atypical for a city neighborhood.

Teplin (1984) analyzed 1,382 police-citizen encounters. However, she eliminated from her study 188 "public service incidents." However, she does not explain what these incidents were. She also eliminated 310 "traffic offenses." She does not explain why she did this. However, in another publication she states that these two categories were deleted because the 310 traffic offenses had an arrest rate of 0.9 percent and public service incidents, involving 324 citizens, had an 0.0 percent arrest rate (1986:18). This is somewhat surprising since traffic stops can produce DUI, warrant, and drug arrests. They can also involve homeless people living in cars, fleeing felons, "rolling domestics" (domestic disturbances in moving vehicles), or "gang banging scum bags" (this is a term commonly used by officers). Some of these traffic stops could have involved a mentally ill person.

Teplin (1984) eliminated 498 of these public service and traffic encounters involving 757 citizens from her analysis. As a result of this, her data included 884 police encounters involving 1,798 citizens. In this sample she found arrests to be "a relatively rare event." It occurred in 110 incidents for a rate of 12.4 percent. My sample of 1,338 encounters (which included traffic, suspicious persons, disturbances, assistance, warrants, and other arrests) had an almost identical rate of 12.6 percent rate.

She ascertained the presence of mental disorder "via a checklist that listed the major characteristics of severe mental illness." This included "confusion/disorientation, withdrawal/unresponsiveness, paranoia, inappropriate or bizarre speech and/or behavior, and self-destructive behaviors" (1984:797). Rather surprisingly, she concluded that "of the 30 suspects defined as being mentally disordered by the field worker, only 15 . . . were detected by the officer" (1984:799). Further, in another publication she stated that "the fieldworker and the police officer agreed on the apparent mental status of the suspect in 491 or 97.0 percent of the cases" (1986:20).

She also states that a "data component [an observational data narrative] detailed the underlying police officers discretionary judgments in relation to their handling of the situations" (1984:798). However, none of this narrative material is presented and no officers are quoted in the 1984 publication. However, in a later publication she states that 1800 pages of qualitative information were recorded (1986:4). Some of it is presented in the 1986 publication and a later one by her (Teplin, 2000). From this narrative material it appears that the officers studied did not handle many of these individuals as "mentally ill." Instead, they handled the incidents as incidents that needed to be solved.

Lastly, Teplin found that the arrest rate for mentally disordered suspects was 46.7 percent. The arrest rate for non-mentally disordered suspects was 27.9 percent. However, her (1984) sample involved only 30 mentally ill individuals in an atypical area of the city.

In another Teplin publication (1986) she discusses the 30 mentally ill individuals encountered by the police. However, she also states that in the sample of 1,072 encounters "85 person involved in 79 encounters were defined by the field-worker to be mentally disordered" (1986:4,27,30). It is not clear where this data comes from. Of these 85 individuals she found that hospitalization was "an exceedingly infrequent event (less than 0.5 percent)." Arrests were also relatively rare. And most incidents with mentally ill individuals were solved informally (71.8 percent) (1986:5, 10). Based on this data, or two sets of data, she concluded:

"This research provides some *preliminary evidence* that the mentally ill are being criminalized." She later states: "In sum, the data presented here provide *some confirmation* that the mentally ill are being criminalized." And, lastly, she asserts that "persons exhibiting signs of mental disorder have a higher probability of being arrested than those who do not show such signs. Clearly, the way we treat our mentally ill is *criminal*" (1986:789-801; emphasis added). This last sentence may be good rhetoric, but it is not supported by the data.

Engel and Silver (2001) did an examination of the criminalization hypothesis using statistical data. In one sample Engel and Silver used data from Indianapolis in 1996 and St. Petersburg in 1997. Over 5,700 field observations were conducted in 24 neighborhoods in both sites by trained observers. In Indianapolis, 1,849 non-traffic encounters were analyzed. A second sample of 5,688 police-citizen encounters was taken from a study in Rochester, St. Louis, and Tampa/St Petersburg. Here, 1,392 non-traffic encounters were analyzed. Engel and Silver state that this data is "directly comparable" to Teplin's 1984 data (2001:233).

Engel and Silver's analysis revealed that in the first data set 17.8 percent of non-traffic suspects were arrested. In the second data set the rate was 13.1 percent. Using officer perceptions, and not an observer's checklist, they found the percentage of mentally ill in the first data set was 3.6 percent and in the second set it was 2.7 percent. A statistical analysis indicated that police officers in the first data set were significantly less likely to arrest mentally ill people than other suspects (7.6 percent versus 18.2 percent). In the second data set mentally disordered individuals were arrested at a higher rate (16.2 percent) than non-mentally ill offenders (13 percent). However, this may have been due to the fact that the mentally ill offenders were involved in almost twice as many felony offenses as non-mentally ill suspects (13.5 percent versus 7.5 percent).

Engel and Silver concluded that there is "little support for the criminalization hypothesis" (2001:241-2). They felt that an important limitation of Teplin's "core findings" was that it lacked statistical controls for extra-legal factors known to influence police discretion (2001:229; see also: Lamb and Weinberger, 1998). They concluded that "the robustness of Teplin's (1984) finding that police disproportionately use arrest to resolve encounters with mentally disordered suspects remain open to question" (2001:229). I agree.

7. Discussion

The police perform many non-criminal functions. In Boston, for example, the police at various time licensed pawnshops, liquor establishments, hackney carriages, and wagons. They also issued building permits, gave holiday donations to the poor, provided beds and soup for the needy, acted as health officers, were concerned with truancy, and tried to reform drunks and prostitutes. Early reformers saw the police as a tool for social betterment. Most politicians, however, saw the police as simply a service agency. Lane notes that "the political ideal in police work was routine municipal housekeeping. Both the watch and members of the marshal's office had always been instructed . . . to remove minor obstructions from the streets and sidewalks, to put out fires, test doors, and turn off running water. While some departments had been split off from the police—street lamps, health—the patrolman continued to serve as `the eyes and ears' of all of them. They rarely did physical labor, but it was still their job to note potholes, smells, and broken lamps, and to report these for reference to the appropriate agencies" (1967: 109). Over the years the police have had various non-criminal functions forced upon them because they were the only governmental agency available 7 days a week, 24 hours a day (Reiss and Bordua, 1967:26). However, other community agencies have been unwilling to provide services in areas in which the police are untrained. The President's Commission on Law Enforcement and Administration of Justice put the issue succinctly: "Because few efforts have been made to develop alternatives to police involvement, the consequence of police not taking action is that drunks would be left to lie where they fall" (The Presidents Commission on Law Enforcement and the Administration of Justice, 1967:14).

Although patrolmen provide social services, they do not act as social workers. In fact, they do not even act as "officials." Rather, they perform their duties as pragmatic craftsmen who are experts in order maintenance. Smith notes:

> The policeman's art . . . consists in applying and enforcing a multitude of laws and ordinances in such degree or proportion and in such manner that the greatest degree of protection will be secured. The degree of enforcement and the method of application will vary with each neighborhood and community. There are not set rules, nor even general principles, to the policy to be applied. Each policeman must, in a sense, determine the standard to be set in the area for which he is responsible. Immediate superiors may be able to impress

upon him some of the lessons of experience, but for the most part, such experience must be his own . . . Thus he is a policy-forming police administrator in miniature, who operates beyond the scope of the usual devices for control. (1960: 19; see also: Bittner, 1970:55)

Most police officers are left on their own in dealing with the average service call. As long as they handle each call expeditiously, they will be allowed to do their job without much administrative interference. Therefore, one might assume that when dealing with service calls the officer's behavior appears to be based upon their personal inclinations (see: King and Dunn, 2004; Ruiz and Miller, 2004). However, in dealing with skid-row alcoholics, Bittner found that "the best among the patrolman, *according to their own standards*, use the law to keep skid row inhabitants from sinking deeper into the misery they already experience. The worst, *in terms of these same standards*, exploit the practice for personal aggrandizement or gain" (1967a:711; emphasis added). Therefore, the police do *not* simply employ their own personal standards in handling the mentally ill. Instead, there are subcultural norms applied to the handling of such cases. For example, police officer's come across people who "need to be arrested." These are people who are disruptive, mentally ill, drunk, vulnerable, or simply, "assholes." When this occurs, questions of justice or injustice are irrelevant. The officer's immediate concern is in solving a problem; that is, he or she wants to avoid injury, end a disturbance, prevent exploitation, or punish an individual. In such cases, the end justifies the means. In these situations the officer is maintaining order, being humane, or doling out just deserts.

In the apprehension of mentally ill persons we find police officers combining order maintenance with humanitarian values. An officer once told me that in dealing with drunks or the mentally ill one can "do the humane thing, or be an asshole, a cop." And, Rock quotes a Chicago policeman as saying: "A mentally ill person is like a thistle berry—when one is on you, you try and get it off as quickly as possible, but when it's on somebody else, it doesn't bother you in the least" (1968:91). In the department that was studied this was not the typical attitude. The officers tried to do the "right" thing when confronted with a mentally ill person. However, the problem was that the officers didn't know what the "right thing" was.[5]

One of the departments that was studied was rated as one of the best for its size in the nation by the International Association of Police Chiefs. The department's directive on the handling of mentally ill persons said that officers should show "every possible . . . courtesy" to a mentally ill individual and the family and that "all avenues" should be explored before a mentally ill person was confined. Further, "all officers . . . should familiarize themselves with all the community organizations that are willing to assist." However, these

---

5. I repeatedly asked the officers I met if anyone knew of an excellent pamphlet put out by the National association for Mental Health entitled, *How to Recognize and Handle Abnormal People: A Manual for the Police Officer* (Matthews and Rowland, 1954). No one, on any of the departments I studied, had ever heard of the booklet. So I wrote to the National Association for Mental Health and asked them what they were doing to get their booklet out to officers on the street. Not much, they replied.

organizations were closed evenings and weekends. The directive went on to explain how to confine and handle the person if necessary and to then call the local mental health center if it was during working hours. If the apprehension occurred after working hours the local mental hospital's admissions office should be called. If they agreed to admit the individual they were to be transported there. However, the critical questions of who is mentally ill, under what circumstances should an officer apprehend a mentally ill person, and when and if a "safekeeping" arrest should be made, were never mentioned (see: Patch and Arrigo, 1991).

The attitude towards such contacts among the officers I rode with was to try and be humane, although they didn't understand mental illness or its treatment. For example, one evening on patrol we drove past a small private psychiatric hospital in a nearby suburb. The officer pointed to the hospital and said that they occasionally assisted on calls at the facility. He said: "We call that place, The Twilight Zone; they fuck in the halls and everything; it's incredible over there." During my initial six months of research not one police officer, from captain to patrolman, knew how to handle a mentally ill person; and all of them either began or ended their comments on the subject with a shrug. For example:

A man called and said his wife who was mentally ill, had locked herself in their hotel room, and he was concerned about her safety. Four officers went to the room and knocked. She answered, but did not open the door. She then began talking to her cat with an English accent. The officers tried for 10 or 15 minutes to get her to open the door but the woman seemed oblivious to the officer's requests. The call had initially been treated as a joke; however, as time wore on the officers became anxious. Finally, one of the officers looked to the other members of the group for assistance, but all avoided his glance. He then shrugged and said, "Well, I guess she won't hurt herself or anybody else, and she hasn't broken any laws, so . . ." with a collective shrug, they left.

The police I rode with went out of their way to be patient and to use restraint in handling the mentally ill.[6] That was because they were perceived to be "sick." To put it in a more formal way: The police operate within the moral consensus of the community. Therefore, they treat sick people as other community members would treat them. A person who is sick is believed to be incapacitated by something beyond his or her power to cope with and is in the need of help in order to recover (Parsons, 1951:428-473).

Usually individuals come to the attention of the police because they have been disruptive. If they are criminals, drunks, or "just kids," the police know how to deal with their behavior. That is because it is understandable. However, a mentally ill person's behavior is not understandable because it is irrational. Since the person is sick and possesses no criminal intent, he or she is not considered to be a criminal, but a *victim*. This conclusion by the officers is the result of them observing that person's irrationality. It is not viewed as any specific psychiatric pathology. The person's irrationality, therefore, becomes, in practice, his or her illness. In other words, the people the police pick up are acting "unreasonable."

---

6. However, the director of a mental health clinic told me that police officers in his area try to get mentally ill persons as excited and aggressive as possible because otherwise the hospitals refused to take them.

And they have pushed past society's tolerance limits (see: Van Vetchen, 1940; Newman, 1965). The police, as well as our society, believe that few persons are saints or devils. However, they do believe that the average citizen should be the Reasonably Rational Man or Woman.

Most people who are arrested for disorderly conduct, or some such similar charge, are usually free on $25 cash bond shortly after the arrest. However, a mentally ill person may be held for long periods of time. The mentally ill person is held so that he or she can get "help." One might argue that this is a gross injustice. The police officer, and most citizens, would respond that a "higher justice" is being served by confining a mentally ill person until he or she is well enough to be released.

References

Abramson, M. F.
  1972   "The Criminalization of Mentally Disordered Behavior: Possible Side-Effects of a New Mental Health Law." *Hospital and Community Psychiatry* 23:101-105.

Adams, Thomas F.
  1963   *Field Interrogations*. Police.

Adlam, K.R.
  1982   "The Police Personality: Psychological Consequences of Being a Police Officer." *Journal of Police Science and Administration* 10: 344-349.

Austin, T.L., et.al.
  1987   "The Effects of Lay-Off On Police Authoritarianism." *Criminal Justice and Behavior* 14: 191-210.

Baldwin, James
  1962   *Nobody Knows My Name*. New York: Dell.

Banton, Michael
  1964   *The Policeman in the Community*. New York: Basic.

Barker, J.C.
  1999   *Danger, Duty and Disillusion*. Prospect Heights, IL: Waveland Press.

Barth, Alan
  1963   *Law Enforcement Versus the Law*. New York: Collier.

Bittner, Egon
  1967a   "Police Discretion in Emergency Apprehension of Mentally Ill Persons." *Social Problems* 14:278-292.
  1967b   "The Police On Skid-Row: A Study Of Peace Keeping." *American Sociological Review* 32:699-715.
  1970   *Functions of Police in Modern Society*. Bethesda, MD.: National Institute of Mental Health.
  1978   "The Functions of the Police in Modern Society." In *Policing: A View from the Street*, P.K. Manning and J. Van Maanen, (eds.) pp.32-50. N.Y.: Random House.

Bonovitz, Jennifer C., and Jay S. Bonovitz
  1981   "Diversion of the Mentally Ill Into the Criminal Justice System: The Police Intervention Perspective." *American Journal of Psychiatry* 138:973-976.
Borzecki M., & Wormith, J. S.
  1985   "The Criminalization of Psychiatrically Ill People: A Review with a Canadian Perspective." *Psychiatric Journal of the University of Ottawa* 10: 241-247.
Broderick, John J.
  1977   *Police in a Time of Change*. Morristown, NJ: General Learning Press.
Brooks, Thomas R.
  1965   "New York's Finest." *Commentary*. 40.
Bureau of Justice Statistics
  1999   "Special Report: Mental Health and Treatment of Inmates and Probationers." U.S. Department of Justice, Bureau of Justice Statistics. Washington, D.C.
Cohen F.
  1996   "Offenders with Mental Disorders In The Criminal Justice-Correctional Process." In *Law, Mental Health, and Mental Disorder,* B. D. Sales and D. W. Shuman, eds. pp. 397-413. Pacific Grove, CA: Brooks/Cole.
Conti, N.P.
  2000   *Creating the Thin Blue Line*. Unpublished Doctoral Dissertation. University of Pittsburgh.
Cooper, Virginia H., Alex M. Mc Learen, and Patricia Zopf
  2004   "Dispositional Decisions with the Mentally Ill: Police Perceptions and Characteristics." *Police Quarterly* 7: 295-310.
Cumming, E., I. Cumming, and L. Eddell
  1965   "Policeman as Philosopher, Guide, and Friend." *Social Forces* 12: 276-86.
Engel, Robin S. and Eric Silver
  2001   "Policing Mentally Disordered Suspects: A Reexamination of the Criminalization Hypothesis." *Criminology* 39: 225-252.
Engel, Robin, James J. Sobol, and Robert E. Worden
  2000   "Further Exploration of the Demeanor Hypothesis: The Interaction Effects Of Suspects' Characteristics and Demeanor on Police Behavior." *Justice Quarterly* 17: 235-258.
Fisher, W. H., Packer, l. K., Simon, L. J., & Smith, D.
  2000   "Community Mental Health Services and the Prevalence of Severe Mental Illness in Local Jails: Are They Related?" *Administration and Policy in Mental Health* 27: 371-382.
Fuller, Lon
  1964   *The Morality of Law*. New Haven: Yale University Press.
Goldstein, Joseph
  1960   "Police Discretion Not to Invoke the Criminal Process: Low Visibility Decisions in the Administration of Justice." *The Yale Law Journal* 69: 543-948.
Green, T. M.
  1997   "Police as Frontline Mental Health Workers: The Decision to Arrest or Refer to Mental Health Agencies." *International Journal of Law and Psychiatry* 20: 469-486.

Gross, P.R.
   1991   "The Structure of Occupational Fears in Police Recruits." *Police Studies* 14:
          176-179.
Harris, R.N.
   1973   *The Police Academy: An Inside View.* N.Y.: Wiley.
   1978   "The Police Academy and the Professional Self-Image." In *Policing. A View
          from the Street*, P.K. Manning and J. Van Maanen (eds.). pp. 273-291. N.Y.:
          Random House.
Hopper, M.
   1977   "Becoming a Policeman: Socialization of Cadets in a Police Academy." *Urban
          Life* 6: 149-170.
Illinois
   1968   *Mental Health Code, Statutes.* As Amended, 1969-71.
Kaminski, Robert J. Clete Di Giovanni, and Raymond Downs
   2004   "The Use of Force Between The Police and Persons With Impaired Judgment."
          Police Quarterly 7: 296-338.
King, William R. and Thomas M. Dunn
   2004   "Dumping: Police—Initiated Transport of Troublesome Persons." *Police Quar-
          terly* 7: 339-358.
Klopsch, J.W.
   1983   *Police Personality Change as Measured by the MMPI: A Fine-Year Longitudinal
          Study.* Unpublished Doctoral Dissertation. Fuller Theological Seminary.
LaFave, Wayne R.
   1962a "The Police and Nonenforcement of the Law—Part I." *Wisconsin Law Review.*
          pp. 104-137
   1962b "The Police and Nonenforcement of the Law—Part II." *Wisconsin Law Review.*
          pp. 179-239.
   1965   *Arrest.* Boston: Little, Brown.
Lamb, H. Richard, and Robert W. Grant
   1982   "The Mentally Ill in an Urban County Jail." *Archives of General Psychiatry* 39:
          17-22.
Lamb, H. Richard and Linda E. Weinberger
   1998   "Persons with Severe Mental Illness in Jails and Prisons: A Review." *Psychiat-
          ric Services* 49: 483-492.
Lane, Roger
   1967   *Policing the City.* New York: Atheneum.
Link, Bruce G., Howard Andrews, and Francis T. Cullen
   1992   "The Violent and Illegal Behavior of Mental Patients Reconsidered." *American
          Sociological Review* 57: 275-292.
Maghan, J. L.
   1988   *The 21st Century Cop: Police Recruit Perceptions as a Function of Occupational
          Socialization.* Unpublished Doctoral Dissertation. City University of New York.
Mastrofski, Stephen D., Jeffrey B. Snipes, Roger B. Parks, and Christopher D. Maxwell
   2000   "The Helping Hand of the Law: Police Control of Citizens on Request." *Crimi-
          nology* 38: 307-342.

Mather, F. C.
  1959 *Public Order in the Age of the Chartists*. Manchester: Manchester University Press.
Matthews, Robert A. and Lloyd W. Rowland
  1954 *How to Recognize and Handle Abnormal People: A Manual for the Police Officer*. Arlington, Virginia: National Association for Mental Health.
McInnes, Colin
  1962 *Mr. Lane and Justice*. London: New English Library.
Menzies, Robert J.
  1987 "Psychiatrists in Blue: Police Apprehension of Mental Disorder and Dangerousness." *Criminology* 25: 429-453.
Muir, William K.
  1977 *Police: Street Corner Politicians*. Chicago: University of Chicago Press
Neiderhoffer, A.
  1967 *Behind the Shield*. Garden City, N.Y.: Doubleday.
Newman, Philip
  1965 *Knowing the Cururumba*. New York: Holt, Rinehart and Winston.
Palermo, George B., Maurice B. Smith, and Frank J. Liska
  1991 "Jails Versus Mental Hospitals: A Social Dilemma." *International Journal of Offender Therapy and Comparative Criminology* 35: 97-106.
Parnas, Raymond
  1971 "Police Discretion and Diversion of Incidents of Intra-Family Violence." *Law and Contemporary Problems* 36: 535-565.
Paoline, Eugene A., III
  2001 *Rethinking Police Culture*. New York: CFB Scholarly Publishing.
Patch P. C., & Arrigo, B. A.
  1999 "Police Officer Attitudes and Use of Discretion in Situations Involving the Mentally Ill." *International Journal of Law and Psychiatry* 22: 23-35.
Piliavin, Irving and Scott Briar
  1964 "Police Encounters with Juveniles." *American Journal of Sociology* 70: 209-211.
Parsons, Talcott
  1951 *The Social System*. New York: Free Press.
Rabkin, Judith
  1979 "Criminal Behavior of Discharged Mental Patients." *Psychological Bulletin* 86: 1-27.
Reiner, Robert
  1999 "Police (Canteen) Culture." *British Journal of Criminology* 39: 287-307.
Reiss, Albert J. and David J. Bordua
  1967 "Environment and Organization: A Perspective on the Police." In *The Police*, David J. Bordua, (ed.) pp. 25-55. New York: Wiley.
Reith, Charles
  1943 *British Police and the Democratic Ideal*. London: Oxford University Press.

Riksheim, Eric and Steven Chermak
  1993   "Causes of Police Behavior Revisited." *Journal of Criminal Justice* 21: 353-382.
Rock, Ronald S. with H. A. Jacobson and R. M. Janopaul
  1968   *Hospitalization and Discharge of the Mentally Ill*. Chicago: University of Chicago Press.
Rubenstein, J.
  1973   *City Police*. New York: Ballantine.
Ruiz, Jim and Chad Miller
  2004   "An Exploratory Study of Pennsylvania Police Officers' Perceptions of Dangerousness and Their Ability to Manage Persons with Mental Illness." *Police Quarterly* 7: 359-371.
Silver, Allan
  1967   "The Demand for Order in Civil Society." In *The Police*, David Bordua (ed.) pp. 1-24. New York: Wiley.
Silver Eric
  2000a   "Extending Social Disorganization Theory: A Multilevel Approach to the Study of Violence Among Persons With Mental Illnesses." *Criminology* 38: 301-332.
  2000b   "Mental Disorder and Violent Victimization: The Mediating Role of Involvement in Conflicted Social Relationships." *Criminology* 40: 191-212.
Skolnick, Jerome
  1966   *Justice Without Trial: Law Enforcement in Democratic Society*. New York: Wiley.
Skull, Andrew T.
  1977   *Decarceration: Community Treatment and the Deviant*. Englewood Cliffs, N.J.: Prentice-Hall.
Smith, Bruce
  1960   *Police Systems in the United States*, 2nd ed. New York: Harper and Row.
Smith, Douglas A. and Christy A. Visher
  1981   "Street-Level Justice: Situational Determinants of Police Arrest Decisions." *Social Problems* 29: 167-177.
Steadman, Henry J., John Monahan, Barbara Duffee, Eliot Hartstone, and Pamela Clark Robbins
  1984   "The Impact of State Mental Hospital Deinstitutionalization on United States Prison Populations, 1968-1987." *The Journal of Criminal Law and Criminology* 75: 474-490.
Steadman, Henry J., Edward P. Mulvey, John Monahan, Pamela C. Robbins, Paul S. Appelbaum, Thomas Grisso, Loren H. Roth, and Eric Silver
  1998   "Violence By People Discharged from Acute Psychiatric Inpatient Facilities and by Others in the Same Neighborhoods." *Archives of General Psychiatry* 55: 393-401.
Steury, Ellen H.
  1991   "Specifying 'Criminalization' of the Mentally Disordered Misdemeanant." *Journal of Criminal Law and Criminology* 82: 334-359.
Sullivan, Ronald
  1968   "Violence, Like Charity, Begins in the Home." *New York Times Magazine*, November 24: 58.

Swanson, Jeffrey W., Charles E. Holzer, Vijay K. Ganju, and Robert T. Jono
    1990   "Violence and Psychiatric Disorders in the Community: Evidence from the Epidemiologic Catchment Area Surveys." *Hospital and Community Psychiatry* 41: 761-770.

Tenerowicz, C.M.
    1992   *A Longitudinal Study of Personality Change in Urban Police Officers: Educational Implications*. Unpublished Doctoral Dissertation. Cleveland State University.

Teplin, Linda
    1983   "The Criminalization of the Mentally Ill: Speculation in Search of Data." *Psychological Bulletin* 94: 54-67.
    1984   "Criminalizing Mental Disorder: The Comparative Arrest Rates of the Mentally Ill." *American Psychologist* 39: 794-803.
    1986   *Keeping the Peace*. Washington, D.C. National Institute of Justice.
    1990   "The Prevalence of Severe Mental Disorder Among Male Urban Jail Detainees: Comparisons with the Epidemiologic Catchment Area Program." *American Journal of Public Health* 80: 663-669.
    2000   "Keeping the Peace: Police Discretion and Mentally Ill Persons." *National Institute of Justice Journal* 8-15.

Teplin, Linda A. and Nancy S. Pruett
    1992   "Police as Streetcorner Psychiatrist: Managing the Mentally Ill." *International Journal of Law and Psychiatry* 15: 139-156.

The Presidents Commission of Law Enforcement and Administration of Justice
    1967   *Task Force Report: The Police*. Washington, D.C.

Travin, S.
    1989   "The Role of the Police With The Mentally Ill." In *Criminal Court Consultation*, R. Rosner & R. B. Harmon (eds.). pp. 137-155. New York: Plenum.

Truncale, J. and T. Smith (Eds.)
    1994   *MDTS: Monadnock Defensive Tactics System*. Fitzwilliams, New Hampshire: Monadnock PR-24 Training Council.

Van Maanen, J.
    1972   *Pledging the Police*. Unpublished Doctoral Dissertation. University of California at Irvine.
    1973   "Observations on the Making of Policeman." *Human Organization* 32: 407-418.
    1975   "Police Socialization: A Longitudinal Examination of Job Attitudes in an Urban Police Department." *Administrative Science Quarterly* 20: 207-228.
    1978a   "The Asshole." In *Policing: A View from the Street*, P.K. Manning and J. Van Maanen, (eds). pp. 221-238. N.Y. Random House.
    1978b   "People Processing: Strategies of Organizational Dynamics." *Organizational Dynamics* 19-36.

Van Vechten C.
    1940   "The Tolerance Quotient as a Device for Defining Certain Social Concepts." *American Journal of Sociology*.

Wachholz, Sandra and Robert Mullaly
    1991   "Pricing The Deinstitutionalized Mentally Ill: Toward An Understanding of Its Function." *Crime, Law, and Social Change* 19: 281-300.
Walsh, James Leo
    1977   "Career Styles and Police Behavior." In *Police and Society*, David H. Bayley, ed. Beverly Hills: Sage.
Westly, William
    1951   *The Police: A Sociological Study of Law, Custom, and Morality*. Unpublished Doctoral Dissertation, University of Chicago.
    1953   "Violence and the Police." *American Journal of Sociology* 59: 34-41.
Wilson, J.Q.
    1968   *Varieties of Police Behavior*. Cambridge, Mass.: Harvard University Press.
Wilson, Orlando W. and Roy C. McLaren
    1972   *Police Administration*, 3rd ed. New York: McGraw-Hill.
Worden, Robert E.
    1989   "Situational and Attitudinal Explanations of Police Behavior: A Theoretical Reappraisal and Empirical Assessment." *Law and Society Review* 23: 667-711.
Worden, Robert E. and Robin L. Shepard
    1996   "Demeanor, Crime, and Police Behavior: A Reexamination of the Police Services Study Data." *Criminology* 34: 83-105.
Worden, Robert E., Robin L. Shepard, and Stephen D. Mastrofski
    1996   "On the Meaning and Measurement of Suspects' Demeanor Toward the Police: A Comment on 'Demeanor and Arrest'." *Journal of Research in Crime and Delinquency* 33: 324-332.

IV Studying Up

The Illinois Department of Mental Health and the Illinois State Legislature and the Governor's Office

5 The Illinois Department of Mental Health
The Mental Health System?

1. Introduction

In the 1970s commitment was primarily a medical decision decided by foreign born permit physicians. An analysis of "the foreign born physician problem" in the 1970s might help explain the functioning of the mental health court. For example, for the last several decades treatment on the wards of the Illinois Department of Mental Health (DMH) has been given by large numbers of foreign-born and foreign-educated physicians. In the 1970s many of these physicians were unlicensed to practice in the State of Illinois outside of the state's mental hospitals. Some of these physicians worked for the department only until they become licensed and then left for private practice. Others never become licensed and remained in the department for years with little training beyond their initial medical education. Some DMH administrators accepted "the problem" with a shrug. Others were more concerned. One DMH official commented: "We once went into the Manteno staff dining room and we were the only ones speaking English!"

Some feel the answer to the foreign physician problem is to increase salaries, which will hopefully then draw the American born and educated physicians into the department. The problem, however, is not simply one of salary. "It's more complicated than just money," an official of the American Psychiatric Association explained several years ago. "California is very attractive for a physician, Illinois isn't. Therefore, Illinois becomes a producer state, and a big loser. As the American physician leaves the foreign physician fills the vacuum. California, Arizona, and Florida have the climate, that's why people leave. The foreign born physician who fills the void is a second or third class citizen in medicine. He's less talented, maybe, and less able to be an effective leader and spokesman. Some, frankly, lack the skills and therefore, make errors in judgment. They're viewed by most as an evil.

"As bad as they might be at least you can get doctors in Chicago. Downstate you can't even get a doctor to staff a mental hospital. For example, Anna State Hospital at the southern tip of the state has no full-time psychiatrists on its staff. The hospital is run like the mental health programs in the 1800s. Little has been done to remedy the situation. Federal legislation has helped. Some new people have been brought in because there's more money. And with health insurance there will be still more, but Illinois will still lose. Illinois is a producer state. That is, a physician in California can still make more money than here, plus he can live a nice lifestyle" (de Vise, 1973; Hines, 1974a, 1974b).

With the elimination of the limited license ("permit") physician all the doctors on the wards of the Illinois Department of Mental Health are now licensed. Overall, about 25 percent of the U. S. physician workforce is foreign medical graduates. However, most of the physicians on the wards of the Illinois Department of Mental Health are still foreign medical graduates. Since they are all now licensed their quality appears to have improved. However, studies find that foreign medical graduates are not as well qualified as U. S. trained medical graduates (Hallock, J., et. al., 2003; Varki, 1992; Ben-David, et. al. 1999).

Recently, a DMH administrator commented that the department's physicians were "good, they provide good services, and they are English speaking." He explained that the reason the department is able to attract physicians is because "inpatient care is a desirable setting. They make about $115,000 a year and they don't have to worry about paying liability. If they worked in an outpatient setting they could make from $120,000 to $200,000, with an average of $150,000 to $160,000 a year. But, they would have to pay liability and be on call 24 hours a day." However, another DMH official lamented the loss of many of the department's best physicians. He commented that "our talent is moving out the door."

Narrowly, the "problem" with commitment in the 1970s was the quality of the foreign born physician in a medically dominated proceeding. However, since the 1970s the number of commitments has fallen dramatically, the hearings have become more legalistic, the quality of physicians has improved, and other mental health professionals are now allowed to testify during the hearings.

However, whether the physicians, or other mental health professionals, dominate, or merely, influence, the hearings, they are all representatives of the Illinois Department of Mental Health. So, let us follow our vertical and contextual analysis. Let us "study up" and examine the functioning of the Illinois Department of Mental Health.[1] However, first let us begin with a brief overview of mental illness in America.

A recent study found that more than half of all Americans will develop a mental illness at some point in their lives. Dr. Thomas Insel, the director of the National Institute of Mental Health concluded that "mental disorders are highly prevalent and chronic." The study found that 20.8 percent of the population will suffer from mood disorders, particularly depression, during their lifetime. Substance disorders, particularly alcohol abuse, effects 14.6 percent of the population. Various anxiety disorders affect 28.8 percent. And, impulse control disorders affect another 24.8 percent (Carey, 2005a, 2005b; see also: Abboud, 2005).

---

1. An examination of the department was undertaker in the 1970s. The department was followed in the 1980s and 1990s. A formal update was conducted in 2005. In this study only mental health services for adults were relevant. Therefore, treatment for children, adolescents, and the developmentally disabled were excluded.

Such statistics, however, should not be overblown. Although a substantial portion of the population has experienced a mental disorder, the major burden of mental illness is concentrated in a fairly small portion of the population. In a one-year prevalence study of mental disorder among adults 18 to 54 it was found that 23.9 percent (44.2 million) had a mental disorder. However, only 5.4 percent (10 million) had a serious mental disorder and 2.6 percent (4.8 million) had a serious and persistent mental disorder. If we add in the homeless and institutionalized individuals with serious mental illness (about 2.2 million) we would have about 17 million seriously mentally ill persons in the U.S. If we include those seen for addiction problems the percentage would rise to 14.7 percent of the U.S. population. (Kessler and Zhao, 1999; Polgar and Morrissey, 1999; Cockerham, 2000)

In any given year 5 to 7 percent of adults have a serious mental illness. This produces an economic loss of $79 billion dollars. This reflects lost productivity, mortality, incarceration, and missed family care. This means that mental illness ranks first among illnesses in the U.S., Canada, and Western Europe. Worldwide suicide causes more deaths every year than homicide or war. In 1997, the latest year comparable data was available, the U.S. spent $1 trillion on health care. Seventy-one billion dollars of this was on mental health. Mental illness accounted for nearly 25 percent of all disability in major industrialized countries. However, only half of all people with mental illness seek treatment (Presidents' New Freedom Commission on Mental Health, 2003).

Although mental illness is a major medical problem, mental health specialists see fewer than 30 percent of all patients with a well defined mental illness. The other 70 percent are seen in primary care settings. Therefore, family practitioners, internists, and pediatricians initially see most individuals with mental illnesses. These primary care physicians often make referrals to specialists. However, between one-third and one-half of these patients do not go on to see a specialist (Cockerham, 2000; see also: Clauson and Yarrow, 1955).

Further, there is an inverse relationship between available treatment resources and the severity of the mental illness. For example, in 1971, 14 percent of the total hours of all psychiatrists were spent in state mental hospitals (where the sickest and most chronic patients were treated). An additional 7 percent of the hours were spent in community mental health centers; and 13 percent in private and general hospitals. However, 41 percent of all the hours psychiatrists spent in treatment were in private practice (where those with the least severe illnesses are seen). Most of those patients seen in private practice have been called "YAVIS"—young, attractive, verbal, intelligent, and successful (Horwitz, 1982: 139). Little has changed since then.

2. A History[2]

Before the 1840s the mentally ill were either kept in their homes or were placed in whatever public facilities were available—jails, almshouses, or private charitable facilities. Some communities established asylums for the insane but most of those persons who were charac-

---

2. Much of the history of the department is taken from personal interviews, as well as, Reidy (1964), Mehr (2002), and Briska (1997).

terized as mentally ill were simply neglected. During the 1840s citizen protest against such treatment reached a peak. In 1847 the first state mental hospital was established in Illinois. It was in Jacksonville, not far from the state capitol in Springfield (Mehr, 2002).

In 1860 Elizabeth Packard was committed to the Jacksonville hospital by her husband. Mrs. Packard waged a battle in the courts and the State Legislature in order to gain her freedom. In 1863 she was released. Mrs. Packard campaigned against the existing commitment laws. In 1867 the state enacted new provisions which made significant changes to the law. These changes were that women and men were equal in their rights to freedom, individuals could only be committed if they were dangerous, and a person could only be committed by juries (Briska, 1997).

In 1869 additional state hospitals were established. That year the Board of State Commissioners of Public Charities was also established and charged with the responsibility of visiting and inspecting state welfare institutions, almshouses, and jails. The Commissioners quickly found that many mentally ill persons were living in deplorable conditions in almshouses and jails. They protested and many of the mentally ill were transferred to the newly constructed state hospitals. In 1888 state hospitals held 3,685 persons. And the Cook County asylum held another 901 (Briska, 1997: 74).

In the 1890s psychopathic or detention hospitals began to be established in some cities. Patients were admitted to these hospitals for a week of evaluation. After the evaluation patients were released or taken for commitment hearings. These hospitals acted as triage centers and provided an early form of crisis intervention therapy. Such hospitals avoided admission to far away state hospitals. In Illinois the first detention hospital was the Cook County Psychopathic Hospital. Half of all the patients who were admitted to state hospitals in Illinois were screened through this facility (Briska, 1997: 155-6).

By the middle at the 1890s only 25% of the mentally ill were still in county almshouses; and by 1909 only 121 persons labeled mentally ill remained in these institutions. In 1907 the state took full responsibility for the care of the mentally ill and ordered that all mentally ill persons should be transferred to state hospitals. In 1912 the state took over the Cook County Insane Asylum near Chicago and renamed it Chicago State Hospital. (To this day it is still sometimes simply called, "Dunning" after the farm on which it was located.) At the time it held 2,000 patients. The part-time Charity Board was eliminated and a new full-time Board of Administration was established to govern the state hospital system. The Board consisted of five members, one of whom was required to be a qualified "alienist" (psychiatrist). The Board was given full control over the hospital system. Since the existing hospitals were overcrowded, three new hospitals were built. The Board acted as a progressive force and attempted to have the mentally ill treated in a "scientific" manner. It also developed policies to eliminate restraints, to expand therapies for disturbed patients, to increase nurses training, to initiate an eight hour work day, and to broadening the merit system (Briska, 1997).

In 1917 the state government was reorganized and most state functions were consolidated in to code departments with directors appointed by the governor. A Department of Public Welfare took over the administration of the state mental hospital system. During the ensuing years more hospitals were built. By the late 1920s Illinois had nine state hospitals. The number of patients in state hospitals rose from 19,456 in 1924 to 30,782 in 1940. By the mid-1930s, 20 to 30 percent of all admissions were for the demented elderly. By 1947 the number of inpatients had increased to 42,000. However, the hospitals were only designed to house 28,000 persons. In 1955 the total reached its peak at 47,956 patients (Briska, 1997: 187, 251; Mehr, 2002: 392). In some cases 180 patients slept in dormitories designed for 45 persons. Because of this over crowding, and the perception of poor care, the public began to label these institutions as "snake pits."

Over the years other changes occurred. In 1917 the Institute for Juvenile Research was transferred to the department. In 1944 the laws concerning commitment, admission, detention, and care of the mentally ill were revised by the passage of the Mental Health Act. This act also provided for the licensing and regulation of private institutions which cared for the mentally ill. A further revision of the Mental Health Act in 1952 created a Mental Health Code which incorporated provisions for the care and protection of the mentally retarded as well as the mentally ill.

In 1952 the state passed a law allowing limited licensed physicians ("permit physicians") to practice only in state mental hospitals. Many of these physicians, who were rarely psychiatrists, practiced for years at state mental hospitals because they were unable or unwilling to pass the state licensing examination. During World War II maintenance was poor and the hospitals began to deteriorate. By 1958 their condition had become so poor that a bond issue for $81 million for the department was proposed. It failed by 200,000 votes. Two years later a $150 million bond issue for capital improvements was passed after a strenuous campaign (Mehr, 2002).

In 1960 Otto Kerner was elected governor. In 1961 he created the Department of Mental Health. The governor appointed Dr. Francis Gerty to head the department. Gerty used the $150 million bond issue to begin planning for a new community-based delivery system. Under this new system the state was divided into eight zones which were served by eight newly constructed zone centers. These centers, costing about $8 million dollars each, were to be located so that no person was more than 90 minutes by car from a zone center (Mehr, 2002: 487-499).

The state hospitals had usually been located in rural areas. The zone centers were placed in cities (Chicago, Rockford, Peoria, Springfield, Decatur, and Champaign) near colleges or universities. Seven centers were eventually built with the southern third of the state being served by the two existing state hospitals (Alton and Anna). The facility in Chester, near St. Louis, served as the Department's security hospital.

In 1963 and 1965 federal legislation was passed that subsidized the construction and staffing of community mental health clinics. The federal government mandated the creation of planning areas consisting of populations between 75,000 and 200,000 people. Each planning area was to have at least one community mental health center. These clinics would focus on preventive care, early intervention, crisis intervention, partial hospitalization, and aftercare (Briska, 1997: 225).

Between 1966 and 1976 the Federal government spent $1.5 billion to create 650 centers. The Federal government funded these centers directly. That was because state governments were viewed as impediments to reform. Later, President Reagan reversed this policy and returned responsibility to the states by consolidating mental health monies into block grants. He also reduced those grants by 25 percent (Frank and McGuire, 1996).

In Illinois one of the major considerations for the establishment of the zone system was to entice personnel away from the Chicago area. At the time, 470 of the 543 members of the American Psychiatric Association in Illinois lived in the Chicago area. Of the 370 physicians who were certified by the American Board of Psychiatry and Neurology only twenty-nine lived outside of the Chicago metropolitan area ("downstate"). Facilities for the mentally ill were also meager downstate. For example, in 1960 forty Illinois hospitals gave some psychiatric treatment outside of emergency care. Almost half of these hospitals were in the Chicago area. The others were concentrated in half-a-dozen downstate cities. Outside of Chicago only three cities had any specifically designated psychiatric beds in their general hospitals. Also, almost half of all hospitals in the state were in the Chicago area (Reidy, 1964). So, one of the prime concerns of the new zone center plan was to improve the medical and psychiatric facilities downstate.

The zone center program was based upon seven principles:

1.) Whenever possible treatment should be available in the community.
2.) Facilities should provide early, intensive treatment to avoid hospitalization.
3.) Hospitalization should be in or near the person's community.
4.) During hospitalization programs should be initiated to ease the patient's return to the community.
5.) Outpatient care should be provided after an acute episode to hasten the resumption of full community living.
6.) A wide range of services should be incorporated to treat all types of psychiatric patients.
7.) Interagency cooperation should be stressed (Reidy, 1964).

The zone centers were intended to herald a revolution in treatment. And, it was hoped that the state hospitals would fade away. In practice, the zone centers treated those who were young and attractive and sent the remainder of the patients to the state hospitals. Because of the flow of money and personnel into the zone centers the thirteen state hospitals deteriorated even further. In state hospitals patient spending was as low as $10-11 per patient per day whereas in zone centers it was as high as $100 per patient per day. A two-tiered system of treatment soon developed in most of the state. In Chicago, however, the old Chicago State Hospital was merged with the new Charles Read Zone Center (Mehr, 2002: 498-501, 520).

After World War II a great deal of research focused upon the negative impact of mental hospitals. Many studies pointed to the apathy, dependence, and depersonalization of patients in such custodial institutions (Wing, 1962: 39; see also: Martin, 1955). Because of this the zone center directors were leery about letting their facilities become miniature state hospitals. Therefore, the zone centers 200 to 400 inpatient beds were seldom more than half full. The consequence of this was that the flow of patients in to the state hospitals continued.

The emergence of the zone center approach was seen as a great innovation by many mental health professionals. Therefore, Dr. Gerty, and his successor, Dr. Harold Visotsky, reigned over the department's "golden age." Innovation was the watchword, and Illinois became the "in" place to work.

During this period of reform the department drew professionals from all over the country. One former DMH official described the period: "Visotsky made Illinois the in place to go. He was charismatic and that had a mushrooming effect. The zone director was the system's stars and Illinois became as good as anyplace. You had very good professionals and very poor ones. And the medical model was no longer very important because Visotsky put all kinds of people in all kinds of jobs. Before the zone centers were established the department was just a collection of facilities and an accounting office downtown. There were thirteen hospitals and two schools for the mentally retarded. Each one of the facilities was run by a superintendent like a feudal kingdom and he reported directly to the director. Now the superintendent reports to the zone director who has a community orientation. Along with the zone centers, two new schools for the mentally retarded were built downstate. The zone centers actually became regional centers with the hospitals becoming old, overcrowded, understaffed, and deteriorated. The zone directors pushed private community services rather than departmental services. The idea was to make the department a resource facility, that is, to backup, and control, local programs. Voluntary, non-profit agencies were set up and the legislature passed a law which allowed local communities to tax themselves, pick a board, and establish local programs. Half of the state's counties passed referenda and established what were called 708 Boards, named after the number of the enabling legislation. The idea was for the department and the local community to contribute to the program and establish community services. It was hoped these services would keep people out of the hospital."

The patient population had reached a height of almost 48,000 inpatients in 1955. The new community philosophy, and later, the use of drugs, led to a significant drop in hospital populations (see: Gronfein, 1985a, 1985b). Under Visotsky's administration hospital populations began to drop dramatically. One of the primary reasons for this was the expansion of the federal Medicaid program in 1965. This extension of welfare benefits to the indigent mentally ill significantly influenced mental health policy. This was accomplished by passing Medicaid monies though the state's welfare system to public aid recipients. This meant that when patients were discharged most of the cost of care was transferred from the state to the federal government. These new benefits included the cost of care in nursing homes. Within a relatively few years nearly half of all state hospital patients, that is, the elderly and infirm, were transferred to nursing homes (Briska, 1997: 226). This depopulation led to a state hospital inpatient population of only about 15,000 by the early 1970s.

After about five years Visotsky's administration ran into trouble. Visotsky had wanted to close three or four state hospitals because of falling patient populations. He tried to close Kankakee State Hospital but was blocked by political pressure. As a result of this, he lost his power and when the Kerner administration ended in 1968 he left his position.

The new governor, Richard Ogilvie, a Republican, was not a devotee of mental health. Although Ogilvie was not anti-mental health he was pro "management" and "efficiency." Ogilvie was interested in establishing a rational planning system. He considered DMH to be chaotic. What had been a "golden age" to some had appeared to be a mess to others.

Ogilvie appointed John Briggs, an accountant, as acting director of the department. One former official explained that when Briggs took over he began to cut out many innovative, though sloppy, programs. The pro-management forces cheered and the professionals began to leave. One former DMH official described the period this way: "Ogilvie was interested in fiscal responsibility and accountability. It wasn't just running a tight ship, but it was that he had a poor orientation towards government services. He felt private organizations should provide the services. Ogilvie believed the department was poorly managed. Actually, it was 'loosely' managed. Briggs was sent to clean up the mess. However, his management approach created antagonisms and almost the entire upper echelon of the department quit. Also, Briggs was brutal with his cuts. He had no mental health training and when he reorganized the department many people didn't like it."

Briggs sped up the depopulation of the state hospitals. In 1968, 25 percent of all inpatients had been in state hospitals for 20 or more years. These people were quickly transferred to community facilities. Some spoke highly of this attempt to get the elderly out of state hospitals. Others were more cynical. One former DMH official commented that "Briggs began pushing people into the community when he realized that the feds would pay for three-quarters of the cost of a patient in the community."

After a year Briggs was replaced by Dr. Albert Glass, a psychiatrist, and former director of the Oklahoma Department of Mental Health. Glass had been the head of the U.S. Army's psychiatric program. He had been praised for having established a decent and humane system of psychiatric care in the Army. In Illinois, however, he was not an activist or innovator and the department continued in its management orientation. One former mental health official criticized Glass for his inactivity and conservative mental health policies. The former official commented that "in 1969 there was generally a breakdown in the department's creative processes." However, in spite of Ogilvie's drive to economize, the department's budget actually went up. In 1969 the length of stay was down to 30 days. However, the department was losing staff due to attrition and patients due to depopulation. Community grants, however, rose.

This trend continued for three years until Ogilvie was defeated for reelection by Daniel Walker, a Democrat. Glass was replaced by Dr. LeRoy Leavitt, a former medical school dean with an excellent reputation. Leavitt was highly regarded among psychiatric professionals and it was believed that the "golden age" would soon return. However, little changed from the Ogilvie to the Walker administrations. Ogilvie had been defeated because he had pushed through a state income tax and Walker was determined not to suffer the same fate. So, Walker, like Ogilvie, focused on bureaucratic efficiency and cutting costs. He began by firing several hundred of the department's middle management who were supposedly "sponging off the taxpayers." He also closed one state hospital and moved towards more purchased care. The results, according to some department employees, were cuts in patient services. Employee unions protested. Also, frequent newspaper exposés of inadequate services put the administration on the defensive and soiled Leavitt's reputation.

In 1972 intense lobbying by parents forced the administration to upgrade services for the developmentally disabled. Also, the department's name was changed to the Department of Mental Health and Developmental Disabilities (DMHDD).

In the mid-1970s hospitals and zone centers became "mental health centers" and the state schools for the retarded became "developmental centers." In 1977 all children's programs in the state were consolidated at the Henry Horner Center in Chicago. In 1981 all alcoholism programs were closed and a new state agency called the Department of Alcoholism and Substance Abuse (DASA) was established. The new department did not run any of its own facilities. Instead, it contracted out all its services.

Budget pressures, as well as a policy preference for community care, led the next governor, James Thompson, to close six major mental health facilities in the early 1980s. By 1985 there were only 3,568 patients in state operated mental health facilities. Meanwhile, 140,000 individuals were receiving outpatient services. During this time funding for community based services dramatically increased. In fiscal year 1981 the department spent $51 million on community services. However, by 1986 spending on community services had doubled to $101 million. Meanwhile, funding at state hospitals rose only slightly from $180 million to $188 million (Briska, 1997: 248-258).

The 1990s brought further change. In 1993 the department organized the community agencies it funded into Local Area Networks (LAN's). The creation of LAN's was to better coordinate community mental health care. It was also to further shift the focus of treatment away from the state hospitals. In 1996 the LAN's were renamed Comprehensive Community Service Networks (CCSN's). The CCSN's were organized with a network manager for the community agencies and a hospital administrator for the state hospital. This model was based upon the National Institute of Mental Health's (NIMH) Community Support Services Program (CSSP). Agencies were to provide case management in order to help individuals connect to needed services. Such services were medication management, crisis intervention, supported housing, day treatment, rehabilitation programs, pre-admission hospital screening, and peer and family support counseling. It was hoped that such an approach would allow those with severe and persistent mental illness to function in the community (Briska, 1997: 274-6).

3. Inpatient Hospitalization: The 1970s

The community mental health system of the 1960s and 1970s was superimposed upon the old state hospital system. Before the zone centers were built the mental health delivery system was dysfunctional. The physical plants were in the wrong places (in rural areas) and the hospitals were run like fiefdoms. "In fact, in the old days," one legislative aide noted, "the superintendent had a house on the grounds and patients served cocktails at five p.m."

The traditional community response to the mentally ill was extrusion. Because of this the state hospital system grew to about 48,000 inpatients in 1955, which represented 10% of the national total. By mid-1974 that number had dropped to 15,200 (Regan, 1974).

In the 1970s when a patient was admitted they began drug treatment (on the acute wards). If they did not improve in 60 to 90 days they were transferred to a hospital which specialized in long term care for the chronically mentally ill. These wards were usually called "back wards." Therefore, some hospitals dealt almost entirely in acute care while others were primarily for chronic patients. On the long term care wards little treatment occurred beyond the continuance of drug therapy. One department administrator commented, "I frequently asked patients what they do on back wards. 'Not much' they usually answer. But then I asked patients on acute wards what they did all day. 'Not much' they would also say."

In spite of the minimal level of treatment given patients there was a strong push by the administration to discharge patients from state hospitals. Ward staff claimed that there were discharge quotas, and if they were not met, staff members were fired.

Hospital population, however, was not simply a matter of treating and discharging patients. There are a certain number of staff positions in a hospital. To maintain those jobs the patient population could not be allowed to fall below a base level. Therefore, as patient population dipped, intake loosened. As wards become overcrowded, admissions tightened.

Although there may not have been much activity on the wards in the 1970s they were much improved over the previous twenty years. For example, a nursing supervisor described the situation on one woman's ward where she worked in the 1950s (before medication came into use). "We used to wake our patients in the morning and lead them in to the ward. We'd push some picnic tables together and close off a large square in the center of the ward. We'd then herd the patients in to the square and have them stay there all day so we could keep the filth in one area. At the end of the day we'd hose them down and send them to bed. It was mostly a big management problem. Now they give them drugs and push them out into the street."

In 1972 a scandal occurred at Elgin State Hospital, which is located on the fringe of the Chicago metropolitan area. A foreign born physician who had been practicing there had been ordering treatments such as the injection of ink and crushed bananas for the hospital's patients. It was eventually discovered that he had forged credentials and was indicted (see: Dublin, 1974; Haug and Martin, 1971; National Science Foundation, 1972; Lavin, 1969). Shortly thereafter, the Charitable Subcommittee of the Legislative Commission to Visit and Examine State Institutions held hearings at the hospital. A few days before the hearings the chairman took an unaccompanied walk through the grounds and saw decrepit and deteriorating physical facilities, sexual promiscuity, and patients inadequately dressed, supervised, and cared for.

The legislators examined the hospitals discharge policy. They found that 50% of the discharged patients returned to the hospital. They called this an "evacuation syndrome." The Subcommittee concluded that although per diem cost per patient had risen from $4 to $21 it appeared that a considerable portion of the per patient increase had been monopolized by costs of an ineffective discharge and aftercare program. Consequently, the custodial and treatment programs for the geriatric and long term care residents who remained at the institution had suffered.

They also concluded that administrators appeared to have little knowledge of what occurred on the wards. In fact, certain administrators had not been on the wards in over six months. The subcommittee also found insufficient security, maintenance, and poor staff morale (Legislative Commission To Visit and Examine State Institutions, 1972).

The push towards community mental health in some cases exacerbated the custodial nature of these institutions. Under Governors Ogilvie and Walker the funds which would have gone to state hospitals were trimmed and the money was channeled into the community grants program. Although there had been a 300 percent increase in the early 1970s for such grants, the hospitals had received only small increases. The result was poor care in the hospitals. One supervising nurse noted that "the linen services and the prepackaged food are both poor. If the food budget were doubled our huge medication costs would certainly go down." A long time critic of the department was more acerbic. "They should separate those with 'nervous disorders' from the lunatics that'll tear them apart. And they should give them some decent food, those people are starving!"

In February 1973, the Chicago Sun-Times began a series of stories on the poor conditions at Tinley Park Mental Health Center, a state hospital in Chicago's southern suburbs. Two reporters, G. Robert Hillman and Nancy Day posed as college students and volunteered in order to gain access to the hospital. The series began with a story about rapes, teenage prostitution, beatings, and poor care at the hospital. On February 12, under the title, "Inside Tinley Park: How They're Suffering For Their Insanity," Ms. Day described overmedicated patients who wandered aimlessly about, disinterested staff, and filthy wards (Hillman, 1973; Hillman and Day, 1973). On February 27 an article entitled, "Mental Expert Tells Tinley Park Chaos" appeared in the Sun-Times. The article, by G. Robert Hillman, described how a mental health specialist had told a legislative investigating commission that the treatment program at the hospital had "broken down."

While the Tinley Park exposé was in progress an article on abuses at Chicago-Read Mental Health Center appeared. The article, on February 15 by Jerome Watson, entitled, "Charges Bungling, Theft, and Loafing At Chicago-Read." Drug abuse and prostitution were reported to have occurred at Read. The administration was seen as complacent. One former administrator was quoted as saying: "When you're in Read, you're condemned to hell."

Such stories were common. For example, on April 4, 1974, Carolyn Toll of the Chicago Sun-Times wrote an article entitled, "Patient Tied To Bed 2 ½ Days," (1974f). She also reported that staff shortages were causing younger patients to be treated with "crowd control" techniques. Two and one-half weeks later Toll closed the series with an article entitled, "Nurse Suspended In Chicago-Read Abuse; Chief Quits," (1974e; see also: Toll, 1973a, 1973b, 1973c, 1974a, 1974b, 1974c, 1974d, 1974e, 1974f, 1974g).

Downstate hospitals were reported to have problems during this period, as well. In the 1970s the Illinois Security Hospital (ISH) in Chester served the statewide security needs for persons who were found to be incompetent to stand trial and patients who were unmanageable at other DMH facilities. In the 1960s the average stay at the hospital was three to five years. By the 1970s this has been reduced to eleven months. The recidivism rate for the hospital was also reduced to a remarkable three percent. However, ISH had problems. A report of the Charitable Subcommittee of the Legislative Commission to Visit and Examine State Institutions (1972) criticized the facility for deficiencies in staffing and excessive drug usage. Further, ISH, which was designed like a jail, had no indoor plumbing, and the buildings were eighty years old. The patients sat in their cells all day. Many of ISH's problems were alleviated when a new 400 bed facility on a 40 acre campus opened in 1974. The new facility resembled a minimum security prison or mental health facility rather than a maximum security prison.

Anna State Hospital in the far southern tip of the state had traditionally been unable to attract staff. For its 700 inpatients in the early 1970s Anna had only one part-time, fully licensed psychiatrist.

In spite of these many failings, the community mental health philosophy, plus the use of medication, had made patients more manageable. And this manageability allowed for the depopulation of state hospitals.

4. Community Mental Health: The 1970s

In the 1970s large numbers of patients were discharged "into the community." In Chicago this meant that many of them were discharged into one poor neighborhood on the north side-Uptown. One community mental health administrator in the neighborhood observed that DMH discharged 15,000 to 20,000 patients into that community. However, even they did not know how many ex-patients were now living there. One agency reported:

"Many of these patients are only tangentially [in the] 'community;' they may have arrived in Uptown because of the discharge policies of DMH, or the patient culture that exists, or the welfare culture that exists, or the rooming house structure that exists, etc. Some disappear for months, only to reappear after a sojourn in a jail, a state hospital, another community like Uptown, or relatives" (Edgewater-Uptown Community Mental Health Center, 1972-3: 24).

The administrator of the agency in Uptown noted that "if people are going to be treated in the community we must know what a community is, but we don't. Uptown is a big slum, it's just a community on paper. Besides, the community concept is only understandable when you understand the total system, and *nobody* does. What frequently occurs is that the legal and mental health systems extrude someone who is deviant and then they dump him back into society in a place like Uptown."

A psychiatric nurse from DMH concluded: "The state is trying to get out of the mental health business. They're funding general hospitals, community centers, and community organizations to provide services. They think it's cheaper. To do this kind of thing you have to have data so that you know what you're doing. But the data is poor from community treatment centers, so the department fudges it. What community psychiatry has become here is nothing more than dumping people into halfway houses. Those places are awful, almost criminal. There's tremendous neglect. In one I know of there are two aides for an entire floor. The patients are herded into two large rooms and just shuffle around all day half dressed and drooling on themselves. The doors are all locked or the patients would end up wandering all over the streets. These places are just back wards" (see: Luhrman, 2000: 127-8).

In 1971 Dr. Murray C. Brown, Commissioner of Health for the City of Chicago told a U.S. Senate Special Committee on Aging that "far in excess of 50 percent" of the seven thousand patients discharged by Illinois state hospitals in 1970 and 1971 were sent to nursing and residential care homes in Chicago without adequate provisions that they would receive decent care. Brown also stated that "we have further learned that such former patients were discharged not only into licensed facilities, but into rooming houses and converted low-class hotels, some of which the Chicago Board of Health has never been able to identify or locate" (quoted in Chu and Trotter, 1974, p. 41).

Similar problems have developed in New York where patients have been dumped into communities on Long Island. Many ex-patients in California too, have suffered a similar fate (Chase, 1973). The California State Employee's Association, which represents the employees of the state Department of Mental Hygiene, estimated that the death rate among transferred patients is from 5 to 10 percent higher than among patients who have remained in the hospital (1972). One of the chief results of the drastic depopulation of California mental hospitals from 22,000 patients in 1967 to 7,000 in 1973 was frequent police involvement with ex-patients. Sergeant Floyd Hatcher of the Los Angeles Police Department's hospital detail reported that calls to pick up people who were wandering down freeways or into someone's kitchen had doubled to 200 a month. "We're getting more repeaters, too," Hatcher added. "We pick up someone and send them to Metropolitan State or County General. If they keep them at all, they keep them for 72 hours and put them back on the street. And we just pick them up over and over." Hatcher told of one woman he had picked up and sent to a hospital 16 times. Her offense was lying down in the street. "Every time they just medicate her and send her home," he said. "She wants to go back to Carillo State Hospital. She says she loves it there." Lieutenant James Burleson, of the Santa Clara County Sheriff's Department commented that "our jail population has at least tripled with the people who require hospitalization or anti-psychotic medication." Most of the mentally ill are picked up for loitering or mischievous behavior (Chase, 1973: 18-19).

Lieutenant Burleson went on to point out that "since Governor Reagan has directed the closing of several State Hospitals for the Mentally Ill and placed the responsibility for their care with the community level, I have noticed a marked increase of mentally ill persons in our jail facilities. Santa Clara County has accepted its responsibility for its mentally ill persons; however, many other communities have not. The net result is that our county seems to be rapidly increasing in out of county mentally ill persons.

"As many of these people have no real friends or relatives they are not only those responsible in many crimes but the victim in a tremendous number of crimes. Many of these people fall prey to the smooth talking con-artists, the rapist, etc.

"Many of the mentally ill who end up in jail are not suitable for this type of detention. They find it difficult to adjust to the surroundings and the other individuals detained with them. The sad part is that we have no place to send them, especially felony suspects" (personal communication).

A nurse from an Illinois state hospital explained that "there's nothing wrong with the theory of community psychiatry, but in practice, it's horrendous. The theory is that as a person begins to get sick, he or she is treated in the community and kept from getting sicker. It's a preventive approach. The reality is that persons are only seen when they become psychotic. Therefore, the only alternative is to hospitalize them and withdraw them from the community. Community psychiatry also assumes the community has been educated and that's not true. The idea's based upon a supply and demand approach. But if information was available, we'd be swamped. We, therefore, are forcing people to deteriorate into hard-core crazies before they can receive treatment."

In the 1970s the department argued that their mental hospitals were community based, and in a sense, they were. One DMH official described an arrangement between the Chicago police and DMH. "On Friday and Saturday night Chicago-Read becomes a dumping ground for Chicago police department freaks. The police dump them at Chicago-Read because it's a state facility and therefore, it saves the city money. If they took them to Cook

County Hospital, which is supported by city and county money, it would cost them more. Anyway, the Friday and Saturday night derelicts are back on the street by Sunday, so it's an O.K. system." However, he went on to add that in spite of this, "relations between the police and the state hospital have often been poor. This is partly because of erratic admissions policies at Chicago-Read." One community mental health center director commented, "Read often turned people away who were actually hallucinating. This has led to mistrust and battles."

In a series of articles by Carolyn Toll of the Sun-Times she highlighted problems between the state hospital and the community mental health agencies, as well. On January 26 and March 13, 1974 (1974e, 1974g), Toll reported that representatives of private agencies were unable to provide service to the increasing number of persons discharged from state mental health programs because they could not get additional funding to meet the needs. However, the department replied that the state only funds on the basis of an agencies willingness to serve "high-risk" patients. Department officials often claimed that professionals only want to serve "interesting" patients and let the others go without services. They frequently pointed to family service agencies becoming "community mental health centers" while still serving a middle class clientele with state money. Some mental health professionals believe that such charges are true.

One DMH psychologist in charge of evaluation for community mental health clinics in Chicago's suburbs angrily charged that "clinics take money, sometimes in seven digits, and then refuse to link with DMH hospitals. It's the 'I don't want to get involved with those dirty, state hospital patients' syndrome. But, I say, 'Not with state money you don't!' "

Addressing this point Ragan has concluded:

> The Department's definition of community mental health has confused and angered many community service providers because they contend that the Department has changed the rules of the game. Previously, they say, the Department placed no restriction on the types of patients to be served in the community. To do so now threatened many of the services which the Department had previously supported. Operationally, their argument was undoubtedly true. However, Department policy for twenty years had been to give priority consideration to patients in greatest need. Mental Health Regulation 74, implemented in 1953, required any facility receiving state grants to treat those former state mental hospital patients and all conditionally discharged patients who were referred to them. In its haste to support new community facilities, the Department may have been lax in enforcing this regulation. (1974: 20)

In May, 1974 Carolyn Toll wrote a major, week long, series on DMH (1974b, 1974d). One long article in that series, entitled, "Mental Patients Suffer In Shift From State Care," continued the controversy on community mental health services. The article recited three "horror stories" concerning patients being unable to secure proper treatment. The article noted that under Governor Walker (1973-77) there was a 23 percent drop in state hospital patients from the previous year. This compared with a 10 percent decline in the preceding year. There were also 1,800 departmental employees laid off and at least three outpatient programs were closed. Also, the Walker administration cut the Chicago-Read Mental Health Center budget by $2.2 million (8.4 percent) while overall administrative costs for 1975 rose by 14.6 percent.

Walker had promoted community care for the mentally ill during his campaign. However, community agencies complained of underfunding and patient dumping once he took office. They said this forced them to ignore many other needy persons. One clinic director commented that "the middle class fellow is now forced to get sicker and enter a hospital or get poor and go on welfare before he is eligible for state psychiatric help." Community clinics also claimed that they were now serving three times as many persons as the department, an 18 percent increase. However, grants to clinics decreased by $3.1 million.

The states outpatient services, which were generally regarded to be good, have also recently drawn criticism. A state law was passed mandating a "reasonable" fee for outpatient services. The department interpreted this to mean the initiation of a $25 per hour fee for therapy or counseling. Although the fees were on a sliding scale, many felt that the fees would be prohibitive to large numbers of middle and lower income families. (Welfare recipients were not affected because their fees are paid by the state.) A DMH employee complained:

"A family could blow $75 to $100 their first day here," said one psychologist. "That could keep a lot of people away who badly need our help." (Toll, 1974b: 14)

The department's director defensively replied: "If we discover these fees are interfering with treatment or excluding people, we'll reconsider them."

The quantity of outpatient service was large: 29,505 active cases at the end of fiscal 1973 in state operated clinics and 64,961 active cases at the end of fiscal 1973 for state aided clinics. However, many former state hospital patients may not have been among those receiving these services. An indirect indicator of this is high state hospital readmission rates. For example, two-thirds of all inpatient admissions were readmissions from the previous year. Many of these were patients who had been released less than 30 days previously (Illinois Department of Mental Health, 1973). Critics believe this indicated poor discharge planning. The most positive statement one high DMH official could muster concerning this situation was that, "we're trying to monitor it."

Another problem has been aftercare. There are three types of community care facilities for the mentally ill in Illinois: skilled nursing facilities (providing skilled nursing care, continuous skilled nursing observations, restorative nursing, and frequent medical supervision); intermediate care facilities (providing basic nursing care and other restorative services under periodic supervision); and sheltered care facilities (providing personal care and assistance, supervision overnight, suitable activities, and medical care as necessary) (Ragan, 1974: 32-3; Kohen and Paul, 1976).

Many felt that individuals did not receive adequate services in these facilities. An attorney commented that "DMH has never bothered to set up regulations for aftercare. They just use public health's—which is an inadequate response to the problem. Also, the law says that patients in aftercare facilities should be visited *at least* once a month. DMH says *only* once a month."

One DMH official described the "problem with nursing homes": "Mental health, public health, and public aid all do the licensing. DMH does the program licensing, public health does the sanitation, and public aid checks for the patient's financial eligibility. There are problems here in coordination between the departments. And, to be frank, lobbyists and provider groups block legislation letting DMH do it all. You can take people out of these places or refuse to put them in but then a legislator calls. The connection between the nursing home operator and legislator works like this. An individual who wants leverage gets on a candidate's 'citizens committee' or such and then pushes his interests. The politician listens because he's been given money by this guy. Somebody says that's the way democracy works and somebody else says it's a bunch of baloney. Also, provider groups give money to candidates. Now, you might ask: How do I find out about these contributions? Well, the answer is, you can't, nobody will tell you the truth. And I can't tell you. I've got to deal with these people. On second thought, I can say that the main one is the Illinois Association for the Mentally Retarded. The other is the lobbyist who works for the Illinois Association for the Mentally Ill and a third is a group of nursing home owners. For example, the bill to split off services for the mentally retarded into a separate department came up. Half of the controlling board for that agency was to consist of provider groups. Is that a good idea? The guy who runs the retarded association kicked up an emotional storm about that bill. He used chicanery and demagoguery.

"And these halfway-houses and nursing homes? Well, there are a lot of snake pits. There are immoral and irresponsible people in the business. And how do you change this situation? It's a 'management problem.' You have to develop 'accountability' in the licensing process. And, how do you develop accountability? Well, it's a political problem; and we can only do so much about it. Besides, some of the inspectors are on the take. And it's fantastically naïve to believe you can catch them. Besides it costs a lot of money to catch them and a smart guy can always get around it. But, show me somebody and I'll hang him! But who checks the checkers? The way to do it is to develop standards and a reporting system and have several independent bodies check them. We're developing a three person team, DMH, public health, and public aid to solve this very problem. Further, we've got a philosophical problem. That is, after release, are ex-patients our concern? The liberals say, yes, the civil libertarians say, no. We have a real philosophical dilemma."

One former DMH official summarized the attitudes of most professionals towards aftercare: "The aftercare program has broken down. They turned out a lot of patients and there's no continued care. They tried to get community clinics to pick up these people. But they're not very attractive patients and so the clinics haven't really served them. What you need to develop are techniques to treat long term hospital patients. 'Halfway-houses' are an answer for these patients, but, in actuality, they're not halfway houses, they're just residential hotels. If you're going to discharge people you really have to take an active interest in them. A lack of interest leads to high readmission rates.

"When we discharge a patient our legal hold vanishes. The problem is that in Chicago you're got a lot of people and few relevant facilities. Downstate there's less pressure and therefore, the system works better. The reason it's so bad in Chicago is because these hotels are run for profit. But profit and mental health are incompatible. Besides, the private sector isn't set to handle a big public health model for mental health. They're still into the fee for service thing. The most productive mental health agencies are non-profit agencies such as hospitals and community mental health centers. Local 708 boards that tax their communities and then receive some state money are good, also. However, the system is currently in flux because DMH sees itself moving towards a granting agency" (see: Emerson, 1985b; Klemens, 1988; Davis, 1997).

An alternative to the current system of aftercare, and a way to prevent admissions generally, is to maintain people in their homes. One former DMH official explained: "It's simply not attractive to go out to a patient's home. Much of the geriatric population could be maintained at home by visitors, but they're not. The closest model to this kind of thing is the public health nurse. It's just that psychiatrists don't make house calls. Besides, psychiatrists don't intervene in crises. Although crisis intervention is new, the attitude that 'you come in to see me' and not vice versa, is prevalent. Besides, tight fiscal controls fight against 'inefficient' home visits."

Political influence also appears to be involved in DMH's relationship with the Chicago Board of Health-Mental Health Division. The city administration has never given mental health a high priority. The development of services has been sluggish and has occurred only with the help of state money. Los Angeles and New York City have commissioners of mental health. Chicago, however, does not. And its mental health services have been chronically underfunded.

During the 1960s and early 1970s the city's Mental Health Division grew to 18 centers which served 13,813 cases in fiscal 1973. This was about half of all the outpatients seen for the year in Cook County by state-aided clinics. The Mental Health Division is supported by approximately $3 million dollars from the city and $2.2 from the state (Golden, 1973). In spite of DMH's oft repeated policy that they serve the sickest and the poorest, the city's clinics serve primarily middle class young adults, some with incomes as high as $60,000 a year. Although a third to a half of the clinic's patients have been discharged from state hospitals only about one-quarter of all the patients seen are poor. The clinic's 45 part-time psychiatrists, 58 full and part-time psychologists, and 300 other workers provide primarily group therapy and medication.

In spite of the Board's uneven performance in serving the sickest and the poorest the state provided it with a $2.2 million grant. However, this did not include the same financial or fiscal controls required of other governmental units and private agencies receiving state mental health funds. This occurred in spite of a state audit in March, 1973 charging that the city had not filled 30 percent of its job openings that the state had funded. The city did not return the unused money. One legislator, upon hearing of the grant, commented that the monies were "the latest evidence of the marriage between Governor Walker and Mayor Daley, as well as the newest nail in the coffin of proper mental health care in Illinois, which has been tragically deteriorating since the beginning of the current administration" (Toll, 1974c).

In conclusion, DMH's success in the 1970s in community mental health was mixed. "Community based" services had little real involvement with the community. Short term hospitalization was distorted through discharge quotas and overly rapid discharges because of financial pressures. And, DMH moved substantial numbers of people into the community but did not provide adequate services to those individuals.[3]

---

3. One judge at the commitment court commented: "Funny things happen when you're dealing with DMH. For example, sometimes I commit people in the morning and I see them walking around downtown that same afternoon. After this happened a few times I called a doctor down at Manteno

In the 1970s there was little effort to form a coherent network of services. There was relatively little contact with non-psychiatric institutions such as the schools, police, and businesses by most DMH facilities in the promotion of preventive services.

The department was characterized by a heavy reliance on the medical model. One former DMH staff member commented. "Prolixin [a long lasting injectable drug] is the universal panacea for mental illness at DMH. Somebody must own stock in the company!" Political influence appeared to interfere with professional decisions. One former DMH staff member commented, "The largest funds seem to be available to South Side blacks in Chicago. The dividing line between Madden Zone Center and Chicago-Read seems to be where the money allocation changes; although the clinics in the Madden area don't have the most work. These South Side clinics do have the most psychotics but I think their money is disproportionately high for their patient loads. I'm sure there are political and racial considerations involved; however, it's a taboo subject at DMH and avoided whenever it's brought up."

This was confirmed by a study of resource allocation between Elgin State Hospital and Madden Zone Center by the Illinois Legislative Investigating Commission (1974). It was found that although Madden had only one-tenth the number of average daily patients (138.7 as compared to 1,326.6) it received 29 percent of the budget Elgin did. Also, per diem cost at Madden was three times higher than at Elgin ($91.33 per patient per day as compared to Elgin's $32.91 per patient per day). This disparity was partly due to Madden's level of staffing which was 2.89 employees per patient whereas Elgin's was 1.1 employees per patient. Although the department denies it, many concede that Madden is Region 2's (the Chicago area's) "showplace."

The initiation of the zone center approach at the beginning of the community mental health movement in Illinois initially evoked excitement from many quarters. The legislature was particularly enthusiastic because the department promised a speedy withering away of the state hospitals. Such a promise brought cheers from conservative budget cutters, as well as, liberals concerned with better treatment. In spite of this wide ranging enthusiasm of the 1960s, the 1970s were characterized by bitter disappointment. One legislator commented that "the original zone centers were to be diagnostic and acute treatment centers. Now they're just another facility." Another legislator added: "In the 60s the department promised the zone centers would 'solve the problem.' But I've become disillusioned. The centers don't seem to be providing services. They don't seem to be doing anything." A third commented: "DMH doesn't care. It ignores its patients. Sixty percent of its discharged patients are back in a year. There's no push to train non-professionals like the police and bartenders. But if a nursing home operator wants help, they get it. Community psychiatry, maybe it's just a slogan."

5. Community Grants: The 1970s

Community groups and agencies are partially funded through the community grants program of DMH. These groups and agencies then provide services to mentally ill and retarded

---

and I said, 'What in hell is going on down there?' The doctor answered, 'It's all political. The social workers are running the place. They make all the decisions'." He shook his head.

persons in their local communities. A high level DMH official has argued: "DMH can't do everything in 'mental health,' whatever that term means. We can't do it efficiently and local agencies can literally do it better. These agencies are locally accountable and tailor their services to meet the community needs whether that community is in the ghetto or along the North Shore. We will fund and coordinate these services, but we will not run them."

Almost 70,000 people were seen in state-aided clinics in fiscal 1973. Although many feel they have provided good, local services, a great deal of controversy has developed concerning their funding. Although the funds going into community grants rose steadily from $250,000 in 1954, to $6 million in 1968, to more than $33 million in 1973, controversy has surrounded the allocation of these funds.

The allocation of funds begins with a formula for determining which portion of DMH's budget would be allocated to the grant program. The Department started with a budget allocation for mental health which was developed in conjunction with the Bureau of the Budget. This allocation was based on previous expenditures for mental health, projected available resources to the state, and mental health's priority in relation to other state funding requirements. The budget allocation was divided by the total state population, resulting in a per-capita budget allocation. The per-capita budget allocation was then multiplied by the population in each of the state's eighty-three mental health planning areas. For each of the planning areas, projected state expenditures for state-operated inpatient and outpatient care, interim care, and purchase of care were then subtracted (Ragan, 1974: 22).

Once this allocation process was completed agencies then submitted grant proposals. These proposals were evaluated in relation to the available services that already existed in the area, the agency's previous performance, and demographic data. The department then funded services on a program by program basis.

Although this was the ideal, the reality was often quite different. One DMH official, who analyzed these applications, felt they were often of poor quality and it was difficult to put staff functions and patient needs together. His office allocated $25 million dollars a year. He observed: "We gave it on personal, non-rational, basis. We tried to cut some of the agencies and they screamed, so we put it back. The agencies asked: 'What were your criteria last year for money?' 'None,' we answered. 'What are your criteria this year?' the agencies asked. 'None,' we answered. It's like walking on jello when you don't have any leadership. The problem is that the only real guideline we have is that the agency sees high risk patients. That is, 'patients in danger of community extrusions.' That's it. And what does that mean?"

One legislative assistant asked: "What is high risk? Nobody but DMH and a few psychiatrists understand what high risk means. And how do you take care of everybody else? What standards do you use? How about nursing homes? And what about those people who don't get any treatment?" One department administrator commented: "The problem is that no one agrees on what mental health is. For example, is it a job, the environment, housing? Mental health can be all things to all people. In talking about mental health one must define a population. The Mental Health Code obligates us to treat everyone who's admitted. That means the mentally retarded who are severely and multiply handicapped, those incompetent to stand trial, severely disturbed kids, and those who are potentially violent. But who needs treatment in the community?"

In order to run a department one must establish goals, and program priorities to reach these goals. One administrator was asked if the department was chronically underfinanced. "Chronically underfinanced? What are your criteria? What do you want to do? What outcomes do you want to measure? The governor now wants to 'cut duplication and extra personnel,' but the real question is: What are your priorities? The governor wants to be known for 'running a tight ship.' That has nothing to do with services. Currently, the big push is to reduce staff. Inevitably this will mean reductions in hospital staffs with the extra money going into community services. The department isn't underfinanced because costs and criteria aren't there. So you can't conclude anything."

An 'old hand' in legislative budgeting commented: "How do they decide who gets a grant? Do they use a point system? Do they have an allocation formula? Do they take into consideration if the area is rich or poor? You tell me. And, what can we do about it? Nothing, really. How can you write into a law the specifics for community grants? How do you measure these things? It's too subjective. What about all the complicating factors? It's just too complicated for us to write into a law, so we have to rely on the good will of the department. But if you ask them how they do it, they just hem and haw and give you a bunch of b.s. The reality of the grant system is that it is haphazard and unscientific. Money is allocated according to *political* influence. The reason it's done that way is to keep people from screaming. That's how they decide who gets grants."

Criticism has also occurred concerning data reporting and the local screening of grants. One former DMH administrator, who now works for a state-aided clinic, commented: "The reporting system is so cumbersome that people are beginning to refuse money because of it. The reporting, it turns out, is not to analyze therapy but to justify the existence of programs. The statistics are really just a body count, which is then a justification for money.

"Another problem is that DMH overfunds certain facilities. This occurs when there's a good personal relationship between the subzone director, who reviews all grant applications for his area, and a community agency director. Subzone directors sometimes fight for more money for their area. This may mean that some agencies receive too much. If the subzone director is savvy about what's going on, grant proposals can be written 'appropriately,' therefore, more money goes out. Just as easily, of course, he can cut come S.O.B. he doesn't like.

"So this is the problem. Somewhere in DMH somebody comes up with guidelines, but they won't tell you the truth if you ask what they are. Then the community agencies rush through a bunch of proposals. Since there's a lack of time there's a lack of systematic review. So even their guidelines aren't followed. Some centers are overfunded, others are underfunded. Also, agencies can't transfer money and can't carry it over to next year. Therefore, a lot of money comes back to DMH. The bedrock problem is that there are no well-defined organizational goals in DMH. They've grown too rapidly and the result has been fragmentation and a lack of coordination. So, what is DMH's function? God, you tell me."

Even the governor's budget analysts have publicly admitted to the failings of the community grant system. Governor Walker's *Illinois State Budget in Brief* for fiscal 1974 concluded:

In recent years, state funding for mental health programs has increased substantially. Although the spirit of these increases was sound, their implementation has sometimes been haphazard. Program administrators have not been held accountable for increased productivity. The Department of Mental Health has not been guided by sound planning or program evaluation. Frequently, resources have been allocated among competing programs on the basis of pressure rather than need. The result has been widely disparate program quality and results. (p. 18)

High department officials admit that "funding review is a mess," but claim they are struggling to do the "right thing." Community groups strongly disagree. They point out that in 1972 the department requested $24 million for community grants. Seventeen million was approved, $14.5 million was funded, but only $12 million was spent.

One legislative aide commented: "The community grant issue is an emotional area, helpless human beings are involved. The community groups claim the department won't fund more than 50% of their budgets. The department denies this. The groups claim they're saving the state bundles of money in reducing hospitalizations. The department agrees, but says it's giving them enough money. The real question shouldn't be about money, though. It should be whether the agency is good. The agencies are listed on a continuum for funding and the department's cutoff point differs from the community groups. That's the real issue. The thing we don't know, and the department won't tell us, is if they're trying to dismantle the department and push everything onto the community groups. That we just don't know."

A DMH official involved in the grant review process explained that "community grants became operational twenty years ago and Illinois is the only state in the country with a grant system. Other states distribute money to their counties and then the counties give it to agencies. When we began in 1954 there was nothing more behind the program than some vague notions. Now we are trying to establish networks of services in order to handle people's problems. We began the programs with seven clinics and a budget of $250,000. In 1974 we'll be distributing about $43 million to clinics serving the mentally ill.

"So, how do you know if these agencies are doing their job? We don't. We try and provide for mental health services in each planning area in the state. However, the quantity and quality of these services are 'highly variable.' The grant system perpetuates itself because you can't stop a grant. For example, the far south side of Chicago was late in developing services, so there are still relatively few services in the area. In other words, there are a lot of black people there who aren't getting the services they need. Should we have pushed for more services? You could say we haven't been as 'responsive' as we should have been.

"Yes, we have problems with the community grant guidelines, but we also have political problems. We have to spend a lot of money because of political pressures in places where the needs really aren't the greatest. For example, we send money to the suburbs, I guess, because its public money and they deserve services. Grant funding is like an accordion, that is, it folds in and out due to 'current conditions.' I don't think that's the proper way to do it. I wanted narrower guidelines, but we get flack from the suburbs and downstate because any tightening of the guidelines would reduce their funding. But they really don't serve many high risk patients. The department claims that they are serving the 'sickest and the poorest.' Well, they're not. In parts of Chicago, the suburbs, and downstate, they're not. Community mental health centers appear to attract a new type of patient. Those who were not very ill and were not candidates for hospitalization in a state institution (see: General Accounty Office, 1977: 73; Gronfein, 1985a, 1985b).

"Then what is DMH's job? That's 'open to interpretation.' I guess you could say we're a 'funding, monitoring, and coordinating body'; and, we run inpatient services in state hospitals. Because the department's job is 'open to interpretation' there are many bitter conflicts about funding and monitoring. For example, one suburban hospital has gotten money for years and saw whomever they wanted. Many old-line programs, and particularly training hospitals, just don't want to see everybody.

"So, why don't we just cut off their grants? We can't, but as a punishment, they may not get substantial increases in upcoming years. Now, however, most hospitals and clinics more or less accept everybody because of the money. Most mental health professionals want to treat people like themselves, that's the crux of the problem. From now on though, we're going to be looking more at the data and being tougher with these agencies. But, to be honest, I don't care what criteria they use. Any criteria would be fine.

"And my job in all this? I 'participate' in the decisions on community grant funding. I take a look at the planning area and examine how much money has previously been spent. One of my responsibilities is to help equalize funding because some areas are very well funded whereas others are not. This has occurred because some areas had preexisting facilities which we could, and did, easily fund.

"And funding the suburbs? There are these junior executives with terrible problems. But should we support them with public money? Well, you must remember there aren't any criteria to define who should be funded. If we didn't fund them, then the wrath of the community would fall upon us. Anyway, how much is enough per city neighborhood? Money is not the answer, because some of the best funded agencies don't do very much. Besides, there seems to be no real relationship between funding and level of services. That is, funding and readmissions. It's just mythology that with money we can cut readmissions. But if we stopped funding these agencies the outcry would be tremendous.

"So, why then don't we establish evaluative measures and fund on that basis? Because DMH isn't willing to do it. DMH will tell you: 'We don't have the money,' 'It won't work,' etc., but when you come right down to it, they just won't evaluate anybody.

"Also, you should keep in mind that we don't control some of the money we pay out. For example, purchased care, in which we pay private hospitals to take care of the working poor or public aid which pays to take care of their clients, is basically unmonitored. I'm told, 'They have peer review,' but I don't think that's adequate. The purchased care is processed through the business office. Therefore, there's no real control over it. The problem is that in Chicago politically powerful hospitals don't want to be 'linked' to us. Downstate that's not true.

"What happens to these patients after discharge? For public aid patients, Medicaid pays for outpatient service, but for the working poor there's no guarantee of services after discharge. Medicaid pays for $300 worth of services after discharge. Because of this, many psychiatrists take these patients on for $300 worth of treatment. The others, we hope, are referred to a clinic after discharge. However, our linkages aren't very good and patients are frequently lost. We don't have control over this thing.

"Also, local communities, through enabling legislation, can tax themselves or divert money, such as revenue sharing, into mental health services. Another means of funding is through local sources. In the suburbs, for example, United Way often contributes for services. And, local fundraising occurs. In Chicago, however, the situation is different. Mayor Daley has always felt that mental health care was the state's responsibility. Therefore, Chicago has been the slowest big city in the nation to develop its own mental health services. We put great pressure on them a few years ago and they finally began to develop their programs.

"There's also federal money going into three community mental health centers in Chicago, and they're disasters. We've never made a commitment concerning their long-term funding. The local community doesn't care about them because the federal money needs matching funds and they don't want to get stuck when the federal money runs out. DMH is also afraid they'll get stuck; but, at least we're currently helping to fund these centers. We also get Medicaid money and some funding from the state's Division of Vocational Rehabilitation for treating adults.

"So, in conclusion, the department doesn't quite know what its doing. But don't say I said so. There's simply no system. They say we operate 'pragmatically;' but it's really just expediency. Of course, that does give us flexibility, but . . . There's simply no systematic planning. In fact, there's enormous resistance to it. If there were a system then you would be held to it. If there was a system you couldn't wheel and deal, favor certain groups. Every time there's a crisis, people yell, 'Do something.' That's the way we 'plan.'

6. DMH: Recent History (1990–2005)

In the 1990s the Department of Mental Health and Developmental Disabilities was sued by the American Civil Liberties Union (ACLU) because of complaints of inadequate mental health care. A study by several experts for the ACLU was conducted. They found that the average daily patient population of the twelve state hospitals was 3,108 patients in fiscal 1994. The total number of admissions during the fiscal year was 13,125. Large numbers of these patients were admitted because of a lack of treatment options in the community. Also over one-third of those who sought admission to Chicago–Read were turned away ("deflected"). The experts felt that this high rate of deflection deterred individuals, mental health professionals, and the police from seeking help for mentally ill persons. Deflection, they argued, was in actuality, the abandonment of the patient. Of those individuals who were admitted a significant number of these patients were discharged to Intermediate Care Facilities (ICF). These facilities often appeared to be sub-standard. It was felt that these facilities just replaced the state hospitals backwards (Report 1; Christian and Parsons, 1995; Experts Report Violence, Neglect, and Poor Treatment In Illinois Mental Hospitals, 1996; Mental Health Case Settled, 1997).

Also, the experts felt that the Local Area Networks (LAN's) of community agencies was merely a loose, voluntary confederation of programs with no governance and formal authority. Further, the LAN's, and its agencies, did not have a mandate to serve high risk patients. And the LAN's and its agencies followed no uniform guidelines on planning. Most significantly, Illinois ranked 44th in the nation in per capita spending on mental health; however, it ranked 12th in personal income (Report 1: 50-1).

All of the state hospitals in Illinois are currently certified by the Joint Commission of Accreditation of Hospitals (JCAHO). However, in 1993 Chicago–Read was decertified by JCAHO. To solve this problem, new programs were created and a new administration was brought in. Eventually, the hospital was reaccredited. On the other hand, in 1993 Elgin State Hospital received an accreditation with commendation.

One administrator explained that state hospitals now primarily provide short-term care. Chicago-Read now has a length of stay of 16 to 18 days. It is seen by the department as a "recovery center." He stated that most patients receive Prolixin and Haldol and are discharged. Many of these patients are MISA (mental illness/substance abuse) patients. He argued that the state hospitals are now actually drug and alcohol treatment facilities. He also believed that the agencies programs have become too 'static'. He thought they should be more "fluid" and adopt programs such as mobile assessment units. And, these units should help with food, housing, and drug treatment. DMH, however, does not directly fund these other needs. So, the department provides short stays. And a lack of community services leads many of these individuals to end up on the street, jail, or hospital emergency rooms (see: Lamb and Shaver, 1993). Further, a significant portion of these individuals are young adult chronic patients. They are often involved in street drug culture, assaultive behavior, and an unwillingness to take medication. These individuals require structured settings. However, these are usually not available (Lamb, 1982).

The department has seen a decline in admissions over the last 10 to 15 years.[4] In the early 1980s community agencies or local hospitals began screening patients before admission to downstate state hospitals. These patients were often directed to private hospitals because they had public aid (Medicaid), Medicare, or emergency funds from the state (the EPS program). Also, the state had initiated a new program—CHIPS (Community Hospital Inpatient Services). This program contracted for bed space in local hospitals. The program began downstate in the 1980s. When it was initiated in the Chicago area in 1990 there was a dramatic drop in admissions (15 to 20 percent).

When this program began in the 1980s the private psychiatric hospital industry was expanding (see: Schlesinger and Gray, 1999). New facilities were being built and old ones expanded. Health insurance was also being expanded to cover more mental health problems. And the stigma of mental illness was decreasing. Therefore, individuals were more willing to come in for treatment. However, in the 1990s there was a downsizing of mental health beds due to cuts by managed care organizations (see: Dorivart and Epstein, 1993). From 1991 to 2003, 51 units or hospitals that provided inpatient mental health care closed. Also, dozens of outpatient programs were eliminated. This produced an increase in emergency room visits by the mentally ill from approximately 37 percent in 1996 to 43.5 percent in 2002 (Data Points, 2003).

---

4. Under Governor Pataki New York cut its state hospital population by more than half to about 4,000 (Perez-Pena, 2006; see also: Hernandez, 1999; Winerips, 1999; Rhode, 1999; Barnes, 2000; Harto-Collis, 2006).

One former DMH official explained that "managed care put the kybosh on stays so the local hospitals were more willing to take state hospital patients. Before that there had been a two tiered system. This broke down some of those barriers. The feeling of the local hospital administrators was that $200 a day was better than nothing. Also, police were trained to bring patients to hospital emergency rooms and not take them to state hospitals."

So, according to a DMH administrator, hospital emergency rooms became "big collectors" of the mentally ill. The ER's were "told, instructed, and encouraged" to accept psychiatric patients. One reason for this was that state hospitals did not want to deal with medical emergencies. The state hospitals wanted patients medically cleared before they saw them. So, the state hospital urged the community to "try anywhere else first."

During this period the state was also economizing. The state legislature passed a bill to promote early retirement throughout the state government. It is estimated that in 2002 half of all middle management employees in DMH retired. One administrator at Elgin State Hospital commented that "the system collapsed. Some smaller facilities were gutted. Elgin went from a bustling beehive to a ghost town."

Since 2003 all state facilities have been cut further. It is estimated that the department's staff has been reduced by 20 percent. Tinley Park Mental Health Center (hospital), which covers Chicago's south side and the south suburbs, is slated to close. The Illinois Hospital Association fears that the closing of Tinley Park will reduce the overall financial support available for mental health services. That is, there will be fewer funds available to hospitals and community mental health centers than are currently being allocated to the Tinley Park hospital (2005: 3). The state now has nine hospitals. But after Tinley Park closes, it is believed that Chicago-Read will also close. Therefore, all Chicago patients will be brought to Madden Mental Health Center. Also, the state is shifting from a grant program to a fee for service model. It is hoped that this will allow more billing of federal agencies, and therefore, the recovery of more federal money.[5] The transition to a fee for service system will take at least two to three years. The result of all this is that the state role in mental health will shrink (see: Graham, 2006).

---

5. The department hopes to recover money from the Federal government's Medicaid program. Medicaid is a means-tested, federal-state, individual entitlement program in which states voluntarily participate. If they do, they receive federal matching funds of 50-90% of the cost of care for specified groups of people. The federal match rate depends on the per capita income in the state in comparison to the national per capita income. Illinois, as a wealthier state, receives a 50 percent match. To obtain matching funds, states must offer basic benefits (medical services) to specific categories of people. The states can also offer optional services to other needy groups and receive matching federal funds.

   To receive matching federal funds, states must offer basic services to "categorically needy" populations such as low-income families with children, Supplemental Security Income (SSI) recipients, Medicaid-eligible pregnant women and infants, some low income children, and some Medicare beneficiaries. Some of the services these individuals must receive are:

   a) inpatient and outpatient hospital services,
   b) physician services,
   c) nursing facility services for adults 21 and over.

In 1997 the Department of Mental Health was merged into the Department of Human Services along with other state social service agencies. The department now runs Comprehensive Community Service Networks (CCSN) (see: Figure 1). Each network administers a state hospital and purchases community based services in the area. Overall, the department purchases care from 162 local agencies. In the state there are also seven private psychiatric hospitals and 34 general hospitals with psychiatric units (Illinois Department of Human Services, Division of Mental Health, 2005a: 16-17).

The network director oversees all mental health services in the region. This includes "core services" such as acute care, outpatient services, inpatient care, and rehabilitation. All these services are premised on the Supreme Court's ruling in Olmstead vs. L.C. in 1999. This ruling held that unjustified institutionalization of people with disabilities is a form of discrimination under the Americans with Disabilities Act (ADA). Thus, individuals should live in the least restrictive environment. That is, not in state hospitals but in the community.[6] Therefore, outpatient services are stressed. As a result of this, admissions to state hospitals have fallen from 21,393 in fiscal year 1987 to 8,844 in fiscal year 2004. One community provider asked: "By limiting admissions are they just providing an excuse for hospital closure. And, is the money saved going back into mental health? Or, is the money that is being saved to bail out the state?" One DMH official commented that "there are serious budget pressures from the governor's office. This is requiring belt-tightening." The length of stay for a patient in a state hospital in fiscal year 2004 has dropped to 14 days. Also, many state hospitals have a census of less than 100. The largest is under 200 (Parker and Dennison, 2005).

Federal matching funds are available for optional services such as:

  a) clinic services,
  b) nursing facilities for individuals under age 21,
  c) intermediate care facilities for the mentally retarded,
  d) prescription drugs,
  e) case-management for the mentally ill,
  f) adult day care services.

Mental health services provided in a clinic or rehabilitation facility are part of these optional services. However, Institutions for Mental Disease (IMD's) for persons 21 to 65 are not covered. (Post, 2001).

6. Munertz and Geller (1993) argue that "in the community" has come to mean any living arrangement that is not in the state hospital. However, they ask: Are mentally ill people in jail living "in the community" and "in the least restrictive environment"?

Figure 1
DHS Regions

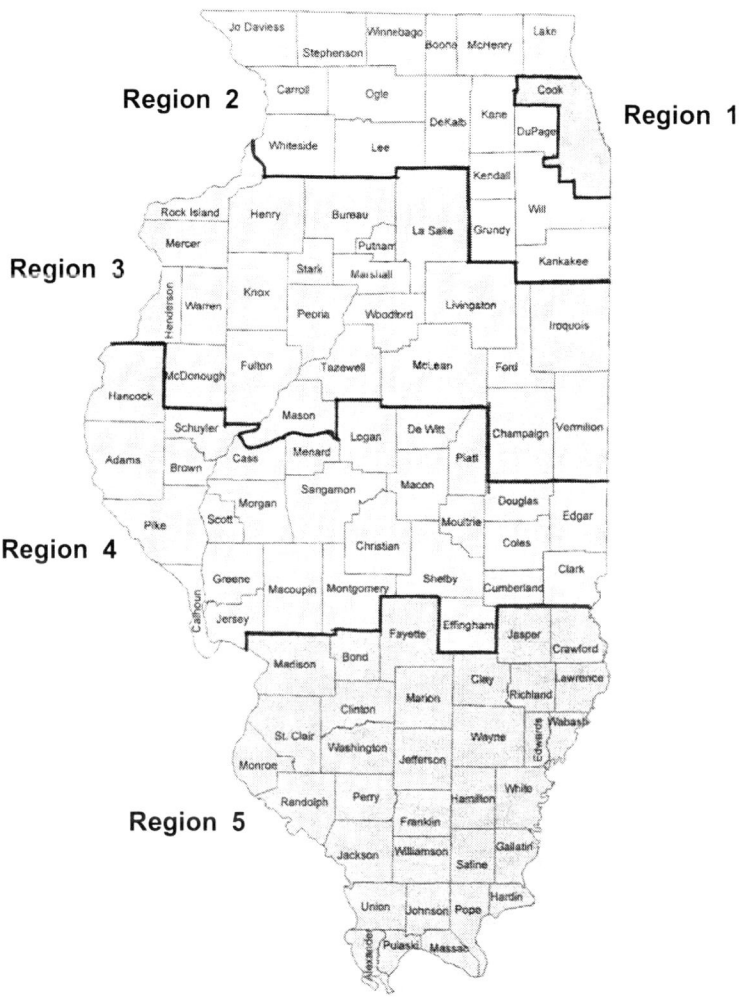

(Illinois Department of Human Services, 2009)

The transition from a grant system to a fee for service system has also created problems. For example, traditionally the state funded agencies via grants. These grants had a "contract maximum" as a ceiling to control costs. Under a fee for service system federal entitlement rules require eligibility determination, proactive contract monitoring, service authorizations, and claims audits. At this time the state is not prepared to do this. According to a department funded consultants report, the providers determine eligibility (need) and determine the target population. The department does not enforce a policy of serving those most at risk. And providers have "very liberal and highly divergent interpretations of medical necessity" (Parker and Dennison, 2005: 10-11). The department itself admits that "Illinois' mental health providers have established idiosyncratic patterns of services and accessibility" (Illinois Department of Human Services, Division of Mental Health, 2005a: 52). Agencies

have been required to have independent financial audits. However, audits and service reporting for community agencies was traditionally done by the contract division after the year
ended. Therefore, accountants, and not mental health professionals, have analyzed the agencies
functioning and priorities "after the fact."

Under the new fee for services system the department must define a consumer benefit
package. It has not yet done so. Also, the department will have to fundamental change from
a funder to a purchaser of services. This would mean shifting its funding from agency grants
to a purchaser of services that follows the consumer. The department must also develop and
implement "evidence based practices" which have proven success.[7] Overall, the consultants
report concluded that "target and eligible population definitions are broad, not uniformly
applied, not audited or reviewed, and there is extremely low penetration in target
population[s]" (Parker and Dennison, 2005: 65-66).

In its change over to a fee for service system the department must ask:

a.) Who do you pay for? (Who is eligible to receive benefits?)[8]
b.) What do you pay for? (What types, standards, and amounts of service do they
   wish to purchase?)
c.) How do you pay for it? (What is the funding source, unit of service, and payment method to be employed?)
d.) How do you determine when to pay? (What are the circumstances of necessity
   [medical or social], consumer choice, and duration of services?)
e.) How are you, and the consumer, sure that you have received what you paid for?
   (What techniques of monitoring of compliance with service requirements, rules,
   standards, quality indicators and outcomes are to be employed?) (Parker and
   Dennison, 2005: 4; see also: Bachrach, 1976: 11).

The department has been unwilling to specify these criteria since the 1970s. Will it be
able to do so now?

Also, the department had originally planned to transition to a fee for service system in a
year. It is now obvious it will take several years to implement the new system. The driving
force to implement this new system was to capture more federal dollars. In fiscal 2005 the
department received $64.5 million in Federal funding (Federal Financial Participation—
FFP) (Illinois Department of Human Services, Division of Mental Health, 2004, 2005a:

---

7. The Institute of Medicine (2006) has pointed out that there is a "quality chasm" in mental
health and substance abuse treatment. This is because treatment in these areas is not based upon the
clinical evidence. Therefore, proven "evidence based practices" should be promoted in these areas.
Evidence based practices such as supported employment and assertive community treatment (ACT)
have also been promoted by various agencies and advocates (National Association of State Mental
Health Program Directors Research Institute, 2004; see also: Wing and Morris, 1981).

8. Federal Rule 132 requires the state to define the services it will pay for. Then the Federal
government will match those funds if they fall within its guidelines.

100, 139, 182-3). It hoped to quickly increase this amount by $25 million. This now appears to be unrealistic.

Further, planning for services is difficult because of insufficient statistical information. For example, the department lacks information on most individuals treated in general hospital psychiatric inpatient units, their outpatient services, and persons served in nursing homes (see: Kiesler and Sibulkin, 1987: 220). Also, the department does not routinely receive information from other state agencies that provide or purchase mental health services. Therefore, the department has concluded that "we do not currently have outcome data that would enable us to know where the system is working and where it is not" (Illinois Department of Human Services, Division of Mental Health, 2005a: 74, 77, 87). This is a particularly troubling problem for the 15,000 residents of nursing homes with psychiatric diagnoses (Illinois Department of Human Services, Division of Mental Health, 2005a: 34, 37, 44, 112).

Also, by its own admission, the department's services have been uneven. For example, in its fiscal year 2006 mental health block grant application the department, indirectly, notes deficiencies in rural, Assertive Community Treatment teams (ACT), employment, homeless, forensic, and long-term care services (Illinois Department of Human Services, Division of Mental Health, 2005b). For example, seventy-six counties in rural Illinois had a census of about 1.5 million in 2000. At a prevalence rate of 5.4 percent it is estimated that about 81,500 individuals are mentally ill in these counties. However, in fiscal year 2005 only about 28,500 individuals received services. The department's consultant concluded that the "data indicates considerable variation and inequity in service provision and availability by county and region" (Parker and Dennison, 2005b: 67; Illinois Department of Human Services, Division of Mental Health, 2005a: 70-73, 87-118). And a DMH administrator admitted that he did not know the amount of penetration of services given to target populations. The primary barrier to such services appeared to be transportation.

Assertive Community Treatment (ACT) teams have proven very successful in providing 24 hour a day services to the mentally ill. Illinois funds 52 ACT teams. The Chicago area has 8 ACT teams, six more teams are planned. They serve 2,952 individuals. However, this is a tiny percentage of the seriously mentally ill in Illinois (Illinois Department of Human Services, Division of Mental Health, 2005b).

Employment appears to be another problem. At intake mentally ill individual's employment rates are about 20 percent. However, vocational placement is only about 3 percent. Further, the Department of Rehabilitation Services (DORS) accepted only 25 percent of all referrals for employment training and assistance from community mental health agencies. And from this group only 11 percent achieved employment (Illinois Department of Human Services, Division of Mental Health, 2005b).

Also, it is estimated that there were over 55,000 homeless individuals in Illinois in fiscal 1992. This number dropped to about 26,900 in fiscal 2004. However, the number of shelter nights for individuals has been increasing. In fiscal 2004 it was 1,738,381. Mental illness is the most common disability in this group (6 percent). The racial makeup of the homeless was 57 percent African American, 29 percent white, and 11 percent Latino. The state received a $10 million grant for the creation of an Access to Community Care and Effective Services Program (ACCESS). The grant ended in 1999. The ACT teams that were funded through this program enrolled 800 homeless mentally ill persons. When the Federal grant expired the program was continued with state funding. However, the program reached only a small percentage of the mentally ill homeless. Overall, 6,190 homeless mentally ill individuals received DMH funded services in fiscal year 2005. This, too, is a small percentage of the homeless population (Illinois Department of Human Services, Division of Mental Health, 2005b).

Treating the forensic population is also a problem. Only 1 percent of persons with mental illness seen at DMH funded providers were forensic outpatients. And about 2 percent had a correctional history. However, the number of mentally ill in jails is increasing. We may conclude from this that few mental health facilities are willing to serve (potentially violent) ex-offenders (Illinois Department of Human Services, Division of Mental Health, 2005b; see also: Steadman, McCarty, and Morrissey, 1989: 142).

Typical of the attitude of most mental health professionals towards such individuals was a story an intern told me: "I took a seminar on how to handle violent patients during my training at the hospital. The seminar was attended by doctors, nurses, social workers, and security officers. The seminar covered aggression, verbal talk-downs, the use of seclusion, the application of leather restraints, and patients' rights. However, early in the program the instructor told us about a nurse who was attacked by a patient. The patient grabbed a handful of her hair and pulled it out. Her scalp went along with it. The nurse had to have surgery in order to place skin grafts on her head to replace the scalp. Because of her injury she was forced to retire. As the instructor told the story everyone's eyes opened wide. And you could see their expression saying, 'I didn't sign up for this!' After the program ended the only part of the seminar the staff talked about was that story."

Lastly, long term care facilities have often been called the "new back wards." Just as in the 1970s no one agency is responsible for the monitoring of those services. For example, the Illinois Department of Public Health (DPH) is responsible for the licensing of nursing facilities. The Department of Healthcare and Family Services (DHFS), formerly The Department of Public Aid, oversees Medicaid funding. And DMH provides program oversight. This includes the mental health pre-admission screening (PAS/MH) that is required by federal statute. The number of individuals in these institutions is expected to grow. Currently, there are 1.6 million persons over the age of 60 in Illinois. It is estimated that 15 to 20 percent of these individuals experience symptoms of mental illness and may need to be institutionalized (Illinois Department of Human Services, Division of Mental Health, 2005a: 20; Miller, 1987: 233-7).

7. New Programs

In our initial study psychiatric treatment by the Illinois Department of Mental Health was our focus. Since that time the department has improved. However, since then treatment has shifted to the community. Services and funding, however, have not followed. Therefore, in order to understand the current system we must explore the plight of patients adrift in the community.

For example, Holcolm and Ahr (1988) argue that the criminal justice system has replaced state hospitals as agents of social control. This is particularly true for young, violent individuals with psychiatric disorders. For example, in 1994 the U.S. had approximately

5.2 million adults under correctional supervision. This included 3 million individuals on probation, 690,159 on parole, 483,717 in jail, and 991,612 in prison (Bureau of Justice Statistics, 1996).

The San Diego County Jail reported that in 1995 14 percent of its 4,572 male inmates and 25 percent of its female inmates received psychotropic medication. The assistant sheriff described the jail as "the bottom-line mental health provider in the county" (Torrey, 1995).

King County Jail in Seattle, Washington, Travis County Jail in Austin, Texas, and Dade County Jail in Miami, Florida all reported that they were the largest mental health provider in their counties. The Los Angeles County Jail treated 3,300 of its 21,000 inmates for mental illness. This made it the largest mental institution in the country. In fact, there may be twice as many mentally ill individuals in jails and prisons today than in mental hospitals (Torrey, 1995; see also: Kagan, 1990).

In order to examine this issue further, the chief psychologist at Cermak Hospital (Cook County Jail) was interviewed in 2004. He explained that his facility is the largest mental health facility in the state and he emphasized that the City of Chicago and the State of Illinois do not provide any funds for mental health services in the jail. "Its all county money!"

The jail's hospital is run by the Cook County Bureau of Health Care Services. The jail screens 325 new admissions each day. That is over 100,000 new inmates per year. A medical and psychiatric screening is conducted for each new inmate. If necessary, a second interview is conducted. If a male inmate who is mentally ill is found to be suicidal or assaultive they are placed on a 50 bed acute care unit. If a male inmate suffers from a mood disorder or is psychotic they are usually placed in a "sub-acute" (intermediate care) dorm (A-tier). If a male inmate is believed to have antisocial or borderline personality disorders they are placed on a third unit (B-tier) (Haywood and Thomas, 1997: see also: Lamberg, 2004; Hayes, 1998). In 2000 18,413 days of patient care were given to male inmates on Cermak's acute care unit (April 2001 Biennial Report, 2001). The acute care female unit contains 16 beds and provided 15,416 patient days of treatment in 2001. In 1981 there were 240 women in the jail, in 2001 there were 1400. The male residential unit had 282 beds and had 103,092 patient days of treatment. In June, 2000 data was compiled for 20 days on the 5,406 inmates that entered the jail. Of these, 85 percent were male and 15 percent were female. Blacks comprised 68 percent, Hispanics 15 percent, and whites 15 percent (April 2001 Biennial Report, 2001).

The chief psychologist at that jail stated that his facility functioned like a hospital emergency room. He felt his screening process was very accurate. And if medical or psychiatric treatment was needed it could be given within the jail's medical facility. The hospital was open 24 hours a day, 7 days a week. Crisis intervention services were available at all times and a psychiatrist was on staff until 9pm daily.

In 1981 the jail had a daily population of 3,200 inmates. The population has now risen to 10,000 inmates on any given day. The chief psychologist estimated that 10 to 16 percent of the inmates were mentally ill. To accommodate this increase the number of acute psychiatric beds rose to 82 in 2004. Sixty-two of these were for males and 22 were for females. The intermediate care unit now has 300 male beds and 120 female beds. There are also 400 to 450 inmates receiving "ambulatory care" (psychoactive medication). Currently, the mental health treatment staff consists of 40 B.A level mental health specialists ("psychiatric technicians"), nurses, psychologists, and physicians (see: Institute of Medicine, 2006: 43-4)

Five to eight technicians conduct the initial and secondary screenings. Each initial screening takes 5 to 10 minutes. The chief psychologist believed that such screening is effective since "we only have 1 or 2 suicides a year, L.A. County Jail has 35" (see: Freeman and Alaimo 2001; Hayes, 1998)

Although there are 1,000 psychiatric patients at the jail at any one time, there is only one licensed social worker on staff. She attempts to link inmates to community mental health services. She only has time to assist 70 inmates per month. However about 9,000 inmates are released per month.

Most mentally ill inmates receive two weeks of medication upon release. Some community mental health agencies come in to the jail to arrange for services for the inmates upon release. Other agencies make telephone contact with the inmates. However, the chief psychologist did not know how many released inmates actually received medication or counseling after release. And he did not know how many former inmates became homeless (see: Steadman and Veysey, 1997: 5).

Recidivism is a major problem among mentally ill inmates. More than half of all mentally ill inmates report three or more prior incarcerations. Further, the Pennsylvania Department of Corrections estimates that it costs $140 a day to incarcerate a mentally inmate, whereas it only costs $80 a day to house an average inmate. And, at New York's Rikers Island Correctional Facility the average stay for all prisoners was 42 days. However, the average stay for a prisoner with mental illness was 215 days (Goin, 2004).

In order to reduce such recidivism Cook County launched a pilot Mental Health Court in 2004. The chief psychologist at the jail explained that the program was created in a manner so that no new funds were needed to maintain the program. In order to facilitate this the state legislature passed a law that allowed Cermak Health Services to access the Illinois Department of Mental Health's records by computer. This allowed the hospital to identify inmates who already were being treated by DMH; that is, they were "open cases." This was done so that the Department of Mental Health would have "no new work" (i.e., no new patients or costs) when the inmates needed service while on probation from the court. In 2005 a $10 fee was added to the fine of every individual convicted in Cook County to finance the mental health court. It is estimated that this will bring in $300,000 a year (Ciohajlo, 2005).

Participation in the mental health court is available only to defendants with a nonviolent felony. If the offense is probationable and the defendant consents to participate in the program they then undergo an assessment. They are then arraigned and their case is assigned to the Mental Health Court. The case is then sent to one of the two judges on the Mental Health Court. Once each case is assigned the judge, states attorney (prosecutor), and public defender met to formulate a treatment program. If the defendant agrees to the treatment program they plead guilty and receive probation. They then begin receiving mental health services. Their progress is monitored by the mental health unit of the court's Adult Probation Department and caseworkers from the TASC agency (Treatment Alternatives for Safer Communities). The program began with 50 inmates who resided in the Department of Mental Health's metro-west area (Chicago's west side and the western suburbs) (Christian 1999; Mental Health Court Ready to Handle Cases, 2004; Kuczka, 2004; Long, 2005; Higgins, 2004; Coen, 2002, 2004; Keeshan, 2008).

The jails chief psychologist pointed out that the program was established for individuals with chronic and persistent mental illness. He noted that some of these individuals had been arrested over 100 times and had been incarcerated 30 to 50 times. The idea of the court was that the probationer would receive treatment and be closely monitored through case management and not merely be shunted in to a poorly supervised diversion program. The Mental Health Court was modeled on drug courts that take a treatment approach.

The treatment process begins when the individual pleads guilty and is put on probation. The TASC caseworker helps to secure day to day services such as medication and housing. In the first year 65 individuals were referred to the program. Initially, 15 males and 16 females were accepted. The males had an average of 5.5 felony arrests each and the women had numerous arrests for prostitution. These individuals were usually given 2 years of probation. This is longer than most other individuals convicted of similar crimes. This was done in order to guarantee a long period of services. However, in an interview the court administrator noted that this is often difficult to provide services because "the community mental health centers don't want them."

Once the mental health court began it was realized that their probationers needed more intensive services than they had anticipated. As a result of this the Mental Health Court staff decided to reduce the number of inmates they would accept to 25. However, the Mental Health Court was recently promised $1.2 million over the next three years from the Federal government. This will allow them to increase the number of individuals in the program to between 80 and 90. Eventually, they would like to expand the number on probation to 300 individuals (Coen, 2005, 2006).

In an interview with a supervisor in the mental health probation unit he explained that his unit has 11 officers and each handles 45 clients. The average parole officer, however, has 120 to 150 individuals in their caseload. The mental health probation officers handle persons convicted of misdemeanors, as well as, felonies. The charges these individuals have been convicted of range from disorderly conduct to murder. Their probation ranges from one to five years. Most parole officers see their role as a "cop." However, the mental health unit parole officers see their job as "clinical case management." That is, they help their probationers receive medication, substance abuse treatment, and other services through community agencies. "We are like an ACT [assertive community treatment] team with a high case load," he explained. He said their goal is to make sure that each parolee fulfills their mandated treatment. By doing this they hope to keep them out of the hospital.

They work with TASC case workers as partners. "TASC does the majority of the work," the supervisor noted, "and we verify that treatment is occurring." They often work with TASC caseworkers as a crisis intervention team. They also help to secure medication, housing, or hospitalization for the parolee. However, he estimated that more than 50 percent of the unit's parolees are homeless and a small percentage of them simply disappear. In spite of this, most parolees successfully complete their probation.

The unit receives referrals from the criminal courts, fellow probation officers, and, now, the Mental Health Court. They have received 1,000 such referrals since 2001. They screen them and then take on individuals who are seriously and chronically mentally ill. Most of the parolees are schizophrenic or have mood disorders. In supervising these probationers the parole officers try to balance their mental health and police roles. "However," the unit's supervisor pointed out that "we are probation officers, first." And if someone breaks the law or violates their probation "we don't look the other way." In their work they try to focus on the criminogenic factors that created the parolee's problem. That is why they try to help the probationers cope with drugs, peer pressure, or a lack of structure in their lives. Generally, they attempt to manage the parolees' symptoms with medication and maintain their stability.

A TASC supervisor explained that his assignment from the Mental Health Court was case management. TASC had been created in the 1970s to conduct substance abuse assessment and case management for the criminal justice system. It began its work with the drug court and now evaluate individuals from the Mental Health Court, as well. He explained that the Mental Health and drug courts were not typical criminal courts that merely meted out punishment. Instead, they were "problem solving courts."

In screening for the Mental Health Court, TASC uses a 22 page assessment tool and they do face-to-face interviews. They also secure consent from the individual to examine their mental health records. And they talk to family members and various treatment providers. However, TASC itself, does not provide any treatment. They also do not diagnose an individual. Instead, their job is to collect information and write "a history." Based on that history they produce a "release plan"

The TASC supervisor pointed out that many of the individuals he assesses have no support networks. So, TASC workers attempt to create such support and find the probationer stable housing. In order to do this they help them acquire identification and apply for Social Security and Medicaid. The TASC supervisor pointed out that since most of the parolees he works with are "street people" they commit "lifestyle crimes" such as theft or prostitution in order to survive. Although they have been arrested for felonies "most are not dangerous." In fact, they are more likely to be the victims of crime rather than the offenders. The parolees tend to have cyclical arrest records based upon the ups and downs of their lives. They often have multiple arrests. Thirty to seventy arrests was not uncommon. One parolee had 147 arrests. He noted that these individuals have been arrested so often that even though their crimes might not be serious they often face long prison time.

He concluded by explaining that there are 107 mental health courts in the U.S. However, the courts varied greatly in their functioning since there is no accepted definition of what is a mental health court. Most of these courts deal with individuals who have committed misdemeanors. Chicago's mental health court, however, is only the fourth in the country to handle felony cases (see: Fields, 2006). However, he pointed out that most of the individuals he dealt with from the Mental Health Court were not typical criminals. Instead, they were "mentally ill people with nowhere to go. So, they're on the street. And, they commit 'street crimes'." Initially, the Mental Health Court is functioning in only two courtrooms. And its initial caseload is drawn from a narrow range of cases. That is, individuals who have committed victimless crimes which are non-violent and non-sexual. However, in the future he hopes the program will expand to include all mentally ill defendants and produce "systemic change."

Thresholds, the premier social service agency in the city, has a number of programs that attempt to assist the mentally ill. One of these is the Short-Term Linkage Case Management Program. This program is designed to work with the Cook County Jail staff in order to connect inmates to their former community mental health providers. They also provide brief services for everyone discharged from a state hospital. Their ACCESS program employs Assertive Community Treatment to provide long-term, flexible support to the homeless or those at risk of becoming homeless. This program consists of six-person teams who serve up to 100 clients per year. Their Mobile Assessment Unit (MAU) actively seeks out individuals on the street who are homeless. It also receives referrals from shelters, the police, or community agencies. The program has two six-person teams that cover the city. The agency also has a Safe Haven program. This is a long-term residential service for the homeless who are treatment resistant and cannot cope with a structured program (Bianchi and Fallon, 2001).

One Thresholds program that has been particularly successful is their jail program. Here, Assertive Community Treatment (ACT) teams work with mentally ill inmates to secure housing, teach budgeting, and assist with medication management. Special emphasis is placed on the reasons for past treatment failure. The clients ("members") receive services for as long as they are needed. Workers even make daily visits, if necessary (Helping the Mentally Ill Break the Cycle of Jail and Homelessness, 2001; Lydersen, 2000).

The program has produced a reduction in jail time and hospital stays for its clients of 80 to 90 percent. This has created savings of $1 million for the state hospitals and more than $250,000 for Cook County Jail. These savings are created because it costs $70 a day to incarcerate an individual in Cook County Jail but only $26 a day to treat them in the community. In the first 2 years of the program 29 individuals received services. Before entering the program these individuals had 2,153 days of hospitalization. After entering the program they had only 321 days of hospitalization. This was over an 85 percent reduction and a savings of $916,000. Incarcerations also fell dramatically. For the first 30 people to complete one year in the program their days in jail fell from 2,741 in the previous year to 489 during the year of the program. This was over an 82 percent decrease and saved $157,640. For the 13 individuals who had completed two years in the program their results were equally dramatic. In the two years prior to the program they had spent 1,546 days in jail. However, for the two years they were in the program this fell to 213 days in jail. This was an 86 percent decrease and a savings of $93,310 (Innovative Aftercare Program Slashes Jail, Hospital Stays, 2001).[9]

One example of a client in the program was a 30-year-old male. He had a total of 3,958 days of public hospitalization and 561 days of jail confinement before he joined the program. At $400 a day the hospital stays totaled over $1.5 million. At $70 a day the jail time totaled over $39,000. During the client's three years in the program there were no hospital or jail days. The program's cost over 3 years was $36,000 (The Cost of Non-Treatment, n.d.; see also: Hafemeister and Petrila, 1994).

In an interview the director of the jail program explained that the mentally ill "make judges nuts." The judges do not know what to do with these individuals. If they are released, most programs will not take them because they are difficult, sometimes violent, and the agencies are concerned about liability (see: Lamb, 1982). He pointed out that many of

---

9. Supportive housing for a year costs $10,000 to $12,000 a year, a homeless shelter costs $25,000, prison costs $47,000, and a mental hospital costs $160,000 for a year (Zerger, 2002:14).

these persons have 2 inch thick files at the jail. In the past they were released without any medication from the jail. Now, if a doctor is available, they receive a two week supply.

The Thresholds jail program tries to deal with the most difficult cases. One individual they worked with had 134 arrests and a 26 inch hospital record. He had no housing and "he was a pain." He had set a fire, stolen a bed, and stabbed his mother. But, the jail program director explained that by treating this person society could save money and help everyone. Their ACT teams have low client per worker ratios and they can provide intensive services. They focus on "aftercare." That is, the workers help to secure housing and income (such as Supplementary Security Income-SSI). However, Medicaid has proven to be a stumbling block because of the application process (see: Morrissey, 1999, Warren, 1973).

The program's director explained his approach: "You have to go after these people" in order to avoid the court, jail, hospital, agency circuit. He has found that there was no coordination between them. But, "if everyone talked to each other, I could fire myself." One of the major problems the program's clients face is securing income. The director explained that "SSI is supposed to take 90 days. But, in actuality, it is often six months to decide eligibility. And then they often turn you down." However, "our success rate is 84 percent, but it sometimes takes several levels of appeals to succeed." After applying for SSI then they help the client apply for Medicaid. "Thresholds pays up front" for these individuals and "then recovers later." He explained that SSI cuts these people off when they go to jail. After they are released Thresholds has to help them get birth certificates and other documentation in order to reapply (see: Post, 2001: 17).

Most social programs "cream" their clients in order to succeed. That is, they take the "cream of the crop" or "skim the cream off the top." However, the jail program does just the opposite. The program's director explained that his target population is not just the "run-of-the-mill homeless." Instead, they are recidivists. And he is "dogged" in pursuit of these individuals. For example, the more clothing a person wears in the summer the more out of touch with reality they are likely to be. So he looks for "people with the most jackets on" and with "some investment" he can help these people. For example, he explained that "a nursing home costs $34,000 a year, jail cost $25,000 to $26,000 a year. If I can get them SSI for $564 a month I can help them." But, when you find a mentally ill person with a long criminal history "you must be decisive and act *now* to help them."

One social service executive said that Thresholds had "thrilling compassion. They are client-centered and they will teach you how to do it" (see: Isaac and Armat, 1990: 287-308). The jail program is highly regarded. A mental health probation supervisor praised their "outreach, intensity, knowledge, and organization." And a social service executive stated that the program had produced "compelling results with next to nothing."

In 2000, the program had a budget of $691,645. The Illinois Department of Mental Health provided $546,305 of this amount. The remainder came from private donations.[10] In the ensuing six years the budget has remained flat. When the program director was asked

---

10. Thresholds budget for 2005 was approximately $48 million. Various government agencies provided approximately $36.4 million of this amount. The Illinois Department of Mental Health contributed $26 million (Thresholds, 2005: 21).

why such a successful program had not expanded, he commented: "There's no money. It's not a priority for DMH. They have no incentive to reach in to the jail." And one DMH official observed: "Recidivism is a problem in criminal justice, not mental health."

Another program to help the mentally ill is the newly created Critical Incident Teams (CIT) within the Chicago Police Department. The program is based on the "Memphis model" for handling the mentally ill. The original program was developed in Memphis, Tennessee after the killing of a mentally ill individual by the police in 1987. The victim was black and the officers were white. After the incident there was an outcry by the black community. In order to avoid another such incident the mayor organized a community task force to devise a program to avoid future incidents. The task force created a 40 hour training program for the police. The goals of the program were to provide immediate response and management for situations involving the mentally ill, to prevent injury to the citizen or the officer, and to find appropriate care for the individual. The department trained 213 of its 900 patrol officers in the program. The program involved training in the recognition of mental illness, instruction on psychoactive medication, verbal de-escalation skills, and defensive weapons training. The program also encouraged the police to bring the mental ill to the hospital and not to the jail (Vickers 2000; Zdanowicz 2001a, 2001b).

In an interview the director of Chicago Police Department's CIT program explained that the Chicago program was based on a crisis intervention model, much like the Memphis system. However, Chicago planned to train officers in every district in the city over the next two years and create a "Chicago model." In this way 20 percent of all the officers in the city could be trained. He explained that the Chicago police culture was initially resistant to the idea. Some said that it would be impossible to train 20 percent of a big city police force. However, he felt that this was an "urban myth." Most cities have a more centralized model for handling mentally ill individuals. For example, New York City receives 70,000 calls to the police each year regarding mentally ill individuals involved in disturbances. However, less than 10 percent are handled by specially trained units (Segall, 2004; see also: Pang, 2004; Nevola, 2002; Wronski, 2001; Kifner and Cooper, 1999; Sachs, 1999; Barnes and Sachs, 1999; Wilgoren, 1999; Bernstein, 1999b).

It is envisioned that the Chicago police will act as gatekeepers for the mental health system. The officers will be trained in the signs and symptoms of mental illness, verbal de-escalation techniques, and the availability of viable alternatives to arrest. There will be an initial 40 hours of instruction. Later, they will be 24 to 30 hours of additional training in the use of less-than-lethal weapons. The initial training will emphasize "good verbal de-escalation techniques." The program director noted that the training will emphasize "people skills" because "as long as you're talking, you're not going to get hurt." Later, there will be training with tasers, shotguns employing bean bags rounds, and nets. The program director hopes to train 40 officers per district (five officers and one sergeant per team) so that there will always be CIT officers on duty. The program director believes that about 20 percent of the officers who have volunteered for the program have a family member who is mentally ill. And, most of the officers in the program are college graduates. He sees the program as a win-win situation. If it works, the community will be pleased, incarcerations will go down, diversions from the criminal justice system will go up, and officer injuries will be reduced. And if they are able to de-escalate dangerous situations officers will not be forced to call the HBT unit (the Hostage, Barricade, and Terrorism unit) with their "heavy weapons."

8. Valley View Jail

Critics of mental policy have complained that jails and prisons have become America's new mental hospitals. For example, the Los Angeles County jail has become the largest mental institution in the country (Torrey, 1995). And Cook County Jail is the largest mental health facility in Illinois.

In order to appreciate the single most important gap in service provided by the Illinois Department of Mental Health an observational study was conducted at a suburban-area Chicago jail in 2005 (Cook County Jail was not available as a research site). The county, "Valley View" is one of the five "collar counties" surrounding Chicago.[11] The county is 500 square miles and has approximately 479,500 residents. In 2003 there were 1,200 violent index crimes (murder, criminal sexual assault, robbery, aggravated assault, burglary, theft, theft of motor vehicle, and arson) in the country. This rate was about 50 percent higher than in the other suburban counties. There were 11,000 property crimes. This was about 15 percent higher than neighboring suburban counties. There were about 2,300 arrests for violent and non-violent index crimes in 2003. Roughly 20 percent of these were for violent crimes and about 80 percent of the violent crimes were for aggravated assault. About 90 percent of all property crimes were for theft. There were over 2,100 drug arrests in 2003. The drug arrest rate was 5 to 10 percent higher than in neighboring suburban counties. There were also 8,000 misdemeanor arrests in 2003. Many of those who were arrested by local police departments posted bond and were released. However, those adults that did not post bail were taken to the Valley View Adult Correctional Facility (County Jail). The jail is one of 91 in the state. Over the last decade its average daily population (ADP) has increased from 400 to 500 inmates. However, because of overcrowding at the jail 80 to 150 inmates are housed in other county jails at any one time and are paid for by contract. In 2003 about 90 percent of the population of the jail were pretrial detainees.[12]

A study was conducted at Valley View County Jail in order to examine its screening of the mentally ill. The research at the jail consisted of a one month observational study. The first week was spent in Central Receiving and Transportation ("booking"). For the following three weeks prisoners were observed in booking and then followed to the medical unit and observed during their medical and mental health screening. The rationale for a spending week in booking was to see if the booking officers (all sworn sheriff's deputies) "picked up" mentally ill offenders and treated them any differently than other prisoners. The medical staff had stated that they had given "some training" in mental health to the booking officers (see: Severson, 2005; Gerson and Bassuk, 1980; Gunn and Taylor, 1993; Stefan, 2006).

The booking officers are responsible for the intake and release of all inmates for adult corrections. The booking office is staffed by twenty officers on rotating shifts, four ser-

---

11. In this section and the next pseudonyms will be used for the county jail, agencies, programs, and individuals in order to protect their privacy. Also, the individual cases cited will be slightly fictionalized to protect the privacy of those individuals.

12. The population data was drawn from the U.S. census. The crime statistics were taken from the Illinois Criminal Justice Authority. The information from both sources was slightly fictionalized in order to maintain the confidentiality of the research site.

geants, and a lieutenant. The jails yearly report lists the duties of the booking officers as computerized booking, the taking of digital photos, digital fingerprinting, medical pre-screening, answering public and law enforcement telephone calls, responding to warrant requests, storage of inmate property, and release of inmates.

Booking officers also transport inmates to and from the courthouse, for medical appointments, and for writs and warrants. The officers are also responsible for transport into and out of the county. During fiscal year 2004, the officers transported about 118,000 inmates. In 2004, booking processed over 16,000 persons into and out of the jail.

The booking office is located in the basement of the jail facility. In order to enter a police officer must press a button on the call box near a ramp and request entry. A corrections officer then opens the entry sallyport door at the bottom of a ramp. The exit remains closed during this time. Only one of the two overhead doors can be opened at a time for security purposes.

Once the overhead door opens the squad car or van drives down the ramp and parks in front of the two large shatterproof windows of the booking office. The overhead door is then closed. The prisoners, all wearing handcuffs or shackles, are then unloaded while the booking officers observe the process. The prisoners and the officer are then buzzed in through a heavy metal door. Once that closes they are then buzzed in through a second door. The males are brought in to the booking office. The females are taken to another area of the jail to be processed. Once the booking officers take custody of the prisoners the arresting or transporting officers leave.

When the prisoners enter they are ordered to wait behind a red line near the windows. Their handcuffs or shackles are then removed. They are usually told to face the windows. Each individual is searched. Their belt and shoes are taken from them and each prisoner is placed in the first of two holding cells across from the booking desk. The holding cell is 10 feet by 12 feel. It has bars in the front and a bench around three walls. The cell has an exposed stainless steel toilet in the back. The toilet is not enclosed so that the prisoners can be watched at all times. The holding cell often holds 20 prisoners.

The booking office is a large 30 foot by 40 foot room. The paint is peeling from the ceilings and the facility looks "worn." (The sheriff hopes to build a new jail in the next few years.) The officers work behind a 40 foot long c-shaped desk. To begin the booking process an officer calls out the name of a prisoner. The holding cell door is opened. The prisoner then steps in to a small area between the two holding cells. When the holding cell door closes an interlock allows the outer door to open. The prisoner is then ordered to approach the booking desk. The prisoners are booked using a computerized booking system. However, one officer keeps a permanent record of each inmate by typing an index card on a manual typewriter and placing it in a small filing cabinet. One officer usually spends their entire shift typing these index cards.

Once the computerized booking is completed an officer takes the prisoner "in the back." There they are given a full body cavity search and are required to take a shower. They are given underwear and a green outfit to wear. Then they are digitally photographed. They are then issued a blanket, towel, socks, and toiletries. The prisoner is then placed in the second holding cell across from the booking desk.

Each inmate usually takes 40 to 60 minutes to process. If there are only a few prisoners, the group may only takes 2 or 3 hours to complete. However, if there are many prisoners, it may take 8 or 10 hours to finish the group.

While some prisoners are angry or upset when they are brought in most treat the booking process as routine. In the holding cells some prisoners boast of their sexual conquests or gang affiliations. However, most just talk quietly or sleep. Occasionally, a fight will break out among the inmates and the officers will have to enter the holding cell to subdue the inmates. Also, occasionally, the officers may believe a prisoner is suicidal or in an emotional crisis. They will then call the nurse to speak with the prisoner. During the research period no fights or mental health emergencies occurred in booking. Therefore, during the research period the mentally ill were handled no differently than other prisoners. However, occasionally an officer would lean over and whisper to the researcher, "This is one for you."

During the one month research period, 238 prisoners were observed in booking. The charges for the inmates were grouped by descriptive category (see: Table 5-1).

Table 5-1[13]
Charges

Type of Charge	Number	Percentage*
Driving under the influence (DUI)	14	6%
Drug possession	41	17%
Alcohol possession	3	1%
Traffic offenses	38	16%
Property crimes	21	9%
Other non-violent crimes	38	16%
Violent crime	50	21%
Weapons charges	6	3%
Sexual offenses	9	4%
Warrants	18	8%

Total: 238   100%
                    * rounded
(Table 5-1 is statistically significant to the .01 level.)

These offenses can be grouped under drug and alcohol offenses (including DUI) (24%), traffic offenses (16%), property and other non-violent crimes (25%), and violent crimes (including weapons and sexual offenses) (27%). Warrants (8%) could be issued for any

---

13. A chi-square (x2) test was applied to most tables. The chi-square test determines if the distribution in the table is a matter of chance (not statistically significant) or is not likely to be the product of chance (statistically significant). If the test was statistically significant it was measured at a 90 percent level of certainty (.10 level), a 95 percent level of certainty (.05 level), or a 99 percent level of certainty (.01 level).

offense. Therefore, we can assume that some of those are for violent crimes. Thus, we can estimate that about 30 percent of the offenses were for violent crimes.

The youngest inmates accepted at the jail are 17 years old. Younger inmates are housed in the county's juvenile detention facility. Of the 238 inmates observed age was available for 208. The inmate population was disproportionately young. Only 4 percent of the county's population was 17 to 19 years old. However, 16 percent of the inmates fell into this age group. Similarly, 20- to 29-year-olds were 14 percent of the county's population but comprised 34 percent of the inmates. The 30 to 39 and 40 to 49 age groupings were also overrepresented in the jail population. Overall, the 17 to 49 age group comprised 48 percent of the county's population but made up 95 percent of its inmates (see: Table 5-2A and 5-2B).

Table 5-2A
Age Distribution of Prisoners

Age	Number	Percentage*
17-19	34	16%
20-29	70	34%
30-39	53	25%
40-49	41	20%
50-59	8	4%
60-69	1	.5%
70-79	1	.5%
Total:	208	100%
		*rounded

Table 5-2B
County Population by Age

Age	Number	Percentage*
Under 17	140,000	29%
17-19	18,000	4%
20-29	67,000	14%
30-39	77,000	16%
40-49	72,500	15%
50-59	52,000	11%
60 and over	53,000	11%
Total:	479,500	100%
		*rounded

Teplin, et. al. (1996) conducted a study of mental health among female jail detainees at Cook County Jail. She interviewed 1,272 women and found that over 80 percent suffered from one or more lifetime psychiatric disorders. Jordan, et al. (1997) found higher rates of borderline personality disorder and mood disorder among female prisoners than the general population. Nationally, approximately 22 percent of those arrested were female in 1999 (Maguire and Pastore, 2001: 365). At the Valley View Jail female inmates constituted 14 percent of the inmate population (see: Table 5-3). However, my sample consisted of only 7 percent females. The reason for this was that Valley View County Jail's female inmates were not processed in booking. Instead, their intake processing occurred at another location in the jail at the same time as the males were being booked. Therefore, female inmates were underrepresented in my sample. However, since there were only 14 females in the sample they are combined with the males and simply listed as "inmates."

Table 5-3
Sex of Inmates

Sex		Number	Percentage*
Male		193	93%
Female		14	7%
	Total:	207	100%
			*rounded

(Table 5-3 is statistically significant at the .01 level.)

The race of the inmates was roughly equal (whites—36%, blacks—33%, Hispanics—31%). However, blacks and Hispanics are heavily overrepresented in the inmate population. That is because whites make up 71 percent of the county population. Blacks were only 5 percent and Hispanics (of all races) were 21 percent of the county population (see: Tables 5-4A and 5-4B).

Table 5-4A
Race of Inmates

Sex		Number	Percentage*
White		75	36%
Black		68	33%
Hispanic		64	31%
Asian		1	.5%
	Total:	208	100%
			*rounded

Table 5-4B
County Population by Race

Sex	Number	Percentage*
White	383,600	71%
Black	28,770	5%
Hispanic	115,080	21%
Asian	9,590	2%
Total:	537,040	100%

*rounded

Once all the inmates are processed they are lined up and walked to an elevator. An officer unlocks the elevator and the inmates file in. One or two officers accompany the inmates. The elevator then goes up to the ground level and the inmates file out. They form a line against a far wall across from a floor to ceiling gate. Beyond the gate is the control room. The control room is a large "box" at the intersection of the jail's hallways.b v Most doors, that is, most movement in the jail, is controlled as the control room remotely opens and closes the jail's gates.

Once the prisoners are lined up the gate is unlocked and the officer brings a prisoner list to the control officer. The prisoners are then walked single file down a long hallway towards the medical office. During this trip they must stay to the right of a red line on the floor. About half the time they are told to stop before they reach the medical office. They are told to place their blankets and towels on the far side of the hall and are ordered to face the wall with their hands at their sides. Then a correctional officer with a drug dog sniffs the blankets and towels. The dog handler then tells the inmates to remain still as he weaves the dog through the group. When he is finished the inmates pick up their blankets and towels and walk down the hall to the medical office. The researcher once asked an officer how often they find drugs during these searches. "Never," he replied, "we think the trustees are bringing it in."

The inmates are then led to a small holding cell next to the medical offices. They are told to sit on the benches and the door is locked.

The medical services are run by a private health contractor, the "Wesmont Corporation." While at the jail all inmates receive a health assessment. This includes a medical and psychiatric history, physical, mental, and dental assessment, and testing for communicable disease within 14 days of arrival. Sick call and urgent health care are available seven days a week, 24 hours a day. A consulting physician is available seven days a week, 24 hours a day. In fiscal year 2004 there were 13,000 nurse sick calls, 2,300 physician visits, 300 physicals, and 5,500 tuberculosis tests.

The corrections officers feel the contractor provides "pretty good care" for the prisoners. That is because the Westmont Corporation has brought in emergency medical technicians (EMT's) to assist the two nurses. The county plans to take over its own health care next year.

Other private medical contractors, however, have performed poorly in jails. At Rikers Island in New York City, and at state prisons throughout New York State, a firm called

Prison Health is alleged to have provided inadequate health care. Investigators found short staffing, underqualified or unavailable physicians, nurses' conducting procedures beyond their training, prescription drugs withheld, lost patient records, and unpunished employee misconduct. In spite of these failings, the corporation has 86 contracts in 28 states and treats 237,000 inmates. This is about 10 percent of the U.S. jail and prison population (Von Zielbauer, 2005b; see also: Cohen, 2006).

In 2001 Prison Health received a $254 million contract for health services at Rikers Island jail in New York City. At the jail as many as 25 percent of the 14,000 inmates have psychiatric illnesses. Investigators found that at the jail patient charts were missing, alerts about suicidal patients were lost or unheeded, and neither medical or correctional personnel were properly trained in preventing suicide. There was a rash of suicides ("hang ups") after Prison Health took over. This was partially due to the employment of unlicensed physicians, the shuffling of staff from jail to jail, a reduction in staff, and a large percentage of part-time mental health workers. One psychiatrist who worked at Rikers summed up the care as triage, buffeted by a sense of non-stop crisis. "The staff does the best they can," he said, "and what's left they sweep under the rug" (Von Ziebauer, 2005d, 2005e; see also: Von Zilbauer, 2005a, 2005c; Pfeiffer, 2004).

At the Valley View medical offices, however, there is no sense of crisis or chaos. Patients are handled in a routine manner. The initial mental health screening is conducted in the medical unit next to the medical units holding cell. On the other side of the holding cell is the infirmary. The medical office is a small office with three desks and a locked medicine room. The inmates are called in individually and are screened by a nurse, social worker, or an EMT. They administer a brief screening instrument to evaluate the mental health of the inmate (see: Form 5-1). This questionnaire is similar to the one used at Cook County Jail. Both are modeled on a form recommended by the National Center for Institutions and Alternatives (Practitioners Guide to Developing and Maintaining a Sound Suicide Prevention Policy, 2005; see also: Luhrman, 2000:25-56).

The primary goal of this screening is to identify homicidal or suicide inmates. This is an important consideration since the suicide rate for men is 15 times greater in jail than in the general U.S. population. And, there may be as many as 20 failed suicide attempts for every successful one. Also, the form is used to identify symptoms of mental illness or drug and alcohol abuse (see: Torrey, 1997:30).

The first part of the form is for a brief medical history. It includes questions concerning present illnesses, a general health history, and individual's functional abilities. The other component of the questionnaire is the mental status examination. This includes evaluating the inmate's physical appearance, behavior, emotions, and thought process. If the inmate admits to a mental illness then its onset, duration, and severity are discussed. If the patient has taken psychoactive medication, then its dosage, duration, side effects, and effectiveness are questioned. For substance abusers or dual diagnosis inmates they are questioned on alcohol and illicit drug use. For drug abusers the frequency, amount, and route of usage (IV, nasal, or inhaled) are explored. Questions concerning recent alcohol or substance abuse are important since the inmate may be currently intoxicated or be suffering from withdrawal (Sanders, Freeman, and Goldman, 1998; Stein and Alaimo, 1998).

Form 5-1
Questionnaire

INTAKE MENTAL HEALTH SCREENING

INMATE NAME	ID#	RACE	D.O.B.

SUICIDE POTENTIAL SCREENING (circle one)

1. Arresting or transporting officer believes subject may be suicide risk.	Yes	No
2. Lacks close family/friends in community.	Yes	No
3. Experienced a significant loss within last 6 months (loss of job, relationship, death of close family member).	Yes	No
4. Worried about major problems other than legal situation (terminal illness).	Yes	No
5. Family member or significant other has attempted or committed suicide (spouse, parent, sibling, close friend, lover).	Yes	No
6. Has psychiatric history (psychotropic medication or treatment).	Yes	No
7. Holds position of respect in community (i.e. professional, public official) and/or alleged crime is shocking in nature. Expresses feelings of embarrassment/shame.	Yes	No
8. Expresses thoughts about killing self.	Yes	No
9. Has a suicide plan and/or suicide instrument in possession.	Yes	No
10. Has previous suicide attempt. (Check wrists and note method)	Yes	No
11. Expresses feelings there is nothing to look forward to in the future (feelings of helplessness and hopelessness).	Yes	No
12. Shows signs of depression (crying, emotional flatness).	Yes	No
13. Appears overly anxious, afraid or angry.	Yes	No
14. Appears to feel unusually embarrassed or ashamed.	Yes	No
15. Is acting and/or talking in a strange manner. (Cannot focus attention; hearing or seeing things not there.)	Yes	No
16. Is apparently under the influence of alcohol or drugs.	Yes	No
17. If "Yes" to #16, is individual incoherent or showing signs of withdrawal or mental illness.	Yes	No

TOTAL YES'S=
If there are any **YES'S** circled in shaded areas, or total of **YES'S** equal **8** or more, alert Shift Commander and refer for Mental Health Evaluation.

PSYCHIATRIC SCREENING (circle one)

1. History of psychotropic medication? Type: Current dosage: Source:	Yes	No
2. History of psychiatric hospitalization? When: Where:	Yes	No
3. History of outpatient mental health treatment? When: Where:	Yes	No
4. History of violent behavior? When: Where:	Yes	No

BEHAVIORAL OBSERVATIONS
Difficulties observed in the following area(s): (circle one)

Eye Contact	Terrified/Crying
Appearance	Orientation
Activity	Concentration
Mood	Speech
Affect	Delusional
Memory	Hallucinations
Intellectual Functioning	Psychotic Symptoms

COMMENTS

SUMMARY	**DISPOSITION**
_____No mental health problems.	_____Approved for General Population
_____Mental health problems require routine follow up.	No Mental Health Referral
_____Chronic mental health problem.	_____Approved for General Population
_____Mental Illness _____Developmental Disability	Routine Mental Health Referral
Other_____	_____Special Housing
_____Acute mental health problem.	Mental Health Referral A.S.A.P.
_____Psychosis _____Suicidal	_____Suicide Precaution Procedures
Other_____	Mental Health Referral A.S.A.P.
_____Potential withdrawal from substance abuse.	_____Psychiatric Referral
	_____Medical Monitoring for Potential Withdrawal

SCREENED BY_____DATE_____TIME_____

REVIEWED BY_____DATE_____TIME_____

Withdrawal from alcohol or drugs can be life-threatening. Alcohol withdrawal can produce seizures, hallucinations, and delirium tremors for up to five days after the last drink. Benzodiazepine withdrawal produces similar symptoms. Barbiturate withdrawal can produce anxiety, seizures, fever, and death. Opiate or narcotic withdrawal (e.g., morphine or heroin) are usually not life threatening. They include tearing, runny nose, sweating, and increased blood pressure and pulse. These may progress to vomiting, diarrhea, and joint pain. Methadone and clonipine are common treatments. However, opiate abusers are notoriously manipulative and drug seeking. Stimulant withdrawal can lead to paranoia, hallucinations, and depression. Hallucinogens may induce psychotic symptoms. Phencyclidine (PCP or angel dust) is popular and may produce severe assaultive behavior (Sanders, Freeman, and Goldman, 1998).

Other inmates manifest personality disorders. These are persistent, maladaptive behaviors. In correctional settings borderline, narcissistic, and anti-social disorders are common. These inmates are frequently involved in fire setting, self-mutilation, the flooding of cells, and fighting. These behaviors can be brought on by feelings of isolation and emptiness. They can be produced by minor slights or interpersonal conflicts (Sanders, Freeman, and Goldman, 1998; Kavitz, et. al, 2001).

The researcher observed 178 inmates undergo the initial mental health screening. When the inmates appeared normal the questions were asked quickly. If the inmate appeared disturbed or suffering from drug or alcohol withdrawal the questions were asked in a slow and methodical manner. However, the staff often noted that a limitation of the screening was that "we only know what the inmates tell us."

Of the 178 inmates screened 138 had "no mental health problem" (see: Table 5-5).

Table 5-5
Mental Health Screening Disposition

Disposition	Number	Percentage*
No mental health problem	138	77.5%
Risk/segregation—mental health	16	9%
Risk/segregation—detoxification	8	4.5%
Follow up—mental health	16	9%
Total:	178	100%
		*rounded

(Table 5-5 was statistically significant at the .01 level.)

However, it was often pointed out that only those inmates who had "an acute or overt" mental illness were treated as mentally ill. For example:

Robert Winston, a 20-year-old white male, was arrested on a parole violation. He was taking Haldol (an anti-psychotic medication) and had suffered from alcohol withdrawal in the past. In June, 2004 he had made a suicide attempt. During the interview he did not appear to be in distress. The interviewer checked, "no mental health problem."

David Olds was a 24-year-old black male. He had spent 2 months at Elgin State Hospital's forensic unit for violent behavior in the past. He appeared calm. The interviewer checked, "no mental health problem."

James Harris was a 27-year-old white male who took Lexapro and Trazadone for depression. The interviewer felt there was "no acute distress" and marked, "no mental health problem."

Samuel Lancing, a 25-year-old white male was arrested for forgery. He admitted to taking heroin and cocaine daily. He also took methadone and suffered from anxiety. He appeared in no immediate distress and did not appear to be suffering from withdrawal. The form was marked, "no mental health problem."

Of the 178 inmates screened 16 (9%) were considered to be mentally ill and "at risk." The males were sent to the RISK unit. There was no RISK unit for females. There were only about 60 females in the jail at any one time. So, the females who were "at risk" were sent to a female segregation unit.

The jail has several different types of cell blocks. Some cells blocks were linear with 2 tiers. Others were dorm units. Some were "pods" with two levels of cells in a C shape and a day room contained within the unit. Most inmates were double celled. There were also single inmate segregation cells. The RISK unit was a pod unit. It usually contained 30 to 40 inmates. Most pods did not have an officer in them. The inmates were checked by the officers through large shatterproof glass windows as they make their rounds. However, the RISK unit had an officer at all times and he or she provided "direct supervision" of the inmates.

The RISK unit contained six "glass boxes" (shatterproof glass walled cells) for suicidal inmates. These were single inmate cells. The cells were bare except for a bed and a mental toilet. To prevent suicide attempts the inmates were not allowed to have any clothing. They were only allowed to have a blanket. The officer in the RISK pod had a control console that faced the center of the 2 tiered C shaped set of cells. The glass walled cells were in the center of the C so that these inmates could be constantly watched. Some of the other mentally ill inmates were locked in their cells if it was felt they were dangerous or too disturbed to be in the day room. These inmates were allowed to wear clothes. The other "at risk" inmates on the unit were physically handicapped, homosexuals, older inmates, or inmates in protective custody who had been threatened by gang members. These inmates were allowed to be out during the day and evening. They spent their time talking, reading, playing board games, or watching television.

In order to guarantee the safety of those on suicide watch the state requires a visual cell check at least every thirty minutes. So, once or twice a half-hour the guard walked along the two levels and checked the cells with mentally ill inmates in them. As he did this he inserted an electronic pen in to sockets in the wall which recorded the time of his rounds.

Some examples of mentally ill inmates who were sent to the RISK unit or female segregation cells were:

Sarah Beckman, a 28-year-old white female, was being held for robbery. She stated that she took Celebrex, Zoloft, Resperidol, Trazadone, and Lithium. She said she was bipolar. She had scars on her arm and she said she was a "cutter." She also admitted to a recent psychiatric hospitalization. The staff felt she was suicidal; they also thought that she had a borderline personality disorder. She was sent to a female segregation cell.

Jesus Aguilar, a 32-year-old Hispanic male, was arrested for burglary. He admitted to using heroin and alcohol. He stated that he was depressed and thought of harming himself. His affect was blunted. He was also HIV positive. He was sent to RISK and put on suicide watch.

Morton Grimes, a 28-year-old black male, was arrested for misdemeanor battery. He smiled throughout the interview. His responses to the questions were slow and his memory was poor. He said that he took Depakote. He was thought to be chronically mentally ill and sent to RISK.

Jerry Jansen, a 32-year-old white male, had been arrested for criminal damage to property. He said he took Zoloft, Zyprexa, and Seroquel. He said that he was schizophrenic and bipolar. He also suffered from obsessive-compulsive disorder. In the middle of the screening interview he suddenly announced that he would refuse to answer any further questions. He was sent to RISK.

Martin Ramirez, a 28-year-old Hispanic male, was arrested for criminal damage to property and aggravated assault. He stated that he took drugs daily. He said that he had attempted suicide on numerous occasions. He said that he had been violent in his home. He heard voices and had made a suicide attempt the previous Saturday. His emotions were flat throughout the interview. He was felt to have an acute mental illness. He was sent to RISK and put on suicide watch.

Of the 178 inmates that were screened 8 (4.5 percent) were sent to risk for drug or alcohol detoxification. For example:

Sam Kopell, a 29 white male, had been arrested for felony drug possession. He told the interviewer that he was bipolar. However, he did not manifest any symptoms of bipolar illness so the interviewer checked, "no mental health problem." However, he then added that he drank liquor and a 12 pack of beer every day. He also took crack cocaine daily. He was sent to RISK for detoxification.

Some inmates do not appear to have an immediate mental health problem. However, since they do describe mental health problems in their past, they are sent to the general population and the staff checks the box for a follow up examination. For example:

Karen Callaghan, a white 48-year-old female, had been arrested for misdemeanor drug possession. She said she suffered from anxiety, depression, and bipolar illness. She stated that she took Xanax, Prozac, and Trazodone. She did not appear in immediate distress. The interviewer checked, "follow up."

Cary Townsend, a 37-year-old white male, was charged with three counts of unlawful possession of a controlled substance and obstruction of justice. He stated that he used cocaine and marijuana daily. He said that he was bipolar and anxious about his current situation. He said that he took Lithium, Prozac, and Trazodone. He did not appear in acute distress or suffering from drug or alcohol withdrawal. The interviewer checked, "follow up."

Of the 178 inmates observed 40 (22.5 percent) were considered to be mentally ill or substance abusers. Of the 40 inmates who went to RISK, female segregation, or had a follow up evaluation, charges were available for 21 (see: Table 5-6). Of these 21, 7 had committed a violent crime (see: James and Glaze, 2006).

Thirteen of the RISK inmates were sent there for mental health problems (see: Table 6-2). Three of those 13 had committed a violent act (battery). And only two had a significant number of previous charges. One had 21 traffic offences and another had 4 arrests for aggravated battery. Of the 8 inmates who were sent to RISK for detoxification only one had a violent charge (aggravated battery) (see: Table 5-7). However, one had 13 earlier arrests on various charges, one had 11 arrests including attempted murder and mob action, one had 4 criminal trespass charges, and one had 2 DUI's and 2 drug charges. In the follow-up group who were thought to be mentally ill charges were available for 10 of the 16 (see: Tables 5-8 and 5-9). One had committed a violent crime. And four had previous charges. Those charges were usually drug or alcohol related. Also, the 23 mentally ill inmates (RISK and follow-up) committed 75 crimes (current and former charges). And if we remove one individual from this group that number drops to 22 individuals committing 54 crimes. However, for those 5 inmates who were sent to RISK for detoxification their current and former charges totaled 37. So, these five (who actually were MISA cases—mentally ill/substance abusers) had a much higher arrest rate. So, although the sample is not large, we may conclude that *violence produced one-third of all the arrests for the mentally ill. And, substance abuse greatly increased the number of arrests for mentally ill with drug and alcohol problems* (see: Ditton, 1999; Monahan, 1992:516; Steadman, et. al., 1989; Butterfield, 1998).[14]

---

14. James and Glaze (2006) in a survey of jail inmates found that 76 percent of jail inmates who were mentally ill were dependent on or abused alcohol or drugs. And 34 percent of the mentally ill inmates in jail had used drugs or alcohol at the time of the offense.

Table 5-6
RISK/Charges

Charge	RISK (number)	Follow-up (number)
Criminal trespass to land	2	
Criminal trespass to property	1	
Traffic Offenses	1	1
Driving under the influence	1	
Drugs	1	2
Theft	1	
Burglary	1	
Robbery	1	
Violent crime	5	2
Warrant	3	1
Total:	17	6

(Table 5-6 was not statistically significant.)

Table 5-7
Charges
RISK-Mental Health

Inmate	Current Charge	Previous Charge(s)
1	Non-violent	None
2	Non-violent	None
3	Non-violent	DUI/non-violent
4	Robbery	None
5	Burglary	None
6	Theft/contempt of court/ traffic offense	21—traffic offenses
7	Criminal trespass to property	None
8	Battery	None
9	Unlawful possession of a controlledsubstance/resisting arrest	None
10	Battery	None
11	Criminal trespass to land	4—aggravated battery
12	Criminal trespass to property/ aggravated assault	None
13	Domestic battery	None

Table 5-8
Charges
RISK/Detoxification

Inmate	Current Charge	Previous Charge(s)
1	Drugs	None
2	Aggravated battery	13 various charges
3	Driving while license suspended	11 (including attempted murder, mob action)
4	Criminal damage to property	4 criminal trespass
5	Driving under the influence (DUI)	2 DUI
		2 unlawful possession of a controlled substance

Table 5-9
Charges
Follow Up/Mental Health

Inmate	Current Charge	Previous Charge(s)
1	Drugs	None
2	Violent	3 various charges
3	Attempted murder	None
4	Retail theft	Retail theft/4 unlawful possession of a controlled substance
5	Contempt	None
6	Warrant	None
7	Retail theft	None
8	DUI	3 DUI
9	DUI/warrant	None
10	Unlawful possession of a controlled substance	3 upcs/obstructing justice

Also, if all of the inmates who went to RISK (21 percent for mental health and 4.5 percent for detoxification) and some of the follow-up patients (9 percent) received psychiatric medication this would mean that 20 to 25 percent of the inmates received psychoactive medication. This is similar to the jails own statistics. The jails daily census for the 2004 calendar year was 483 inmates. The average number taking psychoactive medication was 108. This would be a 22 percent rate of inmates taking such medication.

Robins and Regier (1980) conducted a major epidemiological study on mental illness in the U.S. They found that mental illness among prisoners was two to five times greater than in the general population. They found that 6.7 percent of all prisoners had schizophrenia, 21 percent had an affective disorder, and 28 percent had an anxiety disorder. In another study co-occurring substance abuse was as high as 90% (Weisman, 1998). Bolton (1976) conducted a five county study in California. From his sample of 1,048 adult county jail inmates he found that 6.7% were psychotic. Teplin (1990) interviewed 728 inmates at Cook County

Jail. She found that 6.4 percent had a serious mental illness. Torrey, et. al. (1992) surveyed 1,391 jails in the U.S. He found that 7.2 percent of the inmates had a serious mental illness. In the late 1990s Cook county Jail had 8 to 10 percent of its detainees as active patients (Sanders, Freeman, and Goldman, 1998; see also: Morgan, 1981). A recent survey by James and Glaze (2006) found 64 percent of jail inmates, 56 percent of state prison inmates, and 45 percent of Federal prisoners to be mentally ill. This survey excluded individuals in mental hospitals and those found to be mentally incompetent to stand trail or not guilty by reason of insanity (see also: Human Rights Watch, 2003; Butterfield, 2003; McMahon, 2003; Von Zilbauer, 2003).

After the initial screening at Valley View County Jail some inmates have a second screening by a social worker or psychologist. In 2004 approximately 3,400 individuals had this second screening. Approximately 1,800 of these were diagnosed with a serious mental illness. If these individuals needed to see a psychiatrist he was available twice a week. He was able to see about 20 inmates per day.

If the inmates had a prescription for psychoactive medication at a nearby pharmacy that pharmacy would be called to confirm the prescription. Usually, that medication would then be given to the inmate. If the inmate was "acute or overt" and the nurse felt medication was necessary she would call the physician. If he agreed with the nurses assessment he would prescribe the appropriate medication from the jail's supply of medication.

One evening the psychiatrist at the jail explained to the researcher some of the frustrations he faced. He felt that some of his patients were "spoiled" because they only wanted the newer, and more expensive, atypical antipsychotic medications (with fewer side-effects). He felt the older, and cheaper, antipsychotic medications his firm limited him to were fine. However, he felt that many of the individuals he saw lived on the "periphery of society" and medication was only of limited utility to them. He believed their lives were "truncated" as they circled between mental hospitals and jails. Therefore, they were a "predictable population."[15]

One reason this was a predictable population was because the jail did no discharge planning. Also, the physician was allowed to only give two weeks of medication to an inmate when they were discharged from the jail. However, the jail's psychiatrist pointed out that it took two or three months to get an appointment at a mental health clinic for new medication. So, inevitably these individuals ran out of medication, broke down, and were reinstitutionalized (see: Kupers, 1999:78-83; Steadman, McCarty, and Morrissey, 1989: 125-148; Bernstein, 1990a; Bazelon Center For Mental Health, 2006; Boes and McDermott, 2000).

The most striking example of this is Maria Magdalena, a Hispanic female in her early sixties. (She is not reflected in the statistics since the researcher did not witness her screenings.) She is chronically mentally ill and homeless. From 1993 to 1996 she was arrested 8

---

15. The data supports this impression. The lack of services for the mentally ill, plus their unstable living arrangements, leads to re-arrest rates of 24 to 56 percent. One study found that the overwhelming majority of patients had "repetitive cycles of institutionalization in both the hospitals and prisons" (Hiday, 1999: 523).

times and served a total of 2 to 3 months on those charges. From 1997 until 2002 she was arrested 19 times. The charges ranged from criminal trespass to aggravated assault. She served from one week to six months on each of these charges. From 2002 to 2004 she was arrested 18 times. Most of these were for criminal trespass. She served three two-month sentences during this period. And, in 2005 she was arrested 14 times. (Twice during the month the researcher was present).

The medical staff considers her "treatment resistant." She was frequently hostile and aggressive with the correctional officers and often refused to take psychiatric medication. A number of mental health and Hispanic community agencies had attempted to assist her. They have all been unsuccessful. She was considered to be "hopeless" by the jail staff.[16]

The mental health director felt that the jail staff had a good working relationship with the private firm that managed the medical services for the jail. However, he felt that they were very understaffed. However, several jail officials emphasized that the county board, and not the sheriff, had negotiated the medical firm's contract.

The mental health director felt his services were relatively effective since there had been only 2 suicides in the jail in the last four years. And these individuals were not on suicide watch and had no history of mental health problems.

He explained that the job of the mental health staff was stabilization and crisis intervention. When asked about mental health treatment for the prisoners he laughed. He said, "there is no treatment. My job is to run a *safe place* and make sure *nobody gets killed.*"

9. The Mobile Outreach Van

The other glaring gap in services provided by the Illinois Department of Mental Health is for the homeless mentally ill. However, homelessness, itself, is not easy to define. Experts sometimes argue over whether a cardboard box or an automobile can be considered a home. Further, these individuals lack the human resources and community ties to help them move out of homelessness. Therefore, they also suffer from social isolation (Bachrach, 1992).

In one study 70 percent of the homeless were under age 40. And more than 70 percent were minorities (Susser, 1987). The estimates of the total number of homeless varies widely, as well. Some place it at 250,000, while others claim it is closer to 3 million. The Urban Institute estimated the number in 2000 to be between 440,000 and 842,000 (Kanter, 1989; Jencks, 1994; Torrey, 1997: 3,17, 19, 22, 68; Kasindrof, 2005).

Most research on homelessness is within a narrow time frame. However, if this period were to be expanded the number might increase by 50 percent. Also, mental illness is difficult to establish when an individual is suffering extreme physical deprivation. Further, street subculture, which is saturated with alcohol and drugs, makes any psychiatric diagnosis problematic (Baxter and Hopper, 1982; Barrow, 1989; Kaufman, 2004; Post, 2001; Drake, et. Al., 1989; Linn, et. Al., 1990; Harris and Bachrach, 1990; Belcher, 1988).

---

16. For such cases E. Fuller Torrey, a psychiatrist, has suggested forced medication. To date, such an approach has had limited success (Fritz, 2006; see also: Torrey and Zdanowicz, 1998).

Estimates of the rates of mental illness among the homeless vary widely. They range from 22 percent to 57 percent. However, mental illness is only one of the afflictions of the homeless. They also lack housing, access to toilets, mailboxes, telephones, delousing, privacy, and safety (Bachrach, 1992).

In order to examine this problem further a study of a mobile outreach service for the homeless was conducted in 2005. It was run by The Open Door (TOD), a large social service agency in Chicago. The agency is well regarded and has numerous programs. These include mental health, dual disorder treatment (mental illness and substance abuse), housing, and assertive outreach. One of its programs is the Mobile Outreach Van (MOV). Each van is staffed with two social workers. The outreach vans workers attempt to find homeless mentally ill individuals and provide them with "time limited" services. That is, they search out homeless individuals, meet their immediate needs, and then "hand them off" to long term mental health, housing, or other service workers.

The programs' staff searches for the homeless in abandoned buildings, parks, bus and train stations, public buildings, shelters, or the street. It also receives referrals from citizens, businesses, or city agencies. The outreach workers provide crisis, short-term, or intermittent services to homeless persons. Officially, the program is a mental health program. However, since the homeless often have more pressing needs the outreach workers frequently provide food or clothing and the agency pays for shelter or medical care.

If an individual they encounter is thought to be a threat to themselves or others the worker may initiate an emergency psychiatric hospitalization. In such a hospitalization weather is a consideration. Emergency hospitalization may occur in extremely cold weather as a life saving measure. Alternately, in extremely hot weather heat stroke and dehydration may prompt a hospitalization, as well.

The researcher observed the Mobile Outreach Van workers for five weeks in the fall of 2005. The program had six two-person teams to cover the city. Three teams worked out of a Northside office and three teams used a Southside office. Although they used their offices for paperwork or meetings most of their work was conducted on the street. "Our office is our van" or "Our office is our backpack" were frequent comments by the workers.

Each team usually went out for 2 or 3 hours once or twice a day. They drove to areas where the homeless were known to gather. At other times they drove down streets or alleys looking for homeless persons. Some days they had appointments to meet with clients. On other occasions they had referrals to meet individuals or attempted to find a homeless person at a certain place or in a certain area.

The researcher observed 78 contacts, or attempted contacts, over the five week period. (Since many meetings were brief, the term "contact," rather than the more bureaucratic "case," was chosen to define these interactions.)

Rowe (1999) argues that outreach work is a mixture of "entrepreneurial capitalism" and "bureaucratic people-processing." That is, workers attempt to sell their "product" to wary consumers.

In such work "customers" are identified when they appear to be responding to inner voices or visions, exhibit odd posturing, inappropriate laughter, or withdraw from human contact (Lopez, 1996) (see: Table 5-10). (Virtually all of the individuals contacted by the MOV workers were mentally ill.)

Table 5-10
Principal Diagnosis (Axis 1)[17]

	Number	Percentage*
Schizophrenia/Schizoaffective	110	14
Mood Disorder/Bipolar Illness	179	24
Other Psychotic Disorder	264	34
Other Psychiatric Disorder (unspecified)	30	4
V Codes[18]	184	24
Total:	767	100

* rounded

(Table 5-10 is statistically significant to the .01 level.)

The first step in this process is to locate a homeless person. This could be a time consuming process. The Northside team often drove to the south edge of the Loop (the downtown). This has traditionally been a place for transients and the homeless. Also, the "Atlantic Bible Mission," a large homeless shelter, has been in the area for decades. The outreach team would drive around the area and pull over when they saw someone with whom they wanted to speak. Or, they would park and walk around the area. The workers would look for individuals showing signs of homelessness or mental illness. For example, they would look for people who were dirty, disheveled, and ill-clothed. Or, they would look for people wearing multiple layers of clothing in warm weather. They would also look for people pushing grocery carts loaded with their belongings. Or, they would look for individuals who were talking to themselves, appeared agitated, or were acting in a bizarre manner.[19]

Other methods of locating the homeless was local knowledge that "homeless people hang out at . . ." or "homeless people sit in the doorways in the 2300 block of . . ." Also, referrals were called in to the team. They would then go out "looking for someone sleeping behind a building at . . ."[20]

---

17. Axis 1 diagnoses are the principal diagnosis that lead to contact with the mental health system.

18. V codes involve relational problems (i.e. parent-child, partner, sibling), abuse or neglect (i.e. physical, sexual, child neglect), and other problems (i.e. noncompliance with treatment, adult antisocial behavior, occupational problems) (American Psychiatric Association, 2000: 736-42).

19. According to the agencies statistics the workers made 720 contacts over a two year period. Eighty-one percent of these individuals were listed as homeless and another eight percent were unknown. Therefore, the workers estimate of who was homeless was relatively reliable.

20. Contacts with the homeless were tracked by zip code by the agency. Chicago has 63 zip codes. The Northside unit made 478 contacts over a two year period. Of these, 366 (77%) were in, or near, the Loop or on the Northside in the Uptown/Lakeview area. This Northside area has traditionally been a "dumping ground" for patients from the Illinois Department of Mental Health. The Southside unit made 242 contacts. Of these 146 contacts (60%) were from 5 zip codes near the Loop or on the Southside.

In making their initial contact, the workers usually would walk up to an individual and say, "Hi. I'm from The Open Door, have you heard of us?" or, "Hi. I'm an outreach worker from The Open Door. Can I talk to you?" One outreach worker introduced herself by saying: "Hi. I'm an outreach worker from The Open Door. We help people who are living outside." Other workers thought that this was a good, non-threatening approach.

One outreach worker said the rules for interacting with the homeless were simple. Since many homeless people are found sitting on benches or the ground "you should talk to them at eye level. Even if they won't talk to you, you should talk to them. Look off into the distance if they're looking off into the distance. And, don't wake people up." Also, "don't approach more than one person." This is because it is difficult to interact with several homeless people in a group. And, there are safety concerns in dealing with a group.

The workers, many with master's degrees in social work, describe their job in simple and practical terms. However, there is a great deal of crisis intervention theory behind their interactions with the homeless. These interactions progress through seven steps. First, the worker must ascertain if the situation is dangerous. Second, the worker must establish communication and rapport. Third, the worker must identify the individual's major problem. Fourth, the worker must attempt to offer support and discuss the individual's feelings. Fifth, alternative actions must be explored by the client and the worker. Sixth, a plan of action needed to be formulated. This plan was the product of negotiation between the client and the worker. In these discussions the client's needs were often practical ("I need housing" or "I need a job"). However, the worker was likely to see the problem in clinical terms ("He needs medication for depression" or "She needs alcohol detoxification"). And, seventh, whether a plan is initiated or not, follow-up visits with the client should be undertaken (Roberts, 1991; Ligon, 2000; see also: Kraybill, 2005; Barrow, 1989: ix).

The units approach is to visit the same area day after day so that the homeless recognize them and may be more accepting of any offers of assistance. One worker commented: "You need to be there every day making contacts, gaining trust. It's just like a cop on the beat."

The researcher observed 78 contacts, or attempted contacts, over the five week research period.[21] (The number of contacts is small since each contact is quite time consuming. We will discuss this issue in more detail below.) Of those who were actually contacted, 40 (60 percent) were black, 21 (31 percent) were white, 4 (6 percent) were Hispanic, and 2 (3 percent) were Asian (see: Table 5-11). Of the seventy homeless persons who were actually contacted forty-eight (69 percent) were male and 22 (31 percent) were female (see: Table 5-12). Age was known, or estimated, for 62 of the homeless that were contacted. There were no homeless contacts under 20 years old. There were 3 (5 percent) between 20 and 29. There were 45 (73 percent) between 30 and 59. And, 14 (23 percent) were over 60 (see: Table 5-13). Agency data from fiscal year 2005 is similar (see: Tables 5-14, 5-15, 5-16).

---

21. According to agency statistics the Northside unit made approximately 70 percent of the units new contacts in 2005 (409 of 596 contacts). However, this meant that the Northside unit made only 7.9 new contacts per week.

Table 5-11
Race of the Homeless Individual

Race	Number	Percentage*
Black	40	60
White	21	31
Hispanic	4	6
Asian	2	3
Total: 67		100

* rounded

(Table 5-11 was statistically significant at the .01 level.)

Table 5-12
Sex of the Homeless Individual

Sex	Number	Percentage*
Male	48	69
Female	22	31
Total: 70		100

* rounded

(Table 5-12 was statistically significant at the .01 level.)

Table 5-13
Age of the Homeless Individual

Age	Number	Percentage*
16-19	0	0
20-29	3	5
30-39	13	21
40-49	19	31
50-59	13	21
60-69	7	11
70-79	6	10
80-89	1	2
Total: 62		100

* rounded

(Table 5-13 was statistically significant at the .01 level.)

Table 5-14
Known Race of the Homeless Individual[22]

Race	Number	Percentage*
Black	458	65
White	210	30
Hispanic	27	4
Asian	6	1

	Total: 701	100

* rounded

(Table 5-14 is statistically significant to the .01 level.)

Table 5-15
Sex of the Homeless Individual

Sex	Number	Percentage*
Male	499	69
Female	221	31

	Total: 720	100

* rounded

(Table 5-15 is statistically significant to the .01 level.)

Table 5-16
Age of the Homeless Individual

Age	Number	Percentage*
10-19	1	0
20-29	57	9
30-39	118	18
40-49	239	37
50-59	190	29
60+	76	12

	Total: 650	100

* rounded

(Table 5-16 is statistically significant to the .01 level.)

---

22. The race of 44 individuals was unknown.

In 14 instances workers attempted to find an individual but were unable to do so. There were also 6 persons who refused to interact with the workers (see: Lopez, 1996). For example:

A Northside social service agency called and said that a white, middle-aged male was homeless and loitering in a local park. The workers drove to the park to look for him. (He was known to the workers from previous contacts.) The workers mentioned that he had lost his place to live after his mother had died. He had medical and psychiatric problems and they ran across him at this park from time to time. They drove around the area for 20 minutes but did not find him. They returned to the office. The entire trip took one hour.

One day the Southside team drove to a large park looking for a client. In the park they found a camp with several homeless people living in four tents. A 45-year-old white female and a 45-year-old white male were sitting near the curb drinking alcohol. "Hi," the worker said, "we're from The Open Door. We're looking for Melanie. She has an appointment with us. Have you seen her?" "No," the women said, "not lately. She may be hanging out somewhere else." Near one of the tents a 30-year-old white female was sleeping. By a nearby lake a 50-year-old black male was fishing. A bonfire burned in the middle of the little camp. "We're having grilled cheese," the man at the curb told the workers with a big smile, "my favorite." He paused. "But, last night some Mexican guys in a car drove by and shot us with paint balls." The woman then told us that she was supposed to go to court that day to testify in a case but she had called the lawyer and said she did not feel well enough to go to court. The woman explained that "I was supposed to testify today in a trial of a serial killer. I was to be his twentieth victim." The man then suggested that we check for Melanie a few blocks away. We did, but never found her.

The team went to the Westside office of the city's Department of Human Service to see a client who spent his time near the building's entrance. After speaking with the client they went over to a 70-year-old black female sitting on a bench in the lobby wearing a heavy black coat on a warm day. The workers introduced themselves to her and she waved them off with an angry glare. The workers shrugged and walked off. One commented, "She used to talk to us." After much discussion in the office on how to initiate a conversation with this woman the staff bought a book on Alabama, the state where the woman had been raised. Ten days later they returned to the city facility and found the woman on the center's steps. One worker said, "We bought a book on Alabama." She said, "I'm from Alabama. I know all about it." She angrily waved them off. They left. One worker commented, "She was friendlier this time."

The outreach team went to the main library in the south end of the Loop. Many homeless people spend their days sitting in the library. The workers went from floor to floor looking for homeless people. They found several. One was a 50-year-old black male they knew from previous encounters. He seemed engrossed in a book. They said hello and asked what he was reading. He explained that he was working on his lawsuit against the city. They asked him if he would be interested in getting into a program. He said, "No, programs are too restrictive." He said that he lives in a motel a few days a week when his disability check arrives. Otherwise, he lives outside. They asked if he would be interested in permanent housing. No, he said, he was happy with his current arrangement. They gave him their card and walked away. One worker commented, "Imagine how much money the city spends defending itself from lawsuits from people who are delusional."

One day the Southside team drove to an area under an expressway bridge where homeless people were known to live. They parked and walked into the area. They found the bedding of several individuals but no one was in sight. As they were leaving a couple, each wearing several layers of clothing on a warm day, walked up. The couple, both in their forties, carried bottles of liquor in brown paper bags. The man appeared to be drunk. One of the workers said, "Hi. I'm from The Open Door. We help people who live outside. Could you use any help?" The woman smiled. However, the man asked, "Why are you in my space?" "We're here to help," the worker calmly responded. "That's not right," the man angrily said, "I'm not in your space. It's wrong to be going into someone's space." "Do you want some food?" the worker asked. "O.K.," they replied. She gave them some snacks. After a moment of thought the man became even angrier and started yelling, "You're in my space. That's not right." Fearing for the safety of his partner the second worker then stepped between the man and the other worker. The workers then walked away as the man yelled louder and louder. One worker called to the man, "We'll come back." As the workers drove off one commented: "It's hard to get help for couples. Unless they are married most places won't let them stay together. They don't want to split up, so they won't come in for help."

Although some clients are uncooperative most are willing to engage, to some degree, with the outreach workers. Kraybill (2005) argues that successful outreach work moves through four stages: approach, companionship (the building of trust and the provision of initial services), partnership (where a third person, a social worker, nurse, or physician, joins the dyad), and mutuality (where the client receives a home or job and eventually terminates the relationship with the outreach work).

The first stage of this process is often very brief and tentative. For example:

The workers pulled into a no parking zone downtown to speak with a client who was sitting on the sidewalk. Across the street was a panhandler sitting on the sidewalk. He appeared to be drawing in a notebook. One worker said, "He looks very sad," referring to the second man. They crossed the street and squatted down to speak to him. He said that he had been a printer but had been laid off. He had been homeless for 5 years. They gave him their card and said that it had a toll free number that he could call for help. They said they would see him again. "He looks pretty good for someone on the street for five years," one worker observed as they walked away.

Sometimes the relationship moves to the second stages (meeting basic needs) but stalls. For example:

Two workers drove to the city's Westside office of the Department of Human Services. A number of homeless people were sitting on the steps outside. The workers went up to a 35-year-old black male sitting near the doors. "How are you doing?" they asked. "O.K.," he said. He explained that he sat there during the day but slept in a nearby shelter at night. They gave him some snacks. They said that they had brought the medical form they had discussed on their last visit. They asked if he would like to sign it. "No," he said. Then they asked if he would like to see a psychiatrist to get some medication. "No," he said. Finally, they asked if he would like to go with them for a flu shot. "No," he replied. "O.K. then," they said, "we'll visit you again." "O.K.," he replied. Everyone smiled and the workers left.

Sometimes it is difficult to establish trust since some homeless individuals are very guarded. For example:

The outreach workers drove past a bus shelter in the southern part of the Loop. There was a 50-year-old black female sitting in the shelter talking to herself. She wore several layers of clothing, a heavy black coat, and a knit cap on a warm fall day. "Let's talk to her," one worker said, "pull over." They pulled into the bus stop. One worker got out, introduced himself, and gave her a card. He asked if she wanted a doctor's appointment. She said, "No." He asked if she was homeless. She said, "Sometimes." He asked if he could meet her again. She agreed. They made a date to meet in a few days at the McDonald's at the nearby train station.

The following Monday the workers met her at the McDonald's. She was dressed in the same clothing as before. They offered to buy her a sandwich. She refused. She said, "I have my own money." They asked her if she needed shelter. She said, no. They asked her if she could use some counseling. She said, no. She went on to say that a lot of people had promised her things in the past but hadn't delivered. One worker took some paperwork from his backpack. He asked if he could get her birthday for his records. No, she said, not yet; not until she knew him better. He then asked where she stayed and if she had any money for shelter. She said, "Sometimes I sleep near my mother's house." Other times her mother gets her a room. With a smile, and in a silly tone of voice, she explained that her real problem was that she needed to separate from her parents. She should have done this at birth, but she had not. She said she had been to a lot of counseling but since her father will no longer go, she cannot separate from her parents. She said she had a college degree and had been a teacher. However, she had given up her career. She agreed to meet the workers again the following week. However, she did not think she could make much progress with them until she successfully separated from her parents. The workers appeared frustrated as they walked away. "I think she's schizoaffective," one muttered.

Kraybill (2005) argues that the outreach worker-client relationship gradually moves from the second stage, companionship (building trust) to the third stage, partnership (allowing a third person into the relationship). However, there is often an intermediate step. That is, dealing with another agency. Homeless advocates, as well as The Open Door, promote a "housing first" strategy of services. However, permanent housing can often only be attained if the client has public assistance. Also, ongoing health care can usually only be accessed with the acquisition of public aid (Medicaid). Medicaid may be difficult to acquire. There are a number of reasons for this:

a.   complex Medicaid eligibility criteria,
b.   flawed eligibility determination by automated systems,
c.   confusing rules and documentation procedures,
d.   lack of timely or adequate information of eligibility for services,

   e. negative attitudes of some eligibility workers or services providers toward applicants or service recipients,

   f. lack of outreach to eligible individuals,

   g. faulty redetermination procedures resulting in premature or inappropriate termination (Post, 2001).

This led Post to conclude that far too much effort was expended in keeping "unworthy people from obtaining assistance rather then, increasing access to health care" (2001: 31; see also: Frank and McGuire, 1996; Rich and White, 1996; Gold, 1996).

Another complication is that a successful public aid application can only be completed if the client has identification. And many homeless individuals have no identification. So, the first step in "housing first" is acquiring an ID. For example:

> The team picked up a 45-year-old black female and drove her to the Secretary of State's motor vehicle facility to get a state identification card. After several minutes in line she was told that she did not have enough ID to get an ID. She was told that she needed to send a letter to herself at her residence (which she did not have since she was homeless). She also needed a birth certificate or school record to establish her age. And she needed $20 to pay for the ID. The agency was willing to supply the fee. As they left the workers discussed various strategies to secure the required documents. They then drove the woman to the public aid office to apply for Medicaid or MANG (Medical Assistance, No Grant).[23] After a wait she was told that she had to be there at 8:00 a.m. in order to fill out a MANG application. The client and the outreach workers were frustrated. One worker muttered, "in this job you modify your definition of success" (see: Wing and Morris, 1981:9).

In Kraybill's (2005) third stage a physician, social worker, or case manager is added to the dyad. However, sometimes this does not work out. For example:

> The outreach workers saw a 30-year-old black male standing on the street in the south Loop. They knew him from previous contacts. As they approached him they saw he was crying. He said hello and said that he still had their card. They asked him if he would like an appointment at the mental health clinic. He said, yes. The workers called the clinic and made an appointment with their agency's psychiatrist in 13 days. They said they would pick him up for the appointment. He said, O.K. On the day of the appointment the psychiatrist called the workers and said that he had a family emergency and would have to cancel the appointment. One worker commented, "This is unusual, the doctor is very good." They drove to the south Loop and met the client. They told him the doctor had an emergency and had to cancel the appointment. However, they would call for a new appointment the next day. The client shrugged and began to cry. "I'm here every day," he said. The workers drove off.

---

   23. The Illinois Department of Public Aid is now called the Department of Health Care and Family Services.

Occasionally, contacts are made with a simple offer and the process moves smoothly (see: Rowe, 1999). For example:

The workers drove to the south Loop and parked on a side street. They began to walk around the neighborhood. Within a few minutes they saw a 37-year-old black male digging through a garbage can. The workers introduced themselves and asked the man if he would like a McDonald's sandwich. Yes, he said. As they walked to the McDonald's he told them that he had been living in a nursing home but had walked away. He now lived on the street. He said that he had been living in the nursing home because he was paranoid schizophrenic and bipolar.

When we reached McDonald's they bought the man a sandwich. As they talked he mentioned that he had been in jail. "For panhandling?" the worker asked. "No," he said, "for stealing a car." He added that he was still on parole. The worker asked if he could contact his parole officer. Yes, he said. So, the worker took some forms from his backpack and the man signed them. The worker asked if he had any family in the area. Yes, he said, his mother. The worker asked if he could contact her, as well. Yes, he replied, again. "Am I asking too many questions?" the worker asked. "No, that's O.K.," the man replied. Then the worker asked if he wanted housing or to go to the mental health clinic for help. Yes, he said. So, they drove to a mental health clinic on the Northside. They introduced him to the intake worker. The intake worker said he would see him now and he would make an appointment to see the psychiatrist in a week. The outreach workers gave the man a bus pass so he could return to the south Loop that day and return for his appointment the next week. The outreach workers left.

Sometimes substance abuse interferes with the provision of services (see: Lamb, 1982). For example:

The workers pulled into a bus stop in the south Loop and parked. They walked over to a 45-year-old white male they knew who was panhandling. He told them that he had been sleeping on a heating grate near the Federal Building until the police had chased him off. He said that he was bipolar and suicidal and wanted to get some medication. He also wanted housing. He added that he had been taking illegal drugs. The workers said they would make an appointment at the mental health clinic for him. "After the appointment," one worker said, "we'll work on housing and public aid or disability." They dropped him off. As they drove away one of the workers commented: "I don't know. This substance abuse situation complicates things. In the mid-90s Congress screwed everything up. They kicked substance abusers off disability. But, two-thirds or three-quarters of the homeless mentally ill are dual diagnosis—mentally ill and substance abusers."[24]

---

24. In 1996 Congress rescinded SSI eligibility for persons with a disability caused by addiction. This provision was established after Congress was told that SSI benefits were spent "in liquor stores and with the corner drug dealer." Since SSI and Medicaid eligibility are linked in most states substance abusers also lost their Medicaid benefits (Post, 2001: 11; Associated Press, 1995; see also: Lamb, 1982; Lamb and Shaver, 1993; Butterfield, 1998).

A few days later we picked him up to tell him about his clinic appointment. The worker asked how he was doing with his panhandling. He said that on weekends he only made $3 a day because there were only tourists in the Loop. However, during the week he made $10 to $15 a day because "some people help me out." With that money, and some coupons, he could get double sandwiches at McDonald's. However, he could not afford a room. He said he really needed a shower because he had been wearing the same clothes for a month. He said that what he needed was $15 so he could spend a night at The Palace Hotel and take a shower. The worker gave him some new McDonald's coupons and a bus pass to get to the clinic the next day. We dropped him off. As we drove away the worker commented that "the Palace is the worst of all the hotels in the area. The cheaper ones have a small room that is just big enough for a bed. The more expensive ones are a little bigger. However, the Palace has rooms barely big enough for a bed and chicken wire instead of a ceiling."[25]

The Southside team drove to a motel where one of their clients, a 47-year-old white male, lived. (The agency paid his rent.) He suffered from severe back pain and other medical problems. They drove him to a clinic on the Northside. After a long wait he saw the doctor. The doctor gave him a prescription for epilepsy medication and wrote him a referral to a pain clinic for his back pain. As we drove back to the Southside, the client said he was disgusted because he felt nothing had been accomplished. He said that he needed to get on disability so he could go back to his regular doctors who knew how to help his back pain. The workers offered to put him on a housing list or to help him go to another physician. No, he said, he needed food stamps and an ID. And, he needed to go back to his regular doctors. He said that his back hurt so much that sometimes he thought of killing himself. But, he realized that this was no solution. Near the motel we stopped at a pharmacy to fill the prescription. It cost $200. The agency paid for it. The workers were told it would be ready tomorrow. They drove the client back to the motel and dropped him off. The researcher asked why the workers took him to a Northside clinic. One of the workers said, "There are a dearth of services on the Southside." The trip had taken the two workers four hours.

Three days later they picked the client up again. They drove to the Westside office of the Secretary of State's vehicle testing center to get him a state ID. However, it was Monday and the facility was closed. They only facility he could get an ID on Monday was at the Secretary of States office in the State of Illinois building downtown. So they drove downtown. Since there was nowhere free to park they gave him the $20 fee and dropped him off. While he waited in line they drove around the block repeatedly. Finally, one worker ran in to the building and said another team would pick him up later. That afternoon, after he had gotten his ID, a second team picked him up and took him to the public aid office. After a wait he saw a case worker. When he emerged from the office he was elated. He had lost his LINK card (food stamp credit card) and it had been replaced. He had also turned in all his paperwork for his MANG application. As we drove back to the motel he was jubilant. He said that when he had been a caseworker himself, he had been tenacious in getting his clients services. And, now he had been tenacious again, and he had helped himself. He explained that he had hurt his back and had to quit his job. He had applied for disability and

---

25. One study found that many homeless men were uninterested in housing that was tied to social services. Instead, they wanted housing that was small, private, safe, cheap, and anonymous (Scott, 2006).

was told that it took about 18 months to decide a case. However, so far he had been waiting for two and a half years and he had exhausted his savings. He hoped the hearing would be next year. Also he said his depression, actually bipolar illness, had gotten worse and he was often severely depressed. However, he felt that today had been a good day. He hoped to get his MANG card soon so he could return to his regular doctors. And he said that when he received his disability check he planned to retire to Arizona. We dropped him off at the motel.

One study found 31 percent of the homeless had one or more chronic physical disorders. And, a recent study in New York City found that the homeless die at twice the rate of other New Yorkers. And, homeless persons were 7 times more likely to die of AIDS than other New Yorkers (Zerger, 2002; Santana, 2006).

Kraybill's (2005) fourth and final stage for an outreach worker is to "hand off" a client to another program or agency. For example:

On Tuesday a worker drove to an inexpensive hotel where James Barrington, a white 41-year-old male lived. (The agency paid his rent.) A worker from another program arrived that was to take over his case on a long term basis. The outreach worker went upstairs and picked up Mr. Barrington. He introduced him to the new worker. The client appeared guarded and suspicious. Although Mr. Barrington's emotions were flat, he was cooperative. The outreach worker told the client the new case worker would take over in a few weeks.

On Thursday the outreach worker went to see the client again. In the meantime the client had gotten his LINK (food stamp) card and was waiting for his public aid approval. He had also seen the agency psychiatrist. The worker thought he looked rather paranoid and asked if he had any weapons on him. He said, no. The worker told him that he would drive him to the mental health clinic next Monday. He then asked the client if he wanted housing. He said, yes. However, he only wanted to live in the Lakeview neighborhood on the Northside. The worker said goodbye and drove off.

Three weeks later the outreach worker saw Mr. Barrington again. He told him that he would soon transfer him to the new worker. The client's affect was still flat and he seemed to have no reaction. However, he said he wanted a job. The outreach worker told him that the new worker would help him. The outreach worker gave him $10 in McDonald's coupons and then went in to the hotel and paid his rent. He told the client they would have one more meeting before the new worker took over. He said goodbye and left.

In the five weeks the researcher observed the mobile outreach unit there were 19 unsuccessful attempts to find or make contact with individuals. Fifty-nine individuals were contacted by the workers.[26] In 21 contacts (36 percent) the interaction was only verbal (see:

---

26. The agency statistician was asked for data on the MOV program. "You're not going to get much," he commented, "because most contacts only occur once." For example, for 720 persons contacted by the program 579 (80%) had their education listed as "unknown."

Table 5-17). This may have ranged from a brief introduction to a discussion about available services. In 12 contacts (20 percent) food or food coupons were provided. In 9 contacts (15 percent) medical or mental health services were provided. And for 6 individuals (10 percent) housing was provided. The unit also handled crisis calls in the office but these were usually brief (see: Slagg, et. al, 1994).

Table 5-17
Service Provided

Service	Number	Percentage*
verbal	21	36
housing	6	10
gift	2	3
medical/mental health	9	15
food	12	20
clothing	1	2
permission (signature)	1	2
identification	2	3
calls	5	8
Total:	59	100

*Rounded

(Table 5-17 is statistically significant to the .01 level.)

During the five week research period the outreach workers went out for a total of 45 hours. They attempted to contact, or did contact, 76 individuals. Since they usually worked in pairs this constituted 90 hours of outreach. Some (attempted) contacts lasted only briefly and others lasted several hours. However, on average, each contact took 70 minutes. (This included driving to and from the location.) Further, the workers had field notes to write-up after each contact. Also, there were meetings, training, and other agency business that needed attention. So, two workers spend 400 hours working over a five week period. However, the two person team only spent 90 hours on the street. So, only about a quarter of the time was actually spent conducting outreach work.

We may conclude that the mobile outreach unit is a valiant attempt to treat the homeless mentally ill. However, there a too few workers, too few hours, and too many homeless mentally ill to have a major impact on the problem. One worker commented that as they talked to one client another 100 homeless people passed them by. And, the programs director summed up the situation when he commented that the program was "a drop in the bucket."

10. Services

The function of the mobile outreach van is to connect the homeless mentally ill to services. One of these is Homeless Health Services. Homeless Health Services (HHS) is a large social service agency that provides health care and housing for 55,000 people annually. This included immigrants, survivors of domestic abuse, low income individuals, and the home-less. One of its programs consisted of outreach workers for the homeless. They concentrated their work in Uptown. This was traditionally a "dumping ground" for patients discharged from the Illinois Department of Mental Health. Over the years the area had become a "psychiatric ghetto" with 10,000 to 13,000 former patients living in the area (Emerson, 1985a). (Since HHS's outreach workers covered Uptown The Open Door's workers concentrate on the south Loop and the southside. However The Open Door workers did refer clients to HHS's housing program).

The HHS outreach workers searched for clients in shelters, alleys, or parks. The program's director stated that these are individuals who have "bombed out in all other systems of care." So, "what ever they need, we give it to them." However, different individuals have different levels of "readiness to change." The agency does not demand that the client take medication or seek treatment. However, the agency does believe in harm reduction. That is, if the client wants medication or to "stay clean" they will help them. They are also involved in the "continuum of housing" program. At the most basic level this program provides "safe havens." These are rooms which are clean and safe. It allows their clients to live inside and be off the street. As the client settles in it is hoped that their comfort level will increase their receptivity to treatment. She believed and there should be "housing, first, getting better, later."[27]

The program director noted that as the Illinois mental health system shifted from agency grants to a fee-for-services system she was concerned that outreach services will suffer. That is because there is "no fee for looking for clients." Further, she pointed out that homelessness was not just a "lack of housing." Instead, it was the product of criminal backgrounds, drug or alcohol abuse, mental illness, and the loss of housing due to the gentrification of some neighborhoods. Therefore, homelessness was a complex set of interrelated issues.

The Open Door homeless van helps to get people in to shelters. One "high-end" shelter is the Lake Shore Shelter (LSS). It is located in an upscale neighborhood near the lakefront. The shelter provides beds, food, showers, and storage. There is no time limit on how long an individual can stay at the shelter. The shelter operates out of two churches who donate their space to the shelter.

The shelter accepts male and female adults. (Many shelters do not accept women, couples, or families with children.) In the director's words "we provide a lot of social services." She explained that over 20 percent of their clients are addicts in recovery. About a third have serious physical or mental problems. And about half of these suffer from psychiatric difficulties. For addicts the shelter had an onsite recovery group.

The staff focused on client accountability and goal setting. The director explained that the shelter's case managers act as "navigators." The clients are expected to be self-directed.

Like most shelters they open in the afternoon (2:00 p.m.) and close early in the morning (6:30 a.m.). During the day they try to make sure "everyone has somewhere to go." They

---

27. This point of view is supported by research. Barrow, et. al. concluded that treatment linkages were unlikely to occur in the absence of a stable housing situation (1989:xii; see also: Hartman, 1986: 81; Lamb and Lamb, 1990:303; Geller and Fisher, 1993:1075; Wang, 2006).

want their clients to set tangible goals. So, during the day their clients go to outpatient treatment, training, or jobs. The shelter "requires progress." They feel that they are successful since 80 percent of their clients are working or looking for work. The director noted that "we're the shelter you go to if you want to work."

The director emphasized that they were "pretty strict" about keeping anyone out who was "under the influence." Also, those with acute problems "don't last long here." And those with significant mental health and substance abuse problem "self-select themselves out" of the shelter. In this manner they are able to create a "safe and predictable" environment.

A "middle level" shelter is Shelter for Recovery (SHARE). One of its administrators considers it a "life saving, life preserving facility." It functioned as an emergency shelter. And unlike most shelters, it had a day-time drop in center. The staff considered it a safe place to sleep or shower 365 days a year, 24 hours a day. It was set up to serve people in immediate crisis. A staff member stated that it has 175 beds and "was usually packed." They routinely functioned at 100 percent capacity and sometimes turned away 1,000 people a month. Officially, the shelter's intake workers refuse to accept individuals who are mentally ill or substance abusers. However, a staff member stated that if they are not "blatant, and causing trouble," they are allowed admittance. As a result of this policy the staff estimated that 30 to 40 percent of their clients are mentally ill. The shelter also provided rudimentary health care and clothing. If an individual needed more sophisticated health care they were taken to a nearby clinic run by Homeless Health Services (HHS).

The shelter also had case managers who provided life skills classes, education, job training, and substance abuse treatment. If the client agreed to accept these services they received a guaranteed bed. Then a case plan with specific goals was created. However, most clients were only interested in shelter. The staff estimated that 2,500 new clients entered the shelter each year. But only 350 accept case management services.

According to a staff member the clients arrived at the shelter "for 17 different reasons." Some were recently discharged from hospitals or released from jail. Others were brought to the shelter by the police or the city's Department of Human Services. Some were referred by other service providers. Some simply "come off the (homeless) trail" (see: Getting Housed, Staying Housed, n.d.: 6).

The average client spent 17 days in the shelter. The shelter provided crisis assistance. An administrator observed that "there is a fair amount of turnover"; and "where do they come from, and where do they go? We don't know."

The clients sleep in large dormitory rooms. A staff member explained that the shelter's beds ranged from desirable to undesirable. Beds next to the walls were considered desirable because they provided safety and some privacy. Windows were a desired amenity and were "high rent" areas. However, sleeping in the middle of the room was less safe, less desirable, and "low rent."

If a client accepted services the case manager would try to move that individual from the shelter to a SRO (single room only) hotel. The rooms in these hotels were small. They had no bath or sink. The client had to sign in and out and they could not have any visitors. If the client succeeded at the SRO they might be moved up to a small apartment. These apartments had less stringent rules but one still had to sign in and out at the desk. If the client continued to improve they might be moved to an apartment with no front desk. And, if improvement continued then the client might be moved to "a nice two bedroom apartment." In order to keep such an apartment the client had to keep meeting with their case manager and attend meetings. "Such apartments are fine," stated a shelter worker, "but what is needed is more affordable housing."

SHARE receives $2 million from the City of Chicago and Federal grants. The Federal grants come primarily from the U.S. Department of Housing and Urban Development (HUD). Instead of funding agencies individually HUD requires each geographic area to form a consortium to distribute their funds for the homeless. In Chicago it is called the Continuum of Care (C.O.C.). Proposals are submitted to the consortium and they are ranked. The shelter administrator felt that this was an effective strategy. He stated that the Chicago area received about $35 million in 2004. He felt that this amount was inadequate. He believed that "budgets are moral contracts" and "the current budget does not meet the moral needs of its citizens." And, he added, "homelessness is a city and Federal problem." The State of Illinois provides no money for the homeless.

The Atlantic Bible Mission in the south Loop is considered to be the bottom rung on the shelter ladder. It has 300 beds, but little or no social services. It is sectarian and provides "Bible study." One agency director commented: "They don't believe in psychiatry." It is reported that everyone must be up at 5 a.m. for Bible studies. There are few rules. The clients may be drunk, high, or psychotic when they enter the shelter. Therefore, it is a dangerous and unpredictable environment. It is said that the security guards are gang members and are sometimes violent (see: Confessore, 2006). It is privately funded and they often refuse entry to outsiders. This includes social service providers. One shelter administrator commented that since it is privately funded "there is no oversight. They operate in a vacuum." However, "they do serve a purpose." It is a place to go "so you don't freeze to death" (see: Scott, 2006).

Homeless service providers use shelters as a lifesaving device. However, the hope is that individuals move from emergency shelters, with a 30 day stay, to transitional shelters, with a 120 day stay. Then they would move to "second stage" housing for up to two years; and finally, in to permanent housing. However, this model has not worked. In the past 20 years the number of shelter beds in Chicago has risen to 6,500. However, during this period homelessness has only increased. There may be as many as 15,000 homeless in the city. This has been the result of the reduction in the availability of low-cost housing, reduced employment due to deindustrialization, the erosion of government entitlement programs, the narrowing of eligibility requirements for government benefits, and a lack of services for the mentally ill after hospital discharge (Getting Housed, Staying Housed, n.d; Maxwell, 2005; Pfeiffer, 2004; Washburn, 2006).

The City of Chicago funds two-thirds of the shelter beds available in the city. Approximately 15,000 persons were housed in those shelters from July 1, 2000 to June 30, 2001. On any given night mentally ill individuals occupy 1,750 of the 3,500 shelter beds available for single adults. These chronically homeless individuals (about 10 percent of all the homeless) may utilize 50 percent of the total shelter days. These individuals often suffer from multiple stressors such as inability to pay rent, job loss, substance abuse, family problems, loss of public aid, domestic abuse, or a recent release from an institution.[28] Many homeless advocates felt that the problem with the shelter system was that it attempted to "fix" the individual instead of dealing with systemic problems. So, a new approach that is being implemented. It will attempt to prevent homelessness. If this fails, then agencies would attempt to place the individual, or family, into interim housing. After that, they would attempt to move them into permanent housing with comprehensive social services (Getting Housed, Staying Housed, n.d.). Many homeless advocates feel that this is a good approach.

Homeless advocates point out that studies show that supportive housing in Chicago costs $20.55 per person a day. A shelter costs $22. A prison or jail costs about $61 a day. A mental hospital costs $437 a day and a general hospital costs about $1,200 a day. In New York it is estimated that a homeless person uses about $40,500 a year in public services (in 1999 dollars). However, "service-enriched housing" costs only about $12,145 a year (Costs of Serving Homeless Individuals in Nine Cities, 2004:2; Culhane, Metraux, and Hadley, 2001; see also: Lipton, Nutt, and Sabatini, 1988).

So, housing first, and getting better later, appears to be a good approach.

11. DMH: A Comparative Perspective

Before we reach any conclusions on the functioning of the Illinois Department of Mental Health let us move from a micro to a macro perspective.

Fifty-five state and territorial mental health agencies (SMHAs) manage the organization, funding, and delivery of mental health services in the U.S. These agencies provide acute care, long-term treatment, and community based services. These community services include supportive employment, housing, and rehabilitation services. During the last century these state agencies have shifted from providing long-term custodial care to funding community based services.

In fiscal 2001 state mental health agencies served 5 million people and controlled $24 billion in budgets. Over two-thirds of these funds went to community services. These services treated individuals with the most severe mental illnesses (schizophrenia, bipolar disorder, and severe depression) (Lutterman, 2004b).

State department's of mental health have been reducing the number of beds and closing hospitals over the last several decades. For example, from 1972 to 2004, state and county psychiatric beds decreased from 361,765 to about 54,000. This was an 85 percent decrease. During this time period 60 of the 277 state psychiatric hospitals were closed (Lutterman, 2004b; see also: Dowdall, 1996).

---

28. A 1996 survey found that two-thirds of the homeless are single male adults. And, two-thirds of the homeless have mental health or substance abuse problems. Also, fifty-five percent of the homeless are uninsured. However, 40 percent do have Medicaid or Supplementary Security Income (SSI) (Post, 21001: 5; see also: Rucher, 2005).

Cuts in Federal funding and the impact of managed care have also reduced the number of mental health beds in private psychiatric hospitals, general hospital psychiatric units, and Veterans Administration psychiatric units. Consequently, there is now a shortage of acute psychiatric beds in some states. These shortages result in waiting lists, overcrowding, and resistance to further closings of state hospitals (see: National Alliance for the Mentally Ill, 2006).

Community mental health services are usually provided directly by states. They may also fund local governments or contract with providers. Four states, including Illinois, have begun to privatize their services.

Forty states served 4.7 million unduplicated clients in fiscal year 2002. On average, these states served approximately 1.5 percent of their populations. In fiscal year 2002 states reported that they served 434,838 persons in state hospitals. In fiscal year 2002 twenty-eight states reported that they served 2,951,162 persons in community mental health programs. In fiscal 2004 Illinois admitted 9,349 mentally ill to its state hospitals. Illinois served 290,000 clients in community mental health centers (Lutterman, 2004b; Illinois Department of Mental Health and Developmental Disabilities, 2004; Powers, 2005; Promise Unfulfilled, 2004; Graham, 2006).

Medicaid plays a major role in mental health funding. For example, from fiscal year 1997 to 2001 funds from Medicaid for state mental health agencies grew much faster than funds from other sources. Medicaid revenues (from the Federal government, as well as, the required stat matching funds) grew from $4.97 billion in 1997 to $8.4 billion in 2001. This was an increase of 69 percent. During the same time period state funds for mental health increased from $10.4 billion to $12.4 billion. This was an increase of 19.4 percent. Overall, state funding for mental health services increased during this period from $17.3 billion to $23.5 billion. This was a 36 percent increase. However, if this amount is adjusted for inflation and population growth it is only an 8 percent increase. From 1981 to 2001, however, there was an 8.1 percent decline. Although Medicaid has helped to increase mental health spending it reduces the flexibility of a state's programs. That is, it limits services to a specific consumer group and a limited number of services (Lutterman, et. al., 2004a, 2004b; see also: Meyer, 2004; Rochefort, 1999; Ingoglia, 2004).

State mental health departments expended $7.35 billion for state psychiatric inpatient care in fiscal year 2001. This was an $802 million increase (11.8 percent) from fiscal year 1997. However, if the amount is adjusted for inflation the expenditure is actually a decrease of 3.9 percent. Further, inpatient expenditures by states was 32 percent of the department budgets in 2001; that was down from 62 percent in 1981. Alternately, community mental health spending was $15.4 billion in fiscal year 2001. This was 66 percent of the total state agency expenditures. From fiscal years 1997 to 2001 community mental health services rose by $5.6 billion. This was a 57 percent increase. In 1981 community services received only 33 percent of the budget (Lutterman, et. al., 2004b).

In order to appreciate the current functioning of the Illinois Division of Mental Health in comparison to other state mental health agencies let us examine the budget of the department.

There are ten state operated psychiatric hospitals (SOPH's) in Illinois. There are also "Institutions for Mental Disease" (IMD's) that provide inpatient services. Many of these IMD's are state-funded, but privately owned. By law, persons between the ages of 21 and

64 living in IMD's cannot be funded by the federal government. Therefore, the state shoulders the cost of sustaining psychiatric patients in these IMD's. However, if these individuals were in nursing homes, the state would receive a 50 percent reimbursement. In fiscal year 2004 the state spent $266 million on 1,416 resident in state operated IMD's and $237 million on 4,680 residents in privately owned IMD's. Overall, state hospitals and IMD's accounted for nearly 60 percent of all state expenditures for mental health (Powers, 2005; see also: Treatment Advocacy Center, 2006a, 2006b).

About 6,300 individuals live in group homes. These are residential, rather than institutional, settings. In fiscal year 2004 the state spent about $473 million on group homes. The state also spent $5.3 million on 1,975 persons who resided in short-term (crisis) housing (Powers, 2005).

In fiscal year 2004 the state provided $357 for housing and psychological services. These services included:

a)   assessment,
b)   treatment plans,
c)   case management,
d)   crisis intervention,
e)   assertive community treatment (ACT),
f)   treatment (including psychological therapy and psychiatric medication), and
g)   rehabilitation (including day hospitals, vocational services, and supported employment) (Powers, 2005).

These services were traditionally funded by a grant-in-aid program in Illinois. The state is now transitioning to a fee-for-service system in order to capture more Federal dollars. Under such a system the state pays the provider a fee for each unit of service the agency provides to an eligible client (Powers, 2005).

Until 2005 community mental health agencies were funded almost entirely by state grants. There is general agreement that current grant levels reflected "historical happenstance." That is, the grant level was simply based upon the previous years funding (Powers, 2005: 11).

Beginning with the 2005 fiscal year the community mental health agencies began billing Medicaid for eligible clients. The difference between this amount and the agencies total was supplemented by state grants. The state may also continue some grants in order to cover clients who are not Medicaid eligible. For example, in fiscal year 2004, 95 percent (122,323 individuals) served by DMH funded agencies suffered from a serious mental illness (Illinois Department of Human Services, Division of Mental Health, 2005b: 85, 126). Whether the remaining 5 percent will be funded by the state in the future is unclear.

The State of Illinois spent approximately $790 million in fiscal year 2001 for mental health services. This was $63.54 per capita for mental health services. This spending level ranked Illinois as 31st in the nation (see: Table 5-18, 5-19).

Table 5-18
State Mental Health Agency Expenditures

STATE	Total Spending (In Thousands) FY 2001	Spending Per Capita FY 2001	Spending Per Capita Rank	% Spending Inpatient Services	% Spending on Community Services
Alabama	$253,279	$56.97	38	40.9%	56.3%
Alaska (3,4)	$51,445	$81.36	21	33.3%	60.6%
Arizona (1,3)	$472,342	$89.36	17	9.8%	87.9%
Arkansas (4)	$75,737	$28.25	49	30.7%	65.0%
California	$3,147,793	$91.61	14	18.1%	80.9%
Colorado	$282,615	$64.24	30	29.6%	69.9%
Connecticut (2)	$439,520	$128.85	5	34.7%	56.5%
Delaware (2)	$73,506	$92.70	13	64.5%	33.5%
Florida (4)	$578,266	$35.41	46	43.6%	54.7%
Georgia	$380,647	$45.59	42	45.6%	48.6%
Hawaii (1)	$213,644	$175.21	2	15.8%	71.4%
Idaho (1)	$60,524	$46.01	41	36.4%	61.8%
Illinois	$789,861	$63.54	31	38.8%	59.0%
Indiana	$394,001	$64.70	29	32.7%	66.3%
Iowa	$213,047	$73.18	25	22.4%	77.6%
Kansas	$161,844	$60.31	35	35.5%	63.0%
Kentucky	$196,918	$48.64	40	51.2%	47.0%
Louisiana	$200,926	$45.18	43	57.9%	40.2%
Maine	$137,508	$107.31	10	30.1%	65.1%
Maryland (1)	$677,806	$126.62	6	30.0%	65.6%
Massachusetts (3)	$682,219	$107.38	9	29.9%	67.1%
Michigan (1,3)	$895,066	$89.96	16	33.0%	66.0%
Minnesota	$517,964	$104.60	11	29.9%	69.5%
Mississippi	$246,792	$86.71	20	59.6%	39.2%
Missouri (1)	$336,198	$59.96	36	50.4%	45.0%
Montana	$111,722	$124.04	7	23.3%	73.3%
Nebraska	$86,564	$50.73	39	63.4%	34.7%
Nevada (1,3)	$120,211	$57.31	37	36.2%	62.9%
New Hampshire (3)	$140,484	$112.03	8	29.6%	68.6%
New Jersey (1)	$763,057	$90.31	15	38.9%	59.3%
New Mexico (1,3,4)	$59,378	$32.60	48	36.9%	62.6%
New York (1,3)	$3,331,688	$175.97	1	29.8%	66.3%

(continued)

(1) Includes funds for mental health services in jails or prisons
(2) Does not include children's mental health expenditures
(3) Includes majority of publicly supported housing for mentally ill
(4) Does not include Medicaid revenues for community programs.

Table 5-18 (continued)
State Mental Health Agency Expenditures

STATE	Total Spending (In Thousands) FY 2001	Spending Per Capita FY 2001	Spending Per Capita Rank	% Spending Inpatient Services	% Spending on Community Services
North Carolina	$616,120	$75.57	23	46.0%	52.4%
North Dakota	$49,854	$78.90	22	44.9%	53.7%
Ohio	$692,288	$61.12	33	28.0%	67.8%
Oklahoma	$136,072	$39.49	44	29.9%	64.3%
Oregon	$336,848	$97.39	12	24.0%	74.4%
Pennsylvania (1,4)	$1,859,764	$151.98	3	21.5%	77.8%
Rhode Island (1,2,3)	$92,500	$87.71	19	25.6%	72.1%
South Carolina (1,3)	$299,402	$73.99	24	36.3°%	58.2%
South Dakota (1)	$45,696	$60.65	34	67.0%	31.3%
Tennessee	$395,203	$69.13	27	32.1%	66.4%
Texas(1)	$796,974	$37.53	45	38.4%	58.0%
Utah (1,4)	$73,790	$32.64	47	55.9%	42.5%
Vermont (1,3)	$79,658	$130.46	4	12.0%	85.2%
Virginia (1)	$466,573	$65.18	28	59.5%	34.9%
Washington (1)	$525,565	$88.13	18	31.9%	65.8%
West Virginia (1)	$45,804	$25.52	50	80.6%	15.7%
Wisconsin	$389,417	$72.39	26	20.9%	78.5%
Wyoming	$30,097	$61.12	32	43.4%	53.8%

(1) Includes funds for mental health services in jails or prisons
(2) Does not include children's mental health expenditures
(3) Includes majority of publicly supported housing for mentally ill
(4) Does not include Medicaid revenues for community programs.

(Promise Unfulfilled, 2004: 42).

Table 5-19

State Spending For Mental Health Programs (Fiscal Year 2002)

Geographical Area	Total State Spending[1]			Community- Based Services			State-Operated Psychiatric Hospitals			State Administration and Other		
	Dollars Per Capita	Rank[2]	Per $1,000 Statewide Personal Income Rank[2]	Dollars Per Capita	Rank[2]	Percent of Total	Dollars Per Capita	Rank[2]	Percent of Total	Dollars Per Capita	Rank[2]	Percent of Total
Michigan	$91.14	17	18	$62.38	17	68%	$27.97	22	31%	$0.78	N.A.	1%
Wisconsin	$90.56	18	17	$60.87	19	67%	$29.45	18	33%	$0.24	N.A.	0%
Indiana	$69.40	28	28	$44.60	26	64%	$24.12	29	35%	$0.68	N.A.	1%
Illinois	$68.79	31	35	$45.02	25	65%	$22.29	33	32%	$1.47	N.A.	2%
Ohio	$61.21	35	33	$42.20	28	69%	$16.50	44	27%	$2.52	N.A.	4%
U.S. (Average)	$87.65			$58.80		67%	$26.63		30%	$2.66	N.A.	3%
U.S. (Median)	$70.02	25	25	$44.50	25	64%	$25.210	25	32%	$1.40	N.A.	2%

Source: Lutterman, T., Hollen, V., Shaw, R., 2004. *Funding Sources and Expenditures of State Mental Health Agencies: Fiscal Year 2002.* National Association of State Mental Health Program Directors Research Institute, Inc.

[1] Total spending for mental health programs controlled by the state's principal MH agency.
[2] State's ranking from highest (i.e., "1") to lowest (i.e., "50").
N.A. = Not available.

(Powers, 2005: 16)

If mental health spending were measured against personal income Illinois ranked even lower. Illinois spent $2.06 per $1,000 in personal income on mental health services. This was 27 percent below the national average of $2.82 (see: Table 5-19; Powers, 2005).

Nationally, states provided about half of state mental health funding from their general revenue funds (GRF). Medicaid provided another 23 percent. In Illinois, however, almost two-thirds of mental health spending came from the general revenue fund. Only 16 percent came from Medicaid (see: Tables 5-20, 5-25). In Illinois about one-half of the funding for community-based agencies came from general revenue funds. Nationwide, this average was 41 percent (see: Table 5-21). And, in Illinois state hospitals are almost entirely funded by general revenue funds. Nationally, only 61 percent of state hospital costs come from general revenue funds. Nationally, 18 percent of state hospital costs are paid for with federal funds (see: Table 5-22) (Powers, 2005).

In fiscal year 2002 Illinois provided mental health services to 1.2 percent of its population. This is below the 2 percent level in other states. (It is estimated that as much as 5.4 percent of the Illinois population may be mentally ill. This would be about 500,000 people [Illinois Department of Human Services, Division of Mental Health, 2005b: 83]). In 2001 the state mandated that private insurance cover mental health services (Public Act 92-185). However, the Federal Employment Retirement Income Security Act (ERISA) exempts self-insured firms from state insurance regulations. Since a significant number of large and mid-size business firms are self-insured the law has had only a modest impact (Hamos, 2005; see also: Frank and McGuire, 2000). The majority of those who received treatment in Illinois did so on an outpatient basis. In Illinois about .8 percent receive treatment in state psychiatric hospitals. Nationally, the percentage for hospital treatment was .07 (Powers, 2005).

Spending for the mentally ill in Illinois was approximately $861,000 million in fiscal year 2004 (see: Table 5-23). The department served 297,176 persons in fiscal 2004 with mental health problems. Fifty-nine percent of the mental health funds were spent on institutional care. These institutions served approximately 6,000 persons (see: Table 5-24). This was 2 percent of the total number of persons who received mental health services. State operated IMD's only served .5 percent of all persons receiving mental health care yet consumed 31 percent of the states mental health budget.

Community mental health programs served 291,080 persons in Illinois in fiscal year 2004. They provided services such as crisis intervention, outpatient treatment, group homes, and psychosocial rehabilitation. Therefore, community based programs served ninety-eight percent of all those individuals who received mental health services during the year. However, these services received only 41 percent of the state's mental health funding (see: Table 5-20; see also: Kiesler and Sibulkin, 1987: 24; Cuffel, Wait, and Head, 1994).

Table 5-21 indicates the funding sources for all community mental health agencies in the state. The department of mental health provides just over one-half of all funding to these agencies (this total includes funds disbursed by the department that are ultimately matched by federal funds). Other agencies provide 13 percent of the funding. Local governments directly provide 5 percent of agency budgets. And client fees provide 6 percent. Thus, community mental health agencies receive 81 percent of their total budget from government sources.

Table 5-20

State Revenue Shares for Mental Health MH Services b Source Fiscal Year 2002[1]

Geographical Areas	State General Funds (Percent of Total Revenues)	State Medicaid Funds (Percent of Total Revenue)	Federal Medicaid Funds (Percent of Total Revenues)	Medicare (Percent of Total Revenues)	Federal Mental Health Block Grant (Percent of Total Revenues)	Other Federal Revenues (Percent of Total Revenues)	Local Government Revenues (Percent of Total Revenues)	Client and Third-Party Payments (Percent of Total Revenues)	Other Sources (Percent of Total Revenues)
Illinois	65%	16%	16%	1%	2%	0%	0%	0%	0%
Ohio	60%	8%	26%	1%	2%	2%	0%	0%	0%
Michigan	48%	20%	27%	1%	1%	0%	2%	0%	0%
Indiana	39%	0%	32%	0%	2%	21%	0%	0%	6%
Wisconsin	21%	17%	19%	1%	1%	0%	0%	2%	39%
U.S.	49%	15%	23%	1.9%	1.5%	2.8%	0.7%	1.7%	4.4%

Source: Lutterman, T., Hollen, V., Shaw, R. *Funding Sources and Expenditures of State Mental Health Agencies: Fiscal Year 2002.* National Association of State Mental Health Program Directors Research Institute, Inc. October 2004.

1. Revenue sources to finance mental health programs controlled by the state's principal MH agency.

(Powers, 2005: 17)

Table 5-21
State Revenue Shares for Community-Based Agencies CBAs by Source, Fiscal Year 2002

Geographical Areas	State General Funds (Percent of CBAs Revenues)	State Medicaid Funds (Percent of CBAs Revenue)	Federal Medicaid Funds (Percent of CBAs Revenues)	Medicare (Percent of CBAs Revenues)	Federal Mental Health Block Grant (Percent of CBAs Revenues)	Other Federal Revenues (Percent of CBAs Revenues)	Local Government Revenues (Percent of CBAs Revenues)	Client and Third-Party Payments (Percent of CBAs Revenues)	Other Sources (Percent of CBAs Revenues)
Illinois	49%	24%	24%	0%	3%	0%	0%	0%	0%
Ohio	46%	12%	36%	0%	3%	3%	0%	0%	0%
Michigan	45%	0%	42%	0%	3%	2%	0%	0%	8%
Indiana	34%	27%	36%	0%	2%	0%	1%	0%	0%
Wisconsin	0%	20.5%	20.5%	0%	2%	0%	0%	0%	57%
U.S.	41%	17%	27%	1.4%	2.2%	2.6%	0.6%	1.8%	6.4%

Source: Lutterman, T., Hollen, V., Shaw, R. *Funding Sources and Expenditures of State Mental Health Agencies: Fiscal Year 2002.* National Association of State Mental Health Program Directors Research Institute, Inc. October 2004.

1. Revenue sources to finance mental health programs controlled by the state's principal MH agency.

(Powers 2005: 18)

Table 5-22

State Revenue Shares for State-Operated Psychiatric Hospitals (SOPHs) by Source, Fiscal Year 2002[1]

Geographical Areas	State General Funds (Percent of SOPHs Revenues)	State Medicaid Funds (Percent of SOPHs Revenue)	Federal Medicaid Funds (Percent of SOPHs Revenues)	Medicare (Percent of SOPHs Revenues)	Federal Mental Health Block Grant (Percent of SOPHs Revenues)	Other Federal Revenues (Percent of SOPHs Revenues)	Local Government Revenues (Percent of SOPHs Revenues)	Client and Third-Party Payments (Percent of SOPHs Revenues)	Other Sources (Percent of SOPHs Revenues)
Illinois	97%	0%	0%	2%	2%	0%	0%	1%	0%
Ohio	92%	0%	0%	4%	0%	3%	0%	1%	0%
Michigan	79%	5%	7%	2%	0%	0%	5%	1%	0%
Indiana	66%	10%	14%	3%	0%	0%	0%	7%	0%
Wisconsin	26%	0%	15%	0%	0%	56%	0%	1%	2%
U.S.	61%	11%	18%	3.0%	0%	3.2%	0.9%	1.5%	1.4%

Source: Lutterman, T., Hollen, V., Shaw, R. *Funding Sources and Expenditures of State Mental Health Agencies: Fiscal Year 2002*. National Association of State Mental Health Program Directors Research Institute, Inc. October 2004.

1. Revenue sources to finance SOPHs controlled by the state's principal MH agency.

(Powers, 2005: 19)

Table 5-23
State of Illinois Spending and Clients Served in MH and DD
Program Categories, State Fiscal Year (SFY) 2004

	Expenditures Dollars	**Clients (Number)[1]**
Mental Health	$861,023,155	297,176
Developmental Disabilities	$1,311,838,483	92,011
Total:	$2,172,861,638	389,187
As a percent of 'total'		
Mental Health	40%	76%
Developmental Disabilities	60%	24%
Total:	100%	100%

1. The count of client is unduplicated within the IDHS individual programs (but not across individual programs).

Source: Authors' calculations of data provided by IDHS and IDPA.

(Powers, 2005: 29)

Table 5-24
State of Illinois Spending on MH Programs and Clients Served, SFY 2004

	Expenditures (Dollars)	**Clients (Numbers)[1]**
State-Operated IMDs	$266,034,796	1,416
Privately-Operated IMDs	$237,614,428	4,680
Community-Based MH	$357,373,931	291,080
Total:	$861,023,155	297,176
As a percent of 'total'		
State-Operated IMDs	31%	0.5%
Privately-Operated IMDs	28%	1.5%
Community-Based MH	42%	98%
Total:	100%	100%

1. The count of client is unduplicated within the IDHS individual programs (but not across individual programs).

Source: Authors' calculations of data provided by IDHS and IDPA.

(Powers, 2005: 29).

Table 5-25
Agency Revenue Shares by Source

Agency Type	Federal Revenues (Percent of Total Revenues)	IDHS[1] Payments (Percent of Total Revenues)	IDPA[2] Payments (Percent of Total Revenues)	Other State Payments (Percent of Total Revenues)	Local Payments (Percent of Total Revenues)	Charitable Contributions (Percent of Total Revenues)	Investment Income (Percent of Total Revenues)	Client Payments (Percent of Total Revenues)	Other (Percent of Total Revenues)
All Agencies	4%	55%	13%	3%	5%	3%	1%	6%	10%
Agencies in "Cook and Collar Counties"	4%	57%	11%	3%	5%	5%	1%	6%	8%
Agencies in "Rest of the State"	4%	54%	15%	4%	4%	2%	0%	6%	11
Agencies Providing any MH Service	5%	56%	9%	4%	7%	2%	0%	7%	9%
Agencies Providing Any DD Service	3%	55%	14%	3%	3%	3%	1%	5%	12%

1. IDHS is Illinois Department of Human Services.
2. IDPA is Illinois Department of Public Aid.

Source: Authors' calculations of the survey data.

(Powers, 2005: 55)

12. Conclusions

There are several points to be gleaned from this chapter. First, whenever a mental health professional was asked to describe the mental health system in Illinois they invariably replied, "What system?" Kiesler reflects this point of view by noting that "no planned . . . national mental health policy . . . exists. National policy is an ad hoc aggregate of uncoordinated laws, historical accidents, and . . . practices that almost defies discussion" (1980: 1066; see also: Kiesler, 1982).

Second, whenever an official of a community mental health facility was asked: "What is the job of the Illinois Department of Mental Health?" Inevitably, their reply was: "To go out of business." However, the reality is that in 2004 59 percent of the department's budget went to maintain institutions; institutions that treated only 2 percent of all the patients treated by the department or its grant-funded agencies. However, it appears that some state hospitals will be closing in the next few years. The remaining hospitals, however, will still absorb a large proportion of the states mental health budget.[29]

Third, in the 1970s there were a number of newspaper exposés on conditions in the state hospitals. However, since many state facilities have closed the press has lost interest in mental health. As watchdogs the newspapers were interested in exposing abuses in public facilities. This built public pressure for reform. However, once patients were transferred to nursing homes and other private facilities reporters appear to have lost interest in the topic. Perhaps this is because the mentally ill were now living in "private facilities"[30] (Rogas and Breslan, 2005; Pear, 2008).

Fourth, Illinois, and other state departments' of mental health, have been involved in a "cost-shifting game" in which players lower in the game attempt to shift costs on to higher-level players; that is, local governments and community agencies shift costs to the states, while states shift their costs of treatment to the Federal government (Frank and McGuire, 1996: 144, 2000: 941; see also: Kirk, 1999; Read and Silver, 2002). As a result of this states have come to rely upon the Medicaid program to support their mental health systems. Medicaid is now the largest payer of mental health services in the country. From 20 to 25 percent of all services for non-elderly adult users of mental health are now funded by Medicaid. Between 7 and 13 percent of Medicaid enrollees use mental health service. In

---

29.   There is one caveat here. A fairly large proportion of those in hospitals are forensic patients. That is, individuals found to be Unfit to Stand Trial (UST) or those found to be Not Guilty By Reason of Insanity (NGRI). At Elgin Mental Health Center, for example, 315 of the 400 beds are for forensic patients. And when I interviewed an administrator I asked: "How does your hospital work?" He replied, "Which one?" That is, the civil and criminal divisions were considered to be separate hospitals by the staff (see: Quintanilla, 2008; Morris, 1997).

30.   The state's Tinley Park mental hospital was recently decertified by the Federal government's Centers for Medicare and Medicaid services. Since only "low income" (uninsured patients) are housed there it had little financial impact on the department (Ziemba, 2007: Position of the Illinois Hospital Association, 2005). And, a reform of the mental health code was recently reported in the newspapers. However, it was already well on its way to passage with little or no earlier coverage (Rubin and Walberg, 2007).

1997 Medicaid spent $14 billion on mental health care. This amounted to 20% of all mental health spending in the U.S. and 36% of all public mental health spending in the U.S. (President's New Freedom Commission on Mental Health, 2003).

A complication in the cost shifting strategy is that the states Medicaid matching funds have become a burden on state finances. Overall, states pick up about 43 percent of the costs. This amounts to 17 to 22 percent of the average state budget. This is a larger share than for elementary and secondary education. Because of this burden Tennessee recently dropped 300,000 individuals from the Medicaid rolls to reduce state spending. Similarly, Missouri is dropping 90,000 persons from their rolls. These budget pressures are the result of Medicaid rolls having grown by one-third from 2000 to 2004. Medicaid now covers 52 million people. This has caused Federal and state spending to rise an average of 10 percent a year over the last five years. Medicaid spending now totals more than $300 billion annually. Medicaid has also become the key financing mechanism for long-term care in the U.S. This segment of Medicaid pays for about two-thirds of nursing home residents' care. And this portion of the program covers 41 million elderly and disabled persons. Its costs have also been rising and it is now also a $300 billion program. With the addition of the new drug benefit Medicaid's cost is expected to increase by 30 percent by 2007 (Pear, 2005a, 2005b, 2005c, 2006a, 2006b; Harris, 2005; West Virginia and Kentucky Alter Medicaid, 2006; Solomon, 2006; Carreyrou, 2006; Hynes, 2002).

Because of this payment structure it has been argued that although the mental health system is premised on deinstitutionalization and outpatient care, our actual commitment is to inpatient care (Keisler, 1981: 206). There is some truth to this.

A further complication is that Medicaid funded services are fragmented among various state agencies: housing, corrections, rehabilitation, children's services, and schools. Therefore, state departments of mental health have no control over much of a state's mental health funding or services (Promise Unfulfilled, 2004). Also, monies for mental health services come from various sources: state and local funds, Social Security (Social Security and Social Security Disability), vocational rehabilitation, education, welfare (Temporary Assistance for Needy Families or TANF), juvenile and criminal justice, child welfare, and Federal block grants. And, departments of mental health have no control over income dispensed to patients outside of state hospitals.

Housing is probably the most important factor in a patient's life, after their income. This, too, is not controlled by departments of mental health. Since housing is expensive, government agencies have been slow to create housing for the mentally ill. One agency official pointed out that "there are 4,000 housing units available but 44,000 are needed. Housing is a big problem. The state spends very little on it." Also, departments of mental health have limited control over nursing homes. These facilities provide little mental health treatment beyond medication. In 1990 nursing homes had approximately 1.5 million patients in the U.S. And the proportion of patients with a serious psychiatric disorder or dementia was between 30 and 75 percent, depending on how mental illness is defined. However, few, if any, had a full time psychiatrist on staff (see: Talbot, 1981: 100). Other residential facilities have emerged for housing the mentally ill in the community. Facilities such as board and care homes, halfway houses, supervised apartments, and other residential facilities held 300,000 to 400,000 individuals in 1990 (Mechanic and Rochefort, 1990:

311). This number is now much larger for nursing homes, as well as, these other facilities.. That is why researchers have begun to speak of "reinstitutionalization," "transinstitutional-ization," or simply, "detreatmentization" (Kanter, 1989: 92; Horowitz, 2002a, 2002b; Tal-bot, 1985: 1006). Some view this expansion of institutionalized individuals as a humanistic method by the state to deal with dependency. M. Foucoult (1965) and others have seen such institutions as merely a cover for a profound and malevolent drive for social control (see: Dowdall, 1999). Instead of arguing this point we should study the institutionalized (in all settings), as well as, the non-institutionalized mentally ill (the homeless) (see: Kiesler and Sibulkin, 1987; Bachrach, 1992: 458; Gronfein, 1985a, 1985b; Horowitz, 2002a, 2002b).

Two types of facilities that deserves much more attention, but which we have not had the time to devote to them, are IMD's and nursing homes.[31] One community mental health official explained that "in the 1970s state mental health officials came to these guys, the facility owners, and said, 'Help me get the patients out of the state hospitals.' They said, 'O.K., we'll take them.' So, we asked them to step up, and they did. Now, especially for the IMD's, which are wholly funded by the state, there's pressure to change. And one of the reasons for this is the quality of patient care. Some of it is decent. In others they're doin' shit, they're bad. Also, to fill their beds some of them are trolling the city looking for the homeless. And, when you ask them about this they say, 'We're just trying to give these people a place to live' " (see: Berens, 1998a, 1998b, 2001).[32]

The community mental health official noted that nursing home operators, and some unions, have made large political contributions to recent gubernatorial campaigns. And one of the lobbyists for the nursing home industry was in the "kitchen cabinet" of a recent governor. He added that although the state is strapped for cash, nursing homes received an extra $20 million dollars for "platinum" care this year. He concluded: "The nursing home industry is the most powerful lobby in the world."

---

31. More than five thousand individuals with psychiatric disabilities live in privately owned IMD's in Illinois. These IMD's house dozens, and often hundreds, of people in the same building. Some have argued that although these facilities are "in the community," they are, in fact, segregated from the community. The American Civil Liberties Union (ACLU) has recently filed a suit claiming that IMD's deprive individuals of "countless liberties and choices."
Also, the ACLU argues that they are inadequately staffed and lack psychiatric treatment, therapeutic activities, or social rehabilitation. They also do not prepare individuals to live independently nor do these individuals receive information about alternatives to nursing homes. Most importantly, these individuals are institutionalized in IMD's when they should be in the "most integrated setting pos-sible" (i.e., true community facilities) (Williams vs. Blagojevich, No. 5 c 4673, 2006). (In New York, adult homes for the mentally ill were found to be filthy and the patients abused or neglected. A study found that "services are costly, fragmented . . . and appear . . . to be revenue driven" [Levy, 2002a, 2002b]).
32. Some nursing home employees, known as "bed brokers," are alleged to have offered cash or gifts to shelter officials in exchange for the transfer of homeless individuals from shelters to nursing homes (Berens, 1998c).

Lastly, and most importantly for our analysis, we must ask: Did our examination of the Illinois Department (Division) of Mental Health help us to explain the mental health court? In other words, was our vertical analysis fruitful? The answer is, yes and no. I was aware that Lewis and his colleagues (1987: 43-60) had pointed out nearly twenty years ago that the Illinois mental health system had become a voluntary system. At that time only three percent of the patients in his study were involuntarily committed to one of the state hospitals in the Chicago area (see also: Lewis, et. al., 1988). So, in a narrow sense, this study was unnecessary. However, the study of DMH was productive. That is, in the past critics complained about what the department did to its patients. What I learned in 2005 was what was important was not what the department *did* but what it did *not* do (lack of treatment for the mentally ill in jail, the homeless, and individuals in IMD's and nursing homes). Also, having been a public aid caseworker in the 1960s I was quite aware of the state shifting individuals from state and locally funded programs to Federal funded ones. However, without the study of DMH in 2005 the crucial role of public aid and Medicaid would not have been quite so obvious. So, with this knowledge it would be most fruitful for our vertical analysis to skip the state legislature and governor and jump directly to that Federal program. However, instead, let us continue our step-by-step vertical analysis, as we originally planned, by examining mental health policy and budgeting in the state legislature and the governor's office. In other words, let us see if our original theory makes this a useful step in our analysis.

References

Abboud, Leila
    2005   "Mental Illness Said to Affect One-Quarter of Americans." *Wall Street Journal.* June 7: D1.

American Psychiatric Association
    2000   DSM IV-TR. Washington.

April 2001 Biennial Report
    2001   "Cermak Health Services of the Cook County Bureau of Health Services." mimeo.

Associated Press
    2005   "House GOP Targets Cash to Drug, Alcohol, Addicts." *The Washington Times.* January 27.

Bachrach, Leona L.
    1976   *Deinstitutionalization.* Rockville, MD. National Institute of Mental Health.
    1992   "What We Know About Homelessness Among Mentally Ill Persons: An Analytical Review and Commentary." *Hospital and Community Psychiatry* 43: 453-464.

Barnes, Julian, E.
    2000   "Treatment Awaits Subway Killer, In Cellblock or Mental Ward." *New York Times.* March 24: 17.

Barnes, Julian E. and Susan Sachs
    1999   "Man Killed By Police Feared His Own Violent Impulses, Records Show." *New York Times.* September 3: 15.

Barrow, Susan M., et al.
  1989   *The Effectiveness of Programs for the Mentally Ill Homeless*. New York: New York State Psychiatric Institute.
Baxter, E. and K. Hopper
  1982   "The New Mendicancy: Homeless in New York City." *American Journal of Orthopsychiatry* 52: 393-408.
Bazelon Center for Mental Health Law
  2006   *Best Practices: Access to Benefits for Prisoners with Mental Illness*. Washington.
Belcher, John K.
  1988   "Rights versus Needs of Homeless Mentally Ill Persons." *Social Work* 33: 398-402.
Ben–David, Miriam F., et al.
  1999   "The Performance of Foreign Medical Graduates on the National Board of Medical Examiners (NBME) Standardized Patient Examination Prototype." *Medical Education* 33: 439-446.
Berens, Michael
  1998a   "Dangerous Bedfellows." *Chicago Tribune*. September. 27: 1.
  1998b   "With State Help, Nursing Homes Open Door to Mentally Ill." *Chicago Tribune*. September 23: 19.
  1998c   "State Moves to Separate Mentally Ill, Elderly." *Chicago Tribune*. October 11: 1.
  2001   "U.S. Condemns Placing Mentally Ill In Nursing Homes." *Chicago Tribune*. January 23: 1.
Bernstein, Nina
  1999a   "Back on the Street without a Safety Net." *New York Times*. September 13: 17.
  1999b   "Qualms About Police Rules on Handling the Mentally Ill." *New York Times*. September 1: 18.
Bianchi, Jeannie and John Fallon
  2001   "Developing a Continuum of Services across Illinois Justice and Hospital Systems." *American Jails*. March/April: 64-68.
Boes, Mary and Virginia McDermott
  2000   "Crisis Intervention in the Hospital Emergency Room." In *Crisis Intervention Handbook*, 2nd ed., Albert R. Roberts. New York: Oxford University Press.
Bolton, A.
  1976   *A Study of the Need for and Availability of Mental Health Services for Mentally Disordered Jail Inmates and Juveniles in Detention Facilities*. Sacramento: California Department of Health.
Briska, William
  1997   *The History of Elgin Mental Health Center*. Carpentersville, Illinois: Crossroads.
Bureau of Justice Statistics
  1996   *Sourcebook of Criminal Justice Statistics—1995*. Washington: Department of Justice.
Butterfield, Fox
  1998   "Violence by Mentally Ill Tied to Substance Abuse." *New York Times*. May 15: 10.
  2003   "Study Finds Hundreds of Thousands of Inmates Mentally Ill." *New York Times*. October 22: 16.

California State Employees Association
  1972   *Where Have All The Patients Gone?* Sacramento.
Carey, Benedict
  2005a   "Most Will Be Mentally Ill at some Point, Study Says." *New York Times*. June 7:
           17.
  2005b   "Who's Mentally Ill? Deciding is Often All in the Mind." *New York Times*. June
           12: 16wk.
Carreyou, John
  2006   "How a Hospital Stumbled Across an RX For Medicaid." *Wall Street Journal*.
          June 22: 1.
Chase, Janet
  1973   "Where Have All The Patients Gone?" *Human Behavior*. October.
Christian, Sue Ellen
  1999   "Special Court for Mentally Ill in Talking Stages." *Chicago Tribune*. November
          7: 4-1.
Christian, Sue Ellen and Christi Parsons
  1995   "Mental Health in Spotlight." *Chicago Tribune*. December 24: 4-1.
Chu, Franklin D. and Sherland Trotter
  1974   *The Madness Establishment*. New York: Grossman.
Ciohajlo, Mickey
  2005   "Fee Ok'd to Aid Mental Health Court." *Chicago Tribune*. February 2: 2-9.
Clausen, J. and M. Yarrow
  1955   "Introduction. Mental Illness and the Family." *Journal of Social Issues* 11: 25-32.
Cockerham, William C.
  2000   *Sociology of Mental Disorders,* 5th ed. Englewood Cliffs, New Jersey: Prentice
          Hall.
Coen, Jeff
  2002   "Test is Planned for Court to Work with Mentally Ill." *Chicago Tribune*. Sep-
          tember 26: 2-1.
  2004   "Mental Health Court Offers Hope For Ill." *Chicago Tribune*. May 13: 2-1.
  2005   "Mental Court Has Startling Results." *Chicago Tribune*. August 7: 2-3.
  2006   "Mental Health Court Called Model for U.S." *Chicago Tribune*. April 21: 2-11.
Cohen, Fred
  2006   "Custodial Suicide: Yet Another Look." *Jail Suicide/Mental Health Update* 15:
          1-11.
Confessore, Nicholas
  2006   "At a Brooklyn Hotel, 'A Drug for Every Floor'." *New York Times*. Jan. 1: 15.
Costs of Serving Homeless Individuals in Nine Cities
  2004   The Levin Group. Falls Church: November 19.
Cuffel, Brian J., David Wait, and Tom Head
  1994   "Shifting the Responsibility for Payment for State Hospital Services to Commu-
          nity Mental Health Agencies." *Hospital and Community Psychiatry* 45:460-465.
Culhave, Dennis, P., Stephen Metroux, and Trevor Hadley
  2001   *The New York/New York Agreement Cost Study: The Impact of Supportive Hous-*

ing on Services Use for Homeless Mentally Ill Individuals. New York: Corporation for Supportive Housing

Data Points
2003   Illinois Hospital Association. Chicago. December.

Davis, Jennifer
1997   "Full Circle." *Illinois Issues*. October. 23: 18-20.

Day, Nancy
1973   "Inside Tinley Park: How They're Suffering for Their Insanity." *Chicago Sun-Times*. Feb. 12.

de Vise, Pierre
1973   "Physicians Migration from Inland to Coastal States: Antipodal Examples of Illinois and California." *Journal of Medical Education* 48.

Ditton, Paula M.
1999   *Mental Health and Treatment of Inmates and Probationers*. Washington: Bureau of Justice Statistics.

Dorivart, Robert A. and Sherrie S. Epstein
1993   *Privatization and Mental Health Care*. Westport: Auburn House.

Dowdall, George W.
1996   *The Eclipse of the State Mental Hospital*. Albany: State University of New York.
1999   "Mental Hospitalization and Deinstitutionalization." In *Handbook of the Sociology of Mental Health*, Carol S. Areshersel and Jo C. Phelan, eds. New York: Kluwer/Plenum.

Drake, R.E., et al.
1989   "Housing Instability and Homelessness Among Aftercare Patients of an Urban State Hospital." *Hospital and Community Psychiatry* 40: 46-51.

Dublin, Thomas D.
1974   "Foreign Physicians: Their Impact on U.S. Health Care." *Science* 185: 407-41.

Edwater-Uptown Community Mental Health Center
1972-3 *Progress Report*, July 1972 to June, 1973. mimeo.

Emerson, Judy
1985a   "Homelessness: A Side Effect of Mental Illness." *Illinois Issues*. October: 13-16.
1985b   "Serving the Mentally Ill: The Gordian Knot of State Human Services Policy." *Illinois Issues*. November: 21-25.

Experts Report Violence, Neglect, and Poor Treatment in Illinois Mental Hospitals.
1996   *The Illinois Brief*. Spring. 53: 1.

Fields, Gary
2006   "In Brooklyn Court, a Route Out of Jail for the Mentally Ill." *New York Times*. August 21: 1.

Foucault, M.
1965   *Madness and Civilization*. New York: Random House.

Frank, Richard G. and Thomas G. McGuire
1996   "Health Care Financing Reform and State Mental Health Systems." In *Health Policy, Federation, and the American States*, Robert F. Rich and William D. White. Washington: The Urban Institute.

2000   "Economics and Mental Health." In *Handbook of Health Economics*, Anthony J. Culyer and Joseph P. Newhouse. Amsterdam: Elsevier.

Freeman, Anderson and Carl Alaimo
2001   "Prevention of Suicide in Large Urban Jails." *Psychiatric Annals* 5: 447-452.

Fritz, Mark
2006   "A Doctor Fight: More Forced Care for the Mentally Ill." *Wall Street Journal.* February 1: 1.

Geller, Jeffrey L. and William Fisher
1996   "The Linear Continuum of Transitional Residences: Debunking the Myth." *American Journal of Psychiatry* 150: 1070-1076.

General Accounting Office
1977   *Returning the Mentally Disabled to the Community.* Washington.

Gerson, Samuel and Ellen Bassuk
1980   "Psychiatric Emergencies: An Overview." *American Journal of Psychiatry* 137: 1-10.

Getting Housed, Staying Housed
n.d.   *Chicago Continuum of Care.* Chicago.

Goin, Marcia
2004   *Mental Illness and the Criminal Justice System: Redirecting Resources Toward Treatment, Not Containment.* Arlington: American Psychiatric Association.

Gold, Steven D.
1996   "Health Care and the Fiscal Crisis of the States." In *Health Policy, Federalism, and the American States*, Robert F. Rich and William D. White, eds. Washington: The Urban Institute.

Golden, Harry, Jr.
1973   "City Psychiatrist's 18 Centers are Open to All—Free." *Chicago Sun-Times.* October 7: 12.

Graham, Judith
2006   "Failing Grade for State on Mental Health." *Chicago Tribune.* March 1: 5.

Gronfein, William
1985a   "Incentives and Intentions in Mental Health Policy: A Comparison of the Medicaid and Community Mental Health Programs." *Journal of Health and Social Behavior* 26: 192-206.
1985b   "Psychotropic Drugs and the Origins of Deinstitutionalization." *Social Problems* 32: 438-454.

Gunn, J. and P. Taylor
1993   *Forensic Psychiatry.* Oxford, England: Linacre House.

Hafemeister, Thomas L. and John Petrila
1994   "Treating the Mentally Disordered Offender: Society's Uncertain, Conflicted, and Changing Views." *Florida State University Law Review* 22.

Hallock, James A., et al.
2003   "The International Medical Graduate Pipeline." *Health Affairs.* July/August. 22: 94-96.

Hamos, Julie, State Representative
   2005   *Moving Illinois Toward a Cost-Effective Policy for Deinstitutionalization for Persons with Mental Illness*. Springfield: General Assembly.
Harris, Gardiner
   2005   "See Fixing Welfare Seemed Like a Snap." *New York Times*. June 19: wk 3.
Harris, Maxine and Leona Bachrach
   1990   "Perspectives on Homeless Mentally Ill Women." *Hospital and Community Psychiatry* 41: 253-254.
Hartman, Chester
   1986   "The Housing Part of the Homeless Problem." *New Directions for Mental Health Services* 30: 71-85.
Harto-Collis, Anemona
   2006   "A Subway Nightmare Will be the Focus of Yet a Third Trial." *New York Times*. May 23:13.
Haug, J. N. and B. E. Martin
   1971   *Foreign Medical Graduates in the U.S., 1970*. Chicago: American Medical Association.
Hayes, Lindsay
   1998   "Suicide Prevention in Correctional Facilities: An Overview." In *Clinical Practice In Correctional Medicine*, Michael Puisis, ed. St Louis: Mosby.
Haywood, Thomas W. and Diane Thomas
   1997   "Correctional Officer Conversation with Mental Health Workers." *The Keepers Voice*. 6-9.
Helping Mentally Ill People Break the Cycle of Jail and Homelessness
   2001   *Psychiatric Services*. 52.
Hernandez, Raymond
   1999   "Pataki Outlines Plan to Halt Emptying of Mental Centers." *New York Times*. November 10: 1.
Hiday, Virginia Aldige
   1999   "Mental Illness and the Criminal Justice System." In *A Handbook for the Study of Mental Health*, Alan V. Horowitz and Teresa L. Scheid, eds. New York: Cambridge University Press.
Higgins, Michael
   2004   "Mentally Ill Find Guidance After Jail." *Chicago Tribune*. January 06.
Hillman, G. Robert
   1973   "Mental Expert Tells Tinley Park Chaos." *Chicago Sun-Times*. Feb. 27.
Hillman, G. Robert and Nancy Day
   1973   "Inside Tinley Park Hospital: Who Protects a Patients Rights?" *Chicago Sun-Times*. February 11: 4.
Hines, William
   1974a   "Medical Manpower: Issues of Quantity and Quality." *Chicago Sun-Times*. June 30: 8.
   1974b   "Top Medics Seen Leaving City for 'Glamour' Areas." *Chicago Sun-Times*. June 25: 5.

Holcolm, W. R. and P. R. Ahr
    1988   "Arrest Rates Among Young Adult Psychiatric Patients Treated in Inpatient and Outpatient Settings." *Hospital and Community Psychiatry* 39: 52-57.
Horowitz, Alan, V.
    1982   *The Social Control of Mental Illness.* New York: Academic Press.
    2002a   *Creating Mental Illness.* Chicago: University of Chicago Press.
    2002b   *The Social Control of Mental Illness*, 2nd ed. Clinton Corners, New York: Percheron Press.
Human Rights Watch
    2003   *Ill Equipped: U. S. Prisons and Offenders With Mental Illness.* Washington.
Hynes, Daniel W. Comptroller
    2002   *Cover Story: Medicaid Continues to Challenge State Budgets.* Springfield.
Illinois Department of Human Services, Division of Mental Health
    2004   *System Restructuring Initiative Project Plan.* Springfield.
    2005a   *Final Report on a Strategic Vision and Comprehensive Evaluation of the Illinois Public Mental Health System.* Springfield.
    2005b   *FY 2006 Mental Health Block Grant Application.* Springfield.
2009 HDS Region Map
Illinois Department of Mental Health
    1973   *Mental Health Statistics for Illinois, Fiscal Year 1973.* Springfield.
Illinois Hospital Association
    2005   *Position of the Illinois Hospital Association Behavioral Health Steering Committee Regarding the Closure or Other Restructuring of the Tinley Park Mental Health Center Facility.* Chicago.
Illinois Legislative Investigating Commission
    1974   *Patient Deaths at Elgin State Hospital.* Senator Phillip Rock and Representative Stephen Sevich, Co-Chairmen, Illinois General Assembly, Springfield. June.
Institute of Medicine
    2006   *Improving the Quality of Health Care for Mental and Substance Use Conditions.* Washington: National Academics Press.
Ingoglia, Charles
    2004   *Cuts to Mental Health Funding: A Costly Choice.* Lexington: Council of State Governments.
Innovative Aftercare Program Slashes Jail, Hospital Stays
    2001   *Mental Health Weekly.* January 15: 1-5.
Isaac, Rael, J. and Virginia C. Armat
    1990   *Madness in the Streets.* New York: Free Press.
James, Doris L. and Lauren E. Glaze
    2006   *Mental Health Problems of Prison and Jail Inmates.* Washington: Department of Justice, Bureau of Justice Statistics.
Jencks, C.
    1994   *The Homeless.* Cambridge: Harvard University Press.

Jordan, B., et al.
  1997   "Etiological Factors in a Sample of Convicted Women Felons in North Caro-
          lina." In *Role of Sexual Abuse in the Etiology of Borderline Personality Disor-
          der*, M. C. Zanarini, ed. Washington: American Psychiatric Press.
Kagan, Daniel
  1990   "Landmark Chicago Study Documents Rate of Mental Illness Among Jail In-
          mates." *Corrections Today*. 164-172.
Kanter, Arlene
  1989   "Homeless But Not Helpless: Legal issues in the Care of Homeless People with
          Mental Illness." *Journal of Social Issues* 45: 91-104.
Kasindrof, Martin
  2005   "National Count of Homeless Puts Issue in Human Terms." *USA Today*. Octo-
          ber 12:1.
Kaufman, Leslie
  2004   "Surge In Homeless Families Sets Off Debate On Cause." *New York Times*. June
          29:18.
Kavitz, Howard M., et al.
  2001   "Reducing Recidivism Among Mentally Ill Offenders: The Role of Psychotropic
          Medication in Correction Psychiatry." *Psychiatric Annals* 5: 409-418.
Keeshan, Charles
  2008   "A Caring Approach to Fighting Crime." *Daily Herald*. June 19: 2.
Kessler, Ronald C. and Shanyang Zhao
  1999   "Overview of Descriptive Epidemiology of Mental Disorders." In *Handbook of
          the Sociology of Mental Health*, Carol S. Aneshensel and Jo C. Phelan, eds. New
          York: Kluwer/Plenum.
Kiesler, Charles A.
  1980   "Mental Health as a Field of Inquiry for Psychology." *American Psychologist*
          35: 1066-1080.
  1981   "Barriers to Effective Knowledge Use in National Mental Health Policy." *Health
          Policy Quarterly* 1: 201-15.
  1982   *Public and Professional Myths About Mental Hospitalization* 37: 1323-1339.
Kiesler, Charles A. and Amy E. Sibulkin
  1987   *Mental Hospitalization*. Newbury Park: Sage.
Kifner, John and Michael Cooper
  1999   "Mayor Defends Police Shooting of Violent Man." *New York Times*. September
          1: 1.
Kirk, Stuart A.
  1999   "Instituting Madness." In *Handbook of the Sociology of Mental Health*, Carol S.
          Aneshensel and Jo C. Phelan, eds. New York: Kluwer/Plenum.
Klemens, Michael D.
  1988   "Ann Kiley of DMHDD: Working With the Shreds of A System." *Illinois Is-
          sues*. March: 8-12.

Kohen, William and Gordon Paul
  1976   "Current Trends and Recommended Changes in Extended-Care Placement of
          Mental Patients: The Illinois System as a Case in Point." *Schizophrenia Bulletin*
          2: 575-594.
Kraybill, Ken
  2005   *Outreach to People Experiencing Homelessness*, rev. ed. Nashville: National
          Health Care for the Homeless Council.
Kuczka, Susan
  2004   "Lake County Weighs Mental Health Court." *Chicago Tribune*. June 29: 2-5.
Kupers, Terry A.
  1999   *Prison Madness*. San Francisco: Jossey-Bass.
Lamb, Richard H.
  1982   "Young Adult Chronic Patients: The New Drifters." *Hospital and Community
          Psychiatry* 33(6): 465-468.
Lamb, H. Richard and Doris M. Lamb
  1990   "Factors Contributing to Homelessness Among the Chronically and Severely
          Mentally Ill." *Hospital and Community Psychiatry*. March. 41: 301-305.
Lamb, H. Richard and Roderick Shaver
  1993   "When There are Almost No State Hospital Beds Left." *Hospital and Commu-
          nity Psychiatry* 44: 973-973.
Lamberg, Lynne
  2004   "Efforts Grow to Keep Mentally Ill Out of Jails." *Journal of the American Medi-
          cal Association* 292: 555-556.
Lavin, John H.
  1969   "The Foreign Doctor Influx—'It's a National Scandal.'" *Medical Economics*.
          February 17.
Legislative Commission to Visit and Examine State Institutions
  1972   *Report*. Springfield, Ill.: 77th General Assembly.
Levy, Clifford J.
  2002a   "New York Restricts Confinements of the Mentally Ill." *New York Times*. Octo-
          ber 19: 1.
  2002b   "Pataki Study Cites Failings at Adult Homes for Mentally Ill." *New York Times*.
          September 15: 24.
Lewis, Dan, et al.
  1987   *State Hospital Utilization in Chicago: People, Problems, and Policy*. Evanston:
          Northwestern University, Center for Urban Affairs and Policy Research.
  1988   *Worlds of the Mentally Ill: How Deinstitutionalization Works in the City*. Evanston:
          Northwestern University, Center for Urban Affairs and Policy Research.
Ligon, Jan
  2000   "Mobile Crisis Units: Frontline Mental Health Services." In *Crisis Intervention
          Handbook*, 2nd ed. Albert R. Roberts, ed. New York: Oxford University Press.
Linn, L. S., et al.
  1990   "Substance Abuse and Mental Health Status of Homeless and Domiciled Law."
          Hospital and Community Psychiatry 41: 306-310.

Lipton, Frank R, Suzanne Nutt, and Albert Sabatini
  1988 "Housing the Homeless Mentally Ill: A Longitudinal Study of a Treatment Approach." *Hospital and Community Psychiatry* 39: 40-45.
Long, Jeff
  2005 "Mental Health Court Studied." *Chicago Tribune*. July 15: 2-3.
Lopez, Margarita
  1996 "The Perils of Outreach Work." In *Coercion and Aggressive Community Treatment*, Deborah L. Dennis and John Monahan, eds. New York :Plenum.
Luhrman, T. M.
  2000 *Of 2 Minds*. New York: Knopf.
Lutterman, T., et al.
  2004a *Funding Sources and Expenditures of State Mental Health Agencies: Fiscal year 2002*. National Association of State Mental Health Program Directors Research Institute.
  2004b *Trends in Mental Health Agencies: The Book of the States*. Lexington: The Council of State Governments.
Lyderson, Kari
  2000 "For Jailed Mentally Ill, A Way Out." *Washington Post*. June 28.
Martin, Dennis V.
  1955 "Institutionalization." *The Lancet*. 1188-1190.
Maxwell, Tonya
  2005 "City Says Plan to Help Homeless is Working." *Chicago Tribune*. July 8: 2-6.
McGuire, Kathleen and Ann L. Pastore, eds.
  2001 *Sourcebook of Criminal Justice Statistics*. Department of Justice, Bureau of Justice Statistics. Washington.
McMahon, Shannon
  2003 "Mentally Ill Often Jailed, Group Says." *Chicago Tribune*. October 22: 14.
Mechanic, David and David A. Rockfort
  1990 "Deinstitutionalization: An Appraisal of Reform." In *Annual Review of Sociology*, W. Richard Scott and Judith Blake, eds. Palo Alto: Annual Reviews.
Mehr, Joseph J.
  2002 *Illinois Public Mental Health Services, 1847 to 2000*. Victoria, Canada: Santayana/Trafford.
Mental Health Case Settled
  1997 *The Illinois Brief*. Fall. 54: 1.
Mental Health Courts Ready to Handle Cases
  2004 *Chicago Tribune*. April 30: 3.
Meyer, Jack
  2004 *State of the State*. Health Policy Forum on Mental Health. Santa Fe: May 17.
Miller, Robert D.
  1987 *Involuntary Civil Commitment of the Mentally Ill In the Post-Reform Era*. Springfield: Thomas.
Monahan, John
  1992 "Mental Disorder and Violent Behavior." *American Psychologist* 47: 511-521.

Morgan, Carole
  1981   "Developing Mental Health Services for Local Jails." *Criminal Justice and Behavior* 8: 259-273.
Morris, Grant H.
  1997   "Placed in Purgatory: Conditional Release of Insanity Acquitees." *Arizona Law Review* 39: 1060-1114.
Morrissey, Joseph P.
  1999   "Integrating Service Delivery Systems for Persons with a Severe Mental Illness." In *A Handbook for the Study of Mental Health*, Alan V. Horowitz and Teresa L. Scheid, eds. New York :Cambridge University Press.
Munertz, Mark R and Jeffrey L. Geller
  1993   "The Least Restrictive Alternative in the Postinstitutional Era." *Hospital and Community Psychiatry* 44: 967-973.
National Alliance For The Mentally Ill
  2006   *Grading the States*. Arlington, Virginia.
National Association of State Mental Health Program Directors Research Institute
  2004   *State Profile Highlights*. Alexandria, Virginia.
National Science Foundation
  1972   *Scientists, Engineers and Physicians from Abroad: Trends Through Fiscal Year 1970*. Washington.
Nevola, Amy E.
  2002   "Cops Get Better Training in Dealing With Mentally Ill." *Chicago Tribune*. May 19: 4-1.
Olmstead v. L. C.
  1999   527 U. S. 602-603.
Pang, Kevin
  2004   "Mental Illness Takes Stage For Police." *Chicago Tribune*. October 29: 2-6.
Parker and Dennison Associates, Ltd.
  2005   *Fee-For-Service State Readiness Review: Illinois Division Of Mental Health (DMH)*. Scottsdale, Arizona. December 22.
Pear, Robert
  2005a   "Cut In Medicare Payments to Hospitals is Advised." *New York Times*. January 18: 13.
  2005b   "Rulings Trim Legal Leeway Given Medicaid Recipients." *New York Times*. August 15: 12.
  2005c   "States Proposing Sweeping Change to Trim Medicaid." *New York Times*. May 9: 1.
  2006a   "Bush Administration Plans Medicare Payment Changes." *New York Times*. July 17: 13
  2006b   "Planned Medicaid Cuts Cause Rift with States." *New York Times*. August 13: 16.
  2008   "Serious Deficiencies in Nursing Homes Are Often Missed, Report Says." *New York Times*. May 15: 21.

Perez-Pena, Richard
  2006   "New York Put Mental Patients in Home Illegally, Group Says." *New York Times*. March 8: 23.
Pfeiffer, Mary Beth
  2004   "A Death in the Box." *New York Times Magazine*. October 31: 48-53.
Polgar, Michael F. and Joseph P. Morrissey
  1999   "Mental Health Services and Systems." In *Handbook of the Sociology of Mental Health*, Carol S. Aneschensel and Jo C. Phelan, eds. New York: Kluwer/Plenum.
Position of the Illinois Hospital Association
  2005   *Behavioral Health Steering Committee Regarding the Closure or Other Restructuring of the Tinley Park Mental Health Center*. Chicago: Illinois Hospital Association.
Post, Patricia A.
  2001   *Casualties of Complexity: Why Eligible Homeless People are Not Enrolled in Medicaid*. Nashville: National Health Care for the Homeless Council.
Powers, Elizabeth T.
  2005   *The Adequacy of State Payments to Community Based Agencies for Services Provided to Illinois Residents with Mental Illness and/or Developmental Disabilities*. A Preliminary Report to the Illinois General Assembly Pursuant To Public Act 93-842. March 31.
"Practitioners Guide to Developing and Maintaining a Sound Suicide Prevention Policy"
  2005   *Jail Suicide/Mental Health Update* 13: 1-20.
"President's New Freedom Commission on Mental Health"
  2003   *Achieving the Promise*. Washington.
"Promise Unfulfilled"
  2004   *Governing*. 17: 36-44.
Quintanilla, Ray
  2008   "Sad State of Affairs for Elgin Cemetery." *Chicago Tribune*. March 21: 2-2.
Ragan, James F.
  1974   *Mental Health and Developmental Disabilities in Illinois: An Examination*. Springfield: State of Illinois, Department of Mental Health and Developmental Disabilities.
Reid, William H. and Stuart B. Silver
  2002   *Handbook of Mental Health Administration and Management*. New York: Brunner/Routledge.
Reidy, J. P.
  1964   *Zone Mental Health Centers*. Springfield, Illinois: Thomas.
Report 1
  1995   *K. L., et al. Plaintiffs v. Jim Edgar, et al., Defendants*. Report Submitted Pursuant to the Agreed Order to Appoint Expert Witnesses. Honorable Brian Barnett Duff. No. 92 c 5722. June 26.
Report of the Legislative Commission to Visit and Examine State Institutions, Charitable Subcommittee
  1972   Senator Frank Ozinga, Chairman, June 1.

Rich, Robert F. and William D. White
 1996 "The American States, Federalism, and the Future of Health Care Policy." In *Health Policy, Federalism, and The American States*, Robert F. Rich and William D. White, eds. Washington: The Urban Institute.

Roberts, Albert R.
 1991 "Conceptualizing Crisis Theory and the Crisis Intervention Model." In *Contemporary Perspectives on Crisis Intervention and Prevention*, Albert R. Roberts, ed. Englewood Cliffs, New Jersey :Prentice-Hall.

Robins, L. and D. Reiger
 1980 *Psychiatric Disorders in America*. New York: Free Press.

Rochefort, David A.
 1999 "Mental Health Policy Making in the Intergovernmetal System." In *A Handbook for the Study of Mental Health*, Alan V. Horowitz and Teresa L. Scheid, eds. New York: Cambridge University Press.

Rhode, David
 1999 "Defense Opens for Subway Killer, Documenting His Long Psychiatric History." *New York Times*. Oct 19: 19.

Rhodes, Lorna A.
 1991 *Emptying Beds*. Berkeley: University of California Press.

Rowe, Michael
 1999 *Crossing the Border*. Berkeley: University of California Press.

Rogas, Angela and Meg McSherry Breslin
 2005 "Facility Fined in Rape of Patient." *Chicago Tribune*. December 15: 2-1.

Rubin, Bonnie Miller and Matthew Walberg
 2007 "Mental Care Reform Eyed." *Chicago Tribune*. April 8: 4-1.

Rucher, Patrick
 2005 "City Tracks Hidden Homeless." *Chicago Tribune*. January 29: 1.

Sachs, Susan
 1999 "Man Shot By Police Was on a Troubled Quest." *New York Times*. September 2: 1.

Sanders, Roxanne, Anderson Freeman, and Laurie Goldman
 1998 "Managing the Patient with an Acute Psychiatric Condition." In *Clinical Practice in Correctional Medicine*, Michael Puisis, ed. St. Louis, Missouri.

Santana, Marc
 2006 "Health of Homeless is Worse Than Imagined, New York Finds." *New York Times*. January 31: 23.

Schlesinger, Mark and Bradford Gray
 1999 "Institutional Change and Its Consequences for the Delivery of Mental Health Services." In *A Handbook for the Study of Mental Health*, Alan V. Horowitz and Teresa L. Scheid, eds. New York: Cambridge University Press.

Scott, Jenny
 2006 "Discovering What Makes a Flophouse a Home." *New York Times*. April 30: 30.

Segall, Rebecca
  2004   "Crisis Intervention: New Training Can Help Cops Save Lives." *Newsday*. Oct.
          21.
Severson, Margaret
  2005   "Security And Mental Health Professionals Revisited: Still A (Too) Silent Part-
          nership." *Jail Suicide/Mental Health Update* 14:1-7.
Slagg, Nancy B., et al.
  1994   "A Profile of Clients Served by a Mobile Outreach Program for Homeless Men-
          tally Ill Persons." *Hospital and Community Psychiatry* 45: 1139-1141.
Solomon, Deborah
  2006   "Wrestling With Medicaid Cuts." *Wall Street Journal*. February 16: 4.
Steadman, Henry J. and Bonita M. Veysey
  1997   *Providing Services for Jail Inmates with Mental Disorders*. Washington: Na-
          tional Institute of Justice.
Steadman, Henry J., Dennis W. McCarty, and Joseph P. Morrissey
  1989   *The Mentally Ill in Jail*. New York: Guilford Press.
Stein, Leslie and Carl Alaimo
  1998   "Psychiatric Intake Screening." In *Clinical Practice in Correctional Medicine*,
          Michael Puisis, ed. St. Louis, Missouri.
Stefan, Susan
  2006   *Emergency Department Treatment of the Psychiatric Patient*. New York: Oxford
          University Press.
Susser, Erza, et al.
  1987   "Childhood Experiences of Homeless Men." *American Journal of Psychiatry*
          144: 1599-1601.
Talbott, John A.
  1981   "The National Plan for the Chronically Mentally Ill: A Programmatic Analysis."
          Hospital and Community Psychiatry 32: 699-704.
  1985   "Presidential Address: Our Patient's Future in a Changing World: The Impera-
          tive for Psychiatric Involvement in Public Policy." *American Journal of Psychia-
          try* 142: 1003-1008.
Teplin, Linda
  1990   "Detecting Disorder: The Treatment of Mental Illness among Jail Detainees."
          Journal of Consulting and Clinical Psychology 58: 233-236.
  1996   "The Prevalence of Psychiatric Disorder among Incarcerated Women." *Archives
          of General Psychiatry* 53: 505-512.
"The Cost of Non-Treatment"
  n.d.   *Thresholds Jail Project*. Chicago, Illinois. mimeo.
Thresholds
  2005   *The Thresholds and Affiliated Organization: 2005 Audited Financial Statement*.
          Chicago.
Toll, Carolyn
  1973a   "Cite Under-Supervision in Mental Hospital Rape." *Chicago Sun-Times*. Dec.
          6: 78.

1973b   "Staff Charges Mental Head Used Employee As 'Scapegoat'." *Chicago Sun-Times*. Dec. 9: 32.

1973c   "Youth Care-Straight Out of Dickens." *Chicago Sun-Times*. Dec. 30: 5.

1974a   "Didn't OK 72-Hour Restraint on Teen, Says Hospital Chief." *Chicago Sun-Times*. April 5: 22.

1974b   "Experts Denounce States New Mental Clinic Plan." *Chicago Sun-Times*. May 22.

1974c   "Legislator Hits Mental Health Grant." *Chicago Sun-Times*. January 9: 26.

1974d   "Mental Patients Suffer in Shift From State Care." *Chicago Sun-Times*. May 19: 5.

1974e   "Patients Fears Voiced At Mental Health Hearing." *Chicago Sun-Times*. January 26: 42.

1974e   "Nurse Suspended in Chicago—Read Abuse, Chief Quits." *Chicago Sun-Times*. April 21.

1974f   "Patient Tied To Bare Bed 2½ Days." *Chicago Sun-Times*. April 4: 4.

1974g   "State to Shut 3 Area Mental Care Projects." *Chicago Sun-Times*. March 13: 24.

Torrey, E. Fuller

1995   "Jails and Prisons: America's New Mental Hospitals." *American Journal of Public Health* 85: 1611-1613.

1997   *Out of the Shadows*. New York :Wiley.

Torrey, E. Fuller and Mary Zdanowicz

1998   "Why Deinstitutionalization Turned Deadly." *The New York Times*. August 4: 18.

Torrey, E. Fuller, et al.

1992   *Criminalizing the Seriously Mentally Ill*. Washington: Public Citizen's Health Research Group/National Alliance for the Mentally Ill.

Treatment Advocacy Center

2000a   *Briefing Paper*. Arlington.

2000b   *NAMI Policy Paper: IMD Exclusion: Implications of Repeal*. Arlington.

Varki, Ajit

1992   "Of Pride, Prejudice, and Discrimination." *Annuals of Internal Medicine* 116: 762-764.

Vickers, Betsy

2000   *Memphis, Tennessee, Police Departments Crisis Intervention Team. Practitioner Perspectives*. Washington: Bureau of Justice Assistance. July: 1-11.

Von Zilbauer, Paul

2003   "Report Says Many Inmates in Isolation Are Mentally Ill." *New York Times*. October 22: 25.

2005a   "A Spotty Record of Health Care at Juvenile Sites in New York." *New York Times*. March 1: 1.

2005b   "As Health Care in Jails Goes Private, 10 Days Can be a Death Sentence." *New York Times*. January 27: 1.

2005c   "Inmates Medical Care Failing in Evaluation By Health Dept." *New York Times*. June 10: 21.

2005d   "Missed Signals in New York Jails Open Way to Season of Suicides." *New York Times*. February 28: 1.

2005e   "State Board Calls Rikers Suicide a Glaring Case of Poor Care." *New York Times*. April 4: 23.

Walker, Daniel, Governor
1974   *Illinois State Budget in Brief, Fiscal Year 1974, July 1, 1973-June 30, 1974.* Springfield.

Wang, Andrew
2006   "A Safe Place to Lay Their Heads." *Chicago Tribune*. August 24: 2-1.

Warren, R.
1973   "Comprehensive Planning and Coordination: Some Functional Aspects." *Social Problems* 20: 355-364.

Washburn, Gary
2006   "Plan to Aid Homeless is Working, Daley Says." *Chicago Tribune*. January 20: 2-4.

Weisman, Andrea
1998   "Mental Health Outpatient Services in Correctional Settings." In *Clinical Practice in Correctional Medicine*, Michael Puisis, eds. St. Louis, Missouri.

"West Virginia and Kentucky Alter Medicaid"
2006   *New York Times*. May 24: 23.

Watson, Jerome
1973   "Charges Bungling, Theft, and Loafing at Chicago–Read." *Chicago Sun-Times*. February 15.

Wilgoren, Jodi
1999   "Tribute to a 'Poet' Who Died in Confrontation." *New York Times*. September 3: 15.

Williams vs. Blagojivich
2006   *No. 05 C 4673*. In The United States Court for the Northern District Of Illinois.

Wing, John K. and Brenda Morris
1962   "Institutionalism in Mental Hospitals." *British Journal of Social and Clinical Psychology* 1: 38-51.
1981   *Handbook of Psychiatric Rehabilitation Practice*. New York: Oxford University Press.

Winerips, Michael
1999   "Behind One Man's Mind." *New York Times*. December 26: wk 3.

Wronski, Richard
2001   "Cops Get More Leeway to Aid Mentally Ill." *Chicago Tribune*. April 2: 2-3.

Zdanowicz, Mary
2001a   *A Shift In Care Community Links* 8: 3-5.
2001b   "1st Line of Response." *Community Links* 8: 4.

Zerger, Suzanne
2002   *A Preliminary Review of Literature: Chronic Medical Illness and Homeless Individuals*. Nashville: National Health Care for the Homeless Council.

Ziemba, Stanley
2007   "U. S. Stops Payment to Tinley Park Center." *Chicago Tribune*. March 14.

6 The Legislature and the Governor
Battling the Alligators

1. Introduction

How far up does one study? That is problematic. We are interested in the significant, though indirect, influences on the commitment court. Certainly, one could catalog numerous indirect influences, however, deciding what is a "significant" influence is a matter only (empirical) research can answer. The Illinois Department of Mental Health (DMH) has proven to be such an influence.

However, since the department is an arm of state government one can ask: What influence does the state legislature and the governor have on DMH's functioning? This is just the question we have asked.

2. The Legislature: 1975

In an early study of legislatures Dye argued that socio-economic development may shape the content of public policy rather than the functioning of a particular state legislative system (1965:200). However, later research by Ericson, Wright, and McIver has shown that "the apparent statistical power of state socioeconomic variables is largely an illusion." So, "state politics does exactly what it is supposed to do in theory . . . translate public preference into . . . policy outcomes" (1993:245). However, in state legislatures public opinion seldom demands specific actions. And, V.O. Key's (1961) has pointed out that public opinion creates "opinion dikes" which constrain the boundaries of political discourse.

So, how does public opinion, or rather, the state's political culture, shape state politics? An early, and very useful, descriptive scheme can be used here.

American state politics contains three distinct types of political cultures. They are the individualistic, moralist, and traditional cultures. Individualistic political culture is pragmatic and focuses on personal gain. That is, politics is seen as a form of business. Moralistic political culture places value on virtue and the common good. Free speech and equal opportunity are seem as important. The traditionalist political culture defends the existing hierarchy of society, its current norms, and the current distribution of wealth and power. Here, rewards are distributed according to the traditional hierarchy. And, ties are often to the land (Elazar, 1972; Elazar and Zikmund, 1975).

Illinois is the archetypal individualist state. Such a system focuses on self-interest. Emphasis is on the marketplace and private enterprise. And the public interest lies in preserving an open marketplace. It is believed that government should invest in collective goods (roads, waterways, education) so that the private enterprise system can improve the common man's lot. Also, government can be entrepreneurial. For example, urban renewal or industrial parks are useful investments because they produce good returns. However, social services produce little return and therefore they are of dubious value. In other words, politics is simply another form of business. And, it is best pursued by professionals. Meanwhile, government bureaucracy should be efficient and businesslike. But, it should also favor its "sponsors" with jobs and contracts. Political conflict may occur but it is usually over fractional, ethnic, or social struggles within the political marketplace (Elazar, 1972; Elazar and Zikmund, 1975; see also: Van Der Silk and Redfield, 1986; Nicholson-Crotly and Meier, 2002).

So, with the individualistic perspective in mind let us describe mental health lawmaking and budgeting in Illinois.

The function of the legislature is "lawmaking." These laws, which begin as bills, levy taxes, set agency structures and powers, and appropriate funds for governmental functioning. Thus, the laws of the state are the written instruments by which state government operates (Van Der Silk and Redfield, 1986:123).

In Illinois its two legislative chambers are equal in power. Legislators in both houses craft two main types of bills: substantive and appropriations bills. Substance bills spell out the regulations of the state over its citizens and organizations. These bills may produce major or minor changes in the law in the functions of agencies of the state. There are three types of these bills. Major substantive bills make significant changes such as increasing taxes or changing the school aid formula. These bills are often controversial. "Middling bills" may change an agency program or change government regulations. They produce both support and opposition. Such bills may or may not pass; but, they will not produce major conflict. "Assembly line" bills make minor or technical changes in the law. These bills are usually non-controversial. That is because they do not offend existing interests. Appropriation bills do not contain substantive language and have no statutory content. Their only function is to specify the amount of money that an agency can spend (Van Der Silk and Redfield, 1986:131-3).

When the state legislature was studied in 1975 its 236 members were elected from fifty-nine legislative districts with one senator and three representatives elected from each district. The General Assembly, as both houses of the legislature are known, has powers which are numerous, extensive, and diverse; that is, it enacts, amends, or repeals laws; it authorizes revenue sources for the state and local governments; it appropriates money for each agency of state government; it establishes and prescribes the organization, duties, and procedures of most of the administrative agencies of the state; within constitutional limitations it provides for the organization and functions of local governments; it conducts investigations appropriate to legislative functions; and the Senate must approve most political appointments made by the governor.

The General Assembly's primary function is the passage of legislation. Since it would be impossible for any one legislator to review all the bills submitted in a year committees are established to analyze legislation in substantive areas. However, the four legislative leaders (the House Speaker, the Senate President, and the minority leaders in each chamber) ultimately control the flow of legislation in and out of these committees. Also, the four leaders appoint committee chairs and committee members. Each of the four hires staff, establishes the agenda, assigns bills to the committees, and sets the schedule. Also, they raise large quantities of money and help their members get elected. Thus, the legislators are obligated to follow the lead of the leadership when legislating.

The legislative process begins with the Illinois Legislative Council, which researches a bill, and the Legislative Reference Bureau, which drafts the bill.[1] Once a bill has been written it is filed with the clerk of the appropriate house. With this filing the formal legislative process begins:

> Bills are given the first reading on the floor of the house; just the title of the bill is read and the bills are then numbered and printed. Bills are referred to the appropriate committee by the panel on assignment, in the House, or by the Senate Committee on Assignment of Bills, in the Senate.

> Consideration is given to the bill in committee meetings. The committee hearings are open to the public. Proponents and opponents, both from the legislature and the general public, are allowed to speak. This is the only public opportunity for individuals to express themselves on legislation. The committee may then do one of several things with the bill. It may send the bill to its legislative chamber with a recommendation of "do pass" or "do not pass." It may add amendments to the bill. Present rules also provide that a Senate committee may return a bill with no recommendation. House rules provide that a bill must be heard within 45 days after being sent to committee. In the Senate, if a majority of members so vote, committee hearings on a bill can be by-passed and the bill will go to second reading without going to a committee.

> After committee action the bill is returned to the House or Senate floor and is read for the second time (second reading). At this stage, amendments are debated and accepted or rejected by majority vote. In the House the amendments must be on the desks of the members in written form before they can be heard. Once a bill passes the second reading in the House it will expire in thirty days unless it is favorably acted upon.

---

1. There are four types of staff in the Illinois legislature. Bipartisan staff works for the Legislative Council and the Legislative Reference Bureau. The leadership staff serves legislative committees experts. Personal staff works for individual members. And, chamber staff conduct non-partisan administrative functions.

On third reading, the entire bill is debated and then accepted or rejected on a final, recorded vote.

In both houses a majority vote of all elected members is required for passage of a bill. This means 30 votes in the Senate and 89 in the House regardless of absences or deaths. This is a constitutional majority and not a simple majority of those present and voting.

After a bill passes the house of origin, it goes through the same procedure in the other house. If the second house makes amendments the house of origin must concur or refuse to concur in those amendments. Then a conference committee, made up of members of both houses, attempts to reconcile the differences in the bills. If both houses approve the conference committee report the bill passes. If either house does not approve this report, the bill may go to a second conference committee. If either house does not approve the second conference committee report the bill is dead.

After a bill has passed both houses it is printed in the official and final form and then signed by both presiding officers.

Within 30 days after passage the bill is sent to the governor. He has 60 days within which to act upon it or it becomes law. If he approves the bill he signs it and forwards the signed copy to the secretary of state. It is then numbered as a Public Act. The Public Act number becomes the official title of the bills, such as PA77-55. This indicates the 77th General Assembly's 55th act. If the governor does not approve the bill he can veto all or part of it. If he approves of the basic structure but wishes to make changes, he can return the bill to the legislature with suggested changes. This is an amendatory veto. If both houses accept his recommendations, the bill, incorporating the changes, becomes law. The governor may also reduce or veto appropriation items. This is a reduction veto. Portions of the bill which are not reduced or vetoed become law.

A vetoed bill or a changed bill or an item veto is returned to the house of origin. The legislature may override a veto by a 3/5 vote of each house. It may restore a reduced appropriation or accept recommendations for change by a constitutional majority.

A bill passed prior to July 1 becomes effective on October 1. If it is passed after July 1 it does not become effective until July 1 of the next year unless 3/5 of the membership of each house agree to an earlier effective date. The purpose of this is to encourage passage of most bills during the regular legislative session. (League of Women Voters, 1973:58-9)

Although knowledge of the formal legislative process is essential, one must also understand the informal, but equally essential, influences upon the legislative process. Our analysis of mental health legislation will encompass both of these influences.

The legislative process begins when a senator or representative brings an idea to the Illinois Legislative Council, one of the research arms of the General Assembly. Once the initial research on the legislator's embryonic bill has been completed he or she forwards it to the Legislative Reference Bureau. The Bureau, which is composed of 30 to 40 attorneys, drafts a bill in conformance with constitutional requirements. The Illinois Legislative Council and the Legislative Reference Bureau are neutral steps in the legislative process; neither has a political or policy orientation. In an interview the director of the Legislative Research Bureau described the functioning of his agency:

"A legislator comes in with an order. We pull it together and write a law which seems workable and feasible. We are only a technical bureau. We translate proposals into legislation, that is, after any policy decisions have been made. If there are two or three ways we could write the bill, we go back to the sponsor and let him decide. We function on the confidential attorney-client relationship and we do not even go to an agency for help unless the legislator says it is all right. The essence of our function is that we dispose and not propose."

After a bill has been written it is introduced, given a number, read by title, ordered printed, and referred to committee. Committee referral is the daily responsibility of the Speaker of the House and the chairman of the Committee on the Assignment of Bills in the Senate. Although the assignment of a bill can be a very crucial, and a very political, step in the bill's life, this is usually not the case with mental health legislation. Mental health legislation is routinely referred to the Human Resources Committee in the House (formerly, Public Welfare) and to the Public Health, Welfare, and Corrections Committee in the Senate. These are non-partisan committees. One lobbyist explained that "a lot of women and freshman, those with social science interests, are assigned to these committees." These bill assignments are routinely made at the request of the bill's sponsor. The leadership, which makes the assignments, is relatively unconcerned about these bills since these two committees handle non-controversial matters.

By non-controversial, we do not mean substantively non-controversial, we mean, politically non-controversial. Issues become politically charged when they involve the organization, prestige, and power of the parties. Cohesive party voting occurs when organizational matters concerning government agencies or the legislature are contested. Parties are also interested in legislation concerning elections, the transfer of powers from an office controlled by one party to an office controlled by the other, or bills involving jobs. Bills effecting the organization of local government, state administration, civil service, registration and election laws, and legislative procedure are also of concern to the parties. Party cohesion occurs when conflict develops concerning such substantive issues such as taxation, appropriations, labor, or education. However, as the accompanying chart indicates "health and welfare" legislation ranks twelfth out of thirteen categories which produce party cohesion on roll call votes (see: Chart 6-1) (see: Keefe and Ogul, 1964).

Chart 6-1
Party Cohesion On **Roll Call Votes** *By Issue Category in State Senates*
Mean Index of Cohesion

	Democrats	**Republicans**
Election Administration	78	66
Legislative organization	73	70
State administration	68	63
Local subdivisions	64	58
Judicial and legal	61	58
Appropriations	70	69
Labor	67	79
Education	65	57
Taxation and revenue	63	68
Regulation of business	58	57
Transportation	57	62
Health and welfare	55	66
Natural resources	55	59

(LeBlanc, 1969: 43).

Francis (1967) has conducted a similar issue oriented survey of all state legislatures and has codified his responses as Issue Respondex Values (IRV). These responses examined the significance of twenty policy areas in regards to their impact on people, their ability to attract media and political support, and whether they involved large amounts of money. He then analyzed his data according to partisan, factional, regional, and pressure group conflict. He found that health legislation ranked at or near the bottom in all cases (see Charts: 6-2 through 6-5).

Chart 6-2
Issue Respondex Values for Partisan Conflict in Twenty Policy Areas

Policy Areas	**IRV**
1. Elections-primaries-conventions	.49
2. Labor	.46
3. Land	.44
4. Finance	.42
5. Administration	.42
6. Apportionment	.40
7. Taxation	.39
8. Social Welfare	.38
9. Highways-transportation	.23
10. Water resources	.22
11. Agriculture	.22

Chart 6-2 (continued)
Issue Respondex Values for Partisan Conflict in Twenty Policy Areas

Policy Areas	IRV
12. Civil rights	.20
13. Constitutional revision	.20
14. Education	.18
15. Local government	.18
16. Courts-penal-crime	.16
17. Business	.14
18. Health	.12
19. Gambling	.06
20. Liquor	.02

Chart 6-3
Issue Respondex Values For Factional Conflict In Twenty Policy Areas

Policy Areas	IRV
1. Liquor	.63
2. Constitutional revision	.60
3. Agriculture	.50
4. Civil rights	.50
5. Business	.47
6. Apportionment	.46
7. Gambling	.46
8. Taxation	.40
9. Highway-transportation	.40
10. Courts-penal-crime	.39
11. Water resources	.39
12. Education	.36
13. Local government	.36
14. Administration	.36
15. Labor	.35
16. Elections-primaries-conventions	.33
17. Finance	.32
18. Social welfare	.26
19. Land	.23
20. Health	.16

Chart 6-4

Issue Respondex Values for Regional Conflict in Twenty Policy Areas

Policy Areas	IRV
1. Apportionment	.74
2. Local government	.62
3. Constitutional revision	.50
4. Social welfare	.42
5. Civil rights	.37
6. Gambling	.33
7. Education	.29
8. Agriculture	.28
9. Taxation	.38
10. Elections-primaries-convention	.27
11. Business	.27
12. Liquor	.24
13. Highways-transportation	.22
14. Water resources	.22
15. Land	.21
16. Finance	.15
17. Labor	.14
18. Administration	.11
19. Courts-penal-crime	.06
20. Health	.03

Chart 6-5

Pressure Group Interest and Pressure Group Conflict in the Policy Areas

Pressure Group Interest (IRV)	Policy Areas	Rank	Policy Areas	Pressure Group Conflict (IRV)
.80	Civil rights	1	Labor	.69
.78	Agriculture	2	Liquor	.65
.78	Labor	3	Business	.63
.75	Liquor	4	Civil rights	.59
.73	Gamboling	5	Gambling	.56
.72	Education	6	Water resources	.52
.69	Business	7	Agriculture	.50
.65	Water Resources	8	Taxation	.48
.63	Taxation	9	Social welfare	.42
.62	Social Welfare	10	Apportionment	.28
.60	Land	11	Constitutional revision	.33
.50	Highways-transportation	12	Local government	.33
.47	Finance	13	Education	.32
.47	Constitutional revision	14	Highways-transportation	.32
.45	Elections-primaries-conventions	15	Administration	.30
.45	Apportionment	16	Land	.30
.42	Local government	17	Courts-penal-crime	.27
.39	Administration	18	Elections-primaries-conventions	.27
.39	Health	19	Finance	.27
.35	Courts-penal-crime	20	Health	.17

However, later research qualifies this point. That is, every governor and legislature must deal with "perennial" issues concerning the delivery of "traditional" state services. These services are education, highways, corrections, healthcare, law enforcement, and welfare. In fact, these policy areas account for nearly 75 percent of the average state's expenditures. There is a broad consensus for states to provide these services. However, a second set of policies are "cyclical." These policies grow, peak, and then decline. They are representative of political themes that come and go from time to time. For example, the expansion of government programs for the poor was a "theme" of the 1960s. However, "tax cut fever" replaced it in the 1970s (Herzik, 1991).

A good example of such a cyclical issue is mental health (see: Chart 6-6). In 1970 mental health was not an issue. However, it emerged in 1973 at the peak of the community mental movement. However, by 1976 it had again disappeared. However, it did appear again, indirectly, in 1982 as a fiscal issue under Medicaid. In 1985 and 1988 it also indirectly appeared as a medium to low concern as "human services" or "health care" (Herzig, 1991: 32-3).

Chart 6-6
Gubernatorial Issue Agendas: 1970-1988 (By Rank, Percent Governors Mentioning)

1970		1973		1976		1979	
Environment	65.2	73.2	Tax Relief	61.5	Tax Relief	61.5	Tax Relief
Tax Increases	52.1	66.6	Property	46.0	Property	40.0	Property
Education Aid	47.8	8.6	Income	15.3	Income	32.5	Income
Gov't. Reorg.	39.1	46.6	Education Aid	7.6	Sales	20.0	Sales
Health Care	30.4	35.5	Environment	38.0	Education Aid	55.0	Education Aid
Drug Control	26.0	33.3	Gov't. Reorg	38.0	Law Enforce.	30.0	Energy Dev.
Drunk Driving	26.0	31.1	Consumer Aff.	23.0	Energy Dev.	27.5	Aid to Elderly
Mass Transit	26.0	26.2	Mass Transit	20.5	Consumer Aff.	25.0	Health Care
Highways	26.0	26.2	Tax Revisions	17.9	Corrections	25.0	Economic Dev.
Law Enforce.	21.7	24.4	Mental Health	17.9	Health Care	20.0	Environment
Corrections	21.7	24.4	Highway	15.3	Highways	20.0	Corrections
Local Gov't. Aid	21.7	21.7	Corrections	15.3	Mass Transit	17.5	Law Enforce.
Consumer Aff.	21.7	22.2	Health Care	22.2	Economic Dev.	17.5	Budget Reform
Government Ethics	13.0	20.0	Tax Increases	20.0	Elect. Law Ref.	17.5	Utility Relief
Welfare Services	13.0	20.0	Unemployment	15.3	Gov't Reorg.	15.0	Unemployment
		20.0	Court Reform	15.3	State Employee Reduction	15.0	"Sunset Laws"
		20.0	State Employee Reduction	15.3	Environment	15.0	Elect. Law Ref.
		15.5	Restore Death Penalty	12.8	Medical Malpractice	15.0	Local Gov't. Aid
		15.5	Welfare Services	10.2	Unemployment	12.5	Legalized Gambling
				10.2	Welfare Services	12.0	Welfare
				10.2	Aid to Elderly	10.0	
N=23		N=45		N=39		N=40	

Chart 6-6 (continued)
Gubernatorial Issue Agendas: 1970-1988 (By Rank, Percent Governors Mentioning)

1982		1985		1988	
Employee Pay Hikes	32.5	Education Aid	73.5	Education Aid	53.6
Education Aid	30.2	Groundwater Protection	44.1	Education Reforms	41.4
Corrections	30.2	Economic Development	38.2	Economic Development	39.0
Sentencing Reforms	27.9	Child Protection Laws	32.3	Gov't. Productivity	31.7
Highways	25.5	Hazardous Wastes	32.3	Job Training	29.2
Tax Reforms	25.5	Tax Reform	26.2	Highways	26.8
Tax Incentives for Bus.	23.3	Gov't. Reorg.	26.4	Environment	26.8
Local Gov't. Aid	23.3	Highways	26.4	Rural assistance	21.9
Gov't. Hiring/Spending Freeze	20.9	Sales Tax Increase	23.5	Capital Improvements	21.9
Increased Fuel/Oil Taxes	20.9	Corrections	23.5	Asst. "Children at Risk"	21.9
Increased Teachers Sal.	20.9	Health Care	17.6	Child Health Problems	19.5
Funds for Higher Education	18.6	Employee Hike	17.6	Funding for Child Care	17.0
Increased "Sin" Taxes	16.2	Income Tax Cut	17.6	International Trade	17.0
Environment	16.2	Human Services	17.6	Maintain Balanced Budget	17.0
Drug Crackdown	16.2	Job Training	17.6	Corrections	14.6
Medicaid	16.2	Alternatives to Prison	17.6	Housing	14.6
Job Training	13.9	Local Gov't. Aid	14.7	Health Care	14.6
Drunk Driving	13.9	Soil Erosion	14.7	Human Services	12.1
Off-set Lost Fed. Funds	13.9	Solid Waste	14.7	Growth Management	12.1
"High Tech" Training	11.6	Agricultural Aid	14.7	Drug & Alcohol Abuse	12.1
Housing	11.6	Drunk Driving	14.7		
Welfare/Human Services	11.6	Raise Drinking Age	14.7		
Vocational Education	11.6	Housing	11.7		
Ethics Bill	11.6	Parks	11.7		
N=43		N=34		N=41	

These findings hold true in Illinois. The only exception being pressure group conflict concerning the mentally retarded. We will discuss this later. Although mental health legislation does occasionally get caught up in partisan conflict, it is usually considered a non-partisan (and non-political) issue. Legislators consider mental health as a "mom and apple pie" issue. Some typical comments concerning mental health by legislators was:

"It's too close to apple pie to screw around with very much."

"Mental health is like motherhood. You don't gain friends by being for it, but you lose friends if you oppose it."

"You can't attack the concept of helping helpless people."

Such feelings are pervasive throughout the General Assembly. Mental health is, therefore, treated as a non-partisan, "good government" issue. The leadership, which provides direction on most legislative issue, is relatively unconcerned with mental health legislation. Therefore, on most mental health bills members are free to become as interested, or remain as uninterested, as they wish. However, even for those legislators who are interested, many are unable to effectively scrutinize mental health legislation because of the thousands of bills they must handle each session. These range from the abolition of pay toilets, to the procedures for licensing barbers, to the funding of the state's prison system. Because of the yearly glut of bills on so many diverse topics the General Assembly has established a policy oriented committee system. This systems funnels legislation to committees such as local government, public welfare, judiciary, education, etc. This functional specialization effectively limits a member's ability to analyze legislation beyond the scope of his or her committee assignments. The committee system also creates a diffuse or decentralized decision making structure in both houses in which the committees tend to become relatively autonomous in dealing with most non-controversial legislation. Since the leadership is only occasionally interested in such non-controversial legislation one might expect that the committees would become "the primary source of legislative leadership," as they are in Congress (Jewell and Patterson, 1973, p. 219). However, in Illinois this is not the case.

In Congress legislative committees and subcommittees mesh with administrative agencies and special interest groups. This provides specialization and continuity in policy areas. This creates a policy oriented subsystem (Freeman, 1965). These "sub-governments," as Cater (1964) has called them, were first described by Ernest Griffith and labeled "whirlpools." He commented: "It is my opinion that ordinarily the relationship among these men—legislators, administrators, lobbyists, scholars—who are interested in a common problem is a much more real relationship than the relationship between congressmen generally or between administrators generally. In other words, he who would understand the prevailing pattern of our present governmental behavior, instead of studying the formal institutions or even generalizations in the relationships between these institutions or organs, important though all these are, may possibly obtain a better picture of the way things really happen if he would study these 'whirlpools' of special social interest and problems" (1939: 182; see also: Griffiths, 1961). Similarly, Cater has argued that a sub-government was the product of the coalescing of those with "the interest or the yen" to deal with a complex problem. They were comprised of the expert, the interested, and the engaged. However, within these sub-governments are various factions. These factions contend for power. So, within a sub-government the power balance may be stable or unstable. Cater has argued that the sub-government's tendency is to strive to become self-sustaining in control of power in its own sphere. So, each seeks to aggregate the power necessary to its purposes; and, each resists being overridden. Such sub-governments, in large part, have "been a result of an increasingly fragmented power structure trying to cope with increasingly big and complicated problems. These are working arrangements for the effective exercise of governmental power" (1964: 17, 22).

Sub-governments have become powerful in Congress. The congressional committee usually operates independently of the legislative party and its leadership. It is the focal point of the national legislative process; and its influence may be critical to the success or failure of a piece of legislation. Congressional committee power gravitates to its chairman. The chairman is usually chosen on the basis of seniority. He or she is responsible for scheduling hearings and deciding which bills are to be called and when. The choice of committee staff is largely their prerogative. They also create sub-committees, assign their membership, and decide which proposals they will consider. Then, he or she acts as the floor manager of bills approved by the committee or chooses someone else to do it. By the time a bill reaches the floor it bears the indelible mark of the committee system (Gove and Carlson 1972: 62).

Similarly, Freeman has argued: "Except in the case of issues which...become 'escalated' to the level of compelling national concern, the resolution of most policy questions tends more often to be left to secondary levels of the political setting. Policy-making is often left to . . . subordinate units of the Administration and Congress. Similarly, the parties often leave issue politics to interest groups. In this sense, such sub-units of the political setting, encouraged by diffused power and functional specialization of political expertise, tend to enjoy a relatively wide range of autonomy. Policy tends to be 'farmed out'" (1965: 22). Clem Miller has summarized this by stating: "Congress is a collection of committees that come together in a Chamber periodically to approve one another's actions" (1962: 110).

In Illinois, however, the committee system has encountered "difficulty in becoming a creative legislative force." In fact, "as an independent determinant of the fate of legislative proposals, the standing committee is of scant importance" (Gove and Carlson, 1972: 62-3). Rosenthal, in examining the manner in which committees shape legislation, concluded that "the Illinois House furnishes a good illustration of a passive committee system. Amendments are made by committees to fewer than one-fifth of the bills introduced; when offered they tend to be technical rather than substantive; and those that do affect substantive change are usually offered with the consent of all parties concerned. Controversy is likely to be settled before committee consideration" (1974: 25-6). If conflict does develop "the parties to the dispute are customarily encouraged to come to some . . . agreement so that the bill can be reported out of committee and later amended on the floor" (Gove and Carlson, 1972: 40). Rosenthal, based on his research on Congress, has summarized the legislative process. This includes referral, screening, shaping, passage, and development of legislation. This has little meaning in Illinois. The key steps of screening and shaping legislation are almost non-existent; and the study of problems and the development of legislation during interim periods usually only occurs in the sense that some committees hold hearings and hurriedly write legislation in response to newspaper exposes.

According to former Illinois Republican governor, Richard Ogilvie, the General Assembly functions in the manner it does because the Cook County Democratic Organization "sees the political environment of Illinois as one where the leaders of the political parties are the focal point for the resolution of conflict—a summit conference theory drawn from the parallel experience in foreign policy. This role sees the legislature like the United Nations, important for fixing an image and for setting the scene, but not as the institution or the arena for real conflict resolution." Therefore, "the overall political system in a state may not view the legislature in that state as the proper forum for the resolution of conflicting political objectives" (quoted in Gove and Carlson, 1972: 153).

Because of such attitudes, committee performance has been limited in Illinois. For example, until recently, the committees of the General Assembly have met only sporadically during the regular six month legislative session (see: Charts 6-7 and 6-8). They have been inundated with bills and have usually passed almost all of them routinely. Although sponsors will occasionally withdraw bills and other bills will not be referred to committee.

Chart 6-7
Days in Session, 1953-1972

	1953	1955	1957	1959	1961	1963	1965	1967 -68	1969 -70	1971 -72
House										
regular	66	58	69	59	62	69	76	94	116	132
perfunctory	8	9	12	2	9	1	17	12	10	29
Totals	74	67	81	61	71	70	93	106	126	161
Senate										
regular	61	50	66	54	57	65	81	99	126	142
perfunctory	7	17	15	7	14	7	201	27	35	14
Totals	68	67	81	61	71	72	101	126	161	156

(Gove and Carlson, 1972: 84)

Chart 6-8
Committee Workloads, Regular Sessions, 1961-1971

	Bills Considered[a]		Bills Referred to Committees		Bills Reported Favorably	
	House 1	Senate 2	House 3	Senate 4	House 5	Senate 6
1971	4,579	3,735	4,114 (90%)[b]	3,997 (80%)	2,909 (71%)[c]	1,852 (62%)
1969	3,798	3,130	3,622 (96%)	2,809 (90%)	3,005 (83%)	2,440 (87%)
1967	3,821	3,511	3,055 (80%)	2,765 (79%)	2,585 (85%)	2,331 (84%)
1965	3,328	2,958	2,416' (73%)	1,872 (63%)	2,028 (84%)	1,579 (84%)
1963	2,540	2,243	2,054 (81%)	1,699 (76%)	1,554 (76%)	1,338 (79%)
1961	2,354	2,076	1,886 (80%)	1,358 (65%)	1,498 (79%)	1,107 (82%)

a. Includes bills introduced and bills received from the second chamber.
b. Percentage of all bills considered.
c. Percentage of all bills referred to committee.

(Gove and Carlson, 1972: 64)

Usually 80 percent of all bills referred to committee will pass (see: Chart 6-8). In fact, Gove and Carlson found that "for the 1961-1965 period, only about 4 percent of all bills introduced were killed as a result of an unfavorable committee recommendation" (1972: 64).

Beyond the crush of legislation the committees in the General Assembly must face the problem of high turnover of committee members and the lack of expertise that this turnover produces. An examination of five House committees by Gove and Carlson (1972) indicated that committee turnover ranged from a low of 33 percent to a high of 76 percent between 1959 and 1971 (see: Chart 6-9). In fact, they found that in 1971, the chairmen of three of the five committees studied had not served on the committee during the previous biennium. This occurred because the seniority system is of little significance in the General Assembly.

In Congress, however, the seniority system allows the committee system, and therefore, the Congress itself, to function. It produces stable and continuous committee service because only with longevity comes power. The ultimate prize, the committee chairmanship, usually goes to the member of the majority party with the longest service on the committee. Critics of the system argue that longevity and mediocrity are frequent companions. Defenders of the system, however, counter that only through long service can committee members gain expertise. In spite of the problems that the seniority system has created it does produce chairmen or chairwomen with great knowledge in their committees or subcommittee's area of specialization. Jewell and Patterson have concluded: "The committee chairman is a specialist, viewed by his colleagues as an authority (or *the* authority) on a given subject" (1973: 241).

Chart 6-9*
Membership Turnover In Selected House Committees 1959-1971

Percentage of New Committee Members

Committee	1959	1961	1963	1965	1967	1969	1971	Average
Appropriations	38.5	30.8	41.0	60.0	88.9	46.3	41.7	49.6
Education	25.7	30.6	38.9	48.1	66.7	63.3	48.1	
Executive	51.3	43.6	59.0	63.3	88.9	50.0	62.5	59.8
Judiciary	23.1	25.0	35.0	64.7	55.6	42.8	58.6	43.5
Municipalities	45.7	36.1	27.0	74.1	81.5	46.3	69.7	54.3
Average	36.9	33.2	40.2	62.0	76.3	49.7	56.1	50.6
Percentage of new House Members	12.4	15.2	17.5	40.7	31.1	25.0	16.9	22.7

* The rate of turnover is unusually high for the 1965 and 1967 sessions because of the at-large election of House members in 1964. Many of the new members elected in 1964 served only during the 1965 session. Their presence inflates the turnover rate for that session.

(Gove and Carlson, 1972: 70)

Not only is the chairman in the General Assembly likely to have little substantive expertise in the policy area of his or her committee, he or she is also likely to possess relatively little formal power. His or her role is to receive requests from sponsors and act favorably upon them. The chairperson may not kill or pigeonhole bills; even the scheduling and organizing of hearings are left up to the legislator sponsoring a bill.

Since the leadership is usually uninterested, and the committee chairperson is often uninvolved, the decision making power for each mental health bill is usually left to each legislative sponsor. That is, each legislator must "carry" their bills through the entire legislative process. If they falter, the bill dies. However, only a handful of legislators have had the interest or expertise to become involved in mental health legislation.

Further, time and information limit a legislators ability to carry out his or her legislative functions. For example, time is in short supply because the Illinois General Assembly is a part-time legislature. Legislators in Illinois have traditionally worked only six months a year; and in that six month period many "full" weeks were often only four day weeks. Furthermore, sessions tended to begin slowly and become hectic in May and June as the session approached its traditionally July 1st adjournment date (see: Van Der Silk and Redfield, 1986).

Other political duties also nibble away at a legislator's time. For example, they must conduct oversight over state agencies in order to assess how well that agency is fulfilling its legislative mandate. They must accommodate their constituents by acting as their ombudsman; and, they must assist local governments in formulating legislation and securing funding. Considering all these duties, it is not surprising that legislators end up "trimming" their legislative service. This is particularly true since 90 percent of the bills the General Assembly handles are routine and non-controversial (see: Sharkansky, 1971).

Beyond a legislator's political duties is the pressure of their regular business or profession. Although the legislative salary in Illinois has been above the national average, it has not usually been sufficient to allow members to abandon their careers. Salaries in Illinois have risen from $3,000 per biennium in 1895, to $5,000 in 1937, $10,000 in 1953, $17, 500 in 1971, to its current annual level of $20,000. Only legislators in California currently receive higher salaries.

The insecurity of political life has also been a prime factor encouraging legislators to continue their interests in their private careers. Service in Springfield has been viewed by most members of the General Assembly as merely a "legislative interlude" (Gove and Carlson, 1972: 86). Steiner and Gove (1960) have remarked: "Lawmaking is a part-time occupation for all but a few members of the Illinois General Assembly. Participation in legislative activity is neither sufficiently demanding, sufficiently lucrative nor sufficiently secure for members to abandon professional or business interests." In an interview one legislative aide summed up most legislators' feelings concerning their lack of time when he commented: "We have no time to examine much of anything. Each member has 3 or 4 committee assignments, and time-wise, that's ridiculous. You can't even get a committee together to find out what's really going on. Our job is to take a look at the larger issues and decide which way to go. But there's just not enough time. It's better than 25 years ago, but you can't do anything and it's frustrating. The legislature just doesn't have the time . . . the time for the nuts and bolts!"

The other legislative necessity that is in short supply is information. It is routinely said in the legislature that "knowledge is power." Woll has similarly commented: "To a considerable extent when the administrative branch can control the channels of information to Congress, it can control the policies supported by that body" (1963: 131). In Illinois, however, knowledge concerning mental health is chronically in short supply.

The logical place to look for such knowledge is the Illinois Department of Mental Health (DMH). However, the relationship between DMH and most legislators is poor. One legislative aide commented: "DMH never tells you what they're doing . . . they're secretive. Besides, half of the time their explanations are gobbledygook. It's a 'we know what's best attitude.' They lose sight of the fact that they're public employees. DMH simply won't tell you things. They don't like to air their dirty linen in public. But information is important to us. We want to know. Where's the money going, how many patients are there, details on staff cuts, how many people are on certain wards, the ratio of custodial to professional staff, etc.? DMH just won't tell you. They lie to you . . . it's unbelievable! For example, they told us that all their staff wears name tags. So we went over and found out they were lying. The legislators, they're supposed to be the bosses, and they're slowly getting results, but . . ." He shrugged. "If you just go over to a hospital for a visit, they're on their best behavior. And if you start asking questions, you find out that there are no hard answers. Besides, the whole place is Kafkaesque. You start talking to the patients and they tell you some fantastic stories. You just don't know what to do and who to believe. After hearing some of those stories, you don't know who's crazy. A lot of those patients aren't so crazy!"

Many mental health professionals in DMH have an equally poor attitude towards legislators. A DMH staffer commented that "most legislators just don't understand"; and a high level DMH administrator derisively commented that "legislators don't understand a lot about state government."

In spite of their generally poor relationship with the department some legislators have attempted to understand mental health, but have failed. One legislator commented: "Politicians don't understand mental health and keep away. But then it's not well understood by professionals either. There are conflicting trends in the field. For example, getting people in to hospitals used to be considered success, now getting people out is success. How are politicians supposed to know what's right since they have no professional competence in the area? Anyway, what has Congress done in mental health? Not much. Sure the legislature is indecisive and lacks knowledge in mental health, but we just reflect the attitudes of the professionals. It boils down to this. We take a tour and see some place is horrible. But what can we do? Are there any *real* cures for mental illness and mental retardation?"

Although some legislators are concerned, other legislators actively avoid mental health. One legislative staff assistant observed: "In mental health the legislature is impotent. And most of the legislators don't care, anyway. It's just that most legislators feel mental health is unsavory and repugnant. They don't like the field. It's distasteful to go into a hospital and confront the problems. Considering how distasteful the subject is, the legislature has done pretty well for mental health."

Since the average legislator has little substantive knowledge concerning mental health he or she must secure it from some source in order to make rational decisions concerning their legislative votes. To a degree, they can do this by securing a brief, one paragraph description of any bill from the Bill Digest. However, legislators' decisions are primarily based upon personal advice ("cues") that come from trusted legislative experts in the field. Typical comments concerning such practices were: "The Republicans follow____ and the Democrats follow ____." "Representative ____ has a retarded son and legislators naturally assume he wouldn't do anything to hurt the retarded. So they'd ask him, 'What do you think?' Or, when a mental health bill came up one legislator might turn to another and say, 'Ask ____ seat mate, he must know.' Or they'd see ____ in the hall and say, 'I read such and such in the papers,' or 'I heard this or that rumor' or 'I got complaints from my constituents, what do you think'?"

Matthews and Stimson reviewed a number of different legislative decision making theories and concluded that "cue-taking" was the most realistic one to explain legislative voting. They concluded that when a member is confronted with the necessity of casting a roll-call vote on a complex issue which he or she knows very little, they search for cues provided by trusted colleagues. These colleagues, because of their formal position in the legislature or policy specialization, have more information to make an independent decision. In fact, cue-givers need not to be individuals. When overwhelming majorities of groups which the member respects and trusts, that is, the whole House, the members of his party or state delegations, for example, vote the same way, the member is likely to accept their judgment as his or her own. With the assistance of such cues it is possible for the ordinary Congressman or Congresswoman both to vote in a reasonably rational fashion and to do so on the basis of exceedingly little information. Therefore, outside the areas of their own policy specialization members need only to decide which cue-givers to follow (1970: 22-23; see also: Clausen, 1973).

The General Assembly has no more than a half dozen legislators who are considered mental health experts. Another half dozen legislators become involved from time to time.[2] However, one state senator is considered to be *the* expert in mental health in the General Assembly. In a recent interview she emphasized two bills as proof of the General Assembly's involvement in mental health policy formation. One bill, passed in the early 1960s, authorized a $150 million bond issue which began the community mental health movement in Illinois. The other bill allowed communities to tax themselves as a means of providing local mental health services. However, community mental health and taxing for services was the product of non-legislative policy formation in which the General Assembly merely ratified pre-existing proposals. In fact, she admitted that she is often not "on top" of changing DMH policy. For example, she explained that her first knowledge that DMH was discharging large numbers of patients from hospitals and placing them in community facilities occurred when she found out that nursing homes and halfway houses were suddenly becoming overcrowded. She lamented: "In many instances the mentally ill are handled brutally. But then,

---

2. One legislator pointed out that "mental health bills" may actually have little to do with mental health. For example, a bill on the confidentiality of patient records is, in actuality, a civil rights bill and not a mental health bill. Therefore, legislative experts in civil liberties would be just as concerned with it as would legislators specializing in mental health. Therefore, bill content, rather than bill label, determines who the experts are on any specific piece of legislation.

who cares about a 'crazy person'? They should treat them like members of the family; for there's a little bit of God in all of us." However, she feels that DMH seems to be running itself without legislative controls. "We have a problem in the legislature, that is, not enough information, or staff to get it. Without staff assistance you can't make decisions based on fact and rational analysis. Your responses become emotional. When you come right down to it DMH's problem is mostly one of attitude. They have this ingrained way of life in which they're possessive of their institutions. It's a, 'We're professionals, we know what to do,' attitude. Ultimately this leads to DMH changing arbitrarily, without coming to the legislature."

Since information is such a limited commodity in the General Assembly the technical content of a bill is often of secondary importance in determining the vote of an average legislator. Therefore, the success or failure of a bill is often the result of the sponsor's personal reputation. In such a situation "an intricate network of personal relationships provides the environment within which most daily legislative decisions are made" (Gove and Carlson, 1972: 138).

So, how highly regarded are the General Assembly's mental health experts? In questioning legislators or staff concerning the quality of expertise on mental health in the General Assembly they would invariable reply that such experts were "good" or "pretty good." However, if guaranteed anonymity, most informants were more candid:

"Representative _____ doesn't understand."

"Senator _____ doesn't understand *anything*!"

"The committee, do they really know what they're doing? What do they do?"

"He's just a knee jerk liberal"

"Senator _____ , he's really what you call . . . a fascist pig."

" _____ is a senile old jerk and hasn't the slightest idea of what's going on. The bills he passes are emotional responses and are very damaging at times."

"Representative _____ is a self styled expert on mental health, but in fact, he doesn't understand much. His legislation is conceptually terrible and impractical; and besides, it's all technically incompetent."

"Senator _____ is very, very good. So is Senator _____ . _____ is a very good guy, except when he's politically involved. _____ has a retarded relative and Representative _____ is good. But, unfortunately, they're all powerless."

"Senator _____ and Representative _____ come up with these hair-brained schemes and then refuse to listen to reason. You can usually live with the intent of their bills but over half of their stuff is unconstitutional because of technical problems or because they deprive the mentally ill of their civil liberties,"

" _____ is good when he's sober and not selling his soul."

"I guess they're pretty good, but one reason they're not better is that DMH never tells them anything."

"The legislators are better than Illinois' apathetic constituents deserve. They want to do right."

"There's no good voice for mental health who's got his head screwed on right."

"Representative _____ and Senator _____ , they're not architects of mental health, but they've made constructive comments and have done a little, not a lot, but a little something."

"Some legislators see DMH as a non-political group of experts. Others see no one, including DMH, as knowing what's going on. Furthermore, the legislative experts often, sometimes, discount DMH. In the end most legislators feel caught in the middle and usually follow the legislative experts."

Another source of information legislators rely on is the legislative staff. In Illinois staffs are organized on a partisan basis in each chamber and work for their party's leadership. The primary function that the leadership staff performs is the analysis of legislation. One legislative assistant commented: "Staff is a key to the legislative process. There's 1500 pieces of legislation pending at any one time and the staff does a pretty good job of handling that." Another legislative assistant explained that "special interests ran things until Speaker Arrington got here and hired some professional staff. Originally, there were four or five people. Now there are twenty some people for the Senate leadership and an equal number for the House leadership. In 1969 we had a small staff. They were underpaid and not too effective. When Arrington got here he even paid some of them out of his own pocket. Now salaries are competitive. With our current staff, which ranges from interns to specialists, our amendments are pretty well thought out. When a legislator submits an idea the staff analyzes it. We look at the short and long term implications of it. If it isn't a good idea, or it's too expensive, we won't go for it. If we uncritically accepted all the amendments proposed there would be twice as much money spent as there is now."

In Illinois the staff is divided among budget analysts and program specialists. One legislator commented: "The most competent staff is on the appropriations committee. They do a fairly thorough analysis of the budgets. When we have hearings they give us information and questions for the witnesses." Staff, however, are not merely "assistants" to legislators. They are bright, young, well educated professionals who sometimes possess a missionary zeal for "good government." One staff member who worked on social legislation and had a master's degree in social work commented: "Staff can be instrumental in educating legislators and helping to mold legislation. The key is to identify legislators with an interest in a certain policy area and then to work with, educate, that legislator." In spite of the ability and zeal of the legislative staff the quantity of work they must handle is overwhelming. One legislator lamented: "At the Federal level there's some staff to handle the workload . . . but there's not much here."

Staff analyses are conveyed to the membership through memos from the leadership. Gove and Carlson have commented that these memos "are not considered inviolable directives, but rather loose indications of the leadership position" (1972: 232). In fact, such memos on non-controversial topics, such as mental health, are considered primarily informational, and therefore, are sometimes ignored. One legislator from the Human Resources Committee commented: "We receive memos from the leadership each day in committee. These memo's are quite important; but some legislators haven't even read them. In fact, 80 percent of the committee's membership hasn't even read the entire bill before voting on it. Most members will take a look at the bill digest for a minute and ask a few questions in committee; but some of these guys never even bother to show up!" Inspite of some legislator's indifference and lackadaisical attitude, staff work can be a key resource for members of a legislature. In California, for example, staff is assigned to each of the committees to prepare written analyses of each bill for every member of that committee. "Committee staffing was a vital improvement," the California Senate majority leader stated. "Prior to the time we had committee staffing we were dependent on other people for all the information we got—basically on lobbyists." One offshoot of staffing, according to a California Assembly committee chairman, was that "by virtue of the staff, many of the older fellows discovered how many people had been lying to them and how much they had been misled" (Harsh and Woodlock, quoted in Gove and Carlson, 1972: 96).

In Congress, "committee claims to expertise stem not only from the individual talents of their leaders, but from the abilities of their professional staffs." For "where the desire to use a staff and confidence in it exists, staff members constitute a linchpin of internal committee decision-making"(Fenno, 1965: 54). Congressional staffs are expert in their substantive areas. In Illinois, staffs have limited expertise in mental health. Therefore, they must, just as legislators must, receive their information from the department. One highly respected staff "old hand" lamented: "The legislature just doesn't believe what the DMH director is telling us. We know we're not getting the full truth but we have to 'believe' him because we have no alternative. We don't even know where the knowledgeable doctors are to investigate DMH. We just don't know where to get information. We've made valiant attempts but our staffs are small and we can only do so much. We know mental health treatment in Illinois is awful, but it's hard to get reliable, unbiased, information. How do you prove your case? If only there was an unbiased institute that we could turn to. We just don't know much around here!"

Another important source of information for legislators is the newspapers. However, the newspapers do not have the staff, time, or money to do an overall analysis of the Department of Mental Health. Therefore, they "highlight" issues "of importance." Invariably, the important issues are patient abuse and administrative mismanagement. These are spotlighted through exposes.[3] This focus on exposes leads the newspapers into the classic adversarial relationship with the department. One reporter, accompanying a private group on a tour of half-way houses, commented, "Half-a-dozen people touring some half-way houses isn't much of a story; but I'll be going on the wards soon, after five o'clock when all the administrators have gone home, and I'll dig up something. Then, we'll zap them."

The typical response to a newspaper expose is a legislative investigation. In fact, the Mental Health Commission, which was ostensibly established as a study group, has become a reactive body to newspaper exposes. One legislative staff assistant who worked with the Commission commented:

"We respond to public outcry. We're not an ongoing overseer of the department. We simply don't have the ability to monitor DMH, but then, neither does the governor. The result is that we don't know what's going on. Excluding the budget, if they lie to you you're stuck. At least the newspapers give you some idea of the actual workings of the department."

Another legislative staff assistant put the role of the press within the larger context of legislative oversight:

---

3. "In reporting what happened, the press is significant not so much for the interpretation of specific events but for the selection of what is news and what isn't" (Gove and Carlson, 1972: 113).

"It's not the role of the legislature to run DMH. We function interdependently. They run the programs and we give them the money, in good faith, to do the job. Our role should be concerned with long range planning and issues such as the right to treatment. However, we get caught up in the department's day to day problems and we lose our long range focus. However, when we try to look at some of these problems we don't get the straight story from DMH; so we end up getting our information from the newspapers. Because we don't take the long term perspective, and we lack adequate information, in spite of the papers, we come up a day late and a dollar short. In fact, we have very limited control over services in DMH because they disguise their needs. And I think they hide the mental health needs of the state because they're so immense that it's embarrassing. Besides, the money needed to offer adequate services would probably break the government. To be honest, we're not sure what it takes to get the job done.

"In our attempts to find out the legislature asks: 'What are you doing about this problem (in the newspapers)?' DMH responds, 'There's no problem,' or 'We don't have enough information on that to respond.' They get away with it because no one really knows the answers. So you're caught in the 'Legislature-DMH game.' The reason the department responds so poorly towards the legislature is because the department doctors says 'How can I run the department when I'm always testifying' or 'How can I keep discussing, arguing the merits of restraints versus more staff.' They perceive such questioning as threatening and feel they're being condemned, so they become incensed. The DMH response to legislative questioning then becomes: 'You're too pushy' or 'We're being badgered', so they withdraw.

"Under those kinds of conditions the monitoring is done by the press. The newspaper makes the legislature aware of things. They make things a priority, and they change our emphasis. The reason the press is so important is because the legislators don't have any vivid impressions about DMH. Few legislators have seen a mentally ill or mentally retarded person in a DMH facility; so, their impressions of DMH are vague. Although they do know about the facilities in their own district, they don't appreciate the department's overall problems.

"Legislators are like the average citizen, or possibly a little more knowledgeable, in regards to mental health. The legislators understand they have a responsibility for the programs, but they don't know how to respond, or what to respond to. It's like free floating anxiety. Legislators deal with this anxiety by denying its relevance to them. It's like dealing with someone else's mom and apple pie, or like seatbelts, it always happens to the other guy. But if they saw what those wards and half-way houses were like, they wouldn't tolerate it!

"The problem is that if a legislator serves where there's no *obvious* mental health problem, then he has no immediate concern. It's not that the legislator is unconcerned; it's just that it's not an immediate concern. But there *are* immediate concerns from his own district. There are victims of tornados, floods, crime, etc. So without first-hand knowledge, or even much second-hand information, the legislator ends up putting mental health services in a political context. And when the priorities become political, this allows interest groups to function, and then the thing becomes a mess. If we handled these things rationally, I don't know what we'd do!"

Such sporadic and irregular oversight, which is invariably carried out ex-post-facto to the incident under scrutiny, is hardly any oversight at all. There is, therefore, in practice, only a limited attempt to secure compliance with legislative intent and to hold the department accountable to legislative policy-making. However, it should be remembered that legislative control of executive departments and agencies is primarily applied *prior* to executive action through the passage of legislation authorizing or restricting specific departmental activities, by prescribing departmental organization, and by the analysis and passage of yearly budgets (Harris, 1964). In spite of this, evaluation and assessment of departmental program tends to be minimal (see: Chadwin, 1974).

What is routinely called "legislative oversight" are actually three separate levels of legislative influence over executive departments. Jewell and Patterson define these three levels of legislative influence as oversight, supervision, and control. The most rudimentary level of influence is that of oversight: "When an individual legislator observes . . . and becomes familiar with the organization and policy implementation of an administrative agency, or when a legislative committee . . . itself in the posture of a watchdog over agency activities, we speak of . . . oversight" (1973: 507). In the Illinois General Assembly there appears to be little close observation or familiarity with departmental affairs. Except for the budget, the watchdog appears not to be watching. One legislator lamented: "There's not enough staff and not enough time, so the agency just slips away." Another important source of information for legislators is lobbyists.[4] Lobbyists supply technical as well as "inside" information on governmental agencies that legislators and staff are unable to acquire in any other manner. One legislative assistant commented: "Lobbyists talk to staff and share their views. It's a positive thing, a real help." Such remarks are typical of the informational function of lobbyists. However, providing information is only a technique that lobbyists use to gain entree to legislators and staff. But no matter what technique lobbyists' use, legislators are usually interested in what they say because lobbyists represent people and interests who ultimately translate into constituents and votes (see: Andrews, 1961). One lobbyist commented: "Legislators want to get along with everybody. They try to keep organized groups as happy as possible. They can't always do it, but they try."

---

4. One must differentiate between public and private lobbyists. Public lobbyists, usually titled "legislative liaisons," represent government agencies and are powerful because the agencies are powerful. We, however, we will focus on those who represent private interests. We should also recognize the difference between inside and outside lobbyists. Inside lobbyists, such as other legislators, are influential because of the camaraderie among members in legislatures: "Congressmen tend to have a high regard for one another, and if someone has a pet bill, you tend to make efforts to accommodate him if it is at all possible. When Congressman ____ had his cranberry bill, everybody said, 'Let's do something for good old Nick,' and so they passed the bill. It wasn't a very good bill and probably shouldn't have passed; but the 'good of Nick' slogan was enough to do it. No lobby could have pushed that bill through. It was just a personal hand for a member" (Clapp, 1964: 204). Such inside lobbying, by those wanting to protect mental health facilities in their districts, as well as, by the legislative experts in mental health, does occur. However, we will focus on the outside lobbyist, the lobbyist who represent "special interests" (see: Vogler, 1974).

Jewell and Patterson see lobbyists as an essential connecting link between legislators and interest groups. They represent demands on the legislative system from organized citizens; they participate in the negotiation process leading to their satisfaction; and their involvement in decisional processes facilitates support in the polity for the public (1973: 332).

Therefore, a primary function of lobbying is to allow for the resolution of conflict in the legislature. That is because "conflict is the very life blood of a decision making body in a free society" (Fenno, 1971: 75). Lobbyists, however, are involved in only a tiny fraction of mental health legislation. The overwhelming majority of such legislation is non-controversial and frequently the product of routine problem-solving or budgeting by the department. Therefore, most professional associations, and their lobbyists, are relatively unconcerned with most mental health legislation. Comments such as these by legislators or staff were typical: "The Illinois Medical Association can control legislation by opposing it. Who's going to say a doctor is wrong? But, in mental health, they're not very involved." "The Illinois Psychological Association? They're not too effective." "The Illinois Nursing Association may occasionally swing the balance on specific issues, but generally they're so-so effective. They barter, and take as much as they can get." "The Association of Clinical Directors is potentially powerful because they represent a geographic constituency. But they haven't done much yet." "The nurses association, RN's the practical nurses, the Chicago Medical Society, they protect the living crap in their own areas; they're goddam tough, but they're not that important to mental health; that's because they're more concerned with medical stuff than mental health."

One group of organizations that are somewhat effective in lobbying are the unions. However, they are primarily concerned with jobs and salaries, not policy. One DMH nurse commented: "The Illinois State Employees Association does have some effect on a narrow range of issues such as wages and retirement benefits. But, overall, they don't have much of an effect." One legislator, considered the General Assembly's primary expert on mental health, similarly commented: "DMH's employees have great strength in maintaining the budget. In fact, DMH had to justify some recent firings to the union because of the stink they made. The department got singed, so after that they pretty much laid off the firings." One legislator concluded. "The unions pushed the department on pay and to get union tradesmen; otherwise, they're not really important, except for the crimp they put in your budget!"

The most influential union, with a sizable number of members inside the department, is the American Federation of State, County, and Municipal Employees (AFSCME). They represent many ward level employees. Although they are intensely interested in better patient care most of their lobbying efforts have gone into saving jobs in the last few years. For example, AFSCME, along with a coalition of other mental health organizations, organized a "Conference to Save Mental Health in Illinois." The meeting was attended by two to three thousand persons; it was estimated that about half were union employees. The meetings focus was to support a bill which would have forced the department to take any program cut or hospital closing to a community board. And it was assumed the local board would oppose them, thereby saving jobs. The bill, however, failed when the department, and then the governor, opposed it.

A number of other mental health interest groups are also represented by lobbyists. One lobbyist represents two organizations of varying influence, the Illinois Mental Health Association and the nursing home operators. Although both groups have the same lobbyist, the Mental Health Association is thought of as weak and the nursing home operators are believed to be strong. Comments by a local Federal official were typical of the feelings concerning the Mental Health Association. "The Association tries to be effective but it's not very strong. It just really doesn't do very much. However, in states in which the mental health associations are organized along county lines, like Indiana, they have political clout. In Illinois, however, they don't effect the distribution of money, use of services, or rates of utilization. They're just ineffectual. They're the 'tea and crumpets' crowd." He went on to explain that the lobbying for the nursing home operators is effective because they are able to "control votes through their letter writing and telegram campaigns." They are "pretty effective in pushing for more contract [private] care" for former patients. However, it is questionable how much influence they actually possess since the department has also been pushing for more contract care. For example, one high level DMH official recently commented: "DMH can't do everything in mental health. And if we tried, we couldn't do it efficiently. Local agencies can literally do it better because they're locally accountable and tailor their services to the community. We'll fund and coordinate these services but we won't run them."

One question that has arisen concerns the lobbyist for the nursing home operators. Is it a conflict of interest that he is urging that more money be spent for contract care in the community while he is representing those who would benefit from such a policy? In an interview the lobbyist responded to this charge by saying: "There's no conflict of interest. I represent a whole range of groups: the Illinois Press Association, the Independent Accountants, the Optical Organization, the Wildlife Federation, as well as, the nursing home operators; and I only represent them during legislative sessions, and sometimes, not even then. There's no conflict of interest because most patients upon release are sent to shelter care facilities, not nursing homes; and they're represented by a different association and a different lobbyist. I've never had any problem representing the nursing home operators because they've always supported mental health and good government."

The most powerful lobbying group in mental health is the Illinois Association for the Mentally Retarded (IAMR). They buttonhole legislators as they come off the legislative floor. They also organize grass-roots support for their organization's legislative program. In an interview one of the group's lobbyists described her methods:

"What we try to get are inputs into the legislative process. We begin by asking legislators to sponsor increases in the department's budget. While in committee there are various forces we can apply to help get the bill through. For example, we can have people such as volunteers, staff, professionals, citizens, etc. testify. Once the bill gets to the floor we make sure that legislators have personal letters coming in. We don't overdo it. We focus on three or four major bills for letter writing campaigns. The reason personal letters work is because legislators are influenced by people who can cause trouble in their district. Legislators also don't know their constituents' feelings on these issues so that ten letters on one issue may be extremely influential.

"The way you can be assured of strong grass roots support is to keep the rank-and-file people in your organization informed; that is, by sending out newsletters, even twice a week, if necessary. You also have to establish a good relationship with the legislators. There must be rapport, trust, with the legislator; and he must consider you and your organization as 'responsible people.' One way to do this is to only give legislators good, and not embarrassing, bills."

Another of their lobbyists commented: "The key to the process is to try to get the legislator to trust you, and then most of your job is finished. The personal element can be very effective. But you must also come up with reasonable legislation. It can't be pie in the sky and it can't be expensive. Once you've proposed your legislation you must make a case for it as well as find a source for the money. You must also do 'fine tuning,' that is, you readjust things in the budget so that you don't have to ask for a lot of new money all the time. You also have to let them know during the year that they can't cut your money or programs with impunity."

"That's right," the first lobbyist added, "you've got to keep the pressure on. Legislators have to understand that this is an important issue with grass roots support. For example, your bills must be watched closely and when there's a critical hearing you must bring in people from every legislative district. They then have to be psyched up to follow the process. You get people up, but you don't let them get abusive or you'll ruin your organization's good name. Then you've got to teach your people how to lobby. You get a legislator and give him a good talking to. Then you have your people chant, 'When does the bill come up?' And be sure to get the media focused on your people."

"Yes, the media, the press is the tool," the second lobbyist broke in, "a powerful tool. You can use it for projecting your concern and amplifying an issue. It's good for pushing legislative oversight, too. The press, they sting like gnat, they're gad-flies. They put enough heat and light on things to change them. Oh, they deny they change anything, but we know they do."

The first lobbyist continued: "Not for profit organizations can spend only five per cent of our time on lobbying. But, officially, lobbying is only the time spent pulling legislators off the floor. This brief time, however, can be very profitable. You can pull a legislator out of the House or Senate and give him a good talking to quite quickly. The reason you can be successful is because of your image. You're a 'charitable organization' and he figures 'your cause must be clean.' This is important because it must appear that you're above dirty politics. That's why you get 'real people' to write letters to them. This produces the emotional appeal, and then we make an intellectual one with our data. We used this approach with the bill to limit lead in paints. We made the issue the 'paint lobby' vs. 'kids.' We worked and got a decent compromise out of it.

"Our association has been called the most powerful lobby in Springfield. That's because we use the energy of a lot of grass roots people while making reasonable demands. One thing that has really helped is that mental retardation is a current cause. It's a hot issue and a legislator can be made a hero to the grass roots for his support of our bills. The crucial point to keep in mind, and to keep before the legislator, is that this is not a 'political issue,' it's a 'people issue'."

The reason the IAMR is successful in its lobbying is not just because the group has power, but because many legislators and staff perceive them as a legitimate spokesman for that interest (see: Zeigler and van Dalen, 1971; Zeigler, 1963). One legislator commented: "There's a lot of constituent interest in helping the mentally retarded. Parent's groups push hard on this and so do we. The department is pushing for the mentally ill and the legislature is pushing for the retarded."

Some legislators and staff consider lobbyists an annoyance. One highly respected staff assistant commented: "Lobbyists are important, but they're a big pain in the katute! You vote for their bills just to keep them away. Some babe once slept on a Senator's doorstep until she got $45,000 for some program. What a pain."

Other staff members and legislators have more substantive complaints concerning the legitimacy of the IAMR. One staff member commented: "The reason we hear more about the retarded may be because they're a more middle class group than the mentally ill. But, just like anything else in Springfield, the loudest wheel gets the grease." Another staff member added: "Lobbyists are out for their own special interest, or they should be fired. But they forget who they're representing and become more concerned with maintaining themselves than representing their group's interests. They develop issues in order to keep their jobs. They've become a self-perpetuating bureaucracy. Now, don't get me wrong, the director of the Association [IAMR] is sharp and knows his stuff, and in a pinch he's god-damn tough. If he's got a bill coming up there'll be a telegram onslaught. On second reading you'll hear, 'protect the sanctity of the bill.' Then there are invariably a lot of calls to legislators' homes. There will be a lot of pressure to pass his bill." However, a departmental official commented: "The IAMR tried to get a bill through the legislature to set up a separate department for the retarded. This bill had a board which was to have half of its members appointed from the very service providers the department was to deal with. Is that a good idea? He didn't present this issue to us rationally and ask us to analyze it, but he kicked up an emotional storm full of chicanery and demagoguery. It's simple, he represents the provider groups. Politics is very rational. People's needs are being met, but it's very corrupt. The thing that really burns me up about all this is that the association's director, at the drop of a hat, will bring his ten retarded kids and their mothers to Springfield and parade them all over the place. If you vote against their bill you feel like a louse. It's enough to turn your stomach!"

No matter how one feels about the tactics employed by the Illinois Association for the Mentally Retarded, one must ask whether the interests of the Association are the same as those of state's citizens. One highly respected legislator commented:

"The IAMR is a highly organized group, with an emotional appeal, and no opposition. Since the legislature responds to pressure, the Association is a powerful group. A few years ago they pushed through a bill to build half-a-dozen new residential facilities throughout the state for the retarded. This went against the national trend against institutionalizing people. Therefore, we must ask: Is a group of parents with mentally retarded children the wisest group of persons to decide the deployment of state facilities for the retarded? I firmly believe that few of those children truly needed hospital care. However, a lot of those parents can't, or won't, take their kids back home because they're guilt ridden. The parents say,

'Nothing is too good for my kids,' except to keep them at home. Did you know that there are more people in the state with epilepsy than there are retarded, but none of those people are hospitalized.

"With everyone looking out for their own special interest the result is fragmentation in our mental health policy. These people aren't villains, but you need to remember that it's a private association speaking for a few private citizens and not the public. It just never occurred to anyone that the interests of the IAMR and the public were different."

Gove and Carlson have pointed out that special interest groups and their lobbyists perform four services for legislatures: First, they provide information for legislators. Second, they provide the initiative and impetus for a large share of the legislation that moves through the General Assembly. Third, they promote issues out of which the legislature determines its course in many areas of public policy. Fourth, they help resolve many of the disputes in the legislature (1972: 106). Although private interests groups, including the press, do influence the legislative decision-making process, the most influential interest group, by far, is still the Department of Mental Health.[5]

The Department of Mental Health, or lobbying groups, generates most new policy initiatives. What then, is the legislature's role? It appears that it acts as a broker for public policy rather than an initiator of that policy. In fact, in a study of the Iowa state legislature only 13 percent of the legislators saw themselves as "policy innovators." Another 32 percent saw themselves as masters of the technical routines of legislative work (ritualists); 24 percent felt their job was that of advocating popular demands (tribunes); and another 29 percent felt their role was to compromise conflicting demands and interests (brokers). There was also a "residual" category of legislators who were labeled "opportunists" and who used their legislative positions for non-legislative advancement (Hedlund, 1967; Whalke, et al., 1962: 245-66).

If we now return to the movement of legislation through the General Assembly we can examine just how routine and non-controversial is most mental health legislation. In the Seventy-Eighth General Assembly (1973) thirty-two mental health bills were introduced in the House. (This was the last year for which all votes were available.) Of these, no action was taken on five. These five were routine bills or ones which needed further study. Several other bills were not acted upon since they were identical to bills introduced and passed in the Senate. By the end of the session eighteen bills had been examined in the House. Of those, seventeen were passed. As Chart 6-10 A and B indicates, there was little opposition to any of the legislation. As Chart 6-11 shows the situation in the Senate was similar, although four fewer bills were acted upon. (Even though Senate bills have their own number they are often substantively the same as the House bills because the House sponsor finds a Senator to sponsor the bill in that chamber.)

---

5. One lobbyist commented: "No legislator is anti-mental health. Therefore, I don't really have much of a problem in dealing with the legislature. But DMH, they drive me crazy. It's always, 'We can't do it;' or 'We can't allow this.' It's the department that's antagonistic and not the legislature. I'm getting an ulcer from them."

Even money bills are routinely passed (see: Chart 6-12). The reason for this is the "pass the buck" attitude in the General Assembly. Gove and Carlson have commented: "Perhaps because legislators rely so heavily upon each other in making decisions, they have developed over the years the habit of giving most bills the benefit of the doubt. Bills that do not involve partisan considerations are usually judged innocent until proven guilty. This means that passage will usually be forthcoming if the sponsor can demonstrate that his bill has no significant opposition" (1972: 138).

Legislators commented: "Most bills get out of committee. This happens because a legislator will say 'I disagree, but I'll vote for it so it can get to the floor for a vote.'" "Bills go through the House more easily than in the Senate because many House members feel: 'We'll send it to the Senate. They'll just kill it!'" "There's a lot of 'pass the buck' here. You'll hear: 'Let's send it to the governor and let him kill it.'"

Chart 6-10 A
House Bills

Bill	Content of Bill
HB-1494	Licensing and regulation of facilities for the retarded.
HB-29	Confidentiality of hospital record.
HB-1451	Add powers to the Community Mental Health Center Boards.
HB-1454	Contract mental health services for counties.
HB-1452	Contract mental health services for township.
HB-1493	License and regulate mental health facilities.
HB-831	Patient release procedures.
HB-1784	Qualifications for hospital superintendents.
HB-231	Allows township taxing power for Mental Health.
HB-724	Create Department of Developmental Disabilities.
HB-725	Prevention services for developmentally disabled.
HB-824	Change hospital discharge procedures.
SB-829	Separation of sexes in treatment.
SB-826	Revise patient medication provisions.
SB-827	Clarify rights of admitted patients.
SB-111	Limits the use of money for construction from the Mental Health Fund.
SB-943	Requires reports from Mental Health Zone Centers.

(Illinois, House Journal, 1973)

Chart 6-10 B
House Action

Committee Vote

Bill	Committee Assignment	y(yes)-n (no)-present (p)	House Vote: y-n-p	Action by the Governor
HB-1494	Registration & Regulation (R&R)	17-0	162-0	
HB-29	Human Resources (H.R.)	14-1	104-34-1	
HB-1451	H. R.	13-0	114-11-2	App.
HB-1453	H. R.	13-0-1	114-11-2	App.
HB-1454	H. R.	13-0-1	114-11-2	App.
HB-1452	H. R.	13-0-1	114-11-2	App.
HB-1493	R. & R.	17-0	162-0	
HB-831	H. R.	13-0	121-8	
HB-1784	Executive	16-0	106-10	
HB-231	Counties & Townships	10-3-3	104-28-6	App.
HB-724	H. R.	16-0-2	130-7-1	V
HB-725	H. R.	13-0-2	150-0	App.
SB-824	H. R.	16-0-2	—	
SB-829	H. R.	17	158-0	App.
SB-826	H. R.	16-1	158-0	
SB-827	H. R.	16-0	158-0	
SB-111	H. R.	16-0	115-4	
SB-943	H. R.	14-0	112-0	

V: Vetoed In Full
App: Approved

(Illinois, House Journal, 1973)

Chart 6-11
Senate Actions

Committee Vote

Bill	Committee Assignment	y(yes)-n (no)-present (p)	Senate Vote: y-n-p	Action by the Governor
SB-943	Public Health, Welfare & Corrections (PH, W. & C.)	—	37-1	
SB-824	PH, W. & C	—	37-4-2	
SB-826	PH, W. & C	—	37-2	
SB-829	PH, W. & C	—	31-3	
SB-827	PH, W. & C	—	34-2	
SB-111	PH, W. & C	—	46-1	
SB-828	PH, W. & C	—	29-7	
HB-29	PH, W. & C	—	51-2	
HB-1451	PH, W. & C	—	44-0	Approved
HB-1453	PH, W. & C	—	43-1	Approved
HB-1454	PH, W. & C	—	43-1	Approved
HB-1452	PH, W. & C	—	41-2	Approved
HB-831	PH, W. & C	—	40-0	
HB-724	PH, W. & C	—	49-1-1	
HB-231	Local Gov.	—	43-7	Approved

(Illinois, Senate Journal, 1973)

Chart 6-12

Appropriations and Capitol Development Bills

Appropriations Bills	House Com.	H. Com. Vote	House Vote	Senate Com.	S. Com Vote	Senate Vote	Action by the Governor
SB-297	Approp.	16-4-3	149-0	Approp.	N.R.	50-2	
SB-367	Approp.	24-0	120-0	Approp.	N.R.	37-0	
SB-1191	Approp.	24-0	159-1	Approp.	N.R.	41-0	
HB-245	Approp.	24-0	157-0	Approp.	N.R.	47-0	App.
HB-1928	Approp.	25-2	141-2	—	—	—	App.
HB-1937	Approp.	27-0	124-0	—	—	47-0	App.
HB-1978	Approp.	28-0	168-1	—	—	37-0	App.

Capital Development and Public Welfare Bills

SB-459	Approp.	27-0	166-3	Exec.	N.R.	41-0	
SB-460	Approp.	28-0	166-3	Approp.	N.R.	45-0	
SB-697	Approp.	28-0	149-0	Approp.	N.R.	50-0	
SB-701	Approp.	28-0	158-0	—	—	42-0	
SB-702	Approp.	28-0	158-0	—	—	53-0	

App: Approved
N.R. = Not Reported

(Illinois, House and Senate Journals, 1973)

Such attitudes, and near unanimous votes, indicate that little conflict exists in the General Assembly. When conflict occurs the problem is shunted off to others for a solution. Thomas Dye has observed: "The function of political parties is to offer alternatives where significant conflict exists, and a unanimous vote is evidence that no real demand existed for an alternative decision" (1971: 194). Supposedly, "conflict is the very life blood of a decision-making body in a free society" (Fenno, 1965: 75). However, conflict causes disruption; and in Illinois it is avoided because it interferes with "majority building" (Fenno, 1965). A classic example of this avoidance of conflict came when the Illinois Association for the Mentally Retarded, among others, proposed splitting off a separate Department of Developmental Disabilities from the Department of Mental Health. The bill, HB-724, was bitterly opposed by the Department of Mental Health. The push to pass it was controversial, at least in the press. However, the Human Resources Committee in the House passed the bill 16-0-2. The full House passed it 130-7-1. In the Senate, the bill was advanced without reference to committee and was passed 49-1-1. In fact, HB-724 received the highest vote total of all mental health legislation in the Senate and the seventh highest in the House. It appears that most legislators were unconvinced or unconcerned with the department's point of view, but were moved by the IAMR arguments. After the bill passed the General Assembly, the Governor, on the advice of the department, threatened to veto the bill. However, the Lt. Governor worked out a compromise between the IAMR and the Governor in which the bill was to be vetoed but developmental disabilities was to be given new emphasis within the department. When asked how he was able to get the Governor to go along with the compromise, the Lt. Governor replied, "I called him up and told him we had worked something out. Then I said, 'You'd better not screw this one up!' Well, he didn't."

In such a situation the legislature is passive and merely acts to ratify decisions made elsewhere (see: Steiner and Gove, 1960). One highly regarded legislator lamented:

"In mental health, the decisions are made somewhere else. Probably, most of them are made in the Governor's office, except possibly in regards to the retarded. This is the result of history, as much as anything else. Throughout the country executive power has become enormous and legislatures are in retreat."

If there is any one point at which the legislature has potential power it is in the appropriations process. As one staff member put it: "The budget process is a big, key thing. Money, it's the golden thread." In spite of the significance of appropriations bills many members lack the time to (carefully) analyze them. One of the reasons for this is that legislators receive four to five committee assignments each session. Further, the actual committee workload is unevenly distributed so that five House committees (Appropriations, Executive, Judiciary, Municipalities, and Revenue) usually consider from one-half to two-thirds all the bills referred to committees in both houses (Gove and Carlson, 1972: 64).

Charts 6-13 and 6-14 lists all of the House and Senate committees of the 77th General Assembly, the size of each committee, and the number of bills referred to each during the session. The figures in brackets indicate the party membership of each committee. In 1971 the Republicans controlled the House (90-87) and the Democrats, with the help of a Democratic Lt. Governor, organized an evenly divided Senate.

The disparity in work load between substantive and appropriations committees is quite substantial. In the House the Public Welfare Committee's (the predecessor to the Human Resources Committee) fifteen members handled forty bills; whereas the Appropriations Committee's twenty-four members handled 382 bills. In gross numbers the Appropriations Committee handled almost ten times as many bills as the Public Welfare Committee.

Chart 6-13
Legislative Committees of the House—1972

Committee	Number of Members	Number of Bills Referred
Agriculture [8-7]	15	32
Appropriations [13-11]	24	382
Constitutional Implementation [13-11]	24	66
Education [14-13]		
Elementary & Secondary Education Division [10-8]	18	112
Higher Education Division [10-8]	18	42
Elections [9-7]	16	62
Environment [8-7]	15	29
Conservation & Water Resources Division [8-7]	15	54
Executive [13-11]	24	145
Personnel and Veterans Affairs Division [8-7]	15	17
Financial Institutions [17-16]	33	
Banks and Savings and Loan Association Division [9-8]	17	20
Credit Regulations Division [8-7]	15	19
Insurance Division [8-7]	15	49
Pensions Division [8-7]	15	35
Industry and Labor Relations [8-7]	15	22
Judiciary [15=14]	29	
Division I [8-7]	15	185
Division II [8-7]	15	604
Municipal Corporations [17-16]	33	
Cities and Villages Division [13-11]	24	56
Counties and Townships Division [8-7]	15	99
Public Utilities [8-7]	15	31
Public Welfare [8-7]	15	40
Reapportionment [7-7]	14	2
Registration and Regulation [8-7]	15	54
Revenue [9-7]	16	143
Transportation [8-7]	15	62
Motor Vehicles Division [8-7]	15	56

Service Committees

Challenge Consent Calendar [3-3]
House Affairs [3-2]
Rules [10-9]

(Gove and Carlson, 1972: 66-5)

Chart 6-14
Legislative Committees of the Senate—1972

Committee	Number of Members	Number of Bills Referred[a]
Agriculture [9-6]	15	53
Education [9-6]	15	98
Elections [9-6]	15	38
Executive [13-9]	22	142
Financial Institutions [9-6]	15	44
Judiciary [8-5]	13	914
Labor and Commerce [11-7]	18	103
Local Government [9-6]	15	156
Public Finance [14-11]	25	
Appropriations [11-7]	18	307
Revenue [9-6]	15	91
Transportation [9-6]	15	47
Welfare [9-6]	15	38

Service Committees

Assignment of Bills [2-1]
Committee on Committees [8-5]
Rules [3-2]
Senate Operations [7-4]

(Gove and Carlson, 1972: 66-8)

Although budget bills may not receive enough analysis, they do get more than they used to get. Anton described the situation in the early nineteen-sixties in which committee hearings seldom analyzed substantive issues, were poorly attended, and indiscriminately approved bills:

"General lack of committee interest in the detailed content of appropriations bills results in hearings which normally run for no more than two or three minutes for any given bill, though five-to-ten minute discussions sometimes occur and very rarely, a twenty-to-thirty minute discussion will take place. But the time spent in discussing bills is essentially irrelevant to members of the committees, for whom the issue of 'pass or not pass' already has been decided . . . Legislators look upon committee hearings as occasions to record, rather than make, decisions." Further, "the decisions which the appropriations committees are asked to make have been made already, leaving the committees no task other than the production of a record to prove it. Such a task makes few demands upon information, time, or, thanks to proxy voting, the physical presence of committee members." Therefore, "at best . . . activities of the two appropriations committees are ritualistic in nature, conducted more for their own sake than for any impact they may have. Hearings are held and exchanges take place, not so much to make decisions as to mask the fact that neither committee has the knowledge, time, or interest to make decisions" (1966: 161-2).

Departmental budgets are given much greater attention today than they were ten years ago. Most of this analysis is by the Democratic and Republican leadership staffs attached to the appropriations committees. However, one staff analyst described the problems in attempting to analyze the mental health budget:

"Analyzing the mental health budget is a tough job for a number of reasons. First, the DMH budget is big and it takes a long time to prepare. The smaller agency budgets come in earlier and they get the hell beat out of them. But by the time the mental health budget comes up everyone is weary. Besides, it's such a massive agency that you just can't get a hold of specifics. The result is that it's reviewed without a great deal of understanding. You should also remember that this has traditionally been a strong executive state; and with the governor's impoundment and veto powers it's tough for the legislature to have that much influence on *any* appropriations. To compound the problem the legislature usually over-appropriates, to a considerable degree, which leaves the governor to exercise some cuts. But you've got to remember that budgeting is 'imprecise' and you, as a legislator, have to give leeway unless you're willing to rewrite the budget every three or four months.

"When analyzing the DMH budget only 20 percent of it actually gets inspected. That's because there must be a minimum amount of money spent to maintain the institutions, and you can't quarrel with this 'critical mass.' It's just that costs don't vary a great deal no matter how many patients or staff you have at these institutions. Since so many of these costs are uncontrollable, you end up analyzing the community based programs. They *can* be reviewed, at a level acceptable to the Senator in the district, but it's touchy. Even touchier is the money that goes to financially short private institutions. And, of course, you've got the problem of expanding expectations in the community.

"This leads us to the crux of the problems, who is financially responsible for what? What's the state responsible for? It depends on who you ask. DMH says they're responsible for 'high risk' patients. But what does that mean? The department says that that refers to people who might injure themselves or others. But that's really a very small number of people. Anyway, DMH treats 100,000 people a year. However, the Mental Health Code says that DMH has to treat *everyone* with a mental health problem. The department, however, says they only have to treat a few. So you have to ask, what, really, is the target population?

"Furthermore, how do you evaluate what's going on for those who the department is actually treating? If you forget about evaluation and just look at the reporting of cases, you can't say whether there's anything meaningful occurring. What are the private clinics doing, the department outpatient facilities, and the hospitals? You can't really say. If you ask them about something specific, they'll say, 'We're working on it.' It's an old ploy. You really can't find out what's going on, and when they give you data, it's erroneous or you need a computer to check it out. So you're stuck.

"From our perspective the state's mental health program has three components. First, a fundamental commitment to provide mental health services through zone centers, hospitals, etc. Besides, they're hard to close. It's like owning a house, you can't afford to sell it and you can't afford to keep it. Second, some people need to be in a hospital. Third, people depend on those services. So, no matter how frustrated we get with the department, we don't snipe at the budget or deny services to 'people in need,' whatever that means.

"The issue the legislature must face is, whether the General Assembly, which is the institution of government closest to the people, can change an agency's functioning? The honest answer is that we can do damn little. You can't take a department to court, so . . .? Once the department's director is chosen you really can't control him. If you write highly detailed laws on how the department must be run, you'll just have to rewrite them six months later because the department will thwart them. And then are you going to throw the director in jail? You're just kind of locked in. Anyway, if the legislature tried to run the department, they would just screw it up, anyway. The legislature is a lay board and they can't possibly know how to run the department. So you're stuck. This is the way all government is. The executive officers have the greatest power. In mental health everything the legislature does is second hand. The DMH director is the primary shaper of things.

"You've also got to remember that it's the executive branch that bears the responsibility if the state goes bankrupt. And the legislature understands that. You've got to balance receipts and expenditures. Once that's done the general feeling in the legislature is that you can play around within that range. The budget has been growing in the last five years but now we've got to hold back. Governor Ogilvy was defeated because he instituted an income tax, and that was really a shock. So now there's restraint and there just isn't going to be any tax increases. Everyone is scared to death to raise the income tax, so we have additional restraints.

"The mental health problem really boils down to this: Poverty causes most mental health problems and the role of the state is to show humanity and compassion towards these unfortunate people. However, the way it works out is that poorly paid people have to pass out the compassion for the highly paid ones. If we wanted to increase the money going into mental health in order to improve the situation you would have to cut from schools, which is $1.3 billion this year, higher education, $640 million, or public aid, $700 million. They're all good liberal causes, so what are you going to do? And the old thing about cutting highways won't work because that's mostly federal money. So?

"What's really happening here with the budget is a validation process. By that I mean that the legislature is making a formal commitment of its reasonable intentions of good will and humanity in financial planning."

The place where the General Assembly's good intentions are put to the test is the appropriations committee hearings. This is because the appropriations committee's hearings are the only place where a substantive public budget analysis occurs. It is also here that the validation process is most meaningful. This is because the budget hearing is a public forum in which the Department of Mental Health must explain and justify its programs and operations to the public and their representatives.

In the spring of 1975 the House's Appropriations Committee II met to consider DMH's $400 million budget. The hearing began at 3:35 p.m. when the committee chairman gaveled the committee to order.[6] Nineteen representatives were present. The representatives had

---

6. No transcript or any other type of recording is made of the testimony in committee meetings in the Illinois General Assembly. Therefore, the verbatim transcript presented below was recorded by the author.

spent the morning on the House floor in regular session. Earlier that afternoon they had had a hearing on the appropriations bills for the Human Relations Commission, the Department of Corrections, and an emergency appropriation for the Department of Children and Family Services.

The committee hearing began when the chairman announced to those assembled that "I don't want everybody testifying." The dozen departmental officials and interest group representatives waiting to testify shrugged as Dr. LeRoy Levitt, the DMH director, was called to begin the hearing. After some initial confusion concerning staff prepared amendments an amendment to add $300,000 for drug treatment to the department budget was introduced. There was some question as to whether the money belonged in the DMH budget or in the budget for the newly created Dangerous Drug Commission. However, when one representative commented that assigning the money to DMH was "just a matter of propriety" and that the money could be shifted later, the measure carried by voice vote.

A second amendment was offered which gave the department the power to transfer 2 percent of its $86 million appropriated for community treatment center grants within the budget. One skeptical representative asked why the department wanted "total discretion . . . with the Governor's O.K.," for the transfer of such money. Dr. Levitt explained; "This is only for community money. It has nothing to do with personnel. It's just that the needs for programs and grants differ and all we want is flexibility in the use of the funds." The representatives seemed satisfied with the explanation and passed the amendment by a routine voice vote.

A third amendment was offered which added $2 million for additional staffing for the state's two largest residential care facilities for the retarded. The director of the Illinois Association for the Mentally Retarded was asked to testify. That was because, as one representative put it, "it's really his amendment." The IAMR director testified that the money was needed for additional direct care staff in the two facilities so that they could meet Federal standards by 1977 and qualify for Federal monies. "God knows they need it!" one representative injected. In response, Dr. Levitt commented that "I understand the feelings involved, but we're adding 391 staff and we feel with these additions that departmental staffing is adequate. Therefore, we're opposed." One representative asked; "Did you hire the 60 extra people we gave you last year? Did you know that sometimes there are only two people on a ward with 60 to 70 retardates?" "We may be short sometimes," Dr. Levitt replied, "but it's not common. Therefore, I feel the amendment is not appropriate." There were then several questions concerning patient-staff ratios, declining inpatient census, and the chances of losing Federal money. After Dr. Levitt assured the committee that there was little chance of a loss of Federal funds, one representative asked, "Are you going to impound money again this year? Will the department determine what's 'necessary'? Do you feel you have to spend it? Do you feel you're mandated to spend?" "They don't spend it all," the IAMR director injected. "Except for community grants," Dr. Levitt answered, "which are funded frugally and prudently, we spend. We're mandated. We've got recruitment problems, but we don't have literal discretion." The representative continued: "Except for community grants, will you impound money again?" "We'll put 57 people in that we need, but if you gave me 90, I won't use them; that's inappropriate." The legislators were shocked. There was a long moment of silence. Then one representative lamely remarked: "He hires slow . . . it's based on his judgment." Another representative commented: "It's unusual that you don't want money. And if we added it the governor could always use his reduction veto . . ." "I don't know," Dr. Levitt answered. A vote was taken and the amendment passed with 14 voting yes, 4 voting no, and 4 voting present.

The committee then began analyzing the appropriations bill itself. The first representative to question Dr. Levitt was curious about the number of administrators in the department and asked if the department had any "ghost pay-rollers" who were performing political work for the governor. Dr. Levitt assured the committee the total number of administrators in the department was relatively small, 2,800 out of 20,000 employees. And the administrators were engaged in extra clinical work beyond their administrative duties. He further assured them that the department had no "ghost payrollers." "Ghosts . . ." one representative commented, "remember before [when we caught you with them]." "Er . . ." Dr Levitt replied.

Another representative asked: "Do you know how many employees you have at your various facilities?" Dr. Levitt looked confused. "Specifically, how many barbers do you have at Galesburg?" Dr. Levitt was speechless for a moment. "I don't know," he answered. The representative continued, "I'm not being frivolous, you understand, but one of my constituents has been a barber at Galesburg for 19½ years and he's being fired. What I'd like to know is what criteria you use when you let people go?" Still looking befuddled Dr. Levitt answered, "I'll let you know." The representative continued: "Why are you moving the Galesburg laundry out of the hospital and giving it to a private firm?" "It's more efficient," Dr. Levitt replied, "I'll get you the details."

Another representative, whose district included Elgin State Hospital, asked: "Do you remember the roasting you took in our press concerning Elgin State? I'd like to know how you're making it better?" "Those articles are not worthy of a response," Dr. Levitt indignantly replied. "They were unwarranted and they didn't take into account the progress we've made there. It's just the usual kind of argument. We have a good staff at Elgin and we're trying to improve it." The representative did not pursue the matter further.

"I . . . we . . . hate to get involved in personalities," one representative commented, "but your department responded with a form letter to one of my inquiries . . . And that made me mad. That's all we got . . . just a little clout . . ." "We do all we can," Dr. Levitt mumbled with obvious embarrassment.

Next a representative complained about former mental patients having guns. A second representative broke in and joked that Dr. Levitt and he always discussed such matters in the capitol washrooms or at breakfast. Everyone laughed. The first representative then went on for several minutes concerning the problem of former mental patients who possessed guns. Dr. Levitt explained that because of state and Federal laws concerning confidentiality the matter was out of his hands. The committee chairman finally ended the conversation when he said, "Let's cut it off. If you two want to keep talking about this why don't you go back to the John." Everyone laughed.

Another representative resumed the questioning by asking several questions concerning community placement. He was particularly concerned about some disturbing information concerning "the community I come from." A second representative added: "Readaptation may take a while and everybody is for good community mental health, 'but not on my block.' It's a philosophical and emotional issue." The first representative then asked, "Can they function if they've been placed in the community?" "We have a wonderful staff," Dr.

Levitt patronizingly assured the representative. "We have over 25,000 admissions and discharges each year and occasionally an error is made, but usually they're right. They're an excellent and skilled staff. We don't do this by fiat," he concluded in the same tone. "My constituents are wondering," the representative sarcastically commented. "We're doing it right," Dr. Levitt asserted, "and we'll investigate any problems." "Restrain yourselves . . . time," the chairman broke in as he cut off the discussion.

One representative then spent several minutes questioning Dr. Levitt concerning the delays in the implementation of a decriminalization program for alcoholics. Dr. Levitt replied that there had been problems in setting up the program because of a lack of cooperation from hospitals and police departments. However, he assured the committee that the department would be ready by July 1, if necessary. The representative also asked a number of questions concerning the placement of patients in unlicensed facilities.

Another representative asked why some employees are given lie detector tests. Dr. Levitt replied that in cases of alleged patient abuse, he can order such tests. "They both must have been in my district," the representative lamented.

In an annoyed tone of voice one representative then asked: "Can you get competent doctors?" "Yes." "Well, I saw this program on Channel 11 concerning commitment and I couldn't understand the doctor. He hardly spoke English. How can you have people like that? I understand you have staffing problems, but . . ." "I could take an hour to explain, but . . . but when he's not on television, he's okay," Dr. Levitt lamely countered. "But I heard his testimony and that was awful too!" "I'll defend him . . ." Dr. Levitt stammered, "We have a hiring problem." "Yes," the legislator responded icily, "and we may need legislation to correct it."

"Speed it up," the chairman barked. A legislator then asked about maintenance problems in the state hospitals. He concluded by saying, "I'm concerned about one particular institution, Chester. It's about 12 miles from my home." "We'll look into it," Dr. Levitt assured the representative. Since there were no further questions the chairman called the question. The vote was 20 for the appropriations bill and none opposed. One representative voted present. The representative who had voted present commented, "I want everyone to know I completely support Dr. Levitt and the department in what they're trying to do but my firm does business with the department."

The chairman declared the bill, H.R. 1314, passed. It was just 5 P.M.

There are a number of interesting things to point out in this budget hearing. First, the distinct time limitation the committee chairman felt. The hearing was held late in the legislative year, sandwiched between the morning and evening legislative sessions, and in conjunction with three other major appropriation bill hearings. The department's $400 million budget was given a total of one hour and twenty-five minutes. Certainly, in such a brief period of time the budget could not have been analyzed. But, in fact, a budget analysis was not even attempted. What did occur was that the committee members performed an ombudsman function for their constituents and the general public. For example, the inquiries concerning the firing of the barber and the questions concerning the lie detector examinations were prompted by constituent complaints. The questions concerning movement of the laundry out of one state hospital fell between constituent complaints and a desire for efficiency in government. More general inquiries, such as exploring the administrative problems in the establishment of an alcoholism program, as well as, the legislators' inquiries concerning "ghost payrollers" were the product of the representative's interest in "good government."

Although the role of an ombudsman is to solve people's problems, it is striking how powerless the legislators felt in this role. For example, one representative lamented that all that legislators had was "a little clout." This is untrue because the constitutionally mandated appropriations process provided the General Assembly with immense potential power. However, unless the legislators used this power the executive retained almost complete control over the budget of the agency. One example of this is the form of the budget.

The General Assembly has insisted on the use of a line item budget for every agency. Such a budget lists the exact amounts appropriated for categories such as personnel, printing, travel, etc. (see: Chart 6-15). Although a line item budget provides excellent fiscal control, and minimizes the chances for scandal, it does not provide information concerning programs or policies. Such line item budgets focus on "expenditure control." That is, such budgets enforce spending limitations. Two other types of budgets are management and planning budgets. A management budget, through the use of "activity accounts," ensures the efficient use of staff and other resources in the conduct of authorized activities. The focus of such a budget is agency output; that is, the analysis of performance versus budget goals in order to examine what is being done and at what cost.

The third type of budget is the planning budget. A planning budget is concerned with the evaluation of alternative programs. Such a budgeting system focuses on the effectiveness of programs (Schick, 1971). Although management and planning are tacitly part of a line item budget they are seldom explicitly dealt with. That is, conscious choices are seldom made by the legislature between policy alternatives. In such a system legislative control over administration "is basically control over details, not essentials" (White, et al. 1964: 427).

Appropriations based upon line item budgeting appear to allow careful control of agency expenditures. However, in reality, that is not the case. For example, Fenno points out:

Chart 6-15
Kankakee State Hospital Line Item Budget

For Personal Services	$ 9,670,600
For State Contribution to the State Employees' Retirement System	580,300
For State Contribution to Social Security	341,600
For Contractual Services	761,000
For Travel	6,000
For Commodities	846,500
For Printing	6,000
For Maintenance and Travel for Aided Persons	1,000
For Equipment	119,900
For Operation of Automotive Equipment	28,500
For Telecommunications	71,600
For U. S. Mental Health Fund	53,000
Total:	$12,513,000

(Illinois, General Assembly, 1973: 9)

"An executive agency will have a widely recognized, well-supported, and well-established core program. And what it requests each year from the Appropriations Committee are additions or subtractions from that core program. In the language of the agency budget people, the core program is known as an agency's 'base.' Agency expectations are that the Committee will accept its base and focus decision-making on the increment being requested. It does not . . . expect the Committee should (even if it could-which is quite another question) re-evaluate the agency's entire program" and budget (1966: 266).

Another factor effecting budgetary analyses by members of appropriations committees are their attitudes towards their role in the budgetary process. In Congress, for example, members of the House Appropriations Committee feel they are merely performing a "technical" function dealing with dollars and cents: "The Committee, of course, makes decisions on the same controversial issues as do the committees handling substantive legislation. Committee members know this, and they know that, after all, their ability to affect policy is the root of their influence in American national politics. If their actions had no programmatic consequences, they would hardly merit their reputation as 'the powerful Appropriations Committee.' Yet the decisions Committee members make are money decisions. And a money decision-however vitally it may affect national policy is, or certainly can be perceived as, less directly a policy decision. Members refer to this Committee as a 'business' or 'technical' committee as distinguished from a 'policy' committee. In the words of its chairman, the Committee 'deals with national finance and economics and not with politics.' . . . If this is so, decisions can be reached by bargaining and compromise easier than if the point at issue were acknowledged to be one of social philosophy and differences of opinion with fellow Committee members are not converted into ideological conflicts. Money decisions are continuum decisions rather than dichotomous, yes or no decisions. One does not fight, bleed, and die if he perceives his disagreement with someone as a disagreement over a figure of $100 million or $125 million for the funding of a program already authorized. Besides, every program gets some money and a member can always say honestly that he did support any given program.

"Committee members have their cake and eat it too. Their dollar and cents decisions affect programs. Yet they believe (and they act as if) in the words of one, 'A disagreement on money isn't like a legislative program-it's a matter of money rather than a difference in philosophy.' Or, as another put it, 'Policy has been thrashed out ad lib, in extenso, and ad nauseum in the legislative committees. Our only problem is whether to appropriate $20 million or $15 million or nothing.' 'We consider things in dollars and cents,' said a third member, 'that's what we talk about' " (Fenno, 1966: 194).

Wildavsky (1964) concluded that budgeting turns out to be an incremental process, proceeding from a historical base, and guided by notions of fair shares, in which decisions are fragmented, and made in sequence by specialized bodies. They are "coordinated," in the sense that each year budget "attacks" a problem. Thus, the role of the participants fit together to provide a reasonably stable budgeting process.

One of the problems in Illinois is that legislators base much of their budget analysis upon constituent complaints or newspaper exposes. Seldom during budget hearings will legislators broaden their questioning to include basic policy issues. When policy oriented questions do arise ("How do you make it [Elgin State Hospital] better?" "How can you have people [doctors] like that?") the answers are countered by assertions ("They [the charges] were unwarranted . . ." "We have a good staff at Elgin . . ." "I'll defend him . . ." "They're an excellent and skilled staff.") However, these assertions are seldom challenged by further questioning. The most striking example of this was the addition of the $2 million for extra staff at the two state schools for the retarded. During the questioning Dr. Levitt said that he would not hire additional staff if he felt it was "inappropriate." Although the representatives were stunned by the answer, not one of them pursued the matter. It appears that feelings of powerlessness are pervasive among the committee members. It is also interesting to note that the $2 million dollars, though a large amount in absolute terms, is only about one-half of one percent of the department's budget. Ironically, it is often said that the director of the Illinois Association for the Mentally Retarded "runs MR in the state." This is not true. DMH "runs MR." Further, the additional monies the legislature has added over the years for retardation treatment are relatively small amounts which can be impounded by executive fiat.

The final committee vote on the budget (20-0-1) is also interesting. Although a number of legislators were displeased with the tone and/or the substance of some of Dr. Levitt's answers, all the representatives supported the appropriations bill. In fact, they had little choice. Since the treatment of "sick people" is the direct product of the bill, it served little purpose to vote against the bill. This is especially true since the voters might not understand the reason for a negative vote and turn the legislator out of office. Anton, in his study of the Illinois state legislature in the early 1960s, concluded that "budget bills are approved because there is really no alternative to approval. With little time and no information what can be done . . . ? As one legislator put it, 'We've got to support state government'" (1966: 156-7).

Although what occurred at the hearing was interesting, what did not occur was even more interesting. The committee appeared to be strikingly disinterested in examining the department's budget. In Congress, "cutting out the fat," is their primary goal. In Congress a committee's dominant goal is primarily negative; and, the committee's self-image is "guardian of the federal Treasure." In one appropriations committee members have hung a Calvin Coolidge aphorism on their wall which states: "Nothing is easier than the expenditure of public money. It does not appear to belong to anybody. The temptation is overwhelming to bestow it on somebody." In such an environment "it is a mark of the intensity and the self consciousness with which the consensus on budget-cutting is held that it is couched in a distinctive occupational vocabulary. The workaday jargon of the Committee is replete with negative verbs, undesirable objects of attention, and effective instruments of action." Agency budgets are said to be filled with "fat," "padding," "grease," "pork," and "oleaginous substance." These budgets are then "cut," "carved," "sliced," "trimmed," "whittled," "pruned," "squeezed," or "whacked." The tools of the trade are a "knife," "meat axe," "scalpel," "meat cleaver," and "fine-tooth comb." The accepted attitude is: "There has never been a budget . . . that couldn't be cut" (Fenno, 1966: 100, 104-5). Such attitudes were completely absent from the Illinois House committee. It appeared that the committee had little interest in analyzing the budget or "guarding the treasury."

What was even more striking was the committee's handling of the major change in the department's budget over the previous year. This was the addition of $40 million for the treatment of persons in the community. This new money for outpatient services was considered a major innovation by the department. However, this increase was never even mentioned during the budget hearing. This is somewhat understandable since the General Assembly has no explicit goals in mental health. Only such notions as "decent care" or "good management" are their concern.

This is ironic since a "professionalism index" was developed during the 1960s and Illinois' legislature was rated as "highly professional" (John Grumm in Dye, 1971). Furthermore, the Citizens Conference on State Legislatures ranked the Illinois General Assembly as the third highest ranking state legislature in the country behind New York and California. This was because Illinois had a strong staffing pattern. This staffing "permits the continuous, year-round examination of state resources and expenditures and provides program review and evaluation of executive agencies" (1971a, 1971b).

Although the General Assembly may rank third in the nation on a comparative basis, it appears unwilling or unable to deal the most basic question in mental health policy. Is mental health receiving a fair share of the state's resources? One long-time legislative assistant commented: "Are we giving mental health a 'fair share'? I don't know? We'll give them anything they want, plus. But, the question is, has the governor asked for enough? To tell you the truth, I think this is a chincy budget. Also, you hear about this issue about highways versus social services. This is a phony issue because highways are human services too!" Another staff assistant added: "We're not sure what it takes to get the job done." A third commented; "Mental health generally gets its fair share. Well . . . in terms of need . . . I guess not. However, proportional to the available resources . . . kind of. The department is short-changed some in professional staff. . . . The point is this, 'fair share' implies you know what a 'fair share' is, and we don't." One highly respected legislator concluded: "Fair share? That's an argument for philosophers, preachers, and social scientists!" (see: Easton, 1953, 1965).

The same type of non-substantive treatment of mental health also occurs during floor voting. The researcher observed House proceedings on the day the mental health appropriations bill was brought up for its third reading (final vote) on the House floor. On May 28, 1975 the 177 members of the House were considering appropriations bills during the closing days of the legislative session. They were hurrying to complete their work. As each bill was called by the clerk its sponsor rose and gave a brief description of the bill. Invariably, one conservative representative, who considered himself, "the taxpayers watchdog," rose and questioned the appropriation. He would ask the agency's appropriation for the previous year and the percentage of increase. Usually, the sponsor would reply, "I don't know." When the appropriation for the Illinois Arts Council came up for a vote "the watchdog" was particularly incensed at the "huge" increase the Council was receiving. However, he never asked what was to be funded with the increased monies. Two or three other legislators also rose to attack the bill. Other representatives jumped to the defense of the bill. They explained that the Council had done an exemplary job by supporting some project in their community. After several minutes of heated debate over the bill a vote was taken. The bill passed by an overwhelming majority. As other bills were called, the same representative simply remained standing as he questioned the appropriation on each bill. Other representatives then followed with questions having to do with the technical functioning of each of the agencies whose bills were being considered. Invariably, the sponsor would reply, "I don't know." For example, during consideration for "the ordinary and contingent expenses of the Office of the State Appellate Defender," one representative asked whether certain law enforcement personnel had access to specific state laboratories for the analysis of evidence in criminal cases. Looking dumbfounded the sponsor replied, "I don't know." In fact, the scenario of bill introduction, brief, non-substantive questioning, and routine passage, occurred throughout the session. Such votes were considered so routine that the newspaper reading, coffee drinking, donut munching, and general din of conversation subsided only long enough to punch the buttons of the electronic voting system. However, since many members were out of their seats, those that remained would invariable lean over and press the "yes" button for those members not present. The result was that every bill observed that day passed within a few minutes by margins of 101-7-1, 98-3-2, 107-0, 111-1-1, etc.

Although the Senate is smaller (59 members instead of the House's 177), and more sedate, the results were similar. For example, the mental health appropriations bill (HB 1314) discussed earlier passed the House by a vote of 125-3-4. The Senate committee hearing the bill passed it 17-0. It then went to the Senate floor where it was passed 47-2-6.

In his study of the General Assembly in the early 1960s Anton concluded that "any bill that has not provoked strong opposition or is not otherwise defective, is treated as a 'good thing to do,' and dealt with accordingly, in deference either to a sponsor or to the need to support state government. Budgets, revenues, or total expenditures are all essentially peripheral to a body more concerned with expressing opinions than with making decisions. That the opinions are almost always favorable, is probably due more to the absence of grounds for alternative opinions than to an unusual degree of legislative good nature" (1966: 157). This still appears to be true.

In this regard one legislator commented; "The system kind of hobbles along. Our political system performs a lot of strange antics. There is a lot of neglect and buck passing. The system works, or doesn't work, this way because the people are usually apathetic; and the legislature reflects it. Once in a while the people rise up and demand things get done but usually the system just hobbles along. But, I guess that's better than having a revolution every five years." A legislative aide put it more colorfully: "When I watch the legislature work, it reminds me of a cartoon. It pictures a guy caught in a swamp who is saying; 'When you're up to your ass in alligators, it's hard to remember that you came here to drain the swamp.'"

3. The Governor: 1975

The function of the executive is to act. For a governor these actions are not just as chief executive, but also as chief legislator. A variety of formal and informal powers accrue to the governor that enables him or her to significantly influence the legislative process (Zeigler and Van Dalen, 1971). One of the formal powers the governor possesses is the veto. The traditional veto power of the governor in Illinois has been strong. The General Assembly has usually been closely divided between Republicans and Democrats and it has been exceedingly difficult to overturn gubernatorial vetoes. To override a veto traditionally required a two-thirds majority of all elected members in both houses. To muster this many votes was rare. Before the 1970 Constitution took effect bills were overridden only four times in the history of the state. One of the prime reasons for the veto being so absolute has been the timetable of bill passage in the General Assembly. Since most bills have been passed in the last few days before the legislature's adjournment, there has not been time for the General Assembly to overturn gubernatorial vetoes. For example, 90.3 percent of the vetoes in 1965 occurred after the legislature had adjourned (Illinois Commission on the Organization of the General Assembly, 1967: 15-17). The 1970 Constitution added to the Governor's power by giving him a line item reduction veto. This was to allow him "fine-tuning" over the "throttle" of state government. The new Constitution allowed for such a veto to be overridden by a simple majority of the General Assembly. However, in the first test of this new override provision the legislature failed to overturn even one of the governor's 141 line item reductions for the 1971-2 session (Hanley, 1972: 8). The new Constitution also gave the governor an amendatory veto which allowed him to return a bill with specific recommendations for change to the house in which it originated rather than vetoing the entire measure. These recommendations may then be accepted by a vote of the majority of the elected members of each house. The bill must then be presented to the governor for his certification. If the bill conforms to his recommendations it then becomes law. If the governor refuses to certify the bill, it is returned to its originating house as a vetoed bill.

Under the new constitution, the majority needed to override a bill has been relaxed from two-thirds to three-fifths. As a result of this, overrides of bills have occurred. In fact, Governor Walker suffered a number of overrides. This was partly due to the animus between the legislature and the "anti-politician" attitude of the Walker administration. One legislative aide commented: "We have a unique situation between the governor and the legislature. There are a lot of hard feelings. The usual legislative courtesies of sitting down with the governor's people to work things out so his legislative program goes through just isn't happening. There's hate this time. Walker's deputy governor and former campaign manager wrote an article that said, in effect: 'We're going to do it our way and if you don't go along we'll beat you. We're going to run the state.' The old fashioned courtesies are gone. For example, in some committee hearings the courtliness, deference, respect, and cooperation, has disappeared. Normal bills didn't get through the legislature this year and last. House-keeping bills, like institutional name changes, just usually go right through; now all that's changed." Typical of the negative attitude towards the governor in the legislature was the sarcastic comment a legislator reportedly made in which he referred to "our glorious, but temporary, governor."

Although vetoes have occasionally been overridden, and conflict has marked the Walker administration this has had relatively little direct effect on such "non-controversial" areas such as mental health. The governor and DMH are still in control of the legislative process.

Another formal power the constitution allows a governor is that he may succeed himself or herself. Other governors may face reelection every other year or are limited to only one four year term. In fact, Schlesinger (1971) compiled a General Power Index codifying the strengths of all U.S. governors. These formal powers, such as tenure potential, appointive, budgetary, and veto powers, were rated on a scale so that the maximum possible rating was 20. Only three states received such a rating: New York, Hawaii, and Illinois (see: Chart 6-16).

As chief legislator the governor also possesses potent informal powers over the legislature. His or her use of the media may be as important as any formal power he possesses. His or her ability to create or dramatize an issue may be so powerful that public opinion, to which any legislator must be mindful, can be swayed. Therefore, access to the media becomes a political tool through which the governor may indirectly control much of the legislative process.

Chart 6-16
A Combined Index of the Formal Powers of the Governors

	Tenure Potential	Appointive Powers	Budget Powers	Veto Powers	Total Index
New York	5	5	5	5	20
Illinois	5	5	5	5	20
Hawaii	5	5	5	5	20
California	5	4	5	5	19
Michigan	5	4	5	5	19
Minnesota	5	4	5	5	19
New Jersey	4	5	5	5	19
Pennsylvania	4	5	5	5	19
Maryland	4	5	5	5	19
Utah	5	3	5	5	18
Washington	5	3	5	5	18
Ohio	4	4	5	5	18
Massachusetts	5	5	5	3	18
Tennessee	3	5	5	5	18
Wyoming	5	2	5	5	17
Missouri	4	3	5	5	17
Alaska	4	3	5	5	17
Idaho	5	4	5	3	17
North Dakota	5	1	5	5	16
Kentucky	3	4	5	4	16
Virginia	3	5	5	3	16
Montana	5	3	5	3	16
Nebraska	4	3	4	5	16
Connecticut	5	4	4	3	16
Delaware	4	1	5	5	15
Oklahoma	4	1	5	5	15
Alabama	3	3	5	4	15
Wisconsin	5	2	5	3	15
Colorado	5	1	4	5	15
Louisiana	4	2	4	5	15

(continued)

Chart 6-16 (continued)
A Combined Index of the Formal Powers of the Governors

	Tenure Potential	Appointive Powers	Budget Powers	Veto Powers	Total Index
Georgia	3	1	5	5	14
Oregon	4	2	5	3	14
Nevada	5	2	5	2	14
Arizona	2	1	5	5	13
South Dakota	1	4	5	3	13
Maine	4	2	5	2	13
Vermont	2	4	5	2	13
Kansas	2	2	4	5	13
Arkansas	2	4	3	4	13
Iowa	2	3	5	2	12
New Hampshire	2	2	5	2	11
Rhode Island	2	3	4	2	11
New Mexico	1	1	5	3	10
North Carolina	3	2	4	1	10
Mississippi	3	1	1	5	10
Indiana	3	5	1	1	10
Florida	3	2	1	3	9
South Carolina	3	1	1	3	8
West Virginia	3	3	1	1	8
Texas	2	1	1	3	7

(Schlesinger, 1971: 232).

In addition to the prestige and influence inherent of the office a governor is also an important political figure. Legislators must often run under the party label of the governor and therefore they are concerned with the success of the governor's program. One legislative aide commented: "If an issue becomes political then the governor's party, the 'ins', supports him whereas the 'outs,' fight like hell. Of course most issues are not political, but still the governor is important to the individual legislator. Legislators often need help raising money and pushing to get elected; this gives the governor influence, and votes, later on. Also, the governor is influential with the county chairmen. He has patronage, services, and favors to dispense. He can raise money statewide, and he is simply the state's top politician." Mayor Daley, rather than the governor, is often considered the state's "top politi-cian," However, Daley's interest in mental health has been minimal. It is the governor and the department who control mental health in the state.

The governor has a number of staff members to help carry out the work of his office. This staff gathers information, weighs policy options, implements decisions, and negotiates in the name of the governor. With the staff's assistance the governor then decides how to act on various bills.

Probably the most important staff in the governor's office is in the Bureau of the Budget (BOB). That is because the BOB maintains day to day control over the state's departments. The BOB official charged with monitoring the Department of Mental Health explained his job:

"Until 1969, when the BOB was established, there were no checks and no analyses of the state's budget; it was merely a compilation of the budgets of the various departments. Unless the governor had a particular interest in a department's programs he seldom was involved in the budgetary process. Before 1969 there simply was no overall policy direction to state government. When the BOB was established, along Federal BOB lines, we were charged with three functions. One, planning the establishment and maintenance of an over-all long-term plan for state government. Secondly, we're concerned with management, that is, efficiency. Thirdly, we're charged with maintaining fiscal control so that the governor can have increased control over the fiscal resources of the state government. In practice, we function by requiring the departments to develop quarterly spending plans and then we hold them to those fiscal plans. We also assign analysts to the agencies at the policy level. They look at the alternative policy issues involved in departmental functioning and communicate their evaluation of those alternatives to the governor in a review document.

"In evaluating mental health policy alternatives, we have problems. Mental health is the toughest area in state government. That's because we're unable to say what is quality care. We haven't even been able to decide who is the state's responsibility. Mental health is also overlaid with intense feelings; there are vendors, consumers, and legislators and they all have a strong emotional stake in mental health programs. Also, mental health services are visible, so that further complicates things. Besides the complexity of policy, management, and care levels, there is the political nature of the thing. And that cannot be dismissed. In spite of all this, we try to make sure the governor's policies are being implemented. In specific cases we, as reasonable men, try to see if this or that is logistically feasible. That's our job. For example, should we build a new facility and then transfer patients into it, or should we do something else? Those kinds of questions, plus program analyses, are the things we grapple with. We rely on program analyses as one of our primary tools. However, one of the problems with program analysis is that the legislature won't cooperate by switch-ing to program budgeting. They feel program budgets are 'too vague.' Instead, they use line item budgeting. That gives them terrific fiscal control so that they can analyze budgets minutely. Besides, they feel that's the only way DMH can be held accountable. But even then, you can't throw the DMH director in jail if he shifts some money in the budget. One thing that does help us, though, is that there is program information attached to the budget; but that's not a legal document and you can't hold the director responsible if he doesn't follow it. In fact, without knowing what programs the department is running the legislature doesn't get to the heart of what the department is on earth for. But then they've only got a dozen or so staff for the entire executive branch. They're trying to expand and take over some of our functions, but they haven't so far.

"Getting back to the governor. The governor is the line head of all departments and has to take the fiscal condition of the state into mind in making policy decisions. And when we don't spend, the bottom line reason, is for fiscal control, fiscal integrity. Either we increase taxes, decrease programs, or make some trade-offs. That's often the way policy decisions are actually made. However, I should stress that money isn't everything. For example, Illinois spends almost $14,000 a year per patient. Some places spent $30,000 a year per patient. Menninger's spends only $18,000 per patient per year."[7] A number of legislators and legislative assistants have been concerned with the criteria for such "trade-offs." They have felt that the BOB has acted arbitrarily in making many decisions. An example of such decision making was described by Wildavsky (1964) for the federal government's Bureau of the Budget (now the Office of Management and Budget, OMB) concerning the National Institutes of Health (NIH) budgets. A BOB budget analyst explained how he analyzed the NIH budget:

Analyst: My day to day work was not very effective. It was a desperate attempt at wondering how to grasp ahold of this whole business . . . We couldn't get a meaningful standard to judge as to how much medical research the Government should support.

Interviewer: How did the BOB decide where and how much to cut the NIH request?

Analyst: This is a very good question. I wonder how we did decide. I would say as a generalization that it was some kind of a mechanical factor like "let's hold it to last year's budget" or "last year's budget plus 10 percent of new grants" . . . or just 10 percent increase over last year."

Interviewer: How did you arrive at this figure?

Analyst: We do it on an ad hoc basis. 10 percent sounds right . . . They [the NIHI] may point out that it doesn't demonstrate a 10 percent growth due to certain factors, so we will give them say 12.5 percent . . . We were playing around with graphs and figures. Curves . . . projecting growth to 1965 and say the figure was 1.3 billion. The people in BOB will say, let's reach 1.3 billion not by 1965 but by 1975. So we cut the figure by the percent to reach it by 1975 . . . There was an argument on what to start with as . . . [a] base, the unobligated balance to be included or not. If we take the lower figure we could give them the same rate of growth but it would be say 60 million less than they asked. . . . I would get the [NIH] estimate and come up with my recommendation. This would have to be a little lower than the department request.

---

7. As of July, 1972 Illinois spent $12,063.25 per patient per day for residential patient care in state mental hospitals. Illinois ranked eighth in state spending. Alaska ranked first with spending of $22,929.30 per patient per day for residential care. Illinois spending, however, ran ahead of New York ($7,442.35) and California ($10,282.05) (Clarke, 1975).

Interviewer: Why?

Analyst: Because I didn't think it was appropriate to give the same amount the department asked, so I cut a little. From here my recommendation went to the division review meeting. . . . I would say they [the NIH] asked for say a 32 percent increase and I allowed 23 percent. Comments might go like this. "We have to put a stop to this NIH." "Congress will up it anyway, no matter what we do. . . . " Then somebody else would reply, "No that is no good. That isn't realistic at all. There has to be some increase." Then another would say, "Can we raise them 10 percent and get a rationalization for this?" and "we will try to figure one out."

The President's budget got shot to hell with major increases. The staff [of the BOB] would [then] consider the possibility of a veto. But you can't veto a health bill politically. It makes the President in favor of cancer. But you can't just crawl under a rock. What can you do? (p. 44-5)

The BOB official in Illinois went on to explain:

"What the governor wants to do is to increase the productivity, and therefore, the quality, of patient care. Productivity can be defined in broad terms, within categories such as basic maintenance, diet, or housekeeping. However, if you start playing around with such things as diet, the problem immediately becomes political, and then you don't know what to do. Another example might be custodial services. If you want the place cleaned up, it will cost you money. So you're often stuck even on the most basic questions."

"One way you try and handle these financial considerations is to transfer the costs to Federal programs when patients are moved out of state institutions. But even if you almost empty an institution, you don't receive much offset because of the high cost of maintaining the institution itself. We've also tried reductions in support services and middle management to save money. But in a year or two that plays out and then you have to decide to either increase your budget or reduce programs and close hospitals. Of course, you can almost empty hospitals and then keep them open anyway. Then you're providing welfare for the employees and the town. But then, you could just keep the patients in the hospitals. These are the kinds of real life problems you face.

"The product of all this is that over 80 percent of your budget is tied up in institutions. Therefore, you're left with less than 20 of the budget to mold. In this kind of situation the BOB's creditability comes from pointing out soft spots in departmental budgets.

"All this has come about because the total tax bill over the last decade has become enormous. In the late '60s management and accountability became important. Since then we've been looking at outputs, performance, and accountability. One of the problems with such a management approach is that innovative programs, which are often sloppy, tend to be cut or even decimated. That's a real problem.

"In conclusion, what we're trying to do is ask reasonable man questions and then figure out how to get there. We have to establish time specific plans with measurable milestones. To do this, DMH must make a thorough public definition of its responsibilities. You can oversell mental health, and you have definitional problems with mental health and poverty, but when you come right down to it, DMH should have some planning, and they don't. It seems that rational planning is just not very well received in DMH. Besides, long range plans get people mad, and DMH wants to avoid that.

"Ultimately, what we're concerned about is fiscal management. By that we mean getting money to where it's needed and establishing some accountability in its use. Those are not green eyeshade accountant questions."

Although reasonable men and women in the BOB "ask reasonable man questions" many legislators and legislative assistants are skeptical about BOB's rational approach towards accountability. For example, one legislative staffer commented:

"BOB is very important, but it's hard to say exactly what it does. It belongs body and soul to the governor. It gets into program analysis in regards to spending. They have input into anything fiscal. The result of this is that BOB and the departments end up bargaining over a lot of things. There's just as much politics in BOB as in the General Assembly. What happens is that special interest groups put pressure on the governor, who then leans on BOB. The thing to remember is that BOB decisions are made within a context of political realities.

"In the old days the governor and the departmental director got together and worked things out. Now it's the BOB and the departments. In fact, BOB has *become* the governor. That's because the governor's involvement is pretty limited. For example, if BOB and a department director square off the governor decides, otherwise. . . ? The power of BOB is inversely related to the power of the cabinet member they're involved with. If the cabinet member has the governor's ear, he can tell BOB to 'Go to Hell!' However, the governor may not go along with BOB or the agency director. He can always do what he likes with a budget.

"The BOB, first and foremost, is concerned with dollars. They want to 'cut out the fat.' How many good programs go may well depend on how well the director defends the budget. The governor then makes the decisions. And those decisions may not be based upon departmental needs.

"Like I said, BOB is interested in saving money. It really isn't all that interested in performance. The BOB under the current governor is off to a pretty good start, although they're a little too parsimonious for my tastes. But then, legislators are notorious about appropriating more money than they raise.

"However, BOB just doesn't work the way it's supposed to. One guy gets it set up and then the whole thing changes when a new governor comes in. Then you have a new bunch of bright young men trying to make a record for themselves. BOB is hampered by too many youngsters who are, in effect, dictating policy. The agencies have to run to them for almost everything. Before BOB there was too much freedom, now there's too little. Besides, BOB has become a terrible bureaucracy itself. There is no real mental health expert in BOB now. Most of the people that are working there are totally green, with no experience. It's like in-service training. The result is that you don't get a well rounded appraisal of an agency's needs."

Because of the functioning of the Bureau of the Budget the governor has minimal contact with the details of agency administration. Therefore, the governor has great freedom to define his relation to the departments. His leadership is essentially political. He must be concerned whenever conflict arises, as well as, whenever scandals emerge. But his relationship with day-to-day administration can be very tenuous. Governors find it more important to maintain their political standing than to influence administration directly through daily supervision (Schlesinger, 1971: 25).

Anton has argued that state bureaucracies are perfectly capable of running themselves. This situation forces the governor "to seek changes...as a means of becoming relevant." Unless he or she does so there is nothing for which he or she can take credit. Therefore, a governor becomes a focal point for change. However, this change is problematic because what the governor chooses to do is a personal decision. That is, if the governor does not attempt to exert their influence it is not because he or she cannot, instead, it is because they will not. Therefore, it is the Governor's own perceptions and motivations that determines their behavior in office (1966: 112, 116; see also: Van Der Silk and Redfield, 1986: 153-7). However, even if a governor wishes to influence policy he or she is often trapped by previous commitments, legal constraints, and a lack of available time, resources, and information (Anderson, 1975: 90-93).

In fact, a governor must deal with administrative agencies in the same way he or she deals with the legislature and other interest groups. Woll points out: "He must persuade the bureaucracy to go along with him, for he cannot command it to obey him" (1963: 159). Although a governor or president may have the legal authority to compel action, they are often forced to use persuasion to accomplish a policy objective. President Truman once remarked, "I sit here all day trying to persuade people to do the things they ought to do without my persuading them. . . . That's all the powers of the Presidency amount to" (quoted in Neustadt, 1960: 9-10).

Warren Moscow, a political reporter for The New York Times, has written that compared with being mayor of New York City or President, the job of governor of New York State was a "soft snap. Save in rare emergencies, the press of work is not so much greater than that of a big-business executive. The physical strain is light enough so that any man of sound mind and sound politics with the ability to pick trustworthy subordinates can function adequately as governor. The reason for this is simply that the important part of the job of governor lies in the fields of policy-making rather than in the handling of administrative detail. The Governor is not awakened late at night or early in the morning by recurrent crises in international affairs, nor is his executive domain so vast that the number of minutes in the calendar week is insufficient to permit even abbreviated conversations with each of his lieutenants, a difficulty which plagues a modern president" (1948: 186).

Although governors possess enough time to meet with departmental administrators to discuss policy formation, this often does not occur. Governors spend much of their time involved in personal interviews, correspondence, phone calls, public speeches, and radio, television, and public appearances. In fact, many governors hold two press conferences a day so that both the morning and afternoon papers will have fresh stories. Such time consuming public relations activities often trump governmental management. Although they may be time consuming, public relations are necessary and important for a governor. James Forrestal has said: "The difficulty of Government work is that it not only has to be well done, but the public has to be convinced that it is being done well. In other words, there is a necessity both for competence and exposition, and I hold it is extremely difficult to combine the two in the same person" (quoted in Ransome, 1956: 153). The result of such public relations activities is that it is estimated that governors spend only 10 to 15 percent of their time talking with their department heads (Ransome, 1956). The charts below (see: Charts 6-17, 6-18, 6-19) indicate that governors probably have little time for, and therefore, little control over, the day to day administration of state departments. However, it should not be thought that because a governor meets with an agency director for only a half-hour every week or two they are powerless to control an agency. They are far from powerless because governors exercise strong policy control over departments through their power of appointment. Since 1960, Illinois governors have chosen progressive directors to lead the Department of Mental Health. Although some governors have been personally indifferent to mental health, the department has moved towards a community mental health orientation. In fact, even if "conservative" directors had been chosen it seems likely that the department would have moved with the national trend towards similar goals. This movement towards community mental health has been nationwide and strikingly similar experiences have occurred in other states, particularly New York and California.

Such movement, however, can only occur with the passage of legislation. The proposal of such legislation is invariably the product of the governor's initiative. These proposals form an agenda; and the legislators are forced to deal with the governor's agenda rather than one of their own making. This is because they often are too disunited to formulate one of their own (Neustadt, 1965). However, it must also be realized that within broad policy and budgetary guidelines the department actually are the ones who establish the agenda. Therefore, it is the mental health professionals who actually determine mental health policy.

This situation is analogous to Huntington's (1961) study of defense policy in which the military decided "strategic" questions such as the strength of military forces, their makeup, their deployment, and weapons development. Congress, however, was influential in deciding "structural" questions concerning the amount of money to maintain overall levels of personnel and material and how these force levels should be organized. We might add a third category which could be labeled "parochial." Such parochial concerns for DMH would involve securing mental health services for individual constituents, maintaining institutions and jobs in one's district, and securing grants for local community mental health services. In Illinois, there is intense interest in parochial concerns. There is limited interest in structural questions; and strategic questions are left to the "experts." In practice, these experts are the in-house professionals in the Department of Mental Health.

Chart 6-17
The Governor's Day

Time	Activities
8:30 to 9:30 a.m.	Reading and answering previously screened correspondence.
9:30 to 10:430 a.m.	Conference with department heads or legislators.
10:30 to 11:00 a.m.	Press conference.
11:00 to 12:30 p.m.	Interviews or conferences with public, legislators, and department heads.
12:30 to 2:00 p.m.	Lunch, during which the governor welcomes some group meeting in the city or has luncheon conference.
2:00 to 4:00 p.m.	Conferences with public, legislators, and department heads.
4:00 to 4:30 p.m.	Press conference.
4:30 to 6:00 p.m. or later	Completes correspondence, makes phone calls, plans work with staff, etc.
7:00 p.m.	Frequently attends a banquet or similar gathering where he is either the principal speaker or must "put in an appearance."

(Ransome, 1956: 124).

Chart 6-18
*Analysis of Visits to the Governor's Office in Arkansas**

Purpose	Percent of Time Consumed
Requests for State Positions	23
Requests for Special Favors	13
Requests from Civic, Church or School Organizations	12
Problems of Administrative Officials	10
Purpose Unknown	8
Criticism of Governmental Policy	7
Social Calls	6
Reports of Confidential Information	5
Requests for Executive Clemency	4
Press Conferences	3
Requests for Information	2
Invitations to Board Meetings	2
Board Meeting in Governor's Office	1
Report of Parole Violation	1
Conference with Personal Tax Consultant	1
*Based on 100 visits	100

(Ransome, 1956: 132)

Chart 6-19
Weekly Schedule of the Governor of New Hampshire

Activity		Average Time Spent in Activity
Correspondence		9 hrs. 40 min
Phone Calls		3 hrs. 30 min.
Interviews		20 hrs.
With Members of the Legislature	5 hrs.	
With Department Heads and Officers	4 hrs. 20 min.	
With Citizens	4 hrs.	
With Job Seekers	1 hr. 20 min.	
With the Press	1 hr.	
On Industrial Development	1 hr.	
With Party Leaders	1 hr.	
On State Reorganization	1 hr.	
On Employee Reclassification Study	40 min.	
On Miscellaneous Matters	40 min.	
Meetings		7 hrs. 20 min.
Of Governor's Council	4 hrs.	
With State Boards and Commissions	2 hrs.	
On Political Matters	1 hr. 20 min.	
Making and Writing Speeches		3 hrs. 30 min.
Travel		10 hrs. 30 min.
Dignitary' Matters (Such affairs as christening USS Pickerel, bill-signing ceremonies, meeting groups of school children, acting as honored guests at various meetings		9 hrs.
Total Time Spent on Week's Activities		63 hrs. 30 min.

(Ransome, 1956: 137)

4. The Legislature: 2003-2008

a. An Overview

In 1986 the size of the Illinois House was reduced from three representatives to two for each of the 59 Senate districts. This cut the number of representatives from 177 to 118. Also, cumulative voting, where a voter could give 1, 1½, or 3 votes per representative was eliminated. Instead, two single member districts were created within each Senate district. Structurally, this was the only significant change in the Illinois legislature since my initial study.

Since my original research the legislative process still works in the same way. Ideas are brought to the Legislative Research Unit (formerly, the Illinois Legislative Council) for formulation. The Legislative Reference Bureau then drafts a bill.[8]

In the past most mental health bills were written by the department. Now, many of the mental health bills submitted each session are the product of "providers" (mental health service agencies) or lobbyists. However, the department still prepares its budget. In this regard, one long-time staffer concluded that the legislature is still "responsive" or in a "reactive mode" when it comes to policymaking.

There are half-a-dozen legislators who are currently the mental health experts in the legislature. Some of them see providers and lobbyists as helpful. For example, one legislator stated that lobbyists possessed a great deal of knowledge. However, another felt their information was not balanced. One staffer felt they provided "heavy oversight" and demanded transparency of the department. Because of this the department was defensive. However, other legislators felt the providers were overbearing and did not treat them as "partners." Therefore, their relationship was "somewhat estranged." One legislator , however, found the advocacy of providers to be "compelling" and their "issues resonated." She also felt they were helpful in resolving budget issues. However, another legislator felt there was a lot of squabbling among providers. That was because they were in competition for scarce resources. One legislator stated flatly that "the unions are driving services." Because of this she often received 40 to 50 e-mails a day on mental health topics from the unions or providers. Both staff and legislators agree that the nursing home industry had a strong lobby.

Due to all the competition, and conflicting information, submitted by providers and professional associations one legislator explained: "Five or six years ago I told them to get their act together." As a result of this the providers and associations formed the Mental Health Summit. They meet once a month to formulate policy. One member called it an "organization of organizations—a coalition." He explained that they have no budget or staff. Their priority is to focus on legislation. They hold rallies and once a year they have a "lobbying day." The organization is currently tracking 75 bills. Some of these are substantive bills and others are appropriations bills. Their focus is to expand the money spent for community mental health services while preserving the number of state inpatient beds. Once the fee-for-services system is fully implemented they want to make sure that extra Federal

---

8. The legislative staff numbers several hundred. The staffs of some support agencies, such as the Legislative Research Unit and the Legislative Reference Bureau, are still hired on a non-partisan basis. Individual legislators are also given a budget to hire staff. Much of their work is "casework." This consists of solving constituent problems involving state or local governmental agencies. The most important staff in Springfield are still those individuals employed by the legislative leadership. Their job is to analyze bills. They prepare written summaries and analyses for legislators of each bill. These analyses examine the existing statutes, the proposed changes, and the positions of state agencies and interest groups on each bill. Fifteen to twenty staff are assigned to the substantive committees. Seven to ten staff are assigned to the appropriations committees. When we cite "legislative staff," as before, the leadership staff will be the individuals we will be referring to (see: Gove and Nolan, 1996: 88-9; Van Der Silk and Redfield, 1986: 5, 100-3, 116-7).

money collected by the state stays within the mental health system. However, the Summit avoids civil liberties issues since the associations and providers differ widely on these issues. "We agree on what we agree on," one participant noted; and, they avoid the rest of the issues.

There are two committees that deal with mental health issues in the House. One is Health and Human Services Committee. The other is Developmental Disabilities and Mental Illness Committee. These are both non-partisan committees. There is also a Fee-for-Service Initiative. In the Senate mental health legislation goes to the Health and Human Services Committee. Most of the legislators on these committees have volunteered for them. These legislators have usually had some involvement with mental health issues at the local level or have a mentally ill relative. One representative pointed out that there are 50 committees and 6,000 bills introduced each session; therefore, "you can't know everything about everything." So, she focuses on mental health; and, she is "consumed with her job."[9]

Recently, the Democratic Speaker of the House appointed one of the former Republican minority leaders to a mental health committee chairmanship. This was to emphasize the non-partisan nature of the issue. However, one representative commented that the new chairman "didn't do much when he was in the leadership. Now he's trying to create a 'legacy'."

One representative believed that those on the mental health committees were "good and caring people." However, budget constraints, and "gubernatorial indifference" hampered their ability to make progress. However, another representative mentioned that most reports on bills on mental health are never read by the members. Instead, they receive their information on the subject from a variety of sources—constituents, newspapers, or advocacy groups. However, one legislative expert on mental health emphasized that most legislators have never even visited a mental health facility. Legislators in the mental health area felt that there has been some improvement in the knowledge and the attitude by some legislators regarding mental health. However, in the legislature most mental health experts felt that some legislators still see the subject as distasteful; or a black hole into which one can pour unlimited amounts of money. Others see it as a thankless topic demanding too much effort that produces little political gain.

When voting on mental health bills members usually rely on the legislatures' mental health experts. In Springfield "knowledge is power" (see: Gove and Nowlan, 1996: 53). However, today most of the knowledge in mental health is provided by associations and lobbyists. And a number of staff members and outside experts feel that *no* legislator understood the entire mental health system.

---

9. As we noted before, lawmakers take on four roles in he legislature: district advocates, committee experts, brokers, or issue advocates. The district advocates focus on issues directly relating to their constituents, such as highways. Committee experts usually spend years on a committee and become experts in that area. Brokers stitch together majorities on legislation to overcome partisan, regional, and ideological differences. And issue advocates promote their ideological commitment to an issue (liberal/conservative, populist/elitist, pro/anti gay rights). However, increasing careerism has made legislators more district oriented over the last several years (Gove and Nolan, 1996: 82-3, 103; Dye, 1965: 182-184).

As in the past, not all substantive mental health bills are sent to the mental health or human services committees. One staffer noted that some bills are "randomly assigned." For example, some mental health legislation goes to the civil law committee. Bills that deal with confidentiality, patient rights, and competence are assigned to the state government administration committee. Also, a member of the Human Services Committee felt that bills on parent notification, guns, and stem cell research are "dumped" in to that committee. Therefore, the committee is overwhelmed.

Once a bill arrives at the committee legislators explained that they "sift through it," do some "fact finding," and "amend it later." In the House much of the mental health legislation is dealt with by the Developmental Disabilities and Mental Illness committee. One legislator noted that most of the legislation they produced was in response to crises. Such legislation was written to "throw a bone" to advocates or to show the public that you "feel their pain." She felt that even though these bills were not particularly substantive or important she had to "push them in to the faces of the leadership and the governor to get them passed."

In the past most legislators say they were able to work with the department. Now, they say the department is "uncommunicative." So, one legislator stated that she had to "learn the subject on my own." The legislator explained that when she called the department "they put walls around who you can talk to." For example, when she called a facility director with a question he said that he could not comment on it until he had checked with the department. The department then told her that he could not call her back. However, she did find the department's legislative liaison in Springfield to be responsive.

Today the main legislative focus of the department is the budget. One long-time staffer commented that "the budget is where the action is." The legislature still uses a line item, and not a program, budget. In spite of this the staff tries to take a "macro-view" of the feasibility and affordability of the department's programs. However, a key legislative staffer admitted that they were only able to inspect new increments in the budget. The staff or the legislators rarely looked at ongoing operations except for utilities and middle management (see: Nowlan, 1989: 112).

A legislator explained that the mental health appropriations committee was a "consensus committee." And, another legislator noted that "many issues are all about the money." And, "money is about bargains" (see: Everson and Gove, 1993: 23).

One area which has received a great deal of time and money, proportionately, has been autism. It has become the "in" issue. One staffer observed that legislators spend "an extreme amount of time" on the subject. Another legislator commented that attention on autism has become "huge" and the legislature has been "aggressive" in examining it. However, how much has been accomplished in dealing with this problem is unclear.

One success the legislature has had has been the passing of a mental health parity bill. This bill mandates that all insurance policies give equal treatment to mental, as well as, physical illnesses. One legislator explained that it took 10 years to educate members of the legislature on this issue. However, she felt that once the stigma of mental health was overcome, the bill was easy to pass. However, when it did pass it excluded organizations that had self-insurance. This meant that many medium and large corporations and institutions were exempt from the bill. Therefore, the bill has had only a limited impact.

Another area the legislature has worked on is the shift from community grants to a fee-for-services system. The department wanted to make the shift quickly. However, the Speaker of the House felt this was unrealistic. This was because there was a lack of knowledge in the legislature about how the system was going to be implemented. For example, legislators asked: Would the state pay enough per patient? Would it pay promptly? How much paperwork would be involved? As a result of such questions a legislator commented that "a talented staff person" was assigned to work on the bill. A similar problem occurred two years ago. Funding for child services was shifted from the state to a Federal matching system. Eventually, child advocates had to sue the state because payments for child services were too low. Also, legislators wondered if relying on a fee-for-service system that was Medicaid funded would actually cut out certain patients, reduce treatment, and thus, increase mortality. Because of such question the transition to fee-for-service has been moving slowly.

The legislature has had trouble grappling with four other problems relating to mental health. They are juvenile justice, illegal immigrants, the working poor, and the number of beds the state should maintain in the mental health system. For example, legislators have been unable to determine if the quality and quantity of mental health treatment in the juvenile justice system is adequate. Also, since undocumented workers are ineligible for Medicare or Medicaid private hospitals turn them away. So, they end up in state hospitals. Also, the working poor, that is, those without insurance, often do not receive treatment. And, no legislator is clear on how many inpatient beds should be maintained in the state hospitals.

There are other problems that legislators and staffers find troubling in the mental health system. For example, one staffer felt the mental health system needed to be "rebalanced" because more home and community based services were needed. He also felt that the mentally ill in jail and those that were homeless were "just not a priority." Also, a legislator felt those with a dual diagnosis, that is, mental illness and substance abuse, were not being dealt with by the state or local providers. These problems have been aggravated by the Federal decertification of Tinley Park Mental Health Center, south of Chicago, and the possible closing of Chicago-Read Mental Health Center in Chicago.

Further complicating mental health policy making has been the attitude of the current administration. Their only interest in the department appears to be budgetary. Their relationship with the legislature has been variously described as "constructive," "somewhat estranged," "adversarial," and "insensitive." One staffer commented that the administration does not "openly communicate." Therefore, there is "no transparency on the macro issues." There is also "no closure on issues." And, in regards to the fee-for-service shift the administration simply "stonewalls" the legislature. One staffer concluded that there is simply "not a great deal of confidence in the competence of the administration."

One legislator, however, pointed out that those with influential ties to the governor receive benefits. For example, he pointed out that the governor "hasn't found a big chunk of money to give to mental health." However, he did find $3 million extra for nursing homes. Another legislator felt that the administration is dismissive of the legislature. And one legislator told the administration: "When you've got a plan come back to us." Another legislator lamented that for the governor "mental health is not on his priority list" (see: Crew, 1995).

The role of the leadership (the Speaker of the House, and the House minority leader, the Senate President, and the Senate minority leader) is often crucial to the passage of legislation (see: Gove and Nolan, 1996: 93). In order to guide (control) their members the leadership traditionally sent out memos on how to vote. Legislators felt obligated to follow these memos because the leadership had raised money for their elections. One legislator put it simply: "you depend on the leadership for election" (see: Redfield, 1992; Clucas, 2003: 391).[10, 11]

Mental health however, is mostly non-partisan and there rarely is direction from the leadership. Some argue that the job of the leadership is to help members attain their goals (Clucas, 2001). However, in mental health there appears to be no clear goals. One legislator commented: "The Speaker listens and tries to help but it is not a legislative priority." However, on the "big issues the Speaker controls the agenda"; and his focus is "self-interest." However, the legislator concluded that the Speaker is "brilliant and knowledgeable, beyond anyone" in Springfield.[12]

One advocate explained that important bills go to the rules committee in both houses. These committees are controlled by the leaders. These committees are "fake committees that never meet in public." They are the gatekeepers for the leadership (see: Clucas, 2003: 390). One legislator commented: "If they approve a bill, it passes 116-0."

One area the leadership cares about is the budget. One advocate commented: "There are only three players on the budget: the governor, the House Speaker, and the Senate President." In this regard, implicit in much of the work of the mental health advocates and experts is the question of whether mental health gets its "fair share" of the budget. One

---

10. State parties have become multi-million dollar organizations with experienced executive directors and knowledgeable staffs. Fierce electoral competition has led them to develop training for candidates, write issue papers, polling, and media consulting. (Morehouse and Jewell, 2003: 151; 167; see also: Abbe and Hernson, 203; Moncrief, 1998; Weber, 1999: 619-620).

11. In 1998 candidates for Illinois House seats averaged $92,000 in campaign spending. Candidates for the Illinois Senate averaged $142,000. The most spent by a House candidate was $468,000. The most spent by a Senate candidate was $778,000. The combined spending in one Senate race was $1.3 million.

Much of this money is supplied by the four legislative leaders. Collectively, they raised $18.5 million in 1997-1998. For example, in 16 targeted races in 1998 the House Republican leader donated an average of $215,000 in cash and services. This was 67 percent of the spending in those races by Republicans. The Democratic House leader averaged $171,000, or 68 percent, of the spending in those races for Democrats. The Senate Republican leader averaged $295,000 in cash and services in eight targeted Senate races in 1998 for Republican candidates. . This was 68 percent of what those candidates spent. And the Senate Democratic leaders donated an average of $158,000 in cash and services, or 54 percent, to Democrats in those eight races (Redfield, 2001: 77, 91).

12. Three styles of legislative leadership exist. One is the "command" style. Leaders in this category maintain control by minimizing the participation of legislators. The "coordinating" style seeks control through negotiations among legislators. And "consensus" style leaders encourage participation and conflict resolution among legislators (Jewel and Whicker, 1994: 124-130; Rosenthal, 1998: 265-266). On the big issues Illinois is a command state.

legislator sarcastically commented that "the legislature had a $55 billion agenda; and, that was mostly for bridges." Another observed that with new Federal funding children's mental health was doing "O.K." However, overall, the department was "underfunded and over-whelmed." Besides, she noted that "human services are just not a priority." A third added that except for autism, mental health was not "trendy." And a fourth legislator observed that mental health did not receive its fair share of the budget. However, he added that its "fair share" is "more than we have to give." One highly respected legislator noted that there was only a "very small number of legislators who cared enough to listen" about the issue. Overall, he felt that state's commitment to mental health was "shallow and shabby."[13]

One legislative staffer, who may be *the* legislative expert on mental health in Springfield, commented: "Fair share? I don't know what that means. Illinois gets ranked poorly in state to state comparisons. However, that's not fair, it's apples and oranges. Fair share? It's a black hole; demand is insatiable." A legislator similarly commented: "It's the capacity of the community agencies to treat these people versus the hospitals. These people [the patients] are known to the system. Sure, screening and case management may avoid problems; and yet, they keep going back to the ER. In Springfield we spend millions, billions of dollars. Do we shift more money to mental health? There's more and more demand. But mental health is a black hole. However, jail for the mentally ill is more cost effective. Then there's more money left in the bank for other things."

b. The Legislature and Interest Groups in Mental Health Legislation (2003-2007)

The power of the Illinois Association for the Mentally Retarded has faded over the years. Now the nursing home operators are the most powerful lobbying group in the mental health field. As we mentioned, they are sometimes called "the most powerful lobby in the world." Let us examine their role in more detail.

Interest groups fit neatly into the pragmatic and bargaining political culture of Illinois. Interest groups are widely regarded as legitimate actors in the legislative process. In Illinois "let's make a deal" is the essence of the legislative process. Illinois legislators are continually seeking a consensus among competing groups over specific issues. This produces "agreed bills" in which the legislators "sign off" on bills negotiated by outside interest groups (Morehouse and Jewell, 2003: 81; Thomas and Hrebenar, 2004: 108-9).

Political contributions allow access to these negotiations. A common phrase heard in Illinois politics is that one must "pay to play." Studies show that such resources are the major determinant of long-term political success. Therefore, businesses and other economic interests tend to predominate in the legislative process (Thomas and Hrebenar, 2004: 126-7).

---

13. Similarly, concern with nursing homes has been limited. For example, in 2003 the legislature called for teams of experts to review sexual assaults and deaths in nursing homes. However, the teams were not formed because the state's Department of Public Health claimed they did not have any funds for the teams. In 2006, after the sexual assault of a 23-year-old woman in a nursing home, the legislature passed a bill to shift funds to create such teams (Rozas, 2006; Janega, 2007; see also Pear, 2007).

As the political and economic system in the U.S. becomes more complex so, too, does the political system. For example, in 1980 there were about 15,000 lobbying organizations in the U.S. By 1999 there were almost 37,000 of these groups (Gray and Lowrey, 2003).

Although the number of lobbying organizations has increased, it appears that they only become activated when issues relevant to them arise (Gray and Lowrey, 2003; Leech, et.al., 2002). For example, as state hospitals were depopulated many of their residents were transferred to nursing homes. Once this happened nursing became much more active in their lobbying efforts in Springfield (see: Parsons and Berens, 1999).

As we mentioned, access and influence in politics is gained through campaign contributions. Since money is the "mother's milk of politics" let us examine the campaign contributions of nursing home operators and employees.

The Illinois State Board of Elections (2002, 2004, 2006) lists the top twenty political action committees (PAC's) for each election. In the gubernatorial election years of 2002 and 2006 one of the nursing home industries main lobbying organization, the Illinois Council on Long Term Care, was one of the top twenty contributors. However, it did not rank in the top twenty in the off-year election of 2004 (see: Charts 6-20 and 6-21).

Compared to the expenditures of other PAC's the Illinois Council on Long Term Care's PAC was modest ($303,559.51 in 2002 and $269,236.59 in 2006) (Illinois, State Board of Elections, 1999-2007).

The money it donated was raised from 295 small contributions ranging from $118.31 to $1,975.29 from October 8, 2000 to June 30, 2007. The exception to this was $34,000 from its sister organization, the Health Care Association. The Illinois Council on Long Term Care expenditures from July 1, 2000 to June 30, 2007 were $426,416.30. Overall, from 1999 to 2007 the Council's PAC made 129 political donations. It gave $327,000 to the Democratic governor for his two elections but only $20,000 to his first Republican opponent. It gave nothing to his second opponent. It also gave $73,500 to the Democratic leadership in the legislature and $61,000 to the Republican leadership in the legislature (Illinois, Board of Elections, 1999-2007).

The partner of the Illinois Council on Long Term Care is the Illinois Health Care Association. It took in $134,503.50 from July 1, 2006 to December 31, 2006 from 616 individual contributors in the nursing home industry. Most of these contributions were small—under $1,500, and many were under $100. However, the owner of one nursing home chain contributed over $20,000.[14]

---

14. This particular nursing home chain is privately owned. It has 26 nursing homes and over 3,500 employees. It is ranked 104 in a list of privately held companies in the Chicago area with $225 million in revenue in 2004 (Crain's Chicago Business, 2005).

The owner of the company paid himself $215,400 to be president of one of his nursing homes. His daughter was paid $69,000, his son-in-law was paid $47,000, and the company vice-president received $215,000. Further, the company was paid $675,000 to manage one of its own nursing homes in 2004. A related company was paid $105,000 for its supplies. And the nursing home paid itself more than $1 million in rent for the facility (NBC5.com, 2005).

Chart 6-20
Ranking of Top 20 PACS by Total Funds Expended*

1.	Illinois Political Action Committee for Education (IPACE)	$2,569,375.93
2.	Illinois Federation of Teachers COPE	$1,530,532.26
3.	Roofers' Political Educational and Legislative Fund	$850,482.74
4.	AFSCME Illinois Council 31 PAC	$761,354.74
5.	Personal PAC Inc.	$732,394.99
6.	International Brotherhood of Painters & Allied Trades Political	$661,706.50
7.	FOXPAC	$638,426.40
8.	Illinois State Medical Society PAC	$604,211.11
9.	Leaders For a Republican Majority	$538,060.63
10.	Illinois Trial Lawyers Association PAC	$494,565.91
11.	Illinois Hospital Association PAC (IHA PAC)	$416,132.23
12.	Voters for Choice—Illinois	$376,578.76
13.	RPAC Illinois Association of Realtors	$328,972.94
14.	Manufacturers PAC (MPAC)	$317,775.34
15.	9th Congressional Dist Campaign Victory Fund—Non-federal	$314,309.44
16.	Illinois Council on Long Term Care Committee On Political Education COPE	$303,559.51
17.	American Insurance Association PAC State Corp	$296,754.64
18.	Associated Beer Distributors of Illinois PAC (ABDI-PAC)	$275,131.54
19.	IUOE Local 399 Political Education Fund	$248,790.70
20.	Statesman of the Year State And Local PAC	$242,005.11

*Ranked by: Total funds expended from July 1, 2002, through December 31, 2002.

(Illinois, State Board of Elections, 2002: 24)

The Health Care Association raised $90,954.52 from January 1, 2007 to June 30, 2007 from 532 small nursing home employee contributions. The expenditures of this PAC during this period were $226,255.26. Of this amount $25,000 went to the Democratic governor's campaign. The campaigns of the Democratic House and Senate leadership received $12,500. The Republican House and Senate leadership received $40,000. And $24,000 was transferred to the Illinois Council on Long Term Care. The association also paid $6,000 to a lobbying organization (Illinois, Board of Elections, 1999-2007).

Chart 6-21
Ranking of Top 20 PACS by Total Funds Expended*

1.	Illinois Federation of Teachers COPE	$2,105,988.90
2.	Illinois PAC for Education (IPACE)	$2,065,146.73
3.	SEW Illinois Council PAC	$1,110,626.35
4.	Chicago Teachers Union PAC	$775,400.86
5.	Personal PAC Inc	$741,792.08
6.	Illinois State Medical Society PAC	$696,413.57
7.	JUSTPAC	$566,747.06
8.	Illinois Hospital Assn PAC (IHA PAC)	$524,922.37
9.	Intl Union of Operating Eng Local 150 State	$457,406.15
10.	AFSCME Illinois Council 31 PAC	$432,219.37
11.	The Illinois Chamber PAC	$417,864.70
12.	Associated Beer Distributors of IL PAC (ABDI/PAC)	$406,452.28
13.	RPAC IL Assn of Realtors	$393,324.69
14.	Illinois Trial Lawyers Assn PAC	$329,792.00
15.	Illinois Pipe Trades PEF	$327,890.98
16.	Illinois Laborers' Legislative Committee	$294,238.34
17.	Statesman of the Year State & Local PAC	$282,616.33
18.	Illinois Council on Long Term Care	$269,236.59
19.	Illinois House Victory Fund	$262,026.88
20.	Associated Fire Fighters of IL PAC	$235,665.00

*Ranked by: Total funds expended from July 1, 2006 through December 31, 2006.

(Illinois, State Board of Elections, 2006: 27)

Although these may appear to be large contributions they are relatively modest when one realizes that the Democratic gubernatorial candidate spent $12,761,033.73 in his first campaign and $15,930,027.93 in his second campaign. Also, the Democratic party spent over $6 million in each of the 2002 and 2006 elections and over $3.7 million in the 2004 campaign (see: Charts 6-22, 6-23, 6-24).[15]

15. Redfield has observed: "The free flow of money allows the players to maximize their financial resources and pursue power and advantage without regard to limits or legal distinctions. A free market approach to campaign finance is completely consistent with the market-oriented approach to politics and public policy that is the hallmark of Illinois politics" (2001:37).

Chart 6-22

Ranking of Candidate Associated Committees by Total Funds Expended*

1.	Blagojevich for Governor	$12,761,033.73
2.	Democratic Party of Illinois	$6,899,498.45
3.	Citizens for Jim Ryan	$6,369,905.43
4.	Citizens for Lisa Madigan	$5,273,831.28
5.	Republican State Senate Campaign Committee	$3,339,697.69
6.	Citizens for Emil Jones	$2,928,661.63
7.	Citizens to Elect Joe Birkett	$2,675,875.68
8.	Friends of Dan Hynes	$2,149,364.94
9.	Citizens for Judy Baar Topinka	$2,116,261.43
10.	Friends of Michael J. Madigan	$2,094,732.18
11.	Citizens for Jesse White	$1,771,126.28
12.	Betty Loren-Maltese Committeeman Fund	$1,751,925.39
13.	Illinois Senate Democratic Fund	$1,472,755.29
14.	Friends of Lee Daniels	$1,282,728.15
15.	James Pate Philip Campaign Fund	$1,248,845.20
16.	House Republican Campaign Committee	$1,183,538.57
17.	Illinois Republican Party	$1,145,073.22
18.	Citizens for Dart	$878,396.92
19.	Citizens for Kathy Parker	$846,671.24
20.	Citizens for Susan Garrett	$830,128.13

*Ranked by: Total funds expended from July 1, 2002 through December 31, 2002.
Caucus committees are included in this ranking.

(Illinois, Board of Elections, 2002: 23)

Chart 6-23
Ranking of Candidate Associated Committees by Total Funds Expended*

1.	Democratic Party of Illinois	$7,029,682.83
2.	Illinois Senate Democratic Fund	$3,763,389.16
3.	Illinois Republican Party	$3,122,660.37
4.	Republican State Senate Campaign Committee	$2,576,102.15
5.	Citizens for Emil Jones	$2,143,363.43
6.	Friends of Michael J. Madigan	$1,870,156.86
7.	Citizens to Elect Tom Cross	$1,729,054.10
8.	House Republican Organization	$1,692,241.94
9	Citizens for Karmeier	$1,484,353.29
10.	Gary Forby Campaign Fund	$1,064,452.13
11.	Citizens for Frank Watson	$995,478.39
12.	Patrick Ouimet for State Senate 2	$992,002.52
13.	Citizens for Welch (Patrick)	$956,373.23
14.	Friends of Blagojevich	$889,920.71
15.	Summers for Senate	$757,468.28
16.	Ernst for Senate	$725,138.54
17.	John Sullivan for Senate	$684,851.27
18.	Gary Dahl for State Senate	$661,772.40
19.	Citizens for Slone	$642,023.49
20.	Citizens for Pamela J. Althoff	$638,344.03

*Ranked by: Total funds expended from July 1, 2004 through December 31, 2004.
Caucus committees are included in this ranking.

(Illinois, Board of Elections, 2004: 24)

Chart 6-24

Ranking of Candidate Associated Committees by Total Funds Expended*

1.	Friends of Blagojevich	$15,930,027.93
2.	Citizens for Judy Baar Topinka	$6,286,567.16
3.	Illinois Republican Party	$4,626,556.40
4.	Illinois Senate Democratic Fund	$4,456,020.46
5.	Democratic Party of Illinois	$4,263,899.40
6.	Republican State Senate Campaign Committee	$3,121,971.75
7.	Citizens for Emil Jones	$3,099,332.38
8.	Citizens for Giannoulias	$2,839,286.74
9	House Republican Organization	$2,782,164.73
10.	Citizens to Elect Tom Cross	$2,317,174.67
11.	Citizens for Frank Watson	$1,962,234.95
12.	Citizens for Jesse White	$1,961,186.20
13.	Friends of Todd H. Stroger for President of the	$1,715,969.33
14.	Citizens for Lisa Madigan	$1,689,635.48
15.	Friends of Michael J. Madigan	$1,447,923.45
16.	Citizens for Peraica	$1,194,556.29
17.	Friends of Frerichs	$1,112,883.53
18.	Senator Demuzio Committee	$1,030,812.37
19.	Dan Rutherford Campaign Comm.	$976,400.68
20.	Citizens for Christine Radogno	$882,561.73

*Ranked by: Total funds expended from July 1, 2006 through December 31, 2006. Caucus committees are included in this ranking.

(Illinois, Board of Elections, 2006: 26)

From January 1, 2007 to June 30, 2007 the Long Term Care Council also spent $145,429.71 on "other expenses." Ninety-eight percent of this went to three lobbying organizations in the capitol. However, these three lobbyists did not exclusively represent the nursing home industry. Each represented other business interests. These ranged from AT&T to the Coin Machine Operators Association. So, again, the efforts on behalf of nursing home interests were significant, but modest (see: Thomas an Hrebrenar, 2004: 126).

Unions and business groups gave much more money to Illinois political campaigns (see: Charts 6-20 and 6-21). However, their interests were often varied. This included saving state jobs, propping up state pension funds, improving health care, and raising or lowering taxes (see: Thomas and Hrebrenar, 2004: 111). However, the nursing home industry had a narrow interest and was highly focused on its issue. For example, the Illinois Health Care Association (IHCA) Public Policy Report (2006) noted that they did not just rely on paid lobbyists. Their staff worked with the Illinois Council on Long Term Core and a third group, the Life Services Network on only 190 out of the 11,000 bills or resolutions that were introduced that session.

The ICHA report emphasized that "lobbying involves a great deal more than talking to members of the General Assembly." It involves "monitoring all House and Senate sessions, as well as always maintaining a presence in every meeting of the various committees that hear legislation of interest to the industry." They also provided both oral and written testimony when priority legislation was to be heard before a committee. And they made "personal face to face visits with all members of the committee" which was scheduled to hear the industry's priority legislation. The association's staff also drafted legislative language in their attempt to compromise on regulations that would impact the industry. The report emphasized that in accomplishing all this the IHCA public policy staff spent 850 hours of overtime on legislative issues between January and May, 2006 (2006; see also: Everson, 1985; Gray and Lowery, 1996: 177).[16]

There are another group of lobbyists in all state capitals and Washington that are quite important. They are the legislative liaisons for every department and elected office holder (Thomas and Hrebrenar, 2004). They battle over legislation and budgets with interest groups, lobbyists, and legislators. Usually a deal is struck between these individuals. However, in these battles the legislature is usually only indirectly involved; that is, they referee the struggle and ratify "the victories...and [then] record . . . the terms of surrender . . . compromise . . . and conquest . . . in the form of statutes" (Latham, 1964: 48). So, legislators are not "Moses the law giver," rather, they act as "Moses the registration clerk" (Everson and Gove, 1993: 45; see also: Weber, 1999; Morehouse and Jewell, 2003: 78).

This "dance of legislation" is often long and arduous. Many legislators introduce "shell" or "vehicle" bills that can be used to "carry" legislation late in the legislative session. And conference committees can resurrect "dead bills" as amendments to shell bills. In this way "dead" legislation may have "nine lives." Also, the governor's amendatory veto makes him or her an important legislative player. Since it takes 60 votes to override such a veto in Illinois the legislature is often left with a take-it-or-leave-it choice by the governor (Emerson and Gove, 1993; Dilger, Krause, and Moffett, 1995; Rosenthal, 1993).

As we noted earlier, there is a balkanization in the legislative process. The department, plus a few interest groups, a few legislators, a few staffers, and the governor mold most mental health legislation. However, as before, the key document is the budget; and, the key player in the budget is the department. It initiates the budget and some of the substantive legislation. Then legislators, lobbyists, and the governor make "adjustments" at the margins of the budget or the bill (Gray and Lowery, 1996: 25-31; see also: Heaney, 2004: 256).

Further, it must not be forgotten that legislators represent geographic areas. Therefore, they are prone to respond to local and, not policy, issues.[17] Also, leadership priorities and

---

16. Parties are most interested in increasing the number of seats they hold in the legislature. However, PAC's wish to expand their influence with legislators. Therefore, parties employ a "maximization" or electoral strategy in their campaign spending. Whereas, PAC's spend their funds in order to employ an "access" strategy (Ramsden, 2002: 181).

17. Squire (1988a, 1988b) has identified there types of legislatures: "dead-end," "career," and "springboard." Ambitious individuals are drawn to springboard legislatures and see it as one rung on their political ladder. These members tend to be constituent oriented (Jewell, 1982: 76; Maestes, 2000: 666-67).

interest group pressures influence them. Conversely, most agency administrators are state employees that devote themselves to their professional careers. In DMH they see themselves as "mental health professionals." Or, more narrowly, they are members of the medical, nursing, psychological, or social work professions. So, their orientation is to their professions and to their patients. It is not to the ever-changing winds of politics. Obviously, Governors and legislators have "influence" over them, but it is usually the professionals in the department that prevail. That is, unless an issue rises to the top of the political agenda with "an overwhelming force" (Dometrius, 2002: 253).

Rosenthal argues that legislatures are open and legislation is the product of interest group struggles (1998: 239). However, governors can usually override interest groups and get their way if they place an item on their agenda (Crew, 1995). However, it must not be forgotten that the governor's leadership role is primarily *political*. That is, he or she is concerned with conflict, scandal, poll numbers, and the next election. So, it's not surprising that one study found that governors spent only about 10 percent of their time speaking with department heads (Schlesinger, 1965; Ransone, 1956; Schlesinger, 1965; Schmuckler and Belknap, 1956: 30). So, if the governor is uninterested in a policy area, the department, along with lobbyists and legislators, work things out.

c. Mental Health Legislation (2003-2007)

We have spoken in generalities in regards to legislation. Now let us examine the fate of mental health legislation. However, first, let us briefly review the powers of the legislature. Through its bills the legislature creates the structure of state government, it defines its powers and functions, sets the tax rates, and appropriate money for state government. Thus, the bills the legislature passes are the written instruments by which state government operates (Van Der Silk and Redfield, 1986).

There are three types of bills the legislature considers: First, revisory bills are noncontroversial bills that merely make corrections in state statutes. Second, appropriation bills specify the dollar amounts state agencies may spend. Third, substantive bills spell out the regulations of the state over its citizens or agencies. Substantive bills may amend existing statutes or they may repeal all or a section of a statute. Further, substantive bills can be categorized as major, middling, or assembly line bills. Major bills can raise taxes, change the school funding formula, or mandate seat belt use. They draw high interest. Middling bills make changes in existing programs or agencies. Unless one is interested in a particular area most legislators ignore middling bills. And assembly line bills make minor or technical changes in existing laws. Assembly line bills are narrow and are written to fix a particular problem without stirring up opposition (Van Der Silk and Redfield, 1986).

In each house bills are sent to an assignment committee. From there they go to standing committees to "sift," "screen," "revise," "refine," "weed," "prune," "shape," "develop," "dismiss," "amend," "gut," or, "rewrite" these bills. An important factor in this arrangement is that the majority party usually has a majority on all legislative committees. The size and party ratio of each committee is then determined by the party leaders and approved by the party membership in each house.

The process begins when a bill is written for a member by the legislative service bureaus. As we noted before, each bill "belongs" to its sponsor. A bill does not become a law in Illinois unless the sponsor "carries it." The first action taken on a bill is that it is filed in one of the houses. The bill then receives its "first reading." That is, its title is read. Then it is printed and assigned to a standing committee. The staff then prepares a written analysis of the bill. When the sponsor is ready the bill is called for a "second reading." This may be perfunctory or it may occur after negotiations with other legislators, agencies, or lobbyists. Negotiated amendments may be added at this point. However, bills may be held in committee and die if a sponsor cannot get enough support.

Third reading follows. Some bills are withdrawn before this stage. At third reading the sponsor presents its contents and urges its passage. At third reading a bill can be discussed for up to 10 minutes in the House or 5 minutes in the Senate. Most bills never reach this time limit.

Once the bill passes one house the sponsor must find a sponsor in the other house. If the bill passes the second house it must go to a conference committee if the bills language is not identical in both houses. Usually problems are worked out and conference committee reports are adopted. The bill then goes to the governor. The governor may then sign the bill, veto it, or amend it.

In order to examine how the legislative process works in practice we analyzed all mental health legislation in 2003. This was done by reviewing the 2003 Illinois House and Senate Journals in which almost all legislative actions are recorded. (This was the latest year in which the journals for both chambers were available. The 2003 journals were published in 2005. However, we will refer to them as the 2003 House or Senate Journals.)[18]

We began by reviewing the index of all bills in the last volume of the House Journals. There were 155 mental health bills listed under various topics (see: Chart 6-25). Money bills were sent to the Appropriations Committee. Substantive bills were sent to other committees. However, only ninety-four bills were introduced and ninety-two were referred to a committee. Of these, 51 were reported from a committee. (All bills that received a committee vote are listed on Charts 6-26 and 6-27). Of these bills 47 had a second reading and 39 passed on third reading. (Where information was available these bills are listed.) Overall, 39 bills passed the House (25 percent) but only 9 (6 percent) were acted upon by the governor.

In the Senate 240 mental health bills were listed in the index (see: Chart 6-28). However, only 97 were introduced. Fifty-one of these were referred to a committee and 41 passed the committees (see: Charts 6-29 and 6-30). (Where information was available these bills are listed). Thirty-five bills had a second reading and 26 passed (11 percent). However, the governor acted on only 13 of these bills (5 percent).

---

18. The 2003 Illinois House Journal is eight volumes and contains 9,613 pages. The 2003 Senate Journal is six volumes and contains 6,663 pages.

Chart 6-25
Summary—House—2003
Actions on Mental Health Bills in he House

Committee & Bills	Listed in Index	Introduce First Reading	Refer to Committee	Reported from Committee	2nd Reading	3rd Reading Passed	Acted on by Governor	Percent (%) Passed	Percent (%) Acted on by Governor
Appropriations Committee									
House Bills	46	32	31	12	11	7	0	21%	0%
Senate Bills	0	0	0	0	0	0	0	21%	0%
Substantive Committee									
House Bills	93	57	56	34	31	29	6	31%	6.5%
Senate Bills	16	5	5	5	5	3	3	25%	19%
Totals	155	94	92	51	47	39	9	25%	6%

Chart 6-26
2003—House—Bills Passed

Appropriations Committee (Bill Number)	Committee Votes	House Votes	Actions of the Governor
3261	11-0-2	72-42-5	
3738	P	117-0-0	
3788	12-0-0	117-0-0	
2027	P	71-42-4	
2454	P	103-14-0	
3309	18-0-0	60-53-4	
1108	P	69-44-4	

Health Care: Mental Health and Developmental Disabilities Committee

0057	P	87-1-24	
012	8-0-0	115-0-0	Cert.
SB 0199	7-0-2		App.
SB 0200	8-0-0	115-0-0	App.
1826	P	71-41-5	
0686	P	70-43-4	
1809	P	116-1-0	App.
0075	P	118-0-0	App.
SB 0639	P	114-0-1	AV-NPA
0697	P	70-43-4	
0722	P	69-44-4	
1185	8-0-0	117-0-0	Vetoed
1062	P	70-43-4	
0198	9-0-0	61-42-6	
0199	9-0-0	115-0-0	App.
1827	P	72-42-5	
1828	P	70-42-5	
2900-	P	107-5-1	
0684	P	70-42-5	Cert.
2607	P	81-11-25	
1814	P	71-41-5	
1815	P	71-41-5	
1807		71-41-5	
1808		71-41-5	
1812		71-41-5	

Actions of the Governor:
App: Approved
AV: Amendatory Veto
Cert.: Certified As Revised
V: Veto

Actions of the Legislature:
P: Passed
VO: Veto Overridden
NPA: No Positive Action by the General Assembly

Chart 6-27
2003—Mental Health—Bill Content
Bills in the House Passed and Acted on by the Governor

Health Care: Mental Health and Developmental Disabilities Committee
(Bill Number)

HB 0057	State employee health benefits
HB 012	Mental health code
SB 199	Mental Health Code—authorized involuntary treatment
SB 200	Mental health commitment training
1826	State-operated facilities (changes in technical language)
HB 0686	Mental (changes in technical language)
HB 1809	Health
HB 0075	Disability services
SB 0639	Mental health
HB 0697	Revise mental health code regarding transportation of patients
HB 0722	Mental health
HB 1185	Public employee benefits
HB 1062	Privacy
HB 0198	Correctional facilities
HB 0199	Department of Public Health
HB 1827	Health*
HB 1828	Health
HB 2900	Children
HB 0684	Disabled persons (autism services)
HB 2607	Human services
HB 1814	Health
HB 1815	Health
HB 1807	Health
HB 1808	Health
HB 1812	Health

* Details were not available for every bill cited in the House Journal.

Chart 6-28
Summary—Senate—2003
Actions On Mental Health Bills In Senate

Committee & Bills	Listed in Index	Introduce First Reading	Refer to Committee	Reported from Committee	2nd Reading	3rd Reading Passed	Acted on by Governor	Percent (%) Passed	Percent (%) Acted on by Governor
Appropriations Committee									
House Bills	49	1	7	2	1	0	0	0	0
Senate Bills	1	13	0	0	1	0	0	0	0
Substantive Committee									
House Bills	133	44	14	17	12	10	7	7.5%	5%
Senate Bills	57	39	30	22	21	16	6	28%	10.5%
Totals	240	97	51	41	35	26	13	11%	5%

Chart 6-29
2003—Mental Health
Bills Passed in the Senate

Appropriations Committee	Committee Action	3rd Reading/ Passed	Actions of the Governor
Human Services Committee			
(Bill Number)			
SB 0871	P	32-16-2	
SB 0994	P	36-16-2	
HB 0697	P	42-16	
Health Care Committee			
HB 0088	P	59-0	
SB 0199	P	56-2	App.
SB 0252	P	57-0	App.
SB 0200	P	58-0	App.
SB 0809	P	54-1-1	App.
HB 2221	P	51-2-5	App.
HB 1179	P	53-2-1	V
HB 0684	P	57-0	Cert.
HB 0685	P	38-15-4	Cert.
SB 0742	P	36-16-2	
HB 0684	P	57-0	
Mental Health and Developmental Disabilities Committee			
HB 1809	P	55-0	App.
SB 0808	P	54-1-2	
SB 0809	P	54-1-1	App.
SB 1951		32-16-2	App.

Actions of the Governor:
App: Approved
AV: Amendatory Veto
Cert.: Certified As Revised
V: Veto

Actions of the Legislature:
P: Passed
VO: Veto Overridden

Chart 6-30
2003—Mental Health—Bill Content
Bills Passed in the Senate and Acted on by the Governor

Human Services Committee

(Bill Number)

SB 0871	Amend state finance act regarding Medicaid Trust Fund
SB 0994	Task force on evaluating the Department of Human Services
HB 0697	Revise mental health code regarding transportation of patients

Health Care Committee

088	Health care (change in technical language of bill)
SB 0199	Health (change in technical language of bill)
SB 0252	DHS shall create a database of disabled individuals
SB 0200	Mental health—public employee benefits
SB 0809	Mental health—established trust fund for special needs individuals
HB 2221	Collective bargaining rights for personal attendants for disabled persons
HB 1179	Personal care attendants
HB 0684	Disabled persons (autism services)
HB 0685	Public aid
SB 0742	Rules for budget implementation and payment procedures

Mental Health and Developmental Disabilities Committee

HB 1809	Health
SB 0308	Staffing levels of mental health facilities
SB 0809	Mental health
SB 1951	Screening of children for mental health services

Two points are striking in this analysis. First, in the past "everything passed." In 2003 (almost) "nothing passed." Secondly, no appropriations bills passed. In order to examine these two issues I contacted a House staff member. He explained that at the beginning of each session 1,200 shell bills were introduced for every section of the statutes. Some of these were to make technical or non-substantive changes in previously passed legislation. Other bills were later amended with substantive changes. Many of the shell bills, however, were merely "moved" in case they were needed later. That is, "they were moved in order to remain alive." In other words, there was no real intent to pass them. He concluded that "numbers do not always tell the story."

Further, the staffer explained that the leadership may "admonish members" who introduce their own legislation. That is because "the leaders will introduce all the shell bills needed to do the members work." However, members may introduce legislation as a "press piece" for publicity or to mollify an advocacy group.

He also explained that for the last 10 years one omnibus budget bill was passed to fund the entire state budget. So, he stressed, "numbers do not always tell the story."

5. The Governor: 2003-2008

a. Overview

The governor uses his formal and informal powers in order to fulfill a variety of roles. His major roles include policy development, legislative leadership, party leadership, coalition building, management of the executive branch, and ceremonial functions. In practice, the most important power of Illinois governors is the "keeper of the purse" (Crane, 1980; Rosenthal, 1990; see also: Di Leo, 1997; Fergeson, 2003; Herzig, 1991).

Although legislatures have gained strength in relation to the governors over the last few decades, legislators still often suffer from an inferiority complex. That is because they see themselves as individuals rather than as an institution (Rosenthal, 1990: 51). For example, one former legislative staffer explained:

"A lot of it . . . comes from the fact that most legislators are dependent on the governor and the executive branch for issues and information, and they resent it. Despite all the legislative staff and all the various committees . . . in the end the agencies run the government, and all the legislators and legislative staff can do is try to keep up" (quoted in Carlson, 1982: 24).

Probably the single most important function of the governor is budgeting. However, the governor, and the legislature, as well, do not actually control large portions of the budget. For example, construction based on bonds, income and expenditures of "special authorities" such as housing authorities, port commissions, and tollway systems, are not under the control of the governor and legislature. Also, Federal aid is reflected in the state budget, but is placed in a special section and control of that money is specified by Washington (see: Thompson, 1987: 758). There are also dedicated funds for highways, education, or local aid which are restricted by statute or the state constitution. Therefore, the governor and legislature have control over about only 5 to 15 percent of the state budget. Further, this amount is influenced by the local economy. When times are good extra money comes in to the state. When the economy is weak the state budget must be restrained (Ferguson, 2000). However, the budget is still the "golden thread" in Springfield. Or, as one Kentucky legislator put it: "If you grab them by their budgets, their hearts and minds will follow" (quoted in Rosenthal, 1990: 131-4).

b. Governor Blagojevich (2003-2008)

The amount of money that the legislature and governor can directly allocate is limited. In spite of this there are often conflicts between them. Crane (1980) analyzed the success of several governors: Adlai Stevenson II (1948-1952), William A. Stratton (1952-1960), Otto Kerner (1960-1968), Samuel Shapiro (1968), Richard Ogilvie (1968-1972), Dan Walker (1972-1976), and James Thompson (1976 through 1980).[19] Crane identified several factors

---

19. Thompson served from 1977-1991. He was followed by James Edgar (1991-1999), George Ryan (1999-2003), and now Governor Blagojevich. Blagojevich won his first term in 2003. He is now in his second term.

that produced a "formula for success." They were: a.) bi-partisanship, b.) utilizing political and managerial leadership, c.) cooperation with the legislature, d.) accommodation, rather confrontation, among major interests, and e.) keeping in mind the good of the entire state, rather than, sections, groups, or parties.

The current governor, Rod Blagojevich, appears to have violated all these rules. He has been in constant conflict with the legislature since the beginning of his first term. For example, the governor has avoided important issues such as reforming the school funding formula, reducing state pension indebtedness, shoring up mass transit funding, and tightening campaign spending laws. Legislators point out that the governor likes to go over their heads "to the people." Thus, "instead of making deals," they argue, "he creates dogfights." And because of his unwillingness to raise income or sales taxes he has been unable to deal with the state's budget. Further, a few years ago he browbeat state legislators for spending like "drunken sailors." This infuriated legislators. As a result of such bad blood a tax proposal the governor wanted was voted down 107-0 in the House. After the governor reneged on a budget deal one journalist observed: "In Springfield, the budget is like a holy agreement, and it's entirely based on trust . . . So, when Rod decided he was going to break that agreement, it had a cataclysmic impact. The whole town has never been the same since." As a result of this, the legislators made the governor sign "memorandums of understanding" to force the governor to follow the state budget. In fact, budget impasses have become so intense that the governor has called 36 special sessions of the legislature through early 2008. When the governor proposed a universal health care plan legislators were uninterested. One Chicago reporter committed that his goal appeared to be "face time on CNN" (Bernstein, 2002).

The governor's problems go beyond Springfield. The previous governor, George Ryan, was convicted on Federal corruption charges (Davey, 2008). Blagojevich swept in to office on a promise of ending "pay-to-play" politics. However, he has become embroiled in several corruption cases. In these cases there is frequent mention of "Public Official A." It is believed that that official is Gov. Blagojevich. Several of his fund-raisers have been convicted of bribery. His wife is also under investigation. One of his fund raisers, Antonin "Tony" Resko was recently convicted. A former Federal prosecutor commented: "This is about so much more than Tony Resko." In one of the cases it was revealed that a veteran Democratic fund-raiser was offered his pick of contracts and state business in exchange for helping Blagojevich build a national fund raising machine in order to run for president (Mendell and Long, 2007; Chase and Kidwell, 2008).

In this year's budget battle (2008) the legislature passed a budget bill and the governor made several reduction vetoes. Many of the cuts were from education and social services. This included $600 million in Medicaid-related funds which will cause the state of lose Federal matching funds (Long and Meitrodt, 2008a, 2008b).

One Legislature staffer noted that the governor was not actively involved in the budget process. And his cuts will hurt addiction services, housing for the mentally ill, and community living facilities for the developmentally disabled. The staffer felt that negotiations to create a small across-the-board cut would have been a much better approach. However, the governor had refused to negotiate. The staffer also noted that he had never heard the governor say anything about mental health except in regards to the budget. However, along with the budget cuts the governor used his amendatory veto to alter legislation so that insurance companies would be required to cover diagnosis and therapies for autistic children (Garcia, 2008).

As the investigations and budget battles played out the governor has seldom appeared in public. He rarely goes to his offices in Chicago or Springfield. He reportedly conducts business from his Chicago home via conference calls. His campaign fund, Friends of Blagojevich, has been depleted by nearly $2 million in legal bills. Recently he held a fundraiser which was attended by a number of lobbyists (Chase and Long, 2008). One reporter commented that few people in government listen to the governor any longer since they expect him to be indicted.

Conclusions

We began this chapter with the argument by some analysts that socioeconomic variables are a key factor in policy-making (Dye, 1965). More recent research considers this "largely an illusion" (Erickson, Wright, and McIver, 1993: 252; see also: Thomas and Hrebenar, 2004: 108-109). We leave this argument to the political scientists. However, what does appear to explain the functioning of the legislature, and mental policy-making, in particular, is Illinois' political culture.

Earlier, we mentioned that American state politics contains three distinct political cultures: individualistic, moralist, and traditional. Individualist culture is pragmatic and focuses on personal gain. Moralistic political culture places value on virtue and the common good. And traditional political culture defends the existing hierarchy. Illinois is the archetypal individualistic state. Here, the public interest lies in preserving an open marketplace. Thus, the government should invest in collective goods such as roads, waterways, and education. However, social services, including mental health, are seen to be of dubious value.

In the 1960s and 1970s the state embraced community mental health. Liberals were delighted because they saw this as a long overdue reform that would allow decrepit state hospitals to be closed. Conservatives saw it as a way to reduce state hospital budgets. However, within a few years both groups were disappointed. Soon, mental health faded as a significant issue in Springfield (see: Bardach, 1972; Connery, 1968). Since then, budgetary considerations have been the main focus of mental health. So, phrases such as "budgetary constraint," "cutting middle management," and "wasteful spending." have been the focus of the mental health debate.

As this debate occurred state hospitals were closed and funding was increased for community treatment. However, it has never been clear if the level of community services provided has ever met the needs of former hospital patients. (And it is no accident that Cook County Jail has become the largest mental health facility in the state.)

All this is interesting, but beyond the point. Did our study of mental health legislation and budgeting help explain the mental health court? No. The key player in the functioning of the court was the Illinois Department of Mental Health (and its physicians). At the beginning of our study the court was dominated by medical opinion. Recently, the court has become legalistic and the role of the physician has been reduced. However, the crucial change in the court is that few individuals appear in court anymore. So, as we noted in our last chapter, the Department of Mental Health's response to the new mental health code was to simply stop sending patients to the court. The result of this is that "the commitment court" I began to study no longer exists. This change in the reality of the court is what we will explore in our last chapter.

References

Abbe, Owen G. and Paul S. Hernson
    2003   "Campaign Professionalism in State Legislative Elections." *State Politics and Policy Quarterly* 3: 223-245.
Anderson, James E.
    1975   *Public Policy-Making*. New York: Praeger.
Andrews, James H.
    1961   *Private Groups in Illinois Government*. Urbana: University of Illinois.
Anton, Thomas J.
    1966   *The Politics of State Expenditures in Illinois*. Urbana: University of Illinois Press.
Bardach, Eugene
    1972   *The Skill Factor in Politics*. Berkeley: University of California Press.
Bernstein, David
    2002   *Mr. Un-Popularity*. Chicago. February: 73-128.
biz.yahoo.com
    2007   Sector List—Yahoo! Finance Industry Browser.
Carlson, Richard J.
    1982   "The Office of the Governor." In *Inside State Government*, James D Nowlan, ed. Urbana: University of Illinois.
Cater, Douglas
    1964   *Power in Washington*. New York: Random House.
Chadwin, Mark L., ed.
    1974   *Legislative Program Analysis in the States*. New Brunswick, New Jersey: Rutgers University.
Chase, John and David Kidwell
    2008   "Governor in Middle of Case." *Chicago Tribune*. May 18: 4-1.
Chase John and Ray Long
    2008   "Despite Scrutiny, the Cash Rolls In." *Chicago Tribune*. May 23: 1.
Citizens Conference on State Legislatures
    1971a   *State Legislatures*. New York: Praeger.
    1971b   *That Sometime Governments*. New York: Praeger.
Clapp, Charles
    1964   *The Congressman*. Garden City, New York: Greenwood Publishing.
Clarke, Gary J.
    1975   *Health Programs in the States*. New Brunswick, New Jersey: Rutgers University.

Clausen, Aage R.
   1973   *How Congressmen Decide*. New York: St. Martins.
Clucas, Richard A.
   2001   "Principal-Agent Theory and the Power of State House Speakers." *Legislative Studies Journal* 26: 319-39.
   2003   "Improving the Harvest of State Legislative Research." *State Politics and Policy Quarterly* 3: 387-419.
Connery, Robert H., et al.
   1968   *The Politics of Mental Health*. New York: Columbia University Press.
Crains Chicago Business
   2005   *Crain's List Chicago's Largest Privately Held Companies*. April 18: 50.
Crane, Edgar G.
   1980   *The Office of Governor in Illinois*, Edgar G. Crane, ed., Dubuque: Kendall/Hunt.
Crew, Robert E.
   1995   "Gubernatorial Influence in State Government Policy-Making." *Spectrum* 68: 29-35.
Davey, Monica
   2008   "Ex-Governor Now In Prison, Sees Case End." *New York Times*. May 28: 15.
Di Leo, Daniel
   1997   "Dynamic Representation In the United States: Effects of the Public Mood On Governors Agenda." *State and Local Government Review* 29: 98-109.
Dilger, Robert J., George Krause, and Radolph Moffett
   1995   "State Legislative Professionalism and Gubernatorial Effectiveness, 1978-1992." *Legislative Studies Journal* 20: 553-71.
Dometrius, Nelson
   2002   "Gubernatorial Approval and Administrative Influence." *State Politics and Policy Quarterly* 2: 251-67.
Dye, Thomas R.
   1965   "State Legislative Politics." In *Politics In the American States*, Herbert Jacob and Kenneth H. Vines, eds. Boston: Little, Brown.
   1971   "State Legislative Politics." In *Politics In the American States*. Herbert Jacob and Kenneth Vines, eds. Boston: Little, Brown.
Easton, David
   1953   *The Political System*. New York: Knopf.
   1965   *Systemic Analysis of Political Life*. New York: Wiley.
Elazar, Daniel J.
   1972   *American Federalism*. New York: Crowell.
Elazar, Daniel J. and Joseph Zikmund II
   1975   *The Ecology of American Political Culture*. New York: Crowell.
Erikson, Robert S., Gerald R. Wright, and John P. McIver
   1993   *Statehouse Democracy*. New York: Cambridge University Press.
Everson, David H.
   1985   "Committees in the Legislative Process: The Illinois General Assembly." In *State Government*, Thad L. Beyle, ed. Washington: Congressional Quarterly.

Everson, David H. and Samuel K. Gove

1993 "Illinois: Political Microcosm of the Nation." In *Interest Group Politics in the Midwestern States*, Ronald J. Hrebenar and Clive S. Thomas, eds. Ames: Iowa State University Press.

Fenno, Richard F., Jr.

1965 "The Internal Distribution of Influence: The House." In *The Congress and America's Future*, David B. Truman, ed. Englewood Cliffs, New Jersey: Prentice-Hall.

1966 *The Power of the Purse*. Boston: Little, Brown.

Ferguson, Margaret R.

2003 "Chief Executive Success in the Legislative Arena." *State Politics and Policy Quarterly* 3: 158-82.

Freeman, J. Leiper

1965 *The Political Process*. New York: Random House.

Garcia, Monique

2008 "Bill Offers Help in Autism Battle." *Chicago Tribune*. July 14: 2-3.

Gove, Samuel K. and Richard Carlson

1972 *An Introduction to the Illinois General Assembly*. Urbana: University of Illinois.

Grove Samuel K. and James D. Nowlan

1996 *Illinois Politics and Government*. Lincoln: University of Nebraska Press

Gray, Virginia and David Lowery

1996 *The Population Ecology of Interest Representation*. Ann Arbor: The University of Michigan Press

2002 "State Interest Group Research and the Mixed Legacy of Belle Zeller." *State Politics and Policy Quarterly* 2: 388-410.

2003 *Trends in Lobbying in the States. Book of the States*. Lexington, Kentucky: Council on State Governments.

Griffith, Ernest

1939 *The Impasse of Democracy*. New York: Harrison-Hilton.

1964 *Congress*, 3rd ed. New York: Random House.

Hanley, Williams S.

1972 "The 1970 Constitution and the Executive Veto." *Public Affairs Bulletin* 1.

Harris Joseph F.

1964 *Congressional Control of Administration*. Washington, D.C. : Brookings.

Heaney, Michael T.

2004 "Issue Networks, Information, and Interest Group Alliances: The Case of Wisconsin Welfare Politics, 1993-99." *State Politics and Policy Quarterly* 4: 237-270.

Hedlund, Ronald D.

1967 *Legislative Socialization and Role Orientation*. Ph.D. dissertation. Ames: University of Iowa.

Herzik, Erick

1991 "Policy Agendas and Gubernatorial Leadership." In *Gubernatorial Leadership and State Policy,* Erick B. Herzik and Brent W. Brown, eds. New York: Greenwood.

Huntington, Samuel
  1961   *The Common Defense*. New York: Columbia University Press.
Illinois
  1973   *General Assembly, Department of Mental Health FY 1974 Appropriations Bill*.
          Public Law, 78-82, Senate Bill 1191, Seventy-Eighth General Assembly.
  1973   *Journal of the House of Representatives*. Seventh-Eight General Assembly. Vol.
          I-III.
  1973   *Journal of the Senate*. Seventh-Eight General Assembly. Vol. I-IV.
  2003   *Journal of the House of Representatives*. Ninety-Third General Assembly. Vol.
          I-VIII.
  2003   *Journal of the Senate*. Ninety-Third General Assembly. Vol. I-VI.
Illinois Commission on the Organization of the General Assembly
  1967   *Improving the State Legislature*. Urbana: University of Illinois Press.
Illinois Health Care Association
  2006   *Public Policy Report*. Springfield.
Illinois State Board of Elections
  2002   *Money and Elections in Illinois*. Springfield.
  2004   *Money and Elections in Illinois*. Springfield.
  2006   *Money and Elections in Illinois*. Springfield.
  1999-2007   Reports. Springfield.
Janega, James
  2007   "Mental Patients Torment Elderly In Nursing Homes." *Chicago Tribune*. April
          13: 1.
Jewell, Malcolm E.
  1982   *Representatives in State Legislatures*. Lexington, Kentucky: University of Ken-
          tucky Press.
Jewell, Malcolm E. and Samuel C. Patterson
  1973   *The Legislative Process in the United States*. New York: Random House.
Jewell, Malcolm E. and Marcie L. Whicker
  1994   *Legislative Leadership in the American States*. Ann Arbor: University of Michi-
          gan Press.
Keefe, William J. and Morris S. Ogul
  1964   *The American Legislative Process*. Englewood Cliffs, New Jersey: Prentice-Hall.
Key, V. O.
  1961   *Public Opinion and American Democracy*. New York: Knopf.
League of Women Voters
  1973   *The Key to Our Local Government*, 3rd ed. Chicago: Citizens Information Ser-
          vice.
Le Blanc, Hugh L.
  1969   "Voting in State Senates: Party and Consistency Influences." *Midwest Journal of
          Political Science* 13: 33-57.
Latham, Earl
  1964   "The Group Basis of Politics." In *Political Parties and Pressure Groups*, Frank
          Munger and Douglas Price, eds. New York: Crowell.

Leech, Beth L., et al.
  2002   *Drawing Lobbyists to Washington: Government Activity and the Demand for Advocacy*. Chicago: Midwest Political Science Association.
Long, Ray and Jeffrey Meitrodt
  2008a   "Budget's Winners and Losers." *Chicago Tribune*. July 14: 2-1.
  2008b   "$1.4 Billion Budget Face-off." *Chicago Tribune*. July 10: 2-1.
Maestas, Cherie
  2000   "Professional Legislatures and Ambitious Politicians: Policy Responsiveness of State Institutions." *Legislative Studies Journal* 25: 663-90.
Matthews, Donald R. and James A. Stimson
  1970   "Decision Making By U. S. Representatives: A Preliminary Model." In *Political Decision Making,* Sidney Ulmer, ed. New York: Van Nostrand.
Mendell, David and Ray Long
  2007   "A Governor under Siege." *Chicago Tribune*. December 23: 1.
Miller, Clem
  1962   *Member of the House*. New York: Random House.
Moncrief, Gary F.
  1998   "Candidate Spending in State Legislature Races." In *Campaign Finance in State Legislative Elections,* Joel A. Thompson and Gary F. Moncrief, eds. Washington: Congressional Quarterly Press.
Morehouse, Sarah M. and Malcolm E. Jewell
  2003   "State Parties: Independent Partners in the Money Relationship." In *The State of the Parties*, 4th ed., John C. Green and Rick Farmer. eds., Lanham, Maryland: Rowman and Littlefield.
  2003   *State Politics, Parties, and Policy*, 2nd ed. Lanham, Maryland: Rowman and Littlefield.
Moscow, Warren
  1948   *Politics in the Empire State*. New York: Knopf.
NBC5.com
  2005   "Unit 5: Grandmother Cares for Raped Daughter's Baby." September 13.
Neustadt, Richard E.
  1960   *Presidential Power*. New York: Wiley.
Nicholson-Crotly, Sean and Kenneth J. Meier
  2002   "Size Doesn't Matter: In Defense of Single-State Studies." *State Politics and Policy Quarterly* 4: 411-22
Nowlan, James D.
  1989   *A New Game Plan for Illinois*. Chicago: Neltnor.
Parsons, Christi and Michael J. Berens
  1999   "Nursing Homes Target of Mental Health Bill." *Chicago Tribune*. March 27: 6.
Pear, Robert
  2007   "Oversight of Nursing Homes is Criticized." *New York Times*. April 22: 17.
Ramsden, Graham P.
  2002   "State Legislative Campaign Finance Research: A Review Essay." *State Politics and Policy Quarterly* 2: 176-98

Ransone, Coleman B. Jr.
  1956   *The Office of the Governor in the United States*. University, Alabama: University of Alabama Press.
Redfield, Kent
  1992   "Limited Role of State Political Parties in Financing Illinois Campaigns." *Illinois Issues*. 16-19.
  2001   *Money Counts*. Springfield: University of Illinois at Springfield.
Rosenthal, Alan
  1990   *Governors and Legislatures*. Washington: Congressional Quarterly Press.
  1993   "The Legislative Institution in Transition and at Risk." In *The State of the States*, 2nd ed., Carl E. Van Horn, ed. Washington: Congressional Quarterly Press.
  1998   *The Decline of Representative Democracy*. Washington: Congressional Quarterly Press.
Rozas, Angela
  2006   "Nursing Homes Face New Scrutiny." *Chicago Tribune*. July 6: 2-3.
Schick, Allan
  1971   *Budget Innovation in the States*. Washington, D. C.: Brookings.
Schlesinger, Joseph A.
  1971   "The Politics of the Executive." In *Politics in the American States*, Herbert Jacob, ed. Boston, Little, Brown.
Smukler, Ralph and George Belknop
  1956   *Leadership and Participation in Urban Political Affairs*. East Lansing: Governmental Research Bureau. Michigan State University.
Squire, Peverill
  1988a "Career Opportunities and Membership Stability in Legislatures." *Legislative Studies Quarterly* 13: 65-82.
  1988b "Member Career Opportunities and the Internal Organization of Legislatures." *Journal of Politics* 50: 726-44.
Steiner, Samuel K. and Richard W. Carlson
  1960   "An Introduction to the Illinois General Assembly." Urbana: University of Illinois.
Thomas, Clive S. and Ronald J. Hrebenar
  2004   "Interest Groups in the States." In *Politics in the American States*, Virginia Gray and Russell R. Hanson, eds. Washington: Congressional Quarterly Press.
Thompson, Joel A.
  1987   "Agency Requests, Gubernatorial Support, and Budget Success in State Legislatures Revisited." *Journal of Politics* 49: 756-779.
Van Der Silk, Jack R. and Kent D. Redfield
  1986   *Lawmaking in Illinois*. Springfield: Sangamon State University.
Vogler, David J.
  1974   *The Politics of Congress*. Boston: Allyn and Bacon.
Weber, Ronald E.
  1999   "The Quality of State Legislative Representation: A Critical Assessment." *Journal of Politics* 61: 609-27.

Whalke, John C., et al.
  1962   *The Legislative System*. New York: Wiley.
White, L., et al.
  1964   *The American Legislative Process*. Englewood Cliffs, New Jersey: Prentice-Hall.
Wildavsky, Aaron
  1964   *The Politics of the Budgetary Process*. Boston: Little, Brown.
Woll, Peter
  1963   *American Bureaucracy*. New York: Norton.
Ziegler, L. Harmon Hendrick Van Dalen
  1971   "Interest Groups in the States." In *Politics in the American States*, Herbert Jacob, ed. Boston: Little, Brown.

V Conclusions

7 *Conclusions*

1. The Passing of the Asylum

This study began with the mental health court. We expected to find a "people-processing organization." Such an organization classified and labeled individuals. They were then usually hospitalized. So, in the 1970s people processing was a reasonable theory to begin our analysis. However, when the mental health code was rewritten it changed the nature of the process. Commitment was transformed from a bureaucratic process to a legalistic one. That is, the code was changed from an assembly line process to one with numerous procedural obstacles. This made the process slow and time consuming. The Department of Mental Health's administration concluded that commitment was simply not worth the time or the effort. Therefore, it switched to an almost all voluntary admission's policy.

This change was more than merely a bureaucratic slight-of-hand. What the department did was to redefine its function. In the past it admitted or committed "everyone"; now, it committed "no one." In this regard it was frequently said that the job of the Department of Mental Health "was to go out of business." Although this is an overstatement, there is a kernel of truth in it. In the past state hospitals were "asylums"—a place of refuge for a large numbers of people (Miller, 1987: 47-51). But today, where have all these "refugees" gone?

An explanation is given by Penrose. Penrose (1939) documented an inverse relationship between mental hospital and jail populations in eighteen European countries. This occurred even though the number of people requiring institutional care remained fairly stable. If we add up those in various institutions, as well as, the homeless mentally ill, this appears to be what has happened in the U. S. (Stone, 1978; Palermo, Smith, and Liska, 1991; Kohen and Paul, 1976). However, this is not simply a shift of the population. There is a larger issue involved here.

The department has decided to change its role. However, what we are also seeing is an historical and societal shift. That is, the department is being redefined as larger societal forces change the context of its functioning (see: Bowker and Star, 1999: 96, 86; Prior, 1997: 70; see also: Driori, et al., 2003: 280-308). And, what are these larger societal forces?

Before we answer this question let us briefly review the history and political context of mental health care in the U.S. since 1945. We need to do this because practically all modern organizations are creatures of the modern state and are supported by its legal and political framework (Meyer, 1994: 215).

After World War II the U. S. economy boomed and attitudes towards the mentally ill became more liberal. Robert Felix, William Menninger, and others in the American Psychiatric Association began to promote a Federal mental health institute. They drafted a National Mental Health Act and built a political coalition to support it. The bill was introduced in Congress in the spring of 1946, quickly passed, and signed by President Truman that July. This act created the National Institute of Mental Health (NIMH). This new institute provided grants for research, stipends for training, and financial aid to the states. Over time a powerful, long-term national constituency developed around NIMH. With the emergence of psychoactive medication the treatment of the mentally ill was greatly enhanced (Kirk, 1999).

In 1955, Felix, who had become director of NIMH, urged Congress to pass a Mental Study Act. Congress quickly passed the bill and set up the Joint Commission for Mental Illness and Health. In 1961 the Joint Commission published its report entitled, *Action For Mental Health*. The report called for a "bold new approach" to treating the mentally ill. After negotiations in Congress a community mental health centers act was passed in 1963. It was soon signed by President Kennedy. After Kennedy's death President Lyndon Johnson promoted NIMH's implementation of the act. The hidden agenda in the legislation was to replace decrepit state hospitals with modern community mental health centers. This goal was furthered by the enactment of Medicare and Medicaid in 1965 and Supplemental Security Income (SSI) in 1972. SSI provided money directly to ex-patients and Medicare and Medicaid provided them with healthcare. This allowed many state hospital patients to be discharged and to live in the community. As a result of this the population of state hospitals plunged from 559,000 in 1955 to 125,000 in 1981. Many of these discharged individuals, however, did not actually "live in the community." Instead, they were transferred to nursing homes or other facilities under these new Federal programs. Also, NIMH spent $3 billion in 1981 inorder to fund 700 communities mental health centers (Kirk, 1999).

NIMH's efforts, and funding, were successful in shifting the focus of care away from the state hospitals to the new community mental health centers. However, there was no convincing evidence that these community mental health centers effectively treated the mentally ill or saved any money. Then, in the 1980s homelessness emerged as an issue. This was seen as partly the result of large number of patients being deinstitutionalized from state hospitals. So the depopulation of state hospitals, which had begun as reform, soon became a new problem.

The Reagan Revolution ended the activism of NIMH. It consolidated ten Federally funded alcohol, drug abuse, and mental health programs in to a single block grant to each state. This was the beginning of a much larger American political change in which leadership for an array of social programs was transferred from Washington to the states. Further, by 1980 the conservative mood in the country had chastened NIMH and ended its social activism. As a result of this, NIMH, as well as, much of American psychiatry, turned towards the politically safe harbor of biomedicine. Soon, the focus of NIMH shifted to brain chemistry; and, the new focus came to be called, "The Decade of the Brain" (Kirk, 1999: 550-51).

Now let us return to our earlier question. What does the change in mental health policy tell us about change in our larger society?

The Great Depression of the 1930s led to the emergence of Keynesian economics. This approach promoted government regulation and progressive taxation inorder to ameliorate the excesses of free market capitalism. However, in the 1970s mass production industries in the U.S. and Europe began to collapse. This strained the economic underpinnings of the welfare state. These strains produced a conservative backlash. Eventually, what emerged was a new form of liberalism, neoliberalism. In the past Keynesian economics had applied only to the economic sphere. Under neoliberalism it was extended to the political and social spheres, as well (Hackworth, 2007).

The older form of Keynesian liberalism was characterized by managerialism; that is, an emphasis on national regulation, local participation in Federal programs, strong local ad-ministration, and a decent standard of living for the average citizen. Neoliberalism, how-ever, promoted entrepreneurialism, devolved regulatory power to local authorities, and pushed local authorities into public/private partnerships. All this helped to produced un-regulated growth. The consequence of this was that unfettered markets were promoted and inequality grew (Hackworth, 2007).

Further, after World War II minorities in inner cities became isolated by Federally sponsored highway policies promoting suburbanization for the middle class (Mills, 1987). As a result of this the poor were trapped in cities with inadequate schools and a shrinking pool of manufacturing jobs (Wilson, 1987). Neoliberalism emphasis on the market further isolated and concentrated these people as jobs migrated to the surburbs. Also, direct outlays for social programs to localities were slashed during the 1980s under the guise of returning power to local communities (Hackworth, 2007: 24, 67-69; see also: Fainstain and Fainstain, 1983, 1985).

However, this shift in ideology has been halting and incomplete. What the right hand took away in social service and mental health programs it gave back in health care and disability payments. So, as social and mental health programs shrank, Medicare, Medicaid, and Supplementary Security Income (SSI) greatly increased. For example, in 1999 Medic-aid covered 21.2 million people. Medicare covered another 36.1 million persons in the same year. And, Medicare covered 96 percent of those over 65 (National Estimates of Mental Health Insurance Benefits, n.d.; Post, 2001).

So, state hospitals were depopulated. Then, with funds from SSI and the creation of Medicare and Medicaid a new type of healthcare system emerged—"welfare medicine" (Stevens and Stevens, 1974, 2003). And with welfare medicine came the demise of the asylum.

2. The End of the Exploration

In conclusion, let us return to our original theory, congeneric analysis; and let us see if it has worked. In the early 1970s a vertical analysis seemed reasonable. At that time community mental health centers were new and mental health policy was still primarily a state and local matter (Meyers, 1994: 224). However, by 2000 national programs and funding had radically altered and state and local mental health programs.

The assumption of our initial analogy was to see the court as a platform. Patients were brought up from below (the street) by an "escalator." Meanwhile, power, authority, money, and law came down the "escalator" from above. By 2000 this analogy was obviously too simple. So, how do we now conceive of the connections in the system?

Scott sees organizations as "Chinese boxes"; that is, smaller organizations are contained within larger organizations. However, he sees these boxes as porous. Therefore, it is frequently impossible to say whether a given behavior is in one box or another (1994: 97). Heinz and his associates (1990, 1993) found networks of private elites active in four domestic policy areas. However, these elites only communicated with those of similar interest. This structure was labeled as "a hollow core." Both of these analogies appears to miss the point. That is because they ignore the different levels of power and authority in society. Instead, what our study has taught us is that we must examine the *levels* (contexts) of power and authority. However, we have also learned that contexts, and funding, change over time. Similarly, Holstein and Gubrium have pointed out that there isn't an unchanging realm that is called "the context." Therefore, researchers should be careful not to "freeze" the context "into a static entity." For, "context is emergent, variable, and highly elastic" (2004: 308, 309). Holstein and Gubrium seem to have the point exactly right. Context is *emergent*.

Hall calls his analysis of context "meso-domain theory." He urges us to examine the problematic linkages between social sites in which practices, policies, and actors from other sites constitute the conditions that frames an individuals behavior. Such an analysis, then shifts the focus from the action to "the linked *network* of sites that constitute" the (structural) context (1991: 131; 405 emphasis added; see also: Schinnar, et al. 1992; Hadley, et al., 1992; Heinz, 1990, 1993).

Michael Mann has similarly emphasized linked networks in his research. He has conducted an in depth historical analysis of Western society and concluded that society should be conceived of as a set of multiple overlapping and intersecting "networks of power" (1986: 1-3, 1993).

Today, congeneric analysis is not a viable theory. However, with this network perspective in mind, let us return to our earlier notion of *grounded theory as a replacement for congeneric analysis*. In grounded theory analysis and theorizing begins as soon as one begins to collect data. Sampling is not driven by the need to find representative data. Instead, data collection is driven by our "emergent analysis." As data accumulates we begin to produce "situational maps" of societal networks. These maps then lay out the elements we should analyze. These maps also allow us to capture "the messy complexities" of behavior "in their dense relations and permutations." Then the negotiations between collective actors (in their arenas or social worlds) can be analyzed. Thus, these maps help us "*to decide which stories to tell*" (Clarke, 2003; emphasis added).

Strauss, however, has cautioned us that what we should study is not always clear. Therefore, we need to *discover* the relevant structural linkages (1978: 259). After my initial examination of the mental health court I thought the assignment of judges to the court was important. So, I conducted an examination of the Cook County court system. I found the mental health court to be an apolitical island in a sea of political clout (see: Appendix). So, this proved to be a dead end.

What I now know is that I probably should have jumped to a study of Medicaid, Medicare, and Supplementary Security Income (SSI) as a way of understanding how state hospitals were emptied. However, this may not have produced the answer I had sought. That is because these programs are only one portion of the much larger welfare state. However, "the welfare state" is not a coherent government program. Instead, it is a mélange of numerous programs covering welfare, unemployment compensation, public pensions, public health, and housing (Lindert, 2007).

An attempt to examine the welfare state might lead us to explore an endless series of disjointed programs. Instead, we could shift to a broader perspective and analyze the three types of welfare states that exist: The first type of welfare state is the positivist state. The positivist state focuses on a government-business collaboration to drive economic growth. The primary aim of the positivist state is to protect property holders from the vagaries of unregulated markets and demands for redistribution. The second type of welfare state is the social security state. This type of welfare sate emphasizes full employment. For those unable to secure or maintain employment guaranteed minimum benefits are provided. The third type of welfare state is the social welfare state. This type of state also attempts to provide maximum employment. But it also regulates property through planning to create social amenities. And, ultimately, it attempts to broaden economic equality (Furniss and Tilton, 1977; Snower, 1993).

As an ethnographer such a comprehensive analysis might be fascinating, but it would prove to be impractical and "excessive." So, let us return to a comment we made earlier. We argued that our research should consist of a connected series of ethnographies. However, we have learned that a *connected* series of ethnographies is unnecessary. Instead, we should conduct our initial research. During this study we should *discover* what program, organization, or institution *penetrates* the social organization we are examining. Then we should *jump* to that new site and conduct a second study.

To describe this technique let us use another analogy. Earlier, we spoke of the "escalator." Now, let us use a "stone skipping" analogy. We begin our research by finding an interesting spot at the beach to explore. We should do some digging, get our hands dirty, and stir up some dust. Then we should find a flat stone and skip it across the water. As we watch the stone hop across the waves we should try to discern any pattern in the spray. However, at some point the stone will sink. We should then swim to that spot and dive to the bottom. Just like an underwater archaeologist, we should then conduct a careful excavation. Who knows what we might dig up?

References

Bowker, Geofrey C. and Susan L. Star
  1999 *Sorting Things Out*. Cambridge: MIT Press.
Clarke, Adele E.
  2003 "Situational Analysis: Grounded Theory Mapping After the Postmodern Turn."
      Symbolic Interaction 26: 553-76.

Drori, Gili, et al.
  2003 *Science in the Modern World*. Stanford: Stanford University Press.
Fainstain, N. and S. Fainstain
  1983 "Regime Strategies, Communal Resistance, and Economic Forces." In *Restructuring the City*, S. Fainstain, et al., eds. New York: Longman.
  1985 "Is State Planning Necessary For Capital? The U.S. Case." *International Journal of Urban and Regional Research* 9: 485-507.
Furniss, Norman and Timothy Tilton
  1977 *The Case for the Welfare State*. Bloomington: Indiana University Press.
Hall, Peter M.
  1991 "In Search of the Meso-Domain: Commentary on the Contribution of Pestello and Voydanoff." *Symbolic Interaction* 14: 129-34.
  2004 "Meta-Power, Social Organization, and the Shaping of Social Action." *Symbolic Interaction* 20: 397-418.
Hackworth, Jason
  2007 *The Neoliberal City*. Ithaca: Cornell University Press.
Hadley, Trevor R., et al.
  1992 "Expenditure and Revenue Patterns of State Mental Health Agencies." *Administration and Policy in Mental Health* 19: 213-33.
Heinz, John P. et al.
  1990 "Inner Circles or Hollow Cores? Elite Networks in National Policy Systems." *Journal of Politics* 52: 356-90.
  1993 *The Hollow Core*. Cambridge: Harvard University Press.
Holstein, James A. and Jabar F. Gubrium
  2004 "Context: Working It Up, Down, and Across." In *Qualitative Research Practice*, Clive Seale, et al., eds. London; Sage.
Joint Commission on Mental Health Illness and Health
  1961 *Action for Mental Health*. New York: Wiley.
Kirk, Stuart A.
  1999 "Instituting Madness: Evolution of a Federal Agency." In *Handbook of the Sociology of Mental Health*, Carol S. Aneshensel and Jo C. Phelan, eds. New York: Kluwer.
Kohen, William and Gordon L. Paul
  1976 "Current Trends and Recommended Changes in Extended-Care Placement of Mental Patients: The Illinois System as a Case in Point." *Schizophrenia Bulletin* 2: 575-94.
Lindert, Peter H.
  2007 *Welfare States, Markets, and Efficiency: The Free Lunch Puzzle Continues*. Van Leer Jerusalem Institute. December 17.
Mann, Michael
  1986 *The Sources of Social Power*, Vol. I. Cambridge: Cambridge University Press.
  1993 *The Sources of Social Power*, Vol. II. Cambridge: Cambridge University Press.

Meyer, John
    1994   "Institutional and Organizational Rationalization in the Mental Health System." In *Institutional Environments and Organizations*, W. Richard Scott and John W. Meyer, eds. Thousand Oaks: Sage.

Miller, Robert D.
    1987   "Involuntary Civil Commitment of the Mentally Ill." In *The Post-Reform Era*. Springfield: Thomas.

Mills, E.
    1987   "Non-Urban Policies as Urban Policies." *Urban Studies* 24: 561-569.

National Estimates of Mental Health Insurance Benefits
    n.d.   Department of Health and Human Services, Substance Abuse and Mental Health Services Administration. Washington, D.C.

Palermo, George B, Maurice B. Smith, and Frank J. Liska
    1991   "Jails Versus Mental Hospitals: A Social Dilemma." *International Journal of Offender Therapy and Comparative Criminology* 35: 97-106.

Penrose, L.
    1939   "Mental Disease and Crime: Outline of a Comparative Study of European Statistics." *British Journal of Medical Psychology* 18: 1-15.

Post, Patricia
    2001   *Casualties of Complexity: Why Eligible Homeless People are Not Enrolled in Medicaid*. Nashville: National Health Case for the Homeless.

Prior, Lindsay
    1997   "Following In Foucault's Footsteps: Text and Context in Qualitative Research." In *Qualitative Research*, David Silverman, ed. London: Sage.

Schinnar, A. P., et al.
    1992   "Public Choice and Organizational Determinants of State Mental Health Expenditure Patterns." *Administration and Policy in Mental Health* 19: 235-50.

Scott, W. Richard
    1994   "Institutional Analysis." In *Institutional Environments and Organizations*, W. Richard Scott and John W. Meyer, eds. Thousand Oaks: Sage.

Snower, Dennis
    1993   "The Future of the Welfare State." *The Economic Journal* 103: 700-17.

Stevens, Robert and Rosemary Stevens
    1974   *Welfare Medicine in America*. New York: Free Press.
    2003   *Welfare Medicine in America*. New Brunswick: Transaction.

Stove, A.
    1978   "Comment." *American Journal of Psychiatry* 135: 61-3.

Strauss, Anselm
    1978   *Negotiations*. San Francisco: Jossey-Bass.

Wilson, W. J.
    1987   *The Truly Disadvantaged*. Chicago: University of Chicago Press.

Appendix
The Courts: A Dead End

1. Clout

In my original research the mental health court was staffed by three judges. The chief judge had a masters degree in social work, another judge was the "bright young son" of a senior judge, and the other judge was a "down to earth" Irishman. Other judges and lawyers considered these three judges to be a cut above the mediocrity of the Cook County judiciary. I wondered how three such highly qualified judges had come to serve in the mental health court. In other words, I wanted to "follow my data" to see if this situation had larger significance. So, I began an exploratory study of the Cook County court system. Initially, I conducted some library research. Then I interviewed a number of judges, lawyers, politicians, and political workers.

The modern Illinois court system was created by an amendment to the Illinois Constitution in 1964. The 1964 Judicial Article created a unified, state-wide court system. The 1970 Constitution confirmed this. The system has three tiers. The top tier is the seven-member Supreme Court. Below the Supreme Court are five districts with an Appellate Court in each. And, then there are 21 circuit or trial court districts. Most circuits consist of two or more contiguous counties. Cook County (Chicago and its close-in suburbs) is one circuit.

Cook County is divided in to two departments, County and Municipal. The system is divided in to six geographical districts; and each district is divided in to civil, criminal, traffic, and ordinance sections. The Municipal Department hears minor cases in the county. The County Department hears major cases. It is divided in to seven functional units: criminal, juvenile, county, probate, divorce, chancery, and law. The County Division hears cases involving adoption, elections, inheritance, real estate taxes, municipal organizations, and mental health. The Probate Division handles wills and the administration of estates. The Chancery Court hears matters involving injunctions, wills and trusts, and mortgage foreclosures. And, the Law Division hears suits for the recovery of damages in excess of $15,000 (see: Figure A-1).

The 1964 Judicial Article abolished justices of the peace and police magistrates. Now there are only two types of trial judges—circuit and associate. And, all judges must now be

Figure A-1

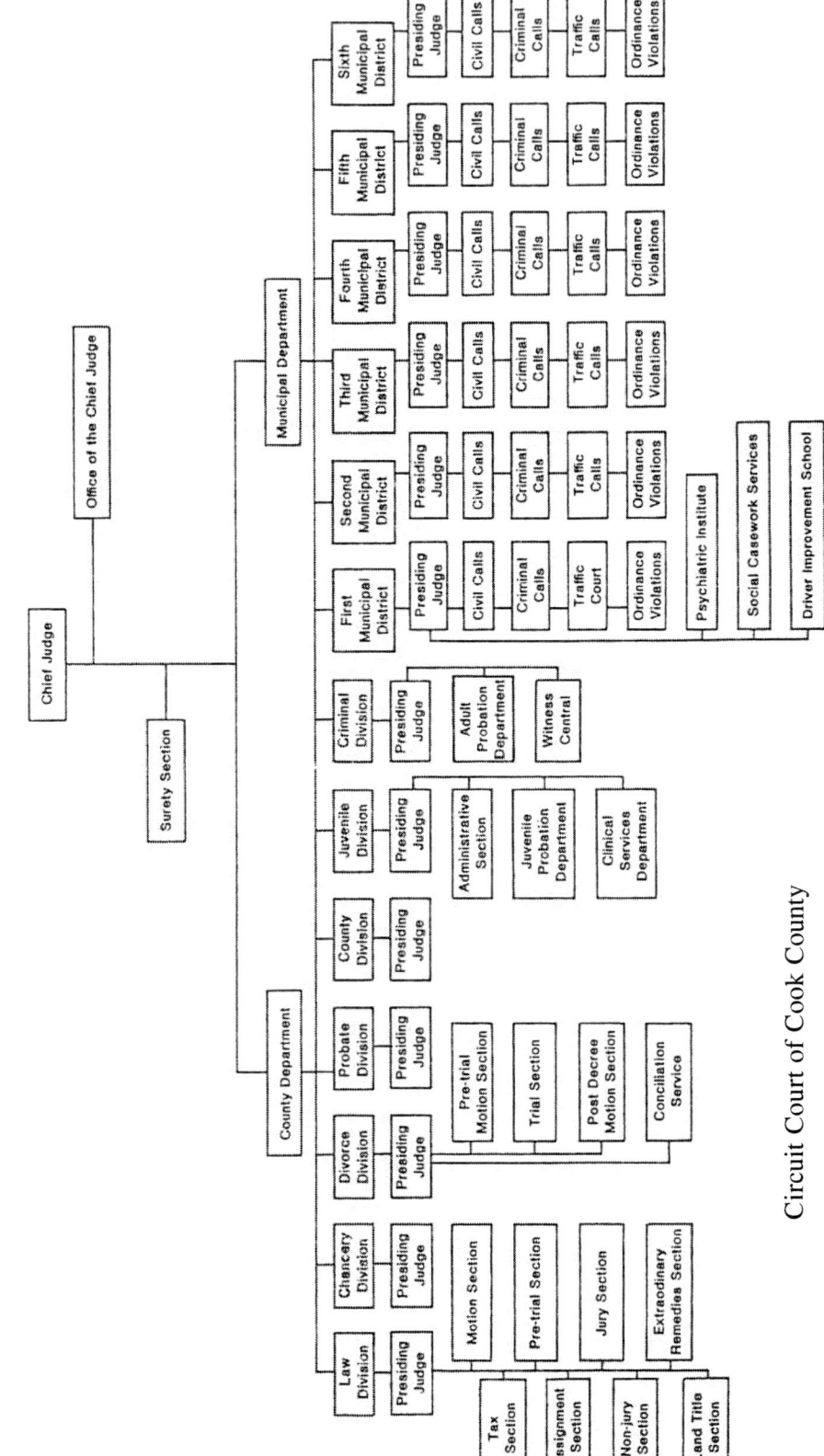

Circuit Court of Cook County

(Daniels and Kopecky, 1980: 133)

lawyers. Circuit judges are elected to six year terms. Associate judges are appointed by the circuit judges of each circuit to four year terms. The chief judge of a circuit may assign associate judges to hear any matters except criminal cases which are punishable by more than one year in prison.

Most of the day-to-day business of Illinois courts takes place in the circuit courts. In 1977 3,524,456 cases were filed in the circuit courts (see: Table A-1). Only 4,381 cases were filed in the appellate courts. About two-thirds of all the cases in the state were filed in Cook County (Daniels and Kopecky, 1980; see also: Mindes, 1980).

Cook County is divided in to six geographic districts. The first district is Chicago. The other five districts are in the suburbs. The first district has various specialized courts. For example, there are two felony courts for preliminary hearings and to weed out minor crimes. There are two narcotics courts. There is also a women's court, a shoplifting court, a domestic relations court, two racket courts (for guns and gambling), three or four alcohol violation courts, a housing court, a tort and contract court, a landlord-tenent court, a personal injury court (for up to $15,000), a paternity court, a probation violation court, and a large traffic court with 22 judges.

This may sound rather ordinary and bureaucratic; but, it is not. It is highly political. Each of Chicago's fifty wards and suburban township has a committeeman. (At this time most of these positions were held by men.) The committeeman is assigned a certain number of patronage workers by the Democratic organization ("politicals"). The workers are expected to "turn out the vote." If they do, they receive a city or county job. (Democrats usually control the city and county while Republicans often capture the governorship and the state jobs.) The committeeman also "slates" (endorses) the alderman or serves as alderman, himself.

Most of the power in the Democratic organization is held by the city committeemen. Suburban committeemen have fewer votes and therefore, receive few patronage jobs. (At one political meeting a suburban committeeman moaned: "We need some juice [jobs] in our township.") Or, as one city worker observed: "Votes equal jobs equal power" (Pallasch, 2005).

It is said that the Democratic organization (the mayor) alots a certain number of judgeships per ward or township. However, at this time Irish wards received a disportionate number of judgeships whereas black wards received relatively few. (Many voters only vote for the major offices. They skip the endless list of unknown judges that are listed on the ballot. This allows the organization to get out the vote for its choices for judgeships. And those tend to be women or Irish-named men [Pallasch, 2005].)

One "well-connected" lawyer who worked for the city explained the four ways lawyers become judges. The first is by donating money. For example, if a lawyer contributes to the ward organization, gives money to campaigns, or gives gifts (directly or through discounts) he gets "noticed." The second way is through political or business activity. If this produces a lot of votes or supports precinct workers the committeeman is "appreciative." The third way is through the influence of labor unions. That is, unions give money and provide workers for political campaigns. Therefore, they can "push" certain lawyers for judgeships. And lastly, newspapers and local television stations, directly or indirectly, promote lawyers

Table A-1
Total Circuit Court Caseload by Area: 1977

Law Over $15,000		Law $1,000 to $15,000							Chancery	Divorce
Jury	Non-Jury	Jury	Non-Jury	Small Claims	Tax	Eminent Domain	Misc. Remedies			
25,652	9,665	13,484	140,099	172,792	113,005	504	6,604		24,282	67,025

Mental Health	Municipal Corporation	Probate	Juvenile	Family	Misd.	Ordinance Violations	Conservation Violations	Felony	Traffic
8,290	147	33,929	25,686	20,188	422,954	57,525	7,192	31,663	2,343,770

Total: 3,524,456

(Daniels and Kopecky, 1980: 139)

who are sympathetic to their positions. The "well connected" lawyer concluded: "There are no clean people in this world." And, "there are no non-political judges."

A long time city worker, "a political," explained the process of becoming a judge. Precinct captains recruit workers. They are often college or law school students. If a law student does well in his or her precinct work they will be appointed to be a law clerk to a judge. That is a position in which he or she runs errands for the judge. If the law student continues to do well with his or her precinct they may get a job as an assistant states attorney (prosecutor) or similar job after graduation. The city worker explained that assistant states attorneys can do "jobs on the side, on the q. t." for cash. Assistant states attorneys can also earn money "under the table" for working out plea bargains with defense attorneys. However, "they have to be careful because of the Republicans or Federal investigators. But," he explained, "there's always a fix; and, if you know somebody you can always straighten somethin' out." After several years as a good precinct captain the lawyer may be considered for a judgeship. That is, if he or she is "on the ball" and "sells himself to the ward."

If the ward or township committeeman decides to push a lawyer for a judgeship the lawyer then submits his or her credentials to the Chicago Bar Association. This begins the official process of becoming a judge. In 1991 237 applications were submitted to the Chicago Bar Association's screening committee. Of these, 217 applicants were considered to be qualified and were forwarded to the Chief Judge. The Bar Association found 50 applicants to be "highly qualified," 140 to be "qualified," and 27 were "not recommended." However, the bar associations influence is "limited." For example, not one of the highly recommended candidates was "slated" (nominated).

Committeemen may push lawyers for judgeships but associate judges are officially chosen by an executive committee of circuit court judges in Cook County. So, whomever is sitting on this committee decides who is appointed to a judgeship. Therefore, the "well connected" lawyer concluded that "whoever is doing the cooking will get to eat" (see: Marin, 2005).

The slating by the executive committee of circuit court judges is done in secret. Sometimes those who are to be slated have already been picked. One former judge commented: "It's a ceremony . . . it's just a ceremony." Other times there is "horse-trading." Judges will openly discuss whether an Italian, a black, a Jew, or a Republican should be slated. In one slating session it was reported that some judges urged that five blacks should be slated. This was considered to be politically unrealistic. However, slating three black candidates was considered to be "a politically do-able thing." One judge commented that judgeships were traded like baseball cards. Another judge explained that in the end clout is what mattered. He described the voting process: "Everybody sits down and says, 'Whose guy is this guy?'" (Gratteau and Lipinski, 1991; Marin, 2005; see also: Chase, 2006; Higgins, 2006).

One reporter described the process in a slightly different manner: "They don't like strangers here. Big-firm lawyers with Ivy League degrees are fine. But if they haven't seen your face at the ward office, the party picnics, or ringing doorbells to get Democrats elected, why should these party bosses work hard to get you elected judge?" The key to becoming a judge is to be "one helluva a Democrat" (Pallasch, 2005; Brown, 2005).

If the judges committee slates the lawyer for a judgeship the candidate must then raise $5,000 to $10,000 to run a campaign. Other lawyers, business people, and corporations donate this money. The city worker explained that they donate because they want favors. He explained: "Nobody gives money to get nothin' in return" (see: Kuczka and Gibbard, 2005; Jones, 2008).

One well known Chicago lawyer explained that lawyers who work hard for the organization may receive a large pay-off in the end—a judgeship. And judgeships are greatly prized because one can earn "extra revenue." For example, he explained that "traffic court is lucrative, but unpleasant." (One police officer noted that "the going rate to get someone off for drunk driving is $1,200. That is, in small bills slipped under the judge's door in a plain white envelope before court.") Personal injury cases also allow judges to make "extra money." Chancery Court is the highest status division in Cook County. That is where many high profile corporate cases are heard. However, the lawyer noted that the Chancery Court also gave judges a lot of patronage. That is, it allowed judges to appoint attorneys to lucrative positions as trustees and receivers. The lawyer explained that there are 35,000 political workers in Chicago. Many of them drove trucks and ran elevators for the city or county. However, "the judicial system is a high paying and prestigious arm of the machine."

The judicial system also plays an important role in the functioning of the machine. If political workers or bosses are indicted sympathetic judges can dismiss their cases on technicalities. If a case attains notoriety it may have to go to trial. If there is a conviction, the judge, months later, can give a light sentence. The lawyer concluded that "the judiciary is an arm of the machine and its front line of defense." Because, "the purpose of the machine is to keep itself in power."

If you wanted to climb the judicial ladder you had to show loyalty to the organization, a highly respected independent alderman and attorney observed. "It's just like the city council," he explained, "they must follow the party line. They perform like trained seals. If they want to move up, they have no choice. They are made in the mold of the machine."

The city attorney explained that once you become a judge you usually have the freedom to pick your own assignment. Many judges want to find a "comfortable branch." For example, "criminal court is easy and you take your gratuities." However, the alderman contradicted this when he commented that new judges are assigned to criminal court as an "unpleasant apprenticeship." There are also a few assignments, such as weekend court, that some judges covet. However, a private practice attorney disagreed. He said that "the quality of clout," and not the preference of the judge, determined a judges assignment. He went on to say that every judge owes his job to a ward committeeman. And that judge has a "perpetual ring in his nose" tied to that committeeman. Because of this corruption seeps in to the judicial system. However, this corruption is often subtle. For example, a phone call may lead to the sympathetic treatment of a defendant by a judge. It may also produce a reduction in a charge. Or, a judge may force the lawyers in a case in to a negotiated settlement. But then he asked: "Is this *really* corruption?"

The original question I had raised was: How did three highly qualified judges come to serve in the mental health court? Also, after all I had heard I also wondered: Were judges exiled to the mental health court? "No," one judge explained. "If you want to get rid of some guy you send him to one of the outlying traffic courts." However, the alderman commented that the mental health court had "no prestige, no brownie points, and no money." Politically, there's "nothin' to it. It's a dead-end assignment." And a lawyer added: "Talent and no clout, right to the mental health court."

However, one prominent judge noted that such comments missed the point. All the judges in the mental health court were there by their own request. That was because they had "a tendency towards that kind of work." He explained that commitment cases are "the most difficult decisions in the world." In fact, he felt that you needed to be "close to God" to make these decisions. And he believed that you needed the best people available in those positions. He pointed out that the chief judge of the mental health court was a "decent and honorable human being. He's the best." And one lawyer saw him as someone with "ambition to advance in the social work field."

2. Conclusions

I have argued that you need to "follow your data." In fact, in this case, my data did not lead me anywhere. I acted on a hunch. And, my hunch was wrong. The mental health court was not driven by politics. In fact, it was an apolitical island in a sea of clout. Certainly, the judges "on the island" were appointed because of their political connections. However, politics stopped at the waters edge. Politics did not help explain the functioning of the mental health court. So, my examination of the courts was a dead end.

References

Brown, Mark
    2005   "System Works Find for Pols Who Really Pick Our Judges." *Chicago Sun-Times*. November 23: 2.

Chase, John
    2006   "Politics a Means to End on Court." *Chicago Tribune*. April 7: 2-1.

Daniels, Stephen and Frank J. Kopecky, Jr.
    1980   "The Illinois Judicial System." In *Illinois*. Edgar G. Crane, ed. Dubuque: Kendall/Hunt.

Gratteau, Hanke and Marie Lipinski
    1991   "Clout Remains Vital to Would-Be Judges." *Chicago Tribune*. January 14: 1.

Higgins, Michael
    2006   "For Judges, Sheahan's Aid Trumps Screening." *Chicago Tribune*. December 4: 1.

Jones, Tim
    2008   "Lobbyist Cash Clouds Judicial Races." *Chicago Tribune*. July 28: 1.

Kuczka, Susan and M. Daniel Gibbard
    2005   "Law Cuts Judicial Circuits, Nerves—Diversity Claim Falls Flat, Republicans Say." *Chicago Tribune*. April 12: 2-1.

Marin, Carol
    2005   "Sure, It's a Done Deal, But Slate-making Retains Appeal: It Was Clear That Everyone in the Room Knew How it Was All Going to Turn Out." *Chicago Sun-Times*. November 23: 51.

Mindes, Marvin, W.
  1980   "Courts, Lawyers and the Reality of the Law." In *Illinois*. Edgar G. Crane, ed.
          Dubuque: Kendall/Hall.
Pallasch, Abdon M.
  2005   "Making the Slate: Proven Loyalty to the Party Outweighs Lofty Credentials for
          Judge Candidates." *Chicago Sun-Times*. November 27: 24.

Index

Note: a *c* following a page number indicates a chart on that page; an *f* following a page number indicates a figure on that page; an *n* following a page number indicates a note on that page; a *t* following a page number indicates a table on that page

About the Author

George C. Klein, Ph.D. is a Professor of Sociology/Anthropology at Oakton Community College in Des Plaines, Illinois. He has served as a part-time police officer. He is a trained hostage negotiator and served as a consultant to a SWAT team. He is also a consultant to the Behavioral Science Unit at the FBI Academy. Dr. Klein has written articles on mental health, criminal justice, hostage negotiation, and terrorism. His first book was *The Adventure: The Quest For My Romanian Babies*, Hamilton/Rowman and Littlefield (2007).